EUROMISSILES

EUROMISSILES

THE NUCLEAR WEAPONS THAT
NEARLY DESTROYED NATO

SUSAN COLBOURN

CORNELL UNIVERSITY PRESS

Ithaca and London

First published 2022 by Cornell University Press

Printed in the United States of America

Library of Congress Cataloging-in-Publication Data

Names: Colbourn, Susan, 1987– author.
Title: Euromissiles : the nuclear weapons that nearly destroyed NATO / Susan Colbourn.
Description: Ithaca, [New York] : Cornell University Press, 2022. | Includes bibliographical references and index.
Identifiers: LCCN 2022001104 (print) | LCCN 2022001105 (ebook) | ISBN 9781501766022 (hardcover) | ISBN 9781501766039 (pdf) | ISBN 9781501766046 (epub)
Subjects: LCSH: North Atlantic Treaty Organization—History—20th century. | Nuclear weapons—Europe—History—20th century. | Arms race—Europe—History—20th century. | Intermediate-range ballistic missiles—History—20th century. | Cruise missiles—Europe—History—20th century. | Cold War. | Europe—Foreign relations—Soviet Union. | Soviet Union—Foreign relations—Europe. | United States—Foreign relations—1977–1981. | United States—Foreign relations—1981–1989.
Classification: LCC U264.5.E85 C65 2022 (print) | LCC U264.5.E85 (ebook) | DDC 355.8/25119094—dc23/eng/20220203
LC record available at https://lccn.loc.gov/2022001104
LC ebook record available at https://lccn.loc.gov/2022001105

For my family

How can you explain to people that you defend peace and freedom with weapons which if they, once they are used will destroy mankind?

—Hans Apel

If there are enough nuclear weapons now in Europe to destroy the continent 30 times over, what does it matter if one side can do it 14 times and the other 16?

—E. P. Thompson

Contents

ACKNOWLEDGMENTS

I have accumulated a whole host of debts in the process of writing this book. Any book of this size and scope would be impossible to write without countless others. I am grateful to the archivists, librarians, and declassification specialists whose hard work and assistance made it possible for me to consult the records cited herein (and many, many more). I am also grateful to the various teachers over the years who kindled my interest in history and encouraged me to follow that curiosity.

Arne Hofmann convinced me that I might have the chops to become a Cold War historian, and his sound guidance and advice put me on a path to always put my own interests and well-being at the top of the proverbial pile. Robert Bothwell plucked me out of a stack of papers and took a chance on me. I will be forever grateful that he did.

At the University of Toronto, Lynne Viola was a constant source of support and wisdom—a true role model as a scholar. Timothy Sayle's arrival partway through my second stint at Toronto could not have been more fortuitous. In Tim, I found a coauthor, a fellow NATO enthusiast, and an unflagging champion. The Bill Graham Centre for Contemporary International History and its first director, John English, offered me an extra intellectual home while in Toronto. At Yale University, I went in new directions and the International Security Studies program proved the perfect place to do so. Paul Kennedy, Nuno Monteiro, Fritz Bartel, Michael Brenes, and Arne Westad all made it an engaging environment that shaped what this book became in meaningful ways, as did my junior seminar students in "NATO in Crisis." A year at Johns Hopkins School of Advanced International Studies (Zoom Campus) helped to sharpen my thinking about transatlantic order thanks to Dan Hamilton, Andreas Rödder, and Mary Sarotte. Last, but by no means least, I have had the great fortune to wrap this project up at the Triangle Institute for Security Studies. I am grateful to Kyle Beardsley, Tricia Sullivan, and Peter Feaver for welcoming me to TISS—and to Duke University—with so much support.

Support from several institutions made archival research possible: the American Council on Germany, the Gerald R. Ford Presidential Foundation, the Scowcroft Institute of International Affairs at Texas A&M's Bush School of Government and Public Service, and the John Adams Center at the Virginia Military Institute all provided funds that made research in Belgium, Canada, France, Germany, the Netherlands, the United Kingdom, and the United States possible. The Department of History, the Joint Initiative on German and European Studies, and the School of Graduate Studies at the University of Toronto all provided funds, as did the International Security Studies program at Yale University.

I have been very fortunate to have had generous colleagues, works-in-progress groups, and conference copanelists over the years who read earlier drafts and talked to me about even earlier ideas. Thanks to Jean-François Bélanger, Michael Brenes, Jasen Castillo, Elizabeth Charles, Andrea Chiampan, Katherine Elgin, Michael Franczak, Mathias Ormestad Frendem, Matthias Haeussler, Louis Halewood, Ashlyn Hand, Ian Johnson, Michael Joseph, John Maurer, Brandon Merrell, Maris Rowe-McCulloch, Rachel Myrick, Erik Sand, Thomas Schwartz, Joshua Shifrinson, Jennifer Siegel, Lauren Turek, Emily Whalen, Anna Whittington, and Claire Yorke. The entire Nuclear Proliferation International History Project community has been a great source of inspiration and ideas; thanks to Leopoldo Nuti and Christian Ostermann for creating such a welcoming home. Tim Sayle helped me figure out major elements of this project's scope and overall shape and Paul Pitman offered invaluable comments on much of the book. The two anonymous reviewers were critical in shaping the book and the final product is undoubtedly better thanks to their suggestions and generous feedback.

The entire team at Cornell University Press has helped make this book possible. Michael McGandy shaped this project in significant ways and gave me advice on how to put my best foot forward in my own dance with the Euromissiles. I would also like to thank Clare Jones, Karen Hwa, and Brock Schnoke for their hard work. Monica Achen and Glenn Novak provided incisive edits that helped to whip the final product into shape, and Katy Balcer did an exceptional job compiling the index.

Lastly, there are yet more friends and family without whom this would not have been possible. Caroline Cormier and Marcel Kloos made stops in Berlin a delight. Leo Brussel and Catherine White shared many postarchive dinners with me in Washington, DC, and Katie, Derek, and Elizabeth Joslin, an excellent time in Munich; I look forward to many more adventures with Annie, too. Charles Pierson has been there at every step, often with a much-needed laugh. Elaine and Marvin Givertz, Arlene Manson, Linda

Manson, Caryl and Dennis McManus, and Murray and Silvia Miles have all been wonderful and supportive champions. My husband, Simon Miles, has been the greatest champion of all. He read countless drafts, listened to me chatter away about arms control minutiae and the wittiest antinuclear protest slogans I could find, made numerous suggestions, and shot down a few of my not-so-great ideas. His love, support, and sharp edits made this a much better book. There aren't proper words to express how grateful I am to my dad, Charlie, my mom, Karen, my stepmom, Violet, and my sister and partner in crime, Sarah. Thanks for always believing this was possible. This one's for you.

Abbreviations

ABM	anti-ballistic missile
CDU	Christlich Demokratische Union, Christian Democratic Union (Federal Republic of Germany)
CFE	conventional armed forces in Europe
CND	Campaign for Nuclear Disarmament
CSCE	Conference on Security and Cooperation in Europe
CSU	Christlich-Soziale Union in Bayern, Christian Social Union of Bavaria (Federal Republic of Germany)
END	European Nuclear Disarmament
FCO	Foreign and Commonwealth Office (United Kingdom)
FDP	Freie Demokratische Partei, Free Democratic Party (Federal Republic of Germany)
FOTL	follow-on to Lance
FRG	Federal Republic of Germany
IKV	Interkerkelijk Vredesberaad, Interchurch Peace Council
INF	intermediate-range nuclear forces
IRBM	intermediate-range ballistic missile
LTDP	Long-Term Defense Program
MAE	Ministre des Affaires Étrangères (France)
MBFR	mutual and balanced force reduction
MLF	multilateral force
MRBM	medium-range ballistic missile
NATO	North Atlantic Treaty Organization
NPG	Nuclear Planning Group
NSC	National Security Council (United States)
SACEUR	supreme allied commander, Europe
SALT	Strategic Arms Limitation Talks
SDI	Strategic Defense Initiative
SED	Socialist Unity Party of Germany, Sozialistische Einheitspartei Deutschlands (German Democratic Republic)
SNF	short-range nuclear forces

SPD   Sozialdemokratische Partei Deutschlands, Social Democratic
        Party (Federal Republic of Germany)
START   Strategic Arms Reduction Talks
TASM   tactical air-to-surface missile
TNF   theater nuclear forces

Note on Terminology

The terminology used to describe nuclear weapons can cause a lot of confusion. Categories and labels were constantly in flux, shaped by new strategic doctrines, new weapons systems, and new arms control agreements that set out and defined new classes of nuclear weapons. For much of the 1950s and 1960s, weapons were divided into two categories: strategic and tactical. Strategic use tended to refer to the prospect of firing on military targets (known as counterforce) or industrial and urban targets (known as countervalue), whereas tactical use remained much more localized and circumscribed to battlefield use. The proliferation of new weapons systems, such as nuclear-capable aircraft, blurred the lines between these two; a nuclear war fought in Europe with tactical weapons would be strategic for Europeans. Advances in technology and the emergence of new weapons spurred another category: theater nuclear forces. After the first use of this term at NATO in the late 1960s, theater nuclear forces remained the common shorthand for the alliance's various nuclear weapons within Europe. That category was divided yet further, sorting systems with different strike ranges, such as longer-range theater nuclear forces. In the early 1980s, the terminology shifted again, replacing the shorthand theater nuclear forces (TNF) with intermediate-range nuclear forces (INF).

Introduction
Security and Survival

E. P. Thompson paced back and forth before a packed hall. At the historic Oxford Union Debating Society on February 27, 1984, the eminent socialist historian and veteran peace campaigner brandished two pamphlets. One was *Soviet Military Power*, the latest glossy overview of Moscow's military might produced by the US Department of Defense. The other was the Soviet rebuttal, *Whence the Threat to Peace*. Waving the two, Thompson reminded his audience that just two men had controlled the vast arsenal cataloged therein throughout the tense autumn of 1983. Neither inspired much confidence. Yuri Andropov, the recently deceased Soviet general secretary, had been "on a kidney machine and half-dead from the neck down." Andropov's opposite number in Washington, Ronald Reagan, Thompson quipped, was "on an autocue machine and half-dead from the neck up."[1]

Thompson's sparring partner for the evening, Caspar Weinberger, looked on, pencil in hand, jotting down notes on a scrap of paper. The sitting US secretary of defense had made the trip across the Atlantic to plead Washington's case before a student debating society. The two men were an improbable pair: a prominent peace activist and a sitting cabinet secretary with a decidedly hawkish reputation. "Nothing like this has happened," the night's host, Edwin Newman, told viewers tuning in from the comfort of their own living rooms.[2]

The resolution being debated that night? That there was no "moral difference" between the foreign policies of the United States and the Soviet Union. "The view of the United States that is implicit in that motion," Newman explained, "is placing the Western Alliance under severe strain, threatening to split it, perhaps even destroy it."[3] This book is about how the North Atlantic Treaty Organization narrowly escaped such a fate.

That story revolves around the rise and fall of three kinds of missiles: SS-20 ballistic missiles, Pershing II ballistic missiles, and Gryphon ground-launched cruise missiles. Together, they came to be known as the Euromissiles. These weapons—usually called theater nuclear forces or, later, intermediate-range nuclear forces—targeted the great cities of Europe on both sides of the divided continent. Armed with these and thousands of other nuclear weapons systems, along with hundreds of thousands of troops, the United States and the Soviet Union could obliterate Europe and bring about World War III.

Typically, the history of the Euromissiles follows a familiar arc. After the Soviet Union began deploying the SS-20s in the mid-1970s, when this story often starts, the Western allies banded together to upgrade their own forces in Europe. With December 1979's Dual-Track Decision, NATO's members planned to deploy a new generation of US missiles to bases across Western Europe—in Belgium, the Federal Republic of Germany, Italy, the Netherlands, and the United Kingdom—starting in 1983. Record-breaking demonstrations across the West tried to derail these deployments, as did a vigorous propaganda campaign by the Soviet Union and its Eastern European allies in the Warsaw Pact. But NATO stood firm. In the autumn of 1983, the first US missiles arrived, and US-Soviet talks collapsed. A mere four years later, the United States and the Soviet Union signed an arms control agreement that embraced the seemingly impossible negotiating position the Reagan administration had first put forward in the autumn of 1981: to get rid of these weapons entirely. Under the terms of the Intermediate-Range Nuclear Forces Treaty signed in December 1987, Reagan and his Soviet counterpart, General Secretary Mikhail Gorbachev, agreed to eliminate an entire class of weapons, dismantling and destroying every land-based missile with a range from five hundred to fifty-five hundred kilometers. To reach that agreement, Gorbachev went much further than Reagan, agreeing to deep cuts far outstripping those required of the United States and leaving Washington's advantages in air- and sea-based systems unchecked. At every step, it seemed the perfect policy outcome for the Western allies.

But it was hardly so smooth in practice. Hindsight—and the certainty it affords—can make what ultimately transpired seem like the most logical or likely outcome, perhaps even one that could be easily replicated.[4]

For the Western allies, the successive decisions to field, deploy, and destroy the Euromissiles involved high-stakes gambles that might not have paid off. In the pages that follow, I tell a transatlantic history of the Euromissiles, from the arms race's origins in the early 1960s to the final days of the Cold War. Revisiting that history is a stark reminder of just how fragile the Atlantic alliance remained, even as communist governments across Europe hemorrhaged money and workers fled the workers' paradise.

NATO's history is not neatly packaged, tucked away in the alliance's archives in Brussels. The Atlantic alliance does not work that way, and any historian of NATO quickly confronts a deceptively simple question. What are we actually talking about when we talk about NATO?

At first glance, the answer seems straightforward: an alliance of like-minded North American and Western European states. But each of those fifteen—and, after Spain's accession in 1982, sixteen—countries had its own national interests, security priorities, and fears. An organizational chart of NATO is a bit like a work of abstract art, covered in boxes and lines denoting dozens of commands and committees and their various offshoots, both civilian and military. The Atlantic alliance has a language all its own, too, its documents replete with technical jargon and acronyms. And yet, despite these deliberative bodies and common shorthands, much of the alliance's decision-making occurs outside NATO's formal councils, taking place in national bodies, bilateral meetings, or ad hoc gatherings. Even within NATO's committees, officials would sit behind a placard bearing a country's name and were expected to represent their countries' interests, not those of the alliance writ large.

NATO's members did not have an equal degree of influence. The United States, with its economic power, superpower status, and nuclear arsenal, was unquestionably first among equals. As a result, we are often tempted to simplify the alliance's political process, casting it as a mere extension of Washington's preferences or the purview of only a few major players. But the premium placed on allied cohesion gave each member a voice, no matter its size or relative power.

Any history of NATO is an attempt to capture—and organize—an unruly web of individual members' foreign policy priorities, domestic political pressures, and jockeying between allied governments.[5] This book is no different. But while NATO occupies center stage, the history covered in the following twelve chapters also extends far beyond the councils of the alliance. Here, I put policymakers in conversation with protestors to show how and why the Euromissiles mattered.

We already know a great deal about the Euromissiles. No shortage of contemporaries followed the twists and turns of the superpowers' arms control talks, fretted over the tensions between the Western allies, and tried to make sense of what those protesting the Euromissiles hoped to achieve. Armed with a growing body of accessible archival evidence, historians have revisited old lines of inquiry and charted new ones, delving into the diplomatic, political, social, and cultural history of the Euromissiles. But few have put these various approaches together.[6]

This book does just that. It is a history of diplomacy and alliance politics, of social movements, and of strategy; it is about nuclear weapons and nagging fears, and about politics, both high and low. Only by putting these various strands back in conversation can we fully appreciate how and why the Western allies made policy as they did, how their adversaries and electorates shaped those calculations, and why those choices mattered. Writing that kind of history took me to archives on both sides of the Atlantic. I use the records of alliance committees, national governments, and antinuclear campaigners from Belgium, Canada, France, Germany, Italy, the Netherlands, the United Kingdom, and the United States to understand why the saga of the Euromissiles captivated so many.

As I pored over meeting minutes, press clippings, and television spots, I became increasingly skeptical of the language we often rely on to make sense of the Euromissiles. Scholars almost instinctively use the language of crisis. The episode is a slow-motion Cuban Missile Crisis or, simply, the Euromissiles Crisis.[7] Yet the contours of that crisis remain ill-defined. Was it triggered, as is often suggested, by Helmut Schmidt's October 1977 speech at London's International Institute of Strategic Studies, when the West German chancellor seemed to publicly question the US military commitment to Europe?[8] Certainly, Schmidt did not think so. He pointed to a "first mistake" much earlier, in the early 1960s, when the United States removed a set of ground-based missiles from NATO's arsenal in Europe.[9] An endpoint is no more certain. Did the crisis wind down when NATO began deploying the Pershing IIs and "glickums" (as almost everyone called the ground-launched cruise missiles) at the end of 1983? Or with the signing of the INF Treaty four years later?[10]

Nor is there any consensus about what, exactly, the essential ingredients of that crisis were. In other words, what made the crisis a crisis? There are any number of potential contenders: the nuclear arms race between the United States and the Soviet Union; the increased risk, both real and perceived, that a nuclear war might break out in Europe; the Cold War's seeming return to Europe and the widespread anxieties triggered by that realization; and the fracturing of the security consensus, to name but a few. Did the crisis pit NATO's members against their adversaries in the Warsaw Pact? Or were the sources of crisis internal to the Atlantic alliance? The more I dug into these questions, the more convinced I became that there were crises of all shapes and sizes everywhere.

Crisis was nothing new in allied circles. NATO's history is one of near-constant crisis.[11] Earlier episodes of transatlantic turmoil had divided the Western allies in public rows (the Suez Crisis), called into question the continued purpose of their alliance (the so-called NATO Crisis triggered by Charles de Gaulle), and threatened to unravel critical components of their defenses (the Offset Crisis).[12] "The NATO crisis," as Schmidt put it, "appears as the Loch Ness monster does—every summer in the British papers."[13]

The obsession with crisis can obscure as much as it reveals.[14] What set the Euromissiles apart was not the nature of the problems plaguing the Western allies, but the severity and frequency of these problems. The various, overlapping struggles over the Euromissiles exposed fault lines and uneasy compromises that had been present in the Atlantic alliance for decades, dating back to its creation in the late 1940s.[15] NATO's structure, in other words, was one virtually guaranteed to produce crises.

Four dilemmas defined NATO's structure of crisis throughout the Cold War. The first flowed from the allies' relationship with the Soviet Union. As long as the Soviet Union posed a clear and present danger to the Western allies, fear of the Kremlin was the glue that bound them together. If and when the threat posed by the Soviet Union appeared to wane, so too would the case for NATO. The second stemmed from the asymmetrical distribution of power among the allies. NATO's arrangements depended on the United States' commitment to protect Europe, yet that protection could easily be called into question. What if the Western allies no longer believed that commitment was credible or, at the other end of the spectrum, that the US weapons used to provide protection made war more, not less, likely? The third of these dilemmas was an extension of that logic. To keep the Soviets out and the Americans in, the Western allies relied on the destructive power of nuclear weapons. NATO's planners touted these terrible weapons as a guarantor of peace, but the human costs should deterrence fail would be catastrophic. The fourth dilemma revolved around the West Germans, who, more than any of the other allies, depended on these arrangements to ensure their security. What if those in the Federal Republic of Germany—its leaders or its voters—lost faith in the transatlantic bargain?

Since the signing of the North Atlantic Treaty in April 1949, the Western allies had struggled to develop a viable strategy that met the political, economic, and military requirements of NATO's members. Nuclear weapons offered a way out, making it possible to endorse a forward strategy as far east as possible without the considerable political and financial costs of matching the massive standing armies of the Soviet bloc.[16] Yet, NATO's reliance on nuclear weapons was a fragile arrangement. Any attempt to project military power to other territories as a form of protective cover—as the United States did through NATO—was more art than science. "To *fight* abroad is a military act," Thomas Schelling observed, "but to *persuade* enemies or allies that one would fight abroad, under circumstances of great cost and risk, requires more than military capability. It requires projecting intentions. It requires *having* those intentions, even deliberately acquiring them, and communicating them persuasively to make other countries behave."[17] But huddled together under the nuclear umbrella held up by the United States, the other allies routinely worried about what would happen if a storm actually came. Would the United States use its nuclear arsenal to defend its allies in Europe? If officials in Washington did follow through on their promises, was that even desirable? Victory in the atomic age might look devastatingly similar to defeat.[18]

After 1967, NATO's strategic doctrine envisioned a concept of escalation often referred to as flexible response. With a greater range of options for the use of force, nuclear and otherwise, the thinking went, the Western allies could respond to Soviet aggression without resorting to all-out nuclear war. But that doctrine relied on a healthy dose of well-placed ambiguity, papering over the fact that NATO's members hardly agreed about when and how escalation might take place. At its most basic, however, flexible response assumed a greater role for nuclear weapons stationed in Europe. If the strategy's primary objective of deterring aggression failed, these theater nuclear forces might be used as part of a limited response.[19]

Even that terminology illustrated the fraught nature of NATO's planning. To refer to theater nuclear forces or tactical weapons ignored what would happen if these capabilities in Europe were ever used. To Europeans, how far a nuclear warhead had traveled before it hit them scarcely made a difference. Helmut Schmidt bemoaned "the peculiar habit" of US policymakers who defined strategic weapons as "only such weapons which could hit their own soil and their own cities." For Schmidt and his fellow Germans, even a strike by a battlefield nuclear weapon would be "a strategic event."[20]

The uncertainties of nuclear strategy only added to these anxieties. Strategists had developed doctrines and war plans that harnessed the awesome destructive power of nuclear weapons in the hope that those same weapons would never be used. The backbone of NATO's defenses—deterrence—relied on making threats in order to protect the status quo. (Its close cousin compellence envisioned the use of threats to revise or restore that status quo.)[21] But the basic principles underpinning that pursuit of peace were themselves uncertain, predicated on intangibles and unprovable assumptions.[22] "An awful lot of strategic doctrine in the Cold War," one US official later summed up, "was mind-playing." Strategies and slogans imposed a sense of order in an attempt to alter the behavior of adversaries and allies alike, but also to reassure their architects about the logic of drafting plans and building weapons with consequences too horrifying to contemplate.[23] "How can you explain to people," one former West German defense minister, Hans Apel, wondered, "that you defend peace and freedom with weapons which if they, once they are used will destroy mankind?"[24]

Those responsible for NATO's defenses struggled with the same question. Could the United States reassure its allies, particularly those on the front lines in Europe, that Washington would protect them? Who needed to be reassured? Was it possible to reassure political leaders without terrifying their constituents? Or without terrifying their adversaries?

In an alliance primarily made up of democracies, strategic policies required a degree of support at the ballot box. Democracy, as no shortage of allied officials appreciated, was a permeable and fragile system. The prospect that their own voters—or finicky constituents in other NATO member states—might reject the alliance's policies constrained their options and colored their choices as they tried to make their policies palatable. In a struggle between rival ideologies, democracy was a double-edged sword. It was a source of considerable strength, used to rally the proverbial troops to defend their freedoms in the face of communist alternatives.[25] Yet it was also an easily exploited weakness. The system's permeability and transparency could be harnessed to turn citizens in the West against their governments—and against NATO.[26] Time and again, frustrated officials on both sides of the Atlantic bemoaned the seeming ease with which the Soviet Union could manage public opinion, certainly compared to their own efforts with unruly electorates.

It was those unruly electorates who took to the streets in record numbers in the early 1980s. Catholic bishops and uniformed soldiers marched alongside punks, hippies, and grandmothers rallying around slogans like "Together, we can stop the bomb."[27] In town squares and community centers, neighbors debated the dangers of nuclear weapons and the point of alliances. As swaths of the electorate questioned the wisdom of NATO's Dual-Track Decision, it became more and more difficult to sustain popular support for the alliance's nuclear addiction. In the face of growing opposition, could NATO preserve the nuclear options its planners still deemed necessary to preserve the peace in Europe? These problems deepened over the decade, the result of a growing rejection of the Cold War's binary logic and of the ordering principles that defined NATO's role.[28] Voters and elected representatives across the Atlantic alliance wondered about the wisdom of nuclear deterrence and questioned the benefits of the United States' continued protection. If NATO remained dependent on protection from the United States, were Western Europeans still willing to live alongside the terrible weapons that seemed to require? In the spring of 1989, the alliance seemed hopelessly divided over this question.

These problems were the product of tensions and structural dilemmas woven into the very fabric of the alliance: the chronic tensions between détente with and deterrence of the Soviet Union; the paradox of providing for Europe's security with weapons that could annihilate everyone they were intended to protect; and the delicate balancing act required to sustain a transatlantic security order that constrained the power of the Federal Republic of Germany without leaving the Germans convinced that they were second-class citizens. What ensured NATO's survival was not the strength of the alliance's policies; it was the boldness of Mikhail Gorbachev's vision and his sweeping program of reforms. Glasnost and perestroika, one observer wryly noted, "bailed out the incredibility of flexible response."[29]

This book is about fear. Policymakers worried that NATO might fall apart, while pundits sounded the alarm over and over, concerned that the latest dust-up or diplomatic row might be the one to finally deal a fatal blow to the Atlantic alliance. At foreign ministries and intelligence agencies, analysts worried that the Soviets might be able to win the Cold War without even firing a shot, by systematically turning voters against their governments and ally against ally. Protestors worried about the dangers of nuclear annihilation, whether on purpose or through some sort of terrible technical malfunction. A placard hoisted by one Göttingen demonstrator spoke for millions: "I'm afraid of a nuclear war."[30]

The Euromissiles—and the dangers they represented—shaped the politics and culture of an era. Their impact was felt at the ballot box, on the streets, and over the airwaves. Listeners tuned in to hear Nena sing about a nuclear war inadvertently triggered by ninety-nine red balloons or Sting's hope that the Russians loved their children too.[31] Even the James Bond franchise got in on the action with 1983's *Octopussy*. The 007 of the day, Roger Moore, foiled the plans of a rogue Soviet general and saved the world from nuclear catastrophe.[32] We now know that the doomsday scenarios that inspired everything from *WarGames* to war-gaming remained the stuff of fiction.[33] But for those living through it, that outcome was far from certain.

These twelve chapters are about these fears, how they evolved, and why they endured. I chart how protestors, policymakers, and pundits tried to make sense of what security looked like in an age defined by nuclear weapons and Cold War competition. That story unfolds in a triptych, divided into three parts.

Part 1, Decide, uncovers the long and diverse origins of NATO's December 1979 Dual-Track Decision. To understand that decision, I begin almost twenty years earlier with the Cold War's stabilization in Europe following the Cuban Missile Crisis. As the contours of a more stable European order took shape, that order transformed the Atlantic alliance and remade world politics. To casual observers, the rise of détente, whether superpower or European, suggested a waning of the Cold War. Throughout the 1970s, the Western allies struggled to pursue détente yet also maintain their defenses in the face of expanding Soviet power. Though by no means the only signal of the Soviets' drive for true superpower status, the SS-20 underscored a multitude of strategic, economic, and political challenges plaguing the Western allies in the 1970s. How to meet these challenges was far from obvious, and the Dual-Track Decision was a classic product of alliance politics, shaped by compromises and political constraints. NATO's members returned to a familiar formula: the parallel pursuit of détente and defense enshrined in the Harmel Report of 1967. Mimicking that parallel structure, the Dual-Track Decision married plans to deploy new missiles to Western Europe with the promise of arms control. It attempted to thread the needle, offering reassurance that the alliance's strategy of flexible response remained remotely credible—and that the United States would defend Western Europe—while trying to limit the political fallout from fielding new nuclear weapons.

If the Dual-Track Decision reassured some, it terrified others. NATO's plans to station new nuclear weapons in Europe quickly became a lightning rod for popular anxieties and brought the politics of alliance and questions of nuclear strategy to new audiences. Part 2, Deploy, zeroes in on these debates to show how they threatened NATO's policies and why the Western allies forged ahead with the Dual-Track Decision in the face of such immense opposition. No longer confined to specialist circles, the debates of the early 1980s spilled out into the streets, the subject of nightly news segments and dinner table arguments. Columnists and concerned citizens had just as much to say about the Euromissiles—and fundamental questions about how to wage the Cold War and the consequences of doing so—as those charged with making foreign policy. Though protestors were often cast in opposition to the officials elected to represent them, the dividing lines were never so neat. It was precisely because this conversation was so wide-ranging that it proved so dangerous. Even as the Western allies cobbled together enough support to begin deploying the Pershing IIs and cruise missiles in late 1983, they appreciated that it had come at the cost of calling into question nearly all of the assumptions on which NATO rested.

Part 3, Destroy, picks up with the Soviet Union's response, walking out of the INF talks. It explains why, within the span of just four years, the Western allies went from deploying Pershing IIs and cruise missiles to dismantling them. That dramatic shift depended on Mikhail Gorbachev. The Soviet general secretary's willingness to reconsider old orthodoxies, and his desire to break free of the arms race, cleared the path to an agreement eliminating the superpowers' intermediate-range nuclear forces. Once an agreement seemed possible, many in allied circles panicked. It turned out that their earlier gambles had come at a cost, and, though they were wary of the strategic and political implications of destroying the missiles, their hands were forced. NATO's leaders had been calling for a solution abolishing the Euromissiles since the autumn of 1981. How could they turn around and disavow that proposal now that it finally seemed attainable? These anxieties only intensified once the United States and the Soviet Union signed the INF Treaty, this time centered on the modernization of NATO's short-range nuclear forces. Even as Germans took chisels to the Berlin Wall and communist regimes across Eastern Europe crumbled, the Western allies agonized over the erosion of their own defenses. But the modernization of NATO's short-range nuclear forces was swept away with the Cold War itself, as the Western allies relegated the earlier doctrine of flexible response to the ash heap of history.

When E. P. Thompson and Caspar Weinberger squared off at the Oxford Union, the resolution made no mention of the Euromissiles. But it was that controversy that had brought the two men together. Thompson envisioned a world in which "two ossified gerontocracies" would no longer hold Europeans "in mortal fear under the protection of their nuclear umbrellas." Weinberger rejected any such equivalence between the two superpowers. He pointed to the Fulda Gap dividing the two Germanys. "Our observation towers face east," he reminded the audience. So too did the Warsaw Pact's. How could there be moral equivalency between an alliance protecting its people and one keeping them prisoner?[34]

Like Thompson and Weinberger, those who debated the Euromissiles confronted much larger questions. Would nuclear weapons make them safer? What about the alliances that divided Europe? How should the Cold War be prosecuted? Was it worth fighting at all? This is a history of how individuals understood the dangers to their world and tried to preserve the peace within it.

PART ONE

Decide

Helmut Schmidt was certain that NATO's strat-
egy needed to change. The alliance's existing arrangements simply no longer
made sense. The balance of power between the United States and the Soviet
Union had shifted, and strategy needed to shift accordingly. "The dilemma
of these next few years," he wrote in 1961, "lies in the fact that a nuclear balance of increasing stability will be achieved between the two major powers,
but that in face of it the West has nothing to put in place of all-out nuclear
retaliation as a deterrent against non-nuclear aggression." The growth of the
Soviet Union's arsenal, in other words, created a dangerous degree of parity
between the two superpowers.[1]

Schmidt's preferred solution, sketched out in 1961's *Verteidigung oder
Vergeltung (Defense or Retaliation)*, was an approach characterized by greater
flexibility and more options. "The strategies devised for the defense of
Europe," Schmidt argued, "must make up a continuous system extending
without gaps from cold war to total and general war." The Western allies
should be prepared to "present the aggressor with intolerable risks at the lowest as at the highest level of possible warfare."[2] Schmidt's thinking reflected
arguments put forward by British strategists in the 1950s, then picked up and
popularized within the United States.[3]

Confident and well-spoken, with a penchant for menthol cigarettes,
Schmidt was a strategist in his own right. And as he considered the onset

of parity in the late 1950s and into the 1960s, he began to develop a strategy of balance.[4] An SPD member of the West German Bundestag, Schmidt had supported the creation of a nuclear weapon–free zone in Central Europe; removing nuclear weapons from the region, he believed, could serve as a precursor to further negotiations to slash the standing armies at the heart of the continent.[5] "Arms limitation," he wrote in *Verteidigung oder Vergeltung*, "must lead to a general balance or equilibrium made up of a series of partial balances at the levels of the various forms of possible warfare."[6]

Constant efforts to maintain balance would prevent war from breaking out in Europe.[7] Starting from that premise, Schmidt continued to develop his ideas throughout the 1960s. His 1969 book, dedicated to exploring the impact that strategic parity would have on the German question, appeared under the title *Strategie des Gleichgewichts* (*Strategy of Balance*).[8] That strategy prioritized balance in multiple forms. Schmidt envisioned not only a military balance at various levels but also a balance of tactics to secure that equilibrium. The constant renewal of the balance would require continued investment in NATO's defenses but also the pursuit of arms control negotiations. "What matters," Schmidt argued, "is to arrive, in addition to the balance in the military field, at a similar balance in the political and psychological fields." Doing so would give "the precarious peace of today a more stable foundation."[9] He took those ideas with him into the top levels of government in the Federal Republic of Germany, becoming defense minister in Willy Brandt's new coalition in October of 1969.

Schmidt's strategy of balance defined the debates of the next decade, most famously in his October 1977 speech at London's International Institute for Strategic Studies. "Strategic arms limitations confined to the United States and the Soviet Union," Schmidt, now chancellor of the Federal Republic, concluded, "will inevitably impair the security of the West European members of the Alliance vis-à-vis [the] Soviet military in Europe if we do not succeed in removing the disparities of military power in Europe." The balance so critical to peace, according to Schmidt, was slipping away.[10]

The five chapters that follow show that the path to NATO's Dual-Track Decision was far from linear. Throughout the 1960s and 1970s, allied officials—not just Schmidt—struggled to find a balance between détente, arms control, and defense policies. Chapter 1 sets the stage, showing how the political stalemate that emerged in the 1960s remade the Atlantic alliance. By the end of that decade, NATO had adopted a more graduated strategy, often known as flexible response, and carved out a political role as an alliance dedicated to more than deterring and, if needed, defending against Soviet aggression. Strong defenses, the allies argued, could underwrite the search for political solutions to the most pressing geopolitical problems. Chapter 2 traces how the Western Europeans and, in particular, the West Germans lost confidence in the protection afforded by the US nuclear arsenal throughout the 1970s. Strategic arms control and the embrace of parity early in the decade left Washington's allies feeling exposed and vulnerable to Soviet political pressure. These anxieties only deepened as the decade wore on and Soviet capabilities multiplied, as chapter 3 shows. The development and deployment of a new Soviet medium-range missile, the SS-20, injected a degree of urgency into these debates, as the Western allies argued about whether these new nuclear weapons would decrease Western Europe's security. Chapter 4 delves into a controversy that dominated NATO's deliberations in 1977 and 1978: the so-called neutron bomb affair. Though ultimately the alliance's schemes collapsed, the deliberations over the neutron bomb laid critical foundations for the Dual-Track Decision. The Western allies hammered out an agreement that would combine plans to deploy new weapons with offers to limit those same deployments. The collapse of the alliance's plans injected a new sense of urgency into the parallel debates regarding the Soviets' SS-20s and NATO's nuclear posture in Europe. Chapter 5 picks up in 1979 to show how the Western allies translated broad ideas into the final Dual-Track Decision. The decision that the Western allies adopted in December 1979 endorsed the very essence of Schmidt's strategy of balance. NATO would deploy a new generation of theater nuclear forces to Western Europe, yet at the same time extend an arms control offer to reduce those systems—and the Soviets' SS-20s. Security could be reached through defense modernization or arms control but, however it was done, the balance needed to be maintained.

CHAPTER 1

The Sixties Stalemate

On October 22, 1962, John F. Kennedy told tele-
vision viewers about an ominous development off the shores of the United
States. He had "unmistakable evidence" of the Soviet Union's build-up on
the island of Cuba. From these missile sites, the Soviets could strike major
cities across the Western Hemisphere, from the northern reaches of Canada's Hudson Bay all the way to Lima, Peru. To bring Soviet construction to
a halt, Kennedy announced plans to impose a naval blockade, quarantining
the Caribbean island.[1]

Determined to find a solution short of escalation, Kennedy entertained
the possibility of a trade with Soviet General Secretary Nikita Khrushchev.
Perhaps, if the United States removed its Jupiter missiles in Turkey, the Soviet
Union would withdraw its missiles from Cuba. Kennedy's advisers balked
at the idea. A trade would unravel the United States' position in Europe.
"We cannot get into the position of appearing to sell out an ally," Kennedy's
national security adviser, McGeorge Bundy, warned. If they did, the Soviets' certain next step would be to demand the complete denuclearization of
NATO territory, another adviser, Paul Nitze, worried.[2]

Kennedy forged ahead, dispatching his brother to sound out the Soviet
ambassador in Washington, Anatoly Dobrynin. The United States was prepared to attack Cuba, Robert Kennedy told Dobrynin, but he could offer a

way out. If the Soviets removed their missiles within the next twenty-four hours, the Americans promised not to invade Moscow's Caribbean client. To sweeten the deal, he mentioned the Jupiters, leading Dobrynin to believe that the president had already ordered those missiles removed months ago, and that they would be gone in a few months' time. Lest the Soviets mistake the situation, the American made clear that this assurance needed to remain a secret. "This is not a deal," he told Dobrynin, "and if you breathe a word of it in public, the deal is off."[3] The next morning, Khrushchev announced that the Soviet Union would dismantle and withdraw its missiles from Cuba.

After the superpowers' close call in Cuba, the Cold War settled into a more predictable pattern. The political situation in Europe stabilized, tempered by recent reminders in divided Berlin and in the Caribbean of what war would mean in the thermonuclear age. The destructive power of nuclear weapons now brought a degree of stability, however uneasy, to the European continent. As the threat of war receded, NATO's success became a liability. In a world where the Soviet Union seemed unlikely to invade Western Europe, what purpose did the alliance serve?

Stability obscured change. Throughout the 1960s, the Soviet Union moved to close the nuclear gap with the United States. As that gap narrowed, the earlier assumptions that had guided NATO's planning no longer held true. The Western powers could no longer rely, as they once had, on a preponderance of nuclear firepower to offset the Soviet Union's enormous conventional forces. But economic pressures and the demands of domestic politics constrained the alliance's options for preserving its position of superiority.

Confronted with this stalemate, a generation of leaders turned to the tools of diplomacy. A degree of rapprochement between East and West could ensure a stable Europe and free up much-needed resources. Perhaps it might even begin to blur the lines of the continent's division as the ties between East and West multiplied. But détente's champions did not come to the policy with the same objectives. For some, like Richard Nixon and Henry Kissinger, détente was a fundamentally conservative strategy, designed to preserve sufficient strength to wage the Cold War over the long haul. Others, such as Willy Brandt and Egon Bahr, saw its potential to transform international politics in the long term and to overcome the Cold War. But in the immediate sense, both of these grand strategies accepted the status quo. Implicitly and explicitly, détente reinforced the message that the West could do business with the Soviets.

At Cold War's End?

Cuba was Nikita Khrushchev's last big bet. The Soviet general secretary had gambled in divided Berlin, attempting to squeeze the Western powers out of their island of capitalism in the East. Thousands of miles away, in Cuba, Khrushchev tried to defend a friendly regime in Havana against the threat of US invasion. Khrushchev had taken the world to the brink—not once, but twice.[4]

Khrushchev's gambits failed. The general secretary tried to cultivate the image of a Soviet Union on the march. Cuba, in particular, proved a stunning blow to that image. Khrushchev's colleagues mobilized to turf the general secretary out of office and replace him with a steadier, more predictable hand.[5] Humiliated by how events had unfolded in Cuba, Soviet leaders ramped up their military spending even further.[6] Khrushchev's successors changed tactics, but they did not abandon his vision of achieving a degree of superpower status that rivaled that of the United States—and was recognized as such.

As Soviet spending skyrocketed, the contours of a political settlement began to take shape in Europe. The Western powers learned to live with the Berlin Wall dividing the city's two halves, just as the Soviet Union did with the presence of British, French, and US forces in West Berlin. Formal agreements followed these tacit compromises. In the summer of 1963, the United States, the United Kingdom, and the Soviet Union agreed to the Limited Test Ban Treaty. To casual observers, the treaty heralded a new era in relations and a breakthrough in world politics. For those steeped in the negotiations, however, it was a joint effort to ensure that the West Germans remained far from a nuclear trigger.[7]

By 1963, a status quo had emerged. With that sense of stability came a diminution of the Cold War's central place in international politics. Shifts in the patterns of power gradually eroded the sharp divisions separating the capitalist world from the communist one. From Paris to Beijing, leaders challenged the strictures of a bipolar order.[8] But there remained a difference between power and the illusion thereof. "While new centers of *ambition* have sprung into existence, no new centers of *power* are visible anywhere on the map of the present world," the political editor of *Die Zeit*, Theo Sommer, concluded in 1964.[9]

Ambition could have easily been the slogan of Charles de Gaulle's France. Under the general's direction, France mounted a systematic campaign against US leadership and the political legitimacy of the Atlantic alliance.[10] De Gaulle pressed steadily against US influence in European affairs, a crusade that set NATO squarely within his sights. Shortly after his return to power in 1958, de Gaulle informed the Americans that the alliance no longer met "the conditions of security in the free world."[11]

The Cuban Missile Crisis all but confirmed de Gaulle's view. He came away convinced that the United States and the Soviet Union would not risk going to war with one another. "The threat," de Gaulle told Charles Bohlen, the US ambassador to France, "had now apparently diminished to the point where virtually no one in Europe, and . . . in the United States, believed in a Soviet attack."[12] De Gaulle, Bohlen concluded, thought that the Cold War was all but finished. He prepared to transcend it—and the alliances it had brought into being.[13] Confident that NATO's military tasks were now complete, de Gaulle insisted that solutions to the underlying problems in world politics would be found outside the structures of alliances, not within their confines. A détente with the East was not, in de Gaulle's estimation, a task to be pursued under NATO's banner.

Though French to its core, the Gaullist challenge capitalized on severe strains within the alliance, as members both large and small sought revisions that would align NATO's procedures with the realities of the 1960s.[14] Gone were the weak, war-ravaged European economies of the alliance's early years. And with the reconstruction of European power came a renewed sense of confidence—and a desire to be treated accordingly. The European allies chafed at Washington's control over NATO's strategy, demanding a greater voice in the process. "Europeans," as Robert Bowie put it, "are not likely to be satisfied for the long run with a solution leaving all decisions to the president."[15] It was not as if the Europeans had a say in who occupied the post.

Demands for greater control came alongside an erosion of faith in the promises and protection afforded by extended deterrence. Since NATO's inception, the Western powers had relied on a "balance of imbalances," wherein the Soviet Union's conventional superiority was offset by overwhelming US nuclear superiority and the promise that this deterrent would be extended to cover Western Europe.[16] The advent of Soviet intercontinental ballistic missiles changed that calculus, and by the early 1960s, few in the capitals of Europe believed that leaders in Washington would defend their territory as if it were the US heartland. The United States' attempts to introduce a new strategy, known as flexible response, only amplified this crisis of confidence. Critics of this new US approach concentrated their fire on the strategy's potential to, in what became popular alliance jargon, "decouple" the defense of Europe from that of North America. If a war in Europe would not immediately escalate to an all-out strategic conflict between the superpowers, then the Soviet Union might come to the conclusion that such a war could be fought—and won.[17] "Either war takes place in Europe and we're destroyed," as de Gaulle put it, "or it's an exchange involving massive retaliation, and that's a matter for America and the Soviet Union. So what's the Alliance for?"[18]

De Gaulle's alternative would be a European project predicated on French power. With the French *non* to British membership in the European Economic Community in 1963, it was clear that project of European integration would be, at least for the time being, confined to the continent. Unlike NATO, it would also exclude the United States. The French logic seemed plain to Paris's neighbors, albeit unpersuasive. "De Gaulle rejects the Atlantic Alliance because there France (and the other states) depends on America's nuclear armory," the West German political scientist Klaus Wehnert concluded, "but he desires a European alliance in which the other partners depend on the nuclear arms of France." If the West Germans had to trust someone else for their defense, Wehnert remained convinced that the Americans were the safer bet.[19] His elected representatives reached the same conclusion.

Defense, Deterrence, Détente

On March 7, 1966, Charles de Gaulle notified Paris's allies that France would withdraw from NATO's integrated command structure. It was the latest in a series of moves to sever France's formal military ties to the alliance, one by one. France intended, as de Gaulle phrased it in his formal notice, to "recover the entire exercise of her sovereignty over her territory."[20] This notice of withdrawal did not mean an end to Paris's participation in NATO's political bodies, only its military arrangements. "They were in and they were out," as one US official summed up the situation.[21]

France's withdrawal forced other problems out into the open. The seeming erosion of the Cold War had left allied officials scrambling to find a new justification for NATO's continued existence. To make matters worse, the North Atlantic Treaty permitted any of the allies to abrogate their membership in the alliance after twenty years, a deadline looming on the horizon in 1969.[22]

Just as de Gaulle believed it was time to move beyond the alliance, so too might voters on both sides of the Atlantic. NATO's successes containing the Soviet menace could spell the alliance's demise. "NATO's Malady Is Its Success," one headline argued.[23] Another asked, "Has Success Spoiled NATO?"[24] "If only the Russians were still frightening NATO, they would provide us with the only sure guarantee of its salvation," the *New York Times*'s diplomatic correspondent Max Frankel wrote as 1965 came to a close. "Unfortunately, for NATO geostrategists, however, the Western nations have never been more prosperous or secure, which is why their formal alliance is having what is ironically called the Crisis."[25] If NATO had been created to deter Soviet aggression, what purpose did the alliance have in a world where the prospect that the Warsaw Pact's armies would sweep westward across the continent seemed to be virtually nil?

This line of argumentation encouraged advocates of arms control, both in the corridors of power and far beyond them. If the Soviet Union no longer posed a meaningful threat to the Western powers, why should they not try to reduce the dangers—and financial burdens—of the arms race?

But this spirit of negotiation need not spell the end for NATO. "Only if the Western nations remain together, even in the absence of an acute threat to Europe's danger point, Berlin, and in the face of seeming Soviet reasonableness," Theo Sommer concluded, "only then can they hope to harvest the fruits of their past labor."[26] A growing number of allied officials began to rely on this same rhetoric, casting the continued strength of NATO as a necessary precondition to negotiate with the Soviets. "Where necessary, we shall defend freedom," Lyndon Johnson vowed in October 1966. "Where possible, we shall work with the East to build a lasting peace."[27] Privately, some officials returned to another justification for the alliance. NATO remained the only plausible mechanism to contain West German power. The "real danger" of the French withdrawal, Bohlen argued, was that it might bring about another Soviet-German rapprochement like that reached at Rapallo in 1922.[28]

Still wedded to the earlier logic of the alliance, Lyndon Johnson and his advisers hoped to put NATO on a more solid footing.[29] In this task, they found an ally in Belgium's foreign minister, Pierre Harmel. In December 1966, Harmel called for a study to reflect on the future of the alliance.[30] The Belgian proposal was a revived and repackaged version of an earlier Canadian initiative.[31] But in 1964, the Canadian proposal seemed an unnecessary bureaucratic exercise. Two years later, in the wake of the French exit, these new political realities demanded a direct response.

Harmel and his colleagues—including France's Maurice Couve de Murville—agreed "to study the future tasks which face the alliance," with explicit reference to how NATO would be "a factor for durable peace."[32] Consultations settled on four areas of study: East-West relations, relations between the NATO allies, the defensive policies of the alliance, and developments outside of Europe and North America. Four subgroups, one dedicated to each of these topics, set to work drafting a report.

The entire exercise was, first and foremost, one of public relations. Pierre Harmel's case for the study admitted as much. The public's impressions were what mattered. The Western allies "must show that the Alliance was looking forward," he implored his fellow ministers, "since this would have a favorable psychological effect."[33] That impulse kept the study on the rails, moving toward a tangible final product even in the face of countless difficulties.[34] Members of the French delegation seemed poised to scuttle the exercise throughout, with representatives speaking openly of how they could let NATO "die in its own sweet time."[35] And the French, though by far the most vocal, were hardly the only source of disagreement.[36]

But the allies could ill afford to lose an opportunity to make a more compelling case for NATO. The widespread perception that the Soviet threat had dissipated stripped the alliance of much of its earlier justification in the court of public opinion. Demographic trends seemed poised to make the problem worse. As a new generation came of age, allied officials doubted that these young people would instinctively come to the same conclusions about the need for an alliance like NATO. Joseph Luns, the Dutch foreign minister, worried about "a growing questioning and scepticism about the meaning and purpose of NATO, especially among the younger generation who had no direct experience of Communist tactics in the post-war period."[37]

The final report, published in December 1967, described an alliance based on twin pillars. NATO's primary function remained the preservation of sufficient military and political strength to deter the Soviet Union. But the alliance's success to date, the allies argued, laid the foundations from which to launch a second task: the pursuit of a more stable and constructive relationship with the Warsaw Pact. "The way to peace and stability in Europe rests in particular on the use of the Alliance constructively in the interest of détente," the report affirmed.[38] That formulation implicitly rebuked the Gaullist line of thinking. Détente was not, as de Gaulle had argued, antithetical to the alliance's functions. Solutions to the political problems that divided East and West, the allies maintained instead, could only come with the continuation of a strong alliance made up of the Western powers. Until those solutions were found, NATO's mission would remain incomplete: "NATO will not have fulfilled its military tasks until its political tasks have also been resolved."[39] Secretary General Manlio Brosio likened this parallel strategy to marching on two legs.[40]

An official endorsement of détente did not signify that the various Western allies had come to any common understanding about what that détente meant. Nor were the report's authors under any illusions about the potential for political trouble. Karl Schütz and Adam Watson, the rapporteurs responsible for the subgroup on East-West relations, warned that the Soviets' interest in détente reflected the continuation of traditional Muscovite objectives: "to weaken the cohesion of the alliance, to drive wedges between the states of Western Europe and open up differences between Western Europe and the United States."[41]

Despite these realistic appraisals of Soviet intentions, the Western allies put détente front and center in NATO's new public image. Simultaneously verbose and anodyne, the Harmel Report was given pride of place at the North Atlantic Council's December 1967 ministerial meeting. The final communiqué lauded the "extensive bilateral contacts made in recent months" between the two blocs and "expressed the hope that these efforts might lead to progress in the settlement of outstanding European problems."[42] NATO's Information Service produced glossy pamphlets dedicated to the contents of the Harmel Report.[43] One such leaflet, 1968's *Why NATO?*, made the case succinctly, as it summed up the alliance's mission with three Ds: defense, deterrence, and détente.[44]

To burnish NATO's credentials as an engine of détente, allied governments turned to the possibility of arms control negotiations to reduce the standing armies of Europe, both East and West. During the drafting of the Harmel Report, the idea of "balanced force reductions" gained traction. In June 1967, the British delegation recommended that the allies create an ad hoc working group to study the idea, seeing it as "a valuable supplement" to the work under way as part of the Harmel exercise.[45] The Harmel Report made mention of this possibility, assuring readers that the allies were "studying disarmament and practical arms control measures, including the possibility of balanced force reductions."[46] These studies continued throughout the spring and summer of 1968, and when allied ministers met in Reykjavik that June, they issued a public declaration calling for talks with the Warsaw Pact to reduce conventional forces in Europe.[47] "Behind NATO's continuing push toward détente," one reporter concluded of this latest overture, "lies the rising wind of public demand in the West—and a cool self-analysis of self-interest."[48] Détente might respond to popular attitudes, but there was always the risk that those attitudes could change.

The Ambiguity of Flexibility

Détente might have provided a new rationale for the alliance, but NATO's other Ds—defense and deterrence—were by no means insulated from change. By 1967, the allies had established a new consultative body, the Nuclear Planning Group, in what Brosio described as "an authentic sharing of nuclear responsibilities."[49] That May, defense ministers endorsed plans to develop a new strategic concept incorporating the ideas of flexible response.[50] France's departure from the integrated command smoothed the path, as it removed the most vociferous critics of flexible response from NATO's military decision-making process. But a series of trilateral talks between the Federal Republic, the United Kingdom, and the United States begun in 1966 in an attempt to defuse the so-called Offset Crisis made it possible to adopt a new strategic doctrine.

The core problem was one of currency, not strategy. NATO's defense arrangements were increasingly untenable, with the financial burdens too high to shoulder. "Without either a break in the European arms race or a willingness on the part of the Western European powers to assume a greater part of the NATO defense burden," one US academic, Betty Goetz Lall, predicted in 1964, "the U.S. will continue to feel the pinch in its balance of payments, resulting from the maintenance of large numbers of troops in Europe."[51] The situation was even worse in London. Staring down acute economic difficulties, the British tried to shift the costs of the British Army on the Rhine to the West Germans through a 100 percent offset. In other words, Bonn would make enough arms purchases from the United Kingdom to cover the full costs of the British forces. When Harold Wilson's government threatened to pare back its troops in the Federal Republic, the potential threat to NATO was clear. Western Europe's defense relied in part on the United Kingdom's continental commitment. Worse still, the Americans might follow suit. Senator Mike Mansfield introduced a resolution calling for cuts to the US forces in Europe in August 1966, concerned about the United States' widening war in Vietnam and its mounting balance-of-payment problems.[52] The West Germans could not meet their existing payment obligations to the United States, let alone shoulder more of the financial burden. Meanwhile, as governments struggled to make payments, their domestic political opponents made much of the other uses to which those funds could be put.[53]

To find a way out, the Johnson administration proposed talks with London and Bonn dedicated to troop deployments and the balance-of-payments problem along with broader questions about NATO's strategy and how best to share the burden. The trilateral nature of these discussions left the other allies aghast—what was the difference between this triumvirate and de Gaulle's earlier schemes for a directorate with the British and Americans? Permanent representatives pressed for this work to be brought into the formal channels of the alliance.[54]

The trilateral talks ensured that the United States and the United Kingdom maintained troops on the continent, albeit with some reductions.[55] But the entire episode revealed how vulnerable the alliance was to both economic and domestic political pressures. NATO's Military Committee came to the same conclusion. Even if the Western allies wished to match the Soviet Union's armies man for man, their parliaments and budgets would not allow it.[56] With the most immediate problems behind them, the Johnson administration appreciated that one of the alliance's smaller members, like Canada, with its own contingent in Germany, could easily trigger a new round of difficulties.[57]

As part of the tripartite deliberations, the Federal Republic, the United States, and the United Kingdom laid down the foundations for a new strategic doctrine that embraced the basic ideas of flexible response.[58] Alongside those discussions, NATO's Military Committee commissioned a draft outline study on strategy in October 1966.[59] With these recommendations in hand, the pursuit of a new strategic concept received political backing in May 1967 when the Defense Planning Committee, made up of the Fourteen—the allies, excluding France—issued guidance calling for the revision of the alliance's strategy to permit "a greater flexibility."[60] The ministerial guidance reflected an uneasy consensus among the allies, "not wholly satisfactory to any NATO member, including the United States."[61]

By year's end, the Fourteen had reached an agreement. The Defense Planning Committee formally endorsed a new strategic concept on December 12, 1967, and the full details were set out in a Military Committee document, "Overall Strategic Concept for the Defense of the North Atlantic Treaty Organization Area," or MC 14/3, dated January 16, 1968. The new strategic concept stressed escalation, not just flexibility. MC 14/3 described the concept's foundation as a degree of flexibility that would "prevent the potential aggressor from predicting with confidence NATO's specific response to aggression" and, as a result, "lead him to conclude that an unacceptable degree of risk would be involved regardless of the nature of his attack." The document went on to describe three possible responses to any aggression against the alliance's territory: direct defense, deliberate escalation, and general nuclear response. Direct defense would respond at the level chosen by the enemy, while deliberate escalation introduced additional possibilities "to defeat aggression by raising but where possible controlling . . . the scope and intensity of combat." As part of that escalation, MC 14/3 proposed a range of potential responses, from the demonstrative use of nuclear weapons to the opening of another front. The final option remained general nuclear response, which MC 14/3 described as "the ultimate deterrent."[62]

NATO's new strategic concept envisioned forward defense and flexibility of response. But beyond these general principles, the strategy left a number of questions unresolved. At what point would the allies decide to use nuclear weapons? When and on what terms would they resort to deliberate escalation, let alone a general nuclear response? How far would they first be willing to let the situation in Europe deteriorate?

The lack of answers to these questions was a critical ingredient to the doctrine's political success in the short term. Ambiguity made it possible for flexible response to address the security needs of NATO's various members "without necessarily conveying the same meaning to each of them."[63] A degree of elasticity left it open to individual interpretation, meaning that the doctrine could be seen as an extension of existing policy preferences, even if the allies did not all come to the same conclusions. Although flexible response was hardly a robust strategic consensus, the Western powers lived with it and "took it seriously," as British prime minister James Callaghan later concluded, "because there was nothing better."[64]

The doctrine of flexible response required a range of forces, both conventional and nuclear. MC 14/3 called for a "full spectrum of capabilities," clustered into three categories: conventional forces, tactical nuclear forces, and strategic nuclear forces. The second of these, tactical nuclear forces, played a critical role in the chain of escalation. These tactical capabilities would, in the words of MC 14/3, confront "the enemy with the prospect of consequent escalation of the conflict" and "deter, and if necessary respond to, the use of tactical nuclear weapons by posing the threat of escalation to all-out nuclear war."[65] Nuclear weapons in the European theater, as a result, fulfilled a critical political function as a tangible coupling link between Europe and the strategic arsenal of the United States.

In an ambiguous strategy, the role that nuclear weapons would play in Europe was even more ambiguous. MC 14/3 was deliberately vague about what role tactical weapons—a blanket term that encompassed everything from battlefield systems to weapons with a longer-range, deep-strike role— would play and their relative importance within the overall strategy. Allied preferences varied widely. Thinking on the matter tended to track with geography; where one sat invariably informed where one stood on the question. Some Americans were willing to entertain warfighting uses for these weapons, but their European counterparts, living on the territory where that war would be fought, shied away from the possibility and preferred to focus on shoring up deterrence at every level. Even the slightest suggestion that a war might be fought in Europe elicited pushback. In one telling instance during the drafting process, Dutch and West German representatives pressed for the revision of a particular passage that "indicated possibility of the acceptance by NATO of a protracted limited war in the center."[66] These concerns were not new, but the ambiguity of flexible response enabled an array of positions to coexist, albeit uneasily, within one strategy.

After the adoption of MC 14/3, the allies remained divided over when, where, how, and why they might use these nuclear weapons.[67] The most immediate priority would be to determine the role of the roughly seven thousand tactical nuclear warheads already stationed in Europe.[68] The Nuclear Planning Group took up these questions with a series of studies, but these consultations did little to create any further consensus.[69] There remained a fundamental disconnect between flexible response in theory and in practice.

That fact was not lost on a new administration in Washington. After Richard Nixon's election in 1968, the incoming Republican administration marveled at just how little of the rhetorical support for flexible response had made its way into operational policy. Nixon rapidly came to the conclusion that the alliance's strategy of flexible response was "baloney."[70] Henry Kissinger agreed. "It is argued that our present flexible response strategy gives us a greater possibility of avoiding nuclear war," he remarked. But when one dug into specific elements of the strategy, there was nothing there: "We simply haven't got it in the NATO context."[71] The administration set out to change that, hoping to make flexible response truly flexible.[72]

Embracing the Status Quo

When Richard Nixon took office in January 1969, he found little to like about the United States' global position. The Vietnam War had sapped the nation's strength and drained its coffers. The Soviet Union, by comparison, was on the rise, at least in the metrics that seemed to matter most. The rapid expansion of Moscow's conventional and nuclear forces gave the Soviet Union a new degree of global influence. In economic terms, new challengers arrived on the scene, as enemies-turned-allies like Japan and the Federal Republic of Germany boomed. Surveying this inheritance, Nixon lamented that he had been left to preside over "the partial dissolution of the American empire."[73]

Nixon was not about to sit idly by and oversee the nation's decline. In this task, he found an unlikely, but ideal, ally in his national security adviser, Henry Kissinger. The two were a political odd couple. The former vice president was a Californian from a lower-class background who chafed at his seemingly perennial outsider status. Henry Kissinger, a German-Jewish refugee, with an appointment at Harvard University, was part of the Ivy League intellectual circles that Nixon detested.[74]

To strengthen the United States' position in the world, Nixon and Kissinger embraced a form of superpower détente. Negotiations with the Soviet Union, if successful, could buy the United States much-needed breathing room. An arms control agreement could constrain the Soviets' rapid military growth while also freeing economic resources tied up in the arms race. Nixon and Kissinger's vision of superpower détente was not a departure from the Cold War, merely a new, more effective means of waging it.[75]

Superpower détente was one part of a larger strategy of retrenchment designed to pare back Washington's commitments and put the United States on a firmer footing. With the announcement of the Nixon Doctrine in 1969, the president tried to lighten the load of fighting communism worldwide. The opening to China could harness the political frictions of the Sino-Soviet split as another check on Moscow's power. Creative diplomacy would enable the United States to retain its preeminent role in global affairs but do so with a much lower price tag.

Nixon and Kissinger did not invent détente. De Gaulle had championed it earlier in the decade, and by the time Nixon and Kissinger arrived on the scene, the Western powers had already endorsed it as the alliance's central political task. But Nixon's talk of "an era of negotiation" and the strategy that he and Kissinger pursued to bring that era into being gave the term new meaning. For better or worse, Nixon and Kissinger's brand of détente became virtually synonymous with the term itself.[76] But alongside superpower détente, another type of rapprochement was also taking shape in Europe.

The primary architect of this European détente was the new West German chancellor, Willy Brandt. The first Social Democrat to hold the post since the Weimar Republic, Brandt articulated a new policy—Ostpolitik— that redefined the Federal Republic's relationship to its neighbors and to the German past. "It is not only a question of moral responsibility because of recent German history," Brandt explained, "but also the fact [that] the peace in Europe is not possible without specific German contributions."[77]

Brandt's diplomatic departures reflected his frustration with the Cold War stalemate. His experience as mayor of West Berlin after 1957 shattered his illusions about the current order. The construction of the Berlin Wall, Brandt later recalled, "forced me to reconsider the external factors" that would form the backdrop for any policy regarding German reunification and the division of Europe.[78] Brandt and his press spokesman as mayor, Egon Bahr, recognized that the division of Germany would not be brought to an end by the superpowers, both seemingly content to live with a "two-state solution."[79] Rather than live with it, Brandt looked for ways to minimize the human costs of the German nation's ongoing division. With 1963's Pass Agreement, West Berliners were granted permission to cross the border into their city's Eastern districts for brief visits. Over just a few short weeks some seven hundred thousand West Berliners headed east to reunite with relatives on the other side of town.[80]

These overtures to the East continued when Brandt became foreign minister in 1966 as part of a coalition with the Christian Democrats under Chancellor Kurt-Georg Kiesinger. Brandt's first steps were tentative, but he did meet with Soviet foreign minister Andrei Gromyko. The constraints of coalition governance stopped him from going further. Kiesinger remained wary, lest he alienate voters who feared that Brandt's overtures might jeopardize the prospects for German reunification.

As chancellor in a new coalition with the Free Democrats after 1969, Brandt could—and did—go further, faster. He found a willing partner in Khrushchev's successor, Leonid Brezhnev, who hoped to consolidate the Soviet Union's position in Europe. Events beyond the continent seemed to demand it. Moscow faced a growing rivalry with the People's Republic of China (now a nuclear power) and erstwhile allies, both within the Warsaw Pact and without. The Prague Spring had undercut the Kremlin's claims to moral and political legitimacy, as Soviet tanks rolled into Czechoslovakia's capital to crush the forces of liberalization. By securing the situation in Europe, the thinking went, the Soviets could focus on other pressing matters. To jumpstart that process, the Warsaw Pact's members issued repeated appeals for a conference on European security.[81]

In his pursuit of Ostpolitik, Brandt discarded many of the principles that had guided his predecessors' foreign policies. He did away with the rigid rules of the Hallstein Doctrine, which proclaimed that the Federal Republic would not maintain diplomatic relations with any state that recognized the German Democratic Republic. (The Soviet Union was the exception.) Bonn's campaign to keep East Berlin diplomatically isolated saw West German officials crisscross the globe to dissuade anyone thinking of recognizing the communist regime.[82] Ostpolitik, as Brandt and Bahr envisioned it, inverted the earlier logic of the Hallstein Doctrine. Rather than isolate the German Democratic Republic, Ostpolitik would accept the current status quo—and recognize East Germany—in the hopes of someday ending Germany's division.[83]

The Ostpolitik of Brandt and Bahr did not start from the same premise as Nixon and Kissinger's détente.[84] The Americans developed a strategy designed to forestall the decline of US power, shedding burdens and reducing pressures. Nixon and Kissinger embraced the status quo so as to continue waging the Cold War over the long haul. Brandt and Bahr envisioned the opposite. By embracing the status quo, the two West Germans intended to transcend the Cold War in the long run.

The 1960s saw a transformation in European politics. The deep fault lines of the high Cold War receded, replaced by a growing network of economic, cultural, and political ties that connected East and West. As détente's fortunes increased, so too did popular impressions that the Cold War's dangers had receded into the past.

Trends suggested otherwise. While the Cold War faded from the public's consciousness, the Soviet Union poured money into its military, investing in improvements to nuclear and conventional forces alike. The Western allies, by comparison, struggled to balance their military requirements with a multitude of economic and political pressures that conspired to keep defense budgets from growing. NATO's members tried to insulate themselves from these pressures with a new political rationale that linked defense and deterrence with the pursuit of détente, along with a new strategic concept that responded to the growing capabilities of the Soviet Union. That strategy's emphasis on providing a range of escalatory options added to the importance of the nuclear weapons deployed in Europe, or theater nuclear forces, as an essential link between conventional troops and the strategic arsenal of the United States.

The dramatic growth of Soviet forces threatened to upend the alliance's strategy and erode confidence in the protection afforded by the United States. Economic constraints encouraged the Nixon administration to tackle this problem through diplomatic means. Through arms control negotiations, the United States and the Soviet Union could limit the costly arms race. But the terms of that agreement, as Nixon and Kissinger would soon find, could easily create their own crisis of confidence within the alliance.

CHAPTER 2

Parity's Problems

Like many in the late 1960s, Richard Nixon recognized that the growth of Moscow's military power meant that the Soviet Union could reach nuclear parity with the United States in short order.[1] On the campaign trail in 1968, the Republican presidential hopeful promised "to restore" the United States' "objective of clear-cut military superiority."[2] Once in office, Nixon abandoned this search for superiority. Strategic "sufficiency" became the administration's stated aim. What constituted sufficiency remained contested—"it doesn't mean a god-damned thing," one aide told reporters—but the president's rhetorical shift and the arms control agreements that followed gave the impression that the United States had embraced parity with the Soviet Union.[3]

Strategic parity had existed in one form or another since the late 1950s, when Soviet advances in intercontinental ballistic missiles stripped the United States of the most obvious advantages of its geography. With the continental United States now vulnerable to a Soviet attack, Washington could no longer credibly threaten a first strike to disarm the Soviet Union. And with US strategic forces exposed to a Soviet first strike, it became all the more difficult to extend a credible deterrent to Western Europe. If the United States were to escalate a nuclear exchange, leaders in Washington might be reluctant to use weapons based in the United States lest it invite Soviet retaliation.

Given the choice, US policymakers might prefer to keep a war—nuclear or conventional—confined to the European continent.[4]

Such hypothetical military scenarios spilled over into the realms of politics and psychology. Superiority, so long as it was there, served as a security blanket for the Western European allies. It provided just enough reassurance that the United States would respond to a Soviet attack with nuclear weapons. In an era increasingly defined by parity, that confidence waned. The hundreds of Soviet medium-range missiles within striking distance of Western Europe now seemed even more menacing.

The arms control negotiations under way threatened to make matters worse. The United States' initial plans to limit the Soviets' medium-range missiles as part of an agreement limiting strategic arms fell by the wayside. An agreement on those terms "could substantially decrease rather than increase Western European real security," one observer concluded in late 1971.[5] The embrace of parity at one level, but not others, could topple the balance.

The superpowers' interim agreement to limit strategic forces, May 1972's SALT I, left these Soviet nuclear forces aside. And as the superpowers' negotiations on strategic forces continued in parallel with talks to limit conventional forces, a gray area opened up between the two. Left unchecked and undiscussed was a loose amalgam of weapons, including medium-range nuclear forces. The Soviet nuclear arsenal threatening Europe was free to grow, even as those missiles aimed at the United States and Canada were capped. By the middle of the decade, the Soviet Union seemed poised to replace its increasingly obsolete weapons covering European targets with the SS-20, a more accurate mobile system boasting multiple warheads.

SALT

If Richard Nixon wanted to usher in his promised "era of negotiation," then talks to secure limits on the superpowers' strategic nuclear forces were the logical place to begin. Nixon's predecessor, Lyndon Johnson, had proposed negotiations with the Soviet Union to curb the growing arms race.[6] But with negotiations not yet under way, any talks that did take place were certain to be seen as a signature initiative of the Nixon administration.[7]

Nixon avoided any early commitments to pursue strategic arms control. The Soviet Union's public statements of support for the negotiations offered the new administration leverage, which Nixon hoped to parlay into concessions on other issues, including the Middle East and the ongoing war in Vietnam.[8] There were also strategic considerations and military requirements to be pinned down before any arms control negotiations began. Although the Nixon administration had inherited a series of studies from its Democratic predecessors, it was hardly the first or the last administration to insist on a review of its own.

The reduction of the superpowers' arsenals, Nixon believed, would not bring about an end to their rivalry. "The adversaries in the world," as the president told one audience, "are not in conflict because they are armed. They are armed because they are in conflict, and have not yet learned peaceful ways to resolve their conflicting national interests."[9] Arms control negotiations might not end the conflict between Moscow and Washington, but they could cap the growth of the Soviet Union's forces. Since Leonid Brezhnev assumed the Kremlin's highest office in 1964, the Soviet arsenal had expanded dramatically. By the late 1960s, Moscow was adding three hundred launchers a year to its intercontinental ballistic missile force alone.[10] For Nixon and his national security adviser, Henry Kissinger, securing limits that halted the expansion of the Soviets' strategic nuclear forces would ensure the United States did not fall behind the Soviet Union. Better yet, it would do so on the cheap. The United States could avert the need to undertake another financially prohibitive and politically costly build-up to match the Soviets'.

Seeking improvements in relations with the Soviet Union, the president predicted, would also make for good domestic politics. "Nixon calculates that if he succeeds in substantially improving relations with the USSR," Kissinger told the Soviet ambassador in Washington, Anatoly Dobrynin, in the spring of 1969, "he will be assured of winning the next elections, since at least 80% of the electorate will then vote for him."[11] That would be a marked improvement on his showing in the 1968 presidential election, which he won by the slimmest of margins.

The Threat to Europe

Any bilateral talks were bound to create problems. If the United States and the Soviet Union headed to the bargaining table, Washington's allies would be stuck on the outside looking in, dependent on US negotiators to protect their security interests. In capitals across the alliance, policymakers chafed at that uncomfortable realization. US-Soviet talks could lead to what the French ambassador to the United States, Charles Lucet, referred to as a "permanent duet or US-Soviet condominium" controlling international politics.[12] The prospect of an agreement that accepted rough parity, as any negotiations on the superpowers' arsenals seemed poised to do, would invariably highlight the distance between the Europeans' broad public statements and, as Kissinger put it, their "gut feelings."[13] Accepting strategic parity could erode the foundations of extended deterrence and diminish Western Europe's security. Parity undermined the earlier premise that US nuclear superiority balanced the Warsaw Pact's superior conventional forces.

Parity also amplified concerns about the Soviets' nuclear forces in Europe. Moscow's arsenal included over seven hundred of these systems, 90 percent of them aimed at Western Europe.[14] Since the early 1960s, NATO had relied on a mix of weapons outside continental Europe to threaten strikes against the Soviet Union and cover Moscow's SS-4s and SS-5s, the medium-range missiles that could strike the capitals of Western Europe. The backbone of the alliance's deterrent remained the intercontinental ballistic missiles dotting the US heartland, and the allies augmented these with offshore weapons like bombers and submarines. But, after the removal of the Jupiter missiles in 1963, NATO had no longer-range nuclear forces in the European theater.[15] In a landscape defined by strategic parity, how could the European allies be sure that Washington's strategic systems would still provide sufficient coverage?[16] "My NATO colleagues are aware that an increasing number of targets on the nuclear list are left uncovered," Gen. Andrew Goodpaster, the supreme allied commander, Europe, warned.[17]

Parity, in other words, raised the old bogeyman of NATO's strategy: decoupling. Western Europe's security could end up separated from that of the United States, and the protection previously afforded by NATO's extended deterrent would be rendered null and void. If the European allies lost faith in extended deterrence, they might seek accommodation with the Soviet Union or gradually drifting toward a kind of neutrality dubbed "Finlandization" (in a reference to the Soviet Union's influence over Helsinki's foreign policy).[18] "The prospect of parity," the Dutch foreign minister, Joseph Luns, claimed, "was one of the most shocking things he had heard."[19]

Though the promise of extended deterrence mattered to all the Europeans, geography and geopolitics left the Federal Republic of Germany—one half of a divided nation, straddling the ideological fault line of Europe—most vulnerable to Soviet pressure. And the Federal Republic's leaders had few truly independent options to provide for the country's security. NATO's arrangements, crafted in the 1950s to make German power acceptable so soon after the war, constrained the Federal Republic's access to atomic, biological, and chemical weapons.[20] The Nuclear Non-proliferation Treaty, which sorted the globe into nuclear haves and have-nots, cemented the Federal Republic's nonnuclear status.[21]

So long as the Federal Republic remained the largest of the nonnuclear allies, it would in effect remain a dependent of the United States. If Washington hoped to keep Bonn within the fold, the continuation of existing arrangements depended on a degree of satisfaction. West Germans needed to believe that they still had the United States' protection. Any negotiations on SALT had the potential to undermine that confidence. "Everything in the field of SALT," acting foreign minister Georg Duckwitz argued in early 1969, "touches on Germany's vital interests, directly or indirectly."[22]

Negotiations to limit strategic nuclear forces could diminish that protection. Though the Western Europeans favored SALT as a way to deepen the process of détente, the Nixon administration predicted that Washington's allies within NATO would have a number of specific concerns about how those negotiations might unfold. Top of the list would be its potential impact on the US deterrent and the restrictions it would place on the Soviet missiles that threatened Western Europe.[23] Early consultations confirmed these suspicions. When permanent representatives exchanged views on the possible implications of SALT in July 1969, the British delegate, Sir Bernard Burrows, underscored the need to preserve the credibility of Washington's nuclear commitment to Europe. "A particular European interest," he warned, "will be that the targets on SACEUR's threat list (at present covered jointly by the external strategic forces of the US and by the forces assigned to SACEUR) and in particular the Soviet MR/IRBMs continue to be covered."[24] Already, the Federal Republic had pressed for the inclusion of the Soviets' medium-range missiles in any arms control negotiations that opened on SALT.[25] Though supportive of the talks as part of the pursuit of détente, West German officials were unsurprisingly adamant that the negotiations could not be permitted to endanger their security.[26]

Sensitive to the potential political problems, the Nixon administration held a series of consultations at NATO over the summer of 1969. In preparation, the president advised his team to prepare an exploratory paper on the likely US negotiating position for SALT, not a "selling" paper designed to bring the allies onside. "Consultation should be therapy," Nixon suggested.[27] The discussions themselves were carefully calibrated to highlight that the Americans appreciated their European allies' security interests and intended to protect them, starting with the inclusion of Soviet medium- and intermediate-range ballistic missiles in their opening negotiating position. "Even though the Soviets might claim that these weapons do not threaten the United States and are thus not strategic," the deputy assistant secretary of state for politico-military affairs, Philip Farley, argued, "they are in fact a major strategic offensive missile system which holds the European NATO countries at risk and threaten NATO forces in the area."[28]

US assurances in hand, the West Germans lobbied for a broader strategy of balance. "We can say that the era of negotiations about negotiations has begun," Helmut Schmidt remarked at a gathering of the Western European Union's defense ministers in December. As countries East and West talked about talking, the term "balance" should be top of mind, Schmidt argued. The West German defense minister expressed complete confidence that the principle of balance would be protected in SALT, with preliminary exchanges now under way in Helsinki. "The United States will continue to provide a strategic cover for Europe, and will include in the negotiations the Soviet MRBM and IRBM missiles which are poised exclusively at targets in Europe." But the principle of balance could not be confined to the superpowers' negotiations alone. There must also be a balance on the continent.[29]

Equal Security?

When preliminary talks on SALT opened in November 1969, the Soviet delegation put forward a broad definition of "strategic" that included all nuclear systems capable of reaching US or Soviet territory. According to the Soviet negotiators' terms, the talks should encompass British and French nuclear forces, as well as US forward-based systems, such as sea-launched weapons and nuclear delivery aircraft. With these weapons, the United States could launch direct strikes against the Soviet Union. In every metric that mattered, then, these were no different than US intercontinental ballistic missiles. All of these weapons could destroy Soviet territory, and so they should all be counted as strategic forces. Only with the inclusion of these British, French, and US nuclear forces, the Soviet line of thinking went, could the superpowers' security be considered equal.[30]

Soviet calls to bring in US forward-based systems struck at the heart of NATO's defenses in Europe. Whether by air or by sea, these weapons formed a critical component of the alliance's efforts to extend deterrence across the continent and sustain sufficient confidence in the protection it afforded. An agreement that limited these forward-based systems in Europe and in Asia would be politically costly. Maurice Schumann, the French foreign minister, worried that if the United States cut back, it might lead to the complete denuclearization of the continent, including putting an end to France's prized *force de frappe*.[31]

But the Soviets' definition of equal security was carefully calibrated and included no such restrictions on their own medium-range missiles. These SS-4s and SS-5s, trained on targets across Western Europe, should be excluded from an agreement, according to the Soviet negotiators.[32] The Kremlin, Kissinger concluded, would retain "an overwhelming advantage vis-à-vis Europe."[33] To avoid such an outcome, the initial US negotiating position took into account these worrisome medium-range systems.

Preliminary exchanges with the Kremlin's negotiators showed just how hard it would be to bring these systems into the talks. If the United States insisted on including Soviet missiles targeting Europe, ones which fell outside Moscow's preferred definition of "strategic," the Soviet delegation was virtually guaranteed to cling to its demands for limits on US forward-based systems that could strike the Soviet Union.

By the spring of 1970, in advance of the next round of negotiations, the Nixon administration prepared to change course. Soviet negotiators were unlikely to abandon their opening position that their medium-range missiles in Europe posed no direct threat to the United States and should be left out of the talks as an essential element of the Soviet Union's defenses against so-called third countries, namely the nuclear-armed powers—the United Kingdom, France, and the People's Republic of China—that would not be party to an agreement between the superpowers.[34] Gerard Smith, the head of the US negotiating team, warned that Washington's NATO allies were likely to have reservations, as it might appear that the threat posed by Soviet missiles in Europe would not be reduced. Another member of the delegation, Paul Nitze, noted that Willy Brandt had expressed concern about the status of Soviet medium-range missiles in the negotiations. Given these reservations, Nixon insisted on absolute secrecy regarding the administration's position lest the allies' fears be whipped up by any speculation in the press.[35]

Designed to reach an initial agreement focused on limiting "the most important strategic weapons systems," the Nixon administration's new proposal set aside restrictions on the Soviet Union's nuclear forces in Europe.[36] Doing so would not only increase the prospects of a deal with the Soviets, it would also protect NATO's forward-based systems, as the United States expected the Soviets would drop demands for their inclusion.

British analysts relished this news. Since 1969, the British had been desperate to protect NATO's forward-based systems, if only to avoid the alternatives. Any agreement that included these dual-capable aircraft and submarine-launched missiles could open the door to cutting Britain's own nuclear arsenal. After all, the country's Polaris submarines were assigned to NATO.

Begrudgingly, the West Germans agreed. The talks' poor prospects to date demanded a change in negotiating tactics. The Western Europeans might have accepted the need for a new negotiating posture, but they were none too pleased that this change was certain to come at the expense of their own security. When the North Atlantic Council met in July 1970, Wilhelm Grewe, the West German permanent representative, noted that the new US negotiating stance would mean "the exclusion, for the time being, from SALT of the very weapons system which, obsolete or not, continues to pose the most specific strategic threat to NATO in Europe." Failure to address this threat would create a "psychological problem," Belgium's Andre de Staercke warned. If an arms control agreement restricted the nuclear weapons that threatened the superpowers but left those menacing Europe untouched, it would stoke suspicions of decoupling.[37]

Any limited agreement could drive the Western Europeans to pursue new arrangements to provide for their defense. If the superpowers reached a deal on SALT that confirmed parity and restricted anti-ballistic missile systems, Kissinger believed, the British and French were almost certain to conclude that their own national nuclear programs had even greater justification. Against this backdrop, the British might also ramp up their efforts at defense cooperation with the French, something that could be made all the more fraught by the "explosive problem of German association with a possible Anglo-French force."[38] SALT could encourage transatlantic drift in at least three different ways, the director of London's Institute for Strategic Studies, François Duchêne, warned. First, if the United States and the Soviet Union concluded an agreement, it would increase the European belief that "détente is under way and there is nothing to worry about." Second, the rise of US-Soviet consultations could lead to suspicion about the creation of a condominium between the two great powers at Europe's expense. Third, fixing attention on the parity between the superpowers might introduce uncertainty about the United States' willingness to defend Western Europe.[39] "In so far as the talks formalize a situation of existing strategic parity," the British international relations specialist Philip Windsor argued, "the strategy of controlled escalation on which the military security of Europe still depends will come into question."[40]

For the time being, forward-based systems still stood in the way of any tangible agreement on SALT. Soviet negotiators rebuffed the Americans' efforts to exclude them, and the talks remained at an impasse. By the autumn of 1970, the negotiations were stuck in a loop, as the Soviet delegation kept repeating the same old arguments about the dangers of US forward-based systems.[41] In early December, the chief Soviet negotiator, Vladimir Semenov, suggested that the two delegations focus their efforts on an ABM treaty, given the Americans' continued intransigence regarding forward-based systems.

As 1971 began, the two superpowers remained far apart. US and Soviet negotiators still could not agree on what counted as a strategic weapon. By May, however, the United States and the Soviet Union seemed poised to sign an agreement. Nixon and Brezhnev broke the stalemate publicly on May 20 with an announcement that the two sides would pursue an agreement to limit ABMs alongside "certain measures with respect to the limitation of offensive strategic weapons."[42] The product of a months-long back channel between Kissinger and Dobrynin, the announcement formed the basis for an interim agreement, signed at the Moscow Summit a year later.[43] In May 1972, Nixon and Brezhnev deferred the question of forward-based systems to a later round of negotiations.

The superpowers' agreement, SALT I, codified a rough strategic parity, at least in quantitative terms. With the embrace of parity came all of the predictable problems. "In retrospect," the US political scientist Andrew J. Pierre concluded, "it is probably unfortunate that United States officials spoke of nuclear 'superiority' as assuring the credibility of the American guarantee to defend Western Europe." That guarantee depended much more on political and strategic calculations than on missile counts and throw weights.[44]

After returning home from Moscow, Nixon heralded the summit as a symbol of détente's successes. "To millions of Americans for the past quarter century," he remarked before a joint session of Congress, "the Kremlin has stood for implacable hostility toward all that we cherish, and to millions of Russians the American flag has long been held up as a symbol of evil." As part of the Moscow Summit, the flag of the United States had flown over the Kremlin—a reminder of just how much had changed under Nixon's watch. The United States had not secured "instant peace," but Nixon assured listeners that he and Brezhnev had laid the foundations of "a new relationship between the two most powerful nations in the world."[45]

As the United States embarked on this new relationship, Nixon vowed that the nation would continue to do so from a position of strength. Rebuffing domestic critics of SALT's embrace of equality, the president insisted that Washington's stature remained undiminished and its strategic forces sufficient for the task at hand.[46] It was a far cry from his earlier assertions that parity would undermine the credibility of US commitments across the globe.[47]

A formal endorsement of parity, SALT I stabilized the strategic situation to the detriment of Europe. "The credibility of the US strategic deterrent is no longer total," the head of the British Foreign and Commonwealth Office's

Western Organisations Department, Crispin Tickell, wrote to a colleague.[48] Nixon's domestic critics latched onto the same arguments. In a speech before the North Atlantic Assembly's military committee, Senator Henry Jackson, a Democrat from Washington State, charged that the United States now lacked "a coherent strategic doctrine." Nixon's nuclear policies seemed to endorse two principles that could not coexist. The administration maintained that the Western Europeans could rely on the US strategic arsenal "to protect them from Soviet threats and intimidation." Nixon's arms control policies and public pronouncements endorsed an entirely different position. They touted a minimum deterrent that reduced the role of strategic forces to "the striking of Russian cities in response to a direct attack against the continental United States."[49] Nixon's commitments abroad did not align with the president's rhetoric at home.

But the public's attention focused on the superpowers' agreement as a tangible sign that the Cold War confrontation was receding. Long before Moscow and Washington reached a deal, Kissinger appreciated that SALT would likely widen the gap between what NATO's defenses required and what allied leaders' constituents would be willing to underwrite. Even if the leaders of Western Europe understood that strategic parity would increase the likelihood of conflict on the continent, Kissinger did not hold out hope that this realization would lead them to spend more on defense. If anything, given the trends of recent years, the opposite seemed more likely. A sense of euphoria about détente would ratchet up pressure to trim defense budgets.[50] So long as East-West relations were improving, NATO's governments found it difficult to secure the funds needed to maintain their defenses.

On the Margins

SALT I established a rough balance between the superpowers' strategic arsenals, but the same could scarcely be said of the arsenals of Europe. Since the late 1960s, the Western allies had conducted studies on the mutual and balanced reduction of the armies positioned throughout Central Europe. Studies alone, however, could not bring the Soviet Union to the table, and the Nixon administration remained reluctant to enter into any negotiations to limit conventional forces too early.

As Washington delayed, the Federal Republic tried to jumpstart talks on conventional forces. The Stiftung Wissenschaft und Politik, a government think tank, had been studying possible reductions since early 1968. And when Brandt became chancellor in the autumn of 1969, limiting troops in Central

Europe seemed a logical choice to advance his policy of détente. In 1970, under the direction of Helmut Schmidt, the defense ministry's planning staff and the NATO desk at the foreign ministry developed criteria for negotiations.[51] The Brandt coalition's enthusiasm was seen as a direct outgrowth of its drive for Ostpolitik.[52]

The West German government saw mutual and balanced force reduction as a mechanism to reduce the military imbalances within Europe. The Soviet Union and its Warsaw Pact allies had clear numerical advantages in troops and tanks, which NATO's members offset with shorter-range nuclear weapons. Only by reducing both, Bonn's thinking went, could the Western allies achieve the requisite balance with fewer weapons. With that goal in mind, the West Germans flirted with more grand plans. MBFR, they argued, should include all of the weapons excluded from SALT I, and should place a ceiling on the deployment of so-called non-central systems like the Soviet Union's SS-4s and SS-5s.[53]

The West German desire to begin negotiations found support within the US State Department, where officials envisioned schemes to bring the Soviets to the table through the inclusion of nuclear weapons in the negotiations, such as US forward-based systems and the Soviets' medium-range missiles.[54] Without backing from Nixon and Kissinger, however, those attempts were destined to go nowhere.

Congress threatened to force Nixon's hand. Senator Mike Mansfield continued to introduce resolutions to scale back the number of US troops stationed in Europe, just as he had in 1966. If realized, Mansfieldism could destroy the already fragile strategy of flexible response. The removal of US troops, British analysts concluded, would leave NATO caught between "two very unpalatable options." Either the Western allies would need to retreat to the trip-wire strategy of years past, or a precipitous drop in European confidence might "persuade Germany to seek safety in accommodation with the Soviet Union."[55]

Under pressure at home, Nixon and Kissinger abandoned their earlier reservations. Negotiations aimed at cutting the standing armies of Europe could be used to neutralize calls for unilateral reductions like those championed by Mansfield. When Nixon and Brezhnev met in Moscow in May 1972, the two injected new life into proposals for talks to limit conventional forces, along with the Soviets' longtime pet project, a conference on European security.[56]

Negotiations to restrict conventional forces finally opened in October 1973, in a forum Western observers referred to as the Mutual and Balanced

Force Reduction talks. The Soviet delegation refused to use that name—the term "balanced," they argued, suggested that the Warsaw Pact's members would reduce their troops far more than NATO's would—and the talks ended up with the official title Mutual Reductions of Forces and Armaments in Central Europe—or MRFACE.[57] These opening deliberations were a sign of things to come, and the negotiations settled into a protracted stalemate almost as soon as they began. The original Western proposal called for phased reductions based on percentages. Given the Warsaw Pact's substantial numerical advantage, the Soviets would be expected to cut their troops by sixty-eight thousand, whereas the United States would remove less than half that.[58] Soviet counterproposals put forward an alternative definition of balance, favoring equal cuts that would leave their relative advantage untouched.

The Western allies had little leverage with which to bring the Soviet Union closer to their position. Whereas economic constraints and parliamentary preferences demanded reductions to their own armies, there were no similar pressures to exploit in the Soviet Union. British negotiators concluded that the Kremlin's delegation needed to drag the talks out to protect their own troops, given that they served a dual role in Soviet security policy: checking NATO's members and preserving "order in their empire."[59] By introducing a handful of nuclear weapons into the negotiations, the Western allies might be able to sweeten the deal for Moscow. In December 1975, the participating NATO states introduced Option III, the so-called nuclear option, hoping that these weapons could be used as bargaining chips to secure reductions in Soviet troops and tanks.[60]

Unchecked

A gap remained. The United States and the Soviet Union continued to debate limits on their strategic arsenals as part of SALT II, while states from NATO and the Warsaw Pact tried to reach an agreement to restrict the armies of Central Europe in the MBFR talks. In the gray area between the two negotiations were a whole mix of weapons and launch modes: strike aircraft, bombers, submarine launchers, short-range missiles, air-launched systems, and medium- and intermediate-range ballistic missiles.[61]

First deployed in the late 1950s, the Soviets' SS-4s and SS-5s were hopelessly inefficient. It took hours to prepare the liquid-fueled missiles for launch and, with many housed on open pads, they remained easy targets, vulnerable to preemptive strikes.[62] The Soviet Union prepared to replace these aging missiles and, in 1974, US intelligence picked up signs of a new weapon being tested at Kapustin Yar, not far from the Caspian Sea.[63] It was the RSD-10 Pioneer, a missile that NATO referred to as the SS-20 Saber.

Fielding a new generation of Soviet medium-range missiles warranted almost no debate, even at the highest echelons of the Kremlin bureaucracy. "The decision to deploy the SS-20s was made in total secrecy," one senior KGB officer, Nikolai Leonov, later recalled. "Even our intelligence didn't know about it. The military-industrial complex was out of control, including the army. We in intelligence learned about it from American sources."[64] Andrei Gromyko, the longtime Soviet foreign minister, later chalked up the decision to the insistence of Dmitri Ustinov. So too did Mikhail Gorbachev.[65]

Politburo politics made the decision possible. Under an increasingly ailing Leonid Brezhnev, men like Ustinov could—and did—gain considerable influence over Soviet decision-making. As the Central Committee's secretary for the defense industry and, after April 1976, as minister of defense, Ustinov made the most of that power to protect his bailiwick: the military and its interests.[66]

The specifics of how and why a small segment of the Soviet leadership decided to deploy the SS-20 remain fuzzy, with critical records still under wraps in Moscow, but the basic logic is clear. Existing Soviet capabilities in the European theater were rapidly approaching obsolescence. Moscow's earlier attempts to include so-called third-party systems (the British and French nuclear arsenals) in SALT had failed. So had Soviet negotiators' efforts to restrict US forward-based systems. After the superpowers opened the SALT II negotiations in November 1972, the lead Soviet negotiator, Vladimir Semenov, pressed for an agreement that would include these US weapons, but the Americans refused. When Brezhnev and Nixon's successor, Gerald Ford, met at Vladivostok in November 1974, the Soviet general secretary agreed to set aside demands that US nuclear weapons in Europe be covered under SALT II.[67] The Vladivostok Accord left the Soviet Union surrounded by NATO's missiles in Europe, a state of affairs made worse by a growing Chinese nuclear arsenal on the Soviet border. "The SS-20 decision was," as one member of the US delegation, Raymond Garthoff, later put it, "a 'natural.'"[68]

Brezhnev's endorsement of the Vladivostok Accord provoked outrage among the senior leaders of the Soviet military.[69] Ustinov's predecessor, Andrei Grechko, fumed; by deferring discussion of NATO weapons capable of striking the Soviet Union, Brezhnev's decision was tantamount to a betrayal of the Soviet Union itself.[70] Faced with that backlash, it hardly seems a stretch that Brezhnev saw the deployment of the SS-20 as a tool of bureaucratic politics to mollify the military men.

The superpowers' negotiations to date permitted the SS-20, and the new weapon conformed to the ideas of strategic stability that the two delegations discussed as part of SALT.[71] It also tracked with the new ideas emerging in Soviet strategic thinking, as Moscow's military planners embraced a concept not unlike NATO's doctrine of flexible response.[72] With more accurate and effective weapons in the European theater, including the SS-20, the Soviet Union and its Warsaw Pact allies would be able to exploit the fragility of their adversary's security arrangements and undermine the credibility of the US nuclear guarantee to Western Europe.

The SS-20s represented "a breakthrough, unlike anything the Americans had," the assistant to the chief of the General Staff's Main Operations Directorate, Andrian Danilevich, later recalled. "We were immediately able to hold all of Europe hostage."[73] A popular rumor circulating through the halls of the Soviet foreign ministry described Brezhnev and Ustinov crawling around on the general secretary's office floor over a map of Western Europe. Armed with compasses, the two men drew circle after circle, covering the western half of the continent. It would take just twenty SS-20s to obliterate the entire territory.[74]

Parity was a double-edged sword. The embrace of a rough equality between the superpowers was politically dangerous. Any acknowledgment that the Soviet Union had caught up left politicians, Richard Nixon chief among them, vulnerable to charges that they had ceded ground to the Kremlin. For NATO's strategy, predicated as it was on extending deterrence across an ocean, parity undercut earlier promises that superiority would provide sufficient firepower to deter the Soviet Union from probing the margins, and perhaps even striking the capitals of Europe.

The arrival of a somewhat stable parity between the two largest nuclear powers introduced a degree of balance, at least at one level. Guided by a holistic grand strategy, the Western powers could secure that same balance at other levels, including within Europe. Balance would, as Helmut Schmidt argued, underwrite the pursuit of détente and open up ways to remake the political landscape of Europe.[75] That strategy of balance guided the West Germans' thinking, from their efforts to see Soviet medium-range missiles taken into account in SALT to their calls for MBFR negotiations that would cap these non-central systems.

But by the middle of the 1970s, that strategy of balance hardly looked so grand. Arms control had only secured a patchy balance. The superpowers' strategic nuclear forces were capped, though qualitative improvements remained unchecked. So too did the rest of their arsenals, with no limits in sight on troops, tanks, and their various nuclear weapons, both large and small, scattered across the continent. The most immediate threats to Western Europe's security were still free to grow. As the Soviet Union began testing the SS-20, the strategy's primary architects began to worry that the entire equilibrium would be toppled. But if Schmidt and his fellow West Germans lost confidence in the protective umbrella of NATO, who could predict where their crisis of faith might take them? In light of Europe's recent history, the possibilities were too unsettling to contemplate.

CHAPTER 3

Shades of Gray

A series of pictures flickered across the projector screen in a dimly lit room, tucked into the vast complex of the Pentagon. Various weapons in the Soviet arsenal appeared on screen: fighters and airfields, followed by bombers, tanks, and the growing surface fleet of the Soviet Navy. Then the briefer turned to the Soviet weapons aimed at Europe, starting with pictures of the aging SS-4 and SS-5. Another image popped up. It showed a new type of missile installation, made up of a series of garages with what appeared to be retractable roofs. Inside were missiles attached to the backs of vehicles—mobile transporter erector launchers. The audience, made up of allied officials, erupted into a flurry of questions. How many of these missiles did the Soviet Union have? Where did Moscow intend to station them? And when would the Soviets start bringing them online?[1]

These missiles were RSD-10 Pioneers, which came to be known in NATO circles as SS-20 Sabers.[2] Intermediate-range ballistic missiles with a range of five thousand kilometers, the Soviet Union's SS-20s could easily strike the capitals of Western Europe, with everything from Reykjavik to Bonn in comfortable striking distance.[3] Alarmed, some of the Western allies began to seek new concepts, perhaps even new weapons, to shore up NATO's position.

Gone were the earlier assurances of nuclear superiority and, in their stead, successive administrations in Washington could offer little that allayed the fears of European policymakers. Arms control left a series of nuclear weapons unchecked. In the gray area between SALT and MBFR was a mix of Soviet missiles capable of striking Western Europe and US systems that could target the Soviet Union from Western Europe.[4] The testing and deployment of new Soviet missiles drew even more attention to the problems of parity and what it would mean for Europe's security, in a contentious debate that ended up known simply as the gray-area problem.

It was a vicious cycle. With the West Germans fixated on the balance in Europe, their allies feared that this obsession might lead them to seek security in other arrangements, even outright accommodation with the Soviet Union. To ward against that prospect, the administrations of Gerald Ford and Jimmy Carter tried to temper West German anxieties about the Soviets' SS-20s and dissuade Bonn from backing concepts like the Eurostrategic balance that seemed to suggest a decoupling of Europe's security from that of the United States. Against that backdrop, a loose coalition of Americans tried to sell the Europeans on a new technology, the cruise missile. Though the Western Europeans were initially skeptical, their interest grew alongside their worries about the SS-20. Shortly after coming to office in January 1977, the Carter administration found itself the target of a European lobbying campaign desperate to protect any and all cruise missile options in Europe. These low-flying, low-cost weapons could be the key to reducing Moscow's leverage over the governments of Western Europe.

Toppling the Balance

The Soviet Union already enjoyed an overwhelming missile advantage in Europe with the SS-4s and SS-5s. After their deployment in the late 1950s and early 1960s, Nikita Khrushchev reportedly boasted that the states of Western Europe were now "figuratively hostages to us and a guarantee against war."[5] If the Kremlin began to replace its aging missiles with another generation of weapons with greater accuracy and multiple warheads, the Soviet Union could turn up the heat on its hostages in Western Europe.

Confronted with this possibility, West German policymakers fixated on the balance of power within Europe. In October 1974, Helmut Schmidt, now chancellor, headed to Moscow. (He had become chancellor in May after Willy Brandt resigned over the news that one of his personal aides, Günter Guillaume, was working for East German intelligence.) During Schmidt's talks with Soviet General Secretary Leonid Brezhnev, he spoke at some

length about the strategy of balance and the blow the SS-20s could deal
to that balance if deployed. "I thought it necessary to stress the balance,"
Schmidt wrote in his memoirs. "I was made uneasy about the new Soviet
SS-20 intermediate-range missiles then being tested. To me they represented
an additional threat to my country."[6] The government's white paper for
1975–76 echoed this assessment. When deployed, the SS-20 would increase
the nuclear threat facing Europe in both qualitative and quantitative terms.[7]

The broad realization that there should be a balance at various levels was
already a core tenet of the Schmidt strategy, visible in the earlier deliberations over SALT and MBFR. "These regional systems are just as important
as [strategic systems] for the stability of the strategic balance and for the
security of the Alliance," the head of the foreign ministry's political division,
Hellmuth Roth, told a group of US officials in early 1971. "We must take the
regional European nuclear balance seriously."[8] This refrain became a staple
of West German diplomats at the Nuclear Planning Group and at NATO's
regular consultations on SALT II. In June 1975, when the Nuclear Planning
Group met in Monterey, California, the West German representative insisted
on the need to establish balance across the board, ensuring that there were
no asymmetries.[9]

With the development of the SS-20, the notion of a distinct balance in
Europe gained currency. The concept, referred to as the "Eurostrategic balance," started from the same premise as the US negotiating team's opening
position in SALT I; Soviet medium- and intermediate-range missiles constituted a strategic threat to Europe. By that logic, there were two different
categories of strategic weapons, the superpowers' long-range forces, covered by SALT, and the non-central systems that played a strategic role in
Europe. This second group of Eurostrategic weapons was an amorphous
one, made up of various nuclear-capable strike aircraft, medium-range
bombers, submarine-based missiles, and intermediate-range ballistic missiles owned by the British, French, Soviets, and Americans. In an age defined
by strategic parity, proponents of the Eurostrategic balance argued that an
imbalance on the continent would make it possible for the Kremlin to blackmail the governments of Western Europe. The introduction of the SS-20
would, Fredo Dannenbring, the head of the West German foreign ministry's NATO bureau, concluded, enhance "the Eurostrategic potential of the
Soviet Union."[10]

This assertion flew in the face of initial US assessments. In September
1975, the Arms Control and Disarmament Agency's Ralph Earle told NATO
experts that the SS-20 in development would not change the basic security
situation in Europe. Even though the missile boasted three reentry vehicles

and far greater accuracy than the SS-4s and SS-5s, Earle remained sanguine. "The European balance," he assured the group, "would not change materially."[11] Despite these early assurances, the West Germans pressed their case. At the Nuclear Planning Group in January 1976, Georg Leber drew attention to the Soviets' missiles in Europe. These capabilities, the West German defense minister argued, needed to be considered as a critical part of any assessment of the overall correlation of forces.[12]

Talk of the Eurostrategic balance aroused suspicion in some quarters of official Washington. At the State Department, policymakers found the thinking behind the entire concept troubling. It threatened to reopen familiar questions about the nature and credibility of the US guarantee to Western Europe and all of the associated problems that might unleash in Washington's relationship with the West Germans. From a purely strategic perspective, even talk of a separate category of forces could foster the impression that the alliance required new weapons to counter the Kremlin's. NATO's military representatives agreed, cautioning against any attempt to isolate elements of the Soviet threat. "It would be unwise to single out any one part of the threat for undue emphasis," one assessment warned, "lest the overall balance of NATO's forces be disturbed, so jeopardizing the flexible response concept."[13]

Elsewhere in Washington, it seemed clear that flexible response was already in trouble. "An overall military balance probably exists in Central Europe," the National Security Council's Stephen Hadley wrote to Brent Scowcroft, Ford's national security adviser, "but in terms of strictly conventional forces NATO is clearly inferior to the Pact." So long as that remained the case, the Atlantic alliance required a credible nuclear deterrent in the European theater. Without it, the Kremlin's leaders might be tempted to press their luck, backed by their advantage in troops and tanks and the knowledge that the only possible US response would be a strategic nuclear attack. "Our allies," Hadley warned, "would undoubtedly see the situation the same way, and the resulting anxiety about their own security might fragment the Alliance and encourage some states to either develop their own nuclear weapons or to seek an accommodation with the Soviets."[14] Secretary of Defense Donald Rumsfeld was preparing to introduce a program to modernize NATO's theater nuclear forces, building on the work of his predecessor, James Schlesinger, to streamline the stockpile, shedding the "junk" without too much damage to the stockpile's symbolic value as evidence— about seven thousand pieces thereof—that the United States was linked to Europe's defense.[15] Much of the debate within the Ford administration boiled down to whether the modernization program would shore up allied confidence in NATO's posture or whether it would raise familiar fears about decoupling.[16] "Here's political trouble," NATO's supreme allied commander Gen. Alexander Haig reportedly remarked on seeing Rumsfeld's proposal.[17]

Until the summer of 1976, the transatlantic debate about what the Soviets' SS-20s might mean unfolded largely behind closed doors, confined to bilateral exchanges and the regular consultative councils of the alliance. That changed in July, when the Arms Control and Disarmament Agency reported that the Soviet Union had started deploying the SS-20.[18] Donald Rumsfeld's office maintained that the SS-20 had yet to be brought online, but that note of caution did little to stem the speculation of politicians and pundits about the latest addition to the Soviet arsenal.[19] "The USSR does not want a balance of power," one press release put out by the CDU/CSU's shadow defense minister, Manfred Wörner, confidently proclaimed, "but rather absolute military superiority in order to be able to intimidate and blackmail free Europe and the West."[20] C. L. Sulzberger of the *New York Times* agreed. Western Europe was "more than ever under the gun."[21] Fred Iklé, the director of the Arms Control and Disarmament Agency, ominously warned that the Soviet Union's "strength in regional nuclear bombers and missiles grows like a towering dark cloud over Europe and Asia." The SS-20, with its multiple independently targeted warheads, was nothing short of "a massive, unwarranted and unexplained expansion" of Soviet power.[22]

Nor was the SS-20 the only source of Soviet strength. Those convinced that the Kremlin was bent on expanding its power found ample evidence to support this thesis. Moscow now boasted a navy that made it possible to project power worldwide. Soviet adventurism continued unabated across large swaths of the globe, in various parts of what contemporaries lumped together as the "Third World." In Africa, where Soviet and Cuban forces were embroiled in Angola, the Kremlin seemed determined to expand its influence through the promotion of socialist ideals.[23] "With or without détente," the NATO International Military Staff's Intelligence Division concluded, "Moscow remains committed to the goal of becoming the world's predominant power."[24]

With the Soviet Union apparently ascendant, détente's benefits no longer seemed so obvious. The policy's ambiguities—and competing definitions—became a liability.[25] Broad swaths of public opinion failed to appreciate that détente did not mean a complete relaxation of tensions with the Soviet Union, but rather a new form of competition.[26] A growing segment of the population in the United States turned on détente, armed with a litany of grievances about the strategic, political, and moral costs of doing business with the Soviets.[27] These arguments gained ground across the alliance, but eroded confidence further and faster in the United States, Canada, and the United Kingdom than they did on the continent.

In the United States, where voters prepared to go to the polls in November 1976, Gerald Ford faced a slew of Democratic and Republican challengers critical of his administration's continued commitment to détente. By the spring, the opposition was so strong that Ford and his advisers abandoned the term, just weeks after Ford had insisted publicly, "It would be very unwise for [the] president—me or anyone else—to abandon détente."[28] Ford stared down critics from across the political spectrum who linked the policy of détente with the decline of US global power. "The evidence mounts," as Ford's Republican primary challenger Ronald Reagan put it, "that we are Number Two in a world where it's dangerous, if not fatal, to be second best."[29] Even the segregationist Democrat George Wallace, effectively a single-issue candidate, lamented the United States' decline relative to the Soviet Union.[30] Ford's own advisers were under no illusions. "The Soviet Union today," Rumsfeld remarked during one news conference, "is clearly militarily stronger and busier than in any other period of its history."[31]

A New Category?

Georg Leber kept the Nuclear Planning Group's attention focused on the security situation in Europe. At the group's ministerial session in June 1976, the West German defense minister requested that his US counterpart provide a dedicated briefing on the Eurostrategic balance at their November session.[32] In early October, a Pentagon official, Donald Cotter, briefed the permanent representatives on the state of the Warsaw Pact's forces. Though the briefing was billed as a "dress rehearsal" for Rumsfeld's presentation to his fellow defense ministers the next month, Cotter made no mention of the Soviet Union's nuclear forces threatening Europe. Secretary General Joseph Luns inquired about this seemingly obvious oversight; these were exactly the systems that the briefing was intended to cover.[33]

Cotter offered vague assurances that the Soviet Union's nuclear forces would be covered in Rumsfeld's briefing. Not content to leave this up to chance, the West German permanent representative to NATO, Rolf Pauls, seized the opportunity to explain what his ministers hoped to get out of the Americans in November. Pauls was adamant. Rumsfeld should give a specific and detailed overview dedicated to Eurostrategic forces. "A comparison," Pauls clarified, "should not be all-inclusive but separate according to different categories." Eurostrategic forces were different from other types of theater nuclear forces, such as battlefield weapons, and should be treated accordingly.[34]

Advances in the Soviet arsenal made this approach all the more urgent. Between the SS-20s in development and the introduction of a swing-wing medium bomber, the Backfire, Pauls concluded that the entire balance in Europe was shifting. In light of these decidedly negative trends, how could the Western allies ensure that the Soviet Union did not build up its capabilities in Europe, making the most of weapons unchecked by SALT to hold the continent hostage?[35]

The Western allies' current arrangements were fragile and easily exploited. For years, Pauls reminded his colleagues, NATO had relied on a combination of US strategic forces and weapons assigned to SACEUR to cover the Soviet missiles targeting Europe. The Western allies lacked any viable alternative, Pauls argued, but how could they maintain this state of affairs in the years ahead if the Soviet Union deployed a sizable force of SS-20s, each equipped with multiple warheads?[36]

Pauls insisted that Rumsfeld's forthcoming briefing tackle this question head on, going far beyond Cotter's dress rehearsal. Rumsfeld's November presentation should include data on the quality and quantity of Soviet intermediate-range ballistic missiles and medium-range bombers, along with information about targeting. That way, Pauls argued, the ministers could focus their discussion on "how to deter [the Soviet Union] from using these systems, which fell outside of SALT, for purposes of blackmail."[37] Sir John Killick, Pauls's British counterpart, agreed. The November briefing needed to focus on nuclear systems that were "strategic for Europe."[38]

Kissinger's team was desperate to avoid a briefing like that. Wary of what the Eurostrategic balance implied, they tried to steer Rumsfeld away from the concept. High-ranking officials at the State Department, including Arthur Hartman, George Vest, and Winston Lord, believed that the best path forward would be to talk "candidly about the current state of NATO and Warsaw Pact systems," including the SS-20, but to do so in a way that set these systems within a global balance, not a regional one. Rumsfeld's briefing should, as the three men recommended to Kissinger, "explicitly reject the logic of single numerical sub-balances."[39] In other words, it should ignore exactly what Leber and Pauls had demanded.

Even the request for a briefing seemed at odds with Bonn's security interests, and Hartman, Vest, and Lord wondered whether the West Germans had "thoroughly thought out the implications of this line of argument."[40] During the autumn, a string of West German military officers took pains to clarify

Bonn's thinking. Pauls's recent remarks at the Cotter briefing, Gen. Jürgen Brandt told a group of US officials, "were intended to reflect FRG concern over the imbalance in European theatre strategic forces which will result from the installation of the Soviet SS-20s." Harald Wust, the acting inspector general of the West German armed forces, promised that the permanent representative's comments were not an attempt to challenge NATO's overarching strategy or to suggest that a separate European strategic balance should exist. The Federal Republic, he assured his US interlocutors, remained "fully committed to the triad and did not wish to imply any interest in decoupling."[41]

Though dismissive of the West Germans' logic, Hartman, Vest, and Lord did recognize the connections between the Eurostrategic balance and a series of other complicated issues, including SALT II, MBFR, and the ongoing deliberations about NATO's theater nuclear force posture. The entire issue, they speculated, was perhaps less about the specific correlation of forces in Europe than "a general malaise" on the part of West German officials "with the course of US and Western nuclear defense deployments and thinking in a period of strategic parity."[42]

Rumsfeld's briefing was a chance to set the record straight. To that end, Hartman, Vest, and Lord insisted that the presentation studiously avoid any language that could be construed as tacit acceptance of the Eurostrategic balance as a concept. "There is no way that the USSR could employ or threaten to employ the [SS-20] against NATO Europe without risking totally unacceptable levels of retaliation by NATO, including US strategic forces."[43] But Kissinger and his aides quickly found that they were operating at cross-purposes with their counterparts at the Department of Defense, where at least one group of officials tried to impress on the West Germans that the SS-20 represented a new threat in both qualitative and quantitative terms.[44]

After the Department of Defense's Office of International Security Affairs circulated a working draft of the November presentation, aides urged Kissinger to intervene. The draft did exactly what Hartman, Vest, and Lord had advised against, giving credence to the notion of a Eurostrategic balance. According to the current plans, Rumsfeld's briefing would be structured around three different categories of weapons: strategic systems, non-central systems, and short-range systems intended for use on the battlefield. That formulation mimicked the division between strategic and Eurostrategic that State Department officials had been trying to avoid, only obliquely obscured by different terminology.[45] The team at State chafed at the complete disregard for its earlier concerns. "We proposed amendments," James

Lowenstein, James Goodby, and Winston Lord wrote to Kissinger a week before Rumsfeld's briefing, "which would have altered this framework by merging the central and non-central systems to avoid the presentation of a distinct European regional sub-balance." But the Department of Defense had rejected these changes, instead claiming that the briefing's script would underscore the message that the allies needed to consider the entire spectrum of NATO's forces, as well as the Warsaw Pact's.[46]

Lowenstein, Goodby, and Lord believed that the Defense Department's charts and script might lead listeners to different conclusions. It remained in the interest of the United States to focus on the integrity of NATO's deterrent, not divide it into separate sub-balances. "It is particularly important," they advised Kissinger, "that we do not allow the introduction of new weapons by the Soviets, such as the imminent deployment of the [SS-20], to create the illusion that Europe is subject to 'blackmail,' or that a major European 'response' is required."[47]

Rumsfeld did modify his final presentation, falling in line with what State wanted. When he briefed his fellow defense ministers at the Nuclear Planning Group in November, Rumsfeld emphasized the "continuum" of NATO's deterrent and pushed back on efforts to subdivide it. Pauls, attending the meeting in Leber's stead, remained unmoved.[48]

The complexity and severity of the problem was inescapable. Confronted with what one Canadian diplomat referred to as "the challenging and uninterrupted build-up of Warsaw Pact forces," NATO's path forward was far from clear. How could the Western allies respond, making the most of new weapons and technological advances to protect against an evolving threat?[49]

A Time to Rebuild

The difficult task of answering that question fell to a new administration in Washington. On November 2, 1976, Democratic challenger Jimmy Carter narrowly defeated Gerald Ford at the polls. The former governor of Georgia, Carter had started the campaign as a relative political unknown. But his outsider status and earnest demeanor resonated in a nation still reeling from the Watergate scandal and the war in Vietnam. Savvy campaign operatives harnessed the support of country music stars like the Allman Brothers to propel the Southerner into the national spotlight and then into the White House.

Carter came to the Oval Office with strong convictions. NATO's current arrangements, he believed, were the product of outdated assumptions about the distribution of power among the allies. To better reflect the realities of

the 1970s, Carter envisioned a more equitable relationship with greater consultation. Adapting to the current circumstances would also require improvements to the alliance's defenses, and NATO's conventional forces topped the
Democrat's agenda. Since the 1960s, NATO strategy had suggested a greater
emphasis on conventional forces as an alternative to the early use of nuclear
weapons. But limited public appetite and a slew of economic constraints sty-
mied efforts to secure any substantial investment in the alliance's nonnuclear
capabilities. A string of proposals in the mid-1970s looked for ways to get
the most bang for the Western buck. Possible improvements might take any
number of forms—from investments in high-tech weapons to changes to
procurement policy—inspired by recent think tank studies on NATO's readiness, reinforcements, and overall military requirements.[50] Many of those
ideas found their way into the administration when RAND analyst Robert
Komer became Secretary of Defense Harold Brown's personal adviser on
NATO issues.

Komer's early studies blended with other reviews set in motion during
the administration's first weeks. At the beginning of February 1977, Carter
authorized a top-to-bottom evaluation of European issues, PRM 9, which
included a look at NATO's military posture, force structure, strategy, and tactics.[51] PRM 9, alongside Komer's studies, laid the foundations for a new initiative to improve NATO's conventional force posture, what became known as
the Long-Term Defense Program.

What underpinned the Carter administration's plans was not a dramatic
departure from or a revision of NATO's accepted strategy, but a search for
efficiencies. Brown and his counterpart at State, Cyrus Vance, assured the
president that the Atlantic alliance was not in dire shape. NATO was not
"dangerously weak," as the two put it in a memo to Carter, and the Western
allies need not deviate from the strategy of flexible response. Instead, they
should focus their efforts on putting the alliance on a sounder footing for
the decade ahead.[52] With that objective in mind, Komer's studies identified a
series of low-cost measures. Even these were too much to stomach in some
quarters. "In our own present situation," Sir John Killick, the British permanent representative to NATO, noted in an oblique reference to his country's
now chronic financial woes, "even low-cost measures, if we wish to respond,
will surely require additional resources."[53]

Alongside these improvements, Brown and Vance suggested a new study,
not unlike 1967's Harmel Report. Devoted to the state of East-West relations, it could review the recent changes in NATO's political and security
situation.[54] Not all were convinced. When Henry Owen, a former Harvard
professor now working on NATO issues on the National Security Council,

mentioned the idea to Joseph Luns, the secretary general scoffed. What the alliance needed in Luns's estimation was "not new studies to produce new information, but the political will to adopt the necessary policies."[55]

Luns's antipathy did not deter the Carter administration, which forged ahead with plans for a summit-level gathering in London. Initially slated to be a foreign ministers' meeting, the decision to upgrade the May 1977 session to the highest level set the stage for Carter to unveil a package of initiatives, all designed to inject new confidence into the Atlantic alliance. Carter's advisers appreciated the symbolic purpose such a meeting could serve. It provided an ideal occasion to showcase the new administration's commitment to NATO and to the defense of Europe, doubling down on the message of reassurance that had inspired Vice President Walter Mondale's visit to Europe shortly after the inauguration.[56] Paired with a gathering of the G-7's leaders, also in London, the president's trip could be used to offset fears that the West was no longer vibrant and dynamic. Economic difficulties, from energy shortages to the curious new phenomenon of stagflation, sapped confidence in the capitalist system. The troubling political effects of that trend already seemed visible in the rising appeal of an independent strand of communism in Europe aptly branded "Eurocommunism."[57] NATO's members and other like-minded partners, such as Japan, needed to make the case for their societal model. It was imperative that "the democratic system in its political and economic manifestations" show itself to be "viable and attractive," Carter's national security adviser, Zbigniew Brzezinski, told one interviewer on the eve of the London summits.[58]

By the spring of 1977, the time seemed ripe for reassurance. Though by no means a new challenge, the Warsaw Pact's steady growth remained cause for concern as it cast doubt on the credibility of the alliance.[59] The Carter administration's initial moves on foreign policy had compounded this sense of uncertainty. From the president's outspoken attacks on the Soviet Union's human rights record to the administration's sweeping arms control proposals, the tone emanating out of Washington left the governments of Western Europe rattled. Leading up to the summits in London, pundits speculated about the tense relationship between Carter and his West German counterpart Helmut Schmidt. Brzezinski freely admitted that there had been friction, though he took great pains to assure one interviewer that Schmidt was "not in any doghouse" in Washington.[60] NATO's summit in London would be a diplomatic stage on which the president could affirm strong, confident US leadership.

Carter's performance hit all the right notes. He gave a "brisk and impressive speech," peppered with the requisite assurances that NATO remained the cornerstone of US foreign policy.[61] Coverage of the summit echoed this refrain, hailing Carter's remarks as a symbol of his continued commitment to NATO.[62] The president's concrete proposals, both the Long-Term Defense Program and the Harmel-inspired study of East-West relations, got the go-ahead.

At NATO's Defense Planning Committee the next week, ministers issued guidance for the Long-Term Defense Program. The bulk was devoted, like Komer's earlier work, to nonnuclear issues ranging from reserve mobilization to maritime posture. Those priorities worried the European allies, who continued to see any sustained emphasis on conventional weapons as an indication that the United States was unwilling to use nuclear ones. Carter's recent remarks reflecting on how difficult a decision to use the bomb would be did little to help. Though the president expressed understandable reservations about the use of nuclear weapons, something many might have seen as a comforting sentiment, his doing so cast doubt on the assumption, implicit in the alliance's arrangements, that Carter (or any other president) would be willing to strike the Soviet Union.

The Americans had been here before, and US officials saw unmistakable parallels to the European arguments put forward in the acrimonious strategic debates of the early 1960s. Attuned to these sensitivities, the United States tacked another issue onto the Long-Term Defense Program: NATO's theater nuclear forces.[63]

"The Alice-in-Wonderland World of SALT"

NATO's nuclear forces in Europe had no coherent rationale. By the 1970s, the alliance's stockpile in Europe included around seven thousand nuclear weapons, made up of a mix of systems skewed heavily toward short-range capabilities intended for use on the battlefield. A series of recent studies had examined the size, purpose, and ideal make-up of the stockpile with an eye toward modernizing NATO's capabilities, but even with these efforts, the overall posture remained, according to one British observer, "an accidental hangover from the 1950s."[64] Theater nuclear force issues, as the British strategist and academic Lawrence Freedman put it, occupied a position akin to "the Holy Ghost in the Christian trinity."[65] The Holy Ghost of NATO's triad was no easier to explain than its theological namesake.

The logic governing longer-range theater nuclear forces was even more muddled. In the late 1950s, NATO had deployed medium-range US missiles to Europe, stationing the Thors in the United Kingdom and the Jupiters in Italy and Turkey. By the mid-1960s, these weapons were gone and the various schemes for a NATO nuclear force collapsed when the Johnson administration finally pulled the plug on the MLF. Over the course of the 1970s, as the realities of rough parity set in, the lack of longer-range, land-based forces to set against the Soviet Union's SS-4s, SS-5s, and, as they came online, SS-20s assumed increasing centrality in NATO's debates. Though still uncertain about how they wished to offset these Soviet missiles, the Western European allies were determined to keep NATO's options open.

European efforts coalesced around a new weapon, the cruise missile. After signing SALT I the Nixon administration, convinced that a bargaining chip strategy had made agreement possible, prepared to repeat the formula, requesting funds to accelerate existing programs and invest in new ones— including cruise missiles.[66] A series of programs developed throughout the 1970s, exploring the options for air-, sea-, and ground-launched cruise missiles. An early proponent of a cruise missile program, Kissinger became increasingly disenchanted after November 1974's Vladivostok Accord. "We've got a problem with these escalating cruise missile programs," Kissinger, now secretary of state, lamented in the autumn of 1975.[67]

Since Vladivostok, US and Soviet negotiators had found little success converting their broad agreement into a final treaty. By 1975, SALT II was bogged down in a dispute over the Soviets' new swing-wing bomber—the Backfire—and the cruise missiles. Frustrated, Kissinger bemoaned the US negotiating position. "We just keep on inventing things to put in the agreement," he griped.[68] But his counterpart at the Pentagon, James Schlesinger, was adamant that the Backfire be covered in the final deal and the cruise missile programs protected. Kissinger believed it to be a fool's errand: "The Backfire issue is a fraud."[69]

Schlesinger talked up the potential benefits of the cruise missile, including to his counterparts within the Nuclear Planning Group. In that task, he had a whole host of allies in and out of government. Senator Henry Jackson, a presidential hopeful determined not to see another SALT agreement like 1972's, latched onto the cruise missile. One of his aides, Richard Perle, pressed the missile's case with the Europeans, arguing that any restrictions to the weapon's potential use on the continent would be a mistake. After all, it might be just the ticket to strengthen the independent nuclear forces of Britain and France.

Cruise missiles were a regular topic of conversation at the European-American Workshop, an informal gathering of defense specialists from both sides of the Atlantic. Made up of prominent strategic thinkers and planners, the workshop included a number of individuals who would prove instrumental in the shaping and implementation of the Dual-Track

Decision, such as Walther Stützle, then head of the West German defense ministry's planning staff, the defense analyst Richard Burt (who went on to join the Reagan administration), and Norway's Johan Jørgen Holst.[70] Alongside these discussions, a glut of articles appeared in foreign affairs outlets and defense journals touting the potential advantages of the cruise missile, namely its affordability.[71] Even those who advocated a negotiated ban on the emerging weapons noted that "in a time of tight military budgets and escalating weapons costs," it was tempting to turn to cheap, effective weapons that harnessed technological advances like terrain-mapping guidance systems.[72]

Western Europeans' enthusiasm for the cruise missile tracked their anxieties about the SS-20. By 1977, Western European governments had begun a concerted diplomatic campaign to protect cruise missile options and ensure the Americans did not negotiate them away as part of a final agreement on SALT II. During the Ford years, Kissinger's State Department had tried to discourage interest in the cruise missile as a weapon for Europe. The new technology would not be suitable as a response to the Soviets' forces in theater because of its slow flight speed.[73] The Americans' negative refrain was so predictable that after one session of the Nuclear Planning Group during which the US delegation proposed to tone down references to the cruise missile, a member of the Canadian delegation reported back to Ottawa with a simple assessment: "No surprise."[74]

US efforts to dissuade the Western European allies backfired. If anything, they stoked interest in what the new weapon could do. After the Nuclear Planning Group met in October 1976, the Italian delegation circulated talking points calling explicitly for the "inclusion of cruise missiles in [the] defence apparatus of [the] Alliance" as part of any updates to NATO's theater nuclear force posture.[75] In early 1977, the West Germans urged their colleagues on the Nuclear Planning Group to discuss the possible options for cruise missiles.[76]

A discussion could only go so far, given that the incoming Carter administration was still sorting out how these weapons would fit into its overall approach for SALT II. The superpowers' negotiations remained bogged down, with cruise missiles and the Soviets' Backfire bombers critical sticking points. Kissinger had made a last-ditch attempt to convert the Vladivostok Accord into a final agreement in early 1976, hoping to get a deal with the Soviets before the presidential campaign was in full swing. His efforts went nowhere. Neither did the Ford administration's ideas for an interim agreement that would take the cruise missile and the Backfire bomber off the table.[77]

Disarmament and arms control ranked high on Carter's list of presidential priorities. After coming to office in January 1977, he moved swiftly. Four days after Carter's inauguration, he called for a halt to nuclear weapons testing. He followed that with proposals for a series of new arms control talks, including on a comprehensive test ban.[78] That same boldness infused the Carter administration's approach to SALT II. In late March, Secretary of State Cyrus Vance headed to Moscow, armed with two possible proposals. The first built on the ceilings the Ford administration had agreed to at Vladivostok in November 1974 but called for additional reductions of approximately ten percent. But the second, Carter's preference, envisioned far deeper reductions.

The deep cuts proposal, as the initiative became known, baffled the Soviets. The Ford administration had indicated that an agreement was almost at hand, and now, the Americans wanted to reopen long-settled questions. The fact that the Carter administration introduced the proposal publicly only added to the Soviets' discontent. "The proposals were extremely one-sided and in fact amounted to a suggestion that the negotiations should start again from scratch," Soviet academician Georgy Arbatov later argued. "This confirmed the impression in Moscow that Carter was not serious."[79] Even the administration's allies were inclined to agree. Vance's mission was "patently unattainable," Helmut Schmidt later wrote.[80]

After Vance's visit to Moscow, the Carter administration tried to pick up the pieces. In late April, it adopted a new, tiered approach to SALT II, with three components: an eight-year treaty, a three-year protocol, and a statement of principles to guide subsequent negotiations for SALT III. The protocol, designed to deal with the most contentious issues, proposed to set short-term constraints on the modernization of Soviet intercontinental ballistic missiles against short-term constraints on US cruise missiles. The United States had no plans to deploy ground- and sea-launched cruise missiles in the near future, and so neither would be affected. But the Carter administration saw air-launched cruise missiles as an attractive alternative to the B-1 supersonic bomber. The proposal, as a result, recommended restrictions on the deployment of ground- and sea-launched cruise missiles, but left air-launched options unrestricted. To Washington's allies, that prospect was unacceptable. If the superpowers agreed to limit cruise missiles with a nonstrategic range, NATO would "give up an essential counterpart" to the Soviet Union's SS-20s, the head of the West German foreign ministry's arms control and disarmament division, Friedrich Ruth, argued.[81]

Under continued European pressure, the Carter administration relented and circulated a paper reviewing the cruise missile question in May 1977. Assistant Secretary of State Leslie Gelb described the paper as "an even-handed look" at the cruise missile, weighing the pros and cons of the weapon.[82] In practice, this approach virtually ensured that the paper would be attacked from all sides. "The paper," in the estimation of one British official, "devotes a great deal of attention to assembling arguments for and against a particular role, but frequently concludes that there is as yet insufficient evidence to reach a firm conclusion."[83] Gelb viewed this ambiguity as an accurate reflection of where the debate stood. Rather than make the case for or against cruise missiles in Europe, the paper acknowledged that there was no consensus view.[84]

After Carter's June decision to cancel the B-1 bomber, it became all the more important to protect the air-launched cruise missile options left unrestricted in the administration's recommended protocol. Yet, this distinction between air-launched cruise missiles and other ground- and sea-launched variants provided even more fodder for those who believed that the Americans were content to foreclose options that the Europeans might want in order to protect their own interests. "In the Alice-in-Wonderland world of SALT," one anonymous US official remarked, "the B-1 cancellation put additional pressure on us to treat the cruise missile as some sort of holy thing."[85]

But the Carter administration remained wary of any endorsement of a distinct Eurostrategic balance. When defense ministers gathered in Ottawa for the Nuclear Planning Group's June meeting, Harold Brown warned his colleagues that gray-area issues—the common shorthand for the constellation of problems related to SALT II and the correlation of nuclear forces in Europe—could easily divide the alliance and discouraged any endorsement of sub-balances within the overall balance of power. Brown assured his fellow defense ministers that, despite the SS-20s, NATO still possessed more total warheads than the Warsaw Pact. Georg Leber held the earlier West German line; any cruise missiles that fell short of intercontinental range should not be discussed as part of SALT II.[86]

To Deploy or Not to Deploy

Harold Brown tried to ascertain what steps the Western European allies wanted NATO to take. On the margins of the Nuclear Planning Group's Ottawa meeting, Brown asked his British counterpart, Fred Mulley, what, if anything, the Europeans thought should be done to counterbalance the Soviets' SS-20s and Backfires.[87] Mulley demurred, taking the question back to London for further study. For the remainder of the summer, the British Ministry of Defence tried to develop a clear answer. The resulting studies reinforced a growing conviction that the cruise missile could be a solution and injected a new sense of urgency into British attempts to protect the alliance's options. British planners deemed it vital to resist the United States' efforts to divert the Europeans away from theater options for the cruise missile.[88]

West German officials shared that objective. Members of the defense staff worried that political pressure to make progress on SALT II might lead the Carter administration to give away Europe's options, foreclosing the possibility of introducing cruise missiles in a deep-strike role.[89] "Our concern at the moment," as Hans-Dietrich Genscher, the West German foreign minister, put it in a letter to Vance, "was that no commitments should be made which might cause irreparable damage to the position of the Alliance."[90]

In Washington, it was clear that a caucus to protect the cruise missile was emerging in Europe. "More evidence accumulates that the Europeans, late converts to cruise missiles, are no less fervent believers for their tardiness," one report to Brzezinski summed up the situation. One anonymous West German defense official, in merely the latest example of this phenomenon, had recommended that if the administration were to strike a deal with the Soviets on cruise missiles, it should be done independent of SALT II as part of a trade for Moscow's medium- and intermediate-range missiles aimed at targets across Western Europe.[91]

The allies traded views again at the North Atlantic Council in late July. Even the chosen allied forum reflected how the issue's importance was changing; holding the discussion at the council, rather than within the Nuclear Planning Group, ensured French participation.[92] Gelb, who delivered the opening briefing, walked the permanent representatives through the current US position on SALT II. The proposed cruise missile restrictions were designed to introduce some limits but keep open the alliance's core options. This approach would ensure that the allies had time to study the possible uses of cruise missiles, Gelb emphasized, while also keeping these systems as a possible bargaining chip for later negotiations on SALT III.[93]

The possible links to the Soviet Union's new systems were front of mind, and Gelb explicitly raised the question of whether the alliance should "demonstrably counter-balance" the SS-20 and Backfire.[94] Felice Catalano, the Italian permanent representative, focused on the potential roles that the cruise missile could play in the alliance's defenses, pressing for more information. Did the Americans think that NATO's current systems were enough to counter the SS-20 and Backfire? Or did the allies need to introduce new, longer-range forces to enhance deterrence?[95] Walter Slocombe, the deputy assistant secretary of defense for international security affairs, returned to a familiar refrain, arguing that the deployment of cruise missiles would not fill a gap but could add to the alliance's already sufficient capabilities. As for the SS-20 and Backfire, these systems "only represented enhancement of a capability possessed by the Soviets since the 1950s."[96]

Not content to leave US arguments unchecked, the British permanent representative, Sir John Killick, intervened. Cruise missiles, he argued, could augment and diversify NATO's systems, not to increase the alliance's options but to maintain them in the face of the Warsaw Pact's rapid growth. Although the Western allies had credible options at present, there was no guarantee that this would remain the case in the future. Why rule out the possibility of a deep-strike weapon, such as the ground-launched cruise missile, which the alliance might need in the years ahead?[97]

NATO's political requirements demanded broad participation in the nuclear deterrent. With that in mind, Killick pointed out the dangers of relying too much on strategic forces, thereby diminishing "the principle of shared risks."[98] Perhaps the allies would decide in the end that cruise missiles were not needed. Militarily, they might be able to live with fewer long-range strike targets in the Warsaw Pact and western reaches of the Soviet Union. But the issue at hand was about far more than targeting requirements. "The Soviet Union," Killick reminded his colleagues, "is about to pose an even greater threat to Western Europe than at present through the imminent deployment of the SS-20 missiles, the increased deployment of Backfire together with strike aircraft, and the Alliance needs to be able to make an effective response." So long as the allies were debating whether the existing systems were enough, they should not rule out a potential option, like the cruise, that could help solve this problem.[99]

Skeptical of Gelb's claims about the temporary nature of the proposed three-year protocol, Killick, now speaking on his personal authority alone, wondered how the Americans could be so confident that it would remain temporary. The Soviet Union was almost certain to agitate for the protocol's extension, if not its transformation into a permanent agreement. "It would be typical if in so doing they invoked all kinds of threats in terms of future progress on arms control and disarmament, not to mention in terms of US-Soviet relations more generally." The result would be the same: to foreclose NATO's options regarding the cruise missile.[100]

It was one thing for the superpowers to restrict the cruise missile's strategic applications, but to accept restrictions on its possible role as a theater weapon seemed to defy standing policy. Killick drew a comparison to the inclusion of forward-based systems in SALT, something the allies had systematically opposed up to that point. SALT II would be followed by another round of negotiations, likely multilateral talks on SALT III, dealing with forward-based systems and the balance in the European theater. To Killick, it only made sense that the alliance preserve a bargaining chip, "some incentive for serious Soviet interest in reducing their inventory of systems capable of striking with strategic effect at the whole of NATO Europe."[101] Reporting back to London, Killick hoped that his intervention could help win supporters in the interagency debates unfolding in Washington. Gelb and the other Americans in attendance, he noted optimistically, would have "a good deal to report back in Washington to those who may be our supporters over the formulation of the cruise missile clauses."[102]

Killick found one well-placed ally. A few days after the council met, Gen. Alexander Haig called Killick directly to express his strong support. After seeing a readout of the council's discussion, Haig assumed that Killick's comments were informed by the ideas about NATO's theater nuclear posture that Mulley and Brown had traded at the Nuclear Planning Group in Ottawa. Killick confirmed Haig's hunch. "I thought you would be amused— perhaps even impressed," Killick wrote to Michael Quinlan, the deputy undersecretary for policy at the Ministry of Defence, after receiving Haig's call. But Killick assured Quinlan that he would not be advertising the conversation. It was "far from self-evident," Killick quipped, "that the endorsement of Al Haig [was] necessarily the passport to glory in all quarters, even in Whitehall!"[103]

Killick's remarks left little doubt about the British desire to protect all cruise missile options in the European theater. London's lobbying of the Americans continued in bilateral talks, held on the heels of the council's discussion. John Wilberforce, the head of the Foreign and Commonwealth Office's Defence Department, focused on the issue's political dimensions. "The Europeans would be unhappy," he argued, "if a process developed whereby the only possible response to a Soviet strike against Europe was the use of elements of the Americans' strategic systems. It was imperative that NATO should retain the capability to strike Soviet territory from within Europe. This did not entail thinking in terms of a regional nuclear balance." His colleague, Clive Whitmore, put British reservations even more succinctly: "We were unwilling to see options closed off in SALT whose effect might be to reduce European involvement in the deep-strike role by increasing NATO's dependence on US systems."[104]

British thinking had coalesced around the potential need for cruise missiles. Nowhere was this more clear than in an early August letter that Mulley sent to Brown, following up on their conversation on the margins of the Nuclear Planning Group earlier that summer. "With NATO Europe having to adjust (sometimes uneasily) to strategic nuclear parity," Mulley argued, "any major reduction in 'theater' target coverage would cause grave disquiet in NATO—and perhaps dangerous misunderstanding in the Soviet Union." Existing allied systems, such as the Polaris submarines or the Vulcan, Buccaneer, and Jaguar aircraft, all of which could strike the Soviet Union, were unlikely to offer sufficient reassurance in the face of the Soviets' rapid growth. For the Europeans, coupling, linking the theater level to the United States' strategic forces, rested "upon the combination of visible European basing and European sharing in control and ownership (through delivery vehicles)."[105] Cruise missiles could play a vital role in addressing the gray-area problem, meeting NATO's political and military needs.

What Mulley laid out was the case for upgrading NATO's longer-range theater nuclear force, introducing a new generation of land-based missiles. It was the first fully formed justification for what would become the deployment track of NATO's Dual-Track Decision.

The Balancer

Gray areas occupied much of the NATO machinery's time, but the Western allies' debates largely unfolded within the regular channels that made sure the alliance worked day to day. That changed on October 28, 1977, when a frustrated Helmut Schmidt decided to go public with his concerns. In a speech at London's International Institute for Strategic Studies, the chancellor underscored the importance of political and military balance in Europe, before offering a sharp warning about the dangers of strategic parity. "SALT codifies the nuclear strategic balance between the Soviet Union and the United States," Schmidt argued. "To put it another way: SALT neutralizes their strategic nuclear capabilities. In Europe this magnifies the significance of the disparities between East and West in nuclear tactical and conventional systems."[106]

Since 1969, successive governments in Bonn had sounded the alarm on what parity would mean for Europe's security. The contours of Schmidt's case were well worn and easily recognized by anyone familiar with his thinking and writing about the strategy of balance. What made the London speech different was Schmidt's willingness to make that case in such a public setting as an elected official.

The speech focused on the nature of security in the 1970s. In it, Schmidt touched on everything from economic development and the social safety net to the threat of terrorism. The speech's timing underscored the need for such a broad definition. Weeks earlier, members of the Red Army Faction, a leftist West German terrorist group, had murdered the president of the German Employers' Association, Hanns Martin Schleyer, and hijacked a Lufthansa passenger plane with the help of the Popular Front for the Liberation of Palestine. The Soviet threat to Europe was but one of many security concerns and not the sole focus of the chancellor's remarks in London.

But lurking just below the surface in Schmidt's remarks was a familiar question about the credibility of the US nuclear guarantee. Would the United States be willing to follow through on its commitments "to commit suicide for Europe"?[107] The fact that the West German chancellor would raise this question publicly, even if obliquely, was a sign of just how far Bonn's confidence had fallen. Schmidt's mounting distrust of Jimmy Carter only amplified these insecurities, as the chancellor concluded that Carter was neither willing nor able to exercise sufficient leadership worldwide, let alone safeguard the Federal Republic's security interests. An early August press leak suggesting that the Carter administration had adopted a new defense strategy, PRM 10, that included plans to concede a third of the Federal Republic's territory should the Soviets invade, was not exactly a boost to morale.[108]

Above all, Schmidt's warning was the product of frustration. He believed that his earlier concerns about SALT's impact on European security had been ignored by the Carter administration, just as they had been during the Ford years.[109] At NATO's May summit in London, for instance, the chancellor had offered a pointed reminder that the Western allies desperately needed to make the doctrine of flexible response more credible. "The equitable distribution of risks" remained critical, but the broader strategic landscape was shifting. To Schmidt, it seemed that the alliance was approaching a new, third stage in its strategy defined by approximate parity between the superpowers. This would, in effect, reduce the role of strategic nuclear forces, which would increasingly be seen as "an instrument of last resort."[110] Warnings like these went unheeded, much to the chancellor's chagrin. "I was seething; I spoke freely," Schmidt later acknowledged.[111]

Nor was parity the only issue irritating Schmidt. Since Carter had taken office earlier that year, the two had squared off over everything from economic policy and nuclear nonproliferation to how to handle the Soviet Union's dismal human rights record. There was no love lost between the two leaders.[112] "The chemistry was just awful," Carter aides later remembered. The president was, according to staffers, "gentle, assuming, [and] very much into the details."[113] Their descriptions of Schmidt were far less charitable.

A know-it-all with an arrogant streak, the chancellor never seemed to miss "an opportunity to bitch, moan, and criticize the president."[114]

Helmut Schmidt's London speech took on totemic status. Observers, including Schmidt himself, referred to his remarks as the genesis of the Dual-Track Decision, and scholars have given it pride of place in their narratives as the beginning of the Euromissiles Crisis.[115] But Schmidt's comments on strategic parity and the threat to Europe were the product of years of West German angst about the erosion of extended deterrence in the face of new Soviet weapons and new arms control agreements between the superpowers. Everything about the Federal Republic's foreign policy, from the security guarantees that it relied on to the pursuit of détente that Schmidt's government championed, depended on the success of the strategy of balance. From the vantage point of Bonn, new and improved Soviet missiles in Europe threatened to topple that balance, exposing the West Germans to political blackmail and threatening the very foundations of the country's security policy.

But could the Western allies shore up the balance in Europe? The prospects for doing so through arms control negotiations seemed slim. Economic constraints limited NATO's ability to invest in its defenses, as did the continued political constraints of parliaments and publics convinced that there were better things to spend their states' precious funds on. The Soviet Union seemingly faced none of the same restrictions, its coffers flush with cash from the boom in oil prices. With Moscow on the ascent, at least in military terms, policymakers on both sides of the Atlantic wondered if NATO's members could still cobble together enough support to make the difficult decisions required to preserve their security.

CHAPTER 4

Fiasco!

Readers who picked up copies of the *Washington Post* on Monday, June 6, 1977, were greeted with alarming news. The Energy and Research Development Administration's budget for 1978 included funds for a new, devastating weapons system that the story's author, Walter Pincus, dubbed a "neutron killer warhead." This enhanced radiation warhead, Pincus warned darkly, would be the first "designed to kill people through the release of neutrons rather than to destroy military installations through heat and blast."[1]

Grim depictions of a weapon designed to kill people but preserve property seared into the public imagination and spurred a new wave of antinuclear activism dedicated to stopping the so-called "neutron bomb." In the face of this opposition, the Western allies struggled to put forward a compelling case for the warhead. Military requirements and jargon-based technical justifications might be sound logic for a weapon, but as the allies soon found, they scarcely made for a good argument to counter images of the neutron bomb as a capitalist superweapon.

That fact was not lost on the Warsaw Pact. Sensing the opportunities afforded by homegrown antinuclear sentiment throughout the West, the pact's members mobilized. Soviet diplomats touted their credentials as champions of détente and protectors of peace, trotting out a steady stream of proposals to ban the neutron bomb and deepen the military détente in

Europe. From Moscow to East Berlin, governments poured funds into activist groups and disinformation campaigns designed to exploit the discontent simmering within NATO.

Faced with mounting popular opposition and a concerted Warsaw Pact campaign to exacerbate and exploit those tensions, NATO's members searched for ways to make the introduction of the enhanced radiation warheads politically palatable. After months of debate, the Western allies settled on a policy that married the warheads' deployment with an arms control offer that, if accepted, would render that deployment unnecessary.

But with the scheme all set, it promptly fell apart. Jimmy Carter pulled his support in March 1978. Carter's move rattled the rest of the Western allies and reinforced already popular conclusions that the American lacked the fortitude to lead. Desperate to offset these impressions, the Carter administration revisited its policy on NATO's longer-range theater nuclear forces with a renewed willingness to entertain Western European arguments that the Soviets' SS-20s threatened Europe's security in fundamentally new ways.

The Neutron Bomb and the Dangers of Escalation

Pincus's reports caught Carter off guard. After the story broke, the president admitted that he knew almost nothing about the enhanced radiation warhead.[2] Carter was hardly alone. Few in positions of power had thought about it in any detail, even though the weapon had been discussed on and off since the 1950s and was part of plans to modernize NATO's nuclear forces in Europe set in motion during the Ford years. Those who did know about the warhead assumed the story would pass quickly. "I figured Pincus's story was such preposterous journalism that any good PR man would make hash of it in two days," Carter's secretary of energy, James Schlesinger, remarked.[3]

The enhanced radiation warhead was a miniaturized hydrogen device, designed to be fitted to short-range missiles and tactical nuclear artillery in Central Europe. There, it could defend against a frontal assault on NATO's position in the Federal Republic, offsetting the Warsaw Pact's numerical superiority in conventional forces. Designers envisioned a weapon that would use enhanced radiation to emit a burst that would take out the enemy tank crews while limiting the damage to the territory, thereby making it easier to take. When the debate entered the public sphere, these promises of reduced collateral damage were quickly translated into more accessible language; it would destroy people, not property.

Laced with sensational language, early reports branded the enhanced radiation warhead as the neutron bomb and painted a picture of a particularly gruesome and destructive type of nuclear weapon. If used, one story told readers, the warhead would unleash "a particularly intense wave of neutron radiation which kills people but does comparatively little damage to property."[4] Grim cartoons reinforced this impression, depicting skeletons vaporized by the neutron bomb, yet sitting in a still standing and perfectly staged home.[5]

Designed for battlefield use, the neutron bomb was a small warhead. Planners touted the usability of these mini-nukes and the promise of controlled escalation, claims that terrified the growing number of opponents. Critics inverted the planners' logic, arguing that flexibility introduced a new type of danger. It would lower the nuclear threshold, making the prospect of nuclear war more, not less, likely.[6]

With more usable weapons, policymakers might be tempted to launch them. "The principal inhibition in the minds of sane politicians and soldiers," the former British defense secretary Lord Alun Chalfont concluded, "is the very nature of the nuclear weapon—its appalling capacity for inflicting massive, indiscriminate death and destruction."[7] This line of attack probed the unresolved ambiguities within flexible response. When, where, and on what terms should NATO go nuclear? Earlier in the decade, when NATO officials considered the possibilities afforded by new technologies and the modernization of the alliance's stockpile in Europe, they danced around these same problems. Critics from the arms control community in the United States worried that these technological advancements would lower the threshold for nuclear use, while their European counterparts tended to stress the dangers of decoupling.[8]

With the debate unfolding in public, a new segment of the population was exposed to the uneasy assumptions implicit in NATO's nuclear planning. Protestors chafed at the idea that the neutron bomb could be used as a tactical weapon in a nonnuclear conflict. "Far from being a way to contain war," one demonstrator at a Belgian protest remarked, "it could be the means to escalate from non-nuclear to nuclear conflict."[9] To adherents of flexible response, that was an intentional choice and a benefit to be touted. Just as generations of European policymakers had worried that the Americans might try to confine a war to Europe, so too did the neutron bomb's critics, though they communicated with a much larger audience stretching far beyond specialist circles.

Carter managed to secure the program's funding in the Senate, but the weapon's production remained an open question.[10] Cyrus Vance, Harold

Brown, and Zbigniew Brzezinski all advised him to move forward with a decision to produce it. Carter demurred, preferring to consult with the Western European allies first. He hoped to secure support for production as well as for deployment, convinced that it scarcely made sense to produce the warheads if the Western Europeans would never deploy them.

Given their intended role in Central Europe, the most logical home for the enhanced radiation warheads would be the Federal Republic of Germany. But, as July 1977 came to a close, it was clear that Helmut Schmidt's government would face an uphill political battle to secure sufficient support for their deployment. News of the neutron bomb touched off a political firestorm.[11] Egon Bahr, the SPD's executive party secretary, took to the pages of *Vorwärts*, the party's weekly paper, to attack the warhead. The veteran Social Democrat, best known as former chancellor Willy Brandt's right-hand man and a key architect of Ostpolitik, decried the dangers of the neutron bomb and cast it as "a symbol of the perversion of thought." The weapon, he argued, would increase the possibility that a limited nuclear war might be fought in Europe. The superpowers could tolerate that kind of conflict, but for Germans straddling the fault lines of the Cold War, the prospect was intolerable. "Is mankind about to go mad?" the story's headline blared.[12]

Bahr's rejection struck a chord. Hundreds of letters poured into his office from West Germans who shared Bahr's sense of outrage.[13] The emotional and public nature of his appeal galvanized opponents, all the more so given the stark contrast between Bahr's unvarnished assessments and the government's cautious position. Helmut Schmidt, Hans-Dietrich Genscher, and Georg Leber made few public statements about the warhead. The fact that Bahr came from the same party as Schmidt and Leber—Genscher headed the governing coalition's other party, the Free Democrats—injected another layer of political uncertainty into the process. To secure the kind of support for the warheads' deployment that Carter needed, Schmidt would have to cobble together and sustain the backing of his own increasingly fractured Social Democrats. Little wonder, then, that Schmidt urged Carter to stick with the model the president's predecessors had pursued; the United States could make a development decision on its own, followed by a separate decision on the weapon's deployment.[14]

The way that the issue entered the public discourse put the Western allies on the back foot. A flurry of emotionally charged news stories reminded readers of the real dangers of nuclear weapons, and the enhanced radiation warhead ended up seared into the public consciousness as the "killer warhead."[15] Story after story described it, in the words of one columnist in the

Guardian, as a "formidable nuclear weapon which destroys human life but leaves buildings and property intact."[16] No matter the military or strategic arguments in favor, that early messaging made the neutron bomb difficult to sell. "Whatever other virtue or rationale the weapon had would never catch up with that awful sloganeering," the US ambassador to the Netherlands, Robert McCloskey, later concluded.[17] Rolf Pauls, the West German permanent representative to NATO, bemoaned the disarray in the alliance's public position on the neutron bomb. Allied governments desperately needed a compelling case to make to their voters, but Pauls worried that the debate in the Federal Republic was "approaching hysteria."[18]

Zbigniew Brzezinski complained that the Western Europeans were petrified of the popular opposition to the neutron bomb, fearful that any support for the warheads would be interpreted as a tacit endorsement of nuclear warfare waged on their own soil.[19] It was a recipe for prolonged stalemate. Carter and his advisers pressed for a strong commitment to deploy the enhanced radiation warhead, hoping that the Europeans would share the political costs of a production decision rather than leave the president to play the "ogre."[20] But those costs seemed to skyrocket on an almost daily basis, as protest groups mobilized and peace campaigners denounced the evils of the neutron bomb.

Thinking in Parallel

Throughout the autumn of 1977 and into the winter, the United States and the Federal Republic went around in circles. The Americans continued to lobby for a firm statement of support for the neutron bomb's deployment. The likely candidates to host the warheads had few incentives to stake out a strong position in favor of deployment. "We are not going to invite deployment—before your president has even made a decision—and make political fools out of ourselves," one of Schmidt's aides argued.[21]

Despite the impasse, the Schmidt coalition and the Carter administration were moving in the same direction: toward arms control. To deal with the controversial warhead, the West Germans began to consider the weapon's potential as a bargaining chip with a link to the stalled negotiations on MBFR.[22] Brzezinski and Schmidt met in late September, when the two discussed a possible link between the neutron bomb and existing arms control negotiations, whether MBFR or SALT.[23]

NATO's supreme allied commander, Gen. Alexander Haig, thought a trade against tanks presented a promising option to circumvent the problems plaguing the MBFR negotiations. The current Western position, still based on what Haig derided as the "less than enlightened" nuclear option, threatened to give up the kind of longer-range theater nuclear forces the allies were currently arguing about in the debate over cruise missile options and in the SALT II negotiations.[24] A connection to the struggling MBFR negotiations could draw the public's attention to the talks' failure to date and the risks that remained, as Schmidt had in his October remarks at London's International Institute for Strategic Studies. After reminding listeners that those negotiations had yet to produce any tangible reductions, Schmidt underscored the implications for Europe. "Up to now the Soviet Union has given no clear indication that she is willing to accept the principle of parity for Europe, as she did for SALT," he reported. Against that backdrop, the Western allies had no choice but to rely on deterrence. "It is in this context and no other that the public discussion in all member states of the Western Alliance about the 'neutron weapon' has to be seen." But the allies could not focus solely on the weapon's role in deterrence. They could not ignore its place in arms control.[25]

Schmidt's case rested on the continued belief that political and military balance remained the basic prerequisite for security, and, in London, the chancellor cautioned his listeners that they could ill afford to neglect that balance. Not only was it the foundation of their security, but it was also the prerequisite for any progress toward détente. He saw their current moment as a time of great paradox. "There is a closer proximity between a hazardous arms race, on the one hand, and a successful control of arms, on the other, than ever before," Schmidt argued. "There is only a narrow divide between the hope for peace and the danger of war."[26]

After Schmidt's remarks in London, the Carter administration tried to discern what kind of connection the chancellor envisioned between the neutron bomb and the MBFR negotiations. Schmidt's thinking retained a degree of ambiguity, and the Americans remained uncertain whether he wished to see the neutron bomb introduced in MBFR or whether he merely wanted to keep that option for use at a later date. The domestic political constraints shaping Schmidt's ambiguous position were not lost on the Americans. It seemed obvious that the chancellor hoped to make it through the SPD's forthcoming convention in Hamburg in November without taking a firm stand.[27]

Guided by the pursuit of balance, Schmidt's government continued to flesh out its preferred policy regarding the neutron bomb. Almost two weeks after Schmidt's speech, on November 9, the Federal Security Council (Bundessicherheitsrat) laid out a basic position. Consistent with Schmidt's earlier arguments, it maintained that the United States should make a decision about whether to go ahead with the weapon's production. As for the arms control dimensions, the enhanced radiation warheads could be rolled into Option III of the Western powers' negotiating position on MBFR and, in exchange, they could demand a sizable reduction of Soviet tanks beyond the current calls for Moscow to slash seventeen hundred. This approach would help to create a degree of conventional-force parity in Europe, something that State Secretary Günther van Well reiterating Schmidt's arguments in London, conveyed to the Carter administration as consistent with a growing need to secure the balance in Europe, given the superpowers' strategic parity.[28]

A trade with tanks found supporters in Washington, but the Carter administration also entertained the possibility of another link. What if the administration offered to set the neutron bomb against the troublesome Soviet SS-20s? Secretary of Defense Harold Brown anticipated that the Kremlin was almost certain to reject the offer, but that did little to diminish its appeal in the secretary's eyes.[29] It would be simple and timely, putting the squeeze on the Soviets' public diplomacy. If the Kremlin rejected a trade with the SS-20, the Western allies could use that refusal to undercut Moscow's regular refrain that the Soviet Union was the true champion of peace, détente, and disarmament. And in technical terms, if the Soviets refused the offer on the grounds that the neutron bomb was too small to set against the SS-20, that line of argument would undermine earlier Soviet claims that the neutron bomb represented a fearsome new type of inhumane weapon.[30]

Brown's logic departed from Schmidt's in pivotal ways. For the secretary of defense, arms control could be used to push back on the Soviets' arguments and highlight the inconsistencies within the Kremlin's case. The chancellor saw arms control and weapons deployment as two roads to the same desirable outcome: a greater degree of balance within Europe. Schmidt would prefer to achieve this result through arms control, but if the deployment was the only option on the table, then the allies should be prepared to carry it out to preserve their overall strategy of deterrence. Brown's more cynical approach could easily turn into a liability. George Vest, who served as assistant secretary of state for European affairs, warned that a trade for the SS-20 could be construed as a "ploy" to sidestep the thorny debates about cruise missile options unfolding alongside those over the neutron bomb.[31]

After a series of deliberations in November, the Special Coordination Committee, which Carter had created to deal with foreign policy issues, primarily arms control, intelligence, and crisis management, recommended a three-part approach. The final decision could link the weapon's production, its deployment, and an offer not to deploy it if the Soviets refrained from deploying the SS-20. To garner support for this course of action, the committee suggested that Carter first reach out to Schmidt to sound out the chancellor's position and propose consultations on broad security issues. Alongside these exchanges, the Americans would raise the possibility of a trade that set the enhanced radiation warhead against the SS-20, though they would not rule out the West Germans' preferred connection to MBFR. "This line," the committee concluded, "would build on Chancellor Schmidt's recent proposals (a) for four-power consultations on SALT and (b) for linking [enhanced radiation warheads] to MBFR."[32]

Carter hit the suggested themes in a late November letter to the chancellor. After acknowledging Schmidt's concerns regarding parity and the gray-area problem, raised publicly the month before in London, Carter proposed broad consultations with the British and the French to discusses these issues. But the president's prior condition remained; he was willing to produce the enhanced radiation warhead if—and only if—the allies expressed "explicit support for the deployment of these weapons in Europe."[33]

At a series of consultations throughout the winter, British, West German, and US officials tried to nail down a final policy package that brought together production, deployment, and an offer to call off deployment in exchange for a Soviet concession. In each of the three allied capitals, policymakers debated the merits of a trade with the SS-20 relative to one set against MBFR. The former would have the benefit of focusing their constituents' attention on the Soviet Union's nuclear power threatening Europe and might assuage some of the alliance's simmering "political-psychological issues" regarding strategic parity and the gray-area problem.[34] From a purely technical standpoint, linking the neutron bomb to MBFR made more sense as a way to achieve symmetrical reductions. Soviet tanks would be set against the enhanced radiation warheads, which were, regardless of the slogans, fundamentally an antitank weapon.[35]

"The Continued Spectacle of Alliance Indecision"

The longer the Western allies delayed a decision, the more difficult the situation threatened to become. Stuck at an impasse as the allies went around in circles about the relationship between development and deployment, Leslie Gelb wanted a way out. "Our inability to make a decision," he complained in December 1977 to Klaus Blech, the director of the West German foreign ministry's political office, "put us in an impossible political and diplomatic position, where it appeared that Alliance force planning decisions were hostage to a Soviet propaganda campaign."[36]

Since the summer of 1977, when the neutron bomb burst onto the scene, the Soviets had made the most of the weapon's public profile. Moscow mounted a massive public campaign to drum up anti–neutron bomb sentiment, matched by what US intelligence referred to as "an orchestrated pattern of private Soviet diplomatic representations."[37] Soviet talking points latched onto the weapon's capabilities and cast it as the ultimate tool of capitalism. The neutron bomb would destroy people, not property. What better reflected the exploitative spirit of the capitalist system?

Carter's public insistence on European support created an ideal opening for the Warsaw Pact. With the president adamant that European attitudes mattered, the Soviets and their allies, whether the intelligence agencies of the Warsaw Pact or a motley crew of front groups, saw leverage. Public opinion across Western Europe could be used to constrain US policy or, at the very least, dramatically increase the political costs of building a new nuclear weapon. To turn Europeans against the neutron bomb, the Warsaw Pact relied on familiar tools of the trade: well-placed press stories, forged documents, covert funding for peace groups, agitation through front organizations, and preying on existing fears of everything from US domination to nuclear annihilation.

The Warsaw Pact's influence operations mixed with genuine homegrown fears about the neutron bomb. Hoping to heighten these anxieties, front organizations like the World Peace Council churned out pamphlets and brochures laced with accusations that Carter wished to accelerate the arms race.[38] The council declared a week of action, timed to coincide with the anniversary of the first use of the atomic bomb in war, filled with antinuclear demonstrations across Europe, Latin America, the Middle East, and Africa. Warsaw Pact governments poured funds into grassroots campaigns.[39] That same week, twenty-eight communist parties in Europe and North America banded together to issue a public call urging Carter to ban the neutron bomb.[40] US estimates concluded that the Soviets spent the equivalent of $100 million on the campaign to stop the neutron bomb, once the rallies, subsidies, direct advertisements, and travel expenses were all tallied.[41] The East Germans, in the span of two years, funneled 120,000 guilders into one Dutch campaign, Stop the Neutron Bomb (Stop de Neutronenbom), just shy of $60,000.[42]

Stop the Neutron Bomb's communist leanings were no secret, with the campaign publicly spearheaded by the Communist Party of the Netherlands. Nor did those ties damage its popularity. "You can expect some people not to

FIGURE 4.1. Artists protest the neutron bomb, Amsterdam, October 1977. Source: Bert Verhoeff/ Anefo/Nationaal Archief (NL-HaNa inventory file no. 929-4132). https://www.nationaalarchief.nl/ en/research/photo-collection/aca55fbe-d0b4-102d-bcf8-003048976d84.

help a campaign if it is communist-led," one of its leaders, Nico Schouten, told reporters. "But so many people here are convinced that the neutron bomb [is] wrong that they are willing to cooperate with us in a businesslike way."[43] A series of noncommunist peace groups in the Netherlands, such as Pax Christi and the Interchurch Peace Council (Interkerkelijk Vredesberaad, IKV), lent their support to the campaign.[44]

Ramping up Soviet efforts, Leonid Brezhnev dispatched letters to the leaders of NATO countries in January 1978, urging them to reject the weapon lest they jeopardize the entire process of détente.[45] These direct appeals were accompanied by a barrage of letters to Western parliamentarians from members of the Supreme Soviet, as well as by overtures from Soviet trade union representatives to union organizers across the alliance.[46] In public, Soviet diplomacy touted a string of initiatives to ensure that the neutron bomb was never deployed. They introduced resolutions at the United Nations for a convention prohibiting weapons of mass destruction, including the neutron bomb, and continued to float proposals that the two superpowers ban the warhead outright.[47]

But the allies remained at an impasse, still trying to figure out whether and how they might share the burdens of production and deployment. On January 20, 1978, the Federal Security Council embraced the three-part approach that had coalesced throughout the autumn. Carter would announce plans to produce the enhanced radiation warheads, after which NATO would offer to halt the weapons' deployment to Europe as part of arms control negotiations with the Soviet Union. If those negotiations yielded nothing within two years' time, some combination of the European allies—including, but not limited to, the Federal Republic of Germany—would host the neutron bomb. This tiered approach made sense in strictly military terms, as it would reduce the Soviet threat through arms control or, should that fail, through the deployment of new weapons. It would also put the Europeans in a much stronger position with their voters, with a new high ground in the court of public opinion.[48]

Time was of the essence. NATO's secretary general, Joseph Luns, hammered home the political costs as the issue dragged on without resolution. It was easy to envision how the neutron bomb might spill over into the alliance's summit in May 1978, a state of affairs certain to undercut the meeting's central message of renewed investment in Western defense with the adoption of the Long-Term Defense Program's final recommendations.[49] NATO's lack of progress created the impression of weakness and uncertainty, what one Carter aide disparaged as "the continued spectacle of Alliance indecision."[50] There were other reasons to move quickly. Any decision to produce the enhanced radiation warhead was sure to cause a stir if NATO decided to do so in advance of the United Nations Special Session on Disarmament, set to open in late May.[51]

Carter supported an arms control offer that would link the enhanced radiation warhead with the SS-20. "The coupling of these two issues," the Americans told their British counterparts, "would provide a sound political basis for countering Soviet propaganda and going ahead with ERWs."[52] The British thought the offer unlikely to succeed. The Soviets, they predicted, were far more likely to trot out their earlier offers for mutual renunciation of the neutron bomb than to accept a link to the SS-20.[53] Some US officials shared these doubts, focused on the clear asymmetry between the two sides of the offer. The deputy chief of the US Mission to NATO, Maynard Glitman, wondered if the allies were trying to mix "battlefield oranges with strategic regional system apples" in a way that might come back to bite them.[54] There was no obvious link connecting the systems, certainly not in any military sense. The Arms Control and Disarmament Agency concluded that the trade was not credible. "This is probably true," Carter conceded in the margins of one such assessment.[55]

David Owen, the British foreign secretary, pressed for a broader formulation that would link a production decision to the general build-up of Soviet forces, both nuclear and conventional.[56] Convinced that most of the arguments circulating about the warhead were "bogus," Owen worried that it could add to public impressions that these weapons might actually be used. Although he accepted the basic doctrinal rationale for these threats in peacetime, he had no interest in encouraging people "to attach too much credibility" to these plans.[57] It was a telling admission that though planning for the use of nuclear weapons might make military sense, it scarcely made for good talking points.

Owen's suggestions for a more general link ran up against staunch opposition in Washington. Brzezinski complained that Owen had "poked a stick into the otherwise smoothly moving machinery in the Alliance" with a proposal that was completely unworkable. If the allies adopted Owen's nebulous link to progress on arms control in Europe, there would be no obvious threshold at which point NATO could—or should—move ahead with the weapon's deployment. The Soviets could string them along with the promise of progress paired with regular threats that deployment of the enhanced radiation warhead would scuttle it.[58]

What form the final arms control offer would take had yet to be nailed down, even as the Americans lobbied for a final decision well in advance of May. Beating back domestic political opposition, the Dutch government vowed to throw its weight behind a link to MBFR.[59] Pockets of the West German defense ministry still supported a similar link to Soviet tanks, whereas their foreign ministry counterparts tended to favor the US-endorsed link to the SS-20.[60]

By mid-March, the Carter administration decided to move ahead with a link to the SS-20. Still conscious of the looming UN Special Session, the Americans wanted to move quickly. The North Atlantic Council, they hoped, would agree to a three-part policy—a production decision, an arms control offer, and a deployment plan should negotiations fail—at a pair of meetings on March 20 and 22. The West Germans remained interested in a trade for tanks, but were willing to drop this preference in the name of agreement. Vance and Brown held out hope that they would do so in the first of the council's sessions, so as not to jeopardize a final consensus.[61]

Carefully constructed, these plans side-stepped some pockets of opposition. Belgian, Danish, Dutch, and Norwegian reservations about the deployment piece of the equation could be bypassed, the thinking went, with West German support. At the very least, the Federal Republic's endorsement would coax the others "to remain silent so a consensus can be expressed." The final agreement would be a triumph of semantics, parsing the distinction between consensus and unanimity.[62] NATO's endorsement would be the former, even without the latter. Only three of NATO's members would explicitly back the plan: the Federal Republic, the United Kingdom, and the United States. The remainder were expected to bite their tongues.[63]

Jimmy Carter Pulls the Plug

The neutron bomb's opponents continued their offensive. The International Forum against the Neutron Bomb, a mass rally largely coordinated by the Dutch Communist Party on the East Germans' dime, drew activists to Amsterdam from across Europe and beyond. Nearly fifty thousand people took to the streets, united in their opposition to the neutron bomb.[64] Daniel Ellsberg, the former US analyst of Pentagon Papers fame, addressed the teeming international crowd.[65]

That same day, Brzezinski notified Carter that NATO was about to take the final steps to secure agreement on the administration's three-part plan. Scribbling in the margins of the memo, Carter asked Brzezinski to hold off for the time being.[66] The North Atlantic Council's consultations were cancelled with just a few hours' notice.[67]

Some of Carter's advisers begged him to stay the course. If the administration were to change tacks, the political consequences would be devastating. The president's decision, the National Security Council's Reg Bartholomew warned Brzezinski, would be understood as yet more evidence of the administration's weakness or as "moralism running rampant over real security needs and concerns."[68] A glut of stories appeared in the press, filled with insider leaks and speculation about the political implications of a delay.[69]

But Carter wanted a stronger commitment to deploy the enhanced radiation warheads. There were few viable candidates to make that commitment. Fierce opposition rocked the Netherlands, where the neutron bomb divided parliamentarians and animated protestors.[70] In neighboring Belgium, demonstrations brought together trade unionists, young people, and religious groups. The Danes and Norwegians clung to standing policies that opposed the stationing of nuclear weapons on their territory. Determined to secure a firmer statement of support, Carter dispatched Warren Christopher, the deputy secretary of state, to Bonn and London.

Schmidt was appalled. "The stunned German leader," *Newsweek* reported of the chancellor's meeting with Christopher, "took a pinch of his favorite snuff and disbelievingly asked his guest to 'double-check' with Washington."[71] After Christopher left, Schmidt requested that no further steps be taken until Hans-Dietrich Genscher visited Washington on an already scheduled trip a few days later.[72] The chancellor had no interest in being left to carry the bag for Carter.[73]

Before Carter met Genscher, Brzezinski, Vance, and Brown recommended that the president come armed with a final decision. But, if that decision remained negative, it would need to be handled carefully. An outright no, the three men warned, would "produce a storm" within the alliance, along with blowback in Congress about the administration's defense policies writ large, as the White House was already under fire over the decision to surrender control of the Panama Canal. Brzezinski instead sketched out two conditional options that could buy the president some breathing room. Across the top of the memo, Carter scrawled a note: "Zbig, I have to say that you never give up."[74]

Rather than cancel the program outright, Carter elected to defer. On April 6, after his meeting with Genscher, the president notified Schmidt that he intended to delay a final decision. The same letter went to the leaders of the United Kingdom and France, James Callaghan and Valéry Giscard d'Estaing.[75] The next day, the White House went public with a formal announcement. Carter left open the possibility of producing the enhanced radiation warhead and linked the weapon's fate to a call for Soviet restraint.[76] "Is President Jimmy Carter going ahead with a decision to defer development of the neutron bomb? Or is he deferring a decision to go ahead with it?," one editorial in Toronto's Globe and Mail wondered. "Is it no to yes, yes to no, or wait-and-see to wait-and-see?"[77]

Carter's nondecision reverberated across the alliance. After months of painstakingly assembling a package, he had seemingly pulled the rug out from underneath the allies. Press coverage carried a litany of barely concealed grievances from anonymous and on-the-record sources alike. "Nothing President Carter has done has brought him such criticism at home and abroad as his decision on the neutron bomb," the US newscaster Robert MacNeil told viewers. "Carter gives in to Brezhnev," blared one headline in Paris's L'Aurore.[78]

Carter's actions, as Bartholomew predicted, reinforced impressions of a vacillating administration easily swayed by a sense of religious-inflected moralism.[79] Genscher dismissed the president as a "religious dreamer," while his political counselor, Klaus Kinkel, griped that the Carter White House was a "leaderless hen-coop."[80] The entire affair, Sir John Killick concluded, was the product of Carter's about-face. Killick griped that the president had forced them all "out on a limb," only to turn around and saw off the entire branch.[81] Even twenty-five years later, Killick seethed, telling one interviewer that Carter "had prayed all night and decided not to deploy the thing."[82]

Widely portrayed as a sudden reversal on the part of the president, Carter's decision was anything but. His thinking tracked with his personal attitudes from the outset. When Carter met Leo Tindemans in the autumn of 1977, for instance, the president told his Belgian counterpart that it was "inconceivable" that the United States would develop the enhanced radiation warheads if there were strong opposition in Europe.[83] "My cautionary words since last summer," Carter confided in his diary at the end of March, "have been pretty well ignored."[84]

Picking Up the Pieces

Joseph Luns worried that the political fallout from the neutron bomb was merely a symptom of a much larger problem facing the alliance. NATO seemed to be losing "the battle for men's minds." Though this was far from a new problem, Luns feared the situation was getting worse, with deleterious consequences for the alliance's ability to maintain a sufficient—and credible—deterrent. "We are failing to focus public opinion more clearly on the threat to our security which is inherent in the impressive and continuing Soviet military build-up," Luns lamented. The allies' seeming failure to make a persuasive case for NATO's continued relevance to a new generation made these public-opinion problems all the more disturbing. So too did the Warsaw Pact's efforts to whip up popular opposition. "In the face of crude, distorted propaganda campaigns," he argued, "our reactions are often too slow and defensive, even timid."[85] Could a toxic blend of public outcry, transatlantic discord, and well-placed Warsaw Pact propaganda make it impossible for the Western allies to reach the kinds of politically difficult decisions needed to defend the West?[86] The aggressive campaign to discredit the neutron bomb seemed to lend credence to the idea that the Soviets now possessed a *droit de regard* over security policy in Europe.[87]

The political and psychological damage done by Carter's deferral made the gray-area problem all the more important. Well into the spring of 1978, the Carter administration discouraged talk of a separate Eurostrategic balance and disputed characterizations of the SS-20 as a new threat. The entire issue, as one internal assessment diagnosed it, was "a question of changed perceptions, not capabilities."[88] By May 1978, as the administration surveyed the damage done by the neutron bomb, it was increasingly clear that perceptions mattered almost as much as capabilities. A firm policy on longer-range theater nuclear forces that addressed allied concerns could reaffirm the US commitment to Europe and shore up confidence in NATO's extended deterrent.[89] Though concerned about the erosion of confidence across the alliance, the Carter administration's primary target was the Federal Republic. Schmidt's dissatisfaction was palpable, and West German confidence in the United States and the protection it afforded remained the critical foundation for the allies' transatlantic security arrangements.

Over the previous autumn and winter, the allies had studied NATO's theater nuclear force posture as part of the work on the Long-Term Defense Program. In October 1977, the Nuclear Planning Group had accepted a US offer to chair a high-level working group that would develop a comprehensive framework for the alliance's theater nuclear posture, an upgraded version of the Long-Term Defense Program's Task Force 10 that ended up known by the creative moniker the High Level Group.[90] (The High Level Group remained a subset of the Nuclear Planning Group.) With well-connected and senior representation, the thinking went, the allies could avoid another episode like that of the neutron bomb, in which defense ministers ended up blindsided and caught unbriefed.[91]

The High Level Group's discussions quickly coalesced around the modernization of the alliance's longer-range theater nuclear forces, as opposed to improving NATO's battlefield options. Requirements for deep strikes dominated the group's exchanges at Los Alamos, New Mexico, in February 1978, with an eye to denying the Soviet Union sanctuary from allied strikes.[92] "It would detract from the continuity of deterrence to suggest that there was an automatic 'firebreak' at the Soviet border," the Norwegian representative, Johan Jørgen Holst, argued. And, given the evolution of Soviet forces, the group concluded that priority should be given to extra longer-range capabilities launched from the European theater, not offshore weapons as had been the case since the early 1960s.[93]

Despite this seeming agreement, those capabilities did not appear in the subsequent report. David McGiffert, the American who chaired the High Level Group, made no mention of longer-range capabilities in theater. The omission frustrated British, Norwegian, and West German readers, who had expected to see a specific reference to in-theater weapons and a firmer position overall.[94] "The Americans have tended to play down the case for increasing long-range in-theatre capability," one British assessment concluded. And the group's subsequent meeting, in March, all but confirmed the US retreat. To preserve the positions agreed on at Los Alamos, the British suggested a series of amendments, "deliberately overstated" to draw attention to the places "where treacle or straightforward [omission] had produced a rather distorted picture."[95]

Frustrated, the British lamented the lack of a cohesive European view. The Danes and the Dutch seemed eager to avoid producing anything that might include a commitment, while the Norwegians and the West Germans aired their grievances about the US position privately but offered little by way of critique in more formal settings.[96] Though the High Level Group's studies had produced a degree of consensus, there was little urgency on the part of the Carter administration to translate these principles into policy. Prior to the High Level Group's April gathering in Frederikshavn, Denmark, the West German permanent representative, Rolf Pauls, tried to inject some new momentum into the process.

In a circulated statement, Pauls dismissed the need for further study of the broad political and military issues at play in NATO's theater nuclear posture. The High Level Group's deliberations had already covered this ground, concluding that, for a mix of political, military, and psychological reasons, NATO needed to strengthen its longer-range theater nuclear forces. To underscore the point, Pauls offered a laundry list of reasons why:

- the continuum of deterrence would be weakened if gaps should occur in the spectrum of options;
- coupling with the strategic US forces can be made particularly clear by TNF options having a long range;
- as opposed to SLBMs, TNF constitute a "visible" potential which, moreover, permits the nonnuclear Alliance partners a share in the provision of nuclear means of delivery;
- the suitability of the strategic forces for selective options is limited, which makes them less flexible;
- the probable development of the balance of power in the strategic and MRBM range (SS20, BACKFIRE) requires the creation of precautionary military options (also to cover the contingency that they may be introduced into arms control arrangements).[97]

What remained to be decided was not whether NATO needed new longer-range theater weapons, but which systems the alliance should adopt.

Coming on the heels of the neutron bomb, the depth of West German discontent and dissatisfaction took on even greater political significance. In May 1978, the Carter administration began a comprehensive reappraisal of US policy regarding NATO's theater nuclear posture.[98] Previously, the National Security Council had resisted such a study, concerned that the inevitable press leaks would damage US efforts to secure an agreement on SALT II. The severity of the neutron bomb affair changed this thinking. National Security Council staffers came to the view that, without a strategic review, the whole issue of longer-range theater nuclear forces could boil over.[99] By responding to the West Germans' security concerns, members of the administration could begin to rebuild trust with a critical ally and show that they were, as Leslie Gelb later put it, "serious guys."[100] But the reference language for the interagency study of long-range theater nuclear capabilities and arms control, PRM 38, illustrated how far the administration's thinking lagged behind that of its allies. Carter asked the Special Coordination Committee to consider *possible* increases to longer-range theater nuclear forces in Europe and the *possible* inclusion of these systems in arms control negotiations going forward.[101] In Washington, it still seemed a question of whether, not what, to deploy.

After months of study, the administration finally produced a paper in August 1978. That report, PRM 38, sketched out a basic US position. Though NATO's High Level Group had already endorsed "an evolutionary adjustment" of the alliance's longer-range strike capabilities in the European theater, PRM 38's authors were quick to note that the United States had not explicitly backed this policy. At NATO's summit in May, for instance, Carter had remained noncommittal.[102]

Surveying the political stakes of the gray-area problem, the authors of PRM 38 offered a blunt assessment. Some of the challenges were the product of perennial tensions. "Because their interests are not identical to ours," the report noted, "our Allies do not necessarily see the problem as we do." If there was any confusion about whose views mattered, the next line reminded readers. The Federal Republic, as "the only major NATO power to have renounced nuclear weapons," had a marked interest in the credibility of the US nuclear deterrent. Echoing familiar arguments, the study's authors pointed to the West Germans' continued concerns about the implications of strategic parity and what those in Bonn viewed as an inordinate US focus on "the homeland-homeland strategic balance" at the expense of the security situation in Europe. Though the credibility of the US deterrent was no means a solely West German preoccupation, PRM 38 left little doubt that it was Bonn's views that mattered most.[103]

At stake were foundational elements of the transatlantic bargain. The United States, as the State Department's Richard Ericson and George Vest advised Cyrus Vance, needed to preserve the alliance-wide consensus that the Americans' nuclear guarantee was, in fact, credible. After all, that guarantee was what bound the entire alliance together. But Ericson and Vest cautioned against moving too quickly. "We don't want to accept [the] German assessment of the problem, since this could feed their anxieties."[104]

Ericson and Vest lobbied for a path forward that blended deployment and arms control, drawing on the same kind of logic as the earlier policies regarding the neutron bomb. Neither deployment nor arms control could responsibly be done in isolation, so if the administration decided to pursue one path, it should be prepared to do both. "Deployments alone are politically unacceptable to the Germans, who see a need for arms control as at least a 'cover,' if not a complement, to NATO deployments." The potential consequences for US-Soviet relations, and East-West relations more broadly, were no more palatable. But, pursued in isolation, an arms control offer was unlikely to bear fruit without something to trade in exchange for constraints on the Soviets' theater nuclear forces.[105]

As the Carter administration debated its policy, many worried about the direction that policy might take. To Sir John Killick, it seemed that the arms controllers were "running away with the ball," while those focused on the overall nuclear posture were unable to sway the administration's decisions. Gen. Alexander Haig grumbled to various allied governments about the worrying direction of US nuclear policy, fearful that the current course of action might leave the allies with no theater nuclear force improvements in the end.[106] But Haig's prejudices and personal ambitions were well-known. "Some here see Haig as a possible future presidential candidate," one dispatch from the British Embassy in Washington cautioned, "and Haig is conscious of this, whether or not he sees himself in the role."[107] But no matter Haig's propensity for exaggeration, the lack of faith in the administration was palpable. "It seems to me hard to deny that Carter's reliability is open to question," John Robinson reported from the British Embassy in Washington. "That is to say, we cannot rely on him. Whether or not we are prepared to admit this to ourselves, it seems to me evident that the Germans are."[108]

With PRM 38's recommendations in hand, the Carter administration embarked on another round of bilateral consultations with the British, French, and West Germans in the autumn of 1978. The Americans shared ideas for an integrated approach, bringing together arms control and weapons deployments into a single package along the lines sketched out in PRM 38.

The Americans found strong support among the British for the consensus already reached within the High Level Group. The central problem was political and military, and the British participants argued that it could be handled through a force-modernization program. An "evolutionary adjustment," in the allies' preferred euphemism, need not be seen as a direct response to the recent Soviet deployments, but rather as routine maintenance of the alliance's capabilities to strengthen the weakest links in the chain of escalatory options. The British worried that the Federal Republic had "overreacted to the situation," placing undue emphasis on the need for arms control talks to cover systems in the gray area.[109] British preoccupations were understandable; any such talks could imperil Britain's own nuclear deterrent.

Talks with the West Germans underscored the "highly psychological and political" nature of the gray-area problem. To address it, Klaus Blech was adamant that the alliance need not meet Soviet capabilities one for one. The difficulty would be if the current adverse trends continued, opening up an even greater gap between NATO's long-range forces in theater and the Warsaw Pact's. But Blech took pains to clarify that the West Germans did not believe an independent European nuclear capability was the solution, let alone a West German one. The basic principle of sharing the alliance's burdens remained, and any shift in the Federal Republic's position could easily upset the delicate political and psychological balance. It was a perennial challenge; the Federal Republic of Germany needed "to be strong enough to beat [the] Russians, but weaker than Luxembourg."[110]

For the time being, in-depth consultations remained restricted to a small circle of allies. Before the North Atlantic Council met on November 20, in a session slated to include discussion of the theater nuclear force question, the State Department instructed the US Mission at NATO to notify their British, French, and West German counterparts that the conversation would not be nearly as detailed as their earlier bilateral exchanges.[111]

Among the Big Four, the consultative process deepened. Helmut Schmidt proposed a discussion at the highest levels, with an informal summit between the four major powers.[112] Valéry Giscard d'Estaing took up the chancellor's idea, happy to play host in the Caribbean at Guadeloupe. Plans for a four-power gathering early in the new year were justified, however tenuously, as consultations on divided Berlin.[113]

The neutron bomb affair was a preview of things to come. Once the warhead's specifications went public, a growing segment of the population came to appreciate the uncomfortable trade-offs and uneasy accommodations that specialists had been grappling with for decades. For some, smaller and more usable weapons would increase the alliance's deterrent. The enhanced radiation warhead could offset the Warsaw Pact's superiority in troops and tanks and, in so doing, ensure that the Soviet Union and its allies would not contemplate an invasion across the plains of Central Europe. Others thought this logic insane. If the Warsaw Pact did invade, itself a seemingly unlikely prospect, these warheads' small size would only tempt NATO's leaders to actually use them. NATO's strategy of flexible response left open the question of when and where escalation would occur, and the reactions to the neutron bomb made it clear that this sense of uncertainty came with political costs. How could governments reassure their constituents that these weapons would not be used when the standing strategy demanded a degree of ambiguity on that same question?

These fault lines were fodder for the Warsaw Pact. Through cash transfers, communist connections, and carefully placed news stories, the Eastern allies amplified homegrown opposition to the neutron bomb. The playbook for the campaigns against the neutron bomb was a model of success as far as the Kremlin was concerned, and one that could be easily duplicated should the opportunity present itself.

But in the short term, the neutron bomb affair proved a critical turning point in the allies' deliberations over the gray-area problem. The solutions devised to deal with the enhanced radiation warhead relied on a package approach that brought together the decision to introduce new weapons with an offer to cancel those same deployments. It was an idea that the Western allies would come back to repeatedly in the years ahead. And, after Jimmy Carter shied away from this package approach, the ensuing political damage changed the conversation about longer-range theater nuclear forces. In the wake of the neutron bomb, it became impossible to ignore how precipitously West German confidence in the president and in the protection of the US extended deterrent had fallen. Carter and his advisers regrouped, determined to win back that confidence.

CHAPTER 5

It Takes Two

James Callaghan sailed a dinghy along the shoreline. Jimmy Carter went for a jog, while Valéry Giscard d'Estaing played a match of tennis. The three men, along with Helmut Schmidt, stayed in beachside bungalows with their wives and met in open-air huts steps from the sea.[1] "At our last luncheon together, with topless women bathers walking on the beach below us," Carter recorded in his diary on January 6, 1979, "Jim complained strenuously that his back was turned to the beach."[2]

Peppered with downtime to enjoy the winter sun in the Caribbean, the Guadeloupe Summit was anything but an escape from the wider world. The leaders of the four largest Western powers tackled issues across the globe in a *tour d'horizon* that spanned from relations with the People's Republic of China and Pakistan's ties to the West to the state of European security.[3] The Big Four's discussions produced broad agreement that any attempt to resolve the gray-area problem must pair a promise to deploy new theater nuclear forces to Western Europe with an offer to undertake arms control negotiations.

After Guadeloupe, the Western allies spent the remainder of 1979 working out the details of this deploy-and-negotiate package. Two committees worked in tandem for much of the year, as the High Level Group decided what to deploy and a newly created committee, the Special Group, hammered out guidance for arms control talks on the same systems. The final integrated decision was a careful political compromise, designed to balance the preservation of NATO's defenses and deterrent with the pursuit of détente. But, in the face of the Soviet Union's continued growth, it was imperative that the Western allies act. "We can sit by hoping we can cope with the consequence of inequality, we can allow ourselves to be lulled into passivity leaving the Alliance in a situation of inequality and growing vulnerability," as Zbigniew Brzezinski put it. "Or we can take effective action now."[4] This public packaging obscured the fact that the Dual-Track Decision had far more to do with the politics of alliance than anything else. But in private, the Carter administration openly admitted as much. As one internal memo noted, "Some TNF modernization may be useful, but this is primarily a political exercise which requires more careful management."[5]

The earlier neutron bomb fiasco and nagging fears that the Western allies could no longer make the tough choices required for their own defense only added to Brzezinski's case. The success of the Dual-Track Decision, as the two-part policy became known, became "a manhood test."[6] If the allies fell short, that failure would do "irreparable political and psychological damage" to an arrangement already wracked by self-doubt.[7] NATO's members remained gloomy about their own circumstances, which appeared all the more grim in the face of a Soviet Union still seemingly ascendant. "The threat to European freedom," Callaghan's Conservative successor, Margaret Thatcher, warned, "is greater now than at any time since 1945."[8]

Agreement at Guadeloupe

The paper trail regarding the Big Four's discussions on the beaches of Guadeloupe is limited. Committed to an informal session that would enable free-wheeling and open discussion, the summit produced almost no detailed records of what was discussed. What historians know about the summit is largely the result of the participants' recollections, released years later in the form of political memoirs and diaries.[9]

Though by no means the only subject on a jam-packed agenda, the so-called gray-area problem occupied much of the leaders' time. Over a series of sessions, Schmidt, Callaghan, Carter, and Giscard discussed the state of strategic arms control, the Soviets' SS-20 deployments, and what these developments meant for the security situation in Europe. Schmidt relished the chance to share his views. He delivered a lengthy lecture on the nuts and bolts of NATO's strategy during which, according to Giscard's memoirs, he expressed visible delight in needling Carter. Schmidt's prodding got to Carter, who reportedly fumed as the chancellor rambled on about the ramifications of the SALT II negotiations.[10] The substance of Schmidt's comments, however, was hardly a new departure. He hit familiar points, as he reiterated that the Soviet Union's growing arsenal of SS-20s constituted "an intolerable instrument of blackmail."[11] After this forty-five minute soliloquy, the crux of Schmidt's case was clear; there was no way he could support an agreement on SALT II if it did not address the problem posed by the SS-20.[12] Carter proposed a possible solution. The United States, he indicated, would be willing to construct and deploy longer-range theater nuclear forces to Western Europe.[13]

Carter's proposal did nothing to deter Schmidt, who pivoted to protest this latest offer. It would be politically difficult to secure the necessary support to station new missiles in the Federal Republic, Schmidt argued, and the introduction of weapons at some point in the future would do nothing to address the immediate threat. The Soviets' deployments were well under way, with SS-20s aimed at targets across Western Europe.[14] Schmidt's reluctance stunned Carter. If the Federal Republic were not willing to accept the deployments, he wondered aloud, why should any of the other allies be willing to do so on Bonn's behalf? "This was somewhat unjust to Helmut, who had personally never shrunk from doing whatever was necessary in defence matters," Callaghan wrote in his later memoirs, "but he had laid himself open to Carter's remarks by an unusual lack of logic."[15]

Over the course of their discussions, the four men moved gradually toward a paired approach. The Western powers, as Giscard later described it, needed to put a choice before the Soviet Union; the Soviets could halt their SS-20 deployments or prepare to be faced with comparable US missiles in Western Europe. But though the four might have reached the broad contours of an agreement, their assessments still diverged. Giscard later described two alliances, one Franco-American and the other Anglo-German.[16] Carter saw a different constellation of three against one. "I am impressed and concerned by the attitude of Helmut toward appeasing the Soviets," he confided in his diary after one round of discussion. "Much more than the other three of us."[17]

Italian and Canadian officials complained that the quadripartite get-together smacked of a directorate not unlike the Gaullist schemes of the past.[18] British officials griped about the steady stream of Italians crowding their offices to air grievances about the meeting and its restricted guest list.[19] The Canadian permanent representative, Joseph Hardy, registered his discontent at the North Atlantic Council's session the week after the summit.

NATO's consultative processes had been in steady decline, and the gathering in Guadeloupe underscored just how far out of favor these mechanisms had fallen.[20]

Adjusting Upward

Another round of studies followed. After Guadeloupe, the High Level Group continued to try to figure out which systems should be deployed and in what numbers. Agreed that NATO should pursue what was obliquely referred to as an "evolutionary upward adjustment," the High Level Group settled on a range somewhere from two hundred to six hundred.[21]

What the alliance needed depended, at least in part, on how the threat was calculated. At the Department of Defense, analysts suggested at least four possible formulas, even after excluding aircraft and shorter-range theater nuclear forces. Counting the number of SS-20 launchers produced a figure of 70, but counting warheads tripled the number to 210. If the SS-4s and SS-5s were added into the mix, then tallying launchers meant 472, while warhead-based arithmetic took the total up to 612.[22] Numbers were scarcely the only way to convey the scale and scope of the Soviet threat, but in presentational terms, the difference between 70 and 612 was vast.

The High Level Group tried to strike a balance. Any NATO deployments needed to include enough weapons to enhance the overall credibility of flexible response. Yet, the number of new systems should not be too high. To that end, the State Department ruled out an option that envisioned matching the Soviets one for one.[23] Such an approach would almost certainly create the impression of a separate Eurostrategic balance. Even if NATO stayed short of matching the Soviets, too large of a deployment could suggest that it possessed a separate theater nuclear capability, thereby undercutting the allies' attempts to strengthen the coupling links between its theater and strategic forces. Careful not to stray too high or too low, the allies settled on 572 warheads.

That Goldilocks figure of 572 reflected the mix of systems selected. Over months of deliberation, the High Level Group considered a series of options: ground-launched and sea-launched cruise missiles, a new medium-range ballistic missile, the extended-range Pershing II ballistic missile, and a new bomber force equipped with air-launched cruise missiles.[24] The group settled on two. The bulk of the deployments—404—would be made up of Gryphon ground-launched cruise missiles. (Gone were earlier US arguments that ground-launched cruise missiles were not a reasonable option to counter the SS-20 because of their slow flight time.)[25] The remaining 108 would be Pershing II intermediate-range ballistic missiles. Both land-based systems, the Gryphons and Pershing IIs would serve as a visible reminder of the coupling links that bound the defense of Europe to that of North America.[26] Symbolism still mattered a great deal in the alliance's planning.

The High Level Group did entertain the possibility of sea-based options. But these were ruled out as a logistical headache riddled with familiar problems. A force made up of US units would likely be seen as an extension of its existing strategic forces—and not as a theater weapon at all. The alternative would be some type of mixed-manned allied force with US control units. In essence, it would be a revamped version of the MLF with all the same difficulties.[27] Despite these drawbacks, Schmidt and Genscher returned to the possibility of sea-based systems from time to time.[28] There were undeniable political benefits to nuclear weapons that would not be stationed right next door to their constituents.

Voters' attitudes colored NATO's deliberations, and both the Gryphon and Pershing II had distinct benefits in public relations terms. Cruise missiles, with their slow flight time, were not deemed to be a first-strike weapon. (Later critics came to the opposite conclusion.) The Pershing II could be billed as a routine upgrade; it was only one numeral higher than weapons that had been in the field since the late 1960s.[29] The United States would replace the Pershing IAs deployed with US forces with the new, extended-range Pershing IIs.[30]

Belgium, Denmark, and Greece refused to automatically back any decision agreed to at the Nuclear Planning Group. The committee was made up of a mix of permanent members and rotating seats; the Belgians, Danes, and Greeks—in the off season—were unwilling to commit to decisions made without their representatives present.[31] To resolve these problems of consultation, the Dutch proposed that the rotation system be abolished.[32] After this proposal was endorsed by the rest of the allies, the Nuclear Planning Group's permanent membership grew to include all of the allies with the exceptions of Iceland and France.

Even after the allies agreed to the particular mix of 572 warheads, the underlying rationale for deployment remained muddled. "I can envisage no situation to release 572 warheads of this type and call this act a deliberate and selective escalation," one anonymous West German official concluded.[33] One school of thought, popular in US circles, understood the Gryphons and Pershing IIs as part of a shift toward warfighting. Europeans, wary of any suggestion that a nuclear war could be fought on their territory, gravitated toward explanations steeped in the logic of flexible response. The Gryphons and Pershing IIs would enhance NATO's ladder of escalation, fill a "gap in the spectrum," or create a "seamless robe of deterrence," depending on one's preferred metaphor.³⁴ Merely the latest iteration of an unresolved debate about flexible response, that ambiguity ended up replicated in the rationale justifying deployment. At the High Level Group, the drafting process reached an impasse. The various representatives could not agree on language to explain what role the Gryphons and Pershing IIs would play in the alliance's overarching strategy.³⁵

What About Arms Control?

The High Level Group concentrated on the size and scope of modernization, but the other half of the paired package—arms control—had no comparable venue. The West Germans called for the creation of a new consultative body dedicated to the arms control side of the equation. Bureaucratic structures could implicitly reinforce the parallel nature of the plans. A committee could by its very existence signal that the Atlantic alliance took arms control as seriously as modernization.

Even the new committee's name mattered. Proposed terms of reference, prepared by the British and the West Germans, suggested that the new committee be called the Special Working Group. The United States pressed for Special Policy Group instead. The Carter administration worried that putting the word "working" in the committee's name would diminish its stature relative to that of the High Level Group. There should be no doubt that the two were equals.³⁶

In early April 1979, the North Atlantic Council approved the formation of the new committee, now known simply as the Special Group.³⁷ Like the High Level Group, the Special Group was chaired by the United States. From its first meeting on April 19, the newly created body went to work studying whether and on what terms the allies should engage in arms control negotiations covering theater nuclear forces.³⁸ The Special Group's conclusions would be combined with those of the High Level Group as part of one integrated document that would be submitted to Secretary General Luns for consideration early that autumn.³⁹

In preparation for the Special Group's consultations, the Carter administration identified a series of political objectives to guide negotiations to limit theater nuclear forces. The first was simple. Talks should constrain and, if possible, reduce the nuclear threat that the Soviets posed in Europe. Beyond this basic aim, the administration's objectives acknowledged how arms control for theater nuclear forces fit within the broader politics of alliance. It was critical to project strong US leadership and shore up European (read: West German) confidence in the security provided by NATO. "The greatest danger," the administration's assessments concluded, "is the FRG could begin to question the reliability of the US and NATO as the basis of its security." US officials emphasized the need to expand and deepen consultations on arms control to ensure that the Europeans remained satisfied that their interests were being seriously considered and protected in any negotiations.[40] US thinking underscored how arms control could produce a more favorable political climate: "Nearly all allied leaders," one internal memo reported, "have told us that a TNF arms control approach which complements—and protects—essential TNF modernization offers the best chance they have to convince their Parliaments and publics that a new and destabilizing regional arms race is not being launched."[41]

With the Special Group chaired by an American, these general principles shaped much of the committee's early work. By July, the Special Group identified five objectives:

i. To respond to the growing disparity in long-range theater nuclear systems, which has been highlighted by Soviet deployments of the SS-20;
ii. To avoid unconstrained competition and increasing instability in the theater nuclear field;
iii. To ensure that the role of arms control has been given due attention by the Alliance at the same time that decisions are reached on TNF modernization;
iv. To counter Soviet efforts to interfere in Alliance decision-making through vague disarmament offers as an alternative to TNF modernization by formulating concrete and realistic arms control proposals; and,
v. To reflect the strategic unity of the Alliance and the coherence of the Alliance's strategy of deterrence and defense.[42]

Building on these priorities, the Special Group also developed a set of twelve principles to guide the United States in any future negotiations regarding theater nuclear forces. As part of this dozen, the Special Group offered guidance on contentious issues, such as the regional scope of any limits and the exclusion of British and French third-party systems.[43]

The Special Group agreed that negotiations should be conducted under the auspices of SALT III.[44] But the order of operations was still up for debate. Some delegations, like the Americans and the West Germans, believed that a broad endorsement of SALT III was sufficient for the time being, but the Dutch, Danes, and Norwegians all pressed for plans that would hold the deployment track in suspense while negotiations took place.[45] Though not officially party to this work, as it fell under the auspices of the integrated command, the French warned from the sidelines that it would be dangerous to make the deployment track contingent on arms control. Doing so would only tip the scales in the Soviet Union's favor, providing the Kremlin's propagandists with a political and psychological bludgeon with which to beat the Western allies.[46]

Sharing the Burden, Obscuring German Power

If the Western allies wanted to introduce missiles in Europe, they needed somewhere to put them. Which of the allies—to say nothing of their parliaments and voters—would be willing to accept these new systems?

As a general rule, NATO sought the broadest possible participation to ensure the greatest degree of shared risk. "The underlying principle at stake here," as the West German defense minister, Hans Apel, put it to an audience at the annual security conference, the Wehrkunde, "is the fair spread of risks and burdens. The Alliance is an Alliance of the free and of the equal."[47] The political burdens were to be shared with all of the allies—nuclear and non-nuclear, regardless of whether they would host the missiles—endorsing the final decision to deploy and negotiate. Some of the financial burden would be shared as well, with each of the allies kicking in funds through NATO's infrastructure program, though the bulk of the costs would be covered by the United States.

There were only so many viable contenders to host the missiles. Norway and Denmark both had standing policies that ruled out hosting nuclear weapons. Neither France nor Greece were part of NATO's integrated command structure, and the French clung jealously to the independence of their nuclear force. Iceland had no standing army, and Portugal was ruled out, in part because of its sheer distance from the Soviet Union. Geography disqualified Canada as well. Turkey, though possible in a theoretical sense, came with so many political problems, especially vis-à-vis its relations with Greece, that Ankara's participation was deemed too difficult.[48] Six plausible candidates remained: the Federal Republic of Germany, Italy, the United Kingdom, and the Benelux trio (though, more often than not, Luxembourg was included because memo writers defaulted to the Benelux shorthand rather than because of any belief that missiles would dot the tiny country). Already, as 1978 came to a close, the High Level Group's deliberations suggested that the main burden would fall on the United States to deploy the weapons and the United Kingdom and Federal Republic of Germany to host them.[49]

Schmidt's government was not prepared to shoulder that burden alone, and the participation of the United Kingdom—already a nuclear power capable of striking the Soviet Union in its own right—was hardly sufficient. Sticking to the conditions laid out in the earlier deliberations about the neutron bomb, the Federal Republic refused to be the only continental ally to host new theater nuclear weapons. West German representatives made these requirements clear in the High Level Group's deliberations starting in 1978, and, at the highest levels, at Guadeloupe.[50]

Schmidt's insistence on nonsingularity stemmed from a belief that West German power continued to be unpalatable, even to Bonn's closest allies. Decades after the Second World War, a militarily and economically strong Federal Republic still posed a problem. "Germany," as Schmidt flatly told his counterparts at Guadeloupe, "was still not trusted by other European nations."[51] Trends in the 1970s heightened these sensitivities about West German power. Shielded from the worst of the decade's economic difficulties, Bonn fared far better than many of the allies.

By almost any metric, the Federal Republic was the most powerful of the European allies, outstripping other big players like France and the United Kingdom. The outlier to that trend was, of course, its lack of a national nuclear weapons program. Acutely aware that this particular political status symbol loomed large in just about everyone's thinking, West German officials repeatedly underscored their desire to keep their own nuclear role circumscribed and contained. "We do not want to give anyone, East or West, any reason to suspect that Germany is gaining increased access to the nuclear trigger," one West German explained, "and these suspicions are easy to provoke."[52] Already, the French foreign ministry saw Bonn's activism on the gray-area problem as an attempt to forge a structure that would allow the Federal Republic to set the terms of Europe's nuclear defense, even without a nuclear arsenal to call its own.[53]

It was a classic paradox of NATO's policymaking. The driving force behind the Dual-Track Decision was the Federal Republic. The West Germans were most exposed to the Soviet Union's SS-20s and most vulnerable to the political blackmail the Kremlin might pursue, emboldened by a more favorable correlation of forces. But the solution to that problem—which the West Germans played a pivotal role in crafting—was one that drew attention to the Federal Republic's existing sources of power, even enhancing that power with new nuclear weapons. The Federal Republic of Germany, as one French foreign ministry memo succinctly noted, was "at the center of the debate."[54]

To make those changes as palatable as possible, both at home and abroad, Schmidt's government sought refuge in numbers, insulating itself from suspicion. The West Germans also agreed to arrangements that kept a German finger off the trigger. With its extended range, the Pershing II could strike the Soviet Union, and so policymakers in Bonn deemed it best that the missiles remain under US control. The Federal Republic would provide only facilities and financial support, despite the fact that some of the missiles' predecessors, the Pershing IAs, were under a dual key arrangement.[55]

A scheme aimed primarily at reassuring the West Germans, the Dual-Track Decision was built on US power. Carter's advisers wanted to make sure that they did not lose sight of that fact. The president had promised to lead this effort and even the slightest suggestion that the administration was backing away from that role would be dangerous. If the Americans wanted to share the burdens of leadership, one of the National Security Council's Western Europe hands, Jim Rentschler, found few options to like. A recent round of wrangling with the West Germans over an aid package to Turkey had not left him confident that Bonn could lead on any issue as charged and sensitive as nuclear modernization. And the optics of any West German leadership role made the prospect not only implausible but unpalatable. The British were not a much better option. The new government, led by Margaret Thatcher, was still trying to hammer out the details of its own participation. "In these circumstances," Rentschler wondered, "can we really expect them to deal authoritatively with our other allies, particularly the more reluctant?"[56] And, despite being part of the consultative process, the French were still outside NATO's integrated military command.

No matter who was responsible for managing, cajoling, and whipping the allies into a common position, the prevailing popular assumption was that it remained a job for Washington. If the alliance's plans unraveled for any reason, the United States would be blamed for that failure. "The Plimsoll Line of burden-sharing has always been elusive," Rentschler concluded, pointing to a litany of alliance difficulties, from massive retaliation to the current deliberations over theater nuclear forces. "We have never been able to fix with any precision (or safety!) the point where our European allies could effectively float the load." Like it or not, there was no meaningful alternative to US leadership.[57]

A Fragile Consensus

The High Level Group and the Special Group submitted their respective reports to Secretary General Joseph Luns in late September 1979. The High Level Group recommended a deployment program with a mix of 572

Gryphons and Pershing IIs to be stationed in five countries: Belgium, the Federal Republic of Germany, Italy, the Netherlands, and the United Kingdom, beginning in 1983. On the arms control side of the ledger, the Special Group suggested a set of parameters for what any arms control negotiations should pursue. These objectives included avoiding unconstrained competition, reducing the significant disparity between NATO and the Warsaw Pact in long-range theater systems, and adopting tangible and realistic proposals in order to combat the anticipated Soviet efforts to use vague promises of disarmament to throw a spanner in the works.[58] Armed with these recommendations, the next step would be to secure a final decision before the end of 1979.

With the committees' studies wrapping up, the political theater of operations moved to the various national capitals. The two tracks of modernization and arms control blended into one package, ready to be debated by parliaments, columnists, and constituents.[59] Each of the allies needed to secure a modicum of support for NATO's plans, though the formality of that approval varied from country to country. No matter the process, the prospect that domestic politics might derail even the best-laid plans was all too easy to imagine in an alliance primarily made up of democracies. For the five prospective basing countries, the stakes were even higher.

Allied planners were under no illusions about how difficult it might be to win popular support. The deployments in particular were almost certain to be controversial. Reservations in one part of the alliance might be contagious. Embassies and foreign ministries kept tabs on the latest twists and turns in political debates, particularly in The Hague. Dutch reservations might spread to neighboring Belgium, then on to Italy, before perhaps even infecting the Federal Republic of Germany.[60] Desperate to avert this outcome, Schmidt urged Carter to move up the entire timeline of the final decision instead of waiting until December. Carter held firm. A truncated timeline, he worried, might precipitate the kind of split that Schmidt wanted to avoid.[61]

The weakest point in the alliance's designs was already clear: the Netherlands.[62] Antinuclear sentiment within the country was well known, made clear by the surge of activity to stop the neutron bomb. The Dutch government, a fragile coalition headed by Dries van Agt, a Christian Democrat, faced immense pressure not to take on a greater nuclear role. Any Dutch participation would depend on the alliance undertaking broader efforts to reduce its dependence on nuclear weapons.[63]

Dutch politicians suggested modifications to the current plans, all of them designed to alter the terms of deployment. In one parliamentary debate in

October, the Christian Democrats and the Labour Party introduced motions to link their deployment decision with the ratification of the SALT II Treaty, signed by Carter and Brezhnev at Vienna in June and awaiting Senate confirmation. Both motions failed—"neither the government nor parliament wants a major test now," one US assessment reported of the incident—but the entire episode underscored how much arms control initiatives would matter to drum up the requisite support in the Netherlands.[64]

Throughout the autumn of 1979, the Dutch churned out possible revisions to the deployment track. At a meeting of the North Atlantic Assembly, NATO's auxiliary organization of parliamentarians, the Dutch introduced a motion to effectively separate the decision's two components. The Dutch proposal envisioned that the United States would try to pursue negotiations with the Soviet Union before the allies decided on the deployments. It failed, eighty-two to four.[65] In another proposed revision, the Christian Democrats suggested that two years of negotiations should take place before the Dutch made any commitment to host the Gryphons. How damaging this proposal might be was far from evident. When this latest Dutch initiative came up in Anglo-German consultations, British Foreign Secretary Lord Peter Carrington concluded that if the Christian Democrats meant that the deployments could not start until two years of negotiations had occurred, then the Dutch position was hardly cause for alarm.[66]

But the political picture in The Hague was far from comforting. Geri Joseph, the US ambassador to the Netherlands, put the van Agt government's chances of survival at 50 percent. Between the coalition's fragile position and the efforts of parliamentarians to avoid the question of nuclear modernization entirely, the chances of securing the desired outcome seemed slim.[67] Luns—no stranger to the Dutch political landscape—warned that if the van Agt government did fall, the entire election campaign that followed would become a referendum on nuclear weapons.[68]

Temptations and Threats

Meddling would be a siren song that the Soviets found impossible to ignore, or so nearly every informed observer in the West predicted. "I have no doubt that the Soviets will seek to exploit TNF for all it's worth," Jim Rentschler concluded in an August memo to Zbigniew Brzezinski, "it will be in their interest to do so."[69] The question was not whether but when the Warsaw Pact would put its propaganda machine into high gear.

Earlier efforts to stop the neutron bomb encouraged the Warsaw Pact's members to try to repeat their successes. "The political campaign against the neutron bomb," the chief of the International Department of the Hungarian Communist Party, Janos Berecz, argued, "was one of the most significant and most successful since World War II."[70] And the model could easily be replicated, used to oppose other elements of the arms race, including NATO's modernization plans.

The opening salvo came in a speech by Soviet General Secretary Leonid Brezhnev, given in East Berlin to mark the thirtieth anniversary of the German Democratic Republic on October 6.[71] A struggling Brezhnev, slurring his speech, indicated that the Soviet Union would welcome negotiations to restrict long-range theater nuclear forces. In a flourish that underscored the Soviets' desired image of reasonableness, the Soviet leader also unveiled plans to unilaterally withdraw twenty thousand troops and one thousand tanks from the German Democratic Republic within the next year.[72] Though this Soviet withdrawal represented a positive step, allied governments quickly noted that it was hardly enough to justify a shift in their position. A reduction of twenty thousand men would barely make a dent in the Warsaw Pact's superiority in Europe.[73] According to West German estimates, Soviet forces in the German Democratic Republic topped four hundred thousand troops with seven thousand tanks.[74]

Seen as a transparent ploy to derail NATO's December decision, Brezhnev's remarks insisted that any deployment of new theater weapons on the part of NATO would upset the balance in Europe.[75] The figures offered as evidence of that existing balance, analysts at the British Foreign and Commonwealth Office noted, were based on missiles launchers (not warhead numbers, let alone target coverage or mobility) and confined to the western districts of the Soviet Union.[76] In other words, the criteria were carefully selected to give the impression of balance.

Brezhnev appealed directly to the Federal Republic of Germany's leaders. Those in Bonn could, as he put it to his East Berlin audience, "help strengthen peace in Europe and develop peaceful, mutually beneficial cooperation among European states in the spirit of goodneighborliness and growing mutual confidence." If they failed to choose this path, the Federal Republic would "contribute to a new aggravation of the situation in Europe and the world by deploying in its territory American missile nuclear arms spearheaded against the USSR and its allies."[77] That binary, pitting deployment against the continuation of détente, was a staple of Soviet diplomacy. And, by casting the decision as a choice between "unnecessary, US promoted TNF modernization and a return to the Cold War" and the continuation of détente, the Soviet Union broadened the issue, making it not just about a specific weapons system but about the US role in Europe writ large. "It plays on European fears going back to at least de Gaulle," one US analyst concluded.[78]

The Soviets' East Berlin offer was repeated in written form, as Brezhnev dispatched letters to leaders across the alliance.[79] As was often the case, the various recipients swapped views and copies of their respective letters to develop talking points. There was no need for a unified line, British officials concluded, but some general guidance could mitigate the risk of replying. If the allies' responses differed too much, it could create fodder for the Soviets to exploit at a later date.[80]

Recognizing the potential appeal of Brezhnev's cuts, the British recommended that the allies rebut the Soviets' claims publicly. The final communiqué of the Nuclear Planning Group's forthcoming ministerial meeting might be used to set the record straight regarding Brezhnev's claims that the number of Soviet medium-range delivery systems had been reduced in number and in warhead yield over the course of the 1970s.[81] Couched in the jargon typical of the genre, the final communiqué of the group's November meeting in The Hague affirmed: "Ministers agreed that recent Soviet statements on nuclear trends in Europe should not be allowed to obscure the disturbing growth in the Soviet long-range theater nuclear capability and the increasing threat to the Alliance."[82] It was a rebuttal of Soviet claims, though perhaps not the kind of bold assertion that would change their voters' views.

How to calculate the balance in Europe was more art than science, easily exploited for presentational purposes and political arguments. The Soviets, who regularly cast the SS-20 and Backfire bomber as an attempt to redress an earlier imbalance, were emphatic that the calculations could not be confined to the superpowers' systems. Echoing the arguments that their arms control negotiators had made for years, Soviet officials insisted on the inclusion of the British and French arsenals.[83] (The British and French did not appreciate the return of this argument.) "It could be viewed as though we are behind, about even, or well ahead depending on the counting rules," the CIA's director, Stansfield Turner, concluded in 1979.[84]

Analysts at London's International Institute for Strategic Studies, which published a well-regarded annual update on the military balance, went to great pains to clarify their calculations after their findings were "repeatedly quoted out of context" to justify opposition to NATO's plans. "The figures show that the Warsaw Pact enjoys a 10 to 1 advantage if American strategic missiles allocated to SACEUR are excluded from the calculation," one of the institute's press release affirmed, followed by a reminder that those US systems were included in SALT, unlike the Soviets' theater forces.[85]

Various attractive calculations of the balance in Europe appeared along-side a rotating cycle of carrots and sticks. The Warsaw Pact's members churned out arms control initiatives, with regular offers to host conferences on military détente interspersed with threats that a deployment decision would destroy the basis for détente and plunge Europe back into the deep freeze of the Cold War. The Soviets hammered these themes in the weeks leading up to NATO's final decision with a global propaganda campaign.[86] During a press conference in Bonn on November 23, Soviet foreign minis-ter Andrei Gromyko reiterated Moscow's willingness to enter into immedi-ate negotiations on medium-range nuclear weapons. Gromyko's offer came with a clear condition; the allies must halt any plans to deploy new nuclear missiles to Western Europe. "If such a decision is taken while our proposal to begin negotiations is rejected," Gromyko cautioned, "the position of the western powers will thus destroy the basis for the negotiations." Eager to shape the public narrative, Gromyko added that, should the West reject Mos-cow's offer, it was because NATO's leaders would prefer to "try their luck through a new spiral in the arms race."[87]

Gromyko's gambit hardened the Soviet stance even further. Prior Soviet statements, including Brezhnev's in East Berlin, had not gone so far as to suggest that a NATO deployment decision would prevent negotiations from taking place. That the Soviet foreign minister adopted an even sharper tone in public was scarcely a surprise, as Klaus Blech reminded a group of allied officials in a debrief on the minister's visit to Bonn. Gromyko needed to speak out, lest he foster the impression that the Soviet Union tacitly accepted NATO's plans. The West Germans anticipated that the campaign against the deployments would continue up to the last minute.[88]

Three or Five

What if the Soviets' mix of browbeating and attractive arms control offers worked? After Brezhnev delivered another speech in early November, Thatcher told Luns that it was nothing more than an attempt to intimidate the already shaky Belgian and Dutch governments into rejecting the Gry-phons. Luns worried that these efforts might succeed. If the alliance failed to follow through on its decision in December as planned, the damage would be catastrophic. Not only would it undermine the credibility of NATO's defenses and of the alliance's nuclear deterrent, but that kind of failure could easily lead to a falling out between the United States and Europe.[89]

Thatcher's concerns about Belgium and the Netherlands were well founded and widely shared. After the previous year's heated debate over the neutron bomb, Belgian foreign minister Henri Simonet assumed that opponents of modernization could force a parliamentary debate in the Netherlands. If it came to that, he had warned Thatcher earlier that fall, the Gryphons would never be stationed on Dutch soil.[90] Simonet believed that the traditionally close ties between Belgium and the Netherlands could spell trouble in Brussels. His own party, the Socialists, might, under pressure from its Flemish wing, end up swayed by the Dutch debates.[91] Belgium's fractured political landscape had countless potential pressure points, not just within Simonet's Socialists. The governing coalition headed by Wilfried Martens included Social Democrats, Socialists, and representatives of a party dedicated to the expansion of French language rights in the Brussels suburbs.

By early November, the Belgians seemed to be the key. The West Germans would hold the line, as would the British. The Italian government vowed to stay firm, no matter what transpired in The Hague.[92] Italy's minister of defense, Attilio Ruffini, informed his British counterpart, Francis Pym, that the entire government would resign if the Italian Parliament rejected the deployments.[93] However difficult it might be politically, the Italians were determined to see the deployments through to secure a place for themselves at the alliance's top tables. There would be no more Guadeloupes.[94]

Belgium's parliamentarians, already divided into an array of parties, split over the missiles. The Liberals backed plans to host the Gryphons, whereas the Flemish People's Union came out against the deployments, arguing that the move was "of a strategic and aggressive nature."[95] Within the ruling coalition, the Socialists divided into two camps on the matter, with Simonet still supportive of Belgian plans to accept the missiles.[96]

The Dutch position was even shakier. The Christian Democrats' parliamentary leader, Ruud Lubbers, flirted with dramatic cuts to the size of NATO's modernization program. The agreed-on figure of 572, he maintained, far outstripped the alliance's needs.[97] These Dutch suggestions that the allies restructure and reduce the deployments were unacceptable. NATO could not afford to settle for a deployment half the size of what was initially recommended, Thatcher complained to Schmidt. Schmidt agreed. The 572 figure might be "an artificial one," but the allies needed to stick with it.[98]

To address Dutch concerns, Carter and Schmidt discussed the possible withdrawal of a thousand US nuclear warheads stationed in the Federal Republic. Already, the Dutch had pursued a series of initiatives designed to reduce the stockpile. At the High Level Group's meeting in September, for instance, Dutch representatives had introduced a paper calling for reductions in short-range systems should the Netherlands agree to host the Gryphons.

The High Level Group agreed that this question should be deferred until after a modernization program had been approved.[99]

After Carter and Schmidt debated the thousand-warhead reduction on October 29, the proposal quickly found its way into the press. Schmidt championed the cuts, seeing an offer as a way to shore up the Dutch position and enable Van Agt's government to resist calls for a reduced deployment. A unilateral reduction of US forces would have, as he indicated to Thatcher when the two discussed the initiative a few days later, the added advantage of counterbalancing the recent Soviet reductions in the court of public opinion. Schmidt believed the proposal had few downsides. The allies could afford to get rid of these missiles comfortably. "NATO had 7,000 nuclear warheads on German soil," he exclaimed to Thatcher, "they probably needed only 700 or possibly 70!"[100]

With the proposal leaked to the press, Schmidt thought any unilateral cuts were a rapidly wasting asset. To Thatcher, he complained that Carter did not wish to move quickly.[101] But Schmidt's grievances proved premature. The next day, Carter did just that. He wrote to Van Agt, asking him to hold the line, and tried to enlist fellow allied leaders to the same cause.[102]

On November 1, Carter suggested the possibility of cutting a thousand warheads from the stockpile. The move made sense in presentational terms. It would illustrate that NATO's members were not engaging in a nuclear build-up, implicitly rebuffing a popular Soviet line of attack, and would provide tangible evidence of their commitment to maintaining their security at the lowest possible number of weapons. A reduction of this sort could also resolve the contradictions within the Western negotiating position at MBFR, still based on Option III, the so-called nuclear option first introduced in 1975.[103] Option III, made up of one thousand US nuclear warheads, thirty-six Pershing I launchers, and fifty-four dual-capable aircraft, would create headaches once the allies officially agreed to a modernization program. NATO's plans assumed that the Pershing I would be replaced with systems that would not be covered by Option III, but as part of an arms control offer for SALT III. Though reluctant to give up anything in the Western arsenal without securing a parallel Soviet reduction, Thatcher came around to Carter and Schmidt's logic. Unilateral cuts to the stockpile could resolve a whole host of allied problems in one fell swoop.[104]

The reductions went some distance to assuage Dutch reservations, but not far enough to bring The Hague's diplomatic initiatives to an end. Determined to explore every possible permutation, the Dutch continued to call for revisions to the deployment track. Their suggestions included everything from sharp cuts to the number of missiles to a final decision that endorsed the weapons' production but not necessarily their deployment. In the final communiqué announcing the decision, they pushed for language that would explicitly recognize that the deployment track could be reduced to zero should the Soviets agree to reduce their own arsenal.[105] As part of this campaign, the Dutch also considered cuts to other parts of their nuclear role at NATO, including the F-16 aircraft and Nike surface-to-air missiles.[106]

As allied governments increasingly worried about the domestic politics of the final decision, even more suggested revisions to the final package. At the North Atlantic Council in late November, Anker Svart, the Danish permanent representative, recommended deferring the entire decision for six months as a way to demonstrate NATO's continued commitment to détente.[107] Svart's proposal collapsed. None of the allies threw their weight behind the Danish initiative, not even the Dutch whose various schemes continued unabated. Despite these hurdles, Vance assured Carter that they remained in good shape for a positive decision on December 12. Thankfully, the Danes and the Dutch remained isolated from one another, each seeking revisions the other found unpalatable.[108]

Dutch and Danish proposals aimed at wholesale changes to the Dual-Track Decision's modernization plans. The Norwegians focused their efforts on the parallel arms control element. Throughout November and into December, in bilateral and multilateral channels, Odvar Nordli's government pressed for a more credible arms control offer, hoping that it would smooth the final decision at home and across the alliance.[109]

Despite the flurry of activity, the Canadians remained confident. The actual decision had already been made. What remained to be seen was what combination of the five prospective basing countries would publicly commit at the joint meeting of foreign and defense ministers on December 12. Would all five pledge their support? Or would the Belgians and the Dutch falter?[110]

Perennially worried about the politics of participation, the Canadian delegation hoped that the Belgians and the Dutch would hold the line. If the final decision only included the British, the Italians, and the West Germans, it could contribute to the belief that NATO was now "a two-tier Alliance," sorted based on the allies' relative size and power. The upper tier would consist of the United States and the large European allies, all of whom would play a leading role in seeing through both tracks of the decision. Without Belgium and the Netherlands, the smaller allies would be left on the sidelines with a diminished voice, a state of affairs that was certain to mean a reduced emphasis on their traditional priorities, such as détente and disarmament.[111]

The Canadians' lingering concerns proved prescient. Neither Belgium nor the Netherlands offered a full-throated endorsement of the Dual-Track Decision. Van Agt concluded that an unqualified endorsement would bring down his government. When Martens and van Agt met in early December, the two were both seeking solutions that would enable them to stick to as much of the integrated decision as possible without destroying their fragile political arrangements at home.[112]

On December 12, 1979, when NATO's foreign and defense ministers gathered in Brussels, the appearance of consensus was paramount. The plan called for all 108 Pershing IIs to be stationed in the Federal Republic, along with 96 Gryphons. The United Kingdom would host a further 160 Gryphons, and Italy would accept another 112.[113] Belgium and the Netherlands, both intended to host 48 Gryphons, adopted a fence-sitting solution, wherein they agreed to the decision in theory, but deferred their final commitment to a later date. Martens's coalition delayed six months, while van Agt's government kicked the can down the road by two years, until December 1981. These Belgian and Dutch reservations were confined to an annex, thereby making it possible for NATO's leaders to tout the decision's "unanimous" nature.[114]

The Dual-Track Decision relied on a series of burden-sharing devices. To obscure the degree of West German influence and power, the United States worked to secure an elaborate web of commitments, even in the face of immense domestic political constraints, as in Belgium and the Netherlands. Each of the allies had a role to play. Even the weakest was expected to lend its political support to show that NATO remained undaunted and undivided.

The political burdens were also distributed over the two tracks. Carefully packaged, the alliance's messaging reiterated that the modernization of its long-range theater nuclear forces was a response to the expansion and enhancement of the Soviet Union's forces including, but by no means limited to, the ongoing deployment of the SS-20s.[115] If the modernization track was defensive in nature, the arms control track was proactive. "We are giving the political signal [to make] the eighties a decade of arms control," Hans-Dietrich Genscher argued.[116]

With its parallel pursuit of deployments and negotiations, the Dual-Track Decision adhered to a familiar script. Its two tracks mirrored the duality of 1967's Harmel Report with promises to deploy—the defense track—and to negotiate—the détente track. Yet, in bringing these tracks together, the December 1979 decision left the relationship between the two loosely defined. In the most general sense, modernization and negotiation would take place in tandem. The Western allies would prepare to deploy the Gryphons and Pershing IIs in 1983, and, at the same time, the United States would embark on arms control talks with the Soviet Union.

PART TWO

Deploy

Pundits could not resist the seeming irony of Petra Kelly's harsh critiques of the United States. Born in Günzburg in southern Bavaria, the founder of the West German Green Party and prominent peace activist had strong ties to the United States. Kelly's mother remarried a US Army officer, and Kelly (her stepfather's last name) completed her undergraduate studies at American University's School of International Service in Washington. "She speaks an American English frozen somewhere in the let-it-all-hang-out 1960s," one profile in the *New York Times* noted, pointing to her "blend of German passion and American pragmatism."[1]

In the span of a few short years, Kelly crisscrossed the globe. She protested in East Berlin's Alexanderplatz, addressed thousands at Los Angeles's Rose Bowl, and appeared on British television. No matter her destination, Kelly was struck by the similarities. "While I sat listening to those men, those many incompetent men in power," she told one British audience, "I realized they are all the mirror image of each other." On both sides of the Iron Curtain, they threatened violence in the name of ensuring that war did not break out, explaining that they were "forced to plan more evil things to prevent other evil things." That similarity, Kelly concluded, was "the heart of the theory of atomic deterrence."[2]

Dismissive of what policymakers and military planners justified in the name of deterrence, Kelly was no less critical of the Federal Republic of

Germany's security policy. During one public appearance in the United States, which coincided with Ronald Reagan's June 1982 visit to Bonn, she poked fun at the absurdity of the situation. The leader of the free world was in the West German capital, but the police were "protecting the protector from those he [was] protecting!"[3]

Kelly's arguments resonated with millions of concerned citizens. Antinuclear activism took the European continent by storm in the early 1980s. Western Europeans of all political stripes, from Kelly's fellow Greens to Catholic bishops and card-carrying communists, mobilized to stop the Euromissiles. Though described in the popular press as a single, monolithic "peace movement," the activism of the early 1980s was in fact sprawling and amorphous. Those active in peace campaigns and antinuclear organizations appreciated that their strength came in numbers and worked to turn out their neighbors and build transnational networks. And yet, at the same time, their efforts were also informed by local and national circumstances. British campaigners fixated on their nation's own nuclear deterrent, not just US weapons under the auspices of NATO. Belgian activists mobilized in two, largely distinct Flemish and Francophone networks. On the other side of the Atlantic, Canadians and Americans organized in solidarity with their European counterparts, linking calls to halt the Euromissiles with their own efforts to stop the nuclear arms race.

Record-breaking rallies were not the only manifestation of public discontent with NATO's Dual-Track Decision. And, as the Western allies tried to preserve sufficient support to see the planned deployments through, they confronted a growing conversation about the central tenets of their security policy: the nature of the Soviet threat; the protection afforded by the United States; the wisdom of defending themselves with weapons capable of unimaginable destruction; and the likelihood that their constituents would continue to live with this system.

Though the erosion of confidence was alarming everywhere, it was seen as most dangerous in the Federal Republic of Germany. Politicians and policy aides panicked at the prospect that West German voters and their elected representatives in Bonn might loosen the ties that bound them to the West, no longer satisfied with the terms of those decades-old arrangements. High-profile calls for the Federal Republic to leave NATO, including Petra Kelly's, did little to assuage these fears.[4] Terrified their neighbors might fall back into old habits, French leaders exhorted the West Germans to avoid the siren song of another deal with the Soviet Union like 1922's Treaty of Rapallo.

With the surge in antinuclear organizing, the Warsaw Pact saw opportunity. Popular opposition could be used to derail NATO's Dual-Track

Decision and weaken the Atlantic alliance. The Western allies tried to burnish their own credentials as peacekeepers and, in doing so, tried to make the most of the December 1979 decision's parallel tracks. Arms control, as they tried to make clear to their alarmed publics, was more than "Christmaspaper wrapping."[5] It was a genuine attempt to reduce the nuclear threat facing Europe, a point governments hammered in the tense years between December 1979 and November 1983.

The four chapters in this part zero in on this tumultuous four-year stretch to show why NATO's deployments were so controversial and how the Western allies managed to preserve enough political support to begin deploying the Gryphons and Pershing IIs. Chapter 6 traces the rise of antinuclear activism throughout 1980 and 1981, focusing on the proliferation of grassroots campaigns and massive rallies as the Cold War seemed to return to Europe in full force. Chapter 7 turns to the connections between arms control and public diplomacy as the United States and the Soviet Union both tried to win hearts and minds in Western Europe. But the negotiating position adopted by the Reagan White House, the so-called zero option that offered to cancel the Gryphon and Pershing II deployments provided the Soviet Union removed its own medium-range systems, illustrated the problems with this entangled approach. Any arms control negotiations were virtually guaranteed to be seen as a cynical ploy for public support and a fig leaf to cover the deployments, not a genuine effort to reduce the number of nuclear weapons aimed at Western Europe. Chapter 8 steps back to show how the Euromissiles triggered a series of debates about foundational elements in NATO's strategy, from the logic of nuclear deterrence and the wisdom of flexible response to the pursuit of détente with the Soviet Union. Chapter 9 covers the final countdown in 1983—the "year of the missile"—as the governments of Britain, Italy, and the Federal Republic of Germany succeeded in securing support for deployment.[6] The center held at the ballot box.

CHAPTER 6

End the Arms Race,
Not the Human Race

The military historian Michael Howard took to the pages of the *Times* in January 1980 to make the case for a concerted policy of civil defense in Britain. The decision to host cruise missiles on the soil of the United Kingdom would make the country a likely target for a limited Soviet preemptive strike. But without a meaningful civil defense program, the Oxford don warned his fellow Britons, their government's parallel efforts to improve "our 'independent deterrent' [would] be no more than an expensive bluff likely to deceive no one beyond these shores, and not very many people within them."[1]

Howard's letter gained prominence as the opening hook in a rebuttal written by his colleague, fellow Oxford historian E. P. Thompson. *Protest and Survive* was a systematic takedown of the specialists' logic. "NATO's 'modernisation' programme, taken together with that of the United States," Thompson argued, "was one of *menace*." He did not dispute the growth of the Soviet Union's arsenal nor the threat that these weapons posed to Western Europe. But the entire conversation about the United Kingdom's security was obscured by jargon and spin. "The whole basis of our information is corrupt," Thompson charged. "Every official statement, on both sides, is either an official lie or a statement with direct propagandist intent which conceals as much as it reveals."[2] Thompson cut through all of that. In a series of essays and pamphlets, he challenged the arguments in favor of NATO's deployments and urged his readers to take action to halt the Euromissiles.

Millions did. Concerned citizens flooded the streets in record-breaking numbers, attending massive rallies and throwing their weight behind an array of campaigns that aimed to stop NATO's deployments—and halt the nuclear arms race. Many of these activities drew on earlier strands of peace organizing and antinuclear campaigning; the opposition to the Euromissiles brought together people who had mobilized to ban the bomb, protested the Vietnam War, and picketed nuclear power plants.[3] Alongside these veterans marched thousands of their newly worried neighbors.

NATO's Dual-Track Decision served as both a lightning rod and a lowest common denominator around which a diverse group could rally. As citizens worried about the Western allies' plans to install new nuclear missiles in Europe, they expressed fears about far more than just the deployments. NATO's plans seemed to be a symptom of a much larger affliction. No matter the earlier promises of détente, the United States and the Soviet Union remained locked in a global struggle, armed to the teeth. The sharp decline in superpower relations and the crisis of détente made that fact all the more worrying.[4] Terrified citizens, both in and out of government, wondered whether leaders in Moscow and Washington would plunge them all into a third world war. Helmut Schmidt warned that the "smell of 1914" was in the air.[5]

Superpower relations only went from bad to worse. After the Soviet invasion of Afghanistan, Jimmy Carter's foreign policy seemed to tack sharply to the right. The SALT II Treaty, already in political trouble in Washington, was shelved entirely. Whatever détente there had been between the superpowers in the late 1970s, observers concluded, had now disappeared. The arrival of a new Republican administration in Washington made matters worse. Ronald Reagan publicly disparaged détente, dismissing it as "a one-way street."[6] Even more worrying was the administration's propensity for flippant remarks about fighting and winning a nuclear war. So long as there were enough shovels to go around, one administration official proclaimed, everyone would survive a Soviet strike.[7] If Reagan administration officials expressed those views in public, millions wondered what they might be planning in private. The prospect that the Americans were willing to fight a war in Europe, whether nuclear or conventional, drove thousands of Western Europeans to take to the streets, camp outside military installations, and protest in other ways.

The Cold War Strikes Back

NATO's Dual-Track Decision virtually guaranteed that any disagreement regarding its implementation would be seen as a threat. Loss of support in any one of the prospective basing countries could have a domino effect. What if the hesitation on display in Belgium or in the Netherlands spread? If governments in Brussels, The Hague, and Rome all refused the missiles, the alliance would end up in precisely the scenario that Helmut Schmidt and his advisers were so desperate to avoid, the singularization of the Federal Republic of Germany.

Détente's fortunes waned over the course of the 1970s. Frustrations about the glacial pace of arms control negotiations eclipsed the enthusiasm of the decade's early diplomatic breakthroughs. As the Soviet Union's power continued to grow, so too did a sense of disenchantment about what détente had—and had not—achieved. This domestic political backlash was particularly strong in the United States, where critics on both sides of the aisle formed new political constellations brought together by their disdain for détente.[8] By the autumn of 1979, relations between the United States and the Soviet Union seemed to have deteriorated so precipitously that Director of Central Intelligence Stansfield Turner warned that leaders in the Kremlin might "be more inclined to gamble on a substantial intervention in Afghanistan" to shore up their now-socialist neighbor, no matter the cost to US-Soviet relations.[9]

Turner's warning proved prescient. On December 12, 1979, a few hours after NATO's ministers had endorsed the Dual-Track Decision, Leonid Brezhnev approved plans to invade Afghanistan.[10] Earlier in the year, when confronted with an uprising in Herat, Brezhnev had refused to intervene lest it jeopardize the SALT II Treaty. By year's end, these concerns had all but evaporated. Washington's policies suggested a shift away from détente, be it the Carter administration's increases in defense spending or the painfully slow pace of the Senate's deliberations on the SALT II Treaty. If the United States moved away from détente, already a blow to Soviet interests, it would be all the more damaging to lose a friendly regime in neighboring Afghanistan.[11]

Carter was already under fire for the steady deterioration of the US position in the world that had seemingly unfolded on his watch. Walter Cronkite's daily reminder that fifty-two Americans remained hostages in Iran was only the most obvious manifestation of a much deeper pessimism about the country's direction. When Soviet tanks rolled into Afghanistan in late December, not only superpower relations came under strain but also Carter's very credibility as commander-in-chief.

At home, critics railed against Carter's failed foreign policy. "In the thirty-odd months since the inauguration of Jimmy Carter," one member of the neoconservative Committee on the Present Danger, Georgetown professor Jeane Kirkpatrick, argued, "there has occurred a dramatic Soviet military buildup, matched by the stagnation of American armed forces, and a dramatic extension of Soviet influence in the Horn of Africa, Afghanistan, Southern Africa, and the Caribbean."[12] Another critic from the right, Ronald Reagan, turned to an ever-popular historical analogy, likening one Carter speech to "the sorry tapping of Neville Chamberlain's umbrella on the cobblestones of Munich."[13]

Domestic politics demanded a firm response to the Soviet invasion. It was an election year, and the Democratic incumbent hoped to secure another term for himself. Carter introduced a series of sanctions against the Soviet Union, including an embargo on the sale of grain and a boycott of the Moscow Olympics that summer. The SALT II Treaty was shelved indefinitely. Ralph Earle, who took over as head of the Arms Control and Disarmament Agency that year, wryly likened his new job to inheriting "the brewery the day after Prohibition went into effect."[14]

SALT II was, in the eyes of one US analyst, Randall Forsberg, a sorry excuse for a treaty. It was "amazing," she later argued, "that a treaty that was that weak could run into that much trouble from the right."[15] Forsberg spearheaded 1979's "Call to Halt the Nuclear Arms Race" with support from a number of organizations; the original pamphlet was jointly distributed by the American Friends Service Committee, the Fellowship of Reconciliation, Clergy and Laity Concerned, and Forsberg's Institute for Defense and Disarmament Studies. This coalition brought together some of the traditional sources of antinuclear organizing, including Quakers and the Catholic Church.[16]

A mutual freeze proposal, the call urged the United States and the Soviet Union to stop the testing, production, and deployment of nuclear weapons, of which the two superpowers already had upward of fifty thousand. "In half an hour, a fraction of these weapons can destroy all the cities of the northern hemisphere," the call reminded readers. "Yet over the next decade, the USA and USSR plan to build over 20,000 more nuclear warheads, along with a new generation of nuclear missiles and aircraft." Rather than allow this growth to continue, signatories urged the superpowers to stop before it was too late. An end to the arms race, they argued, would be the single most important contribution to preventing a nuclear war and the emergence of more nuclear powers. On the foundation of deep cuts to the number of nuclear weapons, the United States and the Soviet Union could take further steps to build "a stable, peaceful international order."[17]

Calls for a nuclear freeze gained momentum among publics beginning in the spring of 1980.[18] What attracted so many to the freeze concept writ large was not a sudden realization of the sheer destructive power of nuclear weapons, but a combination of accessible language and the visible, sharp deterioration in East-West relations. Even as the freeze movement gained ground in the United States, a number of like-minded Europeans criticized the campaign's failure to prioritize the Dual-Track Decision above all other nuclear issues. US activists could—and should—do much more to halt the deployment of the Euromissiles, they maintained. After all, those weapons would be coming from US shores to the European homeland.[19]

Fated to live among NATO's new missiles, concerned Western Europeans tended to endorse more specific campaigns dedicated to stopping the Dual-Track Decision's deployments. The dismal state of US-Soviet relations only added to their sense of urgency, as many concluded that a world war was not only possible but increasingly likely. In one set of Eurobarometer polls from April 1980, over a third of respondents indicated their belief that a world war was probable within the decade. Across the board, these figures represented a marked increase from the autumn of 1977, when pollsters had last posed that question. British figures tripled from 13 to 39 percent. In France, the number skyrocketed from 14 to 42 percent.[20]

Yet, the détente of the 1970s had done little to reduce the real military threat facing Europe. The continent, one British activist, the Bertrand Russell Peace Foundation's Ken Coates, argued, "remains by far the most militaristic zone of the contemporary world." As evidence, Coates pointed to the thousands—ten, maybe fifteen, he hypothesized—of warheads stockpiled in Europe for so-called "tactical" or "theater" use on the continent.[21]

Coates was part of the group behind the "Appeal for European Nuclear Disarmament," launched in April 1980. Drafted in large part by E. P. Thompson and revised by Coates and Mary Kaldor, a professor of international relations at the London School of Economics, the appeal warned of the dangers already on display around the world—and only likely to get worse. In fact, the appeal's authors argued, the 1980s were poised to be the most dangerous decade in human history. The threat to Europe was inescapable—and deadly: "In Europe, the main geographical stage for the East-West confrontation, new generations of ever more deadly weapons are appearing."[22]

END's appeal for a nuclear-free Europe took aim at the logic of the arms race. "As each side tries to prove its readiness to use nuclear weapons, in order to prevent their use by the other side," its authors argued, "new more 'usable' nuclear weapons are designed as the idea of 'limited' nuclear war is made to sound more and more plausible." They urged readers to reject this trend and throw their weight behind the denuclearization of the continent.[23]

Hundreds of signatures poured into the Bertrand Russell Peace Foundation to endorse the appeal. These responses came from a diverse group of concerned citizens, whom the initiative's organizers showcased. In addition to a series of left-leaning Western Europeans, the appeal enjoyed the backing of the Russian historian Roy Medvedev and of Rudolf Bahro, a recently imprisoned East German now working with the Green Party in the Federal Republic. Boasting signatories from both sides of the Iron Curtain, the appeal's backers highlighted their base of support "from Greece up to Finland, and from Ireland to Moscow."[24] END became both an activist organization and an institution, as the campaign arranged annual conventions that brought together antinuclear campaigners from across the continent to build networks and exchange views.[25]

END's success relied in large part on the writings of E. P. Thompson. In 1980 alone, Thompson penned the pamphlet *Protest and Survive* (a riposte to the Thatcher government's civil defense booklet, *Protect and Survive*) and the essay "Notes on Exterminism, the Last Stage of Civilization," along with regular pieces for major outlets like the *Guardian* and the *Times*. Thompson relied on his sharp wit and accessible language to demystify jargon-laden nuclear policy. This steady stream of pieces in print brought countless individuals to the cause. When END asked its supporters how they had become interested in the initiative, 14 percent of respondents pointed to newspaper articles and 15 percent to books, many penned by Thompson. Nearly a third of those who completed END's survey mentioned the Oxford historian by name.[26]

END's permanent staff stayed small, so as not to compete with the largest British peace organization, the Campaign for Nuclear Disarmament. A product of the late 1950s, CND began to slowly emerge from a hibernation of sorts in the late 1970s, spurred at least in part by the popular outcry over the neutron bomb.[27] The organization boomed in the early 1980s, staging a massive rally in London on October 26, 1980. "The Campaign for Nuclear Disarmament," one reporter confidently proclaimed the next day, "came back with renewed vigour yesterday."[28]

The rally was CND's largest gathering in over twenty years, with over sixty thousand demonstrators flooding the streets of London. A giant inflatable mushroom cloud shaded protestors in Hyde Park.[29] Marchers wound their way to Trafalgar Square with placards urging onlookers to "Fight War, Not Wars" and "Send Thatcher on a Cruise."[30] In the shadow of Nelson's Column, politicians and popular activists—what one newspaper described as a mix of "unilateralists, mutual disarmers, a nun, a Communist and a Quaker"—took to the stage, including Labour Party leaders Neil Kinnock and Tony Benn, the actress Susannah York, and of course E. P. Thompson himself.[31] In the weeks and months that followed, membership in CND soared. When asked why they had joined, many of the group's newest members mentioned one of two people as having inspired them: Margaret Thatcher or Ronald Reagan. It was not meant as a compliment.[32]

CND's revival coincided with a shift in the Labour Party's platform in the United Kingdom. For the first time in two decades, Labour chose to back the unilateral renunciation of Britain's nuclear program. These developments, one editorial in London's *Socialist Organiser* argued, were the direct result of the fact that the world had "recently become alarmingly more unstable." A nuclear conflagration was "now again seen by millions as a threatening possibility in the period ahead."[33]

The trends unfolding in the United Kingdom were not outliers; similar sentiment was clear across the continent. In the Federal Republic of Germany, a collection of communist organizers, ex-military officers, and members of the newly established Green Party put forward their own plea to stop the Euromissiles: the "Krefeld Appeal," spearheaded by the German Peace Union (Deutsche Friedensunion), a communist organization with ties to the East Germans. Petra Kelly lent her support to the appeal, as did the general turned activist Gert Bastian. Targeting Helmut Schmidt's government, the Krefeld Appeal's signatories urged their elected representatives to reject the Dual-Track Decision's planned deployments on German soil. Despite its communist ties, the Krefeld initiative received significant public support. By July 1981, nearly a million West Germans had signed their names in support of the call to the halt the deployments.[34]

Like so many in 1980, the authors of the "Krefeld Appeal" pointed to the international situation as a catalyst. They bemoaned the lack of dialogue between the two superpowers, going so far as to suggest, "Not even the commencement of such talks is in sight."[35] That assertion was easily proven false. By the time the appeal appeared in November 1980, the United States and the Soviet Union had already begun holding preliminary exchanges on theater nuclear forces. But the image of two superpowers shouting past one another, not talking, shaped the public narrative as much—if not more—than the far messier realities of US-Soviet relations.

Who Needs More Bombs, Anyway?

As more came to the cause, they brought with them an array of arguments against NATO's planned deployments. Some of these were tried-and-true staples of the antinuclear movement, such as the sheer expense of the nuclear weapons establishment. The funds required to research, produce, and deploy these destructive arsenals could easily be put to better use, whether in health care, education, or assistance to the developing world.[36] A group of women in the London borough of Hackney dramatized the point in a local action, filling a shopping cart with eighteen British pounds' worth of goods—the per capita amount spent each week on defense in Britain—outside an outpost of the grocery chain Sainsbury's.[37] Others linked their critiques to other causes that mattered to them, such as environmentalism, feminism, and opposition to US intervention in Central America. Feminists in particular found easy fodder in the technical terminology of nuclear strategy, poking fun at military men's talk of "deep penetration" and "missile erectors."[38]

But much of the opposition remained focused on the bomb itself. Already, the sheer size of the superpowers' nuclear arsenals was staggering. Pamphlets offered figures that dramatized the destructive power. The United States alone, one booklet argued, had enough weapons to equal 615,000 Little Boys, the atomic bomb dropped on Hiroshima.[39] "Anyone who can count," one Canadian critic quipped, "must conclude that we simply don't need any more missiles."[40] With so many nuclear weapons already deployed, why did the Western allies need even more?

Picking up on earlier arguments that had circulated among specialists in the 1970s, many critics viewed NATO's deployments as the "centerpiece" of a warfighting doctrine.[41] A steady stream of disenchanted former weapons designers and military planners lent legitimacy and at least a veneer of expertise to these arguments, making them accessible and thereby exposing a much broader audience to them. Their message was simple and alarming. Over the course of the 1970s, US nuclear policies had trended toward a warfighting posture—and that war would be fought in Europe.

Opponents of the Dual-Track Decision enthusiastically adopted the argument. One popular protest ditty underscored the dangers of this shift as it urged listeners to reject NATO's new missiles:

What the hell do they want these missiles for?
Refuse the cruise
Do they think they can win a nuclear war?
I believe they do
Whatever happens we're the ones who lose
Refuse the cruise
Refuse the cruise
Refuse the cruise[42]

Even if the United States and the Soviet Union could be trusted to prevent a nuclear war—far from a foregone conclusion for activists motivated by their worries about the frosty state of relations between Moscow and Washington—a conflict might break out anyway. Technological developments had made that all too easy.

A nuclear war might be triggered by accident through equipment malfunction or user error. The slightest miscalculation could be devastating. "One flick of a switch could bring about the destruction of the world as we know it!" blared one flyer urging readers to join a march for disarmament in New York City.[43] Reports of narrowly averted disasters underscored just how plausible that scenario was. In the summer of 1980, major newspapers carried stories of a computer chip failure that dispatched a series of false warnings about an impending Soviet nuclear strike. Even workaday glitches threatened to unleash incredible destruction, as the *New York Times* reported under the headline "Missile Alerts Traced to 46¢ Item."[44]

Strength in Numbers

By the early 1980s, it was nearly impossible to ignore the fact that the Cold War was still on. Much of the competition between the superpowers of the 1970s had unfolded in Asia, Africa, and Latin America. This made it easy for Europeans to ignore the costs of the Cold War and take solace in détente if they so chose. But in the next decade, the return of hostile rhetoric and the growth of nuclear stockpiles forced millions to confront the continued existential threat to their continent. Many latched onto binary interpretations that cast détente as the antithesis of the Cold War. If the Cold War was back, with a new chill some dubbed the "Second Cold War," then détente must be dead and gone.[45]

Motivated by a sense of fear, the Dual-Track Decision's opponents increasingly turned to mass rallies to press their case as pamphlets failed to change the course of policy. By the autumn of 1981, these demonstrations were a staple of weekend news broadcasts. Massive crowds turned out week after week to protest the Dual-Track Decision in cities and towns across Europe, many of them shattering records for size of gatherings in these locales.

Crowds descended on the lawns of Bonn's Hofgarten on Saturday, October 10, 1981, toting signs, balloons, and homemade banners. The event's primary organizers, Action Reconciliation Service for Peace (Action Sühnezeichen/Friedensdienste) and Action Committee Service for Peace (Aktionsgemeinschaft Dienst für den Frieden), chartered three thousand buses and forty-two trains to bring individuals from across Western Europe.[46] "Americans go west," one demonstrator's banner urged—to the Atlantic Ocean, and onward back home.[47] Another, tongue firmly in cheek, exhorted passersby to "Make Liverwurst of Reagan."[48] Two young people, aided by a moped, paraded a giant papier-mâché missile.[49] An array of politicians and public figures addressed a crowd of at least 250,000. Heinrich Böll, a Nobel Prize–winning author active in the Green Party, waxed poetic about the

FIGURE 6.1. Demonstrators descend on Bonn, October 1981. Source: Rob Bogaerts/Anefo/ Nationaal Archief (NL-HaNa inventory file no. 931-7334), https://www.nationaalarchief.nl/en/ research/photo-collection/ado5f4fo-dob4-102d-bcf8-003048976d84.

new pacifist disease sweeping the neighboring Netherlands, "Hollanditis." Coretta Scott King linked the demonstrators' struggle for peace to the earlier efforts of her slain husband, the civil rights activist Reverend Dr. Martin Luther King Jr. Petra Kelly made the political point behind these rallies clear when she called for Helmut Schmidt's resignation as chancellor—if he did not resign, the implication was, everyone in attendance would turf him out at the ballot box.[50]

Organizers relied on diverse coalitions to make these huge rallies possible. Representatives from twenty-two different organizations—pacifists, ecologists, communists, and Christians—banded together to produce the original call for the October 10 rally in Bonn. The momentum only grew from there, as 340 different groups signed up to participate in advance of the day's events.[51] These connections extended far beyond the borders of the Federal Republic. About four thousand Dutch demonstrators marched in Bonn that day, spearheaded by the peace group IKV. The sheer number of organizations involved suggested the breadth and the depth of opposition to the Euromissiles, as did the diversity of intellectual traditions and policy priorities represented.

Journalists latched onto this diversity as evidence of a broad-based movement coalescing. The rally in Bonn, one *Washington Post* reporter wrote, brought together "a colorful mix of groups ranging from Communists and left-wing activists to churchmen, students and even a batch of soldiers."[52] Opposition to the Dual-Track Decision was not confined to one segment of the population, no matter how one sliced it. Demonstrations brought together veteran campaigners and alarmed newcomers all eager to stop the Euromissiles. "It's not just your freaks anymore," one of the peace movement's old guard told reporters at a demonstration in London. "There's a lot of straight people here who have decided to stand up and be counted. And this is one way to do it."[53] News broadcasts underscored that fact as they led segments with video footage of everyday people, young and old, in crowds that extended as far as the camera's eye could see.

Organizers boasted of the staggering turnout at rallies throughout the autumn of 1981. The day after the protest in Bonn, thirty thousand rallied in Comiso, the Sicilian town slated to host Italy's share of the cruise missiles. The next week, fifty thousand marched in Torino, in the country's north. Activists in Rotterdam took to the city's canals to launch a festive ten-day "cruise against cruise." Enormous crowds called on their elected officials to reject the Dual-Track Decision: two hundred thousand in London, three hundred thousand in Rome, and two hundred thousand in Brussels.[54] Almost all of these figures were contested, but even after taking into account the difference between organizers' optimistic estimates and the far more conservative figures of local police forces, the message was clear. NATO's Dual-Track Decision had terrified a great many Western Europeans, and they were not content to sit by in silence.

Time and again, marchers attributed these fears to a growing sense that the superpowers might fight a limited nuclear war in Europe.[55] Only weeks earlier, Ronald Reagan had told a group of reporters that he could envision an exchange of tactical nuclear weapons "without it bringing either one of the major powers to pushing the button" and attacking one another's homeland.[56] Western Europeans, who would not be spared in such a circumstance, unsurprisingly balked at the president's casual comments. "I can't dismiss Reagan's remarks as a gaffe," Michael Foot, the leader of Britain's Labour Party, explained to reporters. "The Western alliance strategy is based on a so-called flexible response . . . in which in some circumstances the West could strike first."[57]

Since taking office in January, Reagan had made a reputation as a tough-talking hawk with a penchant for anti-Soviet rhetoric. Soaring defense budgets in the United States suggested that the administration was willing to put its money where its mouth was. Even before his inauguration, the authors of the "Bielefeld Appeal"—a noncommunist riposte to the "Krefeld

Appeal"—bemoaned the incoming Republican's clear desire "to continue building up arms."[58] By the autumn of 1981, one critic described the Reagan foreign policy as twofold: "To talk tough and spend a lot of money."[59]

Those searching for it found ample evidence of a president willing to use Europeans as "nuclear cannon fodder."[60] On the thirty-sixth anniversary of the bombing of Hiroshima, Reagan announced that he would move forward with the controversial enhanced radiation warhead of the previous decade. The president's decision scored few political points in Western Europe. Polling indicated that a whopping 90 percent of Norwegians opposed the decision. "We simply don't understand the reason for the neutron bomb decision being made now—when the world is hoping arms control negotiations between the United States and the Soviet Union eventually could start again," one Norwegian academic wrote.[61] At demonstrations across Western Europe, placards drove home the message that US policies left those they were ostensibly designed to protect and reassure terrified, bearing slogans like "Yanks Go Home," "We Are Not America's Guinea Pigs," and "US—Traitors to the Human Race."[62]

Protest as Symbolism and the Case of Greenham Common

Mass demonstrations generated striking visuals, especially as protestors came up with new and creative ways to express their discontent. They held mock funerals and die-ins and donned skeleton tunics and grim reaper costumes. They rallied with inflatable mushroom clouds, towering papier-mâché missiles, and caricatures of political leaders like Ronald Reagan. During Peace Week 1981, one group of West German activists even handed out waffles shaped like tanks to drive home their message: "Waffeln statt Waffen!"—waffles instead of weapons.[63]

But perhaps nothing became a more potent symbol of the opposition to the Dual-Track Decision—and the political changes it signaled—than the women's peace camp at Greenham Common. In August 1981, thirty-six women set out from Cardiff to protest the arms race. Women for Life on Earth, as the group styled itself, walked over a hundred miles from Wales to Greenham Common, the Royal Air Force base in the Berkshire countryside slated to host ninety-six cruise missiles. A handful of marchers chained themselves to the base's main gate when they arrived, before setting up a more permanent presence on its periphery: a peace camp. Over time, the women established a series of smaller camps scattered around the installation, each with its own color and personality. The original outpost was the venerable

FIGURE 6.2. Women camped out at Greenham Common, October 1983. Source: James Pearson/ National Archives and Records Administration (NARA Identifier no. 6377437), https://catalog. archives.gov/id/6377437.

Yellow Gate. Green Gate made a name for itself by refusing all male visitors. And the Blue Gate was known for its New Age focus.

The women of Greenham Common devised creative, sometimes audacious antinuclear actions sure to grab journalists' attention. They blockaded the base, occupied sentry boxes, and took bolt cutters to the perimeter fences, raising alert after alert. In June 1982, eighty women from Greenham Common staged a die-in outside the London Stock Exchange, blocking rush hour traffic in the City for a quarter of an hour.[64] To mark the third anniversary of NATO's Dual-Track Decision on December 12, 1982, the women urged visitors to join them and "embrace the base." They would cover Greenham Common in handwritten messages, banners, and what organizers referred to as the "symbols of life," such as flowers and photographs of their loved ones.[65] Some thirty thousand women turned out, forming a nine-mile chain around the perimeter. E. P. Thompson was there, as were countless other men, who served as cooks, drivers, and auxiliaries to the main event.[66] A few weeks later, on New Year's Day 1983, a group scaled the base's perimeter fence and managed to climb atop the missile silos themselves, singing and dancing.[67]

Unorthodox methods attracted attention, guaranteeing that the cause received mainstream media coverage. So too did the fact that the activists were all women. Countless stories focused on their credentials as ordinary women who, in the eyes of sexist critics, should not be interested in weighty questions of foreign and defense policy. Critics, as one journalist put it, disparaged the women of Greenham Common as "naive exhibitionists, militant feminists, headline hunters, [and] communists."[68]

Nevertheless, the Greenham Common Women's Peace Camp came to symbolize the grassroots activism of the day. "A few women sleeping under plastic sheeting in sub-zero temperatures," one British journalist wrote, "have become the unexpected focus for the Western disarmament movement."[69] The women at the camp were not formally affiliated with other, more structured pockets of opposition to the cruise missile's arrival in Britain, be it the party politics of Labour or the activism of CND. The campers operated on a shoestring budget with no electricity, no running water, and no methods of communication more sophisticated than cycling down the road to use the nearest pay phone.[70]

Their ideas and image still traveled. Journalists gravitated toward the camp, filing stories that shared the women's message and gave them notoriety and name recognition. Television panels invited the women to share their experiences. In one, two women from the camp, Ann Pettitt and Helen John, appeared alongside Petra Kelly in a wide-ranging conversation about John's recent arrest, the Thatcher government's efforts to stifle the movement, and the connections between British and West German activists.[71] Women from the camp went on speaking tours to share their stories with new audiences far from Berkshire. In the autumn of 1983, for example, two women set out across Western Canada sharing their stories from Greenham Common as well as its Sicilian counterpart, Comiso, to drum up support for a Canadian outpost at the base in Cole Bay, Saskatchewan.[72]

Activists flocked from around the world to Greenham Common, some for a few days, others a few months, and many much longer still. Women from across the alliance made their own treks to Berkshire. One twenty-three year old West German dropped out of her lectures at the University of Mainz to join the camp. "We're not intellectual," she told a reporter, "but none of us wants the cruise missile, or a Third World War."[73] Those who couldn't make it in person reached out in other ways. Letters of support poured into the camp, sometimes hundreds in a single week.[74]

Greenham Common became a prominent symbol of the resistance, leading other activists to replicate the model. Peace camps sprang up on both sides of the Atlantic. Activists pitched tents at other sites slated to host the cruise missile, like Comiso and the Dutch town of Woensdrecht.[75] Similar outposts dotted the British countryside, at Molesworth (the other cruise missile site in the United Kingdom) and at Faslane (the home of Britain's nuclear submarines), as well as Fairford, Welford, and at least a dozen others. At the Seneca Army Depot in New York, US and Canadian campaigners set up the Women's Encampment for a Future of Peace and Justice to send a message from the "point of departure for nuclear weapons to Europe."[76]

As the Greenham Common women became a household name, some urged the Thatcher government to push back on their arguments with even greater force. "We are dealing with . . . an induced mass-hysteria impervious to argument," one Conservative peer, Lord Max Beloff, argued. Instead of extending general platitudes about the women and their good intentions, the government should go on the offensive with a concerted campaign to discredit the women of in the court of public opinion. Beloff recommended that the government acquire information on the movement's finances (which he suggested included significant funding from the Libyan leader and terrorist financier Muammar Qaddafi) and on the backgrounds of the women camped out at Greenham Common. "We must force the patriotic wing of the Labour Party into the open to denounce this coming together of their Party and Soviet-inspired anti-patriotic groups and their dupes," he argued. As for the ruling Tories, they could make the most of their leader. Beloff urged Thatcher to make a public speech addressing the women of Britain, appealing to themes of motherhood and family. "I shall not be content until it becomes as hazardous to wear a CND badge on the streets of London," he concluded, "as it would be to sport a swastika in Tel Aviv."[77]

The Communist Connection

A great many shared Beloff's outlook. Those active in campaigns against the Dual-Track Decision were regularly accused of pro-Soviet leanings. Protestors were cast as communist sympathizers and traitors, dupes, or useful idiots whose genuine fears of nuclear war played right into the Kremlin's hands.[78] Critics referred to Gen. Nino Pasti, an outspoken former deputy commander of NATO South active in the peace group Generals for Peace and Disarmament, for example, as a "Warsaw Pact General."[79]

Undeniably, some activists preached the gospel of communism. Still more knowingly received funds, directly or indirectly, from Warsaw Pact governments. The Eastern allies, eager to repeat the successes of their campaign against the neutron bomb, seized the opportunities presented by such homegrown opposition to the bomb.[80] The basic tools of the trade remained the same: financial support, forgeries, front organizations, and the target-rich environment of a free and open press.

Western intelligence agencies nevertheless maintained that, for better or worse, "the balance of forces within the peace movement is becoming more unfavorable to the Communists." A far greater percentage of the opposition was made up of noncommunist groups—flush with enough cash from the donations of fellow citizens who feared the superpowers were teetering on the brink—than of Soviet front organizations.[81] Still, disentangling the views of homegrown opponents with no ties to communism and the talking points promoted by Soviet agents proved a difficult task for those in power across the West.

The Kremlin harnessed the benefits of an open information landscape in Western Europe and North America, using it to champion themes that would resonate with a broad swath of the public, regardless of their political leanings. "Any communication channel can be used to disseminate the message," one former KGB disinformation practitioner noted, "but, since the purpose of the message is to trigger a chain reaction in the mass media, choice of the best medium for surfacing the story is most important."[82] These tactics made it difficult for allied governments to rebut the Warsaw Pact's talking points without dismissing the genuine fears of their own voters. Governments across the alliance did try, producing attractive and informative booklets designed to rebut talking points and arguments popular among antinuclear activists. In the summer of 1981, for instance, the West German Press Office released "Aspects of Peace Politics" in collaboration with the foreign and defense ministries.[83]

The sheer complexity of NATO's political landscape made that task even harder. Although allied officials appreciated the importance of making their case publicly, perhaps even through concerted information policies, there was no one-size-fits-all solution. Their electorates differed, and much of the messaging would need to be calibrated accordingly to the local situation.[84] NATO's own deliberations highlighted the need to put forward a positive vision for the future, not just a series of facts and figures that drove home the continued Soviet threat. But the positive vision preferred by many was the same as that of decades past: the combination of defense and détente endorsed in 1967's Harmel Report.[85] With the president of the United States a vocal critic of détente, which played well with his party's base, there were obvious limits to any allied arguments that NATO remained guided by the pursuit of détente. The fact that a significant portion of the NATO leaders' constituents believed, after talks opened in the autumn of 1981, that the superpowers' arms control negotiations were a piece of political theater designed to keep the deployments on track, rather than to reduce the two sides' arsenals, scarcely helped the alliance's case.

Peace groups represented targets of convenience and opportunity, easily exploited to suit Soviet interests. But concerted campaigns to unmask Soviet infiltration of these organizations could easily engender a domestic political backlash. When the Danish government arrested a Dane and expelled a Soviet diplomat, outed as a KGB officer, for extending financial assistance to an antinuclear campaign, peace groups attacked the entire episode as a sham designed to discredit their legitimate activism and their point of view, which represented a consensus of millions.[86]

Though allied governments hesitated to push too forcefully lest they alienate the voters whose support they hoped to win, a small group of vocal individuals felt no such restraint. Counterprotest organizations developed, eager to challenge the arguments put forward by peace activists and discredit their activities. One British group, the Coalition for Peace through Security, went on the offensive against CND. Its members circulated pamphlets emblazoned with "CND: Communists, Neutralists, Defeatists" and likened CND's supporters to the appeasers of the 1930s.[87] Similar groups popped up across the alliance, often with links both informal and formal to conservative political parties and foundations. In the case of the Coalition for Peace through Security, later reports suggested the group had received direct funding from the Heritage Foundation.[88]

Antinuclear campaigners pushed back. One Shropshire resident, a thirty-year veteran of the security services now active in a peace group, expressed little surprise at the "mendacity and ferocity" of attacks on campaigners as alleged communists. "On the other hand," he wrote in a letter to the editor of the *Guardian*, "I can state—hand on heart—that I have observed not the slightest indication of Soviet direction, not a hint that a single kopek has come to hand, and no inkling at all of Marxist inspiration at any level."[89] Aware that these assumptions were commonplace, however, organizations targeted their messaging and rebutted the claims directly. "CND stands for Campaign for Nuclear Disarmament," a flyer from the group's Clifton chapter informed readers, "*not* for let's help a Russian invasion."[90]

Though some activists were willing to collaborate with socialist groups and communist parties, others tried to insulate themselves by severing ties with all things communist. On demonstration weekends in Paris, the French capital often saw two dueling protests, one communist-led, another noncommunist. In Greece, a group of activists banded together to form a new organization, the Movement for Peace, Human Rights, and National Independence (KEADEA), as a viable alternative to the Greek branch of the Soviet-backed front organization the World Peace Council.[91] And when communist organizations were involved in planning actions, some activists were outspoken in their frustration that these parties refused to criticize the Soviet Union's behavior worldwide. In the lead up to large rallies in Bonn in the summer of 1982, set to coincide with Reagan's visit, members of the Green Party griped that the communists blocked resolutions condemning the Soviet invasion of Afghanistan and Soviet involvement in the introduction of martial law in Poland, as well as those expressing solidarity with the Polish labor union, Solidarność.[92] IKV refused to endorse the rally at all, arguing that the organization could not lend its support to the demonstration's anti-NATO tenor, refusal to condemn the Soviets' SS-20s, and what Dutch organizers deemed to be overtones of German nationalism.[93]

The ideological fault lines of the Cold War still shaped the conversation from top to bottom. Some rejected the rigid binaries that cast communists as enemies of the West, willing to collaborate with anyone who shared their broad objective of halting the deployment of NATO's new missiles, whereas others saw a rejection of communist ties as critical to the success of their movement. Only by demonstrating a broad base of support among the mainstream public could they force their elected representatives to change course.

Despite the popular parlance of the day, there was not one, single peace movement in the early 1980s. A veritable kaleidoscope of individuals and groups mobilized, terrified by the prospects of a nuclear war and the Cold War's return to Europe. Antinuclear activism took different forms across the alliance, shaped by domestic politics, national traditions, and preexisting networks and organizations. Those active in campaigns argued among themselves about what tactics to pursue and what issues to prioritize.[94]

No matter these differences, the depth and breadth of popular opposition to NATO's Dual-Track Decision was inescapable. Antinuclear sentiment was sweeping the alliance from Vancouver to Venice, turning against NATO's plans to deploy new missiles to Western Europe. In the face of that opposition, how could allied governments preserve sufficient support to see the deployments through?

CHAPTER 7

Moons and Green Cheese

Chief Soviet negotiator Yuli Kvitsinsky opened the first session of the Geneva talks with a weak attempt at a joke. A rabbit and a bear were riding in a train compartment. Before the conductor made the rounds, checking passengers' tickets, the rabbit's ticket disappeared. "So what?" the bear responded. "So what!" the rabbit retorted. What would happen when the conductor came by and the rabbit had no ticket? The bear offered to help. When the conductor came around, the bear would hang the rabbit out of the window by its ears; the conductor would never know the rabbit was there. The rabbit agreed, confident in the bear's protection. As the train hurtled along the tracks, the conductor stepped into the compartment. The bear handed over his ticket and, when asked what was in his other hand—the one hanging out the window—he pulled it in, empty.[1]

Kvitsinsky's joke was a transparent call for the United States to throw its allies under the proverbial bus (or, in this case, train). These initial exchanges hinted at how complex the superpowers' arms control negotiations would be. US and Soviet negotiators remained far apart, divided over familiar questions of what weapons should be counted in the talks, whose weapons should be included, and how they should calculate the balance within Europe. Despite these challenges, the United States and the Soviet Union remained at the bargaining table after formal negotiations to limit what were now christened intermediate-range nuclear forces—INF—opened in November 1981.

For both the United States and the Soviet Union, the conduct of private arms control negotiations could not be divorced from the broader contours of their public diplomacy. So long as the United States was in talks with the Soviet Union, it left open the possibility that the two superpowers could reach an agreement to reduce the dangers of the nuclear arms race. Arms control could be used to manage public anxieties, a possible benefit already touted by many of the Dual-Track Decision's original architects. The inverse was true of the Soviet Union. The Kremlin could churn out attractive offers, studded with appeals to the preservation of détente and calls to end the arms race, to whip up popular fears in Western Europe about the thrust of US policies and those of the Atlantic alliance as a whole.

Acutely aware that each side's preferred outcome relied on a volatile popular mood, the United States and the Soviet Union played to the crowd. Negotiations took place as much in public as in private while the two sides tried to woo Western European audiences, in particular West German ones. Both superpowers calibrated their policies accordingly, eager to put their best foot forward in what one journalist dubbed "the dance of the Euromissiles."[2]

Time to Talk

It took time to bring the Soviet Union to the negotiating table. In December 1979, just six days after NATO's ministers had endorsed the Dual-Track Decision, Secretary of State Cyrus Vance approached the Kremlin, formally indicating Washington's desire to open negotiations as soon as possible. The Soviets clung to their earlier position, namely that NATO's plans had destroyed the basis for talks. So long as the Western allies planned to follow through on the Dual-Track Decision, they could not talk arms control.[3]

The Western allies took Moscow's intransigence as a sign that the Soviet Union believed the Dual-Track Decision could be prevented by other means. Only when those in the Kremlin came to see negotiations as their sole option to stop the missiles would talks begin in earnest.[4] But that increasingly seemed too long to wait. With superpower relations in the doldrums and antinuclear campaigns gaining traction, the allies could not afford to wait for the Soviets.

In the wake of the Soviet invasion of Afghanistan, a great many doubted whether the superpowers would negotiate at all. US sanctions curbed ties between Moscow and Washington, and, although they did not explicitly target talks on theater nuclear forces, the general state of relations suggested that problems might spill over anyway. Washington's sharp response to the

Soviet invasion, along with the Carter administration's failure to coordinate with the rest of its NATO allies, worried Helmut Schmidt. He remained a staunch advocate of dialogue with Moscow believing that it was imperative that NATO explain its positions to the Soviets lest misunderstanding lead to a conflagration between East and West. To that end, Schmidt planned to visit Moscow for talks with Leonid Brezhnev in June 1980, taking up a longstanding Soviet offer extended once more in March. The move alarmed some of Schmidt's allies, who feared that the chancellor would go too far in the name of insulating détente, particularly with an election coming up in October.

Schmidt's recent policy moves inflamed these fears. In the weeks leading up to his trip to the Soviet Union, the chancellor publicly suggested a halt to all theater nuclear missile deployments. Carter and his advisers balked at Schmidt's vague formulation for a freeze, which seemed to suggest that both sides should halt their deployments for a spell. Schmidt's latest initiative, they concluded, would only add to the Dual-Track Decision's fragility. Already, the Belgians were waffling, grasping for excuses to defer their final commitment once more. If picked up by Moscow, Schmidt's ideas could give the Belgians the cover they needed.[5] Carter sought clarification, concerned, as he put it in a letter to Schmidt, that the proposal was "unequal and inconsistent with the Alliance's Dual-Track Decision."[6] Schmidt was furious. He maintained that the proposal was nothing more than a call for the Soviet Union to exercise restraint and halt its deployment program, just as the Western allies were currently doing.[7] But his formulation had been far more opaque. A later biographer with close access to Schmidt suggested that ambiguity was intentional; Schmidt had tried to obscure the one-sided nature of the proposal in such a way that it would be palatable to the Kremlin, making it possible for Moscow to accept.[8]

Carter's attempts to clarify enraged Schmidt. When the two met at the G-7 in Venice two weeks later, Schmidt's frustrations spilled over. The chancellor objected to the insinuation that he would not stick to the earlier Dual-Track Decision with such vehemence that Zbigniew Brzezinski could not help but jump in. Schmidt and Brzezinski ended up in a heated back-and-forth, each promising a political fight, that Carter tried to defuse to little avail. The president later described it as "the most unpleasant personal exchange" with a foreign leader of his four years in office.[9]

In advance of the visit to Moscow, Schmidt's aides tried to manage expectations. The purpose of the trip was to ensure that a dialogue remained open, and the chancellor took great care to insist he would not be a go-between, trying to broker a breakthrough in relations between the United States and the Soviet Union.[10] The visit's outcome suggested otherwise.

Schmidt's trip shifted Moscow's position. The Soviet Union indicated that talks on theater nuclear forces could open, even though the Kremlin's previous preconditions had yet to be met. NATO's members refused to disavow the Dual-Track Decision and the SALT II Treaty remained unratified.[11] The Western allies greeted this development with a sense of satisfaction. It was vindication of their own earlier policies. NATO's determination to move forward with modernization had swayed the Soviet Union.[12] Sweeping affirmations like these were almost certainly more palatable than the realization that it was Schmidt who broke the deadlock. The Soviets, however, rarely missed an opportunity to drive that fact home. After indicating to Schmidt that they would be willing to enter into negotiations, the Soviets took nine days to share that information directly with Washington.[13] It was the latest reminder that the superpowers would be playing for the hearts and minds of Western Europe, particularly those in the Federal Republic of Germany.

US and Soviet negotiators opened preliminary exchanges in Geneva in October 1980. Members of the Carter administration prepared for a long slog. The Kremlin's willingness to come to the bargaining table hinted at the depth of Soviets' concern about the Dual-Track Decision, but they were certain to draw the talks out for as long as possible. Any preliminary exchanges were unlikely to yield early results.[14] With voters set to go to the polls on November 4, the presidential election in the United States diminished the prospects further. So too did the change of administration that followed. The electorate denied Carter a second term, opting instead to back his Republican opponent, the former governor of California Ronald Reagan.

For the incoming Reagan team, what to do about arms control was a conundrum. Many within the administration's ranks were viscerally opposed to all forms thereof, convinced that the Soviet Union could not be trusted. Others were content to negotiate with the Kremlin, but only if they could do so from a position of strength. Where Reagan fit remained the subject of speculation, even among his closest aides. But given the bleak assessments of the United States' current position circulating among administration staffers, it would take time to rebuild to the point that they could negotiate comfortably and confidently. In the interim, they were saddled with the Dual-Track Decision. After coming to power in January 1981, the Reagan administration set out to study its inheritance.

Within the new administration were critics of both tracks of NATO's December 1979 decision. Some, like Richard Perle and Paul Warnke, questioned the strategic logic behind the deployments. Perle, a former aide to Henry Jackson who became assistant secretary of defense for international security policy, blamed SALT for enabling the Soviets to develop and deploy the SS-20 in the first place. Then, in the hopes of salvaging the arms control process, the Carter administration had simply repeated the same mistakes. "The whole sorry story," he remarked, "is a classic example of how so-called arms control, far from controlling arms, has had the effect of driving the deployment of new weapons."[15] Others objected to the decision's commitment to negotiate. "We should not really sit down to talk just for talk's sake," Secretary of Defense Caspar Weinberger argued.[16] His counterpart and frequent sparring partner at the State Department, Alexander Haig, suggested that any talks should be subject to a form of linkage. The United States could not consider arms control negotiations in a vacuum, separate from the Soviets' objectionable behavior elsewhere in the world.[17]

Uncertain about the direction of the new administration's policies, Western European governments waited nervously. Any sizable delay in negotiations would make their own political situations worse. Before Margaret Thatcher visited Washington in late February 1981, Schmidt urged the British prime minister to make the case for both tracks of the 1979 decision. Reagan, he worried, might stick to the deployments, but drop the arms control component. Should the president do so, Schmidt warned Thatcher, they would face a long and difficult road ahead. Western European publics would not accept the abandonment of arms control. "The essence of NATO defence policy had to be to secure a balance in the military field and then stabilise it by negotiation," Schmidt told Thatcher. If they failed to do so, it could "deal a fatal blow" to the alliance.[18] Thatcher assured Schmidt that she would raise the matter with the president and, in Washington, she made the case for preserving both halves of the original decision. She appeared to have secured what she came for; at a press conference after their meeting, Reagan and Thatcher jointly affirmed their continued commitment "to modernize long-range theater nuclear forces and to pursue arms control efforts at the same time, in parallel."[19] Vague assurances could only do so much to address the problem, however, and various factions of the administration remained at loggerheads over nearly all of the specifics of when, where, and on what terms to negotiate with the Soviet Union.

While the Reagan administration got its bearings, the Soviets kept up the pressure. In February 1981, as part of the Twenty-Sixth Party Congress, Leonid Brezhnev unveiled a new proposal to freeze the number of nuclear systems in Europe at current levels and called for a summit with his new US counterpart.[20] The White House saw this call for a summit as little more than a ploy to derail improvements to NATO's defenses, along with those of the United States.[21] The moratorium proposal fared little better. The first of many such offers, the Western allies saw it for what it was: an offer to "freeze them into inferiority."[22] The entire foreign policy section of Brezhnev's speech, the NSC's Soviet specialist, Richard Pipes, concluded, had been tailored to Western European audiences "to increase allied pressure on the United States to adopt a 'realistic' (read: 'appeasement-like') policy toward the Communist Bloc."[23]

Soviet diplomacy had fallen into a predictable rhythm, cycling through attractive and not-so-attractive offers to ratchet up the costs should NATO follow through on the Dual-Track Decision's deployments. To meet that challenge, the Reagan administration came to the conclusion, albeit grudgingly, that there was little choice but to negotiate. It was too late to reverse course.[24]

When and where negotiations might begin was another matter. An interagency battle raged, as skeptics squared off against officials tasked with managing Washington's allies like Lawrence Eagleburger (who was confirmed as assistant secretary of state for Canadian and European affairs in May). In late March, NATO's Special Consultative Group, the successor to the Special Group, affirmed the critical role of arms control.[25] Securing support for that statement within the administration was no easy feat. Pockets remained openly hostile to negotiations with the Soviet Union. At one breakfast meeting, after it was suggested that the administration would soon need to let the allies know when they planned to negotiate, Weinberger wondered why. There were few items worth putting on the agenda. Haig pushed back. "We might be getting too heroic," he retorted, warning that it would be all too easy to lose Washington's allies on the deployments if arms control fell by the wayside.[26]

At the Special Consultative Group's meeting on March 31, Eagleburger cautioned his counterparts that the administration's studies were still very much under way, meaning that it was difficult to tell when talks might start with the Soviet Union.[27] And the administration remained bogged down in a debate over how any negotiations would relate to SALT. One meeting of the National Security Council in April 1981 went around in circles, as none of the officials present could agree which studies still needed to be completed or whether these studies had to be finished before negotiations began. At one point, the meeting devolved into a lengthy debate as Haig fought with Frank Carlucci, the deputy secretary of defense, over whether the still hypothetical negotiations needed to take place within the "SALT framework" or in the "SALT context."[28]

Haig urged his colleagues to set a start date lest they cede more ground to critics, providing ample fodder for peace groups and the Warsaw Pact alike.[29] Recent polls suggested that 60 percent of West Germans opposed the deployments, as did 53 percent of respondents in the Netherlands.[30] That surge of opposition spilled over into party politics. The rift within the West German SPD, already visible over the neutron bomb, continued to grow as party members distanced themselves from Schmidt's support for the Dual-Track Decision. Local branches came out against the Gryphons and Pershing IIs.[31] A frustrated Schmidt chastised his fellow Social Democrats, telling one audience in Recklinghausen that they needed "to stop letting [themselves] be talked into thinking that the Americans are our enemies and the Russians are our friends." If the party withdrew its support from the Dual-Track Decision, Schmidt warned the SPD's Bavarian branch, he would resign.[32]

Haig came to the North Atlantic Council in May armed with tangible evidence of the president's commitment to negotiating with the Soviets. The "curtain-raiser" was a personal letter to Brezhnev written by Reagan after the attempt on his life earlier that spring.[33] In it, the president had expressed his hope that the two leaders might be able to pursue a meaningful dialogue, pointing to his recent decision to drop Carter's grain embargo on the Soviet Union as evidence the United States was willing to do business.[34]

As NATO's foreign ministers gathered in Rome, Carlucci made a splash when private comments appeared in the *Washington Post*. The United States, Carlucci allegedly told a closed-door gathering, could not allow Schmidt's Social Democrats—and, particularly, the party's left flank—to define NATO's approach to the Soviet Union, running roughshod over the rest of the allies. The question at hand, at least according to the *Post*, was how to handle the West Germans. "Is the United States permitting Schmidt, out of deference to his precarious political position, too much elbow room against President Reagan's defense buildup in Europe and his challenge to Soviet aggression?" the paper wondered, channeling the hardline wing of the Reaganauts. On that question, the administration was divided. Weinberger publicly endorsed Carlucci's comments, but policy cut in a different direction. At Rome, the United States affirmed plans to negotiate with the Soviet Union, a decision that the *Post* attributed to Haig.[35] The implication that State and Defense were at loggerheads was by no means a new one regarding the Reagan White House.[36]

Haig's commitment at Rome reflected the administration's growing appreciation that negotiations mattered, if only as a tool of alliance management. Western Europe's confidence that the United States would negotiate was, in the words of one assessment, "the most important single determinant" of attitudes toward the deployment of the Gryphons and Pershing IIs.[37] Without talks under way, the domestic political situation in the Federal

Republic could deteriorate further, damaging relations between Washington and Bonn and threatening the cohesion of the Atlantic alliance as a whole.[38]

Going for Zero

Schmidt's position within the SPD was crumbling. Fissures between various wings of the party continued to deepen. The authors of the "Bielefeld Appeal," an SPD riposte to the "Krefeld Appeal," lamented the shift away from the party's earlier embrace of peace and détente. Helmut Schmidt's public statements might emphasize the two tracks of NATO's policies, but only one seemed to be viable. "There have been no serious talks," the appeal's authors argued. "Instead, all preparations are being made to introduce the new weapons systems and create a fait accompli."[39] Convinced that arms control would be left behind, the SPD's rank and file began to agitate for negotiations.

Arms control advocates received a boost from high-profile allies. In July 1981, Willy Brandt, still chair of the SPD, seemed to endorse Brezhnev's calls for a moratorium, which the Soviet general secretary had reiterated during Brandt's recent visit to Moscow. Brezhnev's latest offer, Brandt and Hans-Jürgen Wischnewski, the SPD's deputy chair, argued, was not simply another iteration of the earlier February offer, but a promising opening.[40] British officials worried that Brandt's support, coupled with that of Egon Bahr, lent the Soviet ploy "mainstream respectability," making Schmidt's political position even more tenuous. Increasingly, it seemed as though the SPD had two parallel and contradictory foreign policies: one that backed the Dual-Track Decision, spearheaded by Schmidt, and another that aimed to make the SPD the party of peace, with Brandt and Bahr in the vanguard.[41]

In light of Schmidt's political woes, governments across Western Europe redoubled their efforts to secure the opening of US-Soviet talks as soon as possible. Those talks should, many argued, put forward a sweeping arms control proposal that could capture the public imagination. A "politically sexy" negotiating position could do the trick.[42] Some already had such a proposal in mind: a dramatic offer to cancel NATO's deployments, provided that the Soviet Union withdrew its own medium-range forces in the European theater.[43]

The basic principle was not new. Even before the Western allies adopted the Dual-Track Decision, affirming that arms control was "a complement to modernization, not a substitute" for it, some of the policy's architects held out hope that negotiations might render the deployment track unnecessary.[44] At least one standard case for the deployments endorsed this view. If NATO's decision were a reaction to the Soviet Union's buildup, then any solution that removed those new weapons would remove the earlier reasons to deploy.[45]

Since the Dual-Track Decision's adoption, the prospect of calling off the deployments in exchange for Soviet cuts had cropped up repeatedly, with champions in the Netherlands, Italy, the Federal Republic of Germany, and beyond. The Nuclear Planning Group left this option open and, in October 1981, after the United States and the Soviet Union had formally agreed to open talks later that fall, allied ministers affirmed, "The zero-level remains a possible option under ideal circumstances."[46] Now out of office, members of the Carter administration came to regret their earlier choices. Seemingly inconsequential concessions made in the autumn of 1979 had inadvertently left the door open to an all-or-nothing proposal.[47]

A zero-level solution seemed at odds with prevailing assumptions about how the superpowers' talks would unfold. The conventional wisdom held that the Soviet Union would only negotiate in earnest when confronted with new missiles arriving in Europe.[48] With nothing tangible to offer, NATO's current position was akin to trading "a bucket of ashes for a bucket of coal."[49] Within the Reagan administration, some turned to arms control proposals designed not to secure an agreement with the Soviets, but to shore up the support of Washington's allies. It was no coincidence that the backers of these initiatives tended to dismiss the Western Europeans as spineless wimps.

The zero option found two critical champions in Caspar Weinberger and Richard Perle. The two threw their weight behind the idea as a way to convert the Dual-Track Decision's liabilities into advantages. The zero option's genius, Weinberger believed, stemmed from the fact that the Kremlin's response would be irrelevant. If Moscow embraced the proposal, so be it. Should the Soviets refuse, admittedly the more likely outcome, the governments of Western Europe would have no choice but to support the deployments.[50] By the standards of the genre, the initiative was straightforward and easily explained, not bogged down in technical minutiae and jargon.[51] Its slogan was simple: zero for zero.

Haig dismissed the proposal as a transparent public relations stunt.[52] The zero option was not nearly as novel as Weinberger seemed to suggest, and Washington's allies—and their voters—were almost certain to see the cynical logic behind the initiative. Reagan disagreed, siding with Weinberger and Perle. When the National Security Council met on November 12, the president backed the zero option. "We should simply go in and say that we are negotiating in good faith for the removal of these systems on both sides," Reagan declared. "We should say this is what we would like to have, but we will settle for less. One should ask for the moon, and when the other fellow offers green cheese, one can settle for something in between."[53]

What drove Reagan to embrace the zero option remains fiercely debated.[54] Did the president share the views of Weinberger and Perle that it could keep Washington's allies on the straight and narrow, all but forcing them to back the deployments? Or was Reagan inspired by a grander vision and a genuine desire to do away with these nuclear weapons? Reagan left little evidence in his own hand regarding his support for the zero option. In his diaries, all Reagan recorded was that the NSC meeting had taken place.[55] The president's later memoirs, which appeared in 1990 (after the zero option had yielded a deal), described the initial proposal as a genuine offer. "Hoping it would be received in Moscow as a sincere effort to begin the process of arms reduction," Reagan wrote, "I called for the elimination of all intermediate-range nuclear force (INF) weapons in Europe by both sides."[56]

Though the president left precious few indications about the motives behind his November decision, aides and advisers almost universally viewed Reagan as a committed nuclear abolitionist, whether or not they agreed with him.[57] "From the time I knew him," Kenneth Adelman, the deputy US representative to the United Nations who took over as director of the Arms Control and Disarmament Agency in 1983, later recalled, "everything that popped out of his mouth was antinuclear, and then it was doing away with nuclear weapons." For an administration made up of staunch conservatives, the president's leanings were more than a little alarming. "All of us who were conservative thought that when Carter said, 'I want to eliminate nuclear weapons,' that was the stupidest thing we'd ever heard. We all made fun of it," Adelman later said. "Then we have our hero who says things really more extreme than Carter ever does, and he's unstoppable on doing it."[58]

Given the conventional wisdom on when and how talks with the Soviets might bear fruit, Reagan's decision to back the zero option could easily have been shaped by the short-term exigencies of alliance management. But the president's end goal was not the deployment of the Pershing IIs and Gryphons. What Reagan wanted was an agreement to reduce the nuclear threat on terms favorable to the United States. A sweeping negotiating position, appealing to the promise of eliminating an entire class of nuclear weapons, was his opening bid. It was his ask for the moon.

Reagan unveiled the zero option publicly in a speech at the National Press Club on November 18, 1981. He framed the proposal in sweeping terms, recalling his generation's preoccupation with peace after seeing the world plunged into global conflagration not once, but twice. "With Soviet agreement," he declared, "we could together substantially reduce the dread threat of nuclear war which hangs over the people of Europe."[59] The speech's significance was not lost on the president; it was, as he recorded in his diary, "the big day" with "the speech to the world."[60] Carried across the globe by satellite, the speech was timed for midday to make the evening news broadcasts on the other side of the Atlantic.[61] And the choice of November 18 meant that the speech would preempt a state visit to the Federal Republic by the Soviet general secretary, where he was guaranteed to trot out yet more tempting offers. (The Soviets certainly viewed it as a transparent ploy to undercut Brezhnev.)[62] Given the speech's overarching message of peace, Reagan did find a grim irony in delivering it in a bulletproof vest, but such were the realities of the presidency.[63]

Peace campaigners, however skeptical of the president's intentions, took comfort in the impression that their activism was starting to change the conversation.[64] The core premise of Reagan's zero option seemed ripped from their banners: no cruise, no Pershing II, no SS-20.[65] But the proposal itself came under fire. It was widely seen (as Haig had predicted) as a ploy to make deployment palatable. Petra Kelly dismissed it as a voodoo proposal, a jab that recalled George Bush's swipes about Reagan's "voodoo economic policies" during the Republican primaries in 1980.[66] E. P. Thompson urged the administration to go even further in its pursuit of zero, adapting the new slogan to push END's calls for a nuclear-free Europe.[67]

The optics of a proposal that the Kremlin was certain to reject could easily backfire. Skeptics at the State Department derided it as the kind of arms control designed to appeal to anti–arms controllers.[68] At the Foreign and Commonwealth Office in London, officials worried that the proposal could create "unrealistic expectations" in the minds of voters. It was all too easy to see how NATO's members might end up "a hostage to fortune" if negotiations dragged on without a possible agreement in sight. The zero option could tempt the Soviet Union to up the ante, making the most of the proposal as a springboard to even more sweeping calls for a nuclear-weapon-free Europe.[69]

Members of the Reagan administration assured their counterparts across the Atlantic that the zero option would not be Washington's final offer. Those who had argued for a zero-only approach were what Lawrence Eagleburger disparaged as the "insane fringe."[70] Internal British assessments were a touch more diplomatic, noting that the only major backer of this approach was Richard Perle, a man "not noted for his enthusiasm for the role of arms control in security policy."[71] The Reagan administration's other Richard, director of politico-military affairs Richard Burt, lamented the "unholy alliance" that created the zero option. It was a bizarre and improbable meeting of minds between the Dutch and the Department of Defense.[72]

Negotiations and the Politics of Publicity

In late November 1981, US and Soviet negotiators met in Geneva to begin talks covering what the Western allies now referred to as intermediate-range nuclear forces. Gone was the earlier terminology, ripe with the suggestion that a nuclear war could be fought in the European theater. At the West Germans' behest, US policymakers instead embraced new language focused on range, rather than the contentious, almost theological distinctions between strategic and theater nuclear weapons.[73]

The US delegation was headed by a veteran negotiator, the now seventy-four-year-old Paul Nitze. His opposite number was Yuli Kvitsinsky, a forty-two-year-old known as a "German" within the corridors of the Soviet foreign ministry after serving a series of stints in Bonn and in East Berlin.[74] Kvitsinsky's appointment was a not-so-subtle reminder that the issue at hand was, at its core, a struggle over German power and the Federal Republic's place within the European state system.[75]

US negotiators came to the table with the zero option in hand, but the Soviet Union had already dismissed the initiative as the basis for any talks. Brezhnev publicly disparaged the US position as an "absurd demand."[76] The situation went from bad to worse when, after over a year of speculation about whether the Warsaw Pact would intervene to put down the domestic unrest brewing in Poland, that country's leader, Gen. Wojciech Jaruzelski, introduced martial law in December. The Reagan administration responded swiftly, introducing a series of sanctions against Poland and the alleged architect of the crackdown, the Soviet Union.[77] But these new strains in superpower relations did not spell an end to arms control. If the United States were to walk out of the talks, Reagan believed it would only benefit the Soviet Union.[78]

In Geneva, the delegations remained at the negotiating table to swap proposals, but much of the bargaining played out in public as the United States and the Soviet Union tried to win hearts and minds. Playing to a Western European crowd, Moscow relied on "sophisticated and articulate officials" like Vadim Zagladin, the first deputy chief of the Central Committee's International Department, and Georgy Arbatov, the director of the Institute for the Study of the United States and Canada, to ensure Soviet views went mainstream.[79] The Soviets continued to put forward splashy proposals like the one Brezhnev unveiled at the Socialist International in February 1982. There, the general secretary called for a phased reduction, capping intermediate-range nuclear forces in Europe at six hundred in 1985, then three hundred by 1990. That same proposal formed the basis of a Soviet draft treaty, introduced at the INF talks a few months later. The make-or-break element of the Soviet proposal was the inclusion of British and French systems, which meant that under those ceilings, the United States would be left with only a few token missiles.[80] Another Soviet moratorium scheme followed in March 1982. The Kremlin's offer to halt the deployment of medium-range systems in Europe was riddled with problems. With its limits confined to the European parts of the Soviet Union, it would leave Moscow free to deploy in its vast territory stretching to the Pacific. One recommended press line, later deleted from the guidance, likened Brezhnev's offer to "Marie Antoinette calling for a moratorium on protest."[81] The official White House statement dismissed it as "neither unilateral, nor a moratorium."[82]

As they put forward these proposals, the Soviets relied on carefully calculated figures about the current balance of forces. NATO's members, Brezhnev argued in a November 1981 interview with the West German weekly *Der Spiegel*, had approximately one thousand intermediate-range nuclear weapons. So did the Warsaw Pact.[83] Moscow's math was "plainly contrived," as Eagleburger put it in the pages of the *NATO Review*. Soviet figures counted aircraft like the F-4 Phantom but excluded comparable Soviet capabilities on the other side of the ledger.[84] US tallies came to dramatically different conclusions; the Soviet Union possessed a 6 to 1 advantage in Europe—growing by the day as the Kremlin continued to introduce SS-20s.[85] NATO's regular magazine carried charts tracking the growth of the Soviet arsenal while, in advance of 1983, the total of US Gryphons and Pershing IIs remained zero. By April 1982, it showed an imbalance of 1,200 to 0.[86]

Excluding British and French nuclear forces from a deal limiting intermediate-range forces made little sense, Soviet negotiators argued, because their use would be the same as that of any US weapon covered. At one press scrum, Andrei Gromyko asked journalists to imagine a British or French warhead. "Would it, perhaps, carry the label: 'I am English'?" the Soviet foreign minister wondered. Or would it advertise, "I am French, there's no need to count me?"[87] It did not matter whether these missiles could "crawl, float, or fly," they needed to be counted somewhere.[88] So long as the Soviet Union tried to include British and French forces, the public's attention would remain focused on the soft underbelly of the West's negotiating position. West German officials lobbied for a common press line on the continued exclusion of the weapons owned by London and Paris, but there were few compelling justifications. "It is not like selling Ivory Soap where you can have a short catchy slogan," Richard Perle quipped.[89]

"We, Too, Are Activists"

In the spring of 1982, the Reagan administration prepared to go on the offensive. The public mood was shifting and an electorate that had backed the Republican candidate's promises of investing in the nation's defenses now increasingly agitated for dramatic cuts to the US arsenal. "Once in a great while," as Bill Moyers put it in one CBS news broadcast, "public opinion seems to rise up with a singular message, as if a great revelation had come to the common imagination."[90] Americans seemed to have come to the same realization as countless Europeans and Canadians; nuclear weapons still threatened their world.

Support for a nuclear freeze skyrocketed. By March 1982, 74 percent of Americans supported a freeze on the superpowers' production of nuclear weapons.[91] The campaign's popularity grew, receiving the support of liberal Democrats, including two senators, Ted Kennedy and Mark Hatfield, who brought forward a Senate resolution calling for a mutual, verifiable freeze. Ground Zero, a nationwide campaign established in 1980 by a former NSC staffer in the Nixon administration, Roger Molander, coordinated a week's worth of rallies and information sessions in April 1982.[92] Nearly a million Americans attended, taking part in demonstrations, teach-ins, and die-ins, in a turnout that seemed poised to "evolve into the biggest peace movement of the 1980s."[93]

That surge of opposition spurred the administration to act. It was imperative that the president shore up support for his program of "peace through strength," with a strong emphasis on the first half of the equation. To that end, Reagan's second national security adviser, William Clark, recommended a three-part strategy made up of high-profile speeches, meetings with antinuclear activists, and more streamlined messaging tailored to showcase the president's strategy for arms control. It would be critical, Clark warned, to avoid any impression that the administration disagreed with those who supported a freeze. Instead, any administration effort should make clear that "we, too, are activists."[94] It was a question of tactics, not priorities, and to those protesting the dangers of nuclear war, Reagan offered a simple message: "I'm with you."[95] Aides recommended that they make the most of opportunities to create visuals that showed Reagan as "the concerned, caring individual" he was, such as a photo-op with the famous nun and missionary Mother Teresa.[96]

Reagan and his advisers did not let arguments for a nuclear freeze go unchallenged. The administration's objections revolved around two main points. The first of these highlighted the dangers of a freeze. If the Western allies accepted a freeze at current levels, this could unravel the links between Western Europe's defenses and the United States', meaning a freeze could amplify "the very fear" that had led the allies to back the Dual-Track Decision in the first place.[97] The second of the administration's arguments went even further, suggesting that a freeze was not enough. Instead, the United States needed to secure meaningful reductions to lower the risks of nuclear war. "We don't argue with the people that are out there on Ground Zero or [the] freeze," Vice President George H. W. Bush told one NBC interviewer. "We simply say we think we've got the best answer for peace—a verifiable reduction in this madness."[98]

To underscore this commitment to reductions, the Reagan administration pursued a new set of arms control talks with the Soviet Union: the Strategic Arms Reduction Talks (START). The very name underscored the departure; talks would no longer be guided by limitation (the L in SALT), but by the pursuit of real reductions. The proposal was the centerpiece of a speech at Reagan's alma mater, Eureka College, on May 9, 1982. The president's speech, laced with references to the need for dialogue between the two superpowers, was modeled on John F. Kennedy's famous commencement address, "A Strategy of Peace," delivered at American University in June 1963.[99]

Reagan's aides planned for the offensive's next phase: the president's ten-day trip to Europe in June 1982, with stops in France, Italy, the United Kingdom, and the Federal Republic of Germany, as well as two major summits—the G-7 and NATO. Administration officials saw a prime opportunity to change the conversation. The president's appearances should be used to strengthen his leadership of the West and, as one briefing put it, emphasize his "role as a man of peace" to blunt the appeal of the freeze movement at home and of peace campaigners across Europe.[100] Left unchecked, popular opposition at home could threaten the administration's policy agenda, while opposition abroad could stoke isolationist impulses, encouraging some to advocate for the United States to scale back its commitments to Western Europe. British interlocutors agreed. Ideally, Reagan's appearance in London could be used to defang anti-American arguments circulating in the United Kingdom, with the president coming across "more like a friendly uncle than a nuclear cowboy."[101] Schmidt's government, for its part, steeled itself for the protests certain to erupt during the president's visit. These demonstrations, West German officials hoped, would remain peaceful, unlike the crowds that had rallied—and smashed storefronts—when Alexander Haig stopped in West Berlin the previous autumn.[102]

Reagan's trip came at a critical juncture. NATO's governments were desperate to make the case that they took arms control seriously and could be counted on as sober custodians of their constituents' security. But these arguments depended on a degree of allied unity that was by no means evident. The Western allies remained embroiled in a debate over the strategic value of sanctions, brought about by the Reagan administration's decision to back measures that threatened the construction of a gas pipeline to bring Siberian energy to consumers in Western Europe. US restrictions and their extraterritorial provisions threatened contracts already signed. Western European governments chafed at the style and substance of the Reagan administration's sanctions. Not only did those in Washington fail to appreciate the limited energy options available to Europeans, particularly in the wake of the oil shocks of the 1970s, but the administration also seemed more than happy to wield Western Europe's ties to the Soviet Union as a blunt instrument to punish the Kremlin with little to no regard for what it might mean for its allies' interests. The fact that the Reagan administration took few moves that jeopardized the United States' own, already much smaller, trade relationship with the Soviet Union seemed to drive the point home.[103] Against this backdrop, the White House hoped to project an image of unity with the president coming across as the undisputed head of a cohesive and vibrant NATO.

Though the visit's architects wanted to burnish the president's image as a peacemonger, his stops across Europe also created ample opportunities for the Dual-Track Decision's opponents to make their case. Peace groups arranged massive rallies to greet the president. Demonstrators clashed with police in West Berlin's Schöneberg district, where graffiti artists had tagged buildings with anti-Reagan slogans in English and in German. "Send Ray-Gun Home on a Cruise," one implored.[104] In London, conservative estimates suggested that 115,000 Britons took to the streets to express their discontent with the president and with their own government's war under way in the Falklands. Rally organizers from the Campaign for Nuclear Disarmament put the turnout at 250,000.[105] When Reagan addressed members of the British Parliament, the majority of the Labour Party's MPs declined to appear for the speech. Instead, Labour released an open letter denouncing the Reagan administration's "ideological crusade against the Soviet Union" and propensity for seeing the world in black and white.[106]

Touting Reagan's credentials as a man of peace was a critical part of the trip's design. But a few soundbites—and the media sensation they sparked—made that task even more difficult. At London's Palace of West-minster, in an address before the British Parliament, Reagan expressed his hope that "the march of freedom and democracy" would relegate the doctrine of Marxism-Leninism to "the ash-heap of history as it has left other tyrannies which stifle the freedom and muzzle the self-expression of the people."[107] Oft-quoted, then as now, these phrases drowned out other elements of the speech, such as when Reagan spoke of the dangers of global war as a threat every politician must confront. "I don't have to tell you," he remarked, "that in today's world the existence of nuclear weapons could mean, if not the extinction of mankind, then surely the end of civilization as we know it." It was that reality, Reagan told his audience, that drove his administration to negotiate with the Soviets, via the talks under way to limit intermediate-range nuclear forces and the strategic arms reduction talks set to open later that month.[108] Skeptics almost instinctively doubted these professions, seeing them as scripted pablum inserted by speechwriters to strike the right chord, not the sincere beliefs of a president who believed his own rhetoric about building up to build down.

Walking in the Woods

As the United States and the Soviet Union played to public audiences, arms control talks in Geneva remained deadlocked. By the summer of 1982, Paul Nitze was fed up with the stalemate. The zero option left him little room for maneuver, let alone the possibility of reaching an agreement.[109] Frustrated, Nitze took matters into his own hands. On a walk with Yuli Kvitsinsky in the Jura Mountains outside Geneva, the US negotiator pulled out a piece of paper. A brief list, it outlined the various stumbling blocks in their talks to date. Nitze handed the paper to Kvitsinsky, followed by a second sheet that suggested a potential path forward.

Sitting on a log along a mountain service road, the two negotiators developed a package approach, point by point. Nitze and Kvitsinsky agreed to a series of basic principles. In a compromise designed to jump-start further negotiations, the two sides would accept a mutual ceiling in Europe, along with restrictions to cap the number of Soviet systems deployed in Asia. The Soviets would count SS-20s toward that ceiling, while the United States would only deploy Gryphons, not the Pershing IIs slated for the Federal Republic. The package's math excluded British and French systems, a key US demand, but did include limits on nuclear-capable aircraft.[110]

Any success the negotiators' proposal might enjoy in Moscow or Washington would depend on a degree of ambiguity. To obscure where individual pieces of the package had originated, Nitze and Kvitsinsky rolled them all into a single document that they labeled a "joint exploratory package." If the initiative got any traction, they could resume their talks to convert these broad contours into an agreement.

Nitze disclosed the talks to only a handful of people, including Eugene Rostow, the director of the Arms Control and Disarmament Agency. When Nitze returned to Washington at the session's end, he came with the walk-in-the-woods formula in tow. Rostow urged the president to back Nitze's work.[111] Reagan chaired a meeting to discuss the proposal, attended by the senior ranks of the administration. Nitze, Clark, Weinberger, and Rostow were there, as was George Shultz, who had recently replaced Haig as secretary of state, the chair of the Joint Chiefs of Staff Gen. John Vessey, and William Casey, the director of central intelligence. The so-called troika—Edwin Meese, Michael Deaver, and James Baker—rounded out the session. Initial impressions seemed favorable, but nearly all the attendees asked for more time to study the package in greater detail.[112]

As the administration picked apart the proposal, the complaints piled up. Richard Burt worried that the Western Europeans might use it to get themselves off the hook for the deployments. Richard Perle launched a full-frontal assault on the walk-in-the-woods package, claiming that it sacrificed critical aspects of the US negotiating position.[113] Even the fact that Nitze was willing to pursue any options other than zero was a disaster in Perle's eyes, and he missed no opportunity to remind his colleagues that they had promised to consult with their allies on any negotiating positions before raising them with the Soviets.[114] Perle's insinuation was clear; Nitze had gone rogue.

Perle's lobbying met little resistance. The Joint Chiefs of Staff came out against the initiative, as did Weinberger. The plans to give up the Pershing IIs were deemed particularly objectionable; under these terms, the Soviets would be left with intermediate-range ballistic missiles while the United States gave up its own plans to deploy them.[115] Scrapping the Pershing IIs would also have knock-on consequences for the deployment timelines in the Federal Republic, where any delays could suggest that the government in Bonn had chickened out. Reagan turned down the proposal, telling Nitze that if the Soviets asked why, he could tell them that the president was "just one tough son-of-a-bitch."[116]

Even if the walk-in-the-woods proposal had won the support of Washington, the silence from Moscow was a sign that the Soviets had found little to like about the package deal. In September, the administration signed a new National Security Decision Directive, NSDD 56, that stuck with the original zero option.[117] A couple weeks later, when the negotiations resumed in Geneva, Kvitsinsky formally rejected the package.[118] The talks settled into another lull, even more formal and unproductive than the preceding months.[119] Unable to broker an agreement, members of the US negotiating team busied themselves with word games, mock statements, and a comic song about a Soviet SS-20 that escapes the clutches of arms controllers and lives out its days in the Moscow sewers.[120] As for the walk in the woods, the entire package remained secret for the time being.

A New General Secretary and More Attractive Offers

The Soviet refusal to seriously entertain the walk-in-the-woods package reflected a concerted policy choice. The popular opposition to NATO's Dual-Track Decision could force the Western allies to abandon their plans and, so long as that prospect remained, there was little reason to entertain arms control offers that might undercut the arguments of antinuclear activists across the West.[121]

Soviet offers ramped up as 1982 came to a close, spearheaded by a new general secretary: former head of the KGB Yuri Andropov. A few weeks after Brezhnev's death, Andropov unveiled a new proposal promising to slash the number of SS-20s in Europe. But Andropov's suggested figure, 162, was carefully selected to match British and French nuclear forces already deployed. If the inclusion of third-party systems was not enough to elicit Western rejections, the proposal was also restricted to Europe, leaving the Soviets free to expand their arsenal in Asia—and to menace Washington's allies in the region.[122] The Kremlin's latest proposal, Shultz quipped, was akin to an offer for the "sleeves from your vest."[123]

From Moscow, Ambassador Arthur Hartman predicted that the Soviets would continue this onion diplomacy. They would gradually peel back the layers, one by one, extending new and enticing offers in the hopes that their latest initiative would appeal to the Western Europeans.[124] As the formal negotiations dragged on with no end in sight, a growing segment of allied officials worried that their colleagues and constituents could become even more receptive to the Soviets' tempting offers. Moscow's string of proposals might seem even more appealing if the United States remained stubbornly stuck on the lofty but improbable zero option.

Calls mounted privately for the Western allies to adopt a new, more flexible negotiating position. John Nott, the British defense secretary, pressed Thatcher to consider a new arms control initiative. It could, if nothing else, defuse the growing belief among British voters that the government was little more than a "creature of the Americans."[125] But foreign minister

Francis Pym worried about what any proposal might imply. It could suggest the Thatcher government was no longer committed to the Dual-Track Decision. Even the slightest hint to that effect could jeopardize the whole fragile package.[126]

Political realities demanded a degree of flexibility. In the face of tempting Soviet offers, it became all the more important to illustrate that the United States was willing to reach an agreement with the Soviet Union. Increasingly, it no longer seemed possible to do that with the zero option alone.

So long as NATO's deployments remained controversial, the Soviet Union and its Warsaw Pact allies could leverage the popular opposition to try to stop the deployments. That realization guided the Soviets' declaratory diplomacy, along with the policies of the United States and the rest of the NATO allies. The two superpowers both embraced the need to sell their ideas publicly, waging a battle for hearts and minds—above all, those of the Western Europeans. Arms control and public diplomacy became almost impossible to disentangle as a result.

The blurred lines between arms control negotiations and public proclamations made it easy for skeptics to dismiss the superpowers' talks as a public relations stunt, not a genuine attempt to reduce the nuclear threat. This left policymakers in Washington and their counterparts across the alliance stuck in a feedback loop. To preserve sufficient support for their policies among their parliaments and voters, they needed to demonstrate their commitment to negotiate with the Soviet Union. But many of the steps they took to underscore this commitment, whether public proclamations or their presence at the negotiating table, were dismissed by skeptics as mere propaganda.

CHAPTER 8

First Principles

Protests spelled trouble for supporters of the Atlantic alliance. The success of NATO's policies had always relied not just on the approval of leaders and bureaucracies but also on the broader backing of the various member's publics and parliaments; such were the realities of an alliance composed primarily of democracies. Allied leaders had lived through bouts of anti-NATO sentiment before, including ones punctuated by large public demonstrations against nuclear weapons. But the opposition of the early 1980s seemed worse than ever before. "The current movement is new and formidable," the US political scientist Stanley Hoffmann argued in the winter of 1981. "It is a mass movement of continental dimension, which mobilizes and moves people across borders—something quite exceptional even in the partly integrated Western Europe of today."[1]

NATO's champions scrambled to identify the root causes of this dissatisfaction. In so doing, they often turned to the explanatory power of demographics. "We may have also come to overlook the implications of the coming of age in all our countries of a generation who does not share the almost instinctive devotion to trans-Atlantic cohesion that helped give birth to the Alliance," Secretary General Joseph Luns argued.[2] To make a stronger case for NATO, the alliance's supporters in and out of government turned to the language of peace. Those who demonstrated in the streets were not the only individuals interested in preserving the peace. So too were NATO's leaders.

Boosters took solace in the fact that polling still showed strong support for the Atlantic alliance, but what elicited popular opposition was no less alarming. Voters might not have turned against the alliance en masse, but they had begun to question nearly all of its constituent elements. Western publics failed to understand central elements of the alliance's strategy. They were woefully ignorant of the threat posed by the Soviet Union and filled with "considerable disquiet" about the role of nuclear weapons.[3] What the Atlantic alliance confronted was nothing short of what one group diagnosed as a "gradual but accelerating disintegration of the public support on which NATO depends." Unlike so many of NATO's earlier squabbles and dustups, these problems were not just the result of political leaders or strategists at odds. The Western allies instead faced "a crisis of confidence, values, and perceptions" as significant portions of their electorates challenged the assumptions at the heart of the transatlantic bargain.[4]

Much of the debate in the early 1980s fixated on NATO's Dual-Track Decision and its paired program of deployments and negotiations. Opponents questioned nearly all of its—and NATO's—core principles: the wisdom of relying on the United States for protection, the severity of the Soviet threat, and the logic and morality of nuclear deterrence. Left unchecked, this dissent threatened to destroy the Atlantic alliance. "The NATO alliance," Senator Sam Nunn argued in the summer of 1982, "is now in need of major repair—militarily, politically, and economically."[5]

With few signs of meaningful or productive dialogue between East and West, grassroots activists and allied leaders alike took matters into their own hands. That mix of voices mattered. The doubts raised by NATO's Dual-Track Decision were not confined to placards or pamphlets, but also spread among pundits, former policymakers, and sitting officials. The sheer diversity of voices signaled a shift in the making and implementation of security policy, as the conversation broadened and democratized.[6] No longer confined to expert circles and specialist outlets, a growing segment of the population was interested in—and alarmed by—the assumptions that guided NATO's overall strategy. Whether in protest literature or foreign affairs journals, this increasingly heterogeneous group of individuals challenged the principles underlying NATO's security policies and suggested alternative ways that its members might organize their defense, provide for their security, and ultimately order their world.

On Board the *Titanic*

The basics of NATO's strategy required a leap of faith. What the Western allies asked of their publics, at least implicitly, was that they take their elected officials and unelected bureaucrats, civilian and military, at their word that security could be best preserved through the acquisition of weapons that could unleash untold destruction. A growing constituency questioned that logic in the first years of the 1980s. "The name of the game, on both sides, is mendacity," E. P. Thompson alleged in his 1980 *Protest and Survive.* "Indeed, 'deterrence' might itself be defined as the biggest and most expensive Lie in history."[7] Champions of deterrence, one West German charged, were the modern-day equivalent of a man holding lectures about the unsinkable nature of ocean liners aboard the *Titanic.*[8]

Public questioning of NATO's dependence on nuclear weapons went mainstream, given a boost by four prominent ex-officials. McGeorge Bundy, George Kennan, Robert McNamara, and Gerard Smith took to the pages of *Foreign Affairs* with a call to revisit a critical element of the Atlantic alliance's strategy: the possible first use of nuclear weapons. The so-called gang of four brought considerable policy experience to the question; between them, they had served as national security adviser, ambassador to the Soviet Union, secretary of defense, head of the SALT negotiating team, and director of the Policy Planning Staff. For decades, no matter NATO's official strategic doctrine, the Western allies had relied on the promise that the United States would be willing to launch a first strike to defend Europe. By the early 1980s, the gang of four argued, this promise threatened "the safety of the world" and the survival of the Atlantic alliance itself.[9]

The gang of four's arguments touched off a heated debate about the purpose of nuclear weapons and the broader aims of NATO's strategy.[10] "It cannot be forgotten," Italian permanent representative Vincenzo Tornetta, wrote, responding to the four in the *NATO Review,* "that a conventional conflict—such as the Second World War—resulted in more than forty million dead and, since that time, the destructive capability of conventional weapons has greatly increased."[11] Another quartet, this time made up of prominent West German officials, penned a direct rebuttal in *Foreign Affairs.* Rejecting the Americans' arguments, Karl Kaiser, Georg Leber, Alois Mertes, and Franz-Josef Schulze argued that NATO's aim was not to prevent nuclear war, but "to prevent *any* war." The US gang of four held that a policy of no first use would reduce the prospects of war in Europe, but the West German quartet questioned what, if any, evidence they could point to in support of such a claim.[12]

Nuclear weapons, the West Germans argued, had secured the single longest period of peace in Europe's history. They freely acknowledged that the same could not be said of broad swaths of the globe, such as Asia, Africa, and Latin America, where "more than a hundred wars" had been fought over the same time span. Even with this staggering number of conflicts, they touted the security afforded (to them) by the long peace that nuclear weapons made possible.[13] Henry Kissinger concurred. Adopting a no-first-use doctrine, he argued in one May 1982 lecture, could give the impression that the United States would rather be defeated in Europe by a conventional-force attack than resort to the use of nuclear weapons. Doing so could increase the chances of war, inviting Soviet aggression, rather than reduce them.[14]

If NATO elected to reduce its dependence on nuclear weapons, there were any number of ideas circulating about what direction a new defense concept might take, moving beyond flexible response. Was there not another option, perhaps one that would make the Western Europeans less reliant on the United States?[15] One popular argument called for greater emphasis on conventional forces.[16] No less than NATO's supreme allied commander, Gen. Bernard Rogers, advocated for increased investments in conventional options, urging the alliance to increase its defense spending target to 4 percent.[17]

To make that possible, strategists and social scientists debated the merits of emerging technologies. Not for the first time, new, more sophisticated weapons systems seemed to offer a silver-bullet solution that might solve the perennial dilemma of how to craft a strategy that was affordable and acceptable. Many were drawn to the new, high-tech US operational concept known as AirLand Battle, designed to defeat quantitatively superior Warsaw Pact forces with qualitative edges that NATO (and particularly the US military) enjoyed, above all in speed.[18] The alliance's information officials, the experts who shaped its public messaging, cautioned against undue focus on AirLand Battle lest they "lead the public to expect there could be an easy trade-off of Western nuclear weapons for an increased conventional weapons effort." No matter the new concept, nuclear weapons would remain essential to NATO's deterrent. Any emphasis on "Western military inferiority" could also produce problems in the public mind, "frightening or disheartening citizens in NATO countries."[19]

But the prospects of change seemed slim. None of the old constraints, be they political, economic, strategic, or psychological, had disappeared. "There is only one way that the Western allies can markedly improve the conventional balance," the US political scientist John Mearsheimer argued, "and that is by increasing the number of their fighting units. That will not happen."[20]

Suggestions for change all started from the same realization; the current strategy, reliant on early use of nuclear weapons, no longer seemed workable, let alone desirable.[21] The West Germans' 1983 defense white paper seemed to admit as much with its open discussion of the debates unfolding about "alternative strategies."[22] That discussion's participants were an unusual coalition, forming what the influential Senator Sam Nunn referred to as "a slowly emerging consensus [that] runs across the political spectrum—from defense-oriented conservatives to more responsible segments of the anti-nuclear movement."[23]

Flexible response appeared to be on its last legs. Privately, no shortage of allied policymakers had recognized it was more of a wish than a reality; a growing segment of the population came to the same realization in the 1980s as a result of the debates over the Euromissiles. "In its current formulation," the US political scientist Samuel Huntington concluded, "flexible response is seen as inadequate by the strategists, unsupportable by the public, and, one must assume, increasingly incredible by the Soviets."[24]

Common Security and the Palme Commission

The Independent Commission for Disarmament and Security Issues reflected this quest for alternative models of security. In January 1980, Olof Palme, the former (and future) Swedish prime minister, and former British foreign secretary David Owen, inspired by the Brandt Commission on North-South Relations, suggested a similar body dedicated to questions of arms control and disarmament.[25] Palme, like countless others, was spurred to action by the twin shocks of December 1979: NATO's Dual-Track Decision and the Soviet invasion of Afghanistan. Determined to avoid another spiral in the nuclear arms race, Palme hoped to build momentum to bring the Soviet Union and the United States to the negotiating table.[26]

As the commission took shape, well-known politicians gave it additional star power. The SPD's vocal critic of the Dual-Track Decision, Egon Bahr, volunteered his services, as did Joop den Uyl, the head of the Dutch Labour Party. The sixteen-member commission consisted of a combination of politicians and professional diplomats from across the globe, but a strong European contingent from both sides of the Iron Curtain made up its core.[27]

At the commission's deliberations throughout 1981 and into 1982, members tackled the various dimensions of the arms race and the prospects for disarmament, including the Euromissiles. One session in April 1981 was dedicated almost entirely to a discussion of NATO's Dual-Track Decision. It began with a paper from a French expert, Pierre Lellouche. But his

Soviet colleague Georgy Arbatov pushed back on Lellouche's basic premise, insisting that the SS-20s were not upsetting the overall balance of power within Europe. Picking up a common Soviet refrain, Arbatov charged that if NATO's deployments were to go ahead, it would be not unlike the Soviet behavior that had so upset the Americans and precipitated the Cuban Missile Crisis.[28]

The final report released by the commission in the spring of 1982 began to articulate a concept of common security. Bahr, who coined the term, conceived of it as a meaningful alternative to deterrence. Common security began from the argument that security could not be achieved through unilateral actions. "States can no longer seek security at each other's expense," the commission's final report, fittingly titled *Common Security*, maintained, "it can only be obtained through cooperative undertakings."[29]

The commission also called for the creation of a battlefield-nuclear-weapon–free zone in Central Europe. Stripping a corridor at the center of the European continent of nuclear weapons, its members argued, would raise the nuclear threshold, thereby making it more difficult for a conflict to "go nuclear."[30] Throughout the commission's discussions, David Owen had emphasized the threat posed by these particular weapons. "There needs to be an attempt to negotiate a battlefield nuclear weapon free zone in Central Europe," he argued in an October 1981 paper, circulated to his fellow commission members. "These weapons are currently deployed cheek by jowl with inadequate command and control mechanisms."[31] To Owen, the risks seemed self-evident. *Common Security* argued that "doctrines which postulate fighting limited nuclear wars"—NATO's among them—"create the illusion of control and this might tempt political leaders in toward situations 'to risk all in one cosmic throw of the dice.'"[32]

The final proposals stopped short of more radical prescriptions put forward by Bahr. At one point, the West German had touted a three-part plan that envisioned the withdrawal of all nuclear weapons from all nonnuclear states in Europe (including his home, the Federal Republic) along with the creation of an approximate balance in conventional forces between the two military alliances and the preservation of both NATO and the Warsaw Pact. Bahr's vision met strong resistance. Norway's Johan Jørgen Holst, for instance, warned that the any scheme calling for the denuclearization of the Federal Republic was not only impossible to achieve—Helmut Schmidt was certain to reject it, as were the opposition Christian Democrats—but it would also be fodder to those already warning of Western Europe's drift toward neutralism.[33] Even the toned-down version that appeared in the commission's final report elicited such fears. If the recommendations came to pass, the French intellectual Pierre Hassner warned, it would spell the end of NATO.[34]

Protection or Dependence

Pamphlet-writers conveyed their skepticism about the Dual-Track Decision through the liberal use of scare quotes, derisively referring to NATO's program of "modernization."[35] Though the program was often cast as a direct response to the Soviet Union's SS-20s, some critics dismissed this rationale. Returning to arguments made in the debates of the late 1970s, they argued that the Kremlin's SS-20s did not give the Soviet Union any additional leverage over the governments of Western Europe or increase the threat posed by Moscow. One US group, the Cruise & Pershing Project, made this case by invoking the expertise of McGeorge Bundy, quoting his observation that "the SS-20 did not and does not give the Soviet Union any nuclear capability against Europe alone that she did not have in overwhelming measure before a single SS-20 was deployed."[36] Others latched onto the writings of Helmut Schmidt, citing comments from the late 1950s that NATO's plans to introduce land-based, medium-range missiles in Europe would only increase the threat of war. If Bundy and Schmidt were right—and given their positions and expertise, that was no stretch of the imagination—then what was the point in upgrading NATO's own capabilities?

Western Europeans who would live amid NATO's new missiles (should the deployments go ahead) fixated on the possible use of the Gryphons and Pershing IIs. Doing so only underscored the dangers of relying on the United States. If launched, the weapons were intended for "a nuclear exchange at a lower level."[37] That euphemism, along with a strategy that envisioned a chain of escalation, seemed to imply that a nuclear war could be waged in, and perhaps even confined to, Europe. NATO's plans entertained the possibility that a strategic nuclear war might be deferred, perhaps even avoided. Such a strategy, European Nuclear Disarmament cofounder Ken Coates underscored, meant that the superpowers could negotiate while Europe incinerated.[38] That prospect terrified many and inspired some of the protestors' most memorable slogans, like "Visit Europe before It's Too Late" and "No Euroshima!"[39]

In the eyes of countless critics, NATO's planners seemed to default to the acquisition of new nuclear weapons, with little to no interest in policies that could reduce NATO's—and the Warsaw Pact's—stockpiles.[40] It was easy to imagine a few possible outcomes of the current situation, E. P. Thompson

FIGURE 8.1. Protestors worry that the United States will repeat the mistakes of the past, Amsterdam, June 1982. Source: Rob Bogaerts/Anefo/Nationaal Archief (NL-HaNa inventory file no. 932-2078), https://www.nationaalarchief.nl/en/research/photo-collection/ad197e94-d0b4-102d-bcf8-003048976d84.

argued. The superpowers' negotiations in Geneva could break down without a resolution, leaving "the dragon's teeth" sown at sites like Greenham Common and Comiso to become nuclear missiles: "This is the worst case, and we might not long survive it." Perhaps US and Soviet negotiators would reach an agreement, announcing cuts to the numbers of Gryphons and Pershing IIs, but leaving some of the original deployments intact. Such a solution would be a victory for arms control, one that in Thompson's estimation would cover a serious defeat: "The agreement would legitimate a new 'balance' at a higher and more dangerous level, and the superpowers would have got the matter back from the streets and the peace camps and into their own hands again."[41]

European Nuclear Disarmament wanted to go further. Since its launch in the spring of 1980, END's backers, including its originator, Thompson, had called for a nuclear-weapon-free zone spanning "from Portugal to Poland."[42] Supporters described the initiative inverting the continent's place within NATO's defense planning; by ridding Europe of nuclear weapons and atomic installations, END could transform the continent into a "theatre of peace" (rather than one destined for war).[43] "If the powers want to have a bit of a nuclear war, they will want to have it away from home," Ken Coates argued.

"And if we do not wish to be their hosts for such a match, then, regardless of whether they are right or wrong in supposing they can confine it to our 'theatre,' we must discover a new initiative which can move us toward disarmament."[44]

Coates and Thompson tapped into a source of considerable angst among Western Europeans: their reliance on the United States. For people across Western Europe, whether in or out of government, the Dual-Track Decision was a sharp reminder of their own fundamental status as dependents. Europe's security was being negotiated at a bargaining table where Europeans had no direct representation. And, if deployed, the Pershing IIs and Gryphons—like so much of NATO's arsenal—would be owned by the United States. That control arrangement drove accusations that allied governments would have no say in when and where these weapons were used.[45] In the United Kingdom, the Campaign for Nuclear Disarmament pointed to the massive number of US military bases dotting the British countryside, circulating leaflets that asked "Did you vote to become America's largest aircraft carrier?"[46] Summing up these popular sentiments, Stanley Hoffmann argued that Western Europeans had been reminded, once more, that Europe was "a frying pan on a stove" where others controlled the knobs.[47] The veteran SPD politician Egon Bahr put an even finer point on Europe's lack of control when he asked, "Who will protect us from our protectors?"[48]

Confronted with their continued dependence on the United States, activists cast their efforts in the language of liberation. Standing up against NATO's plans could restore their agency in international affairs. "The peace movement," one SPD politician, Erhard Eppler, argued, "shows that the old nations of Europe are more than just chess men on the board of the world powers."[49] Asked to explain the dramatic swell of opposition in the early 1980s, Petra Kelly later argued that it was, above all, a reaction to the realization that a limited nuclear war could easily be fought in Europe without Europeans having a say.[50] The prospect that any public debate about the modernization of NATO's nuclear forces in Europe might focus on the potential for a limited nuclear war did not escape Western policymakers, even before the Dual-Track Decision. In the lead-up to the decision, British defense secretary Fred Mulley had warned that any increased emphasis on the alliance's doctrine of flexible response could easily foster the belief that NATO's members hoped to wage a limited war in Europe.[51] And if the intricacies of an escalatory strategy were not reminder enough, there were always historical antecedents to fall back on. "We fought World War I in Europe, we fought World War II in Europe and if you dummies will let us, we will fight World War III in Europe," the Center for Defense Information's Gene Le Rocque, a former admiral, quipped.[52]

European efforts to cast off perceived US dominance took different forms, inspired by national narratives and existing structures, whether organizational or societal. Peace groups in Greece mobilized to rid the country of US bases. Activists decried their country's status as "the 53rd star in the American flag." (What the Greeks counted as 51 and 52 was not clear.)[53] These types of calls resonated across the Atlantic. Canadian activists, embroiled in their own struggle against the testing of US cruise missiles in their airspace, bemoaned their nation's status as an auxiliary in the US empire.[54] At demonstrations, placards revived an old slogan demanding "no annihilation without representation." But END's Mary Kaldor wondered about the wisdom of that cry. She had no interest in being annihilated, with or without representation![55]

British campaigners called on their countrymen to jettison the old imperial trappings of their self-image. "If we accept that we are now a second-class power," E. P. Thompson argued, "it does not have to follow that we have to be a client state of the USA (nor of a fiction called 'NATO'). Nor do we have to be second-rate."[56] From Brussels to Athens, activists urged their governments to cast off US domination and remove their communities from the arms race. Campaigns proliferated for the creation of local and regional nuclear-weapon-free zones, aiming to ban the weapons from schools and community centers—more a symbolic rejection than anything else—and to outlaw them from whole regions like the Balkans or Scandinavia.[57]

With activists fixated on the role of the United States, press coverage and political analyses speculated about a rising tide of anti-Americanism. Pickets of visits by high-profile US officials provided visual reminders of the depths of discontent with the United States in some segments of European society. Secretary of State Alexander Haig's September 1981 visit to West Berlin brought fifty thousand into the streets.[58] When Vice President George Bush visited Krefeld in June 1983 to mark the three-hundredth anniversary of German emigration to the United States, protestors greeted the vice president with placards demanding "Bush, Go Home" and "USA, Hands Off Nicaragua." As Bush and his entourage returned to their hotel, one group of demonstrators began flinging rocks and bottles at the motorcade, breaking the window of a nearby bus. At a luncheon later that day, Bush joked that the whole scene reminded him of 1968 in Chicago, when police and antiwar demonstrators clashed at the Democratic National Convention.[59] It was a telling reference that echoed a broad sense that the upheavals of the early 1980s were an extension of the spirit of '68. "It's not only the weapons and the war games," one West German told a reporter. "We want to prevent the further Americanisation of life."[60]

"America has to be told that it's Europe's business to decide how to defend itself," one London statistician told reporters. "We need some kind of strictly European defense."[61] What the United Kingdom needed, the British academic Adam Roberts argued, was a defense policy that the average Briton could live with, which likely meant one that reduced the country's dependence on nuclear weapons. "Our present defence policy," Roberts wrote, "consists largely of begging the Americans to promise to escalate a war. This inevitably leads to public disquiet in Europe, and ultimately serves to vitiate the moral acceptability and military credibility of NATO."[62]

The search for some form of European defense flowed to a degree from the direction of US policies. The Strategic Defense Initiative, a ballistic missile defense program, suggested to Europeans that the United States might be willing to entertain a retreat into "fortress America," extending a protective bubble over itself—but not over its allies.[63] The fact that Reagan's March 1983 announcement of the Strategic Defense Initiative came with virtually no advance warning only added to European suspicions about what the program might mean. British officials, for instance, acknowledged that the president's speech had been carefully worded so as not to offend European sensibilities or exacerbate known sensitivities about Washington's commitment to the defense of the continent. But the initiative drew attention to a series of questions "likely to prove less than helpful in the context of maintaining support for national and NATO nuclear policies." Reagan's plans seemed wildly optimistic, if not fantastical. Pundits captured that sense by christening the Strategic Defense Initiative "Star Wars," a reference to the popular trilogy of science fiction films. Beyond the prospect that the initiative could trigger a new arms race in space, its premise indicated a shift away from deterrence toward defense—already unhelpful from the vantage point of shoring up support for NATO's deterrent—coupled with the possibility that the superpowers would be sheltered from nuclear strikes, leaving them free to fight a nuclear war in Europe.[64]

Spurred by these developments, European policymakers began to contemplate alternatives. The process of European integration intensified after a sluggish spell in the 1970s, and a segment of Western European officials began to flirt with options to enhance their own defense capabilities. In France, François Mitterrand's government deepened its strategic dialogue with the Federal Republic, eager to strengthen the bilateral bonds between Paris and Bonn to keep the West Germans bound to the West if confidence in the Americans' protection no longer could.[65]

Equidistance, Neutralism, and Finlandization, Oh My!

US security policies faced a crisis of confidence and, to explain what European opposition might mean, pundits and public intellectuals tried to suss out just how far Europe might move away from the United States. To do so, they offered new diagnoses and described old ailments.

For a segment of vocal critics who spoke out against the Euromissiles, there was little difference between the two superpowers. "We do not wish to apportion guilt between the political and military leaders of East and West," END's appeal for a nuclear-free Europe argued. "Guilt lies squarely upon both parties."[66] Arguments like these became textbook examples of a phenomenon dubbed equidistance. One political cartoon encapsulated the equidistance of the 1980s: Reagan and Brezhnev stood side by side, each pointing down at a general. The US general stood atop a crude caricature of a Latin American (complete with sombrero), while the Soviet general's foot was firmly planted on the back of a protestor from the Polish labor union, Solidarność.[67] In the eyes of many within the Reagan White House, the Dual-Track Decision's opponents were not the only ones guilty of espousing this view. After Pierre Trudeau delivered a commencement address at the University of Notre Dame in May 1982 in which he dared to suggest that the United States might bear some of the responsibility for the recent downturn in East-West relations, the Canadian prime minister found himself in hot water in Washington. Even the Canadian ambassador, Allan Gotlieb, thought Trudeau had taken the argument too far. Gotlieb complained in his diary that the prime minister had harped on "the old 'moral equivalence' theme—the superpowers are both bad boys, endangering world peace by their arms race."[68]

Equidistance was not the only dangerous disease seemingly sweeping the alliance. In the summer of 1981, Walter Laqueur took to the pages of *Commentary* to diagnose a new affliction—Hollanditis. This Dutch brand of neutralism was not the product of an aversion to hosting the cruise missiles, a problem Laqueur was confident could be solved, but reflective of something much bigger and more dangerous: "a desire to keep out of world problems and an aversion to spending money on defense." It was already spreading, according to Laqueur, who pointed to the complaints of Belgian-Flemish Socialists that they were "nuclear hostages" and a "protectorate" of the United States, the unilateralism of Michael Foot's Labour Party in Britain, and the emergence of the Greens in the Federal Republic.[69] Dutch activists made the most of Laqueur's branding. They launched a postcard campaign cheekily asking Londoners, "May I infect you with a disease?"[70]

Finlandization also returned to the popular lexicon. The Soviets' ongoing efforts to drum up antinuclear sentiment in Western Europe and derail the Dual-Track Decision was explained as yet another attempt on the part of the Kremlin to neutralize Washington's allies on the continent, as they had their Finnish neighbors.[71] In some quarters of the Reagan White House, already suspicious about Western Europe's exposure to Soviet pressure through economic ties and energy supplies, it was all too easy to imagine that the continent would slowly drift into a state of neutrality not unlike Finland's.[72]

Valéry Giscard d'Estaing worried that neutralism was sweeping Western Europe, gaining ground everywhere except, mercifully, at home in France.[73] His successor François Mitterrand agreed and made no secret of his fears that the rising tide of neutralism would leave Europe more vulnerable. "If I condemn neutralism," he remarked in a July 1981 interview in the West German magazine *Stern*, "it is because I believe peace is due to a balance of forces in the world. The installation of SS-20s and the Soviet Backfire bomber disrupt this balance in Europe. I do not accept it and I admit the necessity to arm in order to re-establish the balance. After that one will have to negotiate."[74]

Faced with a steady stream of reports touting massive demonstrations at which Europeans expressed a deep aversion not just to US foreign policy

FIGURE 8.2.   A burning US flag left by protestors at Rhein-Main Air Base, Federal Republic of Germany, December 1982. Source: Don Sutherland/National Archives and Records Administration (NARA identifier no. 6366649), https://catalog.archives.gov/id/6366649.

but also to US culture, some proponents of NATO wondered how everyday Americans would react. Would they embrace already popular stereotypes that the Europeans were nothing more than wimpy freeloaders? The US ambassador to the Federal Republic, Arthur Burns, put it in slightly more diplomatic language. "Many Americans are now wondering whether Europeans are sufficiently mindful of the fact that the Atlantic Alliance has made a free, prosperous, and peaceful Western Europe possible during the past thirty years," he warned one audience in Bonn in late 1981.[75] Richard Nixon agreed wholeheartedly. After reading a copy of the speech, the former president wrote to express his support: "If the Europeans believe we are no different from the Russians and if they want us to go home, while you and I would urge us to stay," Nixon wrote, "most Americans would say—good riddance!"[76]

The Lessons of History

Not all the news was bad for the Atlantic alliance. Polling data suggested that NATO still remained popular among voters.[77] But demographic trends seemed to be working against it. As a new generation came of age, these young people seemed to have forgotten the lessons learned by their parents' generation.[78] Pollsters in the Federal Republic found that over half of all West Germans surveyed believed that the Soviet Union posed a threat. When that data was restricted to only those born after 1945, the number dropped precipitously—to just below 30 percent.[79]

The formative experiences of this successor generation were not the ones that their elders had lived through in the 1940s: the Second World War, the Marshall Plan, and the Berlin Airlift. Instead, this latest generation had grown up with the Vietnam War and the Watergate scandal. NATO's boosters, many of whom were themselves shaped by the events of the 1940s, worried that without an instinctive sense of why the Atlantic alliance had come into being in the first place, the youth would not be willing to make the same sacrifices to secure the West.[80] Approximately 30 percent of the population of the Netherlands, the Dutch permanent representative noted with some trepidation, had been born after 1960; they had grown up in a period of détente and, as such, saw the Soviet threat as "less real and more remote" than a generation who had "consciously experienced Soviet imperialist expansion."[81]

Solving this problem would be no easy feat. Since the late 1960s, various committees had studied the potential problems of the generational shift under way. At the Conference of National Information Officials in October

1968, attendees had suggested a series of educational initiatives designed to increase knowledge of the alliance among the youth, though some cautioned that "young radicals" were unlikely to be a receptive audience given their aversion to authority.[82] Five years later, one set of information guidance underscored the difficulties of making the case for NATO when "Western democracy, which the Alliance was set up to protect, is no longer considered so praiseworthy by a widening circle of people, particularly the young generation."[83]

Questions of how to package and explain allied policies to the electorate received minimal attention within the higher levels of the allied machinery. When the North Atlantic Council took up the question of its information policies in October 1980, it was the first time it had done so at that level since 1973.[84] By the early 1980s, these challenges had only deepened, driven by the debates over the Dual-Track Decision. Voters remained broadly ignorant of international institutions, and NATO was no exception.[85] Social scientists speculated about fundamental shifts under way in the body politic, as a new generation gravitated toward "post-materialist" priorities like "belonging, self-expression, and the quality of life" rather than the traditional materialist priorities of "physical sustenance and safety."[86]

NATO's own experts readily acknowledged the enduring nature of the problem they faced. At one discussion in early 1981, the British representative shared a twenty-five-year-old report from the archives: "It is a depressing truth that despite years of effort on the part of the Information Division, National Information Services, and voluntary bodies, knowledge about the structure and aims of NATO remains abysmally small." This problem endured.[87] "NATO's image," one allied official noted, "seemed to have been slowly eroding since 1952." Even those that remained supportive of the alliance tended to see it as a "necessary evil," not a force for good in the world.[88] In times of economic difficulty like the downturn of the early 1980s, it was all the more challenging to make the case for international institutions and the expenditures they demanded.[89]

The structures of democracy posed challenges to any campaign to change that narrative. Allied experts who attended NATO's conferences for information officials remained leery of undertaking an active and organized program spearheaded by the alliance. Although there was no doubt that NATO required a robust program to educate its citizens, the experts believed the primary responsibility for so doing should remain with individual national governments.[90] Should NATO undertake a vigorous public relations campaign all its own, it could easily appear as though the alliance were indulging in the same propagandistic habits as the Warsaw Pact.[91]

A combination of allied organizations, national government initiatives, and civil society campaigns set out to educate the public. NATO's Information Service prepared a special edition of the *NATO Review*, dedicated to the challenges facing the alliance (complete with a cover depicting a crossroads), and arranged a traveling photo exhibition that would contrast "the freedoms characteristic of the Atlantic nations" with the realities of life under communist rule.[92] For the first time in NATO's history, in 1982, the alliance prepared and circulated its own publication with figures on the correlation of forces between NATO and the Warsaw Pact, along with an press kit filled with charts and photographs.[93] At NATO's headquarters in Brussels, officials kept up earlier efforts to welcome visitors with even greater emphasis on "more politically influential groups," including peace groups like IKV.[94]

The formal bodies of the alliance struggled to figure out how they might reach a younger generation. After the Wallonian National Action Committee for Peace and Development (Comité National d'Action pour la Paix et le Développement) arranged a demonstration in Brussels in October 1981, drawing over two hundred thousand protestors, the Belgian representative to the Committee on Information and Cultural Relations bemoaned NATO's dearth of materials aimed at the youngest citizens: school children. Since the demonstration, there had been a general uptick in requests for information, particularly among those still in primary and secondary school. All of NATO's existing materials seemed ill-suited to such a young audience. The French representative agreed, suggesting that the allies invest in outreach materials explicitly aimed at children, such as comic strips and trinkets like T-shirts, pens, and decals that could make an impact at a low price point.[95]

Similar thinking guided the efforts of affiliate organizations whose mission emphasized the maintenance of a strong transatlantic partnership. The Atlantic Council of the United States, for instance, arranged a series of meetings with US high schoolers to discuss what they did and did not know about NATO—the latter being the dominant theme. Members of the council bemoaned the inadequacies of the school curriculum and its tendency to give contemporary history and international affairs short shrift.[96]

Shoring up support among the youth would not solve NATO's most immediate and pressing problems. And, as no shortage of officials acknowledged, the people terrified by the alliance's deployments were not just those coming of age. At one meeting of information officials, the Dutch delegate underscored the plethora of older people involved in the grassroots campaigns and protests targeting the Dual-Track Decision. Public polling supported this anecdotal evidence; fear of another world war was higher among those who had experienced the Second World War than among any other demographic.[97]

The True Peace Movement

When arrested, women at Greenham Common were charged with breach of the peace. But even this language seemed absurd. The whole purpose of their activism, the women argued, was to preserve the peace.[98] Although some elected to spend time in prison, one of the Greenham Common women, Helen John, elected instead to accept the terms offered by the magistrate that she should "keep the peace." "I thought it was a very generous offer they made to me and I accepted it," she told one interviewer. "I now consider myself to be the first legalized peacekeeper."[99]

Demonstrations and civil disobedience were not the only tools available to those who took it upon themselves to secure the peace, something observers of the protests sweeping Europe took great pains to emphasize. "Pacifism, though it is an honourable and courageous tradition," one Briton wrote to the editor of the *Guardian*, "is not the only defensible choice in a world where organised aggression still occurs."[100] Though it was popular to refer to the entire transnational collection of activists as the "peace movement," some politicians and commentators rejected the underlying implications of the label. Those marching in the streets did not have a monopoly on caring about the preservation of peace and, by casting themselves as defenders of the peace, they implied that those who disagreed were somehow in favor of nuclear war.[101] When asked about the women camped out at Greenham Common, one anonymous aide of Margaret Thatcher dismissed their tactics as "naive and misguided," arguing that they played directly into the Soviets' hands. But their broader aims were admirable and easy to share: "Of course, I want peace, too. We all do. I respect the women's motives. I am sure they are sincere."[102]

As the Western allies tried to defuse public anxieties about the possibility of war, they returned, again and again, to the same message; NATO was not only an instrument in case of war but a guarantee that there would be peace. This allied messaging, whether promoted by national governments or through NATO's formal structures, emphasized the common objectives between what activists hoped to achieve and what the alliance's policies provided. It was NATO, officials argued, that was "the *true* peace movement."[103]

Détente from Below

Concerned citizens were not content to leave the work of managing the Cold War's tensions to professional diplomats and elected officials. The tensions in East-West relations were dangerous—and needed to be transcended. Convinced of that fact, peace groups answered the call, determined to build their own form of détente from below.

Efforts to expand the ties crisscrossing the Iron Curtain dated back to the 1950s. Through formal and informal channels, whether cultural exchanges, scientific networks, peace groups, or personal connections, individuals tried to build trust between citizens in the West and their counterparts in the East. In the early 1980s, a diverse group of individuals returned to this task with a renewed sense of urgency. With superpower relations in the doldrums, the pursuit of détente was deemed far too important to be left to governments. It was critical to take action to reduce tensions—before it was too late.

Peace groups spearheaded educational initiatives designed to shed light on the realities of everyday life behind the Iron Curtain. These efforts tended to underscore a message of shared humanity. Those living in the Soviet Union and across Eastern Europe were no different from those in West; they were people with jobs, families, aspirations, and heartbreaks of their own.[104] If more citizens on both sides came to appreciate that fact, they could begin to dismantle the psychological and ideological barriers of the Cold War. One group of US activists, the International Fellowship of Reconciliation, described their educational mission as an antidote to the "constant diet of grim stories" obsessed with the failings of communism; they bemoaned the steady stream of stories about political repression, economic failure, shortages of consumer goods, and terrifying military statistics.[105] Various campaigns tried to transcend these flat depictions through letter-writing campaigns that forged personal connections and photograph exchanges and exhibitions showcasing similarities that transcended political systems and ideological blocs.[106] END drove this message home with lighthearted slogans on the campaign's merchandise, such as buttons that implored readers to "date a Bulgarian" or, in an ode to the latest dance craze, "bodypop in Budapest."[107]

For some activists in Western Europe, these efforts went even further, flowing from their desire to liberate the continent from US domination and to cast off the constraints of the Cold War. END's Mary Kaldor, for instance, articulated a vision of nonalignment. Unlike the variant often associated with the Cold War, Kaldor's conception of nonalignment was not about opting out of the binaries that defined the international order but about transcending them to move "beyond the blocs."[108]

Activists traveled to the Soviet Union, meeting with representatives of various peace groups, both state-sanctioned and so-called "independents." When three women from Greenham Common headed east in May 1983, they insisted on bringing a representative from an independent Soviet group, the Committee to Establish Trust between the USA and the USSR, to their meeting with the official peace committee. "We spent a lot of time explaining to these officials how their treatment of this group takes away from the efforts of their millions of peace activists," one of the women, Ann Pettitt, told reporters. "This makes their own (official) peace movement look less credible."[109] IKV sought similar links to independent peace and human rights activists across Eastern Europe in an effort "to overcome the rigid bloc division" between the two armed camps on the continent.[110] The group's president, Ben ter Veer, spoke of a shared struggle that linked their own efforts to those of Solidarność.

IKV's efforts to build ties with these supposedly like-minded partners ran up against the fact that the two sides espoused divergent world views. Members of the Polish trade union rejected the logic underpinning the Western activists' calls for nuclear disarmament. Far from seeing nuclear weapons as the root cause of instability and insecurity on the continent, they viewed these weapons as a vital check on the Soviet Union's power. Whereas activists in the West tended to oppose US policies, their Polish counterparts shared no such sense of revulsion. "There can be no doubt," one supporter of END reported after traveling across Poland, "about the sympathetic regard felt for the USA, evident in the slogans adorning the walls of Krakow suburb Nowa Huta: 'Reagan is with us.'"[111] Similar views could be found throughout Eastern Europe, where dissidents and human rights campaigners rejected the pro forma language of peace championed by the ruling communist parties. "Our citizens have been required to carry the same old peace placards in mandatory parades," the Czechoslovak dissident Václav Havel wrote. The language of peace meant the struggle against Western imperialists and, in these circumstances, it was little wonder that Havel's fellow citizens were uninterested. Even if they embraced Western visions of the concept, what could they do about it? Press outlets in the West drew up maps of military installations, but no such thing happened within the Warsaw Pact. To reveal their locations would land a person in prison. "And when I try to imagine someone daring to come near a rocket base with an anti-war placard or, perish the thought, trying to interfere with its construction"—not unusual occurrences in the West—"I break out in cold sweat," Havel concluded.[112]

Given the immense restrictions placed on expression across the Warsaw Pact, END's members debated the wisdom of bolstering various peace movements behind the Iron Curtain. How could they be certain they were engaging with truly independent activists?[113] After reports suggested that the Soviet Peace Committee, a state-sponsored organization, had not been invited to END's May 1983 convention in Berlin, Dan Smith wrote to clarify END's position. The committee had been invited, with full speaking rights in the various working groups but not in the plenary session. "This seems a reasonable compromise between the fact that it, not surprisingly, has not signed the END appeal—the basis of all our activities—and the desire of everybody for a dialogue."[114] At subsequent conventions, organizers continued their efforts to bring together activists from both halves of the continent. Before the fourth annual convention in Amsterdam in 1985, END actively courted representatives of independent activist groups in Eastern Europe. These efforts failed; when they gathered in Amsterdam, none of these so-called "independents" were in attendance. As consolation, the convention's coordinators circulated a collection of essays penned by Eastern European dissidents designed, as IKV's Mient Jan Faber put it, to "make them present" in Amsterdam, even if their governments would not permit them to attend.[115]

The dialogue that unfolded in the early 1980s was diverse, sweeping, and increasingly democratic. The breadth of that conversation—and of the participants who took part—rattled those who hoped to preserve NATO's existing arrangements, as it suggested an increasingly tenuous security order under attack on multiple fronts. Protestors who took to the streets rejected their governments' assertions that they could provide an acceptable form of security.[116] "Whenever you go, you find people have mastered the same arguments," E. P. Thompson remarked. Individuals had cast off "the entire framework of deterrence" and, increasingly, focused their efforts on overthrowing "the very logic of the bloc system."[117] Even those who dismissed activists as the fringe of respectable politics could not deny that the challenge to the legitimacy of the existing order also came from within; strategic specialists and policymakers, both current and former, openly questioned the wisdom of the Western allies' policies.

Whatever the earlier logic of NATO's plans to deploy the Pershing IIs and Gryphons, the specialists who crafted the strategic case for their deployment failed to grasp the optics. They were too removed to truly appreciate the political risks. "Such specialists are like theologians," the historian Michael Howard argued in 1983. And, as their analysis became "too complex and remote," their authority diminished. "New teachers will arise," Howard wrote, "Martin Luthers, John Wesleys, pastors whose beliefs may be simplistic to the point of lunacy, but whose message is responsive to popular needs and who can speak in a language that everyone can understand."[118] For NATO, this spelled trouble. It was a tough sales pitch: to make the case for nuclear weapons without appearing too sanguine about the dangers such weapons could unleash if used or, worse still, seeming content to use them.

With a growing, diverse group of individuals willing to question NATO policy, it might not matter that the alliance itself retained strong favorability ratings. Faced with voters calling for a NATO free of nuclear weapons and the liberation of Europe from the United States, it was all too easy to imagine how the West's defenses could unravel. The most immediate and "existential stress-test" would be whether the alliance could see through the Dual-Track Decision's deployments in 1983.[119]

CHAPTER 9

The Year of the Missile

Before the Bundestag on January 20, 1983, François Mitterrand warned against the temptation to erode the foundations of the transatlantic partnership. "Whoever would bet on the decoupling of the European continent and the American one," the French president cautioned, "would put into question the maintenance of equilibrium and thus the maintenance of peace."[1] At a press conference the next day, he returned to this refrain. Mitterrand spoke of his admiration for the Federal Republic's first chancellor, Konrad Adenauer, and especially for his commitment to anchoring Bonn within the West. Adenauer had rejected "a Rapallo policy" with Moscow.[2] The subtext was clear; this generation of West German policymakers needed to follow Adenauer's path.

Pundits delighted in the historical ironies. On the twentieth anniversary of the Élysée Treaty, the 1963 Franco-German agreement that had once seemed poised to break the United States' bond with Europe, the French president was now one of the most staunch and outspoken defenders of the transatlantic partnership. The tides had turned so much that it was a French socialist who exhorted "a Germany tempted by pacifist adventure to get a grip on itself."[3] Could the Federal Republic be trusted to hold the line for another year? Press reports suggested not. The chief US negotiator on INF, Paul Nitze, was "already angling for a deal," one US weekly reported, "because he thinks the Germans will cave."[4]

The fear that West German voters might turn against the Dual-Track Decision's deployments hung in the air in early 1983. "The most reliable ally of the United States," the French political scientist Alfred Grosser argued, "has become the country with the liveliest anti-Americanism."[5] But in a democracy, what tends to turn popular dissatisfaction into actionable policy are the votes cast by constituents and the parties they return to office. Already, events in Belgium and the Netherlands had shown that domestic politics could defer, if not derail, tough choices about the Western allies' defense. Even NATO members not expected to host the missiles faced direct political challenges. In November 1982, Norway's conservative government survived a vote of nonconfidence triggered by the country's financial contributions to the common infrastructure fund that would underwrite stationing the Gryphons and Pershing IIs in Europe.[6] Throughout 1983, the missiles' opponents held out hope that they might achieve even greater successes shaping the choices made in the United Kingdom, Italy, and, above all, the Federal Republic of Germany.

Down to Three (For Now)

In May 1981, Dutch voters went to the polls. It took the remainder of the summer for a government to form. By summer's end, the center-right coalition of Christian Democrats and Liberals was out, replaced by a new coalition made up of Christian Democrats, Labour, and Democrats (D-66). Dries van Agt remained prime minister, but cobbling together a coalition together required a major compromise. There could be no final decision on whether to accept the Gryphons. Labour threatened repeatedly to bring down the entire government should a decision be made to station the cruise missiles in the Netherlands.[7] The earlier deadline set for December 1981 came and went with no decision. Van Agt chalked up the delay to the fact that the United States and the Soviet Union had only just opened arms control talks in Geneva. The final Dutch decision, he affirmed, would depend on the results achieved in those negotiations.[8]

Voters cast their ballots again in September 1982, this time with enough votes for the Liberals and Christian Democrats to form another coalition with a slim majority. But even without Labour in power, this new political configuration did not lead to big moves on security policy. Ruud Lubbers, the newly elected prime minister, was primarily focused on addressing the country's acute economic woes, including an unemployment rate topping 10 percent. With the cruise missiles not scheduled to be deployed in the Netherlands until 1986, those in power had ample time to defer a final decision, given the clear fault lines in the Dutch political landscape over nuclear questions.

Despite these incentives to be cautious, Lubbers pressed ahead with plans to identify a basing site. "We really cannot delay the logistical decisions much beyond the end of this year," an anonymous senior government source told reporters just after the September 1982 election.[9] The next summer, in June 1983, the government announced that, should the country agree to host the missiles, they would be stationed at an air base on the Belgian border, Woensdrecht. "The Americans rule here," one Dutch politician griped about even this small step.[10]

All the while, representatives at the US Embassy in The Hague continued to make the case for deployment, trying to shift the public conversation. William Dyess, who served as ambassador from 1981 to 1983, was particularly active, liaising with nearly all of the political parties—he refused to waste time on the Socialists, seeing them as a lost cause—and touring the country to appear at rallies and universities. "We had to be very careful about the way we did it because we were foreigners," he later recalled, "but we had a very legitimate point of view, one which represented the interests of our own country, the Alliance, and also The Netherlands."[11] But it was clear that the Dutch could scarcely be counted on to take a firm position, let alone an affirmative one, before 1983 was through. "It became clear to us," Hugh De Santis, an analyst at the State Department, later explained, "we couldn't . . . we weren't going to count on the Dutch. We were less certain . . . maybe we could count on the Belgians, and of course no one expected the Italians to be steadfast."[12]

Even if the Belgians did intend to follow through on the deployments, it seemed increasingly unlikely they would decide to do so before the end of 1983. In December 1979, Henri Simonet had indicated that the Martens coalition would defer confirmation of the Dual-Track Decision's deployments on Belgian soil. But the Belgian cabinet's agreement had been more circumspect, with its members insisting that they would make a decision in six months, based on the progress achieved through arms control talks.[13]

After the initial delay, the Belgians had revisited the matter time and again, but with no more solid results. In the spring of 1980, observers at the US embassy in Brussels noted with some worry a rapid rise in calls for a "Dutch option"—a much longer delay until December 1981—from Socialists, both Francophone and Flemish.[14] A government crisis followed in April and the ruling coalition collapsed. It took nearly a month to form a new coalition, again headed by Wilfried Martens, and made up of six different political groups. From the outset, the still-fragile coalition fixated on the country's deteriorating economic situation and linguistic divisions.[15]

In May 1980, when the first six-month delay was nearly up, Jimmy Carter appealed directly to Wilfried Martens to stand firm on Belgium's existing commitments. "A decision by Belgium to further delay the confirmation of TNF deployments," Carter warned his Belgian counterpart, "would be especially unfortunate. It would give the Soviets further reason to continue their political efforts to undo the NATO TNF decision and to avoid negotiating an equitable arms control agreement."[16] Privately, Simonet's successor as foreign minister, Charles-Ferdinand Nothomb, assured US interlocutors the he was determined to press for an early, affirmative decision, though "a temporary easing of Alliance pressures on Belgium" to meet its 3 percent spending target would help the situation.[17] The next month, the government pled for an extension.[18]

By September, the Martens government had converted the six-month postponement into an indefinite one. The official declaration affirmed the Belgians' continued desire to see the superpowers' arms control talks succeed. "Should the negotiations between the United States and the Soviet Union not succeed," the government vowed, "Belgium, in concert with its allies, will take all the measures agreed upon by the NATO partners." To give arms control time to yield results, the Belgian position affirmed that the government would revisit its decision every six months. The declaration's ambiguous formulation made it possible for politicians with an array of views to endorse it, with both champions of the deployments and their opponents claiming victory.[19]

Neither Belgium nor the Netherlands would make a final decision on deployment before 1983 was through. That put enormous pressure on the Italians to hold the line, lest the Federal Republic be left as the only non-nuclear power on the continent to agree to take the missiles. But opponents of the Dual-Track Decision within the Federal Republic saw a more direct path to derail the deployments: at the ballot box.

The First Big Election

Helmut Schmidt's coalition split in the autumn of 1982, largely over economic questions. A new coalition of Christian Democrats and Free Democrats, with the CDU's Helmut Kohl at its head, took power. From the outset, the new government's message was one of continuity on foreign policy. Kohl vowed to pursue a "genuine détente" with the Soviet Union and affirmed that his government would see the deployments through unless the Soviet Union agreed to reduce its SS-20s as part of the INF talks.[20]

Kohl's political challengers tried to turn the general election scheduled for early March 1983 into a referendum on the deployments. The Greens, for instance, put the Dual-Track Decision's deployments at the heart of their campaign. Only a few years old, the Green Party was a "mercurial coalition." Its ranks included environmentalists, feminists, pacifists, and what one US journalist described as "re-treaded Marxist-Leninists."[21] This new political movement blended traditional party politics with the grassroots politics of social movements, its members casting themselves as outsiders operating from within the system.[22]

The Greens' electoral campaign tried to drum up opposition to the missiles with a touring rock concert known as the Green Caterpillar and visceral messaging.[23] "We want to die so that America may live!" one of the party's election posters exclaimed, the phrase imposed over an image of the US flag flying over a bombed-out German city.[24] The prospect of Germans' annihilation became a focal point of the Greens' campaign rhetoric, nowhere more so than at the International Tribunal against First-Strike and Mass-Destructive Weapons that the party organized in Nuremberg in the lead-up to the election. A mock trial, the event harnessed the weight of historic comparisons. Just as Nazi war criminals had been held accountable before the law in Nuremberg, so too would nuclear weapons be. Petra Kelly insisted it was time for another trial, given a nuclear war's unimaginable cost to human life, a nuclear version of the Holocaust unleashed by Adolf Hitler and his generals.[25] Programs for the tribunal laid a degree of blame with both superpowers. The front cover of its program, for instance, featured a figure inspired by Dracula with one eye a US flag, the other the Soviet flag. But coverage in the *New York Times* bemoaned that "three days of testimony let the Soviet Union off the hook while soundly criticizing the United States."[26]

Now out of power, the Social Democrats drifted further into outright opposition to the Dual-Track Decision. Under the leadership of Hans-Jochen Vogel, the party's electoral platform gravitated toward peace and security questions. Schmidt's earlier support for deployment no longer held any sway, even as the ex-chancellor held firm to his earlier position. But Vogel insisted that the superpowers' arms control negotiations needed to make progress. To achieve this, he urged the Americans to accept a key Soviet argument and include British and French weapons, as did Egon Bahr.[27] SPD election posters were not as grim as the Greens', but their message was no less clear. "Make Treaties, Not Arms," one exhorted.[28] Another implored voters: "Stop, Make Peace."[29]

Press leaks revealed that the superpowers had flirted, however briefly, with a negotiated settlement in the summer of 1982, as the walk in the woods went public. In January 1983, Eugene Rostow, recently fired as director of the Arms Control and Disarmament Agency, publicly bemoaned the administration's refusal to pursue Nitze's initiative. It was, he remarked to a reporter from the *New York Times*, "a promising approach and well worth further study."[30]

The leftward drift within West German politics terrified the French. Since coming to power in 1981, François Mitterrand (himself a socialist) had been a staunch supporter of the Dual-Track Decision, despite France's distance from the alliance. But Mitterrand endorsed the decision's underlying logic, championing the need for a global balance of forces and resistance to neutralism, which might give the Soviet Union additional political leverage in Western Europe. Aides urged him to put the case clearly to the German people.[31]

Mitterrand's intervention was one of many, as the high-stakes election encouraged interested parties on both sides to weigh in. Soviet Foreign Minister Andrei Gromyko visited the Federal Republic in January, filling the trip with public appearances where he touted the Kremlin's commitment to a reasonable agreement and dismissed the Reagan administration as mere "gamblers and conmen."[32]

But the Reagan White House remained far more cautious. Throughout the autumn of 1982 and into early 1983, the administration came under increasing pressure from its allies to move away from the seeming rigidity of the zero option, including public calls for a solution short of zero to secure an agreement with the Kremlin. But when the National Security Planning Group debated the possibility in January, the group acknowledged the difficulties that any shift in position might create for Helmut Kohl's coalition in advance of the election. The minister of defense, Manfred Wörner, had requested that there be no changes to the US position before March. "We will go along with what is needed for the (FRG) elections," Reagan insisted, "but if we sit there with 0/0 in our negotiating position, and they then propose some ridiculous scheme, we have to respond."[33] For the time being, US negotiators would stick with zero—and nothing more.

When election day came, Kohl's Christian Democrats carried the day with their strongest electoral showing in decades. The SPD, which had led the country for sixteen years under Brandt and Schmidt, ended up reduced to its lowest support since 1961. The Greens crossed the 5 percent threshold to secure twenty-eight seats.[34] It marked the first time since 1957 that a fourth party had managed to win representation in the Bundestag.[35] "The West is saved!" one Reagan administration official reportedly exclaimed.[36] London's *Guardian* informed readers, "Kohl's victory means setback for Russia's anti-cruise campaign."[37]

Kohl's electoral success did not mean that anxieties about nuclear weapons had subsided in the Federal Republic, nor that there was strong support for the Dual-Track Decision among the West German electorate. Voters had decided that, with the unemployment rate sitting at 10 percent, economic questions trumped all else. If anything, observers cautioned, West Germans had cast their ballots for Kohl in spite of his stance on the missiles, not because of it.[38] "The biggest danger for us," one anonymous official at the State Department warned, "is too much optimism, with the idea that Kohl can come through with the family jewels—that's not the case."[39]

Easter Marches

With the election in the Federal Republic complete, Ronald Reagan unveiled a shift in the US negotiating position in late March. The interim option, the first of two announced that year, envisioned global reductions somewhere above the earlier offer of zero. The total numbers were left undefined, that ambiguity designed to underscore the administration's flexibility and commitment to reaching an agreement. In the months that followed, US negotiators offered an array of figures ranging from 50 all the way to 450. "When it comes to intermediate nuclear missiles in Europe," Reagan remarked, "it would be better to have none than to have some. But if there must be some, it is better to have few than to have many."[40]

Reagan's interim option had been in the works for months. When the National Security Policy Group met in January, the same meeting where the president had prioritized the West German election, they debated the merits and drawbacks of an alternative proposal. George Shultz put forward a tiered proposal. Noting that zero continued to be the best outcome—and one that had "great appeal"—he suggested that the United States could introduce another option on the way to zero. It was clear that the administration could not give up on the original zero option. Should they abandon it, Shultz warned his colleagues, "the peace movement would take it up so fast that your head would swim."[41]

Caspar Weinberger agreed with Shultz's arguments in theory, but worried that if the United States were to introduce a proposal based on equal levels above zero too early, it would imply that the administration had decided to abandon the zero option. He preferred to wait until after the deployments began to shift course. "We are in the best position now," he argued. "We should not show flexibility." But Reagan saw the advantages of a more flexible approach. "Why not go along with an interim reduction of the forces while continuing the negotiations for 0/0?" he wondered.[42] US officials had already touted the administration's flexibility in public. At appearances across Western Europe in early 1983, for instance, Vice President George Bush underscored that the zero option was not "a take-it-or-leave-it proposition." If the administration were "to be any more flexible," Bush quipped, "we'd have to be invertebrates."[43] The March interim option underscored that message, as it responded to mounting pressure for some sort of negotiated settlement between the superpowers. As with so many of the administration's initiatives, the timing of the announcement was chosen for maximum effect: on the eve of Easter weekend, traditionally a popular time for peace demonstrations.[44]

Easter 1983 was no different. Over thirty thousand descended on West Berlin's Tempelhof Airport, where a handful of demonstrators stretched out a banner over the memorial commemorating the Berlin Airlift begging the two superpowers to "leave Germany in peace."[45] In Britain's so-called "nuclear valley," tens of thousands of protestors formed a fourteen-mile human chain, snaking their way from Greenham Common to Aldermaston, the home of the Atomic Weapons Research Establishment and Burghfield's Royal Ordnance Factory. Pundits disputed the turnout at these events, as police figures differed wildly from those of CND, but most suggested that seventy thousand concerned Britons had turned out.[46] Michael Heseltine, the British defense secretary, dismissed the marchers as "naive and reckless" and as only strengthening the Kremlin's hand.[47] To keep press coverage of the rallies limited, Margaret Thatcher's press secretary, Bernard Ingham, turned to a darling Prince William. Pictures of the nine-month-old heir to the throne, on tour with the Prince and Princess of Wales in Australia, could be just the ticket to headline news broadcasts and splash across the front pages.[48] But Ingham's schemes were not enough to keep pictures of massive demonstrations out of the news.

Another Victory at the Polls

Britons prepared to go to the polls for a general election in June. As in the Federal Republic, the Euromissiles loomed large in the campaign. The election pitted Thatcher's Tories, staunch supporters of the Dual-Track Decision, against a Labour Party that, despite having presided over the decision, now rejected the deployments outright. In 1982, more than two-thirds of the party faithful had voted against the deployment of any US nuclear weapons in the United Kingdom, making it a binding position in the party platform.[49] Polling suggested that the public might be inclined to agree. One January 1983 survey indicated that more than 60 percent of the electorate opposed the deployment of cruise missiles in the United Kingdom.[50]

E. P. Thompson concluded that the campaign would be the most important British election of the twentieth century. "The matter which we must decide concerns the defence of Britain and how this may be best conducted," he wrote. Other issues mattered, to be sure, but those questions were trivial when compared to the stakes of defense questions. If British voters refused to defend their liberties and their lives, he warned, "then nothing can be solved. For we will move, with all our human neighbours, toward civilisation's 'final solution.'"[51]

Thompson attacked Thatcher's continued refusal to negotiate any reductions to the nation's nuclear arsenal. Andropov's arms control proposals suggested that the number of SS-20s could be slashed in exchange for cuts to the British (and French) stockpiles. "He was offering Mrs Thatcher his arm," as Thompson put it in one essay, "for a waltz on the multilateral ballroom floor." But rather than take the Soviet general secretary up on his offer, Thatcher balked. "The Polaris, she said, was only a weapon 'of last resort' whereas the SS-20 (one supposes) is an ill-bred sort of weapon which might resort at any time and place."[52] Thompson pilloried the prime minister's policies. "I cannot stand the multilateral homilies which come out of that woman's lips," he wrote. "When she croons in her husky way: 'We are the *trooo* disarmers' I cannot even admire her call. Prime Minister, when have you ever made *any* proposal, in good faith, to disarm *anything* (except, of course, the Russians)?"[53]

But in advance of the election, much of the British debate focused on who would control the cruise missiles, should they be deployed, a thorny question governed by a series of agreements dating back to the 1950s. What they boiled down to was a US commitment to consult the British about nuclear use—but not necessarily a commitment to heed London's advice. Thatcher expressed confidence that these arrangements were sufficient to protect Britain's national interests.

Those assertions came under fire at various points in 1983. The previous autumn, defense secretary John Nott had suggested that the government should leave open a final decision on arrangements like a dual key—which would require Number 10's consent to launch—as a way to offset opposition to the missiles.[54] Nott's successor, Michael Heseltine, publicly defended the choice not to pursue a dual key as the smart financial move. It would have cost the government £1 billion to employ a dual-key system. Britain simply did not have the funds.[55] Critics charged that such an arrangement would not secure a British voice in any decision to fire the weapons stationed on British territory. "My Lords, is the noble Lord aware that no nuclear missile can be fired from French soil without a French finger on the trigger?" one peer exhorted in a May session of the House of Lords. "Is he further aware that no missile can be fired from Australian, Spanish or Swiss soil because there is none? If the Government will not put us in the second category, is it not high time they at least put us in the first?"[56]

One group of parliamentarians endorsed a draft motion, subsequently shelved, calling for an arrangement that would introduce "a mechanism for sovereign physical control of theatre nuclear weapons based in this country."[57] Heseltine continued to cry poor.[58] To advocates for a greater British voice, the price tag mattered little. "Does the Minister agree that, high though it is," one MP pointedly asked Heseltine in the House of Commons, "it is worth it for the defence of the sovereignty of this country?"[59] The flurry of debate regarding dual-key control reflected anxieties not unlike those expressed by CND's campaigners or the women of Greenham Common about the dangers of Britain's reliance on the United States.

Even with the controversy over control of the missiles, the Tories' position improved in the weeks leading up to the election. The Labour Party, under the banner "New Hope for Britain," seemed to be hemorrhaging support. The party's platform called for Britain to reject the cruise missile and cancel the Trident submarine program, all in pursuit of a nonnuclear defense policy that would rid the United Kingdom of its nuclear weapons, US and British alike. Journalists predicted a thrashing at the polls in June. "The evidence mounts that Labour's policies on nuclear weapons are major vote losers," one wrote a few weeks in advance of the election. "Aided and abetted by the CND and the Greenham Women, it has alienated much of the middle opinion which supports nuclear deterrence but opposes both cruise and Trident."[60] Polling data supported this conclusion. According to one Marplan poll from late May, 23 percent thought that Labour had the best policies on nuclear weapons and defense questions. Nearly twice that—45 percent—believed that the Conservatives did.[61] Another poll suggested that 52 percent of the electorate now favored the deployment of the Gryphons, while 34 percent remained opposed.[62]

When the votes were tallied, the Conservatives returned a decisive majority. Securing a whopping 397 seats, it was the largest electoral win since Labour's in 1945. For Labour, the general election was a debacle. The party suffered its worst defeat in over sixty years. Michael Heseltine touted the Tory victory as a ringing endorsement of the party's nuclear policies.[63]

Activists pushed back. Thatcher's government had not secured a mandate "for a programme of massive unilateral escalation in nuclear weapons by Britain, and no mandate for United Kingdom support for Ronald Reagan's fanatical pursuit for nuclear superiority," CND's chair, Joan Ruddock, argued.[64] In the main, the Thatcher government's reelection left activists disenchanted, as it seemed clear that the cruise missiles would arrive in the country before 1983 was through. "Post-election depression," one reporter concluded, "appears to have taken the steam out of the protest."[65]

Another One

Italians also cast their ballots in June 1983, just weeks after the British general election. The Christian Democrats, who dominated the country's politics, suffered their largest electoral setback in over three decades. Critically, the seats lost by the Christian Democrats did not go to the Communists (who opposed the Dual-Track Decision), but rather to a number of smaller parties, including the Socialist Party. The Christian Democrats' poor performance meant that, as in the last two elections, the party could not form a government without the Socialists. Bettino Craxi, who headed the Socialist Party, made the most of the opportunity, leveraging it to become the first member of his party to serve as prime minister. Craxi's government enjoyed an unprecedented degree of stability in the notoriously unstable Italian political landscape. By the time Craxi's government fell in June 1986, his thousand-day rule was the longest since the Second World War.

Craxi affirmed the government's support for the Dual-Track Decision's deployments. His vow to hold the line mirrored the now customary line of politicians in power across Europe. He urged the United States and the Soviet Union to continue to explore all options to reach an agreement in Geneva, before affirming that his government would follow through with the deployments should these talks fail.[66]

Footnotes and Other Revisions

Elections returned staunch supporters of the Dual-Track Decision to critical posts, but even a cursory glance around the Atlantic alliance in the summer of 1983 suggested a delicate political situation. NATO's regular communiqués were covered in footnotes drawing attention to various nations' objections to one clause or another. When the Defense Planning Committee met in June, the meeting's final statement highlighted the ministers' "resolve to modernize their forces and pursue arms control." Appended to this sentence, itself nothing more than an anodyne endorsement of the Dual-Track Decision's two prongs, was a footnote indicating that Greece reserved its position on the matter.[67] It was hardly the ringing endorsement of allied unity for which the communiqué's authors had undoubtedly hoped.

The Athenian offensive did not stop there. Andreas Papandreou, Greece's Socialist prime minister, backed a self-styled "policy of peace," amplifying the arguments of antinuclear campaigners. He threw his weight behind the latest round of calls for a nuclear-weapon-free zone in the Balkans and signed on to the Five Continent Initiative for Peace and Disarmament alongside the leaders of Argentina, India, Mexico, Sweden, and Tanzania.[68]

Papandreou's government suggested a string of initiatives that would revise, restructure, or outright reject the missile deployments. In a June interview on Hungarian television, he broke ranks with NATO to call for the inclusion of the British and French nuclear arsenals within the superpowers' negotiations—a boon to the Soviets, who had been suggesting the same thing for years.[69] Later that summer, Greece's foreign minister, Ioannis Haralambopoulos, appealed to his counterparts at the European Community to defer the deployments. Papandreou's government had used its position as president of the community to promote what British officials denounced as its "maverick views."[70]

Danish representatives also relied on the carefully placed caveats of footnotes scattered throughout NATO's press releases. "Denmark reserves its position because the subject is considered to be the province of Ministers of Foreign Affairs," read one objection on a final communiqué of the Nuclear Planning Group.[71] Another helpfully informed readers, "Denmark places a general reservation on parts of this report."[72]

At home, Denmark's Conservative-led government struggled to cobble together sufficient support for the country's participation in the Dual-Track Decision. The previous fall, parliament blocked appropriations for the common infrastructure fund that would dole out money to construct missile sites. In May 1983, the Social Democrats introduced a parliamentary resolution calling for the deployments to be delayed. So long as arms control negotiations were taking place between the superpowers, they argued, NATO's members should not introduce new weapons in the European theater.[73] When parliament backed the resolution, Prime Minister Paul Schlüter decried the decision as naive. The Kremlin, he quipped, would be "pleased with this victory in a Western parliament."[74] High-ranking Social Democrats insisted that the resolution was compatible with the original Dual-Track Decision. That argument strained credulity. Even in the most charitable reading, a proposal to defer the deployments indefinitely cut against the structure of NATO's December 1979 plan. The decision had two, parallel tracks—and Caspar Weinberger likened the Danish plan to "derailing one of the trains entirely."[75]

Observers were quick to note that although Denmark's political difficulties were unlikely to sway the policies of larger allies like the Federal

Republic or the United Kingdom, the problems were scarcely confined to Copenhagen. What was on display in Denmark reflected, in the words of one US journalist, "the widespread unease about the missiles that pervades Europe."[76] NATO's governments steeled themselves for a hot autumn, guaranteed to be marked by near daily protests and antinuclear actions. Peace groups in the Federal Republic, for instance, had plans for a busy October, packed with blockades, rallies, and marches as part of a pan-European effort to stop the missiles.[77]

Hot and Cold

To kick off a new season of protests, prominent West Germans descended on the US base at Mutlangen on September 1, 1983. Organizers believed that date—the forty-fourth anniversary of the Nazi invasion of Poland—to be a powerful symbol of their opposition to war. High-profile activists and politicians blockaded the base, including household names from the Green Party like Petra Kelly and Heinrich Böll, along with the SPD's Oskar Lafontaine and Erhard Eppler. Americans, too, lent their star power to the celebrity event. Daniel Ellsberg appeared at Mutlangen, as did Philip Berrigan, a Roman Catholic priest made famous after he broke into a General Electric facility, destroying two missiles and pouring blood on a stack of paperwork.[78]

But it was another event that same day that changed the conversation: the Soviet downing of a passenger aircraft, Korean Airlines flight 007. Soviet Air Defense Forces, mistaking the aircraft for an espionage overflight, launched air-to-air missiles bringing the plane down in the Sea of Japan. All 269 passengers and crew on board were killed.

Soviet press releases insisted that the commercial flight had been in "flagrant violation" of Soviet airspace. Predictably, the Kremlin laid blame for the incident with Washington.[79] These outright denials, coupled with the tragedy itself, dealt a blow to the Kremlin's image as the protector of peace. Outraged at this latest act of seeming Soviet aggression, Caspar Weinberger recommended that the president walk out of the negotiations in Geneva.[80] Reagan refused. It was "too dangerous" for the superpowers not to talk.[81]

Who in Moscow they might be able to talk to was another question. The thrust of Soviet foreign policy seemed increasingly difficult to discern, as did the Kremlin chain of command. Andropov's poor health was the subject of considerable speculation, and Western intelligence agencies and press outlets alike resorted to the bluntest instruments to determine the general secretary's overall fitness. (A flurry of stories appeared when he missed a Kremlin rally to mark the sixty-sixth anniversary of the October Revolution.)[82] With

Andropov out of the limelight, the Soviet position seemed to be a veritable grab bag. At once, the Kremlin's talking points suggested that an agreement on INF must cover British and French forces and that a deal could happen without including them at all.

Despite the contradictory signals emanating from Moscow, the Reagan administration forged ahead with plans for another interim option. The proposal built on the exploratory proposal recommended in March and, in late September, Reagan unveiled this latest sign of his flexibility.[83] He laid the groundwork with a radio address on September 24 in which he lamented the superpowers' failure to reach an agreement. "What could possibly be better than to rid the world of an entire class of nuclear weapons?" the president wondered aloud.[84] Two days later, at the United Nations General Assembly, Reagan went even further. After reminding his audience of the various negotiating positions that the US delegation had already pursued in Geneva, the president offered yet more evidence of Washington's flexibility, suggesting a series of general principles that could help the two sides reach an agreement.[85] Predictably, the Soviets dismissed this latest overture as yet more of the same.[86] The prospects of an agreement before year's end were virtually nil. Nitze told a gathering of Western legislators that it would be impossible to reach a deal before December.[87] On the Soviet side, Georgy Arbatov was no more optimistic, telling one Hungarian television interviewer that the United States wished "to deploy and not to reach an agreement."[88]

Arbatov's view found plenty of sympathy. Though peace activists were increasingly convinced that the deployments would begin in a few months' time, no matter the size and scope of their demonstrations, they redoubled their efforts to bring their fellow citizens out into the streets. Over three million Western Europeans turned out in the week of October 22 alone as part of a flurry of events billed as an international week of action. In the Federal Republic, twenty-six different groups collaborated to arrange marches, blockades of US military bases, human chains, and at least three different "people's assemblies." Demonstrators in Hanover staged a mock funeral procession where a set of Pershing IIs carried Europe in a coffin.[89] A rally in Bonn attracted nearly half a million in an affair that boasted speeches from major political figures including Willy Brandt and Petra Kelly.[90] Protests in Madrid saw one hundred thousand snake their way through the Spanish capital, armed with placards calling for the denuclearization of Europe and an end to Spain's membership in NATO (itself barely a year old).[91] Crowds flooded the streets of other capitals across Western Europe: five hundred thousand in Rome, three hundred thousand in Brussels, even a massive pair of dueling rallies, one communist and one noncommunist, in Paris. Capping off the week of action was a massive demonstration in The Hague, where 550,000—a whopping 4 percent of the entire Dutch population—turned out, including the queen's sister, Princess Irene.[92] Peace groups across Canada and the United States arranged solidarity rallies. Some seventy-five thousand Canadians rallied, many linking the struggle in Europe with their own efforts to resist the testing of US air-launched cruise missiles in the country's western provinces.[93] US activists, for their part, banded together in a nationwide call to stop the deployments alongside local actions to oppose the US role in the arms race. The Campaign to Stop the Euromissiles, based in Cambridge, Massachusetts, organized civil disobedience actions at local defense installations involved in making the cruise missile.[94]

That same week, the Nuclear Planning Group announced massive cuts to NATO's nuclear stockpile. Meeting at Montebello, in the woods outside the Canadian capital, the Western allies pledged to remove fourteen hundred warheads from Europe. These cuts would shrink the stockpile to its smallest figure in two decades.[95] Ministers touted the cuts as evidence of their desire "to preserve peace through the maintenance of forces at the lowest level capable of deterring the Warsaw Pact threat."[96]

Slashing the stockpile could, somewhat paradoxically, shore up the credibility of NATO's deterrent by making it more palatable to Western publics. The removal of outdated and unnecessary weapons could strengthen the allies' case that they were not engaged in an out-of-control arms race, but rather retained the bare minimum required to keep their citizens safe.[97] Like the reductions to the stockpile announced in December 1979, this latest round of cuts could serve as tangible evidence of the Western allies' restraint. But almost all of the attention generated by the proposal ended up swamped in the news cycle as journalists scrambled to cover the week's other events: the bombing of the US Marine barracks in Beirut, Lebanon, and the US invasion of the tiny Caribbean island nation of Grenada.

War Scares

Capping off that tumultuous week, Pierre Trudeau launched a whirlwind diplomatic initiative to defuse the now "ominous rhythm of crisis" in international affairs. The superpowers' communication, such as it existed, was a dialogue of the deaf according to the Canadian prime minister. It was all too easy to imagine how the United States and the Soviet Union might stumble their way into a nuclear war, even if only through a catastrophic technical glitch. "The risk of accident or miscalculation," Trudeau argued, "is too great for us not to begin to repair the lines of communications with our adversaries."[98] The Soviet downing of Korean Airlines flight 007 was a stark reminder of how easy it might be for one of the superpowers to make a fatal blunder. Trudeau resolved to act, doing whatever he could with his remaining political power before it was too late.[99]

How close the superpowers came to fulfilling Trudeau's worst nightmares in the autumn of 1983 has only come to light in subsequent decades. In late September, a duty officer at the Soviet Union's Oko nuclear early-warning system complex, Stanislav Petrov, received reports that the United States had launched a missile. Moments later, he received an update; the United States had fired five more. Petrov, ignoring protocol, concluded that the warnings were nothing more than a false alarm and that the satellites were malfunctioning. "When people start a war," he later remarked, "they don't start with only five missiles."[100] Convinced that it was a glitch, Petrov deviated from his standing orders. The Soviet Union did not fire off a nuclear strike of its own.

In retrospect, the autumn of 1983 has taken on almost mythical status as a time of misfires and miscalculations. Historians routinely describe it as the most dangerous point since the Cuban Missile Crisis, if not of the entire Cold War.[101] The textbook evidence for this is a November 1983 NATO exercise, Able Archer 83, which many allege brought the superpowers to the brink as the Soviet Union mistook the allies' rehearsal of nuclear launches as cover for a surprise nuclear attack.[102]

Archival records paint a far more complex picture of how NATO's adversaries viewed Able Archer. The Soviet Union did take steps in certain military districts, but leaders in the Kremlin, familiar with the exercise's script, did not see it as a smokescreen for actual aggression. "We knew that NATO was doing an exercise, not really planning for the nuclear blow," one Soviet official, the chief of staff of the Soviet Strategic Missile Forces, Viktor Esin, later argued, before going on to acknowledge, "We couldn't fully eliminate the possibility that the nuclear strike might have been delivered."[103] Similar assessments could be found in capitals across the Warsaw Pact. East German observers stressed that the exercise's rehearsal of the transition from conventional to nuclear war should not be seen as a commentary on NATO's views of the current situation in international politics.[104]

The real tensions in superpower relations did, unsurprisingly, linger in the minds of Warsaw Pact observers. "The international situation is at present white hot," one member of the Politburo, Grigory Romanov, reminded his colleagues.[105] And there was little doubt that the Soviet leadership had played its part in whipping up that sense of anxiety, creating the atmosphere of a war scare in order to terrify the Soviet public, justifying high levels of defense expenditure—and most citizens' commensurately low standard of living. In fact, Soviet officials admitted as much to their US counterparts in the autumn of 1983.[106]

Talk of a war scare did not mean that Able Archer was a near-brush with nuclear annihilation. The fact that subsequent Western assessments, whether in the United States or the United Kingdom, came to the conclusion that the Soviet Union did entertain a strike is no smoking gun. They provide vivid evidence of how tense the autumn of 1983 was, to be sure, but do not—and cannot—confirm what policymakers across the Warsaw Pact believed to be the exercise's true intentions.[107]

For those living through the autumn of 1983, the prospect that the superpowers might miscalculate and plunge the world into nuclear war remained the stuff of fiction. November 1983's made-for-TV movie, *The Day After*, saw a war break out between NATO and the Warsaw Pact after a showdown over Berlin boiled over.[108] Millions tuned in to ABC to watch the two alliances trade nuclear blows. The film's graphic depictions of mushroom clouds over the US heartland—what one viewer called a "simplistic but searing vision of nuclear annihilation"—left viewers with an inescapable conclusion. Next time, it might not be fake.[109]

Viewers who stayed on ABC once the film came to an end were greeted by Ted Koppel. "If you can take a look out the window," he opened the show, "it's all still there. Your neighborhood is still there, so is Kansas City." A veritable who's who joined Koppel that night for a discussion of deterrence and the dangers of the nuclear age. There was the predictable cast of current and former government officials: George Shultz, Henry Kissinger, Robert McNamara, and Brent Scowcroft. Conservative intellectual William F. Buckley Jr. appeared, as did physicist Carl Sagan, who had popularized the concept of nuclear winter. The fireballs viewers had just seen on their television sets, Sagan argued, paled in comparison to the destruction an actual nuclear strike would unleash. "The nuclear winter that will follow even a small nuclear war," he explained, "involves a pall of dust and smoke which would reduce the temperatures of not just in northern and mid latitudes, but pretty much globally to sub-freezing temperatures for months." Rounding out the panel was the author and Holocaust survivor Elie Wiesel.[110]

A German Question

As viewers in the United States and Canada tuned in to watch the world be blown up, the Gryphons were already arriving in Western Europe. Two of the three major parliamentary debates on the issue had already taken place, one in the United Kingdom, the other in Italy.

The debate in the House of Commons litigated many of the arguments of the past four years once more. Michael Foot, who had recently stepped down as Labour's leader, offered his colleagues a synopsis of Helmut Schmidt's position throughout the affair, while others focused on more recent history, concerned about their own sovereignty in the wake of the Americans' unilateralism in Grenada. The deployment's supporters, too, appealed to the lessons of the past, reaching a little further back in time. "In two world wars," the Conservative Cecil Franks argued, "our allies have played a critical part in the defence of our freedom and independence, and our future freedom and independence lie in the preservation of a strong and united partnership with our NATO allies." Franks exhorted his colleagues to follow this path; it was the only option.[111] A majority of the chamber agreed, and the House of Commons voted to station the Gryphons on British soil.

As members debated, the women of Greenham Common staged a Halloween party, complete with witches' hats and spider-web face-painting. More than a thousand women gathered at the base, in an event that saw part of the perimeter's fencing breached and destroyed.[112] British press outlets carried photographs of a "nuclear tug-of-war" between the soldiers of Greenham Common and the women camped outside.[113] Michael Heseltine caused a stir when he suggested that the government had a responsibility to protect the base, even if that meant shooting the demonstrators.[114]

With the arrival of the Gryphons now guaranteed, some activists bemoaned the lack of meaningful debate on the matter. E. P. Thompson complained that the cruise missiles had not featured as a major issue of the election and that the views of critics like CND were given short shrift within the popular press. CND's opposition to the cruise missiles, the Trident program, and the SS-20 went unreported, Thompson charged, "because it was in the Tory interest to caricature the policy of the peace movement as a total unilateral unreciprocated floparoo."[115]

Even after the missiles were given the go-ahead in Parliament, Britons continued to clamor for dual-key control. Grenada reinvigorated the national conversation about British sovereignty, as observers in and out of government were confronted with the Reagan administration's failure to undertake any meaningful consultations with London before invading a fellow member of the Commonwealth. One November opinion poll suggested that a whopping 94 percent of Britons wanted dual-key control of the Gryphons.[116] Observers across Western Europe came to similar conclusions. Grenada was what one Canadian diplomat termed a "test-tube illustration" of why Washington's allies worried about the United States' attitude toward its commitment to consult.[117]

Two weeks later, on November 14, Michael Heseltine announced in the House of Commons that the first Gryphons had been delivered. Labour backbenchers greeted the news with cries of "Shame!"[118] But the defense minister took great pains to note that the missile's arrival at Greenham Common should in no way be construed as a sign that the Western allies' commitment to arms control had subsided. NATO's deployments were slated to take place over five years and could be "halted, modified or reversed at any time" if progress at the negotiating table warranted such a shift. That outcome seemed far from likely. Even as the Soviets implored Western allies to cancel their deployments—and attempted to browbeat governments into doing so—Moscow's own arsenal grew apace. From December 1979 to November 1983, the number of SS-20s in the European theater nearly tripled.[119]

The Italian parliament opened debate on the Euromissiles in mid-November. Craxi, in assurances not unlike Heseltine's, pledged to do everything in his government's power to promote an arms control agreement between the superpowers that might make the deployments unnecessary. But barring such a deal, he insisted that Italy accept its share of the Gryphons. After three days of debate, the final vote returned a strong endorsement of the Craxi government's plans to deploy the cruise missiles, with 351 in favor and 219 opposed.[120]

Soviet negotiators nevertheless remained at the negotiating table in Geneva. US missiles might be arriving in Western Europe, but the make-or-break moment had yet to come. The West German Bundestag still needed to make its final decision on whether to accept the Gryphons and Pershing IIs. On the margins of the talks in Geneva, Yuli Kvitsinsky hinted that the Soviet Union might be open to a proposal based on equal reductions to 572, the same size as NATO's deployment plans. As part of this trial balloon, the lead Soviet negotiator dropped the question of British and French forces, but kept an earlier Andropov offer to freeze deployments to Asia. West German officials went public with the offer. Almost immediately, the Kremlin tried to spin the incident, claiming the proposal had actually come from the Americans.[121] This episode, dubbed the walk in the park (in an echo of the previous year's walk in the woods), was a convoluted offer based on equal reductions, but the Soviet effort to spin it as an initiative from Washington was little more than an attempt to paint the United States as cynical, looking for a spot of good press to cover the missile deployments that had begun.[122]

Soviet negotiators still hoped to influence the final debate in the Federal Republic, scheduled for November 21 and 22. At the SPD's conference on the eve of that debate, now-familiar rifts between the party's various wings loomed particularly large. Already, the SPD executive had voted to oppose

the deployments by a margin of twenty-seven to five. But at the conference itself, the debate was still acrimonious and at times heated. Helmut
Schmidt, now firmly in the minority, offered a sweeping justification for the
Dual-Track Decision in a speech that clocked in just shy of an hour and a
half. In it, the former chancellor expressed his dismay that the superpowers' negotiations had not borne fruit, airing his grievances about the Reagan
administration's refusal to seriously entertain the previous summer's walk-
in-the-woods proposal—or even share specifics about the deal with its allies,
including him. No matter this frustration, Schmidt held firm to his earlier
conviction; without a suitable arms control agreement, the deployments
must go ahead.[123] But Schmidt persuaded few. Out of four hundred delegates
present at the party's conference, only fourteen voted against the motion,
with a further three abstaining.[124]

Though the SPD's rank and file opposed the missiles, even the combination of the Social Democrats and the Greens—also staunchly opposed—could
not derail the deployments. The governing coalition of Christian Democrats
and Free Democrats had a fifty-eight–seat majority. Even with the outcome
virtually guaranteed, the Bundestag's debate was a dramatic affair.

The battle lines were drawn in predictable patterns. Kohl expressed strong
support for the decision, casting it as a litmus test of the Federal Republic's
loyalty as a NATO ally. Manfred Wörner warned that failure to deploy the
Gryphons and Pershing IIs would enable the Soviet Union to blackmail the
governments of Western Europe with the SS-20s. The Greens' Petra Kelly
exhorted her colleagues to realize that the enemy was not the Kremlin but
the atomic age itself; the source of fear should be the "greatest of all possible
dangers—the destruction of all life." The SPD's spokesman, Willy Brandt,
opposed the deployments as destabilizing. Instead, he called for the continuation of détente and promoted a new model of security partnership to rede-
fine relations between East and West. Brandt took pains to clarify that the
Social Democrats' opposition did not imply a rejection of NATO or of the
leadership role the United States played within the alliance. Schmidt made
his case for deployment one last time, before contenting himself with lob-
bing a paper airplane with Pershing II scrawled on it out into the Bundestag
chamber as the debate raged around him.[125]

November 1983—and the Bundestag's decision to accept the Gryphons and
Pershing IIs—marked the end of four tumultuous years. Protestors joined
pundits, professors, policymakers, and planners to grapple with the uncertainties of nuclear deterrence and what these terrifying weapons meant for
their own security, that of their country, and that of the planet. An open

conversation about nuclear weapons crisscrossed the Atlantic, but at the ballot box, the center held and voters elected governments that would see the deployments through in the Federal Republic of Germany, Italy, and the United Kingdom. NATO's members had survived the most immediate test, weathering a violent political storm. But any calm on the horizon was likely to be fleeting. In the years ahead, the Western allies would need to make yet more difficult defense decisions, including whether or not to modernize their shorter-range nuclear systems in Europe. Just because the NATO allies had seen the contentious deployments through did not mean that they could repeat that success.

Pundits, meanwhile, tried to identify lessons learned. In retrospect, it was clear that the Western allies had failed to predict major transformations in international politics and to fully consider the possible repercussions of the Dual-Track Decision in the lead-up to December 1979. Former NSC staffer Gregory Treverton, now teaching at Harvard, identified no fewer than five: the Soviet invasion of Afghanistan, the US Senate's failure to ratify the SALT II Treaty, the arrival of a new administration in Washington, the significant shifts in European politics, and a fundamental miscalculation about how the Soviet Union would respond to the deployment track, particularly the plans to introduce the Pershing II. Not all of these developments, Treverton conceded, could have been easily predicted.[126]

But the Western allies had also suffered from a failure of imagination. NATO's governments proved themselves to be incapable of envisioning the possibilities—and potential problems—of a plan that included such a long lag time between decision and deployment. The fact that they had survived the past four years with the December 1979 decision intact was as much a testament to their luck as to their fortitude. The Italians, for instance, had stayed the course and, in so doing, had ensured that the Federal Republic's chief condition was met; another nonnuclear, continental power would house the missiles, even as the Belgians and the Dutch balked.[127]

Though a mess from a strategic standpoint, the zero option was a political masterstroke. "It out-disarmed the disarmers," as Treverton put it, making it all but impossible for antinuclear activists to oppose the US negotiating position, even if they instinctively doubted the president's sincerity.[128]

PART THREE

Destroy

Nuclear weapons were an article of faith for Margaret Thatcher. However dangerous and destructive they might be, the threat of annihilation had guaranteed the peace in Europe for decades. "Wars are caused when an aggressor believes he can achieve his objectives at an acceptable price," she wrote in an April 1986 open letter responding to CND's Bruce Kent. Nuclear weapons made it such that this price was unbearable. "This is deterrence. And it has worked."[1]

Thatcher freely admitted that "in an ideal world there would be no weapons of mass destruction." But she did not live in an ideal world, and the bomb could not miraculously be uninvented.[2] Here, the British prime minister's views differed from those of her close ideological counterpart, Ronald Reagan. Thatcher later described the role of nuclear weapons in international politics as "the only real divergence" between the two. For Reagan, the desired outcome was a world without nuclear weapons. Thatcher's objective was to secure a world without war. That goal made nuclear weapons indispensable, according to her; they were what secured the peace in Europe.[3]

More worrying still were the similarities between the president's position and that of his opposite number in the Kremlin, General Secretary Mikhail Gorbachev. "I don't accept this," one Soviet Foreign Ministry spokesman, Gennadi Gerasimov, remarked of Thatcher's fidelity to the British nuclear deterrent, "because we want to see the world nuclear-free and we cannot see it nuclear-free if Britain is going to keep her nuclear forces." The Soviets would have to convert the erstwhile British "to our faith."[4]

Thatcher refused to abandon the tenets of hers. Asked about Gerasimov's remarks in a press conference, she returned to her own foundational principles: "I want a war-free Europe. A nuclear-free Europe I do not believe would be a war-free Europe." It was scarcely a surprise that Gorbachev wished for a Western Europe free of nuclear weapons, Thatcher quipped. He was perfectly poised to make the most of it: "the enormous superiority he has got in men, in tanks, in aircraft, in all conventional weapons, and the colossal superiority in chemical weapons, would mean that if he got the nuclear weapon out of Europe, we would never be able to deter an aggressor."[5]

Desperate to guard against that outcome, Thatcher cautioned against moving too far, too fast to reduce the size of the Western powers' nuclear arsenals. Gorbachev might boast of his new thinking, but the old threats were still there. It would be dangerous to presume that relations between East and West had miraculously changed course overnight and, time and again, Thatcher urged her colleagues to respond not to Gorbachev's appealing rhetoric, but to his deeds.[6] But no matter what the British prime minister said, the arms control offers that Gorbachev churned out at a blistering pace were almost too tempting to refuse.

Gorbachev was something of an enigma to Thatcher. After an April 1987 visit to Moscow, the British prime minister noticed he spoke with "almost messianic fervor" about reforming the Soviet economy. But he also seemed unwilling, perhaps unable, to appreciate the full scope of the economic challenges plaguing the Soviet Union over which he presided. In the face of acute problems, Gorbachev's ideas seemed rudimentary, even "simplistic." He rallied around the need for reform, and yet left Thatcher stunned by his staunch commitment to the orthodoxies of the system. "If I ever had any doubts whether Gorbachev is a true believer in the communist system," she wrote in a letter to Reagan, "my talks with him dispelled them."[7] Summing up the prime minister's "somewhat paradoxical view," one Reagan aide described a duality between Thatcher's respect for Gorbachev's boldness and her deep anxiety that he is "a very skillful and even dangerous challenger of the West."[8]

From the Soviet walkout from the INF talks in the final weeks of 1983 to NATO's London Summit in 1990, Thatcher's fidelity to the long peace held. Thatcher was not always in the majority, but her anxieties about a steady slide toward denuclearization encapsulated the tensions, contradictions, and uncertainties of doing business with Gorbachev. Could the savvy Soviet leader's new thinking be genuine? Or were his professions little more than a smokescreen to achieve long-held Soviet objectives and destroy NATO's defenses, if not the alliance itself?

These three chapters follow the negotiations to destroy the Euromissiles, culminating in the signing of the INF Treaty in December 1987, and the forces that threatened to destroy NATO's deterrent in the wake of the superpowers' historic agreement. Chapter 10 considers how the Western allies brought the Soviet Union back to the negotiating table, setting this within a broader effort in 1984 to jumpstart East-West dialogue after the doldrums of the early 1980s. Chapter 11 explores the challenges, both old and new, posed by the new general secretary, Mikhail Gorbachev. In Gorbachev, Reagan found a partner with whom he was willing and able to negotiate. But the results of those negotiations, whether the near-deal at Reykjavik in 1986 or the INF Treaty the two signed a year later, set the cat among the pigeons in NATO circles. In 1981, the Western allies had wholeheartedly endorsed the zero option. In 1987, the superpowers' embrace of zero left governments across Western Europe terrified about what would happen to NATO's defenses. Chapter 12 examines the political fallout from the INF Treaty and the Western allies' arguments over whether to modernize their remaining short-range nuclear weapons in Europe and when they should negotiate with the Soviets on these systems, if they should do so at all. The struggle over short-range nuclear forces was not just about the continuation of NATO's nuclear deterrent but also about the Federal Republic of Germany's place within the alliance. In the summer of 1989, policymakers in Washington, London, and beyond worried more and more about a resurgent and increasingly assertive Bonn, willing to challenge even the most fundamental elements of their alliance. Before 1989 was through, even the unthinkable seemed possible: the reunification of Germany's two halves. As Germans looked to the future, Margaret Thatcher looked to the past. In one exchange with Helmut Kohl, she allegedly dug into her trusty handbag to pull out a map of Europe, hand-colored to identify all the territories that had fallen victim to German aggression during the Second World War. "We have beaten the Germans twice," she fumed. "Now they're back."[9]

CHAPTER 10

The Empty Chair

Paul Nitze prepared three sets of speaking notes for the negotiating session on November 23, 1983, the day after the Bundestag's final vote. Per protocol, his Soviet counterpart, Yuli Kvitsinksy, would open the session. Depending on what Kvitsinksy said, Nitze wanted to be ready. The US side drafted talking points for various contingencies, whether the Soviet negotiators planned to remain at the negotiating table, set out conditions designed to force the United States to break off their exchanges, or call off the talks immediately.[1]

Kvitsinsky's opener left little room for maneuver. The head of the Soviet delegation declared that, as the strategic situation was now changing rapidly, the current round of talks was over. The Soviets would not set a date for negotiations to resume. Nitze responded accordingly and on script. Laying blame for the talk's collapse with the Soviet Union, he affirmed the United States' continued commitment to negotiate. The two delegations stood up, shook hands, and walked out of the session. The INF talks were over.[2]

The next day, Yuri Andropov released a blistering statement that hardened the Soviet position further. "The United States has torpedoed the possibility of reaching a mutually acceptable accord at the talks on questions of limiting nuclear arms in Europe," the general secretary declared. The Soviet Union could no longer participate in the negotiations—and would not return to the talks until the United States withdrew the missiles being installed in Europe.[3]

Andropov's statement adhered to the script laid out by the Soviet Union in the months prior. Commentators described the outcome as the predictable end to the sweeping political drama that was 1983.[4] Even with this air of inevitability, the international situation seemed increasingly uncertain, given the apparent absence of leadership within the Soviet Union. Andropov had not been spotted in public for ninety-eight days, leading Western diplomats and press outlets alike to speculate about who was calling the shots in the Kremlin.[5]

Throughout 1984, the Western allies tried to create conditions that would bring the Soviet Union back to the bargaining table. But for the time being, the Kremlin's chair remained empty. So long as the Soviets remained absent from the negotiations, NATO's governments invested their energies in attempts to reinvigorate East-West dialogue—and to shore up the alliance's image, returning to familiar formulas to do so. As in the late 1960s, when they had faced skepticism regarding their continued relevance in a changing international landscape, the Western allies championed defense and détente as the pillars of their strategy.

Success and Failure

The arrival of US missiles in Western Europe was a source of disappointment for many who had mobilized to stop the bomb. Leading figures like Petra Kelly publicly acknowledged a sense of "exhaustion" alongside the dissatisfaction that, despite their best efforts, antinuclear groups had failed to derail the Dual-Track Decision.[6]

Once unified by a common enemy, the various groups and campaigns that had opposed the Euromissiles splintered after the autumn of 1983. Some opponents lost interest in the cause entirely. The number that turned out for demonstrations in 1984, for instance, paled in comparison to the figures from 1983, let alone to the surge of opposition seen in the autumn of 1981. Organizers in the Federal Republic of Germany concluded that some seventy thousand of their countrymen had shown up at the 1984 Easter rallies. Police estimates pegged the total at a fraction of that, somewhere between fifteen thousand and eighteen thousand.[7] Press coverage suggested much higher figures, with the *Washington Post* reporting that organizers boasted of three hundred thousand at one October 1984 demonstration to build a human chain, though the same basic pattern held. According to local police, the number was about half that.[8] Only the highest of these figures matched the scale seen earlier in the decade.

Those activists who stayed the course often poured their energies into other causes. For some, these priorities remained closely linked to the Euromissiles, such as widespread campaigns to interrupt NATO's military maneuvers in the Fulda Gap. But others followed the interests that had brought them to the Euromissiles in the first place, such as feminism, antimilitarism, or ecological concerns.

Campaigns did continue to focus on the missiles arriving in Europe. A human chain organized in October 1984, for instance, stretched from Hasselbach (a planned cruise missile depot in the Federal Republic) up to Duisberg, nearly 130 miles away.[9] The next spring, over Easter weekend, tens of thousands gathered at missile sites in the United Kingdom, Italy, and the Federal Republic. Protestors at Mutlangen, a Pershing II base not far from Stuttgart, encircled the facility. At the Sicilian outpost of Comiso, a handful of protestors scaled the base's fence, hoping to deliver an Easter cake to the installation's commander.[10] Peace groups also spoke out against the Soviet Union's response to the Dual-Track Decision deployments: the introduction of new nuclear weaponry across Eastern Europe. CND organizers, for instance, launched Operation Christmas Card, a campaign to raise awareness about the Soviets' deployments by sending letters to counterparts in the East. "As well as making a protest," the operation's backers argued, "we hope to open up a dialogue between the British peace movement and ordinary citizens and officials in Eastern Europe."[11] Transcending the Iron Curtain remained a critical dimension of many activists' thinking about how they could break down the barriers of the Cold War, moving beyond what their elected representatives seemed willing to do.

In the basing countries in particular, campaigns and dedicated actions changed course to focus on the missiles already there. CND latched onto the fact that the Gryphons, mounted on road vehicles, left their bases as part of regular exercises. Organizers jumped at the opportunities afforded by this travel and established a network of protestors they named Cruise Watch. A neighborhood watch–type group for cruise missiles, the program was designed to turn out opposition whenever the missiles left their home and greet the missiles with paint and other small obstructions. "It was tough," the deputy commander responsible for the ground-launched cruise missile wing's logistics at Greenham Common later recalled. "We had to 'protestor proof' the vehicles."[12] Tracking the weapons, the program's architects argued, represented yet another means to take back power at the grassroots level. State power relied on secrecy, and so transparency could be "somewhat disarming."[13]

FIGURE 10.1. Graffiti tags at RAF Greenham Common, April 1986. Source: Patrick Nugent/ National Archives and Records Administration (NARA identifier no. 6413550), https://catalog. archives.gov/id/6413550.

Though actions continued to target the Euromissiles, the political power of these demonstrations waned. Press coverage regularly described a peace movement disenchanted and disaffected. Even when organizers did manage to turn out respectable crowds, these were cast as efforts to breathe new life into the movement and return to the heyday of the decade's earlier years. Paul Nitze later marveled at just how quickly "the steam seemed to go out of the German and British movements."[14]

Activists concluded that, paradoxically, they had been too successful. Because they had changed the nature of the conversation about security, their own campaigns no longer seemed so urgent. "The peace movement has been told for the last several months that they have in fact failed very much," Petra Kelly remarked to one interviewer in late 1986. "I don't think we have failed. I think that the consciousness-raising in the public was done by the peace movement, was done by the Greenham Common women, by the people in [Mutlangen], by the people in Hassel, it was done by them, the people in Comiso."[15]

Talks about Talks

After the Soviet Union walked out of the arms control talks in Geneva in late 1983, the Western allies responded by affirming their commitment to negotiations. The Reagan White House underscored its willingness to resume talks "at any table anywhere in the world."[16] Month in and month out, NATO's Special Consultative Group, the body dedicated to allied consultations on arms control, repeated this mantra.[17] It published an interim progress report providing audiences with a comprehensive overview of the negotiations to date, clocking in at just over forty pages. Since NATO's December 1979 decision, the report argued, the Soviet Union had failed to put forward any meaningful proposals that addressed the allies' minimum security needs "while compiling an unbroken string of rejections" of US offers.[18] Even though negotiations were not under way, the Special Consultative Group continued to meet regularly, implicitly underscoring that same message. The Soviets might not be willing to talk arms control, but the Western allies were—and would do so among themselves until the Kremlin was ready.

Even before the deployments began, a growing swath of Western leaders had conceded that their current approach to East-West relations needed to be revised. "The West has been staggering from decision to decision without an overall concept," Margaret Thatcher lamented in the summer of 1983.[19] Pierre Trudeau's peace mission started from that same premise. Without meaningful dialogue between East and West, the Canadian prime minister believed, they could blindly stumble into a nuclear conflagration.[20]

Trudeau's efforts to reinvigorate the dialogue had come at an inopportune time in the eyes of his fellow leaders, as he had launched the peace mission before the final parliamentary votes on deployment, rather than waiting until after the missiles had begun arriving in Europe. But now that the deployments were under way, Trudeau's counterparts flocked to the Canadian's cause. Helmut Kohl's government spearheaded a campaign to emphasize the alliance's desire to improve relations between East and West. Before NATO's foreign ministers met in Brussels in December, the West Germans pressed for the meeting to illustrate the allies' commitment to dialogue. Writing to Reagan in early December, Kohl insisted that they should make the most of the meeting to "set the necessary political accents" for their policies in the months ahead. Kohl pointed to three major areas of concern: arms control and East-West relations, consultations among the Western allies, and questions of overall strategy.[21]

The December meeting's final product, dubbed the Declaration of Brussels, pledged that the United States remained ready to negotiate on intermediate-range nuclear forces at any point. "The deployment of US missiles can be halted or reversed by concrete results at the negotiating table," the communiqué affirmed. "In this spirit we wish to see an early resumption of the INF negotiations which the Soviet Union has discontinued."[22]

The Soviet line remained consistent. The parliamentary votes to approve the deployments had undercut the basis for negotiations. If the Gryphons and Pershing IIs were arriving at bases across Western Europe, Soviet negotiators would not return to talk arms control. The United States and the Soviet Union could resume negotiations if—and only if—the missiles already deployed were removed.[23] Needless to say, the Kremlin's threats applied only to the United States' new missiles, not the Soviets' own.

The Kremlin's refusal to hold talks on nuclear weapons seemed out of step with other elements of the Soviet position on East-West dialogue. The decade-old talks on mutual and balanced force reductions continued to take place, as did new rounds of negotiations on confidence-building measures, chemical weapons, and upgrading the communications between the United States and the Soviet Union. The Special Consultative Group's chair, Richard Burt, made sure to tout these inconsistencies in his regular press releases. There was, as his February statement put it, "no reason why the Soviet Union should not agree to resume negotiations on nuclear forces."[24]

Yuri Andropov's death in February 1984 created a glimmer of hope that the Soviet position might soften up. Perhaps the change in leadership would crack open a "window of opportunity" in which to restart the INF talks.[25] Konstantin Chernenko, Andropov's already ailing successor, dashed those hopes. Under Chernenko, the same preconditions remained. Through the spring and summer of 1984, as Soviet officials charged that the Western allies had destroyed the basis for talks, they followed through on earlier threats to introduce new missiles of their own in Eastern Europe, above and beyond the SS-20s: shorter-range SS-21s and SS-22s. "The Soviet nuclear build-up," the Nuclear Planning Group warned, "continues unabated at all levels."[26]

The Soviet Union's refusal to negotiate also came under fire from within the Warsaw Pact. The Romanian leader Nicolae Ceaușescu, a perennial thorn in Moscow's side, publicly opposed the installation of new Soviet missiles in Czechoslovakia and the German Democratic Republic.[27] Ceaușescu's Hungarian counterpart, Janos Kádár, urged the small and medium states of Europe to come together to "limit the damage" in East-West relations.[28] Even the German Democratic Republic pushed back against the seeming deep freeze in East-West relations. The country may have hosted new Soviet nuclear weapons, but Erich Honecker also touted East Berlin's "coalition of reason" with the Federal Republic and accepted another massive loan from the Kohl government, this time to the tune of DM950 million.[29] Economic realities trumped the bonds of socialism.

Financial ties could insulate relations between Bonn and East Berlin, protecting them from the broader downturns in East-West relations. Yet, the continued connections between the two Germanys were greeted with skepticism and a degree of trepidation in both alliances. On the eve of Hans-Dietrich Genscher's May 1984 visit to Moscow, the Soviet Union launched a vigorous campaign attacking the Federal Republic's "revanchism" in what *Pravda* deemed "a process of almost open rehabilitation of Nazism."[30] (Contemporaries deduced that this was an oblique attack on Honecker's German Democratic Republic, using the government in Bonn as a scapegoat to criticize East Berlin's recent attempts to exert a degree of foreign policy independence.)[31] Italy's foreign minister, Giulio Andreotti, all but endorsed this point of view. "Everybody agrees that the two Germanys should have good relations," he remarked to one Roman crowd in the fall of 1984, but "there are two German states and two German states must remain."[32]

Favorable Trends and Shifting Attitudes

Even in Washington, there were signs of an administration now willing to openly engage the Soviet Union. On January 16, 1984, Ronald Reagan delivered a dramatic public address in which he affirmed his desire to build a more constructive relationship with his counterpart in the Kremlin. In a memorable closing, the president asked his audience to imagine two couples in a chance meeting, one Soviet and one American. What would the four discuss? Would they argue about the differences between capitalism and communism? Or would they talk about their lives, professions, and families? To Reagan, the answer seemed obvious. His hypothetical quartet, Jim and Sally, Ivan and Anya, would talk not of ideology, but of their shared humanity.[33]

"I have openly expressed my view of the Soviet system," Reagan admitted in that same speech. "I don't know why this could come as a surprise to Soviet leaders who've never shied away from expressing their view of our system." But Reagan was adamant that none of this rhetoric, however heated, should prevent the United States and the Soviet Union from entering into a serious dialogue; it was imperative that the two powers do so, given the immense dangers of a world with nuclear weapons.[34]

Reagan's January 16 speech marked the end of a yearlong effort to recalibrate the administration's policy toward the Soviet Union. It was not, as some cynics suggested, merely a public relations move geared toward the president's bid for reelection later that year.[35] Nor was it a sudden reversal on the part of the president, spurred by viewing the made-for-TV movie *The Day After*, or by NATO's November 1983 exercise, Able Archer.[36] If anything, these events encouraged him to double down on his existing strategy. "It's very effective and left me greatly depressed," he confided in his diary after a White House screening of *The Day After*. "My own reaction: we have to do all we can to have a deterrent and to see there is never a nuclear war."[37]

Since the beginning of 1983, Reagan and key foreign policy advisers, including George Shultz, William Clark, and George Bush, had been developing a strategy to ramp up their direct dialogue with the Soviet Union. Shultz spearheaded much of that effort, lobbying for an "intensified dialogue" with the Kremlin as a way to take the temperature in Moscow.[38] Clark recommended that these overtures take place in private, worried that if they went public, it would merely whet the public appetite for concessions and hand the Soviets another lever with which to ratchet up pressure on the Americans.[39] But Shultz's line found critical backers within the president's inner circle. Nancy Reagan wholeheartedly endorsed the secretary of state's position, eager to see her husband dial down his inflammatory rhetoric.[40]

As 1983 came to a close, Reagan's advisers thought it time for a public address designed to dispel popular misconceptions about the tenor and thrust of the administration's Soviet policy. Jack Matlock, who had joined the National Security Council in the autumn of 1983, envisioned a speech that would serve as "a basic document for both our public and private diplomacy." Matlock insisted there was no need to announce new initiatives. Should the president do so, these proposals would likely backfire, making it even easier for observers, whether in Moscow or any other foreign capital, to dismiss the entire speech as a mere public relations stunt.[41]

Behind the scenes, the Reagan administration continued earlier efforts to open additional channels of dialogue with Andropov's Soviet Union. "We're trying to engage them in some dialogue right now," Reagan informed his former publicist, Barney Oldfield, in early 1984. "If he asks about me," the president requested, referring to Oldfield's regular correspondent, the influential Soviet academician Georgy Arbatov, "tell him I don't eat my young."[42]

What underwrote these efforts was a growing sense of confidence about the United States' position in the world; NATO's deployments catalyzed that new sense of confidence. "The United States was in its strongest position in two decades to negotiating with the Russians from strength," Reagan later wrote. The economy was booming, and the feelings of weakness that permeated the late 1970s were cast off. "In spirit and military strength," Reagan argued, "America was back."[43]

But, despite this push to intensify the superpowers' dialogue, the president still moved with a degree of caution. When Andropov died in February 1984, Reagan elected not to attend the general secretary's funeral, instead sending the vice president in his stead (again).[44] The funeral provided a rare opportunity for low-cost, high-level dialogue between East and West. Andropov's successor, the seventy-two-year-old Konstantin Chernenko, held one-on-one talks with Bush, as well as with Thatcher, Kohl, Trudeau, and Italy's Sandro Pertini.

Thatcher's presence at the funeral belied a shift in her own policy toward the Soviet Union. Her trip to Moscow was only her second voyage east of the Iron Curtain since becoming prime minister in the spring of 1979—and the first had taken place mere days earlier, when she made a state visit to Hungary. These two trips were not, as Thatcher took great pains to clarify, a "sudden, unexpected development," but rather a concerted effort on the part of her government to improve relations with the Warsaw Pact's members.[45]

The evolution of Thatcher's thinking followed a similar trajectory to that of Ronald Reagan. The previous autumn, in September 1983, she had convened a team of Soviet specialists at the prime minister's country residence, Chequers, to discuss the government's handling of foreign policy, including its approach to East-West relations.[46] Much of the meeting revolved around whether British policy should seek "the gradual evolution of the Soviet system towards a more pluralistic political and economic system." (That formulation was cribbed from George Shultz.) The prospects for meaningful change in the Soviet Union were deemed slim, but the discussions roundly endorsed the need to build up high-level dialogue with the Kremlin. Thatcher resolved to do so.[47] The government would do this quietly, with no public announcement that such a shift was under way. Instead, in the prime minister's public appearances, she increasingly referred to the need for greater dialogue with the East—provided that the West remained strong and unified.[48]

These shifts in Anglo-American tactics brought a degree of unity to the Atlantic alliance's approach. No longer divided as to whether the time was right to engage the Soviet Union in dialogue at the highest levels—a source of considerable acrimony in the preceding years—top-ranking officials from across the alliance now descended on Moscow in rapid succession throughout the spring and summer of 1984.[49] Calls for expanded dialogue found no shortage of vocal backers. The already outspoken Greek prime minister, Andreas Papandreou, banded together with leaders from five other nations to build global momentum behind arms control under the auspices of the Five Continent Initiative for Peace and Disarmament.[50]

"A Successful Alliance for Peace"

As individual allied governments rushed to demonstrate their commitment to dialogue, so too did the formal structures of the Atlantic alliance. The Declaration of Brussels had urged the Warsaw Pact's members to take up the opportunities presented by NATO's policies for "a balanced and constructive relationship and for genuine détente."[51] At that same session of the North Atlantic Council in December 1983, the Western allies also backed a proposal from Belgium's foreign minister, Léo Tindemans, to complete a new study of East-West relations on the model of the earlier Harmel Report.

The drafting process was far from smooth. Delegations argued over how much the study should dwell on the problems of the past and who should bear the blame for the deterioration of East-West relations that had marked the last decade. Whereas the Americans tended to press for a hard-nosed appraisal of the Soviet Union's behavior, the West Germans urged the allies to adopt a more balanced outlook that acknowledged the benefits, as well as the drawbacks, of the alliance's pursuit of détente since 1967. Missteps were not an indication that détente was the incorrect policy. Instead, the West German permanent representative, Hans-Georg Wieck, urged colleagues to see the policy's shortcomings as a sign that "insufficient attention had been paid to the needs of defence" during the 1970s.[52]

The final product was a strong endorsement of the status quo. The Washington Statement on East-West Relations, unveiled at the North Atlantic Council in May 1984, reiterated the parallel formula laid out in the Harmel Report; the Western allies' efforts should continue to be guided by the preservation of their defenses and the corresponding pursuit of détente with the East. Over the long term, only military strength and allied solidarity would make it possible to forge a new relationship with the Warsaw Pact.[53] "The lesson to be drawn from what has been termed détente, and also from the renewed tension of recent years," one of the Belgian representatives, Alfred Cahen, argued, "seems to be that our policy of dialogue, negotiations, and bridge-building with the East is basically the right one and serves our interests." But the success of that policy required "acute vigilance in the preservation of the military balance," along with continued allied resolve to check the Soviet Union's expansionism.[54]

Alongside these efforts, the Western allies tried to make a broader case for their continued partnership. The March 1984 issue of the *NATO Review*, adorned with a glossy hot pink and lemon yellow cover that fit the trends of the 1980s, was emblazoned with a massive slogan: "A Successful Alliance for Peace."[55] In its less visually arresting pages, the lead article, penned by Michael Heseltine, touted an agenda for 1984 that opened by asserting, "A common strategy for European defence depends upon a partnership between North America and Western Europe."[56]

Heseltine's case was a direct rebuttal of the arguments put forward by activists and opponents in recent years. "The Atlantic Alliance is not based on one-sided American idealism and self-sacrifice," he wrote, "nor is it—as a vocal but wholly unrepresentative fringe presents it—one based on power and domination."[57] It remained a partnership that united Western Europeans and North Americans in a common mission.

As the Western allies made this case, proposals abounded for the greater Europeanization of the alliance. "Practically everyone now seems to favor a larger role for West European nations within NATO," one article blared in the autumn of 1984.[58] Governments in Western Europe turned to old institutions like the Western European Union.[59] Seeking to reinvigorate the body, foreign and defense ministers gathered to mark the organization's thirtieth anniversary in October 1984.[60] Intelligence analysts in the United States credited the renewed interest to a growing European desire to develop a more independent role within NATO's security policy, in response to the brouhaha over INF.[61]

Henry Kissinger took to the pages of *Time* to call for a fundamental shift in the balance of power within the transatlantic partnership. Diagnosing "unprecedented and unsettling" divisions between the allies, a state of affairs Kissinger blamed on "neutralists, pacifists, and neo-isolationists," the former secretary of state urged the allies to restructure their existing arrangements. Kissinger's suggestions included shifting more of the burden for conventional defense to the Europeans, including the threat of massive US troop withdrawals to encourage an agreement, and appointing a European as supreme allied commander (a post reserved for Americans).[62] Senator Sam Nunn, working on much the same logic, introduced a resolution to cut the number of US forces in June 1984. The Nunn Amendment was not an attempt to slash the commitment to Europe, but an ultimatum to secure greater European contributions to allied defense.[63] In the United States, NATO's boosters worried about a sharp uptick in press stories about how little the European allies contributed to US foreign policy goals.[64] The fact that final deployment decisions were still outstanding in two of the five prospective basing countries, Belgium and the Netherlands, provided ample fodder for a segment of US neoconservatives fed up with "pacifistic 'Eurowimps' hopelessly addicted to welfare-state socialism."[65]

Dutch Delays

After announcing that the missiles would be stationed at Woensdrecht in June 1983, the Dutch government confirmed that no further decisions would be taken until a new white paper on defense appeared later that year. When it appeared in October, the document included a curious omission. All of the sections related to the country's nuclear role were absent, with publication delayed until the beginning of 1984.

Throughout the spring of 1984, the Dutch tried to engineer a compromise that would make it possible to adopt a final decision after years of delay. Familiar divisions remained. The Labour Party, now in opposition, threatened to reverse any support for the deployments if reelected. The Christian Democratic Appeal, the largest of the ruling coalition's partners, was itself internally fractured on the matter. And with the deployments still an open question, the pressures that deflated and divided activists elsewhere in the alliance mattered little in the Netherlands. IKV's activities continued to attract large crowds, and polling suggested a broad base of opposition to the Gryphons. According to one March 1984 poll, 63 percent of Dutch citizens objected to the deployment of cruise missiles in their country.[66]

What Ruud Lubbers's government adopted in June 1984 was a dual-track decision of its own.[67] The Dutch tried to leverage their plans to deploy to secure a degree of Soviet restraint that might render the deployments unnecessary. To that end, the Lubbers coalition developed a decision tree of options based on the state of affairs in November 1985. If, by that point, the United States and the Soviet Union had reached an agreement to limit intermediate-range nuclear forces, the Dutch vowed to deploy their share of what weapons would remain in Europe under the terms of that deal. If the superpowers failed to reach an agreement, Soviet unilateral restraint could prevent the deployments; the Dutch government pledged that it would not accept the Gryphons provided the total number of Soviet SS-20s remained static. But if by November 1985 the Soviet Union had fielded more than 378 SS-20s (the deployment figure as of June 1984), then the Dutch would go ahead and accept the Gryphons.[68] This complex and convoluted agreement was an appeal to the Soviet Union to back its peaceful professions with deeds. Lubbers made as much clear. "Today's decision," he announced, "is primarily an invitation to the Soviet Union to put a radical stop to the deployment of SS-20 missiles."[69]

Lubbers effectively outsourced The Hague's hard choices. By basing the outcome on progress in the superpowers' talks and the Soviet Union's deployments, Lubbers sidestepped the fraught debate still unfolding within Dutch society about the role that nuclear weapons should play in defense policy. The terms of the June agreement made the final choice to go ahead with the deployments, scheduled for November 1985, dependent on the behavior and policies of others, not those of the Dutch government.[70] After two days of heated parliamentary debate, the cabinet's formula received sufficient support to remain standing policy, by a margin of seventy-nine to seventy-one.

Back for Another Round?

In late June 1984, the Soviet Union proposed a new set of arms control talks dedicated to the "militarization of outer space."[71] The proposed negotiations aimed at stopping the Strategic Defense Initiative, the ballistic missile defense program first unveiled by Reagan in early 1983. Star Wars, as the program came to be known, preoccupied the Soviets, and increasingly, the Kremlin's leaders seemed desperate to stop it.

Reagan's team pounced on the Soviet offer. The Senior Arms Control Policy Group, known to most US insiders as the Sackpig, had but one condition; any negotiations on space should take place alongside resumed talks on offensive nuclear weapons, both strategic and intermediate-range forces. Gromyko refused. The Soviets did not know how "to take yes for an answer," Geoffrey Howe, the British foreign secretary, quipped.[72] The Kremlin leadership had put its reputation on the line to stop the Dual-Track Decision and had failed to see that policy through. Soviet stonewalling seemed an attempt, however misguided, to preserve some semblance of prestige.

As summer stretched on, it seemed unlikely the Soviets could sustain this intransigent position for much longer. A growing body of evidence suggested that Gromyko's critics at home were gaining power. "If we play our cards right we may be able to achieve a breakthrough," Matlock advised in early July. The Soviets' recent arms control proposal—and the Americans' quick response—had given the White House "a very strong tactical position."[73]

To bring Moscow back to the negotiating table, the Reagan administration looked for ways to make a return more palatable. The United States "might need to forge some kind of face-saving device," Reagan remarked to Canadian prime minister Brian Mulroney in September.[74] What the administration had in mind was an umbrella concept that would bring together offensive weapons and outer space in one set of omnibus talks. This umbrella approach could address areas of critical Soviet concern. The prospect of merging the superpowers' talks on strategic and intermediate-range nuclear forces had long been floated. When the Soviets walked out of the talks, press reports indicated that, if and when Moscow returned to negotiations, they would likely be in a new forum that merged the two.[75] The US concept was not an outright merger—each issue would remain distinct underneath the umbrella—but it could leverage Soviet concerns about the Strategic Defense Initiative to get the Kremlin's negotiators to come back to Geneva.

Reagan went further after his landslide reelection in November 1984, eager to spend that political capital. But Shultz was adamant that, to achieve any breakthroughs, change needed to start in Washington. Much of the president's existing team did not share the president's outlook on arms control—the director of the Arms Control and Disarmament Agency, Kenneth Adelman, had just lauded the possibilities of "arms control without agreements" in a *Foreign Affairs* article—and Shultz was fed up.[76] The only way he could turn the president's vision into policy was with a competent team. "I'm frustrated and I'm ready to step aside," Shultz told the president.[77] Reagan sided with Shultz. The president dispatched a letter to Chernenko that suggested broader umbrella talks on nuclear weapons and outer space. Chernenko accepted and proposed that Shultz and Gromyko meet in early January to work out the details.[78] On November 22, the United States and the Soviet Union publicly announced that arms control negotiations would resume.[79]

Arms control topped the agenda when Shultz and Gromyko met in January 1985. Opening the meeting, the Soviet foreign minister offered a comprehensive presentation on the need for it. "If we do not find ways to halt the arms race," he stressed to Shultz, "it will be impossible to correct our relationship." But Gromyko was adamant that individual arms control issues could not be separated from one another and addressed in isolation. In other words, neither strategic arms reductions nor limits to intermediate-range forces could be considered distinct from what Gromyko described as "the problem of preventing the militarization of space."[80] These three components needed to be resolved as part of a single package.

Shultz recommended an alternate label for the third element of the talks: defensive nuclear arms. Gromyko balked. "If your position is that space research programs are to be continued and sometime later can be discussed," the Soviet foreign minister warned, "then this is not acceptable." He reaffirmed the basic Soviet position that the space component of any talks must focus on stopping the militarization of outer space, speculating that the two sides were on a collision course over ballistic missile defense and the Strategic Defense Initiative. "Since all three fora are interrelated," he reminded Shultz, "if the third bursts like a soap bubble, the other two would go down with it."[81]

At Geneva, Shultz secured an agreement from Gromyko that US-Soviet negotiations would resume under this new umbrella framework. Gromyko bristled at Shultz's suggested order for the talks' components, in which the secretary of state had space listed last. The United States, he charged, was "relegating space to the backyard." Shultz instead likened it to baseball. Space would bat clean-up.[82] These new omnibus negotiations were dubbed the Nuclear and Space Talks. Not only had the Soviets agreed to resume negotiations, walking back the objections they had used to stymie talks throughout 1984, but they had also acknowledged a clear link between offensive and defensive systems. For the first time in over a decade, the superpowers' arms control talks would address both.[83]

A package approach came with its own risks. The Italian Foreign Ministry warned that the Soviet Union could easily exploit the umbrella approach to secure points in the court of public opinion. Singling out the contentious Strategic Defense Initiative as an example, Italian analysts concluded that the Soviets could easily insist on the need for negotiations on the research and development of defensive systems as a precondition to serious discussion of other topics like intermediate-range nuclear forces. When, invariably, minimal progress was made, Soviet leaders could pin the blame on the United States and its intransigent attitude.[84] The structure ultimately adopted was a hybrid; the two sides agreed that each delegation would include three autonomous negotiating squads. One would be dedicated to INF, another to strategic forces (still referred to as START), and the third to defense and space. Ambassador Max Kampelman took over as head of the US delegation and as the chief negotiator for defense and space issues. Maynard Glitman became the lead on intermediate-range forces. At Geneva on March 11, 1985, US and Soviet negotiators resumed talks to limit nuclear weapons.

A Belgian Commitment

Just days after the Nuclear and Space Talks opened, the Belgian government agreed to host its share of the cruise missiles. That commitment took time to secure. As early as October 1983, Belgium's prime minister, still the Flemish Christian Democrat Wilfried Martens, had indicated that his government would adhere to NATO's December 1979 decision, even if it meant the collapse of his latest coalition.

Martens indicated that the final decision lay with the government, not with parliament. "Any deployment decision," he argued, "will be communication by the government to parliament, where it will be put to a vote of confidence." Should parliament reject the government's position, his coalition would resign. But this would do nothing to change the country's position on the Gryphons. Martens maintained that it would stand even if the government fell.[85] Parliament debated the procedure in late 1983, but a bill demanding parliamentary approval of the deployments failed, as did another resolution calling for the complete denuclearization of Belgium.[86] Before 1983 was through, the Martens government announced that the deployments would go ahead as scheduled unless the superpowers reached a negotiated settlement in Geneva.

Despite these affirmations, Belgium's allies worried that the government might try to escape its commitments. Martens seemed to be searching for a new compromise in early 1985, perhaps even seeking the postponement of the first deployments into 1986.[87] (NATO's plans called for the deployments to begin in March 1985.) Michael Heseltine and Manfred Wörner contemplated a "concerted private approach" to the Belgian government by the other basing countries to express their dismay.[88] With the Dutch decision postponed until November 1985, another delay would undercut the United States' position at the negotiating table. "Two out of five countries hesitating doesn't look too good," one anonymous NATO official quipped to reporters, "except to the Soviets."[89] Privately, Belgian diplomats assured their allies that the government would deploy, but nothing was guaranteed. "Belgium is unpredictable," one official in Brussels observed to a Canadian counterpart.[90]

Strong pockets of antinuclear sentiment could be found across Belgium. The town of Florennes, the home of the air base where the cruise missiles would be deployed, declared itself to be a nuclear-free zone. So did over three hundred other towns and cities across the country. But the fragility of the Belgian position stemmed more from the country's own fractious politics, particularly the linguistic divide between its Flemish and Francophone communities, than from the politics of the bomb. Those fault lines meant that Belgian elites were often pulled in two opposing directions. Whereas the Flemish might look to the Netherlands for inspiration, Francophones naturally looked to France, where antinuclear activism remained minimal and policymakers expressed staunch support for NATO's deployments and the dogma of deterrence.

After months of hesitation and years of delay, on March 15, 1985, the Belgian cabinet agreed to accept the forty-eight Gryphons initially called for in the Dual-Track Decision. The first set of sixteen arrived at Florennes just weeks later. Of the initial five basing countries, only the Netherlands remained an open question. "And even if the Netherlands never accepts its quota," one US journalist concluded, "the damage to NATO won't be all that great."[91]

Throughout 1984, the Western allies stuck with their tried-and-true two-track diplomacy. Following the Soviet walkout at the end of 1983, NATO's members affirmed their continued commitment to dialogue with the Warsaw Pact to forge what allied representatives now routinely referred to as a "genuine détente"—distinguishing it from the détente of the 1970s which, it now seemed clear, the Soviets had exploited to get ahead.

The West appeared ascendant. A newfound sense of confidence underwrote the allies' outreach to the East. NATO's deployments had restored a degree of balance to the situation in Europe. Even more important was the psychological boost the Dual-Track Decision's initial deployments brought. "The turning point in the Cold War came when we deployed Pershing missiles in Germany and that let [the Soviet Union] say that we were serious," George Shultz later argued.[92] Optimism prevailed, even as domestic political debates raged in the Netherlands and Belgium over whether to refuse the cruise.

The empty chair did not remain so for long. The rigid objections that had marked the Soviet position in the spring and summer of 1984 faded. Moscow's position was simply untenable. Before year's end, the Reagan administration had succeeded in bringing the Soviet Union back to the negotiating table, making the most of the Kremlin's fears of the Strategic Defense Initiative. The arms control circus was headed back to Geneva.

CHAPTER 11

Who's Afraid of Gorbachev?

In February 1984, NATO's leaders descended on Moscow for a funeral. The funeral was Konstantin Chernenko's putative coming-out party as leader of the Soviet Union. Even so, Chernenko could barely carry on a coherent conversation. The seventy-two-year-old struggled through a long, prepared statement in his tête-à-tête with Pierre Trudeau, "unable to respond spontaneously" to any of the Canadian prime minister's comments.[1] Margaret Thatcher, after seeing Chernenko on television during the proceedings, quipped to her entourage that they might as well stay in Moscow for the next funeral—his.[2]

Before dawn on March 11, 1985, just days before the Nuclear and Space Talks opened in Geneva, Ronald Reagan woke to the news that Chernenko was dead.[3] Chernenko had lasted a mere thirteen months in power. For the third time in as many years, the Soviet Union got a new general secretary. "Chernenko has received the standard tributes and honours," one British diplomat cabled from the embassy in Moscow, "but obsequies have been so telescoped as to produce the impression he is being disposed of in some hurry and with little regret."[4]

The man who took the Kremlin's top post next was a significant departure from his immediate predecessors. Mikhail Gorbachev was sharp, articulate, and confident, traits that quickly made him seem dangerous in Western eyes. He was "bound to be more active and more formidable than his predecessors," one US assessment concluded, mere weeks after Chernenko's death.[5] The arms control proposals he put forward at breakneck pace in the months and years that followed confirmed that early assessment, often leaving the Western allies reeling, scrambling to make their own case in the court of public opinion.

In Gorbachev, the Western allies found a Soviet leader increasingly willing to talk arms control. But as Reagan and Gorbachev worked toward the reduction of nuclear weapons, the terms on which the two superpowers seemed willing to do so sent shockwaves through the Atlantic alliance. After the superpowers' summit at Reykjavik in October 1986, it appeared the president might be willing to embrace radical cuts to the West's nuclear arsenal, so much so that it could unravel the alliance's defenses.

The Reykjavik Summit also suggested that it might be possible to sign a treaty governing intermediate-range nuclear forces. That slipped away when the rest of the superpowers' potential deal collapsed, but the episode confirmed suspicions that INF would be the easiest place for the two sides to forge an agreement. What made that possible was a shift in Gorbachev's position.[6] In February 1987, he untied the Soviets' existing arms control package and indicated that he would be willing to sign a separate deal on INF. Soviet objections to the Strategic Defense Initiative would no longer block the path to an agreement. Over the rest of 1987, the United States and the Soviet Union hammered out the final details of an agreement and, at the Washington Summit in December, Reagan and Gorbachev signed the INF Treaty.

That agreement embraced the position championed by Reagan six years earlier, based on the global elimination of intermediate-range weapons. The United States and the Soviet Union agreed to a historic deal, the first to eliminate a whole class of nuclear weapons.

A New Man in Moscow

Chernenko's successor was a far younger man, the fifty-four-year-old Mikhail Gorbachev. The youngest member of the Politburo by over a decade, Gorbachev had been born to a peasant family in Privolnoye, in southern Russia, in 1931 and began his rise through the Communist Party's ranks under Nikita Khrushchev. After a string of positions in Stavropol, where he met vacationing Politburo members like Leonid Brezhnev and Yuri Andropov, he headed to Moscow in 1978 to take over as agriculture secretary. He became a full member of the Politburo two years later.[7]

Western policymakers had some exposure to Gorbachev already. He traveled to Canada in May 1983 on an official visit as agriculture secretary. The next year, in December 1984, he made a parliamentary visit to the United Kingdom, where British interlocutors found him friendly, relaxed, and willing to exchange in meaningful debate—traits that set him apart from many of his fellow Soviet officials in British eyes. Gorbachev left his British counterparts with the impression that he was "someone with whom they could do business."[8] The French came to the same conclusion after François Mitterrand visited Moscow in June 1984. Gorbachev was candid and charismatic, at one point quipping that his country's pressing agricultural problems had first emerged in 1917.[9]

Gorbachev's appointment to the top of the Soviet Union's government marked a changing of the guard. The first leader to be born after Vladimir Lenin's death, he had a markedly different educational background than many of his predecessors, having attended the prestigious Moscow State University in the 1960s. Despite these departures, initial predictions expected little of substance to change with the Gorbachev foreign policy. At home, he faced a stagnant economy, with little room for maneuver to ameliorate the situation. British analysts, for their part, predicted that foreign policy would remain focused on building a more stable relationship with the United States and seeking to "avert technological developments in the arms race which the Soviet Union could not match or could match only at severe economic cost."[10]

The opening Soviet position in the Nuclear and Space Talks, now under way in Geneva, confirmed these estimates. Soviet negotiators fixated on the Strategic Defense Initiative and the talks quickly settled into a predictable pattern. The Soviet stance on INF looked much like that of 1983. It was, in the words of Richard Burt, "predictable if depressingly familiar."[11] British and French weapons remained a sticking point, with Soviet negotiators adamant that any agreement must account for these third-party systems in some way. Their continued interest in constraining the British and French arsenals came as no surprise, Gromyko had made that expectation clear when he and Shultz met in January.[12]

With the Reagan administration determined to protect its options in space, pockets of the State Department pressed for a more forthcoming position on offensive weapons. When the talks opened, the US position remained the same as the autumn of 1983. In other words, the zero option continued to form the basis of the US position, but negotiators were willing to entertain an agreement "to reach the goal of equal global limits."[13]

Arms control was only one part of a much larger choice facing Reagan in 1985. Should he assume that the new Soviet general secretary would refuse to make any substantive changes to policy and focus his own efforts on managing the alliance and putting forward the Western case in public? Or should the president put out feelers to see if Gorbachev might be willing to change course?[14] Jack Matlock warned that the United States could ill afford to sit back and wait. If it refused to engage the Soviet Union, the administration was almost certain to face immense political pressure at home and abroad, all of which would undermine the president's public diplomacy efforts and his ability to manage the alliance.[15] NATO's exchanges on arms control reinforced Matlock's message. When the Special Consultative Group met in April, the Belgian and Dutch representatives urged the United States to go beyond what it had offered in September 1983. "This flexibility should be made more visible and complete," the West German representative urged.[16]

Richard Burt resisted these calls. The US negotiating position had not received a fair hearing in prior rounds, and the chair of the Special Consultative Group maintained that it was not "inflexible" to return to the talks with the same proposal.[17] After all, Burt reminded his colleagues, the zero option continued to reflect the president's "broader goal of the elimination of nuclear weapons."[18]

But the style and substance of Soviet initiatives seemed calibrated to leverage public opinion, designed to turn voters across the alliance against their governments and NATO's policies.[19] On March 29, Gorbachev released an open letter addressed to a local peace council in Heilbronn, one of the Pershing II deployment sites in the Federal Republic. In it, the Soviet leader decried the United States' propensity to use arms control as a smokescreen to obscure the build-up of weapons. A new threat of war was emanating from German soil, he warned, just as it had forty years earlier.[20] The next week, Gorbachev announced a six-month moratorium on the deployment of Soviet medium-range missiles in Europe. The offer, timed for Easter Sunday, was seen as yet more of the same. Ed Rowny, the chief US negotiator on strategic arms, dismissed it as "nothing more than a warmed-over version of offers the Soviets had made in 1982 and 1983."[21]

Gorbachev kept up the pace. In late July, he unveiled another moratorium, this time on nuclear tests, scheduled to begin on the fortieth anniversary of the Hiroshima bombing on August 6.[22] And when he headed off to Paris in October on his first trip to the West as general secretary, Gorbachev described Soviet objectives in vastly different language than his predecessors. He dropped the popular concept of equal security, speaking instead of the need for "reasonable sufficiency." In the French capital, he appealed to a shared heritage, speaking about a common home in Europe, and raised the possibility of separate negotiations with the British and French on intermediate-range nuclear forces.[23] One French commentator likened the general secretary's appearance in Paris to a "three-stage rocket" zeroed in on the various fault lines within the Atlantic alliance.[24]

The timing of Gorbachev's proposals seemed carefully calibrated to exploit NATO's weaknesses. Some of the Soviet initiatives appeared tailor-made to ratchet up pressure on the Dutch government, for which the deployment of the Gryphons remained an open question. As part of a compromise the previous year, the Lubbers government had agreed that it would not accept the missiles if the total number of Soviet SS-20s did not increase by November 1, 1985. The Soviet total needed to remain below 378.[25] Ruud Lubbers reiterated that condition in a July letter to Gorbachev. But the general secretary countered, affirming that the number of SS-20s facing Europe remained the same as June 1984: 243. During Gorbachev's visit to Paris, just weeks before The Hague's self-imposed deadline, he announced publicly that the Soviet Union had just 243 SS-20s in Europe. It was widely interpreted as "an eleventh-hour attempt" to sway the impending Dutch deployment decision.[26] A Soviet offer that the Dutch foreign minister, Hans van den Broek, could visit Moscow provided the government had not voted to accept the Gryphons was even more transparent. But however obvious, Soviet offers added to political pressure from domestic opponents of hosting nuclear weapons on Dutch soil. A people's petition, spearheaded by the No Cruise Missiles Committee (Komitee Kruisraketten Nee), received three-and-a-quarter million signatures.[27] The day it was delivered to the government, some twenty-five thousand rallied in The Hague. Another hundred thousand marched in a solidarity rally in London.[28]

Gorbachev's gambit failed. Despite public professions to the contrary, the Soviet Union had not dismantled or destroyed its SS-20s and a freeze on the Soviet missiles targeting Europe was not enough. The Dutch position, consistent with the alliance's, ruled out regional limits that would leave the Soviet Union's systems in Asia unchecked. The general secretary's case disintegrated in public when, during his trip to Paris, one Dutch journalist inquired how many SS-20s were deployed in total. Gorbachev, eager to tout the magic figure of 243, insisted that there was not enough time to share the total number deployed in the Soviet Union.[29] On November 1, 1985, the Lubbers government stuck with its earlier position and agreed to deploy the Gryphons. Pundits were quick to declare it a "Pyrrhic victory." The struggle over the deployments had cleft the Dutch political landscape in twain and made it virtually impossible to secure support not just for a nuclear defense but also for improvements to conventional forces.[30] Polling showed a nation divided

FIGURE 11.1. Soliciting signatures for the People's Petition against cruise missiles in the Netherlands, 1985. Source: Rob C. Croes/Anefo/Nationaal Archief (NL-HaNa 933-4046), https://www.nationaalarchief.nl/en/research/photo-collection/ad499746-d0b4-102d-bcf8-003048976d84.

nearly in half, with 50 percent of the population opposed to the deployments and another 40 percent in favor.[31]

Gorbachev's blistering pace rattled Western nerves. The substance of his proposals seemed eerily familiar, made up of sweeping pronouncements on disarmament and one moratorium proposal after another. This style was a hallmark of Soviet diplomacy, designed to seize the moral high ground and drive a wedge into the Atlantic alliance. Gorbachev, it seemed, was cut from the same cloth. "No sign of any new directions," analysts at the Foreign and Commonwealth Office concluded, predicting few improvements in East-West relations in the months ahead.[32] Gorbachev's new foreign minister, Eduard Shevardnadze, tackled skeptics head on. If Gorbachev's initiatives were public relations stunts, the West ought to "try some of [the] same propaganda."[33]

Western observers might have been wary of Gorbachev's familiar proposals, but his style seemed to signal a departure from his geriatric predecessors. Members of the Reagan administration still discerned some of "the blunt, sometimes browbeating style" of the past, but Gorbachev's flair and instincts increasingly set him apart.[34] Gorbachev's move against Gromyko, Matlock argued, was a prime illustration of his political savvy. By elevating the long-time Soviet foreign minister to an even higher post, as chair of the presidium of the Supreme Soviet, Gorbachev secured "the real power lever" over foreign policy for himself and, in Eduard Shevardnadze, a tough-minded partner who shared his "flair for PR."[35] Shevardnadze all but confirmed that assessment in a late July meeting with Shultz. As the two men wrapped up their discussion, the new foreign minister turned to his staff, asking, "Okay, fellows, how did I do? How many bloopers did you count?"[36] Gorbachev's appearances alongside his charming wife, Raisa, likewise broke the Soviet mold.[37] "It is a whole new ball game," one anonymous US official told the New York Times. "He is casting himself as the peacemaker. He is a real Pied Piper. Who can be against stopping the arms race?"[38] Wary of Gorbachev's charms, allied officials lamented that the Soviet system made it all too easy for the general secretary to make the most of these skills. Lord Carrington, now NATO's secretary general, quipped that the Soviet leader's post shared two characteristics with the British House of Lords: "No retirement age, and immunity to the electoral process."[39]

The style might be different, but the substance was the same. Observers in the West saw little in Gorbachev's proposals that distinguished the new general secretary's priorities from those of his predecessors. But in retrospect, there were hints that Gorbachev's outlook might also be different. When Gorbachev met Egon Bahr in April 1985, he indicated his support for the premise of common security, which the Palme Commission's Georgy Arbatov had brought to his attention.[40] Some Gorbachev aides later suggested that the general secretary had used the old staples of Soviet diplomacy to conceal a more radical program. From the outset, they argued, his proposals were policy prescriptions, not pablum.[41] But others maintained that early Gorbachev was not the radical of later years. In 1985, he was still "swimming with the stream."[42] No matter Gorbachev's intentions, those in the West worried that he was now in command of events. The Western allies needed to wrest the initiative back from the Soviet Union. That refrain became a mantra, repeated ad nauseam in the years ahead.

The Start of Something New

When Ronald Reagan and Mikhail Gorbachev met at Geneva in November 1985, the summit marked the first such gathering of the superpowers in six years. The very fact that the two leaders were willing to sit down was a sign that the times were changing. "I'm not going to let myself get euphoric," Reagan wrote to Suzanne Massie, who advised him on Soviet issues, "but still I have a feeling we might be at a point of beginning."[43]

There was not much more to tout. The Strategic Defense Initiative dominated Reagan's conversations with Gorbachev, as the two leaders went around in circles arguing about the program's implications. The general secretary warned that it would export the arms race to space, whereas Reagan maintained that the program was a peaceful one. None of these positions were a departure from earlier US-Soviet exchanges on the matter. In advance of the summit, Reagan's aides warned that Strategic Defense Initiative would be a major sticking point. The president's advisers stressed the need for a cohesive message. The Soviets, Shultz predicted, could be expected to trot out something "simplistic yet seductive," casting the entire issue in binary terms, pitting Star Wars against star peace.[44]

Gorbachev kept up the pressure following the Geneva Summit. In January 1986, he unveiled a three-stage plan for the global elimination of nuclear weapons by the year 2000. Under his plan, the United States and the Soviet Union would agree to a comprehensive ban on nuclear testing, slash their strategic arsenals by half, and scale back their intermediate-range forces. The first stage of Gorbachev's ambitious offer envisioned the removal of all intermediate-range missiles from Europe.[45] "My impression is that he's really decided to end the arms race no matter what," Gorbachev's aide, Anatoly Chernyaev, confided in his diary.[46] Although he had initially intended to announce his plans at the Twenty-Seventh Party Congress in February, Gorbachev moved up the date and announced them in a press conference dedicated to the subject. The general secretary wanted to be sure that his ideas were not dismissed as boilerplate but taken as a serious plan put forward by the leader of the Soviet Union.[47] "At the very least," the president confided in his diary after Gorbachev's big speech, "it is a [hell] of a propaganda move. We'd be hard put to explain how we could turn it down."[48]

Gorbachev's call for a nuclear-free world had obvious presentational value. Sweeping and bold, he had adapted the basic premise of the president's zero option. Soviet hardliners, in a striking parallel to Weinberger and Perle, maintained the entire package would be unacceptable to their US interlocutors; Reagan would reject Gorbachev's grand gesture and the Soviets would score a major victory in the court of public opinion. If Reagan defied expectations and accepted the proposal, the Soviet Union could always fall back on its comfortable conventional force advantages.[49] But the proposal's primary architect, the chief of the General Staff of the Soviet Armed Forces, Sergei Akhromeyev, was no hardliner. Akhromeyev appreciated the dangers of an ever-growing stockpile of nuclear weapons.[50] From Gorbachev's vantage point, the bold initiative could clear the negotiating table. It would sweep aside all of the various arguments and counterarguments, what Gorbachev disparaged as the "mothball trash" accumulated over years of haggling.[51]

Gorbachev's timing chafed in Washington. When he went public with the proposal, he gave the White House only a day's notice of its contents. Matlock, who drafted a response, tried to strike a delicate balance. In what he described as "various subtle but unmistakable ways," he hoped to make clear that the public reveal of Gorbachev's proposals made it difficult to negotiate. But Matlock stopped short of criticizing its substance.[52] Reagan insisted on giving the general secretary's latest offer a full hearing.[53]

A call to rid the world of nuclear weapons appealed to Reagan's own sensibilities. Aides worried about what that might mean in practice, but Shultz fiercely protected the president's priorities. "I know many of you and others around here opposed the objective of eliminating nuclear weapons," he told members of his arms control group a few days after Gorbachev's address. But the president did not share this view: "he thinks it's a hell of a good idea."[54] The Reagan administration set out to study the possible paths forward.

In early February, the White House settled on two courses of action. One would focus on the general framework of a process leading to the elimination of all nuclear weapons, not just the US and Soviet arsenals. The second prong, based on the assumption that INF was the most promising candidate for a breakthrough, envisioned a new initiative to limit these forces. Because the Soviet Union refused to accept a global zero-zero solution, the United States would extend another offer to eliminate US and Soviet intermediate-range missiles in Europe, alongside significant reductions in Asia that would gradually bring the deployments down to zero.[55]

Gorbachev's rhetoric indicated that a separate deal covering intermediate-range nuclear forces might be possible. Breaking the missiles in Europe out of the rest of the package was the obvious follow-on from his calls for a common European home. With Gorbachev's shift away from a unified package, he extended the possibility that the United States and the Soviet Union could dramatically slash the missiles threatening Europe.[56]

Despite these shifts, the negotiations limped along. When the Soviet delegation tabled another treaty on intermediate-range forces in May 1986, the brief draft ignored longstanding areas of concern for the United States, including systems in Asia. Official Soviet statements touted INF as the best possible chance for an agreement, but the latest draft treaty suggested that the Kremlin was more optimistic in public than in private diplomatic overtures.[57]

Gorbachev was no less frustrated with the Americans than they were with the Soviets. In September 1986, he reached out to Reagan with an offer for another face-to-face meeting. The two could have a "quick one-on-one" that fall in London or Reykjavik. Gorbachev stressed that there was already sufficient agreement for the two sides to make progress. To illustrate the point, he laid out the commonalities in their positions on intermediate-range forces; he wished to see the elimination of US and Soviet systems in Europe, as did the United States. The United States might have "discovered" a new obstacle in the Soviet weapons in Asia (though US concerns were far from new), but an acceptable compromise could be found. The British and French arsenals need not be counted in an agreement.[58]

Shultz and Matlock advised Reagan to accept Gorbachev's offer. In advance of the summit, the National Security Council anticipated that Gorbachev likely expected any progress to be limited to INF. Accordingly, Reagan's advisers recommended that the president should seize the opportunity to narrow the gap between the Kremlin's position and their own. To do so, Reagan could explore specific ceilings to reach an interim agreement or try to secure Soviet support for elements of the US position, like effective verifications or reductions in Asia, where the Soviet Union had yet to agree.[59]

Seeing Ghosts

What Gorbachev planned for Reykjavik was not a relaxed affair to swap views. The Soviet general secretary instead planned to "sweep Reagan off his feet" with a new approach that the president would be unable to resist.[60] To pull together such a package, Gorbachev was willing to make concessions, including accepting the zero option in Europe and corresponding reductions on intermediate-range forces in Asia. But any breakthrough on INF could only come as part of a larger package. The earlier tight linkage had returned, meaning that the fate of an agreement was tied to the

Strategic Defense Initiative. And, at the Reykjavik Summit on October 11 and 12, 1986, it was this connection that ultimately blocked the superpowers' agreement on limits to intermediate-range nuclear forces from becoming a full-fledged reality.

Reagan and Gorbachev agreed on a great deal at Reykjavik. US negotiators marveled at the concessions Gorbachev seemed willing to make. "This is the best Soviet proposal we have received in twenty-five years," Paul Nitze remarked after the leaders' first session wrapped up.[61] Few could have known better than the veteran arms control negotiator—Nitze had seen virtually all of them. In their second session later that afternoon, Reagan pressed Gorbachev on intermediate-range forces. It seemed as though the general secretary had backed away from his earlier conviction that an agreement was close at hand, Reagan noted, before urging Gorbachev that they could "settle on 100/100 now"—a hundred warheads in Europe and another hundred outside the continent.[62] That evening, US and Soviet advisers convened to try to close the differences. Marshal Sergey Akhromeyev, the chief of the General Staff, surprised the Americans around the table, proving a far more flexible negotiating partner than they had anticipated. Working well into the night, the Americans and the Soviets agreed to a draft that included a 50 percent reduction in strategic offensive weapons, as well as the removal of all intermediate-range nuclear forces in Europe, with a ceiling of a hundred missiles in Asia.

The next morning's session was scheduled to be the summit's last, but, when it yielded no agreement, Reagan and Gorbachev continued their negotiations. The two men were on the cusp of an incredible and sweeping agreement. The stumbling block remained the Strategic Defense Initiative, which Gorbachev still hoped to confine to the laboratory but which Reagan hoped to bring to fruition, rendering all nuclear weapons defunct. Frustrated by their circular negotiations, the president asked Gorbachev to clarify his final offer. Was the general secretary suggesting that "beginning in the first five-year period and then going on in the second we would be reducing all nuclear weapons—cruise missiles, battlefield weapons, sub-launched and the like"? "It would be fine," the president continued, "if we eliminated all nuclear weapons."[63]

Gorbachev pounced. "We can do that. We can eliminate them," he insisted. "Let's do it," Shultz chimed in. Then, just as quickly, the whole package fell apart. Gorbachev circled back to the Strategic Defense Initiative, insistent that any agreement confine the program to the laboratory. Reagan refused. "There is research in the lab stage," he told Gorbachev, "but then you must go outdoors to try out what has been done in the lab." The Reykjavik Summit collapsed without agreement.[64]

Turning to his chief of staff, Don Regan, Reagan held up his hand, thumb and index finger apart slightly. They had been impossibly close to an agreement, the gesture suggested. Under his breath, the president kept muttering to himself, "laboratory, laboratory, laboratory."[65] After flirting with the total elimination of nuclear weapons, Reagan and Gorbachev left Reykjavik empty-handed.

As news trickled out of Reykjavik, the full weight of what Reagan and Gorbachev had nearly agreed to do terrified the Western Europeans. "Thank God for Gorbachev and SDI," one British official reportedly exclaimed.[66] Only the Soviet general secretary's insistence that the United States restrict its ballistic missile defense research had stopped Reagan from abolishing nuclear weapons and eroding the very foundations of the Atlantic alliance. "This is not serious," one anonymous senior French official exclaimed to reporters. "My reflection on all of this is that you should not allow two men to negotiate on a Saturday night in a haunted house."[67] James Schlesinger disparaged the president's performance. "It combined the worst aspects of earlier summits," he wrote. "It was as ill conceived as the Vienna summit of 1961; it had the worst outcome since the blowup of the Paris summit of 1960; and it rested upon utopian expectations not seen since the Yalta conference of 1945."[68] Helmut Kohl, in a particularly unfortunate choice of analogy, cautioned against taking Gorbachev too seriously: "He is a modern communist leader who understands public relations," the chancellor remarked in an interview with *Newsweek*. "Goebbels, one of those responsible for the crimes of the Hitler era, was an expert in public relations, too."[69]

Reagan's performance at Reykjavik confirmed old fears that the president might sell out Washington's allies or withdraw the United States from Europe. Scholars of international relations chalked up the near universal Western European angst to the predictable patterns of NATO's security dilemma: a recurring cycle of abandonment and entrapment.[70] After Reykjavik, the Western European allies were squarely in the abandonment phase. That speculation was further inflamed by the fact that the common line on what Reagan and Gorbachev had nearly agreed to do seemed to be perennially in flux. "Yet another version," one British official scribbled in the margins of a postmortem telegram summarizing the superpowers' deliberations at Reykjavik.[71]

Even in broad strokes, what Reagan had been willing to entertain was unthinkable to many of his counterparts in Western Europe.[72] "My own reaction when I heard how far the Americans had been prepared to go," Margaret Thatcher later recalled, "was as if there had been an earthquake beneath my feet." Reagan's willingness to eliminate all ballistic missiles would spell the end of "the whole system of nuclear deterrence which had kept the peace for forty years."[73] In a telephone conversation shortly after the summit, she urged Reagan to consider the implications. Nuclear weapons remained critical to NATO's defenses, not least because of the Soviet Union's advantages in troops and tanks. What Reagan said in response depended on the note taker. According to the British record, the president replied that the "imbalance could be managed," but the US version conveyed Reagan's skepticism that the imbalance was as great as the conventional wisdom suggested before noting, "What the Soviets do not want is a war."[74] How were NATO's military planners and member governments supposed to convince their voters that nuclear deterrence remained a sound and responsible basis for their policies if the superpowers kept flirting with the possibility of doing away with nuclear weapons entirely?[75]

The president's unmistakable embrace of a nuclear-free world could embolden antinuclear activists and breathe new life into their campaigns. It could also strengthen the arguments of opposition parties across the alliance. For Thatcher, staring down a general election against a Labour Party still committed to a nonnuclear Britain, the parallels between Reagan's position and that of her domestic political opponents were far too close for comfort.[76] In the Federal Republic, the president's stance could easily boost the SPD's existing efforts to develop its own shadow diplomacy with the ruling SED in the German Democratic Republic.

For the most part, Washington's allies were no more enthusiastic about the near-deal to limit intermediate-range nuclear forces. Though they had championed the zero option since 1981, the prospect that the initiative could actually form the foundation of an agreement left allied governments and strategists scrambling. The implications for NATO's defense posture were alarming. The removal of the Pershing IIs and Gryphons would eliminate a rung in the ladder of escalation, weakening the coupling of Europe's defenses to the United States. If the superpowers eliminated all longer-range INF, the Soviet Union would still retain advantages in Europe, be it shorter-range missiles, conventional forces, or chemical weapons. Gen. Bernard Rogers, NATO's supreme allied commander, agonized over the zero option. Rogers made no secret of these concerns, telling reporters that the news from the superpowers' summit had sent "shivers down my back."[77] If the United States and the Soviet Union were to strike a deal based on the zero option, it would, Rogers warned, "put us back to where we were in 1979, and in some areas it would have been worse than it was in 1979."[78]

Jean-Bernard Raimond, the French foreign minister, warned publicly that the removal of US missiles "would be inopportune for the Alliance and would reduce the security of Europe." The Western allies, he argued, invoking Schmidtian logic, could not lose sight of "other factors of disequilibrium."[79] But, as Reagan's remarks to Thatcher shortly after the summit indicated, the Western allies were not agreed that the Warsaw Pact still had a meaningful advantage in conventional forces. Quantitative tallies still favored the pact. By those metrics, the Soviet Union and its allies had a "formidable margin of superiority."[80] In qualitative terms, the balance was much more difficult to calculate.[81] No matter where allied governments came down on this question, political realities demanded that they stick to the zero option. They were "politically inextricably committed" to zero.[82]

Gorbachev Unties the Package

After the Reykjavik Summit, Moscow's messaging was muddled. Victor Karpov, the veteran Soviet negotiator who now headed Moscow's newly created Directorate for Arms Control and Disarmament, suggested that the superpowers could reach a separate deal to restrict intermediate-range nuclear forces. But Gorbachev's own remarks suggested otherwise. INF remained part of the Soviet arms control package, along with strategic forces and outer space.[83] Gorbachev's Politburo colleagues backed him; the strength of the Soviet position at Reykjavik had come from their insistence on the linkage between issues. "We do not need any cheap tricks," Gorbachev argued, "only the package."[84]

By early 1987, Soviet thinking began to evolve. A growing segment of the leadership questioned the wisdom of deploying the SS-20s, convinced that their predecessors had miscalculated the political costs. Even Gromyko admitted the decision had been a "gross error."[85] The Soviet Union now faced an acute threat in the Pershing IIs. Soviet officials likened it to "a revolver put to our temple."[86] The missiles' short flight time meant that they could easily be used to carry out a decapitating strike against the Soviet Union.[87] Kremlin policymakers had made no secret of these concerns; since the early 1980s, they had been churning out a steady stream of public pronouncements condemning the Pershing II as a destabilizing, first-strike weapon capable of destroying Soviet targets within five minutes of launch.[88]

One of Gorbachev's close foreign policy advisers, Aleksandr Yakovlev, penned a lengthy memo to the general secretary in late February, arguing that it was time to decouple the arms control package. Yakovlev's reassessment came on the heels of a visit from high-profile ex-officials including Henry Kissinger, Cyrus Vance, and Harold Brown. Conversations with these visitors inspired Yakovlev, who now made the case for abandoning the package and isolating INF. The prospects for an agreement remained slim and, now over halfway through Reagan's second term, time was running out. The Reykjavik Summit had confirmed that INF represented the best hope for progress in the short term. The advantages, Yakovlev argued, were plenty; the Soviet Union could remove "a very serious threat," while also reaping the benefits of an agreement in Western Europe. "The fact of untying," he reminded Gorbachev, "does not in any way signify the automatic conclusion of agreements on conditions that are unfavorable to us." Yakovlev's case inverted the earlier logic; the strength of the package came not from its format, but from the ideas therein. Bundling them would only limit the Soviets' room for maneuver. But if they planned to change course, Yakovlev was insistent that they act before the 1988 presidential campaign was in full swing.[89]

Yakovlev's case was strengthened by developments within the Soviet Union. The previous December, the Politburo had agreed to let the prominent Soviet physicist and dissident Andrei Sakharov return from exile in Gorky. Gorbachev hoped that Sakharov's release would serve as tangible evidence that his policy of openness and transparency, glasnost, meant more than a change in rhetoric. Sakharov wasted little time. After his release, he levied sharp critiques against the Soviet approach to arms control, including the Reykjavik package. Moscow's obsession with the Strategic Defense Initiative, Sakharov argued, was narrow-minded; the likelihood that the United States could produce anything worth worrying about was negligible. But in the name of stopping the Strategic Defense Initiative, Gorbachev had given up a chance to secure cuts in other weapons. Sakharov's arguments echoed those of Gorbachev advisers like Yevgeny Velikhov, the director of the prestigious Kurchatov Institute for nuclear research, and the head of the civilian space program, Roald Sagdeyev.[90]

The day after Yakovlev's exhaustive memo, on February 26, 1987, the Politburo decided to untie the arms control package.[91] The arguments in favor ran the gamut from concerns about the threat posed by the Pershing IIs to the economic benefits of an agreement, made all the more important by the recent slump in the Soviet economy. Time continued to work against the Soviet leadership, and their various earlier efforts to get rid of the missiles had failed. Dismantling the arms control package, most concluded, was the only viable option remaining. But this shift was not without its critics. Defense minister Sergei Sokolov denounced plans to abolish so many missiles, exclaiming on one occasion that it would be "a state crime!"[92] To counter this opposition, Gorbachev made the most of an incident caused by an unlikely accidental ally: an amateur pilot from Schleswig-Holstein. On the evening of May 28, 1987, eighteen-year-old Mathias Rust landed a small Cessna aircraft on Moscow's Bolshoi Moskvoretskii Bridge before taxiing out onto Red Square. Rust's flight provided the perfect pretext, and Gorbachev moved swiftly to purge the ranks of the Soviet military. Sokolov lost his post, as did countless others in the largest changing of the guard since the Stalinist purges of the 1930s.[93]

Gorbachev's decision to break intermediate-range forces out of the arms control package injected new momentum into the superpowers' negotiations. In March 1987, US negotiators introduced a revised draft treaty, based on the principles Reagan and Gorbachev had agreed to at Reykjavik the previous autumn; longer-range missiles would be capped at a global ceiling of a hundred, with zero in Europe. Other intermediate-range nuclear forces, shorter-range weapons with ranges between five hundred and a thousand kilometers, would also be constrained. The draft US treaty included stringent verification measures, including the exchange of baseline data, onsite monitoring, permanent monitoring, and short-notice inspections.[94]

Soviet negotiators responded with a draft of their own in late April, accepting this verification regime. It was a significant departure from standing Soviet policy, which had long dismissed inspections as cover for espionage, but Gorbachev's new thinking was at work. Verification fit squarely within the general secretary's case for transparency. Eager to secure an agreement, Gorbachev sweetened the deal further. When George Shultz visited Moscow in April, the general secretary offered to remove all Soviet shorter-range INF, more than meeting the United States' earlier demands.[95]

Western European governments panicked. A double zero solution, removing both shorter-range and longer-range INF, could easily be the first step toward the complete denuclearization of Europe.[96] One of Thatcher's foreign policy advisers, Charles Powell, concluded that it was a gamble on Gorbachev's part. "Once people in the West have tasted reductions in nuclear weapons," Powell argued, "their appetite for more will grow and government will be unable to resist."[97] Powell's colleagues grudgingly respected the general secretary's savvy strategy. Gorbachev had regained nearly all of the ground lost at Reykjavik the previous autumn.[98]

There were few options for the Western allies but to accept the Soviets' double zero offer. Shultz was blunt about that fact when he stopped at the North Atlantic Council on the heels of his visit to Moscow. In the secretary of state's estimation, there were three viable options to move forward. The allies could accept the Soviet proposal, accept the first zero on longer-range systems but decline the second, or introduce a counterproposal with ceilings on the shorter-range systems that would bring down the size of the Soviet arsenal, though not all the way down to zero.[99] If Washington's allies preferred either the second or third of these options, Shultz warned, they must also be prepared to deploy new shorter-range missiles. There was no point in turning down an offer to remove 122 Soviet nuclear weapons just to keep open the prospect that NATO might, at some point in the future, wish to upgrade its own meager capabilities.[100] Should the allies rebuff the Soviets' double zero offer, it was certain to make any modernization program a political lightning rod.

Shorter-Range Struggles

Gorbachev's double zero offer found considerable support in the Federal Republic of Germany. The Free Democrats, the Social Democrats, and the Greens all came out in favor of the proposal, as did an array of peace groups. But reactions from Helmut Kohl's government were far more muted. The Christian Democrats split on the question, with one wing of the party furious about what double zero might mean for their security. The proposal included substantial risks for the Federal Republic that could not be ignored. Alfred Dregger, the chair of the CDU/CSU's parliamentary group, pressed for the inclusion of even shorter-range systems, capable of striking targets between 150 and 500 kilometers, that threatened both halves of divided Germany.[101] Dregger, part of the Christian Democrats' right-wing faction, the so-called steel helmets, found allies in other parts of the party. Manfred Wörner, a staunch Atlanticist (who would go on to become NATO's secretary general later that year), appealed directly to Kohl. Double zero, the defense minister argued in one letter, would leave the West Germans "in the worst of all nuclear worlds." The Federal Republic would be unduly exposed, isolated as a prospective nuclear battlefield while the longer-range systems that threatened its neighbors were abolished.[102] What alarmed Dregger and Wörner was a variation on a familiar theme: the prospect of the Federal Republic's singularization within the alliance.

Kohl favored a solution that fell short of double zero. Ideally, he believed, under the terms of an INF treaty, some shorter-range missiles would remain. But that outcome was hardly politically viable. In allied circles, Shultz's warnings were a sharp reminder that the price to avert double zero was a modernization that the West Germans did not want: the conversion of the Pershing IIs into Pershing IBs, reducing the weapon's overall range and downgrading its capabilities to make it a shorter-range intermediate-range nuclear weapon, rather than a longer-range one. At home, with peace groups and every other political party clamoring for dramatic reductions, the pressure was sky-high. And the optics of being the only party desperate to keep these nuclear weapons were awful.

The Christian Democrats' concerns were a logical outgrowth of NATO's standing strategy. Should the Western allies embrace the double zero option, it would rip the seamless robe of deterrence. The old bogeyman— decoupling—was back. Kohl bemoaned that the Americans no longer seemed to care, preferring instead to parrot antinuclear activists' claims that the United States' strategic arsenal provided sufficient coverage to defend Western Europe.[103]

Given the politics at home and abroad, the meaningful political chances of stopping double zero were virtually nil. Some Christian Democrats courted the French, pursuing schemes of a European Security Union based on Franco-German cooperation—and the nuclear firepower of Paris's *force de frappe*. Other segments of the party dreamed of an alliance with the British, given Thatcher's known opposition to the double zero offer. Neither enjoyed much traction. Mitterrand was embroiled in coalition politics of his own, a Socialist in a government filled with Conservatives who detested the double zero. But Mitterrand himself remained open to the proposal and was eager not to box in Kohl. The overtures to Paris went largely ignored. As for those courting London, Thatcher's government elected to back the two zeros, despite strong reservations at Number 10. London's change of heart left the Federal Republic the sole remaining obstacle to double zero within the alliance.[104] In early June, Kohl's coalition grudgingly endorsed the proposal.[105]

That support, however lukewarm, paved the way for the Western allies to publicly endorse a deal based on double zero, and when NATO's foreign ministers met at Reykjavik a few weeks later, they expressed strong support for such an agreement. This formal consensus masked lingering divisions about when and on what terms any further reductions, moving beyond these intermediate-range weapons, should take place.

An agreement that would abolish both shorter-range and longer-range missiles implicated not only US and Soviet systems but also a group of shorter-range intermediate-range nuclear forces stationed in the Federal Republic: the seventy-two Pershing IAs owned and operated by the West Germans but fitted with US-owned nuclear warheads. Kohl hoped to keep these missiles outside the superpowers' talks, even as the Soviets pressed for their inclusion. When the coalition announced its position in early June, the Pershing IAs remained squarely outside the scope of the superpowers' deal.

Kohl's was a nearly impossible position to sustain. When the Soviets had pressed for the weapons' inclusion in late April, US negotiators refused. But the issue was almost certain to come back, as the Soviet delegation tried to count these systems or, at the very least, restrict their modernization through noncircumvention clauses.[106] Soviet proposals called only for the destruction of the nuclear warheads, not the rest of the delivery mechanisms, in a move that highlighted uncomfortable questions of ownership and control. Whereas the earlier case for the exclusion of British and French relied on the fact that these were part of independent, national nuclear arsenals, any similar argument regarding the West Germans was a political and public relations nightmare. In theory, the United States could argue that the Pershing IAs were solely the property of the Federal Republic and, as such, outside the scope of the superpowers' bilateral talks. But doing so would strain arguments that the Federal Republic was a nonnuclear power. Even the slightest insinuation to that effect could be damaging, if not dangerous.[107]

The Pershing IAs were another source of friction within Kohl's coalition. The day after the government announced that the Pershing IAs would remain outside the talks, a condition agreed to by both the Christian Democrats and the Free Democrats. But Hans-Dietrich Genscher changed course. The West German foreign minister quickly abandoned this position and, instead, sent private diplomatic signals to interlocutors in East Berlin (where they were sure to be passed on to Moscow) that he would be happy to see the missiles junked.

Soviet officials picked up the hints. In July, Eduard Shevardnadze griped that the Americans and the West Germans kept passing the buck on the Pershing IAs, each citing the other as the reason they could not discuss the missiles. The Pershing IAs, the Soviet foreign minister charged, were now the single largest obstacle standing in the way of an agreement to do away with intermediate-range nuclear forces. Ratcheting up the pressure yet further, Gorbachev announced that the Soviets would agree to a complete and global double zero, dropping the token hundred-missile ceiling outside Europe that had remained up to this point.[108]

Predictably, Christian Democrats opposed that outcome. Dregger insisted that the missiles be protected lest the Federal Republic lose one of the few items left in its arsenal to protect its territory. To shore up support for their position, some Christian Democrats appealed to the British and French, drawing direct comparisons between the exclusion of their national nuclear forces and of the Pershing IA, flirting with arguments sure to terrify a generation of policymakers still fearful about a German finger on the nuclear trigger.

The Soviets kept up the pressure. In August, Yuli Kvitsinsky informed Genscher that, given the current West German position on the Pershing IAs, the entire deal to abolish intermediate-range nuclear forces was in jeopardy.[109]

To solve this problem, the Federal Republic could make a move on its own. The decades-old Pershing IAs were nearly obsolete; Martin Marietta, the firm that built them, had already made clear that they would not produce any more spare parts for the systems after 1992. What if the government made a unilateral offer to give up the Pershing IA missiles?

Kohl did just that. On August 26, he announced that the Federal Republic would give up the Pershing IAs should the United States and the Soviet Union reach an agreement to eliminate their intermediate-range missiles.[110] To finesse the delicate political situation at home, including within his own political party, Kohl exhorted the governments of the Warsaw Pact to match his gesture with one of their own: the removal of tactical nuclear forces.

Kohl's public call cut against decades of NATO planning. Should the Warsaw Pact take the chancellor up on his offer, allied planners could confront the scenario they had been trying to avoid for decades: staring down the pact's conventional forces without the benefit of nuclear weapons to balance the scales. The Western allies needed to fight to avoid this outcome. "We should establish a firebreak," one diplomat told reporters, referring to a point below which NATO's members would refuse to negotiate. Without one, the Soviet Union would appear with yet another tempting offer of zero. Such a proposal would "be instantly popular in the West," the allied representative concluded, "and eventually we'll have to accept it."[111]

The Road to Washington

Most of the major elements of a treaty had been sorted out by autumn. Gorbachev's endorsement of a global zero eased some of the verification process, but there were still countless details to be sorted out, including provisions for the Soviets to inspect missile sites in Western Europe. Doing so took up most of the autumn.

Regardless of this progress, the United States continued to deploy missiles to Western Europe. NATO's initial plans had called for Gryphons and Pershing IIs to be introduced in stages, and missiles still had yet to be deployed to Molesworth in the United Kingdom, as well as to Woensdrecht in the Netherlands. A batch of Gryphons was scheduled to arrive at Molesworth in December 1987, meaning that even the slightest delay to the superpowers' talks could saddle Thatcher's government with an undesirable scenario wherein the missiles should still be delivered, despite the public knowing that Moscow and Washington were on the verge of signing an agreement.[112] The Campaign for Nuclear Disarmament seized on these seeming contradictions.

"As the superpowers come to agreement on the *removal* of cruise and SS20 missiles from Europe, *MORE* brought to the new base which has just been built," one flyer read. One local chapter exhorted Sheffield residents to act now, as their city was in danger, a message flyers drove home with a map of the cruise missiles' dispersal area.[113] Peace activists in the Netherlands stepped up their campaigns at Woensdrecht. "It's not logical to build the base when it's likely not to have the missiles," one campaigner camped outside the base told a reporter.[114] In October, Gorbachev floated the prospect of a joint moratorium on missile deliveries in advance of the treaty's conclusion, but Shultz refused. It did not make sense to impose a moratorium until the ink was dry on the final treaty.[115]

Pesky details remained to be resolved, with dozens of items still outstanding before an INF agreement could be finalized. But the big picture of US-Soviet relations was rosy, at least in Shultz's eyes. "It is increasingly clear," he argued, "that the Soviet Union is going to be seen by history as Ronald Reagan's 'China.'" To sustain that momentum, Shultz set out a series of principles to guide relations with Gorbachev moving forward. "Our interest is to keep the Russians well behind us but not so far behind that they become desperate and dangerous," the secretary argued. To do so, Shultz focused on the need to manage the changes in US-Soviet relations, as well as those within the Soviet Union, clustered around six guiding principles. The secretary's list read:

- Keep holding out the vision of the future that the Soviets are not capable of handling without change (the information age).
- Keep making it clear that their old policies just will never work (regional intervention, attempts to limit SDI, non-market economics, etc.)
- Don't urge better relationships (it will be read as though we are reaching) but always be quick to act to build them when the opportunity comes.
- Give Gorbachev all the chances he seeks for greater exposure and attention. The more he talks up his programs the higher the expectations he arouses among his people and the world's.
- Keep our role of being the "psychologically superior" party. So far, we have brilliantly allowed Gorbachev to posture as the innovator and take the credit for moves that come in our direction and follow our agenda.
- And when we make trade-offs, be sure they tend to lock in our positions and our version of the future. We are doing this with INF. We can do it with SDI too.[116]

Shultz headed to Geneva a few days later for the final push to secure the kind of INF agreement the Reagan White House wanted. By the afternoon of November 24, Shultz and Shevardnadze had resolved the issues outstanding on INF. Gorbachev would head to Washington for a summit a few weeks later, capped off with the signing of the first true disarmament treaty between the superpowers.[117]

The terms of that agreement were unmistakably advantageous to Washington. The Soviet Union would dismantle and destroy some fifteen hundred weapons already deployed. The United States would eliminate just over 20 percent of that. The verification procedures were stringent—by far the strictest to that point in US-Soviet arms control agreements—and a considerable concession given the Soviets' historic opposition to inspections. What was left outside the treaty also played to Washington's advantage. The two superpowers dismantled all land-based weapons, nuclear and conventional, with a range between five hundred and fifty-five hundred kilometers, but the deal included no such restrictions on air- or sea-launched missiles, where US programs far outstripped those of the Soviet Union. Even with these advantages, the Reagan administration came under fire for supporting such a treaty in the weeks leading up to the Washington Summit.

At the Summit

Side by side, Reagan and Gorbachev strolled into the East Room of the White House on December 8, 1987, for a signing ceremony, the undisputed centerpiece of the Washington Summit. Reagan opened the ceremony, reminding the assembled dignitaries about the zero option he had introduced six years earlier. "It was a simple proposal, one might say disarmingly simple," the president joked, as laughter spread through the crowd.[118]

Reagan turned to Gorbachev, repeating an old Soviet adage: "Doveryai, no proveryai—Trust, but verify." Gorbachev chuckled, before exclaiming, "You repeat that at every meeting!" The entire room broke into laughter once more, along with a round of applause.[119] The rapport between the two men was easily spotted.

Reagan's comfort with the Soviet leader stoked domestic opposition to the treaty. Howard Phillips, who chaired a right-wing public advocacy group, the Conservative Caucus, charged that the president had become "a useful idiot for Soviet propaganda."[120] Phillips banded together with Richard Viguerie, a specialist in direct-mail fund-raising, to spearhead a campaign against the treaty's ratification under the banner of the Anti-Appeasement Alliance.[121]

Eugene Rostow picked up the same analogy. The INF Treaty, he charged, was "a new Munich."[122] Other conservatives objected not to the specifics of the agreement, but to the fact that the president had agreed to anything at all. "I really think the whole arms-control thing is a waste of time," one Idaho Republican, Steven Symms, concluded. "The only way to keep the peace is to be strong and to protect ourselves. You can't do it by signing a piece of paper with a bunch of liars, cheats, and murderers."[123] North Carolina's Jesse Helms was even more blunt: "They are communist proposals, and I don't trust *any* communist proposals."[124]

Helms tried to derail the ratification process in the Senate. He bogged down the treaty with a series of amendments proposing to make its approval contingent on other concessions from the Kremlin, such as the withdrawal of Soviet forces from Afghanistan or a reduction in Moscow's conventional forces. Helms's first offensive failed. At the end of March, the treaty made it out of the Senate Foreign Relations Committee by a comfortable margin of seventeen to two.

A dispute over the technical protocols to implement the treaty threatened to provide the agreement's critics with a blunt instrument to wield in the ratification fight. But Shultz and Shevardnadze defused the issue with a new set of agreements in May. With Reagan's planned visit to Moscow only weeks away, the White House urged the Senate to pick up the pace. On May 25, the day the presidential delegation was set to leave for the Soviet capital, Jesse Helms conceded that he could not defeat the treaty. Two days later, the Senate ratified the agreement. It passed with resounding support. Of the five senators who voted against the treaty, four were members of the president's own party.[125]

Four days later, on May 31, Reagan and Gorbachev strolled through Moscow's Red Square. One of the reporters assembled for the occasion asked whether the president still believed that the Soviet Union was an "evil empire." Reagan demurred. He had been "talking about another time, another era."[126] Later that day, before a giant bust of Vladimir Lenin at Moscow State University, Reagan marveled to the assembled students about how much progress had been made in a few short years. The United States and the Soviet Union would exchange the ratification protocols for the INF Treaty the next day, concluding what Reagan hailed as "the first true nuclear arms reduction in history."[127] At least one member of the audience that day came to the conclusion that the Cold War was now over.[128]

Within the span of a few short years, relations between the United States and the Soviet Union transformed dramatically. In March 1985, when Mikhail

Gorbachev rose to the Soviet Union's top post, negotiators were heading back to the bargaining table in Geneva on the most contentious nuclear issues. Three years later, observers found ample evidence to argue that the superpowers' decades-long confrontation was now a relic of the past. The INF Treaty was not the only sign of a relationship transformed, but it was a powerful one.

It was Gorbachev who made the INF Treaty possible. He dropped the earlier Soviet conditions, insisting that any deal governing intermediate-range nuclear forces be linked to a broader arms control package including the thorny question of the Strategic Defense Initiative. Gorbachev made significant concessions to secure a deal with the Reagan White House. But Gorbachev believed it was a price worth paying to reduce the dangers—and economic burdens—of the nuclear arms race.

Gorbachev's intentions remained hard to discern. For a generation of policymakers familiar with the diplomacy of the 1960s and 1970s, it was all too easy to imagine that Gorbachev was repeating the tried-and-true formulas of the past. Indeed, the general secretary sought breathing space in order to shore up the Soviet Union, echoing Leonid Brezhnev's strategy. But some within the Atlantic alliance were already confident that Gorbachev was different. Hans-Dietrich Genscher implored his colleagues to "take Gorbachev at his word."[129] Uncertain how deep or durable the transformations taking place would be, the Western allies found themselves divided once more.

CHAPTER 12

Blast from the Past

The cover of the February 1988 issue of *END*, European Nuclear Disarmament's regular magazine, featured a giant cartoon of cruise missiles in a garbage can. But underneath the weapons slated to be destroyed by the recently signed INF Treaty were another set of missiles, underwater and decked out in snorkeling gear. "Cruise Is Dead," the cover's headline blared, "Long Live Cruise!"[1]

Though the INF Treaty eliminated an entire class of nuclear weapons from Europe, the reductions amounted to a mere 3 percent of the superpowers' total nuclear arsenals.[2] That figure looked dismal to many still concerned about the sheer number of nuclear weapons in the world. The prominent Australian disarmament campaigner Helen Caldicott disparaged the superpowers' agreement perhaps most trenchantly of all; it was akin to offering a cancer patient aspirin and claiming it would cure the patient's ailments.[3]

Even that 3 percent reduction was seen by some as dangerous. In the months leading up to the treaty entering into force, Gen. Bernard Rogers, recently retired as NATO's supreme allied commander, charged that the loss of the Pershing IIs and Gryphons would severely damage the alliance's defenses. "I am concerned," he remarked in early 1988, "the long-term credibility of NATO's deterrent is being sacrificed by this treaty on the altar of short-term political expediency."[4] The removal of the Gryphons and Pershing IIs suggested that NATO was sliding toward complete denuclearization of its defenses in Europe. Against that backdrop, the nuclear weapons that would remain in Europe, at least for the time being, took on even greater strategic, political, and psychological significance. Those short-range nuclear forces were already slated to be replaced and upgraded, but their modernization became all the more urgent in the eyes of NATO's strategists with the signing of the INF Treaty. SNF was now, as one US journalist quipped in December 1987, "the hottest acronym at NATO."[5]

Soviet advantages in that domain were striking. Whereas NATO had just eighty-eight Lance surface-to-surface missiles, the Soviet Union had over a dozen times that, a mix of Scuds, SS-21s, and Frogs. Any attempt to modernize NATO's short-range forces was certain to be contentious. The signing of the INF Treaty—and the political breakthrough in US-Soviet relations it symbolized—produced political pressures certain to make the introduction of any new nuclear weapons an unpopular course of action. By concluding an agreement that did away with an entire class of nuclear weapons (an oft-repeated refrain of the treaty's champions), the INF Treaty set a precedent that could be difficult to overcome. Would voters now assume that the purpose of arms control was to abolish entire groups of weapons in one fell swoop?

Upgrading the short-range forces remaining in Europe was deemed critical to ensure the continuation of the alliance's strategy of flexible response. Failure to do so could lead to the steady withdrawal of all nuclear forces from Europe and, with them, the US ground troops committed to the continent. In agreement—at least in theory—that modernization was necessary, the Western allies split over when those upgrades should happen and how they might relate to efforts to secure a balance in short-range forces through arms control negotiations. Yet again, disputes about tactics served as proxies for much larger questions about the wisdom and direction of NATO's security policies. To some, like Margaret Thatcher, the preservation of short-range weapons was critical to ensuring that NATO remained a nuclear alliance in Europe. But for others, such as Hans-Dietrich Genscher, the desire to push ahead with modernization could jeopardize the prospects to remake relations with the Soviet Union and, with it, the entire European order.

SNF brought the Atlantic alliance to the brink. The range of the weapons in question, under five hundred kilometers, meant that the entire issue—where they were based, where they would be fired, and where they would detonate—revolved around the Federal Republic of Germany. As a result, the controversy over short-range forces sharpened earlier dilemmas, exposing the most essential tensions of the transatlantic bargain. Could NATO preserve its nuclear defenses in Europe and, with it, the US commitment of troops to the continent? Would the Federal Republic of Germany continue to accept security on the other Western allies' terms? Could the Western allies find a solution that managed to achieve both of these outcomes?

In the spring of 1989, that was far from certain. But by autumn, the entire political landscape in Europe seemed in flux. Cracks had begun to appear in the Iron Curtain and, by year's end, the possibilities appeared limitless. The collapse of the Berlin Wall opened the door to new political solutions, including the unification of the two Germanys, which sidelined the earlier struggles over SNF. For NATO, enduring strategic concerns ran headlong into a profoundly new—and ever-changing—European landscape.

Montebello and the Case for Modernization

At Montebello, Quebec, in October 1983, NATO's defense ministers agreed to slash the stockpile in Europe. The Atlantic alliance would not exceed forty-six hundred land-based nuclear warheads in Europe, a sharp reduction in a stockpile that once topped seven thousand. To make those cuts possible, ministers endorsed the modernization of a series of short-range weapons systems, including nuclear artillery and the Lance, a tactical surface-to-surface missile.[6]

What ministers approved at Montebello was an abstract commitment to upgrade NATO's short-range forces, not a concrete program of modernization.[7] For the Reagan administration, even this broad endorsement was sufficient backing to pursue congressional funding for specific short-range weapons programs, including a follow-on to the Lance and a tactical air-to-surface missile. Subsequent allied assessments, including NATO's Nuclear Weapons Requirement Study, NWRS 85, affirmed the need to modernize these capabilities and recommended steps that the alliance might take to ensure a credible stockpile well into the 1990s.[8]

Technology was key. By investing in and harnessing new scientific advances and the creation of more sophisticated weapons systems, the thinking went, the Western allies could pursue further reductions to the number of systems deployed—sure to be a politically popular position—without sacrificing military effectiveness. Publicly, NATO's planners touted the novelty of this stance. "For the first time in the history of the Alliance," Rogers remarked to one Dutch audience in late 1985, "we have a plan that describes precisely the minimum required non-strategic forces—by number of each weapon type and by location—which assures deterrence."[9]

Within NATO's existing strategic doctrine, deterrence relied on a mix of weapons, conventional and nuclear. SNF formed part of the politically sensitive coupling links between strategic weapons and conventional forces, not unlike longer-range nuclear forces like the Pershing II and Gryphon. Flexible response might have been more myth than reality, but sustaining that myth was pivotal to the psychological and political functioning of the alliance.[10] There remained no meaningful, viable alternatives that ticked the requisite strategic, economic, and political boxes for the Western allies. "You either revert to the strategy of 'massive retaliation,' which makes no sense," Rogers argued, "or you say, 'if we are attacked conventionally, we will have to capitulate because we are not going to resort to the use of nuclear weapons'; that makes no sense either."[11] In October 1986, after nearly twenty years of trying, the Nuclear Planning Group produced a series of general political guidelines (always referred to as the GPGs) for the follow-on use of nuclear weapons. These guidelines shifted the focus of allied planning toward weapons with a deep-strike role, such as the Pershing II, and away from shorter-range battlefield options. In so doing, the Western allies affirmed—largely at the Federal Republic's insistence—that short-range nuclear weapons would not be an acceptable substitute for any eliminated longer-range systems.[12]

But the Reagan administration pushed for just that. As part of the ratification debate over the INF Treaty in the spring of 1988, the White House made clear that the United States planned to move forward with the modernization of NATO's short-range forces in accordance with the Montebello decision. Failure to modernize these forces, some well-placed Americans argued, could cast doubt on the arrangements that kept US troops on the European continent. At the annual security conference in Munich, the Wehrkunde, Secretary of Defense Frank Carlucci made clear that the United States alone could not shoulder the burdens of the alliance.[13] If the Atlantic alliance failed to modernize its short-range nuclear forces, it was unlikely US ground forces would remain in Europe.

Creeping Denuclearization?

Since the superpowers' October 1986 summit at Reykjavik, Margaret Thatcher had worried that the Atlantic alliance was slowly but steadily creeping toward an unpalatable outcome: a nuclear-free posture in Europe. The denuclearization of NATO's defenses in Europe would leave the allies exposed to Soviet power, rendering them incapable of fending off the Kremlin's political pressure, let alone its massive armed forces should it attack westward.

Reagan's flirtations with a world without nuclear weapons were too close for comfort for Thatcher. At home, Thatcher pressed the case for nuclear deterrence in the face of a political opponent, Neil Kinnock's Labour Party, that backed a nonnuclear Britain. During the 1987 election, Thatcher charged that her challenger would destroy NATO and leave Britain in danger. Kinnock returned fire, arguing that Labour's policies were simply an extension of the Reagan administration's moves toward the "denuclearization of Europe." "When President Reagan is very actively engaged in the clearing of Europe not only of long and short range intermediate weapons but also of battlefield weapons," Kinnock argued, "then we are with the grain of that ambition."[14] Reagan's enthusiasm for a world without nuclear weapons put Thatcher—and those who shared her convictions about the long peace provided by nuclear weapons—in a political bind. How could they make a compelling case for nuclear deterrence in public when the president of the United States openly disagreed? Even if they convinced their constituents, did it matter if the president succeeded in slashing the superpowers' stockpiles? For policymakers in London and Paris, the question was exceptionally fraught, as any questioning of nuclear deterrence not only threatened NATO's strategy but also their own national nuclear weapons programs.

To avert a steady slide toward the removal of NATO's nuclear weapons from Europe, the British urged their allies to adopt a ceiling under which they would not negotiate with the Soviet Union. This firebreak point was designed to protect the alliance's nuclear arsenal, but for many West Germans, it smacked of discrimination. Perched off the coast of the continent, the British were more than content to set the firebreak point far from their borders, at five hundred kilometers. For the West Germans, living within that radius, these schemes suggested a growing separation between their security and that of the remainder of the allies. Confronted with the Soviets' offer for a double zero solution, then, Helmut Kohl's Christian Democrats were already sensitive to their exposed position.

By the summer of 1987, Hans-Dietrich Genscher had turned against the earlier logic of upgrading NATO's short-range nuclear forces. When NATO's foreign ministers gathered in Reykjavik in June, he pressed for arms control negotiations to limit the short-range weapons threatening Europe as soon as possible. Genscher and his fellow foreign ministers instead endorsed a set of basic principles to guide future arms control negotiations. The Reykjavik formula put short-range forces last on the list, behind reductions to strategic nuclear forces, a ban on chemical weapons, and drastic cuts to Europe's standing armies. Only then would the allies entertain restrictions on short-range nuclear missiles.[15] In the interim, the Western allies would move forward with their existing plans to upgrade these weapons.

With the successful conclusion of the INF Treaty later that year, the entire process of modernization became even more contentious. A feeling of "arms control/detente euphoria" generated by the superpowers' agreement could easily derail NATO's plans going forward.[16] Gen. John Galvin, who had replaced Rogers as supreme allied commander, underscored the dangers should the Western allies let jubilation stand in the way of good policy. "We must not allow, through denuclearization or the failure to modernize, the military balance between NATO and [the] Warsaw Pact to deteriorate to the point that NATO members become susceptible to pressures to accommodate Soviet interests," he urged readers of the *NATO Review*, nor "to the point where credible deterrence is jeopardized."[17] Galvin duly pressed for a firm statement in favor of modernization at the alliance's March 1988 summit in Brussels.[18]

He did not receive the endorsement for which he hoped. The summit's final communiqué skirted around the question, falling back on a repackaged version of the previous year's Reykjavik formula.[19] Predictably, allied leaders spun the outcome as an endorsement of their preferred policy outcomes. Margaret Thatcher, though privately disappointed that the summit's statement had not gone further, touted it as a victory for modernization. Her government, she informed the House of Commons, "got precisely what we wanted out of the summit." The British had secured all of their major objectives, which the prime minister described as an affirmation of NATO's continued relevance to the defense of the West, of the continued wisdom of its strategy of flexible response and the need to modernize the alliance's forces to keep that doctrine operational, and of the Western allies' resolve "in the face of Soviet attempts to separate Europe from the United States and to denuclearise Europe."[20]

What the Soviet Union hoped to achieve through negotiations formed the basis of this cautious attitude toward talks. Any negotiations were, in the words of one British analyst, "likely to take 5 minutes—which was as long as it would take the Russians to come up with the third zero."[21] No matter the deep cuts such an initiative would require Moscow to make to its own arsenal, allied officials assumed that the presentational and political benefits of a third zero option outweighed the costs. It was an offer that would be too tempting for the Kremlin to pass up.

A third zero sounded like the ideal option in theory, repeating what the United States and the Soviet Union had already done regarding intermediate-range forces. In practice, it would mean the removal of yet more nuclear systems from Europe, something adherents of flexible response feared would unravel the alliance's deterrent entirely. "By maintaining credible deterrence the Alliance has secured peace in Europe for nearly forty years," NATO's leaders affirmed when they met in Brussels in March 1988. "Conventional defenses alone cannot ensure this; therefore, for the foreseeable future there is no alternative to the Alliance strategy for the prevention of war." That strategy required "an appropriate mix of adequate and effective nuclear and conventional forces," all of which needed to be kept up to date in order for NATO's deterrent to preserve the peace.[22]

"The Shorter the Range, the Deader the German"

The INF Treaty unraveled years of work on the part of successive governments in Bonn to shift NATO's nuclear strategy away from an undue reliance on short-range, tactical, and battlefield nuclear weapons—the weapons most likely to destroy their homeland. With the elimination of every missile with a range between five hundred and fifty-five hundred kilometers, what remained in Europe were exactly the short-range systems West German planners had hoped to move away from—but that West German citizens could not. The prospect that the Western allies might modernize these weapons, introducing new, more effective systems as they were removing all intermediate-range forces, struck a nerve in the Federal Republic. Both the range and the intended targets seemed to suggest that the Federal Republic's security was increasingly divorced from that of the rest of the Western allies. Against that backdrop, the concept of singularization returned to the popular lexicon. It was, as the *Süddeutsche Zeitung* put it, "a specter . . . stalking Europe."[23]

After Reagan and Gorbachev's near deal at Reykjavik in October 1986, Helmut Kohl had warned that the Western allies could end up repeating the mistakes of the past, creating a "new gray area."[24] These fears multiplied over the course of 1987 as the United States and the Soviet Union moved closer to a deal that would eliminate all intermediate-range forces. Conservative members of Kohl's Christian Democrats balked at the double zero solution.

Kohl's decision to give up the West German Pershing IAs was the breaking point. Christian Democrats chafed at the seeming disregard for their own national security. Franz-Josef Strauss, the longtime head of the CDU's sister party in Bavaria, the CSU, warned that a "zone of differential security" was emerging within NATO.[25] Repeated British calls for a firebreak reinforced this belief. So too did the January 1988 release of a US government paper, *Discriminate Deterrence*. "We and our allies," the report's authors, Fred Iklé and Albert Wohlstetter, argued, "would rather deter than defeat an aggression, but a bluff is less effective and more dangerous in a crisis than the ability and will to use conventional and, if necessary, nuclear weapons with at least a rough discrimination that preserves the values we are defending."[26] Richard Burt, now the US ambassador in Bonn, warned colleagues at the State Department, "Nothing will faster break up the Atlantic Alliance than the perception that the present or any future administration would seriously entertain the concept of central strategic 'decoupling' contained in this report."[27] Readers in Western Europe derided the report's recommendations as tacit acceptance of a limited nuclear war on their continent.[28]

The suggestion that even close allies were willing to entertain such disastrous scenarios added to the growing anxiety in Bonn about what the modernization of NATO's short-range forces would mean for Germans in particular. Short-range missiles raised painful questions about their intended targets should they be fired, pointing at Germans on both sides of the Iron Curtain. Critics summed up the potential costs in a crass, yet pithy popular slogan: "The shorter the range, the deader the German."[29]

Christian Democrats were not alone in raising these concerns. The possible modernization of NATO's short-range nuclear weapons galvanized champions of continental denuclearization and defenders of flexible response alike. Confronted with this coalition of unusual political bedfellows, pundits speculated about a resurgence of German nationalism. "From right to left," Pierre Lellouche of the Parisian think tank Institut français des relations internationales argued, "German nationalists are uniting against NATO's nuclear posture."[30] And a surge of pacifism, perhaps even neutralism, might encourage the West Germans to seek accommodation with the Soviet Union.

Convinced that the security debates earlier in the decade had fractured the old consensus, worried observers throughout NATO wondered whether the West Germans would be willing to bear the brunt of SNF modernization.[31] After all, if the Western allies were to deploy new short-range systems, they would need to be stationed on the Federal Republic's territory. Prominent Christian Democrats cautioned that the current political situation was so fragile it might not bear such a strain. Volker Rühe warned that the entire consensus behind nuclear deterrence could collapse in the Federal Republic.[32]

Helmut Kohl Zigs

Throughout 1988, the Western allies entertained a variety of options to deal with short-range nuclear forces, including a series of schemes that could link modernization with some type of arms control offer. Perhaps the allies could combine the work being done by the High Level Group with that of the North Atlantic Council to create an integrated decision document like the one produced in 1979 as part of the Dual-Track Decision.

Few of those who had weathered the political storms of the early 1980s, carrying fresh memories of record-breaking public protests, were keen to repeat the experience. A new two-track decision would create easy leverage with which to hold the deployments of new short-range systems hostage.[33] British observers concluded that there was little appetite in Washington to extend any good will to the West Germans on arms control questions. "The worst aspects of the INF experience continue to leave deep scars," the deputy head of mission at the British embassy in Washington, Brian Fall, concluded.[34]

NATO's deliberations were stuck in a holding pattern. Kohl's government continued to push for more studies, while the Reagan White House, increasingly distracted by other issues, such as the scandal over US arms sales to Iran and illegal redirecting of the profits to right-wing Latin American guerrillas, seemed to do nothing. British diplomats despaired. "For nine months," one memo concluded, "they (I am not exactly sure who!) have been preventing any progress with the comprehensive concept beyond the reaffirmation of existing arrangements—which was effectively completed at the turn of the year and enshrined in the Summit Declaration in March." It was difficult, if not outright impossible, to sustain any momentum, especially with a presidential election on the horizon. If the Republican candidate, George Bush, prevailed in November, there might be a hope that the vice president would appoint a national security adviser already familiar with the ins and outs of the SNF issue. But if the Democratic challenger Michael Dukakis won, the whole affair would invariably be drawn out even longer.[35]

For the time being, the NATO allies stuck to nebulous reaffirmations that they would modernize the existing short-range weapons. When the Nuclear Planning Group met in October 1988, defense ministers endorsed a "step-by-step approach" to modernization to ensure "a credible and effective contribution" to deterrence.[36] But even at this glacial pace, British officials worried that problems already extended far beyond the Federal Republic of Germany. After the Nuclear Planning Group's meeting at The Hague suburb of Scheveningen in November, it seemed clear that Wilfried Martens's government in Brussels had gone wobbly, no longer willing to risk being seen as pro-NATO or pronuclear. There was little doubt that this hesitation reflected the chronic weakness of nearly every Belgian government—this was the eighth coalition with Martens at the helm—and that the current government's leaders were desperate to survive long enough to push through necessary fiscal and constitutional measures before it collapsed. But the British worried that the Belgians' reservations could be contagious, part of "a more dangerous virus" infecting NATO's body politic.[37] If Brussels wanted to postpone a decision on the modernization of NATO's short-range nuclear forces, it was almost certain to pick up support in the Federal Republic, with the Danes, Italians, and Norwegians soon to follow. Perhaps even the Spanish would turn against modernization.[38]

NATO's members showed no signs of developing a common position anytime soon. "It would be nice to think that we shall have within a few months some kind of game-plan to which the Germans, the Americans and we would all be working," John Boyd, the British deputy undersecretary of state, opined in late November 1988. But that seemed unlikely to transpire. "What I fear," Boyd wrote, "is that uncertainty over just what Chancellor Kohl wants, or is prepared to do, will persist well into 1989."[39] And persist it did.

A new administration in Washington wasted little time. On George Bush's first day in the Oval Office, January 23, 1989, Thatcher walked him through a series of pressing problems that the Western allies needed to tackle in short order, including the modernization of NATO's short-range systems.[40] Two days later, Bush laid out his basic position in a letter to Kohl. The modernization of short-range nuclear forces, he argued, was critical for NATO's deterrent and the overall strategy of flexible response. Any modernization decision needed to be set within a broader comprehensive concept, as the allies' plans already envisioned. Bush believed it would be a mistake to pursue arms control talks to limit SNF. Gorbachev was almost certain to introduce a "third zero." If he did, the alliance would have little choice but to accept.[41]

A few weeks later, in an interview with London's *Financial Times*, Kohl pushed back publicly. There was no need to make a final decision on the production of a follow-on to the Lance until 1991 or 1992; after all, the existing Lance systems would be operable until 1995. Kohl's language was deliberate, zeroing in on a production decision. Reporting from the US Embassy in Bonn suggested that this formulation had been carefully crafted, inserted by Kohl's close adviser, Horst Teltschik, during the prepublication edits to the interview.[42] This rhetorical hair-splitting was merely Bonn's latest attempt to express sufficient support for the new weapons so as not to jeopardize congressional funding for the program while also avoiding any public commitments that could stir controversy at home about the production and deployment of these short-range warheads. Genscher reiterated this position when Secretary of State James A. Baker III visited the West German capital on February 12.[43]

Politicians across the alliance feared the issue could easily be exploited by those who sought to undermine NATO, because it played on West Germans' sensitivities about their place within the Cold War, both in a geographic and a psychological sense. An adroit tactician like Gorbachev, for example, could make the most of the issue to create problems in transatlantic relations and increase the political pressure on Kohl's government. Not only was the Federal Republic exposed to the Soviets' short-range nuclear weapons, it was also, as Italy's president, Francesco Cossiga, put it to Bush, the "most exposed to the psychological offensives of Gorbachev."[44]

Soviet diplomats missed few opportunities to apply pressure. On December 7, 1988, at the United Nations, Gorbachev announced sweeping unilateral cuts to Soviet forces, including the withdrawal of fifty thousand troops from Eastern Europe.[45] NATO's foreign ministers responded, highlighting their own proposed ceiling on total armaments in Europe, but these statements lacked the drama and imagination of Gorbachev's. "Mr. Gorbachev spoke in bright colors," one US journalist, Jim Hoagland, wrote. "NATO's foreign ministers uttered mud."[46]

The Kremlin's overtures continued into the new year. In late February 1989, Kremlin arms control negotiator Viktor Karpov floated the possibility that talks to restrict short-range forces could be held parallel to those on conventional forces in Europe.[47] (A new forum, the CFE talks, was set to open in March, replacing the earlier MBFR negotiations.) The Bush administration rebuffed these overtures. It was too soon. "Arms control negotiations on short-range nuclear forces," Bush argued in an early March letter to Thatcher, "is an idea whose time has not yet come; nor is it likely to come anytime soon, certainly not before we see a dramatic change in the threat we face."[48] Reducing the imbalance in conventional forces in Europe remained Bush's top priority.

While the Soviets extended one attractive offer after another, Kohl's coalition deliberated. On April 18, 1989, the government finally nailed down a position on the modernization of short-range forces and arms control negotiations on those same systems. The coalition agreed that the Federal Republic should not be involved in a decision to develop the weapons; that was the sole responsibility of the United States. As for the modernization of NATO's forces, the government adhered to the position that Kohl had staked out in his February *Financial Times* interview; the earlier obligation to modernize where needed remained, but a vote on the deployment of a follow-on to the Lance need not be made until 1991 or 1992. In the interim, the West Germans insisted that NATO should back negotiations with the Soviet Union to secure equal ceilings on nuclear weapons with a range up to five hundred kilometers in parallel with talks to limit conventional forces—as opposed to waiting until after a deal on conventional forces was finalized.[49]

Preferred policy in hand, Genscher and his counterpart at the defense ministry, Gerhard Stoltenberg, headed to Washington for talks. Their meetings were rocky, with the West Germans and the Americans sharply divided. Gorbachev made the most of the widely reported rift between allies. When Baker visited Moscow in May, the Soviet general secretary "dropped his customary 'surprise'" in the form of an offer to withdraw five hundred short-range systems from Eastern Europe before 1989 was through. If the United States were forthcoming, Gorbachev vowed to go even further. The Bush administration might not see the issue as a pressing one, Gorbachev lectured Baker, but "we in Europe"—a phrase Gorbachev deliberately intended to exclude the United States—put the matter at the top of the diplomatic agenda.[50]

Baker did not need the reminder. The next day, at a gathering of NATO's foreign ministers, Genscher lobbied for the entire SNF question to be deferred. As the allies squabbled, they winced at reminders that NATO's fortieth anniversary was mere weeks away, and the show of unity that would be demanded of them to mark the occasion.

George Bush Zags

Observers across the alliance worried that it would be impossible to reach an acceptable solution before NATO's fortieth-anniversary summit in Brussels, already scheduled for late May. Hans van den Broek, the Dutch foreign minister, suggested that it might make more sense to defer and "leave everything undecided at the summit."[51] It seemed the Western allies were on a collision course. Kohl's domestic political position appeared to be deteriorating rapidly. Polling put him at his lowest level of support since he took office in the autumn of 1982.[52] The chancellor was caught between two undesirable options, both with obvious political risks. "On the one hand," as one West German newspaper summed up Kohl's dilemma, "he does not want to disappoint the Americans, who rely on West Germany's blind loyalty to the Alliance. On the other hand, Kohl must trust in the historic changes in East-West relations."[53]

Coalition politics made Kohl's position all the more precarious. Hans-Dietrich Genscher's Free Democrats propped up the coalition, and the longtime West German foreign minister was a staunch advocate for negotiations to limit short-range nuclear forces as soon as possible. Genscher spoke in sweeping and emotional terms about the possible introduction of new, short-range weapons. Before the Bundestag on April 27, he laid out the stakes in plain language: "We are talking about systems which can reach the territory of Poland and Czechoslovakia, nations who suffered so terribly during the Second World War. And we are talking about short-range nuclear weapon systems which reach the other part of our fatherland." No German could be expected to forget that fact, least of all Genscher, who had fled the German Democratic Republic in the early 1950s.[54]

Though still far apart on the substance of a solution, Bush and Kohl shared a commitment to finding one before the summit.[55] By early May, various allied governments, including the Canadians and the Dutch, were already hard at work trying to bridge the divide between the British and the Americans on the one hand and the West Germans on the other. Ruud Lubbers and Hans van den Broek went to Bonn, armed with a compromise text they hoped could be inserted into the comprehensive concept. What the Dutch proposed was the quintessential NATO solution: a new committee.[56]

Thatcher opposed the Dutch initiative, a fact she made clear even before Lubbers and van den Broek shopped the draft language around Bonn.[57] A working group dedicated to studying the prospects for arms control talks on short-range systems would do nothing to halt the momentum behind getting straight to the negotiating table with Moscow. "We would find ourselves driven inexorably towards the negotiations themselves, and thence to a third zero," Thatcher's top foreign policy adviser, Charles Powell, wrote to Bush's national security adviser, Brent Scowcroft.[58] Even the prospect of a compromise was anathema to Thatcher and her closest aides. There was a fundamental divide within the alliance. With both her government and the Bush administration opposed to negotiations, the only viable option was to hold the line. "She favors telling Chancellor Kohl he is totally wrong and that there will be no negotiations," Bush confessed to Lubbers when the Dutch prime minister visited Washington in early May.[59]

Though Thatcher hoped an Anglo-American united front would do the job, most of her advisers assumed a compromise with Bonn was in the offing. No matter the firm rhetoric emanating out of Washington, Powell concluded that the Bush administration would shift from its hardline position and reach a compromise agreement with the West Germans before NATO's summit later that month. He predicted that the Americans would vastly prefer that course of action to the alternative: letting the issue fester and derail the entire summit, the first such NATO gathering of Bush's presidency.[60] Constituencies at home seemed certain to push the president toward a compromise solution. Bush's "encouragingly robust" line had already come under fire in the press and from powerful critics like Paul Nitze. Influential senator Sam Nunn endorsed early negotiations on short-range nuclear forces, provided the West Germans ruled out a third zero, agreed to a link with talks to limit conventional forces, and backed a decision to deploy the follow-on to the Lance.[61] Already, Bush had created a small opening through which to maneuver, suggesting at one press conference, "We're not going to go for any third zero . . . but certainly, I'll be willing to discuss these issues."[62]

The summit's success, the US mission at NATO had argued months earlier, would depend on a decision that both preserved "the essentials of Alliance nuclear deterrence" and avoided "pushing the Germans into a corner."[63] Throughout May, the Bush administration worked to engineer such a solution. After Baker and Genscher met on May 12, the minister at the US Embassy in Bonn let slip to a British counterpart that the two had discussed a number of possible compromise formulas to reach a common position before the summit. Scribbling in the margins of a telegram reporting this development back to London, Powell seethed. The British had been "treated cavalierly."[64]

Desperate to avoid any compromise that included an explicit commitment to early negotiations, Thatcher implored Bush to stand firm. It would be all the more difficult to secure support to deploy the follow-on to the Lance once they had endorsed negotiations. Already, it would be an uphill battle in the face of Gorbachev's appealing offers. The general secretary continued to churn out proposals, including the unilateral withdrawal of five hundred short-range nuclear warheads from Eastern Europe followed by plans to remove all of the Soviet Union's warheads stationed in the region by 1991—provided the United States did the same with its weapons in Western Europe. The Soviet general secretary also called for mutual conventional force reductions based on an equal ceiling, embracing the approach long championed by Western negotiators.[65] In London, officials picked apart these latest Soviet overtures. Gorbachev's offer envisioned the withdrawal of short-range systems, not their destruction (meaning they would likely be relocated from Eastern Europe to the Soviet Union proper), and the number of warheads was a drop in the proverbial bucket. British estimates assumed Moscow had upward of fifteen thousand such warheads.[66] Sprung on the Western allies mere weeks before NATO's summit, Gorbachev's latest initiative was widely interpreted as an attempt to exploit the rift visible within the alliance, strengthening Genscher's hand against Kohl.[67]

Gorbachev's bold initiatives forced Bush onto the defensive. Mere months into his presidency, he seemed to be struggling to respond to the Soviet leader and losing ground by the day. Bush tried to change the narrative with a series of speeches in May. At Texas A&M University on May 12, he sketched out a policy that would move "beyond containment," urging the Soviet Union to slash its massive conventional forces and resuscitating an Eisenhower-era proposal for regular flyovers of military installations called Open Skies.[68] Reanimating a thirty-year-old initiative hardly seemed like the breath of fresh air or visionary thinking policymakers yearned for in order to wrest the initiative back from Gorbachev. As the Kremlin abounded in new thinking, the new president's seemed stuck in the past.[69]

Behind the scenes, the Bush administration and the Kohl government continued their search for a solution in advance of the critical summit. The two sides swapped a series of papers with possible paths forward. Horst Teltschik bemoaned the United States' ongoing pressure, convinced that the Bush administration had all but ignored the concessions already made by Kohl.[70] British officials felt similarly ignored. The latest paper circulated by Washington included none of the substantive amendments and changes suggested by Whitehall. Increasingly marginalized from the entire process, Thatcher assumed that any further concessions to Bonn would be interpreted as a sign of weakness and wondered "where the bottom line would be."[71] Her advisers contemplated various overtures to "stiffen" up the Americans, but these were dismissed as a waste of time and effort. The fundamental problem, Powell concluded, was not that the Thatcher government had failed to share its ideas and views with the Bush administration. It was that Bush and his advisers were "hell-bent on reaching accommodation with the Germans ahead of the NATO Summit," no matter what their other allies said.[72]

But Bonn and Washington remained divided over the timing of any negotiations. The Bush administration stayed with the earlier formula. SNF negotiations should only take place after an agreement on conventional forces. Kohl's coalition refused to accept this order of operations. If the alliance waited until a treaty was not only signed but also being implemented, it could easily take over a decade before any talks on short-range weapons opened.[73] That the timing of negotiations was the major obstacle indicated just how much the US position had already shifted to accommodate the Federal Republic—a fact Bush was sure to emphasize to Kohl. The United States had already met critical West German conditions: agreeing to endorse negotiations on short-range forces (albeit only in principle) and to defer a final decision on the follow-on to the Lance until 1992.[74]

To break the impasse, Bush made Kohl another offer on May 23, just six days before the summit. He suggested a broad commitment to negotiations covering short-range nuclear weapons as well as a delayed production decision. The latter would be pushed back to 1992, provided that the allies ruled out a third zero and accepted that talks would not start until after an agreement limiting conventional forces had been concluded.[75]

Italian prime minister Ciriaco De Mita greeted the initiative as at least a solution to Helmut Kohl's precarious position at home. If Kohl and his Christian Democrats lost the next election, De Mita warned Bush, NATO would be faced with significant problems. The allies should do everything in their power to prop up Kohl, given what the return of the nuclear-shy SPD might mean for NATO's policies.[76]

Reactions in London were far more muted. At the Foreign and Commonwealth Office and the Ministry of Defense, officials disparaged the latest US initiative as another public relations stunt. Assessments of the proposal's substance were scathing—the proposal "bore all the marks of having been hastily put together"—matched only in acerbity by those of the other allies' support. One dismissive cable from the British embassy in Rome chalked up the Italian government's endorsement to the fact that the Italians were "bound to find the wrapping attractive" and had clearly not bothered to do any further thinking on the matter.[77]

On May 29, the first day of NATO's fortieth-anniversary summit in Brussels, Bush unveiled a new proposal designed to jumpstart negotiations on conventional force reductions. An initiative aimed at shortening the time to agreement on conventional force reductions could finesse the outstanding questions about when and on what terms talks covering short-range systems would take place by bringing them closer.[78] What Bush introduced was a four-part proposal, including the existing Western proposals for tank ceilings, an expanded NATO offer to reduce helicopters and aircraft, a manpower ceiling, and an accelerated timeline so as to reach and implement an agreement by 1993 at the latest.[79]

Margaret Thatcher Despairs

At the Brussels Summit, NATO's foreign ministers hammered out an agreement. All sixteen ministers crammed around a round table, staff huddled behind them, trading language back and forth for hours to reach an acceptable formula on short-range nuclear forces. The final product postponed a decision on the deployment of the follow-on to the Lance until 1992, which was coupled with a declaration that the United States would pursue arms control talks "to achieve a *partial* reduction" of US and Soviet short-range nuclear missiles once the implementation of a final agreement on conventional forces began.[80] That emphasis on "partial" was the key to the compromise; implicitly, it ruled out the prospect of a dreaded third zero.

The "effect," one British reporter gushed, "was electric." The summit's success transformed Bush's reputation from that of "a do-nothing president into an imaginative statesman."[81] Bush's conventional force proposal and the ensuing success at the summit, coming on the heels of weeks of speculation regarding an alliance hopelessly divided and adrift, offered fresh evidence of an assertive, forward-looking partnership. "Your Move, Gorbachev," blared a triumphant headline in London's *Daily Mail*.[82]

Bush capped off the summit with a visit to the Federal Republic. In Mainz, the president affirmed that the two nations were "partners in leadership," a formulation that ruffled feathers in the United Kingdom.[83] Bush tried to paper over the problem, assuring Britons that the special relationship was no less special; they, too, were partners in leadership. But the entire SNF experience suggested otherwise. Bush's remarks in Mainz only confirmed what Thatcher already knew; increasingly, the triangle that had shaped so much of NATO's policy since the 1960s was becoming a line—and the British were the odd man out.[84]

London was not alone in identifying disturbing trends; the Bush administration was in fact no more optimistic. In August 1989, Brent Scowcroft warned Bush that the Kohl government's "unprecedented" repudiation of the standing NATO position on short-range forces was a harbinger of trouble to come. "Managing our relations with Germany," he argued, "is likely to be the most serious geopolitical challenge our country faces over the next decade."[85]

The Ash-Heap of History

Scowcroft's warning came with a caveat. US relations with the Federal Republic would be the White House's single greatest challenge unless the Soviet Union began to unravel.[86] Stirrings across Eastern Europe in 1989 suggested that prospect might not be so far-fetched. The Polish government entered into talks with the labor union Solidarność and, in April, the two agreed to a series of free elections. The barbed wire dividing neutral Austria from socialist Hungary came down. Hungarians availed themselves of the chance to buy Western products in Austrian shops—and more and more never made the return journey. Countless East Germans followed suit in "a summer-long exodus." Thousands took refuge at the West German embassy in Prague until the ruling SED relented, extending permission for convoys to transit the German Democratic Republic en route to the other Germany. "It was like Christmas and Easter in one shot," one East German told reporters before hopping aboard a westbound bus.[87]

Soviet intervention had been the norm in earlier decades, a tool to shore up faltering regimes and strengthen the Communists' hold on power. But now, Gorbachev refused. "The Brezhnev Doctrine is dead," one Soviet analyst remarked publicly in August 1989, "even if the official obituary had not yet been published."[88] Across the German Democratic Republic, those who remained took to the streets in massive numbers throughout the autumn of 1989. Crowds in Leipzig asserted their own power under a common slogan: "Wir sind das Volk"—We are the people.[89]

A bumbling East German dealt the regime its fatal blow. On the evening of November 9, 1989, the SED Politburo's Günter Schabowski appeared at a regular press conference with a set of new travel guidelines. As the session wrapped up, he mentioned these change in regulations in the broadest of terms. The assembled journalists peppered Schabowski with questions, which he fielded with a few disjointed sentence fragments that suggested East Germans were free to exit the German Democratic Republic effective immediately. Schabowski's remarks were carried on news broadcasts across the globe, including West German ones beamed back into East German living rooms. Curiosity brought East Berliners into the divided city's streets and to crossing points all along the Berlin Wall. An especially animated crowd gathered at Bornholmer Straße, and that checkpoint's guards decided to let a few through to the West. The trickle soon became a flood. Guards at other border crossings made similar decisions, electing to let their fellow citizens into the West rather than fire on them for trying to go.[90]

Events changed quickly and dramatically. By the end of December 1989, the dissident playwright Václav Havel had been elected president of Czechoslovakia. Demonstrations in Bulgaria ousted the country's longtime leader, Todor Zhivkov, who was replaced by a more reform-minded (though still Communist) successor, Petar Mladenov. In Romania, protests turned violent when Nicolae Ceaușescu ordered security forces to fire on demonstrators. The next day, Ceaușescu fled Bucharest, only to be arrested in the countryside. He and his wife were quickly put on trial and executed on Christmas Day. As communism crumbled across Eastern Europe, a whirlwind of diplomacy ensued. Before November 1989 was through, Helmut Kohl had sketched out a ten-point plan to unify the two Germanys. Days later, in early December, George Bush and Mikhail Gorbachev met at Malta to take stock.

The pace and scope of the transformations sweeping across Europe weakened the arguments in favor of modernizing NATO's short-range nuclear forces. How could the United States justify the deployment of short-range missiles equipped with nuclear warheads aimed at countries undergoing massive political changes like the German Democratic Republic, Czechoslovakia, and Poland?[91] "What do we need these missiles for," one senior West German official allegedly asked members of the Bush administration, "to bomb Lech Wałęsa?"[92]

Congressional budgeting made any modernization even more uncertain. Advisers in the Bush White House anticipated that Congress would strike the funds—about $126 million for fiscal year 1991—allocated to the follow-on to the Lance program as part of a review in April. Doing so would effectively kill the program. Faced with that prospect, the National Security Council's Michael Fry and Philip Zelikow recommended two possible options to move forward. Either Bush could preemptively announce the program's termination, or he could try to keep the program afloat. Cancellation could enable Bush to collect political credit, along with Kohl, though any boost the chancellor got would probably mean little by the time the next West German elections rolled around in December. But there were also clear risks in a ploy that could focus the public's attention on NATO's other short-range systems, such as nuclear artillery, and would prevent the allies from using the follow-on to the Lance as a bargaining chip in any future negotiations with the Soviet Union. Should Bush cancel the program, he would also almost certainly infuriate Thatcher. Despite all these drawbacks, cancellation was the only viable option. The other option, Fry and Zelikow concluded, "does not even sound plausible as we write it. The real question, therefore, is how to get the most out of the virtually certain demise of FOTL."[93]

When Helmut Kohl visited the presidential retreat at Camp David in February 1990, he raised the future of NATO's short-range nuclear forces, curious how Congress would approach the programs. "FOTL is dead as a doornail," Bush responded. But even Kohl, who had pressed for the issue to be deferred, worried about how any cancellation might be perceived. He did not want it to appear as though the United States had caved to public pressure and, though modernization appeared less and less likely by the day, it was still intimately linked to the question of preserving US ground forces in Europe.[94] Congress was likely to balk at the prospect of keeping US troops on the continent without a nuclear arsenal at their disposal.

In May 1990, Bush publicly announced the cancellation of programs critical to the modernization of NATO's short-range nuclear forces, including nuclear artillery shells and the follow-on to the Lance.[95] The forty-first president's announcement, according to one Democratic senator, Delaware's Joseph Biden, was textbook Bush. It fit "the administration's familiar pattern of making a virtue out of necessity," as it was clear that neither Congress nor the Germans would lend their support.[96] But privately, the Bush administration worked to protect at least one short-ranged system, the tactical air-to-surface missile, which, by virtue of not being land-based, was seen as less controversial. "We are flexible and want to be helpful," he told Kohl during one meeting in May. "I want to protect TASM—not to talk about it but to reach an understanding." What Kohl and Bush both sought was an agreement that would keep any discussion of these weapons out of the limelight.[97] "We agreed on SNF to kick the can down the road by studying the appropriate mix," Baker informed Kohl a few weeks later. "Push it until after your elections. We should avoid taking up TASM."[98]

As May came to a close, Gorbachev came to accept the principle of a Germany unified within NATO. The Soviet general secretary had little leverage with which to prevent that outcome, however undesirable it may have been from Moscow's point of view. He presided over a Soviet Union that was in dire need of hard cash—funds Kohl was more than happy to supply—and had forsworn the old blunt instruments of outright intervention. Bush's decision to cancel programs critical to the modernization of NATO's short-range forces, effectively admitting that these controversial upgrades would never take place, removed one of Gorbachev's shrinking number bargaining chips: using negotiated reductions in the Soviet Union's immense arsenal of short-range nuclear weapons to extract concessions, however small.

Securing Gorbachev's backing for reunified Germany's membership in NATO required a shift in the alliance's overall image, as did public expectations of a NATO transformed in light of the changes clearly under way in Eastern Europe. At the 1990 London Summit, as tangible evidence of NATO's adaptation to these new realities, the Western allies jettisoned their old strategic concept. NATO's members indicated that they would move away from the old doctrine of forward defense and flexible response to what they touted as "new force plans consistent with the revolutionary changes in Europe."[99] Flexible response was tossed onto the ash-heap of history, and with it went the logic that underpinned any modernization of NATO's short-range nuclear forces.

The changes sweeping Europe did away with the need for nuclear modernization in the nick of time. Making the case for a strategy based on weapons of mass destruction had become a precarious political balancing act for NATO—all the more so as the Cold War seemed to recede. A combination of arms control agreements and a growing aversion to all things nuclear made NATO's standing strategy—and the weapons it required—increasingly unpalatable. All of the dithering and delay over short-range nuclear forces, not least the debate in the Federal Republic of Germany, seemed to suggest that the Atlantic alliance might not survive another round of upgrades to its members' forces. Even if it could, what would the political costs be? Were they worth paying?

Across NATO, analysts parsed public speeches, polling data, and snippets of private conversations to discern just how unhappy the West Germans were with the alliance's arrangements. The Warsaw Pact's troubles spared them from finding out for certain. What saved the Atlantic alliance was not the wisdom of its policies nor the strength of its arguments, but the fact that the pact's problems turned out to be even more acute.[100] Since NATO's creation four decades earlier, the Western allies had been in a race to the bottom. Would support for NATO and its policies disappear faster than the Soviet threat it was designed to ward off?[101] In the end, the Soviets bottomed out first.

Conclusion
Time and Chance

The ground shook as a Pershing II's motor ran. Nearly a minute passed before it burned out like a "mammoth Roman candle." Huddled in a bunker, looking on at the Longhorn Army Ammunition Plant in Karnack, Texas, was the Soviet monitoring team. George Bush was there too, peering through binoculars to watch the fireball from nearby, as were an assortment of representatives from across the Atlantic alliance. Bush went back to Washington with two pieces of the now-destroyed ballistic missile in tow—one for himself, another for Ronald Reagan.[1] This was the first of the US missiles destroyed to fulfill the terms of the INF Treaty; countless versions of that same scene would play out over the next three years as the United States and the Soviet Union dismantled an entire class of weapons.

The next day, on September 9, 1988, the first Gryphons departed the base at Molesworth, headed for Davis-Monthan Air Force Base just outside Tucson, Arizona. A few dozen protestors assembled to see the missiles off, their placards wishing the cruise "good riddance."[2] The next month, Soviet inspectors filled the bleachers at Davis-Monthan to watch Air Force technicians break down the cruise missiles, sawing them into pieces. From the autumn of 1988 to the spring of 1991, US and Soviet inspectors crisscrossed the globe to oversee ceremonies like these. At times, it made for an unusual sight. "How strange it seems to an English Christian priest refused ten paces into the [US Air Force] base, while the Communist Russians have the freedom of the place," one Molesworth activist mused after the Soviet inspection team came to make their rounds.[3]

That improbable outcome was far from certain, even just a few years earlier. The debate over the Euromissiles nearly destroyed NATO. The fault lines that divided the Western allies were not new: tensions between détente with and deterrence of the Soviet Union; the paradox of guaranteeing Western Europe's security with weapons that would destroy the continent (and likely much more of the planet); and the delicate balancing act of maintaining a security system that constrained the Federal Republic's power without alienating the West Germans. Even as the superpowers turned their intermediate-range missiles into scrap metal, these perennial problems persisted.

After the United States and the Soviet Union signed the INF Treaty in December 1987 and ratified it the next spring, NATO's governments continued to argue about the role nuclear weapons should play in the defense of Europe and what their strategy of flexible response demanded. The removal of an entire class of nuclear weapons left strategists and planners convinced that it was critical to modernize the weapons that remained in Europe, the short-range, tactical, and battlefield weapons left outside the US-Soviet agreement. But for Helmut Kohl's government, it was far from obvious that its constituents would continue to tolerate policies that depended on stationing weapons that could destroy them and their homeland.

As the communist grip on power across Eastern Europe loosened in the autumn of 1989 and into 1990, the case for modernizing NATO's short-range nuclear forces evaporated. When the Western allies gathered in London in July 1990, they shied away from the strategy of flexible response that had guided them since 1967. In its place came a new formulation: a promise that nuclear weapons would only be used as a "last resort."[4]

What made these rapid transformations in European politics possible, at least in the eyes of many Western policymakers, was the triumph of NATO's policies. Helmut Kohl drew a straight line from the Dual-Track Decision in December 1979 to the fall of the Berlin Wall nearly a decade later, on November 9, 1989.[5] Margaret Thatcher, in one conversation with Hans-Dietrich Genscher, credited Ronald Reagan's commitment to a strong defense (a position she shared) and lauded the Atlantic alliance's effort to counterbalance the Soviets' SS-20s. Genscher did not miss the opportunity to remind her that his coalition with Helmut Schmidt had laid the groundwork for the Dual-Track Decision and that his subsequent coalition with Helmut Kohl that had seen those contentious deployments through.[6] Genscher did not go the extra step of reminding the long-serving British prime minister that the president who had forged the Dual-Track Decision was not Reagan, but rather Jimmy Carter.

It is little wonder that those involved touted their own role. Policymakers were not alone in indulging in this congratulatory rhetoric. Col. Doug Livingston, the former head of the 868th Tactical Missile Training Group, which trained US Air Force personnel to operate the Gryphons, argued that the weapons they rehearsed using were "one of the key elements that helped win the Cold War."[7] Peace activists, too, claimed credit as they lauded their own role in transforming and transcending the Cold War. According to Sarah Hipperson, who played an active role in the women's peace camp at Greenham Common, the INF Treaty reflected the principles that peace campaigns had championed.[8] E. P. Thompson certainly agreed. "We repeatedly crossed East/West frontiers, entered into dialogue with official and unofficial voices and prised open the doors through which the events of 1989 came," he insisted.[9] These debates, often personal and partisan, continue—a reminder of just how high the stakes were.[10]

The Cold War did not disappear overnight. It eroded gradually in fits and starts, punctuated by dramatic moments of sudden and sweeping change. Mikhail Gorbachev later referred to the INF Treaty as the first significant step out of the Cold War.[11] It is easy to see why. The agreement signaled how far US-Soviet relations had come and held out the hope that more breakthroughs would follow. The Moscow Summit, with Reagan and Gorbachev strolling side by side in Red Square, was a visual, almost visceral reminder of the changes taking place. Before a group of students at Moscow State University, the president touted the benefits of free enterprise and free elections with a giant bust of Vladimir Lenin looming over him.[12]

The terms of the INF Treaty indicated that Gorbachev was running out of time and willing to make a deal on asymmetrical terms that benefited the United States. When all was said and done, the Soviets had destroyed 1,846 weapons, whereas the United States did away with 846. And the final agreement was not only lopsided in numerical terms. The two superpowers did not limit all intermediate-range forces, only land-based weapons. Areas of comparative advantage for the United States like air- and sea-launched missiles were left unrestricted.[13] Gorbachev's willingness to sign off on so imbalanced a deal was not just the product of the Pershing IIs and Gryphons aimed east but also of severe economic challenges, his own struggles in alliance management, and a group of Soviet officials around him willing to rethink Moscow's place in the world.[14]

But the Cold War was losing ground long before Reagan and Gorbachev signed the INF Treaty. In the 1960s, as the tense atmosphere of the conflict's early years receded and the situation in Europe stabilized, some began to envision a world beyond the ideological divide. Activists returned to many of these same arguments in the early 1980s. Rejecting the atmosphere of crisis that permeated superpower relations, they tried to move past the binaries that defined so much of the Cold War. Individuals in the West amplified the voices of dissidents in the East and worked to break down the stereotypes and barriers that divided citizens in the West from their counterparts on the other side of the Iron Curtain. That there were dissidents in Eastern Europe with whom they could make common cause, or at least attempt to, was largely the product of other developments: the signing of the Helsinki Final Act and the emergence of human rights activism.[15]

As the Cold War receded from the popular imagination, its absence created problems for NATO's boosters. Fear of what the Soviet Union might do was the glue that bound the Atlantic alliance together in the eyes of Western publics. The diminution of the Soviet threat, whether real or imagined, undercut the most obvious case for NATO's continued existence that could be made to voters from White Horse to Wiesbaden.

Paradoxically, the gradual dissolution of the Cold War also created the conditions that proved vital to the alliance's survival and, indeed, its expansion. There was not, as the conventional wisdom sometimes suggests, a single moment in which it was obvious that NATO had fulfilled its mission and should be disbanded. The Western powers did dismantle seemingly superfluous institutions like the quadripartite military structure, Live Oak, that had stood guard over divided Berlin.[16] But two of NATO's core tasks remained unchanged, even as the threat posed by the Soviet Union receded rapidly and dramatically. The Atlantic alliance continued to bind the United States and Canada to Europe and to constrain German power. The SNF episode had underscored the fragility of both arrangements, and as the two Germanys moved toward unification in 1989 and 1990, policymakers on both sides of the Atlantic repeatedly affirmed the value of the alliance and German membership within it.

At London in July 1990, the Western allies invited the states of Central and Eastern Europe, including the Soviet Union, to dispatch representatives to NATO.[17] An overture to the East, this move was also a direct response to Central and Eastern Europeans already seeking admission to NATO as the formal structures of the Warsaw Pact dissolved. Those clamoring to join the Atlantic alliance ramped up their calls in the wake of the London Summit. Czechoslovakia's new leader, the former dissident Václav Havel, inquired in

August 1990 how the Western allies might respond should Prague seek membership.[18] The United States, Bush assured Havel when the two met later that fall, had no interest in seeing Poland, Hungary, and Czechslovakia left "in a European no man's land."[19]

Prior to NATO's November 1991 summit in Rome, the Bush administration had recommended deepening the connections and consultations between NATO's members and their former adversaries. Though by no means a formal invitation to join the alliance, such arrangements would leave the door open to some form of NATO membership at a later date. That thinking formed the foundation for a new body: the North Atlantic Cooperation Council. Within weeks, the scope of the council changed, as did the environment in which it operated. At the council's first session, on December 20, 1991, the Soviet representative in attendance, Nikolai Afanassievskiy, announced that his country would formally dissolve within days, not weeks. News of the Soviet Union's imminent collapse was reduced to a footnote in the meeting's final communiqué.[20]

Without a Soviet Union left to handle delicately, many of the arguments against expanding NATO eastward no longer held as much sway. NATO's current arrangements, including the North Atlantic Cooperation Council, were little more than temporary solutions. Central and Eastern European leaders were not likely to accept a permanent state of limbo, waiting patiently to be let into the alliance at some point in the distant—and uncertain—future. Adding former members of the Warsaw Pact, not just the East Germans grandfathered into the Federal Republic's existing membership, could also solve perennial problems of how to sustain public support for the defense of Europe. With Germany now unified, it seemed improbable that the country would be willing to play host to a large contingent of US forces, even after the inevitable cuts of the peace dividend. Should a spate of new members join the alliance, former Warsaw Pact states like Poland would be far more likely to embrace the presence of US troops than unified Germany.[21] The scars of earlier debates were still fresh; for a group of policymakers in the Bush White House, it was hardly a stretch to imagine a scenario in which German voters turned against US weapons and their continued presence on German soil.

NATO's ranks did not grow on George Bush's watch, though they did under his successors, Democratic and Republican alike. In 1999, the Czech Republic, Hungary, and Poland joined NATO, making it a group of nineteen. Successive rounds of expansion in 2004, 2009, 2017, and 2020 have brought the alliance's current membership up to thirty. NATO's expansion to include former members of the Warsaw Pact and ex-Soviet republics remains among the most contested features of the post–Cold War world, and serious study of the historical record is only starting to become possible as various allied governments declassify files from the 1990s.[22]

The fact that NATO had even managed to survive until 1989 was a triumph of time and chance. The boldness of Gorbachev's vision brought the Atlantic alliance to the brink, but the severity of the Soviet Union's economic, social, and political problems, along with those of Moscow's increasingly erstwhile allies, proved too much for even Gorbachev to control. In the Western allies' race to the bottom with the Soviet Union, Moscow plummeted further and faster.

The INF Treaty is now itself consigned to the history books. As early as 2013, the United States warned that Russia was in violation of the treaty as a result of a new generation of medium-range missiles in production.[23] The administration of Barack Obama went public with these charges in the summer of 2014.[24] The Kremlin denied these accusations, returning fire with claims that the United States had violated the treaty on at least three different counts.[25]

The Russian president, Vladimir Putin, had no great affection for the 1987 agreement. In one October 2016 appearance, he railed against the unequal deal to which "the naive former Russian leadership" had agreed. "What we ultimately got," Putin argued, "was a clear imbalance." The United States retained its air- and sea-launched missiles (of which the Soviet Union had none) and the advantages of a friendly neighborhood. The Russians were not so fortunate. "Almost all of our neighbors make such weapons, including the countries to the east of our borders and Middle Eastern countries as well," Putin exclaimed, "whereas none of the countries sharing borders with the United States, neither Canada nor Mexico, manufacture such weapons."[26]

On October 20, 2018, Obama's successor, Donald J. Trump, announced that the United States would withdraw from the INF Treaty. "Russia has violated the agreement. They have been violating it for many years," Trump said after a rally in Elko, Nevada. "And we're not going to let them violate a nuclear agreement and go out and do weapons and we're not allowed to."[27] The next February, Secretary of State Mike Pompeo gave formal notice that, unless Russia came back into compliance within the next six months, the United States would withdraw from the agreement.[28] The Trump administration followed through on that promise and, on August 2, 2019, Pompeo announced the United States' withdrawal.[29] The Russian foreign ministry followed up Pompeo's announcement with an unsentimental eulogy; the INF Treaty was "formally dead."[30]

With the collapse of the INF Treaty came a boom in competing narratives about how and why the agreement came into being in the first place. As part of this search for a usable past, foreign policy watchers have argued about whether Reagan's vision of "building up to build down" forced the Soviets to negotiate and whether the formula can be repeated without another Gorbachev. Calls abound for another "dual-track strategy" to bring Moscow back to the negotiating table.[31] Even the Trump administration turned to the lessons of history as evidence to support its preferred policy. The 2018 Nuclear Posture Review quoted George Shultz's assertion that "if the West did not deploy Pershing II and cruise missiles, there would be no incentive for the Soviets to negotiate seriously for nuclear weapons reductions."[32] The review's authors marshaled this as evidence to support a new cruise missile program, but Shultz's original remarks could easily be read in multiple different ways. They could be interpreted as a commentary on the threat the Pershing IIs and Gryphons posed to the Soviet Union. But Shultz's comments might just as easily be read as a reference to the psychological implications of the deployments: the Western allies' ability to see a difficult decision through and the Warsaw Pact's corresponding failure to stop it.

Hindsight can dull the edges of old crises and convince us that the option that ultimately won out was the most probable outcome all along. NATO's history, punctuated as it was by crisis, can make it even easier to ignore how close-run some events really were. Like Chicken Little's warnings that the sky is falling or the boy who cried wolf, repeated assertions of an alliance in crisis can obscure the fact that not all of the crises plaguing NATO were created equal.[33]

True, card-carrying historians, if popular stereotypes are to be trusted, insist that their subject of study is more complicated than initially meets the eye and defies the chronology by which it is typically bounded. If that is the case, my professional dues are all paid up. Too often, the history of the Euromissiles is described as one crisis, but there was no single overarching source of crisis. What the Western allies confronted cast doubt on the very foundations of the transatlantic bargain: whether the Americans would remain in Europe, whether the Soviets would keep out, whether the (West) Germans would remain down, and whether their publics and parliaments would continue to accept that their security was best protected with weapons that could destroy humankind.

NOTES

CRF   Condoleezza Rice Files
MT   Memoranda of Conversation and Memoranda of Tele-
           phone Conversation
VP   Vice Presidential Records

DGF   Donald P. Gregg Files

FTF   Foreign Trip Files

GFL   **Gerald R. Ford Presidential Library**

NSA   National Security Adviser's Files

PCFEC   Presidential Country Files for Europe and Canada

RBCF   Richard B. Cheney Files
RNP   Ron Nessen Papers
RTHF   Robert T. Hartmann Files
WHSF   White House Special Files

HIA   **Hoover Institution Archives, Stanford University**

ACUS   Atlantic Council of the United States Records

IISG   **International Institute for Social History**
ISCAP   **Interagency Security Classification Appeals Panel**
JCL   **Jimmy Carter Presidential Library**

RAC   Remote Access Capture
ZBC   Zbigniew Brzezinski Collection

SF   Zbigniew Brzezinski's Subject Files

ZBM   National Security Adviser—Zbigniew Brzezinski Material

CF   Country Files

JFKL   **John F. Kennedy Presidential Library**
LAC   **Library and Archives Canada**

MG27 I 218 Voice of Women Fonds
MG28 I 445 Operation Dismantle Fonds
RG25   Department of External Affairs Fonds

LBJL   **Lyndon Baines Johnson Presidential Library**

AH   Administrative Histories
NSF   National Security Files

IMTF   International Meetings and Trip Files

LOC   Library of Congress

PHNP   Paul H. Nitze Papers

**LSE   British Library of Political and Economic Sciences,
            London School of Economics and Political Science**

CND   Campaign for Nuclear Disarmament
5GCC   Greenham Common Collection

MTFA   Margaret Thatcher Foundation Archives
**MUL   William Division of Archives and Research
            Collections, McMaster University Library**

CPC   Canadian Peace Congress Fonds
MTF   Murray Thomson Fonds

NARA   National Archives and Records Administration

AAD   Access to Archival Databases
RG59   Records of the Department of State

AL   Records of the Policy Planning Staff, Director's Files
            (Anthony Lake), 1977–1981
WL   Records of the Policy Planning Staff, Director's Files
            (Winston Lord), 1969–1977

NATO   Archives of the North Atlantic Treaty Organization

AC/52   Committee on Information and Cultural Relations
AC/124   Conference of National Information Officers
C-M   North Atlantic Council Memoranda
C-R   North Atlantic Council Records
DPC   Defense Planning Committee
HR   Future Tasks of the Alliance—Harmel Report
IMSM   International Military Staff Memoranda
IMSWM   International Military Staff Working Memoranda
LOCOM   Liaison Office Communication
LOM   Standing Group Liaison Office Paris Memoranda
M   Press Releases and Communiqués
MCWM   Military Committee Working Memoranda
NPG   Nuclear Planning Group

PO	Private Office of the Secretary General
PR	Private Record of the Secretary General
NSA	**National Security Archive**
EBB	Electronic Briefing Books
OSA	**Vera and Donald Blinken Open Society Archives**
RFE/RL	Radio Free Europe / Radio Liberty Records
PA-AA	**Politisches Archiv des Auswärtigen Amts**
B150	Deklassifizierte Dokumente für die Edition der Akten zur Auswärtigen Politik der Bundesrepublik Deutschland
PPP	**Public Papers of the Presidents of the United States**
RNL	**Richard M. Nixon Presidential Library**
NSC	National Security Files
CFE	Country Files—Europe
RRL	**Ronald Reagan Presidential Library**
DBF	Dennis Blair Files
DGF	David Gergen Files
DTRF	Donald T. Regan Files
ESNSC	Executive Secretariat, National Security Council
CF	Country Files
HOSF	Head of State Files
MF	Meeting Files
JFMF	Jack F. Matlock Files
MBF	Morton Blackwell Files
REPF	Richard E. Pipes Files
RLF	Ronald Lehman Files
WACF	William A. Cockell Files
WPCF	William P. Clark Files
RROHP	**Ronald Reagan Oral History Project, Miller Center of Public Affairs, University of Virginia**
SCPC	**Swarthmore College Peace Collection**
CSE	Campaign to Stop the Euromissiles
END	European Nuclear Disarmament
IKV	Interkerkelijk Vredesberaad

TNA   National Archives of the United Kingdom

DEFE 70   Ministry of Defence (Army): Registered Files and
           Branch Folders
DEFE 24   Ministry of Defence: Defence Secretariat Branches and
           Their Predecessors
FCO 28   Foreign Office and Foreign and Commonwealth Office:
           Northern Department and East European and Soviet
           Department (and Succeeding Departments)
FCO 46   Foreign Office and Foreign and Commonwealth Office:
           Defence Department and Successors
PREM 16   Prime Minister's Office: Correspondence and Papers,
           1974–1979
PREM 19   Prime Minister's Office: Correspondence and Papers,
           1979–1997

VTNA   Vanderbilt Television News Archive, Vanderbilt
        University
WCDA   Wilson Center Digital Archive
WPNA   War and Peace in the Nuclear Age, GBH Archives
YUA   Yale University Archives

CRGSVP   Cyrus R. and Grace Sloane Vance Papers

Introduction

1. "Great Confrontations at the Oxford Union: Caspar Weinberger vs. E. P. Thompson," February 27, 1984, https://www.youtube.com/watch?v=wMdTJJa3kVo. Thompson's remarks were reprinted in E. P. Thompson, *The Heavy Dancers* (New York: Pantheon, 1985), 49–60.

2. "Great Confrontations at the Oxford Union." An earlier iteration of the debate, planned for the previous spring, had been canceled. Rumors swirled that Michael Heseltine, the British defense minister, had intervened to stop Thompson and Weinberger from facing off on the eve of a British general election. R. W. Apple Jr., "Weinberger Drops Debate at Oxford," *New York Times*, April 20, 1983; Melvin Maddocks, "Debaters Who Play Hardball," *Christian Science Monitor*, April 28, 1983.

3. "Great Confrontations at the Oxford Union."

4. For a discussion of hindsight and how it shapes our understanding of the past, see Francis J. Gavin, "Thinking Historically: A Guide for Strategy and Statecraft," *War on the Rocks*, November 19, 2019, https://warontherocks.com/2019/11/think ing-historically-a-guide-for-strategy-and-statecraft/.

5. This characterization of NATO's history is inspired by Timothy Andrews Sayle's observation that the alliance's history is "a kaleidoscope of domestic politics and national foreign policies." Timothy Andrews Sayle, *Enduring Alliance: A History of NATO and the Postwar Global Order* (Ithaca, NY: Cornell University Press, 2019), 7.

6. The notable exception is Leopoldo Nuti et al., eds., *The Euromissile Crisis and the End of the Cold War* (Washington, DC, and Stanford, CA: Woodrow Wilson Center Press and Stanford University Press, 2015). A similar approach, focused on the German experience, can be found in Christoph Becker-Schaum et al., eds., *Entrüstet Euch! Nuklearkrise, NATO-Doppelbeschluss und Friedensbewegung* (Paderborn, Germany: Schöningh, 2012), published in English as Christoph Becker-Schaum et al., eds., *The Nuclear Crisis: The Arms Race, Cold War Anxiety, and the German Peace Movement of the 1980s* (New York: Berghahn Books, 2016).

7. For a comparison to the Cuban Missile Crisis, see Leopoldo Nuti et al., "Editors' Introduction," in Nuti et al., *Euromissile Crisis*, 1. The terms "Euromissile Crisis" and "Euromissiles Crisis" are widely used, and the most obvious example is the title of Nuti et al., *Euromissile Crisis*. That shorthand is not without its critics. Christoph Becker-Schaum, Philipp Gassert, Martin Klimke, Wilfried Mausbach, and Marianne Zepp explicitly referred to the "nuclear crisis" as an alternative to the "Euromissile crisis," in order "to stress that the debate about NATO's Double-Track Decision involved far more than questions of international security and foreign relations." See Christoph Becker-Schaum et al., "Introduction: The Nuclear Crisis, NATO's Double-Track Decision, and the Peace Movement of the 1980s," in Becker-Schaum et al., *Nuclear Crisis*, 2. For a contrary view, taking issue with the crisis characterization, see Wallace J. Thies, *Why NATO Endures* (Cambridge: Cambridge University Press, 2009), 175–99.

8. For a strong rebuttal of this assertion, see Andrea Chiampan, "The Origins of the Euromissile Crisis, 1969–1979" (PhD diss., Graduate Institute of International and Development Studies, 2017).

9. Interview with Helmut Schmidt, n.d. [1982], YUA, CRGSVP, box 35, folder "Palme Commission on Disarmament and Security Issues meeting (at Seven Springs Center, NY) (12–21 Feb) 1982."

10. The chapters in Nuti et al., *Euromissile Crisis*, hint at the problems surrounding chronology.

11. Stanley Hoffmann, "Nuclear Weapons and NATO: Reasons and Unreason," *Foreign Affairs* 60, no. 2 (1981): 327.

12. There are numerous works covering each of these episodes. On the Suez Crisis and its significance in transatlantic relations, see, for starters, Winfried Heinemann, "'Learning by Doing': Disintegrating Factors and the Development of Political Cooperation in Early NATO," in *NATO and the Warsaw Pact: Intrabloc Conflicts*, ed. Mary Ann Heiss and S. Victor Papacosma (Kent, OH: Kent State University Press, 2008), 43–57; W. Scott Lucas, *Divided We Stand: Britain, the US and the Suez Crisis* (London: Hodder and Stoughton, 1991). For the Gaullist challenge and its impact on NATO, see Frédéric Bozo, *Deux stratégies pour l'Europe. De Gaulle, les États-Unis et l'Alliance atlantique 1958–1969* (Paris: Plon, 1996). Its connections to strategic policy are treated in Helga Haftendorn, *NATO and the Nuclear Revolution: A Crisis of Credibility, 1966–1967* (Oxford: Oxford University Press, 1996). The Offset Crisis is covered in Hubert Zimmerman, *Money and Security: Troops, Monetary Policy, and West Germany's Relations with the United States and Britain, 1950–1971* (Washington, DC, and Cambridge: German Historical Institute and Cambridge University Press, 2002), 209–38; Thomas A. Schwartz, *Lyndon Johnson and Europe: In the Shadow of Vietnam* (Cambridge, MA: Harvard University

Press, 2003), 115–32. All three episodes are covered in Sayle, *Enduring Alliance*, which is the natural starting point on NATO's Cold War.

13. Brent Scowcroft to Gerald R. Ford, "Chancellor Schmidt Interview on NATO and Detente," April 30, 1976, GFL, NSA, PCFEC, box 6, folder "Germany (10)."

14. Mario Del Pero termed this scholarly affliction "transatlantic crisology." Mario Del Pero, "Henry Kissinger's Three Europes," *Journal of Transatlantic Studies* 17, no. 1 (2019): 11. On the importance of perceptions, see Robert Jervis, *Perception and Misperception in International Politics*, new ed. (Princeton, NJ: Princeton University Press, 2017).

15. For an early assessment highlighting the fundamental continuities between the Euromissiles and earlier allied defense questions, see David N. Schwartz, *NATO's Nuclear Dilemmas* (Washington, DC: Brookings Institution, 1983).

16. On NATO's early strategy and the alliance's reliance on nuclear weapons, see, as starting points, Timothy Ireland, "Building NATO's Nuclear Posture 1950–65," in *The Nuclear Confrontation in Europe*, ed. Jeffrey D. Boutwell, Paul Doty, and Gregory F. Treverton (London: Croom Helm, 1985), 5–43; Marc A. Trachtenberg, *History and Strategy* (Princeton, NJ: Princeton University Press, 1991), 153–68; Robert A. Wampler, "Ambiguous Legacy: The United States, Great Britain and the Foundations of NATO Strategy, 1948–1957" (PhD diss., Harvard University, 1991); Jeffrey H. Michaels, "Visions of the Next War or Reliving the Last One? Early Alliance Views of War with the Soviet Bloc," *Journal of Strategic Studies* 43, nos. 6–7 (2020): 990–1013.

17. Thomas C. Schelling, *Arms and Influence with a New Preface and Afterword* (New Haven, CT: Yale University Press, 2008), 36.

18. On the contradictions and tensions within NATO's strategy, along with the calculations underpinning it, see Michael Howard, "Deterrence, Consensus and Reassurance in the Defence of Europe," *Adelphi Papers* 23, no. 184 (1983): 17–26; Francis J. Gavin, "NATO's Radical Response to the Nuclear Revolution," in *Charter of the North Atlantic Treaty Organization: Together with Scholarly Commentaries and Essential Historical Documents*, ed. Ian Shapiro and Adam Tooze (New Haven, CT: Yale University Press, 2018), 177–92.

19. J. Michael Legge, *Theater Nuclear Weapons and the NATO Strategy of Flexible Response* (Santa Monica, CA: RAND Corp., 1983), 1. On the strategy's evolution after 1967, see Ivo H. Daalder, *The Nature and Practice of Flexible Response: NATO Strategy and Theater Nuclear Forces since 1967* (New York: Columbia University Press, 1991). On the strategy's clear limitations, see Francis J. Gavin, *Nuclear Statecraft: History and Strategy in America's Atomic Age* (Ithaca, NY: Cornell University Press, 2012), 30–56.

20. Helmut Schmidt interview, November 12, 1987, WPNA.

21. Jon R. Lindsay and Erik Gartzke, "Introduction: Cross-Domain Deterrence, from Practice to Theory," in *Cross-Domain Deterrence: Strategy in an Era of Complexity*, ed. Jon R. Lindsay and Erik Gartzke (Oxford: Oxford University Press, 2019), 14.

22. On the logic of deterrence, the standard entry point remains Schelling, *Arms and Influence*. The evolution of early nuclear strategy is covered in Lawrence Freedman, "The First Two Generations of Nuclear Strategy," in *Makers of Modern Strategy: From Machiavelli to the Nuclear Age*, ed. Peter Paret (Princeton, NJ: Princeton University Press, 1986), 735–78.

23. Robert M. Hunter interview, August 10, 2004, FAOHP, 68–69.

24. Hans Apel interview, October 20, 1987, WPNA.

25. James D. Fearon, "Domestic Political Audiences and the Escalation of International Disputes," *American Political Science Review* 88, no. 3 (1994): 577–92.

26. Jeffrey Herf described this as an "asymmetric strategic interaction," focusing on the Soviet Union's ability to influence the West German discourse. See Jeffrey Herf, *War by Other Means: Soviet Power, West German Resistance, and the Battle of the Euromissiles* (New York: Free Press, 1991), esp. 7–13. Herf focused on only one element of the equation—the weaknesses of democracy in an ideological struggle—and overstated the case for the success of Soviet diplomacy. For a recent discussion of the strengths and limitations of Herf's arguments, see Holger Nehring, "The Last Battle of the Cold War: Peace Movements and German Politics in the 1980s," in Nuti et al., *Euromissile Crisis*, 310–11. Contemporary critiques of Herf's arguments, which illustrate the broader significance of these scholarly debates, along with Herf's response, can be found in Gert Krell et al., "Correspondence," *International Security* 11, no. 2 (1986): 193–215.

27. Ed Barber, "Westminster, May 1983," photograph, in Zoë Fairbairns, James Cameron, and Ed Barber, *Peace Moves: Nuclear Protest in the 1980s; Photographs by Ed Barber* (London: Chatto & Windus, Hogarth, 1984), 23; Hulton Deutsch, "CND Protestors on March in London," photograph, October 22, 1983, Corbis via Getty Images.

28. My argument about the decline of popular support for the Cold War's binary logic draws on Jan Hansen, untitled review in H-Diplo Roundtable 28, no. 30 (June 23, 2017), https://networks.h-net.org/system/files/contributed-files/round table-xviii-30.pdf.

29. "Summary of Remarks by R. C. Richardson," in Robert L. Rinne, ed., *The History of NATO TNF Policy: The Role of Studies, Analysis and Exercises Conference Proceedings* (Livermore, CA: Sandia National Laboratories, 1994), 2:55.

30. "Göttinger Bürger für den Frieden," August 1981, AGG, PKA 3438.

31. Nena, "99 Red Balloons," track 1, on *99 Luftballons*, Spliff Studio, 1984; Sting, "Russians," track 3 on *The Dream of the Blue Turtles*, Sony Music, 1985.

32. John Glen, dir., *Octopussy* (Eon Productions and United Artists, 1983).

33. John Badham, dir., *WarGames* (United Artists and Sherwood Productions, 1983). On the proliferation of doomsday scenarios in early 1980s popular culture, see Philipp Baur, "Nuclear Doomsday Scenarios in Film, Literature, and Music," in Becker-Schaum et al., *Nuclear Crisis*, 322–37.

34. "Great Confrontations at the Oxford Union"; "The Oxford Debate That Weinberger Won," *Washington Post*, March 6, 1984; Caspar Weinberger to Ronald Reagan, February 29, 1984, RRL, ESNSC, CF, box 20, folder "United Kingdom 11/01/83-06/30/84 1."

Part One. Decide

1. Helmut Schmidt, *Verteidigung oder Vergeltung: Ein deutscher Beitrag zum strategischen Problem der NATO* (Stuttgart, Germany: Seewald, 1961), 57. The English translation appeared as Helmut Schmidt, *Defense or Retaliation: A German View*, trans. Edward Thomas (New York: Praeger, 1962).

2. Schmidt, *Verteidigung oder Vergeltung*, 215.

3. Schmidt credited a veritable who's who of strategic thinkers with shaping his views on NATO's strategy. The foreword to *Verteidigung oder Vergeltung* listed Robert Bowie, Alastair Buchan, Anthony Buzzard, Basil Liddell Hart, Denis Healy, Roger Hilsman, Pierre Gallois, James King, Henry Kissinger, Thomas Schelling, John Slessor, and Arnold Wolfers. See Schmidt, *Verteidigung oder Vergeltung*, 10. For an overview of these debates, see Lawrence Freedman and Jeffrey Michaels, *The Evolution of Nuclear Strategy*, 4th ed., rev. (London: Palgrave Macmillan, 2019), 135–53.

4. Kristina Spohr, *The Global Chancellor: Helmut Schmidt and the Reshaping of the International Order* (Oxford: Oxford University Press, 2016), 33–59.

5. Deutscher Bundestag, Stenographischer Bericht, 20. Sitzung, 3. Wahlperiode, March 22, 1958, 1037–48.

6. Schmidt, *Verteidigung oder Vergeltung*, 153.

7. Schmidt, *Verteidigung oder Vergeltung*, 239.

8. Helmut Schmidt, *Strategie des Gleichgewichts: Deutsche Friedenspolitik und die Westmächte* (Stuttgart, Germany: Seewald, 1969). The English translation appeared as Helmut Schmidt, *The Balance of Power: Germany's Peace Policy and the Super Powers*, trans. Edward Thomas (London: W. Kimber, 1971).

9. Schmidt, *Balance of Power*, 18.

10. Helmut Schmidt, "The 1977 Alastair Buchan Memorial Lecture," *Survival* 20, no. 1 (1978): 4.

1. The Sixties Stalemate

1. "Radio and Television Address to the American People on the Soviet Arms Build-Up in Cuba," October 22, 1962, JFKL, JFKWHA-142-001.

2. "Summary Record of the Seventh Meeting of the Executive Committee of the National Security Council," October 27, 1962, *FRUS 1961–1963*, vol. 11: *Cuban Missile Crisis and Aftermath*, ed. Edward C. Keefer, Charles S. Sampson, and Louis J. Smith (Washington, DC: Government Printing Office, 1996), doc. 90.

3. Quoted in Marc A. Trachtenberg, *A Constructed Peace: The Making of the European Settlement, 1945–1963* (Princeton, NJ: Princeton University Press, 1999), 355. On how details of this trade became public knowledge, see Jim Hershberg, "Anatomy of a Controversy: Anatoly F. Dobrynin's Meeting with Robert F. Kennedy, Saturday, October 27, 1962," *Cold War International History Project Bulletin* 5 (1995): 75–80.

4. On the Berlin Crisis, see Francis J. Gavin, *Nuclear Statecraft: History and Strategy in America's Atomic Age* (Ithaca, NY: Cornell University Press, 2012), 57–74. On the Cuban Missile Crisis, see Aleksandr Fursenko and Timothy Naftali, *"One Hell of a Gamble": Khrushchev, Castro, and Kennedy, 1958–1964* (New York: W. W. Norton, 1997). For Khrushchev's thinking, see Vladislav M. Zubok and Constantin Pleshakov, *Inside the Kremlin's Cold War: From Stalin to Khrushchev* (Cambridge, MA: Harvard University Press, 1996), 236–74; William Taubman, *Khrushchev: The Man and His Era* (New York: W. W. Norton, 2003), 529–77.

5. For a nuanced discussion of how Khrushchev's policies contributed to his ouster, see Joseph Torigian, "'You Don't Know Khrushchev Well': The Ouster of the Soviet Leader as a Challenge to Recent Scholarship on Authoritarian Politics," *Journal of Cold War Studies* 24, no. 1 (2022): 78–115. On the impact of the Khrushchev

ouster, see Simon Miles, "Envisioning Détente: The Johnson Administration and the October 1964 Khrushchev Ouster," *Diplomatic History* 40, no. 4 (2016): 722–49

6. Taubman, *Khrushchev*, 579.

7. Trachtenberg, *Constructed Peace*, 352–402.

8. Jeremi Suri, *Power and Protest: Global Revolution and the Rise of Détente* (Cambridge, MA: Harvard University Press, 2003), 3, 44–87.

9. Theo Sommer, "For an Atlantic Future," *Foreign Affairs* 43, no. 1 (1964): 113.

10. Frédéric Bozo, *Deux stratégies pour l'Europe. De Gaulle, les États-Unis et l'Alliance atlantique 1958–1969* (Paris: Plon, 1996).

11. "Letter from President de Gaulle to President Eisenhower," September 17, 1958, *FRUS 1958–1960*, vol. 7: *Western Europe*, ed. Ronald D. Landa et al. (Washington, DC: Government Printing Office, 1993), doc. 45.

12. "Telegram from the Embassy in France to the Department of State," *FRUS 1964–1968*, vol. 14: *Soviet Union*, ed. David C. Humphrey and Charles S. Sampson (Washington, DC: Government Printing Office, 2001), doc. 53. See also Maurice Vaïsse, "De Gaulle's Handling of the Berlin and Cuban Crises," in *Europe, Cold War and Coexistence, 1955–1965*, ed. Wilfried Loth (London: Routledge, 2004), 70.

13. Frédéric Bozo, "Détente versus Alliance: France, the United States and the Politics of the Harmel Report (1964–1968)," *Contemporary European History* 7, no. 3 (1998): 345–46; Garrett Martin, "Towards a New Concert of Europe: De Gaulle's Vision of a Post–Cold War Europe," in *Visions of the End of the Cold War in Europe, 1945–1990*, ed. Frédéric Bozo, Marie-Pierre Rey, Bernd Rother, and N. Piers Ludlow (New York: Berghahn Books, 2012), 94–97.

14. A solid overview of the various issues straining the Atlantic alliance in the early 1960s can be found in Andreas Wenger, "NATO's Transformation in the 1960s and the Ensuing Political Order in Europe," in *Transforming NATO in the Cold War: Challenges beyond Deterrence in the 1960s*, ed. Andreas Wenger, Christian Nuenlist, and Anna Locher (Abingdon, UK: Routledge, 2006), 223–31.

15. Robert R. Bowie, "Tensions within the Alliance," *Foreign Affairs* 42, no. 1: 65.

16. Karl Kaiser et al., *Western Security: What Has Changed? What Should Be Done?* (New York: Council on Foreign Relations, 1981), 17. Walter Slocombe described the extension of deterrence as threefold: a national extension (from the United States to other nations), a geographic extension (from the United States to other territories closer to the Soviet Union), and a threat extension (not just to respond to the largest threats to the United States but also to discourage lesser attacks). See Walter Slocombe, "Extended Deterrence," *Washington Quarterly* 7, no. 4 (1984): 93–94.

17. See, for example, Kai-Uwe von Hassel, "Organizing Western Defense: The Search for Consensus," *Foreign Affairs* 43, no. 2 (1965): 211; Henry A. Kissinger, "The Unsolved Problems of European Defense," *Foreign Affairs* 40, no. 4 (1962): 515.

18. Quoted in Jean Lacouture, *De Gaulle*, vol. 3: *Le souverain, 1951–1970* (Paris: Éditions du Seuil, 1986), 376.

19. Klaus Wehnert, February 7, 1964, quoted in Sommer, "For an Atlantic Future," 115.

20. "Letter from President de Gaulle to President Johnson," March 7, 1966, *FRUS 1964–1968*, vol. 13: *Western Europe Region*, ed. Charles S. Sampson (Washington, DC: Government Printing Office, 1995), doc. 137.

21. John Leddy interview, January 31, 1990, FAOHP, 13.

22. The provision in question was Article 13, which read: "After the Treaty has been in force for twenty years, any Party may cease to be a Party one year after its notice of denunciation has been given to the Government of the United States of America, which will inform the Governments of the other Parties of the deposit of each notice of denunciation." North Atlantic Treaty, April 4, 1949, https://www.nato.int/cps/en/natolive/official_texts_17120.htm.

23. Otto Zausmer, "NATO's Malady Is Its Success," *Boston Globe*, June 6, 1965.

24. C. L. Sulzberger, "Has Success Spoiled NATO?," *Atlanta Constitution*, November 25, 1965.

25. Max Frankel, "The Twilight of NATO," *New York Times*, December 5, 1965.

26. Sommer, "For an Atlantic Future," 113.

27. Lyndon B. Johnson, "Remarks in New York City before the National Conference of Editorial Writers," October 7, 1966, *PPP: Lyndon B. Johnson 1966*, vol. 2, ed. Warren R. Reid (Washington, DC: Government Printing Office, 1967), 503. On the origins and background to Johnson's address, see Thomas A. Schwartz, "Moving beyond the Cold War: The Johnson Administration, Bridge-Building, and Détente," in *Beyond the Cold War: Lyndon Johnson and the New Global Challenges of the 1960s*, ed. Francis J. Gavin and Mark Atwood Lawrence (Oxford: Oxford University Press, 2014), esp. 85–87.

28. Bohlen to Rusk, June 3, 1966, *FRUS 1964–1968*, vol. 13, doc. 172.

29. Thomas Alan Schwartz, *Lyndon Johnson and Europe: In the Shadow of Vietnam* (Cambridge, MA: Harvard University Press, 2003), 92–139; James Ellison, "Defeating the General: Anglo-American Relations, Europe and the NATO Crisis of 1966," *Cold War History* 6, no. 1 (2006): 85–111.

30. US Embassy Brussels to State Department, November 22, 1966, LBJL, NSF, IMTF, box 35, folder "NATO Ministerial Meeting, Paris December, 1966 [1 of 3]."

31. Anna Locher and Christian Nuenlist, "What Role for NATO? Conflicting Western Perceptions of Détente, 1963–65," *Journal of Transatlantic Studies* 2, no. 2 (2004): 197.

32. "Resolution on Future Tasks of the Alliance," December 27, 1966, NATO, C-M(66)145.

33. Untitled extract from C-R(66)68, December 15, 1966, NATO, HR/02-V1. The full text of the resolution approved by the North Atlantic Council is in "Resolution on Future Tasks of the Alliance," December 27, 1966, NATO, C-M(66)145.

34. Timothy Andrews Sayle, *Enduring Alliance: A History of NATO and the Postwar Global Order* (Ithaca, NY: Cornell University Press, 2019), 160.

35. Alan Harvey, "Political Aim for NATO Is Accepted," *Globe and Mail*, December 14, 1967.

36. Helga Haftendorn, *NATO and the Nuclear Revolution: A Crisis of Credibility 1966–1967* (Oxford: Oxford University Press, 1996), 320–74.

37. "NATO and Public Opinion," *NATO Letter* 16, no. 1 (1968): inside cover.

38. *Report on the Future Tasks of the Alliance* (Brussels: NATO Information Service, 1968), 5.

39. Assistant Secretary General for Political Affairs to Secretary General, "Reports on the Future Tasks of the Alliance," October 2, 1967, NATO, HR/02-V9.

40. Secretary General to Permanent Representatives, "Future Tasks of the Alliance," November 16, 1967, NATO, PO/67/832.

41. Assistant Secretary General for Political Affairs to Secretary General, "Reports on the Future Tasks of the Alliance."

42. "Final Communique," December 14, 1967, NATO, M4(67)3.

43. *The Future Tasks of the Alliance* (Brussels: NATO Information Service, 1968); *Why NATO?* (Brussels: NATO Information Service, 1968). NATO's Information Service also printed full copies of the report, packaged for public circulation.

44. *Why NATO?*

45. Henry Newcomer to Director, International Military Staff, "East-West Force Reductions," June 27, 1967, NATO, LOM 145/67. An overview of the idea's emergence can be found in Christoph Bluth, "The Origins of MBFR: West German Policy Priorities and Conventional Arms Control," *War in History* 7, no. 2 (2000): 181–206.

46. *Report on the Future Tasks of the Alliance*, 7.

47. "Mutual and Balanced Force Reductions," June 24–25, 1968, NATO, M2(67)4.

48. David K. Willis, "Why NATO Talks of Détente," *Christian Science Monitor*, June 26, 1968.

49. Manlio Brosio, "NATO and East-West Détente," *NATO Letter* 15, no. 12 (1967): 9. On the origins of the Nuclear Planning Group, see Timothy Andrews Sayle, "A Nuclear Education: The Origins of NATO's Nuclear Planning Group," *Journal of Strategic Studies* 43, no. 6–7 (2020): 920–56.

50. Flexible response had been the subject of considerable transatlantic debate for most of the 1960s. For background on NATO's debates, see, for starters, David N. Schwartz, *NATO's Nuclear Dilemmas* (Washington, DC: Brookings Institution, 1983), 136–92; Jane E. Stromseth, *The Origins of Flexible Response: NATO's Debate over Strategy in the 1960s* (Houndmills, UK: Macmillan, 1988).

51. Betty Goetz Lall, "A NATO-Warsaw Détente?," *Bulletin of the Atomic Scientists* 20, no. 9 (1964): 38.

52. S. Res. 300, August 31, 1966, *Congressional Record* vol. 112, pt. 16 (1966), 21442.

53. Sayle, *Enduring Alliance*, 132–33.

54. "Accelerated Defence Planning Procedures," October 12, 1966, NATO, LOCOM 7294.

55. For details on the outcome of the trilateral talks, see Sayle, *Enduring Alliance*, 143–46.

56. "Statement by Field Marshal Sir Richard Hull Chief of Defence Staff United Kingdom to 37 MC/CS: NATO Strategy," December 13, 1966, NATO, UKR-203-66, enclosure to MCWM-91–66.

57. "NATO Ministerial Meeting, Luxembourg, June 13–15, 1967: Position Paper," June 5, 1967, LBJL, NSF, IMTF, box 35, folder "NATO Ministerial Meeting, Luxembourg June 13–14, 1967."

58. "Trilateral Talks between the Governments of the Federal Republic of Germany, the United Kingdom and the United States: Progress Report by the Three Governments to the Defence Planning Committee," November 30, 1966, NATO, LOM 307/66.

59. A. Struckman memorandum for the members of the Military Committee, "NATO Strategy," October 17, 1966, NATO, MCWM-26-66.

60. Defence Planning Committee, "Decisions Taken at the Meeting of the Defence Planning Committee in Ministerial Session held on 9th May, 1967," NATO, Annex I to DPC/D(67)23. See also "Final Communique," May 9, 1967, NATO, M1(67)1.

61. "4. Revision of NATO Strategy," n.d., LBJL, AH, box 1, folder "Chapter 3 Europe Sections A and B."

62. Military Committee, "Overall Strategic Concept for the Defense of the North Atlantic Treaty Organization Area [MC 14/3(Final)]," January 16, 1968, in *NATO Strategy Documents 1949–1969*, ed. Gregory W. Pedlow (Brussels: Historical Office, Supreme Headquarters Allied Powers Europe and NATO International Staff Central Archives, 1997), 357–59. See also Gregory W. Pedlow, "The Evolution of NATO Strategy, 1949–1969," in Pedlow, *NATO Strategy Documents*, xxiv–xxv.

63. "Paper Prepared in the Department of State and the National Security Council," n.d., *FRUS 1969–1976*, vol. 41: *Western Europe; NATO, 1969–1972*, ed. James E. Miller and Laurie Van Hook (Washington, DC: Government Printing Office, 2012), doc. 28.

64. James Callaghan interview, November 26, 1987, WPNA.

65. Military Committee, "Overall Strategic Concept," 364.

66. "Strategy and NATO Forces—DPWG Meeting, 24–25 Apr 1967," April 26, 1967, NATO, LOCOM 7948.

67. Ivo H. Daalder, *The Nature and Practice of Flexible Response: NATO Strategy and Theater Nuclear Forces since 1967* (New York: Columbia University Press, 1991), 70.

68. "Telegram from the Mission to the North Atlantic Treaty Organization and European Regional Organizations to the Department of State," December 10, 1966, *FRUS 1964–1968*, vol. 13, doc. 225.

69. In the late 1960s and early 1970s, the Nuclear Planning Group conducted studies on the initial use of tactical nuclear weapons, the follow-on use of these weapons, the use of atomic demolition munitions, and the concept of a theater nuclear strike force. A detailed treatment of these studies can be found in J. Michael Legge, *Theater Nuclear Weapons and the NATO Strategy of Flexible Response* (Santa Monica, CA: RAND Corp., 1983), 17–28.

70. "Notes of National Security Council Meeting," February 14, 1969, *FRUS 1969–1976*, vol. 34: *National Security Policy*, ed. M. Todd Bennett (Washington, DC: Government Printing Office, 2011), doc. 7.

71. "Meeting of a Combined Review Group and Verification Panel Meeting," August 31, 1970, *FRUS 1969–1976*, vol. 41, doc. 46.

72. On the Nixon administration's search for greater flexibility and options in its nuclear strategy, see Terry Terriff, *The Nixon Administration and the Making of U.S. Nuclear Strategy* (Ithaca, NY: Cornell University Press, 1995); William Burr, "The Nixon Administration, the 'Horror Strategy,' and the Search for Limited Nuclear Options, 1969–1972." *Journal of Cold War Studies* 7, no. 3 (2005): 34–78.

73. Quoted in Stephan Kieninger, *Dynamic Détente: The United States and Europe, 1964–1975* (Lanham, MD: Lexington, 2016), 77.

74. Thomas A. Schwartz, *Henry Kissinger and American Power: A Political Biography* (New York: Hill & Wang, 2020), 61–64.

75. Jussi M. Hanhimäki, "Conservative Goals, Revolutionary Outcomes: The Paradox of Détente," *Cold War History* 8, no. 4 (2008): 506; Daniel J. Sargent, *A Superpower Transformed: The Remaking of American Foreign Relations in the 1970s* (Oxford: Oxford University Press, 2015), 59–62. The fundamentally conservative nature of the détente pursued in the late 1960s, including the Nixon-Kissinger iteration, is the central thrust of Suri, *Power and Protest*.

76. Richard M. Nixon, "Inaugural Address," January 20, 1969, *PPP: Richard Nixon 1969*, ed. Dorothy G. Chance and Peter J. Haley (Washington, DC: Government Printing Office, 1971), 3.

77. "Builder of Bridges for Peace: Willy Brandt," *New York Times*, October 21, 1971.

78. Quoted in Arne Hofmann, *The Emergence of Détente in Europe: Brandt, Kennedy and the Formation of Ostpolitik* (London: Routledge, 2007), 41.

79. Carole Fink and Bernd Schaefer, introduction to *Ostpolitik, 1969–1974: European and Global Responses*, ed. Carole Fink and Bernd Schaefer (Washington, DC, and Cambridge: German Historical Institute and Cambridge University Press, 2009), 2.

80. Hofmann, *Emergence of Détente*, 93–94.

81. On Soviet support for a conference on security in Europe, see Michael Cotey Morgan, *The Final Act: The Helsinki Accords and the Transformation of the Cold War* (Princeton, NJ: Princeton University Press, 2018), 76–85.

82. On the lengths that West German governments went to in order to enforce the Hallstein Doctrine, see William Glenn Gray, *Germany's Cold War: The Global Campaign to Isolate East Germany, 1949–1969* (Chapel Hill: University of North Carolina Press, 2003).

83. Gottfried Niedhart, "Ostpolitik: Transformation through Communication and the Quest for Peaceful Change," *Journal of Cold War Studies* 18, no. 3 (2016): 32.

84. For a discussion of the similarities, differences, and overlap between the two policies, see Gottfried Niedhart, "U.S. Détente and West German Ostpolitik: Parallels and Frictions," in *The Strained Alliance: U.S.-European Relations from Nixon to Carter*, ed. Matthias Schulz and Thomas A. Schwartz (Washington, DC, and Cambridge: German Historical Institute and Cambridge University Press, 2010), 23–44.

2. Parity's Problems

1. Richard M. Nixon, "Asia after Viet Nam," *Foreign Affairs* 46, no. 1 (1967): 122.

2. Quoted in Raymond L. Garthoff, *Détente and Confrontation: American-Soviet Relations from Nixon to Reagan*, rev. ed. (Washington, DC: Brookings Institution, 1994), 61.

3. Quoted in James Cameron, *The Double Game: The Demise of America's First Missile Defense System and the Rise of Strategic Arms Limitation* (New York: Oxford University Press, 2017), 110. See also Garthoff, *Détente and Confrontation*, 61.

4. Gregory F. Treverton, *Making the Alliance Work: The United States and Western Europe* (Ithaca, NY: Cornell University Press, 1985), 29.

5. James S. Finan, "Europe, the Super Powers and SALT," *Queen's Quarterly* 78, no. 3 (1971): 458.

6. Cameron, *Double Game*, 79–106.

7. Garthoff, *Détente and Confrontation*, 146.

8. "Memorandum of Conversation," January 2, 1969, *FRUS 1969–1976*, vol. 12: *Soviet Union, January 1969–October 1970*, ed. Erin R. Mahan (Washington, DC: Government Printing Office, 2006), doc. 1; "The President's News Conference of January 27, 1969," *PPP: Richard Nixon 1969*, ed. Dorothy G. Chance and Peter J. Haley (Washington, DC: Government Printing Office, 1971), 17.

9. Richard M. Nixon, "America's Role in the World," June 4, 1969, *Department of State Bulletin*, June 23, 1969, 525.

10. David Tal, *US Strategic Arms Policy: Negotiations and Confrontation over SALT, 1969–1979* (London: Routledge, 2017), 5.

11. "Telegram from Ambassador Dobrynin to the Soviet Foreign Ministry," April 15, 1969, *Soviet-American Relations: The Détente Years, 1969-1972*, ed. David C. Geyer and Douglas E. Selvage (Washington, DC: Government Printing Office, 2007), doc. 19.

12. State Department to US Embassy Paris, "Secretary's Conversation January 31 with Ambassador Lucet: Part III—SALT," February 3, 1969, RNL, NSC, CFE, box 674, folder "France, Vol. I (20 Jan–11 Apr 1969)."

13. "Minutes of a Review Group Meeting," June 12, 1969, *FRUS 1969–1976*, vol. 32: *SALT I*, ed. Erin R. Mahan (Washington, DC: Government Printing Office, 2010), doc. 17.

14. Figures are from "Summary Record of a Private Meeting of the Council Held on Tuesday, 8th July, 1969," NATO, PR(69)34.

15. Gregory F. Treverton, "Nuclear Weapons and the 'Gray Area,'" *Foreign Affairs* 57, no. 5 (1979): 1075.

16. "Ministerialdirektor Ruete an die Botschaft in Washington," April 28, 1969, *AAPD 1969*, ed. Franz Eibl and Hubert Zimmerman (Munich: Oldenbourg, 2000), doc. 139; "Aufzeichnung über die Besprechung im State Department," August 7, 1969, *AAPD 1969*, doc. 258. In June 1970, US estimates concluded that there were between 718 and 727 Soviet medium-range systems, a mix of SS-4s, SS-5s, SS-11s, and SS-12s. See CIA Directorate of Intelligence, "The Changing Shape of the Soviet Peripheral Ballistic Missile Force," June 1970, CREST, 0000969860.

17. "Minutes of a National Security Council Meeting," November 10, 1969, *FRUS 1969–1976*, vol. 32, doc. 39.

18. James E. Dougherty, "The Atlantic Community—the Psychological Milieu," in *Atlantic Community in Crisis: A Redefinition of the Transatlantic Relationship*, ed. Walter F. Hahn and Robert L. Pfaltzgraff Jr. (New York: Pergamon, 1979), 46.

19. "Minutes of a Review Group Meeting," June 12, 1969, *FRUS 1969–1976*, vol. 32, doc. 17.

20. "Protocols to the Brussels Treaty," October 22, 1954, *FRUS 1952–1954*, vol. 5, pt. 2: *Western European Security*, ed. John A. Bernbaum, Lisle A. Rose, and Charles S. Sampson (Washington, DC: Government Printing Office, 1983), doc. 197.

21. Andreas Lutsch, "In Favor of 'Effective' and 'Non-discriminatory' Non-dissemination Policy: The FRG and the NPT Negotiation Process (1962–1966)," in *Negotiating the Nuclear Non-proliferation Treaty: Origins of the Nuclear Order*, ed. Roland Popp, Liviu Horovitz, and Andreas Wenger (London: Routledge, 2017), esp. 48–50.

22. US Embassy Bonn to State Department, "Strategic Arms Limitation Talks," January 20, 1969, RNL, NSC, CFE, box 681, folder "Germany, Vol. I [2 of 2]."

23. "Paper Prepared by the Interagency SALT Steering Committee," May 30, 1969, *FRUS 1969–1976*, vol. 32, doc. 14.

24. "Summary Record of a Private Meeting of the Council held on Wednesday, 16th July, 1969," NATO, PR(69)36.

25. "Botschafter Pauls, Washington, an das Auswärtige Amt," February 17, 1969, *AAPD 1969*, doc. 66.

26. "Ministerialdirektor Ruete an die Botschaft in Washington," April 28, 1969, *AAPD 1969*, doc. 139.

27. "Minutes of a National Security Council Meeting," June 25, 1969, *FRUS 1969–1976*, vol. 32, doc. 22.

28. "Summary Record of a Private Meeting of the Council Held on Tuesday, 8th July, 1969." See also "Vorlage für den Bundesverteidigungsrat," July 12, 1969, *AAPD 1969*, doc. 232.

29. Helmut Schmidt, "Perspectives of the Alliance," *Survival* 12, no. 2 (1970): 44–45.

30. Aleksandr' G. Savel'yev and Nikolay N. Detinov, *The Big Five: Arms Control Decision-Making in the Soviet Union*, ed. Gregory Varhall and trans. Dmitry Trenin (Westport, CT: Praeger, 1995).

31. Stephan Kieninger, *Dynamic Détente: The United States and Europe, 1964–1975* (Lanham, MD: Lexington, 2016), 136.

32. US Embassy Helsinki to State Department, "Thinkpiece re: Present Position of Preliminary SALT," December 1, 1969, NSA EBB139: "The Master of the Game": Paul H. Nitze and U.S. Cold War Strategy from Truman to Reagan, ed. William Burr and Robert Wampler, October 27, 2004, doc. 7; Gerard Smith, *Doubletalk: The Story of SALT I* (Lanham, MD: University Press of America, 1995), 91.

33. National Security Council, January 28, 1970, quoted in "Editorial Note," *FRUS 1969–1976*, vol. 32, doc. 50.

34. "Special National Intelligence Estimate," February 19, 1970, *FRUS 1969–1976*, vol. 32, doc. 53.

35. "Memorandum of Conversation," April 11, 1970, *FRUS 1969–1976*, vol. 32, doc. 69.

36. "National Security Decision Memorandum 69," July 9, 1970, *FRUS 1969–1976*, vol. 32, doc. 94.

37. "Sitzung des Ständigen NATO-Rats in Brüssel," July 16, 1970, *AAPD 1970*, ed. Ilse Dorothee Pautsch et al. (Munich: Oldenbourg, 2001), doc. 312, fn. 3.

38. "Memorandum from the President's Assistant for National Security Affairs (Kissinger) to President Nixon," 13 July 1970, *FRUS 1969–1976*, vol. 32, doc. 95.

39. François Duchêne, "SALT, the *Ostpolitik*, and the post–Cold War context," *World Today* 26, no. 12 (1970): 509.

40. Philip Windsor, "Current Tensions in NATO," *World Today* 26, no. 7 (1970): 289.

41. David Nathaniel Vigil, "Elusive Equality: The Nuclear Arms Race in Europe and the History of the INF Treaty, 1969–1988" (PhD diss., Emory University, 2014), 83–84.

42. "Remarks Announcing an Agreement on Strategic Arms Limitation Talks," May 20, 1971, *PPP: Richard Nixon 1971*, ed. Ernest J. Galdi (Washington, DC: Government Printing Office, 1972), 648.

43. Henry A. Kissinger, *The White House Years* (Boston: Little, Brown, 1979), 819–21.

44. Andrew J. Pierre, "The SALT Agreement and Europe," *World Today* 28, no. 7 (1972): 288.

45. "Address by President Nixon to a Joint Session of the Congress," June 1, 1972, *FRUS 1969–1976*, vol. 1: *Foundations of Foreign Policy, 1969–1972*, ed. Louis J. Smith and

David H. Herschler (Washington, DC: Government Printing Office, 2003), doc. 117. For a discussion of the Moscow Summit and its significance, see James Cameron, "Moscow, 1972," in *Transcending the Cold War: Summits, Statecraft, and the Dissolution of Bipolarity in Europe*, edited by Kristina Spohr and David Reynolds (Oxford: Oxford University Press, 2016), 67–91.

46. "Address by President Nixon to a Joint Session of the Congress," June 1, 1972, *FRUS 1969–1976*, vol. 1, doc. 117.

47. Cameron, *Double Game*, 159.

48. "Minute from Mr. Tickell to Mr. Wiggin," March 6, 1972, *DBPO* ser. 3, vol. 2: *The Conference on Security and Cooperation in Europe, 1972–75*, ed. Gill Bennett and Keith A. Hamilton (London: Stationery Office, 1997), doc. 2.

49. US Embassy Bonn to State Department, "SALT: NAA Speech by Senator Jackson," November 21, 1972, CREST, CIA-RDP80T00294A000300050025-0. See also Dusko Doder, "Jackson Urges W. Europe to Push U.S. on SALT," *Washington Post*, November 21, 1972.

50. "Memorandum from the President's Assistant for National Security Affairs (Kissinger) to President Nixon," July 13, 1970, *FRUS 1969–1976*, vol. 32, doc. 95.

51. Helga Haftendorn, "The Link between CSCE and MBFR: Two Sprouts from One Bulb," in *Origins of the European Security System: The Helsinki Process Revisited, 1965–75*, ed. Andreas Wenger, Vojtech Mastny, and Christian Nuenlist (London: Routledge, 2008), 241–42.

52. See, for example, "Note by the Defence Policy Staff of the Chiefs of Staff Committee DP Note 215/72," April 12, 1972, *DBPO* 3, vol. 3, doc. 1.

53. Kieninger, *Dynamic Détente*, 134–35.

54. Kieninger, *Dynamic Détente*, 135.

55. "Note by Trend, Hunt and H F T Smith," April 12, 1973, *DBPO* 3, vol. 4: *The Year of Europe: America, Europe and the Energy Crisis, 1972–1974*, ed. Keith A. Hamilton and Patrick Salmon (London: Routledge, 2006), doc. 65.

56. "Nixon, Brezhnev Relaxed Tensions," *Ottawa Citizen*, May 31, 1972; Roger Hill, "MBFR Prelude: Explorations before Negotiations," *NATO Review* 20, nos. 7–8 (1972): 3–4. On the connections between MBFR and the CSCE, see Haftendorn, "Link between CSCE and MBFR."

57. The MBFR talks included four members of the Warsaw Pact—Czechoslovakia, the German Democratic Republic, Poland, and the Soviet Union—and seven NATO members—Belgium, Canada, the Federal Republic of Germany, Luxembourg, the Netherlands, the United Kingdom, and the United States. On the MBFR negotiations, see Christoph Bluth, *Two Germanies and Military Security in Europe* (Basingstoke, UK: Palgrave Macmillan, 2002).

58. "Draft Steering Brief for the British Delegation to the MBFR Talks," October 11, 1973, *DBPO* ser. 3, vol. 3, doc. 9.

59. "Draft Steering Brief for the British Delegation to the MBFR Talks," October 11, 1973, *DBPO* ser. 3, vol. 3, doc. 9.

60. Option III included a mix of nuclear-capable F-4 attack aircraft and Pershing I ballistic missile launchers, along with the withdrawal of a thousand US nuclear warheads. "Telegram from the Delegation to the Mutual and Balanced Force Reduction Talks to the Department of State," n.d. [December 1975], *FRUS 1969–1976*,

vol. 39: *European Security*, ed. Douglas E. Selvage (Washington, DC: Government Printing Office, 2007), doc. 367.

61. For a rough picture of the deployments in 1976, see "Nuclear Delivery Vehicles: Comparative Strengths and Characteristics," *The Military Balance* (1976): 73–74.

62. Raymond L. Garthoff, "The Soviet SS-20 Decision," *Survival* 25, no. 3 (1983): 112.

63. National Photographic Interpretation Center, "SS-X-16/-20-Association Command and Control Activity, USSR (TSR)," November 1977, CREST, CIA-RDP78T05162A000500010037-6.

64. *Cold War*, season 1, episode 19, "Freeze," dir. Tessa Coombs, aired 1998, on CNN.

65. David Holloway, "The Dynamics of the Euromissile Crisis, 1977–1983," in Nuti et al., *Euromissile Crisis*, 11–12. See also Henry H. Gaffney, "The History of the Euromissiles," World Security Network, March 25, 2004, http://www.worldsecuri tynetwork.com/NATO/Gaffney-H.-H/The-History-of-the-Euromissiles, fn. 1.

66. Holloway, "Dynamics," 12.

67. Gerald Ford, *A Time to Heal: The Autobiography of Gerald R. Ford* (New York: Harper & Row, 1979), 216.

68. Garthoff, "Soviet SS-20 Decision," 112.

69. Jonathan Haslam, "Moscow's Misjudgment in Deploying SS-20 Missiles," in Nuti et al., *Euromissile Crisis*, 35.

70. Holloway, "Dynamics," 13.

71. US negotiators had suggested a set of criteria for strategic stability, including mobility, reduced vulnerability, and reductions in throw weight. The SS-20 met them all. Garthoff, "Soviet SS-20 Decision," 112.

72. Haslam, "Moscow's Misjudgment," 36–37. On the broader shift under way in the Warsaw Pact's doctrine, see Oliver Bange, "SS-20 and Pershing II: Weapon Systems and the Dynamization of East-West Relations," in Becker-Schaum et al., *Nuclear Crisis*, 78–80.

73. Andrian Danilevich interview, September 21, 1992, in *Soviet Intentions 1965–1985*, vol. 2: *Soviet Post–Cold War Testimonial Evidence*, ed. John G. Hines, Ellis M. Mishulovich, and John F. Shull (McLean, VA: BDM, 1995), 33.

74. Oleg Grinevsky, "The Crisis That Didn't Erupt: The Soviet-American Relationship," in *Turning Points in Ending the Cold War*, ed. Kiron K. Skinner (Stanford, CA: Hoover Institution, 2007)," 76.

75. Schmidt, "Perspectives of the Alliance."

3. Shades of Gray

1. Maynard W. Glitman, *The Last Battle of the Cold War: An Inside Account of Negotiating the Intermediate-Range Nuclear Forces Treaty* (New York: Palgrave Macmillan, 2006), 3–5.

2. Prior to the weapon's deployment, the NATO allies referred to the SS-20 as the SS-X-20, with the X indicating that it was experimental.

3. For a map of the SS-20's range according to Western estimates, see *Soviet Military Power* (Washington, DC: Government Printing Office, 1981), 26.

4. MAE note, "Le problème de la zone grise: La question et les réponses," September 6, 1978, AD, 1929INVA/3966.

5. C. L. Sulzberger, "Through Détente's Looking Glass," *New York Times*, August 8, 1976.

6. Helmut Schmidt, *Menschen und Mächte* (Berlin: Siedler, 1987), 39–40. See also "Helmut Schmidt on Those Missiles," *Washington Post*, February 13, 1983.

7. "Aufzeichnung des Vortragenden Legationsrats I. Klasse Dannenbring," August 6, 1976, *AAPD 1976*, ed. Matthias Peter, Michael Ploetz, and Tim Geiger (Munich: Oldenbourg, 2007), doc. 259.

8. "Aufzeichnung des Botschaftsrats Sönksen, Washington," March 12, 1971, *AAPD 1971*, ed. Martin Koopmann, Matthias Peter, and Daniela Taschler (Munich: Oldenbourg, 2002), doc. 91.

9. "Record of NPG Ministerial Meeting," June 16, 1975, TNA, FCO 46/1269.

10. "Aufzeichnung des Vortragenden Legationsrats I. Klasse Dannenbring," August 6, 1976, *AAPD 1976*, doc. 259.

11. US Mission NATO to State Department, "SALT: NATO Experts Meeting, September 12," September 17, 1975, CREST, CIA-RDP80T00294A001200090019-3.

12. "Aufzeichnung des Ministerialdirektors van Well," January 26, 1976, *AAPD 1976*, doc. 20.

13. "Improving the Effectiveness of NATO's Theatre Nuclear Forces," April 13, 1976, NATO, IMSWM-102-76.

14. "Memorandum from Stephen Hadley of the National Security Council Staff to the President's Assistant for National Security Affairs (Scowcroft)," January 10, 1976, *FRUS 1969–1976*, vol. E-15, part 2: *Western Europe, 1973–1976*, ed. Kathleen B. Rasmussen (Washington, DC: Government Printing Office, 2014), doc. 80.

15. Henry H. Gaffney, "Euromissiles as the Ultimate Evolution of Theater Nuclear Forces in Europe," *Journal of Cold War Studies* 16, no. 1 (2014): 186. James Schlesinger had begun studying NATO's theater nuclear force posture in 1974 as part of a broader evaluation of the doctrine, deployment, and use of these weapons. Schlesinger's studies were given a further boost when Senator Sam Nunn (D-GA) pressed for a reduction of the stockpile in Europe with the Nunn Amendment. On these debates, see "Sixteenth Meeting of the Nuclear Planning Group," December 10, 1974, ISCAP Release 2010-072-doc 1.

16. "Memorandum from Stephen Hadley of the National Security Council Staff to the President's Assistant for National Security Affairs (Scowcroft)," January 10, 1976, *FRUS 1969–1976*, vol. E-15, part 2, doc. 80.

17. Gaffney, "Euromissiles as the Ultimate Evolution," 188.

18. State Department to US Mission NATO, "Press Questions on ACDA Report on Soviet IRBMs," July 31, 1976, AAD, 1976STATE190411.

19. "Possible Deployment of Soviet SS-20 MIRV IRBM's," September 14, 1976, GFL, WHSF, box 2, folder "Second Debate: Defense Department Briefing Book (2)."

20. US Embassy Bonn to State Department, "CDU/CSU Reaction to Reported MIRV-ing of Soviet IRBM's," August 10, 1976, AAD, 1976BONN13370.

21. Sulzberger, "Through Détente's Looking Glass."

22. David Binder, "U.S. Aide Accuses Soviet on New Missile," *New York Times*, September 1, 1976.

23. "The Situation in Africa South of the Sahara," March 19, 1976, NATO, C-M(76)11.

24. Intelligence Division, International Military Staff, "Warsaw Pact Military Developments and Trends," December 9, 1975, NATO, IMSM-671-75.

25. French foreign ministry officials pointed this ambiguity over détente's definitions as "the greatest reservation observed in the West" regarding the policy of détente. MAE note, "Les relations Est-Ouest," May 25, 1976, AD, 1928INVA/3699.

26. "Conseil de l'OTAN—Session Ministerielle d'Oslo (1) Séance Restreinte Relations Est-Ouest—Declaration de M. Kissinger," May 21, 1976, AD, 1928INVA/3699.

27. On détente's waning popularity in the United States, see Julian E. Zelizer, "Détente and Domestic Politics," *Diplomatic History* 33, no. 4 (2009): 653–70; Sarah B. Snyder, "'Jerry, Don't Go': Domestic Opposition to the 1975 Helsinki Final Act," *Journal of American Studies* 44, no. 1 (2010): 67–81.

28. Bernard Gwertzman, "President Vows to Back Détente," *New York Times*, January 4, 1976.

29. Ronald Reagan, "To Restore America," March 31, 1976, https://www.reaganlibrary.gov/archives/speech/restore-america.

30. George Wallace campaign appeal, n.d. [1975], GFL, RTHF, box 24, folder "Democratic Presidential Candidates (1)."

31. "News Conference by Secretary of Defense Donald Rumsfeld at the Pentagon, Monday, September 27, 1976," GFL, RNP, box 7, folder "Defense-Rumsfeld News Conferences and Interviews."

32. Arthur Hartman, George Vest, and Winston Lord to Henry Kissinger, "Nuclear Balance Issues at NPG Ministerial," October 18, 1976, NARA, RG59, WL, box 367, folder "WL Sensitive Non-China 11/76."

33. Canadian Delegation NATO to External Affairs, "NPG Perm Reps Mtg Oct5—Briefings on Eurostrategic Balance," October 6, 1976, LAC, RG25, vol. 22103, file 27-4-NATO-1-16, part 27.

34. Canadian Delegation NATO to External Affairs, "NPG Perm Reps Mtg Oct5—Briefings on Eurostrategic Balance," October 6, 1976, LAC, RG25, vol. 22103, file 27-4-NATO-1-16, part 27.

35. Canadian Delegation NATO to External Affairs, "NPG Perm Reps Mtg Oct5—Briefings on Eurostrategic Balance," October 6, 1976, LAC, RG25, vol. 22103, file 27-4-NATO-1-16, part 27.

36. Canadian Delegation NATO to External Affairs, "NPG Perm Reps Mtg Oct5—Briefings on Eurostrategic Balance," October 6, 1976, LAC, RG25, vol. 22103, file 27-4-NATO-1-16, part 27.

37. Canadian Delegation NATO to External Affairs, "NPG Perm Reps Mtg Oct5—Briefings on Eurostrategic Balance," October 6, 1976, LAC, RG25, vol. 22103, file 27-4-NATO-1-16, part 27.

38. Canadian Delegation NATO to External Affairs, "NPG Perm Reps Mtg Oct5—Briefings on Eurostrategic Balance," October 6, 1976, LAC, RG25, vol. 22103, file 27-4-NATO-1-16, part 27.

39. "Memorandum from the Counselor (Sonnenfeldt) to Secretary of State Kissinger," October 18, 1976, *FRUS 1969–1976*, vol. E-15, part 2, doc. 98.

40. "Memorandum from the Counselor (Sonnenfeldt) to Secretary of State Kissinger," October 18, 1976, *FRUS 1969–1976*, vol. E-15, part 2, doc. 98.

41. US Embassy Bonn to State Department, "FRG-NATO Military Matters," November 3, 1976, NARA, RG 59, WL, box 367, folder "WL Sensitive Non-China 11/76."

42. Hartman, Vest, and Lord to Kissinger, "Nuclear Balance Issues at NPG Ministerial," October 18, 1976, NARA, RG 59, WL, box 367, folder "WL Sensitive Non-China 11/76."

43. Hartman, Vest, and Lord to Kissinger, "Nuclear Balance Issues at NPG Ministerial," October 18, 1976, NARA, RG 59, WL, box 367, folder "WL Sensitive Non-China 11/76."

44. William Burr, "A Question of Confidence: Theater Nuclear Forces, US Policy toward Germany, and the Origins of the Euromissile Crisis, 1975–1976," in Nuti et al., *Euromissile Crisis*, 131.

45. James Lowenstein, James Goodby, and Winston Lord to Henry Kissinger, "NPG: Rumsfeld Briefing on Nuclear Balance," November 10, 1976, NARA, RG 59, WL, box 367, folder "WL Sensitive Non-China 11/76."

46. Lowenstein, Goodby, and Lord to Kissinger, "NPG: Rumsfeld Briefing on Nuclear Balance," November 10, 1976, NARA, RG 59, WL, box 367, folder "WL Sensitive Non-China 11/76."

47. Lowenstein, Goodby, and Lord to Kissinger, "NPG: Rumsfeld Briefing on Nuclear Balance," November 10, 1976, NARA, RG 59, WL, box 367, folder "WL Sensitive Non-China 11/76."

48. "Aufzeichnung des Vortragenden Legationsrats I. Klasse Dannenbring," November 19, 1976, *AAPD 1976*, doc. 331; Burr, "Question of Confidence," 132–33.

49. Canadian Delegation NATO to External Affairs, "NPG-Future Work Program," November 5, 1976, LAC, RG25, vol. 22103, file 27-4-NATO-1-16, part 27.

50. Roger L. L. Facer, *Conventional Forces and the NATO Strategy of Flexible Response* (Santa Monica, CA: RAND Corp., 1985), 36–38.

51. Presidential Review Memorandum/NSC-9, "Comprehensive Review of European Issues," February 1, 1977, JCL, https://www.jimmycarterlibrary.gov/assets/documents/memorandums/prm09.pdf.

52. Cyrus Vance and Harold Brown to Jimmy Carter, "May NATO Ministerial Meetings," n.d. [1977], JCL, RAC, NLC-23-19-6-3-7.

53. UK Delegation NATO to FCO, "NAT Summit," May 12, 1977, TNA, FCO 46/1482.

54. Vance and Brown to Carter, "May NATO Ministerial Meetings," n.d. [1977], JCL, RAC, NLC-23-19-6-3-7. See also Michael Palliser note, "The Possibility of President Carter Attending the Ministerial Meeting on 10/11 May," March 10, 1977, TNA, FCO 46/1481.

55. Washington to FCO, "NATO Summit," April 12, 1977, TNA, FCO 46/1481.

56. Vance and Brown to Carter, "May NATO Ministerial Meetings," JCL, RAC, NLC-23-19-6-3-7; Palliser note, "The Possibility of President Carter Attending the Ministerial Meeting on 10/11 May," March 10, 1977, TNA, FCO 46/1481.

57. Silvio Pons, "The Rise and Fall of Eurocommunism," in *The Cambridge History of the Cold War*, vol. 3: *Endings*, ed. Melvyn P. Leffler and Odd Arne Westad (Cambridge: Cambridge University Press, 2010), 45–65.

58. Radio Four broadcast, "NATO—the Politics of an Alliance," May 11, 1977, TNA, FCO 46/1482.

59. Vance and Brown to Carter, "May NATO Ministerial Meetings," n.d. [1977], JCL, RAC, NLC-23-19-6-3-7.

60. Radio Four broadcast, "NATO—the Politics of an Alliance," May 11, 1977, TNA, FCO 46/1482.

61. FCO to UK Delegation NATO, "NATO Ministerial Meeting: Morning of 10 May," May 10, 1977, TNA, FCO 46/1482. See also UK Delegation NATO to FCO, "NAT Summit." For the full text of the speech, see Jimmy Carter, "NATO Ministerial Meeting," May 10, 1977, *PPP: Jimmy Carter 1977*, vol. 1, ed. Margaret M. Donohoe et al. (Washington, DC: Government Printing Office, 1977), 848–52.

62. Washington to FCO, "NATO Summit," May 13, 1977, TNA, FCO 46/1482.

63. Maynard Wayne Glitman interview, April 24, 2001, FAOHP, 40; "High Level Group (HLG) History," December 9, 1981, NATO, IMSM-0612-81.

64. "Improving the Effectiveness of NATO's Theatre Nuclear Forces: UK Comment on the US Paper BMC 10 of 15 December 1975," n.d., TNA, FCO 46/1373.

65. Lawrence Freedman, "The Wilderness Years," in *The Nuclear Confrontation in Europe*, ed. Jeffrey D. Boutwell, Paul Doty, and Gregory F. Treverton (London: Croom Helm, 1985), 44.

66. Nixon seems to have shared this view, later writing in his memoirs: "I am absolutely convinced that had we lost the ABM battle in the Senate, we would not have been able to negotiate the first nuclear arms control agreement in Moscow in 1972." Richard Nixon, *R.N.: The Memoirs of Richard Nixon* (New York: Grosset and Dunlap, 1978), 418.

67. "Memorandum of Conversation," September 18, 1975, *FRUS 1969–1976*, vol. 33: *SALT II, 1972–1980*, ed. Erin R. Mahan (Washington, DC: Government Printing Office, 2013), doc. 106. On the cruise missile program, see Andrea Chiampan, "The Origins of the Euromissile Crisis, 1969–1979" (PhD diss., Graduate Institute of International and Development Studies, 2017), esp. 146–54.

68. "Memorandum of Conversation," September 18, 1975, *FRUS 1969–1976*, vol. 33, doc. 106.

69. "Memorandum of Conversation," September 18, 1975, *FRUS 1969–1976*, vol. 33, doc. 106.

70. Leopoldo Nuti, "The Origins of the 1979 Dual Track Decision—a Survey," in *The Crisis of Détente in Europe: From Helsinki to Gorbachev, 1975–1985*, ed. Leopoldo Nuti (London: Routledge, 2009), 59.

71. See, for example, D. E. Richardson, "The Cruise Missile: A Strategic Weapon for the 1980s," *Electronics & Power* 23, nos. 11–12 (1977): 896–901; Robert L. Pfaltzgraff and Jacquelyn K. Davis, *The Cruise Missile: Bargaining Chip or Defense Bargain?* (Cambridge, MA: Institute for Foreign Policy Analysis, 1977).

72. Kosta Tsipis, "The Long-Range Cruise Missile," *Bulletin of the Atomic Scientists* 31, no. 4 (1975): 12–26, quotation on 16. See also Kosta Tsipis, "Cruise Missiles," *Scientific American*, February 1977, 20–29; Alexander R. Vershbow, "The Cruise Missile: The End of Arms Control?," *Foreign Affairs* 55, no. 1 (1976): 133–46.

73. "Aufzeichnung des Botschafters Roth," January 26, 1976, *AAPD 1976*, doc. 21.

74. Canadian Delegation NATO to External Affairs, "NPG-Future Work Program," October 21, 1976, LAC, RG25, vol. 22103, file 27-4-NATO-1-16, part 27.

75. Canadian Delegation NATO to External Affairs, "NPG-Future Work Program," October 28, 1976, LAC, RG25, vol. 22103, file 27-4-NATO-1-16, part 27.

76. Canadian Delegation NATO to External Affairs, "NPG: Future Work," January 12, 1977, LAC, RG25, vol. 22103, file 27-4-NATO-1-16, part 27.

77. Scowcroft to Ford, "Outstanding SALT Issues," February 15, 1976, GFL, RBCF, box 11, folder "Strategic Arms Limitation Talks—General."

78. Raymond L. Garthoff, *Détente and Confrontation: American-Soviet Relations from Nixon to Reagan*, rev. ed. (Washington, DC: Brookings Institution, 1994), 626.

79. Quoted in Garthoff, *Détente and Confrontation*, 626.

80. Schmidt, *Menschen und Mächte*, 224.

81. "Aufzeichnung des Botschafters Ruth," May 31, 1977, *AAPD 1977*, ed. Amit Das Gupta et al. (Munich: Oldenbourg, 2008), doc. 140.

82. Leslie Gelb to Cyrus Vance, "Strategy for NATO and Bilateral Consultations on Cruise Missiles," July 20, 1977, JCL, RAC, NLC-15-124-3-14-0.

83. "Cruise Missiles—a UK Assessment of US NATO CTS-77-4," July 26, 1977, TNA, DEFE 24/1343.

84. Gelb to Vance, "Strategy for NATO and Bilateral Consultations on Cruise Missiles," July 20, 1977, JCL, RAC, NLC-15-124-3-14-0.

85. Quoted in Strobe Talbott, *Endgame: The Inside Story of SALT II* (New York: HarperCollins, 1979), 106.

86. "Aufzeichnung des Vortragenden Legationsrats I. Klasse Dannenbring," June 15, 1977, *AAPD 1977*, doc. 155.

87. UK Delegation NATO to MOD, "Cruise Missiles," July 19, 1977, TNA, DEFE 24/1343.

88. UK Delegation NATO to MOD, "Cruise Missiles," July 19, 1977, TNA, DEFE 24/1343.

89. Extract from COS1254/11, July 11, 1977, TNA, DEFE 24/1343.

90. Hans-Dietrich Genscher to Cyrus Vance, July 4, 1977, JCL, ZBM, BCC, box 34, folder "NATO 5-7/77."

91. Europe to Zbigniew Brzezinski, "Evening Report," June 20, 1977, JCL, RAC, NLC-10-3-4-9-4.

92. "Cruise Missiles—a UK Assessment of US NATO CTS-77-4," July 26, 1977, TNA, DEFE 24/1343.

93. CommCen FCO to MODUK, "Council Discussion on Cruise Missiles," July 28, 1977, TNA, DEFE 24/1343.

94. "Cruise Missiles—Personal Comments by Sir J Killick at NAC Meeting on 28 July," TNA, DEFE 24/1343.

95. CommCen FCO to MODUK, "Council Discussion on Cruise Missiles," July 28, 1977, TNA, DEFE 24/1343.

96. FCO to Ministry of Defence, "Council Discussion on Cruise Missiles," July 28, 1977, TNA, DEFE 24/1343.

97. "Cruise Missiles—Statement by Sir J Killick at North Atlantic Council on 28 July," n.d. TNA, DEFE 24/1343.

98. "Cruise Missiles—Statement by Sir J Killick at North Atlantic Council on 28 July," n.d. TNA, DEFE 24/1343.

99. "Cruise Missiles—Statement by Sir J Killick at North Atlantic Council on 28 July," n.d. TNA, DEFE 24/1343.

100. "Cruise Missiles—Personal Comments by Sir J Killick at NAC Meeting on 28 July," TNA, DEFE 24/1343.

101. "Cruise Missiles—Personal Comments by Sir J Killick at NAC Meeting on 28 July," TNA, DEFE 24/1343.

102. John Killick to Michael Quinlan, "Cruise Missiles," July 29, 1977, TNA, DEFE 24/1343.

103. John Killick to Michael Quinlan, "Cruise Missiles," August 1, 1977, TNA, DEFE 24/1343.

104. "Record of Anglo-US Consultations on Cruise Missiles Held on Friday, 29 July, at the Foreign and Commonwealth Office," August 4, 1977, TNA, DEFE 24/1343.

105. Quoted in Kristan Stoddart, "Creating the 'Seamless Robe of Deterrence': Great Britain's Role in NATO's INF Debate," in Nuti et al., *Euromissile Crisis*, 179–80.

106. Helmut Schmidt, "The 1977 Alastair Buchan Memorial Lecture," *Survival* 20, no. 1 (1978): 2–4.

107. Robert M. Hunter interview, August 10, 2004, FAOHP, 66.

108. Rowland Evans and Robert Novak, "Conceding Defeat in Europe," *Washington Post*, August 3, 1977.

109. Helmut Schmidt interview, n.d., YUA, CRGSVP, box 35, folder "Palme Commission on Disarmament and Security Issues Meeting (at Seven Springs Center, NY) (12–21 Feb) 1982."

110. FCO to UK Delegation NATO, "NATO Ministerial Meeting: 10 May," May 11, 1977, TNA, FCO 46/1482.

111. Helmut Schmidt and Giovanni di Lorenzo, *Auf eine Zigarette mit Helmut Schmidt* (Cologne, Germany: Kiepenheuer and Witsch, 2010), 196.

112. The difficulties between Carter and Schmidt are well covered in Klaus Wiegrefe, *Das Zerwürfnis: Helmut Schmidt, Jimmy Carter und die Krise der deutsch-amerikanischen Beziehungen* (Berlin: Propyläen, 2005). For a specific focus on the transatlantic nuclear dimensions, see Kristina Spohr, "NATO's Nuclear Politics and the Schmidt-Carter Rift," in Nuti et al., *Euromissile Crisis*, 139–57.

113. Susan M. Klingaman interview, May 1, 1998, FAOHP, 61.

114. William M. Woessner interview, November 29, 1999, FAOHP, 56.

115. Schmidt, *Menschen und Mächte*, 230.

4. Fiasco!

1. Walter Pincus, "Neutron Killer Warhead Buried in ERDA Budget," *Washington Post*, June 6, 1977. The enhanced radiation warhead was also referred to as the enhanced radiation/reduced blast weapon.

2. Jimmy Carter, "The President's News Conference," July 12, 1977, *PPP: Jimmy Carter 1977*, vol. 2, ed. Margaret M. Donohoe et al. (Washington, DC: Government Printing Office, 1978), 1231.

3. Quoted in Vincent A. Auger, *The Dynamics of Foreign Policy Analysis: The Carter Administration and the Neutron Bomb* (Lanham, MD: Rowman & Littlefield, 1996), 36.

4. Mark Frankland and Nigel Hawkes, "Bomb That Respects Property," *Observer*, July 17, 1977.

5. "In The Name of Life Itself, Ban the Neutron Bomb," n.d. [1978], MUL, CPC, box 11, folder "Correspondence—Ban the Neutron Bomb."

6. See, for example, Rudiger Moniac, "Koschnick furchtet verstärkte Spannungsgefahren," *Die Welt*, July 21, 1977.

7. Lord Chalfont, "New Dimensions of Nuclear Madness," *Times* (London), July 25, 1977.

8. Sherri L. Wasserman, *The Neutron Bomb Controversy: A Study in Alliance Politics* (New York: Praeger, 1983), 32.

9. John Palmer, "NATO Opposition to Neutron Bomb Worries Pentagon," *Guardian*, March 17, 1978.

10. Carter, "The President's News Conference," July 12, 1977. The congressional debate is covered in Auger, *Dynamics*, 35–48; and Robert A. Strong, *Working in the World: Jimmy Carter and the Making of American Foreign Policy* (Baton Rouge: Louisiana State University Press, 2000), 129–32.

11. "Les Allemands et La Bombe N," July 28, 1977, AD, 1929INVA / 3887.

12. Egon Bahr, "Ist die Menschheit dabei, verrückt zu werden?," *Vorwärts*, July 21, 1977.

13. Kristina Spohr-Readman, "Germany and the Politics of the Neutron Bomb, 1975–1979," *Diplomacy & Statecraft* 21 (2010): 269–70.

14. See, for example, Zbigniew Brzezinski to Jimmy Carter, "Stoessel's Conversation with Schmidt," n.d., JCL, RAC, NLC-6-24-3-22-2.

15. Pincus, "Neutron Killer Warhead."

16. Palmer, "NATO Opposition."

17. Robert McCloskey interview, May 8, 1989, FAOHP, 23.

18. US Mission NATO to State Department, "Permreps Luncheon, July 20, 1977," July 21, 1977, JCL, RAC, NLC-8-12-1-5-4.

19. Lawrence S. Wittner, *Toward Nuclear Abolition: A History of the World Nuclear Disarmament Movement, 1971–Present* (Stanford, CA: Stanford University Press, 2003), 48.

20. "Dr. Brzezinski's Meeting with British Prime Minister James Callaghan," September 27, 1977, JCL, RAC, NLC-23-22-3-3-6.

21. Michael Getler, "No Bonn Bar Seen to Neutron Arms," *International Herald Tribune*, September 28, 1977.

22. "Aufzeichnung des Ministerialdirigenten Pfeffer," September 1, 1977, AAPD 1977, ed. Amit Das Gupta et al. (Munich: Oldenbourg, 2008), doc. 232; "Allied Views on Enhanced Radiation Weapons and MBFR," November 1977, JCL, RAC, NLC-17-6-12-36-5.

23. "Gespräch des Bundeskanzlers Schmidt mit dem Sicherheitsberater des amerikanischen Präsidenten, Brzezinski," September 27, 1977, AAPD 1977, doc. 257.

24. Alexander Haig, Zbigniew Brzezinski, and Gregory Treverton, memorandum of conversation, September 27, 1977, JCL, RAC, NLC-23-22-3-6-3.

25. Helmut Schmidt, "The 1977 Alastair Buchan Memorial Lecture," *Survival* 20, no. 1 (1978): 4.

26. Schmidt, "1977 Alastair Buchan Memorial Lecture," 3.

27. "Allied Views on Enhanced Radiation Weapons and MBFR," November 1977, JCL, RAC, NLC-17-6-12-36-5.

28. State Department to White House, "Neutron Bomb," November 10, 1977, JCL, RAC, NLC-17-6-12-37-4.

29. SCC summary of conclusions, "Enhanced Radiation Warheads," November 16, 1977, JCL, ZBC, SF, box 27, folder "Meetings—SCC 41, 11/16/77."

30. Harold Brown to Jimmy Carter, "Getting Something for the Neutron Bomb: ER for SS-20?," November 8, 1977, ZBC, SF, box 27, folder "Meetings—SCC 41, 11/16/77."

31. SCC memorandum of conversation, "Special Coordinating Committee (SCC) Meeting on Enhanced Radiation Weapons," November 16, 1977, JCL, RAC, NLC-31-129-6-1-7.

32. SCC summary of conclusions, "Enhanced Radiation Warheads," November 16, 1977, JCL, ZBC, SF, box 27, folder "Meetings—SCC 41, 11/16/77."

33. Jimmy Carter to Helmut Schmidt, November 23, 1977, JCL, ZBC, SF, box 22, folder "Defense—Enhanced Radiation Warhead (3/78–8/78)." See also Zbigniew Brzezinski to Jimmy Carter, "Enhanced Radiation Weapons," November 18, 1977, JCL, RAC, NLC-15-124-7-7-4.

34. "Botschafter Pauls, Brüssel (NATO), an das Auswärtige Amt," February 24, 1978, *AAPD 1978*, ed. Daniela Taschler, Amit Das Gupta, and Michael Mayer (Munich: Oldenbourg, 2009), doc. 62.

35. "Botschafter von Staaten, Washington, an das Auswärtige Amt," December 21, 1977, *AAPD 1977*, doc. 374.

36. State Department to White House, "Consultations with Blech: Enhanced Radiation," December 22, 1977, JCL, RAC, NLC-16-110-3-28-9.

37. National Foreign Assessment Center memorandum, "USSR Weekly Review," December 22, 1977, CREST, CIA-RDP79T00912A000100010058-5. For an overview of the Soviet campaign, see Thomas Rid, *Active Measures: The Secret History of Disinformation and Political Warfare* (New York: Farrar, Straus and Giroux, 2020), 255–62.

38. See, for example, World Peace Council, *In The Name of Life Itself Ban the Neutron Bomb!* (Helsinki: Information Centre of the World Peace Council, 1977), 7.

39. See, for example, "Nhan Dan Supports Campaign against Neutron Bomb," October 5, 1977, FBIS-APA-77-193; "Organizations Rally, Condemn U.S. Neutron Bombs," October 17, 1977, FBIS-APA-77-200.

40. "Bomb Unites the Left," *Guardian*, August 9, 1977.

41. "CIA Study: Soviet Covert Action and Propaganda," in *Soviet Covert Action (the Forgery Offensive): Hearings before the Subcommittee on Oversight of the Permanent Select Committee on Intelligence, House of Representatives, Ninety-Sixth Congress, Second Session, February 6, 19, 1980* (Washington, DC: Government Printing Office, 1980), 76.

42. Beatrice de Graaf, "Stasi Operations in the Netherlands, 1979–89," *Studies in Intelligence* 52, no. 1 (2008): 6.

43. Jonathan Kandell, "Neutron Issue Sparks Wide Dutch Protest," *New York Times*, April 16, 1978.

44. "The Dutch Anti-N-Bomb Newsletter," January 5, 1978, MUL, CPC, box 11, folder "Conferences–International Forum 'Stop the N-Bomb.'"

45. Later US assessments of the Soviet campaign against the enhanced radiation warhead identified three phases: one in the summer of 1977, a second begun in January 1978 with Brezhnev's letter to Western heads of state and government, and a third with Soviet-backed conferences and workshops designed to build momentum in advance of the UN Special Session on Disarmament. See State Department Bureau of Public Affairs Special Report no. 88, "Soviet 'Active Measures': Forgery, Disinformation, Political Operations," October 1981, CREST, CIA-RDP84B00049 R001303150031-0.

46. "Report on Soviet Use of the Media," in *The CIA and the Media: Hearings before the Subcommittee on Oversight of the Permanent Select Committee on Intelligence, House of Representatives, Ninety-Fifth Congress, First and Second Sessions, December 27, 28, 29, 1977, January 4, 5, and April 20, 1978* (Washington, DC: Government Printing Office, 1978), 556.

47. For some examples of Soviet calls for a ban, see "Gromyko Calls for a UN Ban on the Neutron Bomb," *Guardian*, September 28, 1977; "Soviet, at Geneva Parley Asks Neutron Bomb Ban," *New York Times*, March 10, 1978.

48. UK Embassy Bonn to FCO, "ERWs," February 8, 1978, TNA, FCO 46/1812.

49. Holmer to Patrick Moberly, "Enhanced Radiation Warheads (ERWs)," February 8, 1978, TNA, FCO 46/1812.

50. Extract of record of Anglo/US consultations on military nuclear issues, January 31, 1978, TNA, FCO 46/1812.

51. "Secretary of State's Meeting on Military Nuclear Matters: 27 January 1978," TNA, FCO 46/1812.

52. FCO to UK Embassy Bonn, "ERWs," February 3, 1978, TNA, FCO 46/1812.

53. Note by the Secretary of State for Defence, "Enhanced Radiation/Reduced Blast Warheads," 1978, TNA, FCO 46/1813.

54. Maynard Glitman to Cyrus Vance, "Preparations for NAC Consultation on SALT," March 2, 1978, JCL, RAC, NLC-16-23-5-20-2.

55. Harold Brown and Cyrus Vance to Jimmy Carter, "ERW and Alliance Consultations," n.d. [March 1978], JCL, ZBC, SF, box 22, folder "Defense—Enhanced Radiation Warhead (3/78–8/78)."

56. William Wilberforce to Christopher Mallaby, "ERW and SS-20," March 3, 1978, TNA, FCO 46/1813.

57. "Secretary of State's Meeting on Military Nuclear Matters," January 27, 1978, TNA, FCO 46/1812.

58. Brzezinski to Carter, "Neutron Bomb," March 7, 1978, JCL, RAC, NLC-7-17-2-7-7.

59. UK Embassy The Hague to FCO, "Enhanced Radiation/Reduced Blast Weapons (ERWs)," March 1, 1978, TNA, FCO 46/1813.

60. UK Embassy Bonn to FCO, "Enhanced Radiation Warheads (ERWs)," March 3, 1978, TNA, FCO 46/1813.

61. Brown and Vance to Carter, "ERW and Alliance Consultations," n.d. [March 1978], JCL, ZBC, SF, box 22, folder "Defense—Enhanced Radiation Warhead (3/78–8/78)."

62. This careful distinction reflected the conditions set out by Harold Brown at the Nuclear Planning Group in Bari, Italy, in October 1977. On this, see David Haworth, "Europe Stays Cool on Neutron Bomb Plans," *Guardian*, October 13, 1977;

"Ministerialdirektor Blech an Bundesminister Genscher, z.Z. Peking," October 14, 1977, *AAPD 1977*, doc. 286.

63. Cyrus Vance, *Hard Choices: Critical Years in America's Foreign Policy* (New York: Simon & Schuster, 1983), 93–94.

64. "Neutron Bomb Protested," *New York Times*, March 20, 1978.

65. "Tegen neutronenbom tienduizenden in actie," *NRC Handelsblaad*, March 20, 1978.

66. Zbigniew Brzezinski to Jimmy Carter, "Enhanced Radiation Warhead Implementation," March 18, 1978, JCL, ZBC, SF, box 22, folder "Defense—Enhanced Radiation Warhead (3/78–8/78)."

67. "Entwicklung der bilateral und der Bündnisdiskussion," April 2, 1978, PA-AA, B150/390.

68. Reginald Bartholomew to Zbigniew Brzezinski, "Your Meeting on ERW Tonight," March 20, 1978, JCL, ZBC, SF, box 22, folder "Defense—Enhanced Radiation Warhead (3/78–8/78)."

69. See, for example, Hella Pick, "Carter 'to Order N-bomb'" *Guardian*, March 29, 1978.

70. Ruud van Dijk, "'A Mass Psychosis': The Netherlands and NATO's Dual-Track Decision, 1978–1979," *Cold War History* 12, no. 3 (2012): 381–405.

71. David M. Alperin, "Furor over the Neutron Bomb," *Newsweek*, April 17, 1978.

72. Warren Christopher to Jimmy Carter, "Your Meeting with West German Foreign Minister Hans-Dietrich Genscher, Tuesday, April 4 at 2:45p.m.," April 3, 1978, JCL, RAC, NLC-6-24-4-40-1.

73. Friedrich Ruth to Hans-Dietrich Genscher, "Gesprächsführung in Washington," April 2, 1978, PA-AA, B150/390.

74. Zbigniew Brzezinski to Jimmy Carter, "ER Weapons," April 4, 1978, JCL, ZBC, SF, box 22, folder "Defense—Enhanced Radiation Warhead (3/78–8/78)."

75. Jimmy Carter to James Callaghan, April 6, 1978, JCL, ZBC, SF, box 22, folder "Defense—Enhanced Radiation Warhead (3/78–8/78)"; Jimmy Carter to Valéry Giscard d'Estaing, April 1978, JCL, ZBC, SF, box 22, folder "Defense—Enhanced Radiation Warhead (3/78–8/78)"; Jimmy Carter to Helmut Schmidt, April 6, 1978, JCL, ZBC, SF, box 22, folder "Defense—Enhanced Radiation Warhead (3/78–8/78)."

76. Jimmy Carter, "Enhanced Radiation Weapons," April 7, 1978, *PPP: Jimmy Carter 1978*, vol. 1, ed. Katherine A. Mellody, Kenneth R. Payne, and Brian L. Hermes (Washington, DC: Government Printing Office, 1979), 702.

77. "All Clear?," *Globe and Mail*, April 12, 1978.

78. "Carter and the Neutron Bomb," *MacNeil/Lehrer Report*, April 10, 1978, AAPB, cpb-aacip/507-4m91834q7c.

79. Alexander M. Haig Jr., *Inner Circles: How America Changed the World—a Memoir*, with Charles McCarry (New York: Warner, 1992), 533.

80. Julian Bullard to FCO, April 11, 1978, TNA, PREM 16/1577; Bonn to FCO, "Enhanced Radiation Weapons (ERWs)," April 11, 1978, TNA, FCO 46/1816.

81. "NATO: Annual Review for 1978," TNA, FCO 46/1959.

82. John Killick interview, February 14, 2002, BDOHP, 34.

83. Memorandum of conversation, "President's Meeting with Belgium Prime Minister Léo Tindemans," October 19, 1977, JCL, RAC, NLC-7-35-8-4-4.

84. Jimmy Carter diary entry, March 20, 1978, *White House Diary* (New York: Farrar, Straus and Giroux, 2010), 179.

85. Joseph Luns, "Annual Political Appraisal 1978," May 22, 1978, NATO, C-M(78)44.

86. "Mögliche Konsequenzen der Entscheidung des amerikanischen Präsidenten," April 2, 1978, PA-AA, B150/390.

87. "The Situation in the Soviet Union and Eastern Europe," April 4, 1978, NATO, C-M(78)25.

88. "III. A. Europe," n.d., JCL, RAC, NLC-12-33-7-1-4.

89. James E. Goodby interview, December 10, 1990, FAOHP, 82.

90. Memorandum for the members of the Military Committee, "Report on the High Level Group Meeting, 13/14 May 1981," May 19, 1981, NATO, IMSM-0281-81.

91. Henry H. Gaffney, "The History of the Euromissiles," World Security Network, March 25, 2004. http://www.worldsecuritynetwork.com/NATO/Gaffney-H.-H/The-History-of-the-Euromissiles.

92. SHAPE's definition of deep strike included the western military districts of the Soviet Union, extending to 55 degrees east.

93. "Theatre Nuclear Force Modernisation: Task Force 10 Record of NPG High Level Group Meeting, Held at Los Alamos, 16/17 February 1978," TNA, FCO 46/1925. The High Level Group included officials from Belgium, Canada, Denmark, the Federal Republic of Germany, Greece, Italy, the Netherlands, Norway, the United Kingdom, and Turkey, and was chaired by the United States; France, Iceland, Luxembourg, and Portugal were not represented.

94. "Detailed Commentary," n.d. [1978], TNA, FCO 46/1825; Clay to Kevin Tebbit, "Task Force 10," March 13, 1978, TNA, FCO 46/1825.

95. Loose minute, "NATO TNF Modernisation Task Force 10," March 21, 1978, TNA, FCO 46/1825.

96. Loose minute, "NATO TNF Modernisation Task Force 10," March 21, 1978, TNA, FCO 46/1825.

97. "Statement by the Permanent Representative of the Federal Republic of Germany," annex 3 to E. G. Luff note, "Nuclear Planning Group Theatre Nuclear Force Modernisation," April 11, 1978, NATO, NPG/N(78)2.

98. Brzezinski to Carter, "Your Private Luncheon with the NATO Heads of Delegation, Plus Secretary General Joseph Luns (May 30)," May 1978, JCL, RAC, NLC-133-179-3-3-0.

99. James A. Thomson, "The LRTNF Decision: Evolution of US Theatre Nuclear Policy, 1975–9," *International Affairs* 60, no. 4 (1984): 606.

100. Leslie Gelb interview, September 24, 1990, KCL, TNA11/49.

101. Presidential Review Memorandum/NSC-38, "Long-Range Theater Nuclear Capabilities and Arms Control," June 22, 1978, JCL, https://www.jimmycarterlibrary.gov/assets/documents/memorandums/prm38.pdf.

102. "Response to PRM-38 Long-Range Theater Nuclear Forces," August 19, 1978, NSA EBB301: Thirtieth Anniversary of NATO's Dual-Track Decision: The Road to the Euromissiles Crisis and the End of the Cold War, ed. William Burr, December 10, 2009, doc. 1. For an overview of US policy in the lead-up to the Dual-Track Decision, see Stephanie Freeman, "The Making of an Accidental Crisis: The

United States and the NATO Dual-Track Decision of 1979," *Diplomacy & Statecraft* 25 (2014): 331–55.

103. "Response to PRM-38 Long-Range Theater Nuclear Forces," August 19, 1978, NSA EBB301, doc. 1.

104. Richard Ericson and George Vest to Cyrus Vance, "SCC Meeting on PRM-38, August 23," August 16, 1978, NSA EBB301, doc. 2.

105. Ericson and Vest to Vance, "SCC Meeting on PRM-38, August 23," August 16, 1978, NSA EBB301, doc. 2.

106. "US Nuclear Policy," August 16, 1978, TNA, FCO 46/1826.

107. John Robinson to Antony Duff, "US Nuclear Policy," August 30, 1978, TNA, FCO 46/1826.

108. Robinson to Duff, "US Nuclear Policy," August 30, 1978, TNA, FCO 46/1826.

109. State Department to US Embassy London, "TNF Bilateral with UK," October 11, 1978, NSA EBB301, doc. 3.

110. State Department to US Embassy Bonn, "Bilateral with FRG on TNF Issues," October 16, 1978, NSA EBB301 doc. 4.

111. State Department to US Mission NATO, "Statement for the November 20 NAC on TNF Issues," November 17, 1978, NSA EBB301, doc. 5.

112. Zbigniew Brzezinski, *Power and Principle: Memoirs of the National Security Adviser 1977–1981* (New York: Farrar, Straus and Giroux, 1983), 294.

113. Valéry Giscard d'Estaing, *Le pouvoir et la vie*, vol. 2: *L'affrontement* (Paris: Cie 12, 1991), 366.

5. It Takes Two

1. White House photograph, "Jimmy Carter and Leaders of Western Europe, Giscard d'Estaing, James Callaghan and Helmut Schmidt meet in Guadeloupe, 1/5/1979," JCL, NLC-WHSP-C-08902-22A.

2. Jimmy Carter diary entry, January 6, 1979, *White House Diary* (New York: Farrar, Straus and Giroux, 2010), 275.

3. Jimmy Carter diary entry, January 5, 1979, *White House Diary*, 273.

4. UK Embassy Washington to FCO, "U.S. Reactions to the Brezhnev Speech," October 11, 1979, TNA, PREM 19/15.

5. Philip S. Kaplan to Anthony Lake and Paul H. Kreisberg, "The Next 18 Months," July 13, 1979, NARA, RG59, AL, box 18, folder "Next Eighteen Months 8/9/79-9/10/79."

6. Planning Staff memorandum, "Managing Russia," July 1979, TNA, FCO 46/1965.

7. Peter Carrington, Hans-Dietrich Genscher memorandum of conversation, October 31, 1979, TNA, FCO 28/3695.

8. Quoted in Leonard Downie Jr., "Brezhnev Appeals to U.S. Allies," *Washington Post*, October 17, 1979.

9. For the participants' recollections, see Jimmy Carter diary entries, January 5–6, 1979, *White House Diary*, 272–76; James Callaghan, *Time and Chance* (London: Collins, 1987), 541–53; Valéry Giscard d'Estaing, *Le pouvoir et la vie*, vol. 2: *L'affrontement* (Paris: Cie 12, 1991), 363–85; Helmut Schmidt, *Menschen und Mächte* (Berlin: Siedler, 1987), 231–35. An overview of the summit can be found in Kristina Spohr and David

Reynolds, "Bonn, Guadeloupe, and Vienna, 1978–9," in *Transcending the Cold War: Summits, Statecraft, and the Dissolution of Bipolarity in Europe*, edited by Kristina Spohr and David Reynolds (Oxford: Oxford University Press, 2016), 126–30.

10. Giscard, *Le pouvoir et la vie*, 2:375.

11. Giscard, *Le pouvoir et la vie*, 2:375–77; Zbigniew Brzezinski, *Power and Principle: Memoirs of the National Security Adviser 1977–1981* (New York: Farrar, Strauss and Giroux, 1983), 295.

12. Giscard, *Le pouvoir et la vie*, 2:376.

13. Giscard, *Le pouvoir et la vie*, 2:378.

14. Giscard, *Le pouvoir et la vie*, 2:378.

15. Callaghan, *Time and Chance*, 548–49.

16. Giscard, *Le pouvoir et la vie*, 2:379.

17. Carter diary entry, January 5, 1979, *White House Diary*, 274.

18. UK Delegation to NATO to FCO, "NATO Ministerial Meetings 4–8 December 1978," December 11, 1978, TNA, FCO 46/1697.

19. Michael Palliser to Patrick Moberly, "Grey Areas and Modernization of Theatre Nuclear Force (TNF)," February 2, 1979, TNA, FCO 46/2104. See also Western Europe to Zbigniew Brzezinski, "Evening Report," January 12, 1979, JCL, RAC, NLC-10-17-6-13-2.

20. "National Intelligence Daily (Cable)," January 24, 1979, CREST, CIA-RDP79 T00975A031000150002-9.

21. *SALT and the NATO Allies: A Staff Report to the Subcommittee on European Affairs of the Committee on Foreign Relations, United States Senate, October 1979* (Washington, DC: Government Printing Office, 1979), 7; "High Level Group (HLG) History," December 9, 1981, NATO, IMSM-0612-81. To some degree, these figures predated Guadeloupe. When the High Level Group met in late 1978, the group's chair, David McGiffert, suggested a cost-effectiveness study that would evaluate three force sizes: two hundred, four hundred, and six hundred. US officials touted the evolutionary approach as a mechanism designed to avoid decoupling. On this, see MAE note, "'Zone grise'. Travaux du Groupe Spécial," June 25, 1979, AD, 1929INVA/3966.

22. "Arms Control and Deployment Options," June 1979, JCL, RAC, NLC-17-16-16-20-7.

23. Lynn E. Davis, "NATO's Requirements and Policy for LRTNF," in *The History of NATO TNF Policy: The Role of Studies, Analysis and Exercises*, ed. Robert L. Rinne (Livermore, CA: Sandia National Laboratories, 1994), 1:179.

24. James A. Thomson, "The LRTNF Decision: Evolution of US Theatre Nuclear Policy, 1975–9," *International Affairs* 60, no. 4 (1984): 607.

25. See, for example, Simpson memorandum, "Cruise Missiles—Meeting 29th July 1977," August 1, 1977, TNA, DEFE 70/434.

26. *Report of the Special Committee on Nuclear Weapons in the Atlantic Alliance* (Washington, DC: Government Printing Office, 1985), x.

27. *Report of the Special Committee*, 13. On mixed-manning and the MLF, see Andrew Priest, "'In Common Cause': The NATO Multilateral Force and Mixed-Manning Demonstration on USS *Claude V. Ricketts*, 1964–1965," *Journal of Military History* 69, no. 3 (2005): 759–88.

28. See, for example, Zbigniew Brzezinski to Jimmy Carter, "Daily Report," July 18, 1979, JCL, RAC, NLC-1-11-5-22-9; US Embassy Bonn to State Department,

"ACDA Director Rostow's Discussion on Arms Control Aspects of TNF/SALT/ Strategic Weapons with FRG Foreign Minister Genscher," October 13, 1981, RRL, ESNSC, CF, box 14, folder "FRG 09/01/81-12/31/81 2."

29. Strobe Talbott, *Deadly Gambits: The Reagan Administration and the Stalemate in Nuclear Arms Control* (New York: Vintage, 1985), 34–35.

30. Only the Pershing IAs deployed with US forces would be replaced by the Pershing IIs. The shorter-range Pershing IAs, under dual control with US and West German forces, remained in place.

31. "National Intelligence Daily," April 24, 1979, CREST, CIA-RDP79T00975A0 31300200002-0.

32. In 1979, the Nuclear Planning Group had four permanent members—the Federal Republic of Germany, Italy, the United Kingdom, and the United States—and seven temporary members that rotated participation—Belgium, Canada, Denmark, Greece, Norway, the Netherlands, and Turkey. Though listed as an NPG member, Portugal had not participated in the body since 1974. Luxembourg participated as an observer. Neither Iceland nor France participated at all, though a permanent seat was reserved for France should the French wish to rejoin the integrated command structure. Iceland was not a member of the Nuclear Defense Affairs Committee, of which the Nuclear Planning Group was a subset, because it did not provide military forces to the alliance. On the origins of this rotating seat arrangement, see Timothy Andrews Sayle, "'We Do Not Wish to Be Obstructionist': How Canada Took and Kept a Seat on NATO's Nuclear Planning Group," in *The Nuclear North: Histories of Canada in the Atomic Age*, ed. Susan Colbourn and Timothy Andrews Sayle (Vancouver: UBC Press, 2020), 40–64.

33. Quoted in *Interim Report on Nuclear Weapons in Europe, Prepared by the North Atlantic Assembly's Special Committee on Nuclear Weapons in Europe: A Report to the Committee on Foreign Relations, United States Senate, December 1981* (Washington, DC: Government Printing Office, 1981), 16.

34. For "gap in the spectrum," see "Communique," December 12, 1979, NATO, M2(79)22. For "seamless robe of deterrence," see Kristan Stoddart, "Creating the 'Seamless Robe of Deterrence': Great Britain's Role in NATO's INF Debate," in Nuti et al., *Euromissile Crisis*, 176–95.

35. Davis, "NATO's Requirements," 181.

36. "Principal Differences between US and UK/FRG TORs for a NATO Special Group on TNF Arms Control; and US Positions," 1979, JCL, RAC, NLC-17-15-10-12-3.

37. Briefing note, "SCC Meeting, 12 April 1979," April 11, 1979, CREST, CIA-RDP81B00401R001500010001-7. The Special Group included arms control specialists from each of the allied states except France.

38. "Work Program for the Special Group," April 1979, CREST, CIA-RDP81B0 0401R001500010001-7.

39. "High Level Group (HLG) History," December 9, 1981, NATO, IMSM-0612-81.

40. David C. Gompert to Reginald Bartholomew et al., "TNF Arms Control Objectives/Principles," April 5, 1979, CREST, CIA-RDP81B00401R001500010001-7.

41. Gompert to Bartholomew et al., "TNF Arms Control Objectives/Principles," April 5, 1979, CREST, CIA-RDP81B00401R001500010001-7.

42. "TNF Arms Control Objectives/Principles," July 11, 1979, JCL, RAC, NLC-31-148-4-10-9.

43. A complete list of the Special Group's principles can be found in Annex A, enclosure to Carrington to Thatcher, "TNF Arms Control," November 23, 1979, TNA, PREM 19/15.

44. "TNF Arms Control Objectives/Principles," July 11, 1979, JCL, RAC, NLC-31-128-4-10-9.

45. Peter Carrington to Margaret Thatcher, "Theatre Nuclear Arms Control," July 6, 1979, TNA, PREM 19/15.

46. "Modernisation des Forces de Theatre de l'Alliance et Zone Grise," August 1979, AD, 1929INVA/3966.

47. Quoted in "General Report on the Security of the Alliance: The Role of Nuclear Weapons," in *Twenty-Fifth Meeting of the North Atlantic Assembly Held at Ottawa, Canada, October 22 to October, 1979. Report of the U.S. Delegation* (Washington, DC: Committee on Foreign Relations, 1980), 35. The Wehrkunde was the predecessor of the Munich Security Conference.

48. Any Turkish agreement would have also depended on US financial support, which Washington was reluctant to extend. Bonn to MAE, "RFA et Modernisation des Armes de Théâtre," June 27, 1979, AD, 1929INVA/3966.

49. Kevin Tebbit minute, "NPG High Level Group on the TNF Modernisation," November 10, 1978, TNA, FCO 46/1828.

50. Tebbit note, "NPG High Level Group on the TNF Modernisation," November 10, 1978, TNA, FCO 46/1828. See also Henry H. Gaffney, "The History of the Euromissiles," World Security Network, March 25, 2004, http://www.worldsecuritynetwork.com/NATO/Gaffney-H.-H/The-History-of-the-Euromissiles.

51. Carter diary entry, January 5, 1979, *White House Diary*, 274.

52. Quoted in *SALT and the NATO Allies*, 23.

53. "La politique allemande de défense et les relations avec les États-Unis," January 27, 1978, AD, 1929INVA/3962.

54. MAE note, "Entretiens franco-allemands. La RFA et la modernization des armements de théâtre," November 9, 1979, AD, 1929INVA/3966.

55. "General Report on the Security of the Alliance," in *Twenty-Fifth Meeting*, 36.

56. James Rentschler to Zbigniew Brzezinski, "TNF and US Leadership," August 7, 1979, JCL, RAC, NLC-23-5-4-1-6.

57. Rentschler to Brzezinski, "TNF and US Leadership," August 7, 1979, JCL, RAC, NLC-23-5-4-1-6.

58. "Executive Summary of the Special Group Report to Ministers," n.d. [September–October 1979], JCL, RAC, NLC-17-17-1-16-7; Annex to A. C. Davies memorandum for members of the Military Committee and the chief of the French Military Mission, "Briefing on High Level Group and Special Group," October 9, 1979, NATO, IMSM-373-79.

59. A. C. Davies to Military Committee, "Briefing on High Level Group and Special Group," October 9, 1979, NATO, IMSM-0373-79.

60. "Extract from Record of Discussion between PM + Chancellor Schmidt, 31 October 79," TNA, PREM 19/15.

61. "Extract from Record of Discussion between PM + Chancellor Schmidt, 31 October 79," TNA, PREM 19/15.

62. "Entretien au Département d'État: Modernisation des T.N.F.," October 4, 1979, AD, 1929INVA/3887.

63. On the fragility of Dries van Agt's government and the nuclear dimensions, see Ruud van Dijk, "'A Mass Psychosis': The Netherlands and NATO's Dual-Track Decision, 1978–1979," *Cold War History* 12, no. 3 (2012): 381–405.

64. "Theater Nuclear Forces Debate," October 15, 1979, JCL, RAC, NLC-31-127-4-33-7.

65. "Extract from a Record of a Discussion between the Prime Minister and the Secretary General of NATO, Dr. Joseph Luns at No. 10 Downing Street on 7 November at 1210 Hours," TNA, PREM 19/15.

66. "Extract from Record of Discussion between PM & Chancellor Schmidt, Bonn, 31 October 79," TNA, PREM 19/15.

67. Western Europe to Zbigniew Brzezinski, "Evening Report," October 24, 1979, JCL, RAC, NLC-10-24-6-14-3.

68. "Summary of the President's Meeting with NATO Secretary General Joseph Luns," October 12, 1979, JCL, RAC, NLC-23-6-3-9-8.

69. Rentschler to Brzezinski, "TNF and US Leadership," August 7, 1979, JCL, RAC, NLC-23-5-4-1-6.

70. Quoted in Ladislav Bittman, *The KGB and Soviet Disinformation: An Insider's View* (Washington, DC: Pergamon-Brassey's, 1985), 147.

71. In advance of the speech, allied officials predicted that Brezhnev would make the most of it to press the Soviet case against TNF modernization. "Entretien au Département d'État: Modernisation des T.N.F.," October 4, 1979, AD, 1929INVA/3887.

72. John Vinocur, "Brezhnev Says Soviet Will Cut Forces in East Germany," *New York Times*, October 7, 1979.

73. "President Brezhnev's Berlin Speech," October 1979, TNA, PREM 19/15.

74. Vinocur, "Brezhnev Says Soviet Will Cut Forces."

75. Vinocur, "Brezhnev Says Soviet Will Cut Forces."

76. FCO brief, "Brezhnev Proposals, 6 October," October 16, 1979, TNA, FCO 28/3694.

77. Vinocur, "Brezhnev Says Soviet Will Cut Forces."

78. "The Soviet TNF Blitz—Playing the European Card?," n.d. [1979], JCL, RAC, NLC-23-13-7-2-3.

79. Downie, "Brezhnev Appeals to U.S. Allies."

80. Paul Lever to Michael Alexander, "Soviet Ambassador's Call," October 18, 1979, TNA, PREM 19/15.

81. Paul Lever to Michael Alexander, "President Brezhnev's Letter to the Prime Minister," November 5, 1979, TNA, PREM 19/15.

82. NPG final communiqué, November 14, 1979, NATO, M-NPG-2(79)19.

83. "Possible Soviet Responses to an Affirmative NATO Decision on TNF Modernization," December 4, 1979, JCL, RAC, NLC-23-48-5-2-7.

84. Stansfield Turner to [redacted], "Your Memorandum on 4 December on TNF," December 7, 1979, CREST, CIA-RDP80B01554R003300190039-8.

85. International Institute for Strategic Studies press release, November 8, 1979, TNA, PREM 19/15. Analysts at the Foreign and Commonwealth Office also

questioned some of the Institute's assumptions. See Roderick Lyne to Michael Alexander, "'The Military Balance,'" September 24, 1979, TNA, PREM 19/15.

86. FCO to Priority Certain Missions, "Theatre Nuclear Force (TNF) Modernisation: Soviet Propaganda," November 20, 1979, TNA, PREM 19/15.

87. "Andrei Gromyko Repeats Offer of Immediate Talks on Medium-Range Nuclear Weapons," November 1979, TNA, PREM 19/15.

88. UK Embassy Bonn to FCO, "Gromyko's Visit to Bonn," November 26, 1979, TNA, PREM 19/15.

89. "Extract from a Record of a Discussion between the Prime Minister and the Secretary General of NATO," n.d., TNA, PREM 19/15.

90. "Notes of the Prime Minister's Talk with the Belgian Prime Minister, M. Martens, at 10 Downing Street on Wednesday 12 September 1979," TNA, PREM 19/15. These assessments were shared in other allied capitals. See, for example, "Entretien au Département d'État: Modernisation des T.N.F.," October 4, 1979, AD, 1929INVA/3887.

91. "Notes of the Prime Minister's Talk with the Belgian Prime Minister, M. Martens, at 10 Downing Street on Wednesday 12 September 1979," TNA, PREM 19/15.

92. Allied reporting from Rome throughout the fall of 1979 underscored this confidence. See, for example, "Entretien au Département d'État: Modernisation des T.N.F.," October 4, 1979, AD, 1929INVA/3887.

93. Robert Armstrong to Margaret Thatcher, "TNF," November 2, 1979, TNA, PREM 19/15.

94. Leopoldo Nuti, "The Nuclear Debate in Italian Politics in the Late 1970s and Early 1980s," in Nuti et al., *Euromissile Crisis*, 234–35; Thomson, "LRTNF Decision," 610.

95. "VU Chairman Opposes NATO Missile Deployment Plans," November 10, 1979, FBIS-WEU-79-222.

96. Vincent Dujardin, "From Helsinki to the Missiles Question: A Minor Role for Small Countries? The Case of Belgium (1973–1985)," in *The Crisis of Détente in Europe: From Helsinki to Gorbachev, 1975–1985*, ed. Leopoldo Nuti (London: Routledge, 2009), 75.

97. Brian Norbury to George Walden, "Visit of Dutch Defence Minister," October 25, 1979, TNA, PREM 19/15.

98. "Extract from Record of Discussion between PM & Chancellor Schmidt, Bonn, 31 October 79," TNA, PREM 19/15.

99. "High Level Group (HLG) History," December 9, 1981, NATO, IMSM-0612-81. This approach was consistent with the line taken by the Carter administration. On this, see SCC meeting, "Theater Nuclear Forces," August 16, 1979, JCL, RAC, NLC-7-47-4-8-1.

100. "Extract from Record of Discussion between PM & Chancellor Schmidt, Bonn, 31 October 79," TNA, PREM 19/15.

101. "Extract from Record of Discussion between PM & Chancellor Schmidt, Bonn, 31 October 79," TNA, PREM 19/15.

102. Jimmy Carter to Margaret Thatcher, November 1, 1979, TNA, PREM 19/15.

103. Carter to Thatcher, November 1, 1979, TNA, PREM 19/15.

104. Brian Norbury to Michael Alexander, "Theatre Nuclear Forces," November 6, 1979, TNA, PREM 19/15; Margaret Thatcher to Jimmy Carter, November 9, 1979, TNA, PREM 19/15.

105. Cyrus Vance to Jimmy Carter, November 28, 1979, JCL, RAC, NLC-128-14-13-20-8; "LRTNF-Modernisierung," December 4, 1979, PA-AA, B150/434.

106. Defense Policy Coordination to Zbigniew Brzezinski, "Evening Report," November 27, 1979, JCL, RAC, NLC-10-25-5-6-2.

107. Canadian Delegation NATO to External Affairs, "TNF Modernization and NAC: Perm Reps Mtg Nov 28," November 29, 1979, LAC, RG25, vol. 22105, file 27-4-NATO-1-16, part 40.

108. Vance to Carter, November 28, 1979, JCL, RAC, NLC-128-14-13-20-8.

109. US Embassy Oslo to State Department, "More from Holst on Norway on TNF," December 10, 1979, JCL, RAC, NLC-7-47-4-9-0. See also Helge Danielsen, "Norway and the Dual-Track Decision: The Role of Johan Jørgen Holst," in Nuti et al., Euromissile Crisis, 223–24.

110. Canadian Delegation NATO to External Affairs, "TNF Modernization and Arms Control," November 22, 1979, LAC, RG25, vol. 22105, file 27-4-NATO-1-16, part 40.

111. Canadian Delegation NATO to External Affairs, "TNF Modernization and Arms Control," November 22, 1979, LAC, RG25, vol. 22105, file 27-4-NATO-1-16, part 40.

112. Van Dijk, "'Mass Psychosis,'" 397.

113. The United Kingdom had agreed in September to take an additional flight of sixteen Gryphons initially slated for the Federal Republic. See Francis Pym to Margaret Thatcher, "United States Ground Launched Cruise Missiles in the United Kingdom," September 20, 1979, TNA, PREM 19/15.

114. Michael Getler, "Belgians, Dutch Qualify Approval of Missiles," Washington Post, December 13, 1979.

115. "Communique," December 12, 1979, NATO, M2(79)22.

116. "Genscher Reports to Bundestag on Government Vote at NATO Meeting," December 14, 1979, FBIS-WEU-79-249.

Part Two. Deploy

1. James M. Markham, "Germany's Volatile Greens," New York Times, February 13, 1983. On Petra Kelly's career, see Saskia Richter, Die Aktivistin: Das Leben der Petra Kelly (Munich: Deutsche Verlags-Anstalt, 2010).

2. Petra Kelly, Fighting for Hope, trans. Marianne Howarth (Boston: South End, 1984), 37.

3. Petra Kelly, "No Euroshima!" June 6, 1982, AGG, PKA 212.

4. See, for example, William Drozdiak, "More Than a Million Protest Missiles in Western Europe," Washington Post, October 23, 1983.

5. Quoted in SALT and the NATO Allies: A Staff Report to the Subcommittee on European Affairs of the Committee on Foreign Relations, United States Senate, October 1979 (Washington, DC: Government Printing Office, 1979), 23.

6. For "year of the missile," see Strobe Talbott, "Playing Nuclear Poker," Time, January 31, 1983.

6. End the Arms Race, Not the Human Race

1. E. P. Thompson, *Protest and Survive*, 2nd ed. (Nottingham, UK: Russell, 1980), 2.

2. Thompson, *Protest and Survive*, 10.

3. On the connections between the earlier opposition to nuclear power and the campaigns against the Euromissiles, see Stephen Milder, "The 'Example of Wyhl': How Grassroots Protest in the Rhine Valley Shaped West Germany's Antinuclear Movement," in *Nuclear Threats, Nuclear Fear and the Cold War of the 1980s*, ed. Eckart Conze, Martin Klimke, and Jeremy Varon (Cambridge: Cambridge University Press, 2017), 167–85.

4. Thomas Risse-Kappen, *The Zero Option: INF, West Germany, and Arms Control*, trans. Lesley Booth (Boulder, CO: Westview, 1988), 70.

5. "Secretary of State's Discussion with the President of the European Commission," 6 February 1980, TNA, PREM 19/223.

6. Ronald Reagan, "The President's News Conference," January 29, 1981, *PPP: Ronald Reagan 1981*, ed. Wilma P. Greene et al. (Washington, DC: Government Printing Office, 1982), 57.

7. "The Talk of the Town," *New Yorker*, August 30, 1982; Sam Roberts, "T.K. Jones, 82, Dies; Arms Official Saw Nuclear War as Survivable," *New York Times*, May 13, 2015.

8. Justin Vaïsse, *Neoconservatism: The Biography of a Movement*, trans. Arthur Goldhammer (Cambridge, MA: Belknap Press of Harvard University Press, 2010).

9. Stansfield Turner to NSC, "Alert Memorandum on USSR-Afghanistan," September 14, 1979, JCL, ZBM, CF, box 1, folder "Afghanistan, 4-12/1979."

10. Anatoly Dobrynin, *In Confidence: Moscow's Ambassador to America's Six Cold War Presidents (1962–1986)* (New York: Random House, 1995), 437–38; Aleksandr Antonovich Lyakhovskiy, "Inside the Soviet Invasion of Afghanistan and the Seizure of Kabul, December 1979," trans. Gary Goldberg and Artemy Kalinovsky, Cold War International History Project Working Paper 51 (Washington, DC: Woodrow Wilson Center for International Scholars, 2007), 20–21.

11. Artemy Kalinovsky, *A Long Goodbye: The Soviet Withdrawal from Afghanistan* (Cambridge, MA: Harvard University Press, 2011), 19, 24.

12. Jeane Kirkpatrick, "Dictatorships and Double Standards," *Commentary*, November 1, 1979.

13. Adam Clymer, "GOP Presidential Aspirants Tour Nation to Denounce Carter's Foreign Policy," *New York Times*, February 20, 1979.

14. Ralph Earle II interview, February 1, 1991, FAOHP, 39.

15. Randall Forsberg interview, November 9, 1987, WPNA.

16. Claudia Kemper, "More Than a FREEZE: Political Mobilization and the Peace Movement in 1980s U.S. Society," in *The INF Treaty of 1987: A Reappraisal*, ed. Philipp Gassert, Tim Geiger, and Hermann Wentker (Göttingen, Germany: Vandenhoeck & Ruprecht, 2021), 246.

17. "Call to Halt the Nuclear Arms Race: Proposal for a Mutual US-Soviet Nuclear-Weapon Freeze," 1.

18. Forsberg interview.

19. Kyle Harvey, "The Promise of Internationalism: US Anti-nuclear Activism and the European Challenge," in *Making Sense of the Americas: How Protest Related to*

America in the 1980s and Beyond, ed. Jan Hansen, Christian Helm, and Frank Reichherzer (Frankfurt: Campus, 2015), 235.

20. "Public Opinion in the European Community," *Eurobarometer* 20 (1983): 18. See also Maria Eleonora Guasconi, "Public Opinion and the Euromissiles," in Nuti et al., *Euromissile Crisis*, 279–81.

21. Ken Coates, *No Cruise, No SS-20's: European Nuclear Disarmament* (Nottingham, UK: Russell, 1980), 9.

22. European Nuclear Disarmament, "A Nuclear Free Europe," insert in Thompson, *Protest and Survive*.

23. European Nuclear Disarmament, "A Nuclear Free Europe."

24. "Support for END," insert in Thompson, *Protest and Survive*. See also Coates, *No Cruise, No SS-20's*, 3, 22–25.

25. On the links between END's various structures, see Patrick Burke, "European Nuclear Disarmament: Transnational Peace Campaigning in the 1980s," in Conze, Klimke, and Varon, *Nuclear Threats*, 227–50.

26. Burke, "European Nuclear Disarmament," 232.

27. "The neutron bomb campaign could have been, and should have been *gigantic* by now. Its success has been almost despite us," one CND member argued in May 1978. "Report: For Discussion on 20/5/1978," LSE, CND/2008/8/4/14.

28. Alan Rusbridger, "Marchers Revive CND's Golden Years," *Guardian*, October 27, 1980.

29. Andrew Wiard photograph, printed with "Fight the Bomb, Fight Capitalism!," *Socialist Organiser*, November 8, 1980.

30. Rusbridger, "Marchers Revive."

31. "CND Rallies Its Forces," *Observer*, October 19, 1980. See also Rusbridger, "Marchers Revive."

32. Lawrence S. Wittner, *Toward Nuclear Abolition: A History of the World Nuclear Disarmament Movement, 1971–Present* (Stanford, CA: Stanford University Press, 2003), 132.

33. Wiard photograph, "Fight the Bomb, Fight Capitalism!"

34. Neal Acherson, "Foundations of Post-war Europe Begin to Crumble," *Observer*, July 26, 1981.

35. "Krefelder Appell," November 1980, in *Positionen der Friedensbewegung: Die Auseinandersetzung um den US-Mittelstreckenraketenbeschluß: Dokumente, Appelle, Beiträge*, ed. Lutz Plümer (Frankfurt: Sendler, 1981), 64.

36. See, for example, Campaign to Stop the Euromissiles flyer, n.d. [1983], SCPC, CSE; "Women's Peace Camp: Greenham," August 27, 1982, LSE, CND/2008/8/3/8.

37. "Some Actions Happening on May 24 in Britain and Northern Ireland," 1983, LSE, CND/1993/2/2.

38. A popular version of this argument can be found in Helen Caldicott, *Missile Envy: The Arms Race and Nuclear War* (New York: William Morrow, 1984).

39. Harold Freeman, *This Is the Way the World Will End, This Is the Way You Will End, Unless* (Cambridge, MA: Schenkman, 1982), 21.

40. "Enough Is Enough," n.d., LAC, MG28 I 445, vol. 11, folder "Operation Dismantle Action on Cruise Missile Testing Corr Notes Minutes of Meetings and Related Material 1982–1985."

41. Peter Binns, *Missile Madness: The New Weapons Systems and How They Threaten Your Life*, 2nd ed. (London: East End Offset, 1981), 9. For a recent discussion of US policy and its warfighting capabilities in this period, see Austin Long and Brendan Rittenhouse Green, "Stalking the Secure Second Strike: Intelligence, Counterforce, and Nuclear Strategy," *Journal of Strategic Studies* 38, nos. 1–2 (2015): 38–73.

42. Song sheet, "Refuse the Cruise," n.d., LSE, 5GCC.

43. Flyer for June 12 rally, "March for Nuclear Disarmament," n.d. [1982], MUL, CPC, box 18, folder "Disarmament–Demonstrations–12 June, NYC."

44. "Missile Alerts Traced to 46¢ Item," *New York Times*, June 18, 1980.

45. Fred Halliday, *The Making of the Second Cold War* (London: Verso, 1983). Whether or not there was a second Cold War remains the subject of considerable debate. For a survey of the debate and a rejection of the concept, see Oliver Bange and Poul Villaume, introduction to *The Long Détente: Changing Concepts of Security and Cooperation in Europe, 1950s–1980s*, ed. Oliver Bange and Poul Villaume (Budapest: Central European University Press, 2017), 1–15.

46. Bradley Graham, "250,000 in Bonn Protest Stationing of NATO Missiles," *Washington Post*, October 11, 1981.

47. Joseph B. Fleming, "Denounce U.S. in Biggest West German Demonstration," United Press International, October 10, 1981.

48. John Vinocur, "250,000 at Bonn Rally Assail U.S. Arms Policy," *New York Times*, October 11, 1981.

49. Vinocur, "250,000 at Bonn Rally."

50. "Bonn, halb Festung halb Festival. Beobachtungen beim Aufmarsch der 250 000 im Hofgarten," *Die Welt*, October 12, 1981.

51. Christoph Becker-Schaum, "The Institutional Organization of the Peace Movement," in Becker-Schaum et al., *Nuclear Crisis*, 163.

52. Graham, "250,000 in Bonn Protest."

53. Leonard Downie Jr., "Thousands in London Protest Nuclear Arms," *Washington Post*, October 25, 1981.

54. "The Europeans Who Stayed at Home Are Pretty Scared Too," *Economist*, October 31, 1981.

55. A number of influential leaders active in various high-profile campaigns and national peace groups believed that this sense was what brought most demonstrators to antinuclear rallies or drove them to participate in other peace work. See, for example, Forsberg interview.

56. Ronald Reagan, "Remarks and a Question-and-Answer Session at a Working Luncheon with Out-of-Town Editors," October 16, 1981, *PPP: Ronald Reagan 1981*, 956–57.

57. Downie, "Thousands in London Protest."

58. "Bielefelder Appell," December 1980, in *Positionen der Friedensbewegung*, 35–37.

59. "Reagan Policies May Bring War, Admiral Says," *Michigan Daily*, October 9, 1981, clipping in AGG, PKA 3469 2/2.

60. Geoffrey Godsell, "Limited Nuclear Warfare—Why Reagan Worries Europe," *Christian Science Monitor*, October 21, 1981.

61. Berge Furre, letter to the editor, *Bulletin of the Atomic Scientists* 37, no. 9 (1981): 61.

62. Downie, "Thousands in London Protest."

63. Thomas R. Rochon, *Mobilizing for Peace: The Antinuclear Movements in Western Europe* (Princeton, NJ: Princeton University Press, 1988), 120.

64. "The Greenham Factor," 1983, LSE, CND/2008/8/3/8 [1 of 2].

65. Jean Stead, "Ring of Resolve to Stop Cruise," *Guardian*, December 10, 1982.

66. E. P. Thompson, *The Heavy Dancers* (New York: Pantheon, 1985), 82.

67. Rebecca Johnson, in "Return to Sender," British Library, https://www.bl.uk/collection-items/return-to-sender.

68. David K. Willis, "Profiles in Protest: Women at Missile Base in Britain," *Christian Science Monitor*, January 25, 1983.

69. Stead, "Ring of Resolve."

70. Shyam Bhatia, "Festival Fights Missile," *Observer*, March 14, 1982; Stead, "Ring of Resolve."

71. "Petra Kelly Interview / Helen John / Ann Pettitt / Nuclear Disarmament / Part 2 / 1982," November 25, 1982, Thames TV, https://www.youtube.com/watch?v=GAbKZ5JroRo.

72. Press release, n.d. [1983], LAC, MG28 I 218, vol. 43, folder "Cold Lake Peace Camp—Correspondence—Press Releases—Newsletters 1983–1984."

73. Bhatia, "Festival Fights Missile."

74. Willis, "Profiles in Protest."

75. "Al Magliocco: Third International Edition of the Information Bulletin of the International Peace Camp at Comiso, Italy," 1983, IISG, Bro 1471/20 fol.; International Fellowship of Reconciliation (IFOR) pamphlet, "Peace-Camps blühen in Europe," AGG, PKA 3438.

76. *Women's Encampment for a Future of Peace & Justice Resource Handbook*, Barnard Center for Research on Women, http://bcrw.barnard.edu/archive/militarism/womens_encampment_handbook.pdf.

77. Max Beloff note, "The Anti-CND Campaign," n.d. [December 1982], MTFA, doc. 122590.

78. NBC Evening News, June 7, 1981, VTNA, 517762.

79. Carolyn Friday, "Italian Peace Movement Facing an Uphill March to Block Missile Sites," *Christian Science Monitor*, May 23, 1983.

80. For an in-depth look at how one Warsaw Pact government tried to shape public opinion in the West, see Vladimír Černy and Petr Suchý, "Spies and Peaceniks: Czechoslovak Intelligence Attempts to Thwart NATO's Dual-Track Decision," *Cold War History* 20, no. 3 (2020): 273–91.

81. CIA Directorate of Intelligence paper, "Peace Groups and Leaders in INF Basing Countries," November 1982, CREST, CIA-RDP84B00049R001403510021-0. The degree of communist influence and infiltration remains a source of considerable debate. For an approach emphasizing Warsaw Pact influence, based on Stasi documents, see Gerhard Wettig, "The Last Soviet Offensive: Emergence and Development of the Campaign against NATO Euromissiles, 1979–1983," *Cold War History* 9, no. 1 (2009): 79–110. For a series of rebuttals, see Benjamin Ziemann, "A Quantum of Solace? European Peace Movements during the Cold War and Their Elective Affinities," *Archiv für Sozialgeschichte* 49 (2009): esp. fn. 11.

82. Ladislav Bittmann, *The KGB and Soviet Disinformation: An Insider's View* (Washington, DC: Pergamon-Brassey's, 1985), 56.

83. Tim Geiger and Jan Hansen, "Did Protest Matter? The Influence of the Peace Movement on the West German Government and the Social Democratic Party, 1977–1983," in Conze, Klimke, and Varon, *Nuclear Threats*, 297–98.

84. "Summary Record of a Meeting of the Council Held at NATO Headquarters, Brussels on Tuesday, 3rd February 1981 at 10.15 and 16.15 hours," February 20, 1981, NATO, C-R(81)4.

85. "Conference of National Information Officials," March 3, 1982, NATO, C-M(82)17.

86. John Vinocur, "K.G.B. Officers Try to Infiltrate Antiwar Groups," *New York Times*, July 26, 1983.

87. Coalition for Peace through Security, "CND: Communists, Neutralists, Defeatists," n.d., https://www.lse.ac.uk/ideas/Assets/Documents/project-docs/cnd-archives/CND-044-0001-0003.pdf.

88. Richard Norton-Taylor and David Pallister, "A Nasty Little Operation," *Guardian*, February 22, 1992.

89. Tim Hardy, letter to the editor, "Why We Must Talk Peace to Soviet Power-mongers," *Guardian*, January 15, 1983.

90. Clifton CND flyer, n.d., LAC, MG28 I 445, box 8, folder "Operation Dismantle Campaign for Nuclear Disarmament Corr. + Related Material, 1983–1986."

91. Eirini Karamouzi and Dionysios Chourchoulis, "Troublemaker or Peacemaker? Andreas Papandreou, the Euromissile Crisis, and the Policy of Peace, 1981–86," *Cold War History* 19, no. 1 (2019): 49–50.

92. Clive Rose, *Campaigns against Western Defence: NATO's Adversaries and Critics* (New York: St. Martin's, 1985), 172.

93. *Second Interim Report on Nuclear Weapons in Europe, Prepared by the North Atlantic Assembly's Special Committee on Nuclear Weapons in Europe: A Report to the Committee on Foreign Relations, United States Senate, January 1983* (Washington, DC: Government Printing Office, 1983), 53.

94. Holger Nehring, "A Transatlantic Security Crisis? Transnational Relations between the West German and the U.S. Peace Movements, 1977–1985," in *European Integration and the Atlantic Community in the 1980s*, ed. Kiran Klaus Patel and Kenneth Weisbrode (Cambridge: Cambridge University Press, 2013), 179.

7. Moons and Green Cheese

1. Maynard W. Glitman, *The Last Battle of the Cold War: An Inside Account of Negotiating the Intermediate-Range Nuclear Forces Treaty* (New York: Palgrave Macmillan, 2006), 61.

2. "The Dance of the Euromissiles," *New York Times*, November 7, 1983.

3. "Soviet 'Non-Paper,'" January 4, 1980, LAC, RG25, vol. 25121, file 27-4-NATO-1-16, part 42.

4. Canadian Delegation NATO to External Affairs, "TNF Arms Control—PermReps Mtg 24Jan," January 25, 1980, LAC, RG25, vol. 25121, file 274-NATO-1-16, part 42; Joseph Luns to Permanent Representatives, "Special Consultative Group (SCG) Progress Report," June 20, 1980, NATO, PO/80/58.

5. Washington to MAE, "ANT—Déclarations du Chancelier Schmidt," April 30, 1980, AD, 1929INVA/3966; Harold Brown to Jimmy Carter, "Schmidt Proposal for a Freeze on LRTNF," June 13, 1980, JCL, RAC, NLC-12-55-8-19-0.

6. "Aufzeichnung des Vortragenden Legationsrats I. Klasse Citron," June 13, 1980, *AAPD 1980*, ed. Tim Geiger, Amit Das Gupta, and Tim Szatkowski (Munich: Oldenbourg, 2011), doc. 170.

7. Brown to Carter, "Schmidt Proposal for a Freeze on LRTNF," June 13, 1980, JCL, RAC, NLC-12-55-8-19-0. After Schmidt first floated the idea in April, the West Germans churned out clarifications maintaining their fidelity to the Dual-Track Decision. See "Déclarations du Chancelier Schmidt au Sujet de la Modernisation des T.N.F.," April 22, 1980, AD, 1929INVA/3966.

8. Jonathan Carr, *Helmut Schmidt: Helmsman of Germany* (London: Wiedenfeld & Nicolson, 1985), 134.

9. Jimmy Carter, *Keeping Faith: Memoirs of a President* (New York: Bantam, 1982), 538. Zbigniew Brzezinski likely agreed. In his own memoirs, a photo insert includes an image of him and Helmut Schmidt with the caption "One of the rare amiable encounters with Chancellor Schmidt." Zbigniew Brzezinski, *Power and Principle: Memoirs of the National Security Adviser 1977–1981* (New York: Farrar, Strauss and Giroux, 1983), second photo insert.

10. Bradley Graham, "Schmidt's Moscow Trip Worries U.S.," *Washington Post*, June 30, 1980.

11. "Deutsch-sowjetisches Regierungsgespräch in Moskau," July 1, 1980, *AAPD 1980*, doc. 193.

12. "Verbatim Record of the Meeting of the Defense Planning Committee in Ministerial Session Held on Wednesday 10th December 1980 at 11.00 a.m. at NATO Headquarters, Brussels," December 10, 1980, NATO, DPC-VR(80)20 2.

13. National Foreign Assessment Center memorandum, "Likely Soviet Approach to Preliminary Exchanges on TNF," October 3, 1980, JCL, RAC, NLC-23-58-2-2-9.

14. National Foreign Assessment Center memorandum, "Likely Soviet Approach to Preliminary Exchanges on TNF," October 3, 1980, JCL, RAC, NLC-23-58-2-2-9.

15. Quoted in Strobe Talbott, *Deadly Gambits: The Reagan Administration and the Stalemate in Nuclear Arms Control* (New York: Vintage, 1985), 44.

16. "Memorandum for the Record," March 26, 1981, *FRUS 1981–1988*, vol. 3: *Soviet Union, January 1981–January 1983*, ed. James Graham Wilson (Washington, DC: Government Printing Office, 2016), doc. 36.

17. Tom Mathews with Fred Coleman, "Reagan Changes the Rules," *Newsweek*, February 9, 1981.

18. "Telephone Conversation with Chancellor Schmidt," February 25, 1981, TNA, PREM 19/762.

19. "Remarks of the President and Prime Minister Margaret Thatcher of the United Kingdom Following Their Meetings," February 26, 1981, *PPP: Ronald Reagan 1981*, vol. 1, ed. Wilma P. Greene, Katherine A. Mellody, and Kenneth R. Payne (Washington, DC: Government Printing Office, 1983), 166. On British efforts to secure the Reagan administration's support for negotiations in the spring of 1981, see Oliver Barton, "'The Most Staunch and Dependable of the Allies'? Britain and the Zero Option," in *The INF Treaty of 1987: A Reappraisal*, ed. Philipp Gassert, Tim Geiger, and Hermann Wentker (Göttingen, Germany: Vandenhoeck & Ruprecht, 2021), 98–99.

20. "Brezhnev Proposed Talks with Reagan to Mend Relations," *New York Times*, February 24, 1981.

21. William Stearman to Richard Allen, "Approaches to a Summit Meeting," February 24, 1981, RRL, REPF, box 9, folder "02/05/1981-02/28/1981"; Richard Pipes to Richard Allen, "Approaches to a Summit Meeting," February 26, 1981, RRL, REPF, box 9, folder "02/05/1981-02/28/1981."

22. NAC final communiqué, May 5, 1981, NATO, M-1(81)5.

23. Richard Pipes to Richard Allen, "26th Party Congress," February 26, 1981, RRL, REPF, box 9, folder "02/05/1981-02/28/1981."

24. Paul H. Nitze, *From Hiroshima to Glasnost: At the Center of Decision—a Memoir*, with Ann M. Smith and Steven L. Rearden (New York: Grove Weidenfeld, 1989), 368.

25. "Third Progress Report to Ministers of the Special Consultative Group on Arms Control Involving Theater Nuclear Forces," March 31, 1981, NATO, PO/81/37.

26. "Memorandum for the Record," March 26, 1981, *FRUS 1981–1988*, vol. 3, doc. 36.

27. "Text of Report by D/AD (AC&D), P&P Division on SCG Meeting, 31 March," April 3, 1981, NATO, IMSM-160-81.

28. NSC minutes, "Theater Nuclear Forces—Negotiations Timing," April 30, 1981, RRL, ESNSC, MF, box 1, folder "NSC no. 8 2."

29. "Memorandum for the Record," April 23, 1981, *FRUS 1981–1988*, vol. 3, doc. 45.

30. US International Communications Agency (USICA) briefing paper, "Many West Europeans Oppose TNF," April 1, 1981, RRL, DBF, RAC box 4, folder "NATO-North Atlantic Treaty Organization 1981 (August 1981)."

31. Hilary Synnott to Robin Janvrin, "TNF: FRG Views," March 31, 1981, TNA, FCO 46/2715.

32. UK Embassy in Bonn to FCO, "Schmidt on TNF," May 18, 1981, TNA, FCO 46/2710.

33. NBC Evening News, May 4, 1981, VTNA, 517128.

34. "Letter from President Reagan to Soviet General Secretary Brezhnev," n.d., *FRUS 1981–1988*, vol. 3, doc. 46. On the drafting of Reagan's letter to Brezhnev, see James Graham Wilson, *The Triumph of Improvisation: Gorbachev's Adaptability, Reagan's Engagement, and the End of the Cold War* (Ithaca, NY: Cornell University Press, 2014), 12–13; Simon Miles, *Engaging the Evil Empire: Washington, Moscow, and the Beginning of the End of the Cold War* (Ithaca, NY: Cornell University Press, 2020), 33–34.

35. "Too Much Elbow Room for Schmidt?," *Washington Post*, May 8, 1981.

36. On the administration's infighting and its impact on the policy process, see William Inboden, "Grand Strategy and Petty Squabbles: The Paradox and Lessons of the Reagan NSC," in *The Power of the Past: History and Statecraft*, ed. Hal Brands and Jeremi Suri (Washington, DC: Brookings Institution, 2015), 151–80.

37. Acting National Intelligence Officer for Western Europe to Director of Central Intelligence, "Monthly Warning Assessment: Western Europe," August 21, 1981, CREST, CIA-RDP83B01027R000300050039-1.

38. Fritz Ermarth paper, "TNF and Arms Control," July 1981, RRL, SKF, box 90556, folder "NATO-TNF-Arms Control-State Conference (1)."

39. "Bielefelder Appell," December 1980, in *Positionen der Friedensbewegung. Die Auseinandersetzung um den US- Mittelstreckenraketenbeschluß. Dokumente, Appelle, Beiträge*, ed Lutz Plümer (Frankfurt: Sendler, 1981), 35–37.

40. Bradley Graham, "Schmidt, Brandt at Odds on Soviet Missile Proposal," *Washington Post*, July 5, 1981.

41. David Goodall to David Gladstone, "Brandt Visit to Moscow: The Aftermath," July 24, 1981, TNA, FCO 46/2715.

42. "Visit of Horst Ehmke with Richard Perle," March 27, 1981, CREST, CIA-RDP84B00049R001403560044-0.

43. On the connections between Schmidt's political woes and the zero option, see Jean-Pierre Brunet to Claude Cheysson, "'L'Option Zéro' et la RFA," September 30, 1981, AD, 1930INVA/4894.

44. David C. Gompert to Reginald Bartholomew et al., "TNF Arms Control Objectives/Principles," April 5, 1979, CREST, CIA-RDP81B00401R00150001 0001-7.

45. *Interim Report on Nuclear Weapons in Europe, Prepared by the North Atlantic Assembly's Special Committee on Nuclear Weapons in Europe: A Report to the Committee on Foreign Relations, United States Senate, December 1981* (Washington, DC: Government Printing Office, 1981), 14.

46. NPG final communiqué, October 20-21, 1981, NATO, M-NPG-2(81)15.

47. James Thomson indicated that the Carter administration's analyses appreciated that a solution at the level of zero would be "politically and strategically unsound," and, as a result, US policymakers advocated for the broad principle that arms control would be a complement to force modernization, not a substitute for it. "But," as Thomson later argued, "concessions that seemed minor at the time led the alliance down the 'zero option' road." "From NATO's 1979 Two-Track Decision to the Present," in *The History of NATO TNF Policy: The Role of Studies, Analysis and Exercises*, ed. R. L. Rinne (Albuquerque, NM: Sandia National Laboratories, 1994), 1:60. For a recent detailed discussion of how the Integrated Decision Document left open the possibility of the zero option proposal and the implications thereof, see Andreas Lutsch, "The Zero Option and NATO's Dual Track Decision: Rethinking the Paradox," *Journal of Strategic Studies* 43, nos. 6–7 (2020): 957–89.

48. Eugene Rostow to William Casey, "Reflections on My Trip to Brussels, SHAPE, Bonn, and London, September 24 to October 13, 1981," October 26, 1981, CREST, CIA-RDP83M00914R002100110083-0.

49. Glitman, *Last Battle of the Cold War*, 74.

50. "Minutes of a National Security Council Meeting," October 13, 1981, *FRUS 1981–1988*, vol. 3, doc. 92.

51. US Embassy Bonn to State Department, "ACDA Rostow's Discussion on Arms Control Aspects of TNF/SALT/Strategic Weapons with FRG Foreign Minister Genscher," October 13, 1981, RRL, ESNSC, MF, box 14, folder "Germany, FRG 9/1/81-12/31/81 (2)."

52. NSC minutes, November 12, 1981, RRL, ESNSC, MF, box 3, folder "NSC no. 25"; Alexander M. Haig Jr., *Caveat: Realism, Reagan, and Foreign Policy* (New York: Macmillan, 1984), 229.

53. NSC minutes, November 12, 1981, RRL, ESNSC, MF, box 3, folder "NSC no. 25."

54. Reagan's support for the zero option has been widely dismissed as a hard-line position designed to avoid reaching an agreement. See, for example, Marilena Gala, "The Euromissile Crisis and the Centrality of the 'Zero Option,'" in Nuti et al., *Euromissile Crisis*, 162; Andrea Chiampan, "The Reagan Administration and the INF Controversy, 1981–83," *Diplomatic History* 44, no. 5 (2020): 863.

55. Ronald Reagan diary entry, November 12, 1981, *The Reagan Diaries*, vol. 1, ed. Douglas Brinkley (New York: HarperCollins, 2009), 84.

56. Ronald Reagan, *An American Life: The Autobiography* (New York: Simon & Schuster, 1990), 293.

57. See, for example, Max Kampelman, *Entering New Worlds: The Memoirs of a Private Man in Public Life* (New York: HarperCollins, 1991), 339; Kenneth Adelman interview, September 30, 2003, RROHP, 14.

58. Adelman interview, 38.

59. Ronald Reagan, "Remarks to Members of the National Press Club on Arms Reduction and Nuclear Weapons," November 18, 1981, *PPP: Ronald Reagan 1981*, 1062–67.

60. Reagan diary entry, November 18, 1981, *Reagan Diaries*, vol. 1, 85.

61. Marc A. Genest, *Negotiating in the Public Eye: The Impact of the Press on the Intermediate-Range Nuclear Force Negotiations* (Stanford, CA: Stanford University Press, 1995), 1.

62. Canadian Embassy Moscow to External Affairs, "Soviet Reaction to Zero Option," November 20, 1981, TNA, FCO 46/2707.

63. Reagan diary entry, November 18, 1981, *Reagan Diaries*, vol. 1, 85; Reagan, *American Life*, 293.

64. Wim Bartels and Ben Schennink, "The Dutch Peace Movement (IKV): Work, Results, Dilemmas and March for New Alliances," n.d. [1981], SCPC, IKV; Martin to Peter Brown, March 9, 1982, LAC, MG28 I 445, vol. 39, folder "Operation Dismantle Municipal Referendum Winnipeg-corr. + related material nd 1979–1983."

65. Lawrence Freedman, "Zero Is a Plus," *Sunday Times*, November 22, 1981. One pamphlet, circulated by the Campaign for Nuclear Disarmament in the late 1980s, quoted Richard Burt: "We took the slogans from your banners." See CND pamphlet, "One Day, This Could Be a Nuclear-Free Zone," LSE, CND/1993/6/7 [1 of 5].

66. Petra Kelly, "No Euroshima!," June 6, 1982, AGG, PKA 212.

67. E. P. Thompson, "Europe Should Demand All Nuclear Weapons Out," *Guardian Weekly*, December 6, 1981. For similar arguments, see Bruce Kent to George Bush, February 9, 1983, LSE, CND/1993/2/2.

68. Avis Thayer Bohlen interview, February 28, 2003, FAOHP, 41.

69. Richard Hastie-Smith to PS/S of S, "The 'Zero Option,'" December 4, 1981, TNA, FCO 46/2708.

70. David Gillmore to Weston, "TNF: The Zero Option," November 20, 1981, TNA, FCO 46/2707.

71. David Gillmore to Richard Hastie-Smith, "The Zero Option," November 16, 1981, TNA, FCO 46/2707.

72. Note for the record, "UK/US Pol/Mil Talks: 3 December," December 1981, TNA, FCO 46/2709.

73. Helmut Schmidt had long taken issue with using the term "theater" to describe nuclear weapons in Europe. See, for some examples, "Schmidt Disclaims Nuclear Weapons Plan for European Theater, Ascribes It to Carter," *Baltimore Sun*, clipping in TNA, FCO 46/2717; US Embassy Bonn to State Department, "Chancellor Schmidt Briefs Ambassador November 15 on the Brezhnev Visit," November 16, 1981, RRL, ESNSC, CF, box 14, folder "FRG 09/01/81-12/31/81 4." On West German efforts to shift Washington's language, see US Delegation to State Department, "Breakfast Meeting between Secretary Haig and German Foreign Minister Genscher," September 25, 1981, DDRS, CK2349530790. Arms control specialists found the new terminology baffling. US officials defined intermediate-range nuclear forces as everything between battlefield and strategic systems, confusing British analysts. "I have never heard this definition before," one British defense official wrote, "and I have been able to find no basis for it." See "'Intermediate' Nuclear Forces," November 26, 1981, TNA, FCO 46/2708. See also "UK Summary Record of Special Consultative Group Meeting in Brussels on 20 November 1981," December 2, 1981, TNA, FCO 46/2708; "Botschafter Ruth, z.Z. Brüssel, an das Auswärtige Amt," February 12, 1982, *AAPD 1982*, ed. Michael Ploetz, Tim Szatkowski, and Judith Michel (Munich: Oldenbourg, 2013), doc. 53.

74. "Memorandum of Conversation," November 18, 1981, *FRUS 1981–1988*, vol. 3, doc. 104.

75. US Embassy Bonn to State Department, "ACDA Director Rostow's Discussion on Arms Control Aspects of TNF/SALT/Strategic Weapons with FRG Foreign Minister Genscher," October 13, 1981, RRL, ESNSC, MF, box 14, folder "Germany, FRG 9/1/81-12/31/81 (2)."

76. "President Brezhnev's Speech to the 17th Congress of Soviet Trade Unions (Excerpts)," March 16, 1982, *Survival* 24, no. 4 (1982): 184.

77. On the Reagan administration's response to the introduction of martial law in Poland, see Tyler Esnos, "Reagan's Economic War on the Soviet Union," *Diplomatic History* 42, no. 2 (2018): 281–304; Alan P. Dobson, "The Reagan Administration, Economic Warfare, and Starting to Close Down the Cold War," *Diplomatic History* 29, no. 3 (2005): 531–56; David S. Painter, "Energy and the End of the Evil Empire," in *The Reagan Moment: America and the World in the 1980s*, ed. Jonathan R. Hunt and Simon Miles (Ithaca, NY: Cornell University Press, 2021), 43–63. For the transatlantic dimensions, see Andrea Chiampan, "'Those European Chicken Littles': Reagan, NATO, and the Polish Crisis, 1981–2," *International History Review* 37, no. 4 (2015): 682–99; Susan Colbourn, "An Interpreter or Two: Defusing NATO's Siberian Pipeline Dispute, 1981–1982," *Journal of Transatlantic Studies* 18, no. 2 (2020): 131–51.

78. "Gespräch des Bundeskanzlers Schmidt mit Präsident Reagan in Washington," January 5, 1982, *AAPD 1982*, doc. 3

79. CIA Directorate of Intelligence paper, "Peace Groups and Leaders in INF Basing Countries," November 1982, CREST, CIA-RDP84B00049R001403510021-0.

80. Eugene Rostow, "Nuclear Arms Control and the Future of U.S.-Soviet Relations," *Department of State Bulletin*, November 1982, 19–20.

81. "Brezhnev's Moratorium Proposal," n.d. [1982], RRL, DGF, box OA9422, folder "Nuclear [Freeze] (3 of 8)."

82. "White House Statement on President Brezhnev's INF Announcement (Excerpts)," March 16, 1982, *Survival* 24, no. 4 (1982): 185.

83. "Breschnew-Besuch: 'Der hat noch was im Hut,'" *Der Spiegel*, November 1, 1981. See also Dusko Doder, "Brezhnev Seeks Edge in Europe with Interview on Nuclear Arms," *Washington Post*, November 5, 1981.

84. Lawrence S. Eagleburger, "The US Approach to the Negotiations on Intermediate-Range Nuclear Forces," *NATO Review* 30, no. 1 (1982): 10.

85. *Report of the Special Committee on Nuclear Weapons in the Atlantic Alliance* (Washington, DC: Government Printing Office, 1985), 25.

86. The chart tracked five systems: the Soviets' SS-4s, SS-5s, and SS-20s, along with the US Gryphons and Pershing IIs. "Key INF Missile Systems—April 1982," insert in Günther Gillessen, "Countering Soviet Nuclear Supremacy in Europe: Security Policy with Intermediate-Range Missiles," *NATO Review* 30, no. 2 (1982): 21.

87. Quoted in Jonathan Haslam, *The Soviet Union and the Politics of Nuclear Weapons, 1969–87: The Problem of the SS-20* (London: Macmillan, 1989), 33.

88. London to PMO, "Callaghan Visit to USSR," October 25, 1983, LAC, RG25, vol. 25336, file 28-6-1-TRUDEAU PEACE MISSION, part 3.

89. "Ruth/Perle Meeting—6 January 1983," January 12, 1983, RRL, RLF, RAC box 9, folder "INF Materials for Lehman (2 of 6)."

90. Quoted in J. Michael Hogan and Ted J. Smith III, "Polling on the Issues: Public Opinion and the Nuclear Freeze," *Public Opinion Quarterly* 55, no. 4 (1991): 535.

91. Aaron Donaghy, *The Second Cold War: Carter, Reagan, and the Domestic Politics of Foreign Policy* (Cambridge: Cambridge University Press, 2021), 144.

92. Jamie Kalven, "Ground Zero Week 1982," *Bulletin of the Atomic Scientists* 38, no. 4 (1982): 57.

93. Thomas Ferrero, "Ground Zero Week Is Only in Day Three, but . . . ," United Press International, April 20, 1982.

94. William Clark to Edwin Meese, James Baker, and Michael Deaver, "Policy Offensive on Arms Control and the Anti-nuclear Movement," April 22, 1982, RRL, DGF, box OA9422, folder "Nuclear [Freeze] (1 of 8)."

95. Ronald Reagan, "Radio Address to the Nation on Nuclear Weapons," April 17, 1982, *PPP: Ronald Reagan 1982*, vol. 1, ed. Wilma P. Greene, Katherine A. Mellody, and Kenneth R. Payne (Washington, DC: Government Printing Office, 1983), 487.

96. "Possible Activities regarding the Anti-nuclear Movement," n.d. [1982], RRL, DGF, box OA9422, folder "Nuclear [Freeze] (1 of 8)."

97. "A Freeze Would Undermine American Leadership of NATO," n.d. [1982], RRL, MBF, box 15, folder "Nuclear Freeze (2 of 16)."

98. Ferrero, "Ground Zero Week."

99. Michael Wheeler to Paul Bremer et al., "President's Trip to Europe—Public Affairs Campaign," May 10, 1982, CREST, CIA-RDP83M00914R003000110011-9.

100. Paul Bremer to Nancy Bearg Dyke et al., "NATO and Versailles Summits: Paper on Linkage and Speech Strategy," April 8, 1982, CREST, CIA-RDP83M00914R000500120020-6.

101. Sydney Giffard to Nicholas Henderson, "The 'Transatlantic Crisis,'" March 5, 1982, TNA, FCO 28/4719.

102. On Haig's visit, see John Vinocur, "Violence in Berlin Marks Haig's Visit," *New York Times*, September 14, 1981.

103. On NATO's debates over the Siberian pipeline, see Chiampan, "'Those European Chicken Littles'"; Colbourn, "Interpreter or Two."

104. John Tagliabue, "Thousands of Anti-Reagan Protesters Clash with the Police in West Berlin," *New York Times*, June 12, 1982.

105. "Anti-Reagan Protest Draws 115,000 in London," United Press International, June 6, 1982.

106. R. W. Apple Jr., "President Urges Global Crusade for Democracy," *New York Times*, June 9, 1982.

107. Ronald Reagan, "Address to Members of the British Parliament," June 8, 1982, *PPP: Ronald Reagan 1982*, vol. 1, 743, 747.

108. Ronald Reagan, "Address to Members of the British Parliament," 743.

109. Nitze, *From Hiroshima to Glasnost*, 374–75.

110. "Memorandum of Conversation—July 16, 1982," RRL, WPCF, box 3, folder "Intermediate-Range Nuclear Forces (INF): Nitze Meeting 'Walk in the Woods'—07/29/1982-07/31/1982."

111. Memorandum to the president, "INF Package," June 30, 1982, RRL, WPCF, box 3, folder "Intermediate-Range Nuclear Forces (INF): Nitze Meeting 'Walk in the Woods'—07/29/1982-07/31/1982."

112. Nitze, *From Hiroshima to Glasnost*, 386.

113. "Farewell Dark Prince," *Time*, March 23, 1987.

114. Matthew J. Ambrose, *The Control Agenda: A History of the Strategic Arms Limitation Talks* (Ithaca, NY: Cornell University Press, 2018), 202.

115. George P. Shultz, *Turmoil and Triumph: My Years as Secretary of State* (New York: Charles Scribner's Sons, 1993), 120.

116. Thomas Graham Jr., *Disarmament Sketches: Three Decades of Arms Control and International Law* (Seattle: University of Washington Press, 2002), 115.

117. NSDD 56, "Private INF Exchange," September 15, 1982, RRL, https://www.reaganlibrary.gov/public/archives/reference/scanned-nsdds/nsdd56.pdf.

118. Nitze, *From Hiroshima to Glasnost*, 388–89.

119. Nitze, *From Hiroshima to Glasnost*, 389.

120. A collection can be found in LOC, PHNP, box 114, folder 3.

121. Nitze, *From Hiroshima to Glasnost*, 389.

122. "US State Department Statement on Soviet INF Position (Excerpts)," December 21, 1982, *Survival* 25, no. 2 (1983): 88.

123. Steven Strasser, Robert B. Cullen, and John Walcott, "Andropov Aims at the Zero Option," *Newsweek*, January 3, 1983.

124. US Embassy Moscow to State Department, "US/Soviet Relations," January 25, 1983, RRL, JFMF, box 22, folder "USSR Diplomatic Contacts 2/8."

125. John Nott to Margaret Thatcher, "Nuclear Issues," October 20, 1982, TNA, PREM 19/979.

126. Francis Pym to Margaret Thatcher, October 25, 1982, TNA, PREM 19/979.

8. First Principles

1. Stanley Hoffmann, "NATO and Nuclear Weapons: Reasons and Unreason," *Foreign Affairs* 60, no. 2 (1981): 328.

2. Joseph Luns, "Annual Political Appraisal 1981," April 24, 1981, NATO, C-M(81)27.

3. "Conference of National Information Officials," March 3, 1982, NATO, C-M(82)17.

4. Christopher Jon Lamb, "Public Opinion and Nuclear Weapons in Europe: A Re port on the 27th Annual Session of the North Atlantic Assembly," *NATO Review* 29, no. 6 (1981): 28.

5. Sam Nunn, "NATO: Saving the Alliance," *Washington Quarterly* 5, no. 3 (1982): 19.

6. On the broadening of the security conversation, see Wilfried Mausbach, "Vereint marschieren, getrennt schlagen? Die amerikanische Friedensbewegung und der Widerstand gegen den NATO-Doppelbeschluss," in *Zweiter Kalter Krieg und Friedensbewegung: Der NATO-Doppelbeschluss in deutsch-deutscher und internationaler Perspektive,* ed. Philipp Gassert, Tim Geiger, and Hermann Wentker (Munich: Oldenbourg, 2011), 283–304; Holger Nehring, "A Transatlantic Security Crisis? Transnational Relations between the West German and the U.S. Peace Movements, 1977–1985," in *European Integration and the Atlantic Community in the 1980s,* ed. Kiran Klaus Patel and Kenneth Weisbrode (Cambridge: Cambridge University Press, 2013), 180.

7. E. P. Thompson, *Protest and Survive,* 2nd ed. (Nottingham, UK: Russell, 1980), 8.

8. Wilhelm Bittorf, "Was den Krieg möglich macht," *Der Spiegel,* October 9, 1983.

9. McGeorge Bundy et al., "Nuclear Weapons and the Atlantic Alliance," *Foreign Affairs* 60, no. 4 (1982): 753–68. See also McGeorge Bundy, "'No First Use' Needs Careful Study," *Bulletin of the Atomic Scientists* 38, no. 6 (1982): 6–8; Robert S. McNamara, "The Military Role of Nuclear Weapons: Perceptions and Misperceptions," *Foreign Affairs* 62, no. 1 (1983): 59–80; George F. Kennan, *The Nuclear Delusion: Soviet-American Relations in the Atomic Age* (New York: Pantheon, 1982), 185.

10. See, for some examples, Julian Critchley, "Should the First Use of Nuclear Arms Be Renounced?," *RUSI Journal* 127, no. 4 (1982): 32–34; Michael Carver, "No First Use: A View from Europe," *Bulletin of the Atomic Scientists* 39, no. 3 (1983): 22–26; *No First Use: A Report by the Union of Concerned Scientists* (Cambridge, MA: Union of Concerned Scientists, 1983).

11. Vincenzo Tornetta, "The Nuclear Strategy of the Atlantic Alliance and the 'No-First-Use' Debate," *NATO Review* 30, no. 5 (1982): 2.

12. Karl Kaiser et al., "Nuclear Weapons and the Preservation of Peace: A Response to an American Proposal for Renouncing the First Use of Nuclear Weapons," *Foreign Affairs* 60, no. 5 (1982): 1158–60. The article also appeared in *Europa-Archiv* 12 (1982).

13. Kaiser et al., "Nuclear Weapons and the Preservation of Peace," 1158–60. Historians continue to debate the applicability and limitations of the Cold War's long peace, highlighting the sharp differences between Europe and much of the rest of the world. The classic statement of the long peace argument is John Lewis Gaddis, *The Long Peace: Inquiries into the History of the Cold War* (Oxford: Oxford University Press, 1987). For a recent argument on the limits of the long peace thesis, see Paul Thomas Chamberlin, *The Cold War's Killing Fields: Rethinking the Long Peace* (New York: HarperCollins, 2018), esp. 1–19.

14. Tornetta, "Nuclear Strategy of the Atlantic Alliance," 3.

15. Walter Slocombe, "Extended Deterrence," *Washington Quarterly* 7, no. 4 (1984): 97.

16. See, for example, European Security Study, *Strengthening Conventional Deterrence in Europe: Proposals for the 1980's* (London: Macmillan, 1983).

17. *NATO: Can the Alliance Be Saved? Report of Senator Sam Nunn to the Committee on Armed Services, United States Senate, May 13, 1982* (Washington, DC: Government Printing Office, 1982), 8.

18. On the origins and adoption of AirLand Battle, see Wayne E. Lee, *Waging War: Conflict, Culture, and Innovation in World History* (Oxford: Oxford University Press, 2016), 430–36.

19. Joseph Luns to permanent representatives, "NATO Information Symposium," October 28, 1982, NATO, PO(82)118.

20. John J. Mearsheimer, "Prospects for Conventional Deterrence in Europe," *Bulletin of the Atomic Scientists* 41, no. 7 (1985): 162.

21. Adam Roberts, "The Trouble with Unilateralism: The UK, the 1983 General Election, and Non-nuclear Defence," *Bulletin of Peace Proposals* 14, no. 4 (1983): 308.

22. Gert Krell, "The Controversy about 'Flexible Response,'" *Bulletin of Peace Proposals* 17, no. 2 (1986): 131.

23. *NATO: Can the Alliance Be Saved?*, 3.

24. Samuel P. Huntington, "Conventional Deterrence and Conventional Retaliation in Europe," *International Security* 8, no. 3 (1983): 34.

25. The Brandt Commission, formally known as the Independent Commission on International Development Issues, brought together a group of twenty global leaders to discuss the challenges of global inequality and of the economic and social disparities between the developed and developing world. Started in 1977, the commission issued a public report in 1980.

26. Wolfgang Schmidt, "The Euromissile Crisis, the Palme Commission, and the Search for a New Security Model," in Nuti et al., *Euromissile Crisis*, 349.

27. The commission's sixteen members were Georgy Arbatov (Soviet Union); Egon Bahr (Federal Republic of Germany); Gro Harlem Brundtland (Norway); Jozef Cyrankiewicz (Poland); Jean-Marie Daillet (France); Robert Ford (Canada); Haruki Mori (Japan); C. B. Muthamma (India); Olusegun Obasanjo (Nigeria); David Owen (United Kingdom); Shridath Ramphal (Guyana); Alfonso Garcia Robles (Mexico); Salim A. Salim (Tanzania); Soedjatmoko (Indonesia); Joop M. den Uyl (Netherlands); and Cyrus Vance (United States).

28. Schmidt, "Euromissile Crisis, the Palme Commission," 351.

29. Independent Commission for Disarmament and Security Issues, *Common Security: A Blueprint for Survival* (New York: Simon & Schuster, 1982).

30. David Owen and Cyrus Vance to George Shultz, September 29, 1982, YUA, CRGSVP, box 36, folder "Palme Commission on Disarmament and Security Issues Vance-Owen Letter to NATO Foreign Ministers 1982."

31. "Recent Article by Dr David Owen MP Circulated for the Information of Commission Members," October 1981, YUA, CRGSVP, box 35, folder "Palme Commission on Disarmament and Security Issues Meeting (in Paris) (23–25 Oct) 1981."

32. *Common Security*, 105.

33. Johan Jørgen Holst to Cyrus Vance, December 4, 1981, YUA, CRGSVP, box 35, folder "Palme Commission on Disarmament and Security Issues Meeting (in Japan) (4–6 Dec) 1981."

34. Pierre Hassner, "Pacifism and East-West Relations," in *European Peace Movements and the Future of the Western Alliance*, ed. Walter Laqueur and Robert Hunter (New Brunswick, NJ: Transaction, 1985), 128.

35. See, for a few examples, Thompson, *Protest and Survive*, 10; IKV statement, "World Conference: Religious Workers for Saving the Sacred Gift of Life from Nuclear Catastrophe, Moscow 10–14 May 1982," May 1982, SCPC, IKV; Aachner Friedensgruppe press release, October 17, 1981, AGG, PKA 3426.

36. Cruise & Pershing Project paper, "Soviet SS-20s: Background and Issues," May 1983, SCPC, CPP.

37. David Hobbs, *Cruise Missiles: Facts and Issues* (Aberdeen, UK: Centre for Defence Studies, 1982), 13.

38. Ken Coates, *No Cruise, No SS-20's: European Nuclear Disarmament* (Nottingham, UK: Russell, 190), 13.

39. Henry Muller, "Disarming Threat to Security," *Time*, November 30, 1981. One West German band, Geier Sturzflug (Vulture nosedive), recorded a 1983 song, "Besuchen sie Europa (solange es noch steht)" (Visit Europe as long as it's still around), with a graphic depiction of the destruction of Europe, including the bombing of the Cologne cathedral, the Eiffel Tower, and Big Ben. See Martin Klimke and Laura Stapane, "From Artists for Peace to the Green Caterpillar: Cultural Activism and Electoral Politics in 1980s West Germany," in *Nuclear Threats, Nuclear Fear and the Cold War of the 1980s*, ed. Eckart Conze, Martin Klimke, and Jeremy Varon (Cambridge: Cambridge University Press, 2017), 119.

40. See, for example, John Nott to Margaret Thatcher, "Nuclear Issues," October 29, 1982, TNA, PREM 19/979.

41. E. P. Thompson, "We Must Strike Directly at the Structures of the Cold War Itself . . . ," *Guardian*, February 21, 1983.

42. "Statement on a European Nuclear-Free Zone," *Security Dialogue* 11, no. 2 (1980): 109.

43. E. P. Thompson, "Conference on Nuclear War in Europe," April 1981, AGG, PKA 3466 (2/2).

44. Coates, *No Cruise, No SS-20's*, 14.

45. CIA Directorate of Intelligence paper, "Peace Groups and Leaders in INF Basing Countries," November 1982, CREST, CIA-RDP84B00049R001403510 021-0.

46. "The Greenham Factor," 1983, LSE, CND/2008/8/3/8 [1 of 2]. For better or worse, that honor went to Japan, which was fifty thousand square miles larger than the United Kingdom and had a larger US military presence.

47. Hoffmann, "NATO and Nuclear Weapons," 343.

48. "Egon's Quotes," n.d. [September 1981], RRL, SKF, box 90100, folder "NATO–Countries–FRG 9/18/81–9/24/81."

49. Bradley Graham, "250,000 in Bonn Protest Stationing of NATO Missiles," *Washington Post*, October 11, 1981.

50. Petra Kelly interview, December 16, 1986, WPNA.

51. "NPG: The Balance of Nuclear Forces," March 24, 1977, LAC, RG25, vol. 22103, file 27-4-NATO-1-6, part 28.

52. "The Greenham Factor," 1983, LSE, CND/2008/8/3/8 [1 of 2].

53. Quoted in Eirini Karamouzi, "'Out with the Bases of Death': Civil Society and Peace Mobilization in Greece during the 1980s," *Journal of Contemporary History* 56, no. 3 (2021): 628.

54. M. V. Naidu, "Cruise Missiles in Canada: Suffocation through Rejuvenation?" *Peace Research* 15, no. 1 (1983): i. For an overview of Canadian opposition to cruise missile testing, including concerns about Canada's ties to the United States, see Susan Colbourn, "The Elephant in the Room: Rethinking Cruise Missile Testing and Pierre Trudeau's Peace Mission," in *Undiplomatic History: The New Study of Canada and the World*, ed. Asa McKercher and Philip van Huizen (Montreal: McGill–Queen's University Press, 2019), 253–76.

55. Mary Kaldor, "The New Movement in Britain," *Fellowship* 48, nos. 1–2 (1982): 4.

56. E. P. Thompson, "The Defence of Britain," in *The Heavy Dancers* (New York: Pantheon, 1985), 100.

57. For an overview of grassroots campaigns to create nuclear-weapon-free zones in this period, see Susanne Schregel, "Global Micropolitics: Toward a Transnational History of Grassroots Nuclear-Free Zones," in Conze, Klimke, and Varon, *Nuclear Threats*, 206–26.

58. Elizabeth Pond, "Haig Gives Fighting Talk in W. Berlin," *Christian Science Monitor*, September 14, 1981.

59. William Drozdiak, "Protestors Pelt Bush's Motorcade," *New York Times*, June 26, 1983; "Wie in Chicago," *Der Spiegel*, July 4, 1983.

60. "How Deep Does German Hostility to America Run?," *Economist*, September 19, 1981.

61. Leonard Downie Jr., "Thousands in London Protest Nuclear Arms," *Washington Post*, October 25, 1981.

62. Roberts, "Trouble with Unilateralism," 308.

63. Jane M. O. Sharp, "Reshaping NATO Nuclear Policy," *Bulletin of the Atomic Scientists* 41, no. 4 (1985): 38.

64. Enclosure to Richard Mottram to Arthur John Coles, "President Reagan's Speech on Defensive Technology," March 29, 1983, TNA, PREM 19/1188.

65. Frédéric Bozo, "The Sanctuary and the Glacis: France, the Federal Republic of Germany, and Nuclear Weapons in the 1980s (Part 1)," *Journal of Cold War Studies* 22, no. 3 (2020): 138.

66. European Nuclear Disarmament, "A Nuclear Free Europe," insert in Thompson, *Protest and Survive*, 18.

67. Peter Lege, "Unterdrückung der Menschenrechte, dort!," AGG, PKA 647 (2/2).

68. Allan Gotlieb diary entry, May 14, 1982, *The Washington Diaries, 1981–1989* (Toronto: McClelland & Stewart, 2007), 61.

69. Walter Z. Laqueur, "Hollanditis: A New Stage of European Neutralism," *Commentary*, August 1981.

70. Sebastian Kalden, "A Case of 'Hollanditis': The Interchurch Peace Council in the Netherlands and the Christian Peace Movement in Western Europe," in Conze, Klimke, and Varon, *Nuclear Threats*, 251.

71. See, for example, *NATO's Future Role: Hearings before the Subcommittee on Europe and the Middle East of the Committee on Foreign Affairs, House of Representatives, Ninety-Seventh Congress, Second Session, May 20, June 3, and 9, 1982* (Washington, DC: Government Printing Office, 1982), 15, 39.

72. For US suspicions about Europe's dependence on the Soviet Union and talking points designed to rebut European arguments, see William Casey to Ronald Reagan et al., "Siberian Pipeline," July 9, 1981, CREST, CIA-RDP84B00049R000601570020-6. The connections between energy and transatlantic relations are well covered in Werner D. Lippert, *The Economic Diplomacy of Ostpolitik: Origins of NATO's Energy Dilemma* (New York: Berghahn Books, 2011).

73. John Palmer, "Dutch May Turn Back Atlantic Arms Tide," *Guardian*, March 9, 1981. On the French as an outlier to the trends of the 1980s, see Ilaria Parisi, "'Pacifism Does Not Ensure Peace': Explaining the Low Profile of the French Pacifist Movement," in *Making Sense of the Americas: How Protest Related to America in the 1980s*, ed. Jan Hansen, Christian Helm, and Frank Reichherzer (Frankfurt: Campus, 2015), 89–108; Katrin Rücker, "Why Was There No 'Accidental Armageddon' Discourse in France? How Defense Intellectuals, Peace Movements, and Public Opinion Rethought the Cold War during the Euromissile Crisis," in Conze, Klimke, and Varon, *Nuclear Threats*, 316–34.

74. Quoted in *Report of the Special Committee on Nuclear Weapons in the Atlantic Alliance* (Washington, DC: Government Printing Office, 1985), 132.

75. Arthur Burns, "How America Looks at Europe," December 1, 1981, DRRBL, ABP, box 11, folder "Formal Speeches 1981–1982 (5 of 10)."

76. Richard Nixon to Arthur Burns, December 28, 1981, DRRBL, ABP, box 2, folder "Richard Nixon to Arthur Burns 1981 Dec 28–1986 June 23."

77. "Conference of National Information Officials," March 3, 1982, NATO, C-M(82)17.

78. Walter Laqueur and Robert Hunter, introduction to *European Peace Movements and the Future of the Western Alliance*, ed. Walter Laqueur and Robert Hunter (New Brunswick, NJ: Transaction, 1985), 8.

79. Jeffrey D. McCausland, "German Politics and Alliance Unity," *Parameters* 13, no. 4 (1983): 74.

80. "Summary Record of a Meeting of the Council Held at NATO Headquarters, Brussels on Tuesday, 3rd February 1981 at 10.15 and 16.15 hours," February 20, 1981, NATO, C-R(81)4.

81. "Summary Record of a Meeting of the Council Held at NATO Headquarters, Brussels on Tuesday, 3rd February 1981 at 10.15 and 16.15 hours," February 20, 1981, NATO, C-R(81)4.

82. "Information Work in the Academic Community," September 11, 1969, NATO, AC/124-D(69)6.

83. "Co-ordination of Military and Political Information Activities, Including NATO Information Service Co-operation with National Authorities," June 6, 1973, NATO, AC/124-D(73)2.

84. "Summary Record of a Meeting of the Council Held at NATO Headquarters, Brussels on Tuesday, 3rd February 1981 at 10.15 and 16.15 hours," February 20, 1981, NATO, C-R(81)4.

85. "NATO Information Service Survey of Output 1982," January 15, 1983, NATO, AC/124-D(83)1.

86. Ronald Inglehart, "Postmaterialism in an Environment of Insecurity," *American Political Science Review* 75, no. 4 (1981): 880. The concept of postmaterialism originated with Inglehart. See also Ronald Inglehart, "The Silent Revolution in Europe: Intergenerational Change in Post-industrial Societies," *American Political Science Review* 65 (1971): 991–1017; Ronald Inglehart, *The Silent Revolution: Changing Values and Political Styles among Western Publics* (Princeton, NJ: Princeton University Press, 1977).

87. "Summary Record of a Meeting of the Council Held at NATO Headquarters, Brussels on Tuesday, 3rd February 1981 at 10.15 and 16.15 hours," February 20, 1981, NATO, C-R(81)4.

88. "Summary Record of a Meeting of the Council Held at NATO Headquarters, Brussels on Wednesday, 17th March 1982 at 10.00 a.m. and 4.00 p.m.," April 13, 1982, NATO, C-R(82)16.

89. "NATO Information Service Survey of Output 1982," January 15, 1983, NATO, AC/124-D(83)1.

90. "Conference of National Information Officials," March 3, 1982, NATO, C-M(82)17.

91. "Conference of National Information Officials," March 3, 1982, NATO, C-M(82)17.

92. "NATO Information Service Survey of Output 1982," January 15, 1983, NATO, AC/124-D(83)1.

93. "NATO Information Service Survey of Output 1982," January 15, 1983, NATO, AC/124-D(83)1. The special issue appeared as *NATO Review* 30, no. 2 (1982). The cover slogan was "Peace and Security: Choosing the Right Way."

94. "NATO Information Service Survey of Output 1982," January 15, 1983, NATO, AC/124-D(83)1.

95. "Meeting Held at NATO Headquarters, 1110 Brussels, on Thursday, 12th November 1981 at 3 pm," November 27, 1981, NATO, AC/52-R(81)10.

96. Atlantic Council of the United States memorandum, "Successor Generation Student Meeting," January 21, 1981, HIA, ACUS, box 253, folder "Successor Generation Student Meetings." See also "Atlantic Council's Atlantic Educational Program: Mission," n.d., HIA, ACUS, box 253, folder "Successor Generation Student Meetings." For more on US efforts to target this successor generation, see Giles Scott-Smith, "Searching for the Successor Generation: Public Diplomacy, the US Embassy's International Visitor Program and the Labour Party in the 1980s," *British Journal of Politics and International Relations* 8, no. 2 (2006): 214–37; Giles Scott-Smith, "Maintaining Transatlantic Community: US Public Diplomacy, the Ford Foundation and the Successor Generation Concept in US Foreign Affairs, 1960s–1980s," *Global Society* 28, no. 1 (2014): 90–103.

97. "Conference of National Information Officials," March 3, 1982, NATO, C-M(82)17.

98. Rebecca Johnson interview, "Return to Sender," British Library, https://www.bl.uk/collection-items/return-to-sender.

99. "Petra Kelly interview | Helen John | Ann Pettitt | Nuclear Disarmament | Part 2 | 1982," ThamesTV, November 25, 1982, https://www.youtube.com/watch?v=GAbKZ5JroRo.

100. Michael Randle, "Women Alone but in a Common Protest," letter to the editor, *Guardian*, January 11, 1983.

101. James E. Dougherty, "Strategy, Politics, and Ethical Feelings: A Perspective of the Protest Movement," in *Shattering Europe's Defense Consensus: The Antinuclear Protest Movement and the Future of NATO*, ed. James E. Dougherty and Robert L. Pfaltzgraff Jr. (Washington, DC: Pergamon-Brassey's, 1985), 3.

102. David K. Willis, "Profiles in Protest: Women at Missile Base in Britain," *Christian Science Monitor*, January 25, 1983.

103. "Conference of National Information Officials," March 3, 1982, NATO, C-M(82)17.

104. John Lofland, *Polite Protestors: The American Peace Movement of the 1980s* (Syracuse, NY: Syracuse University Press, 1993), 56.

105. Richard Baggett Deats, "Seeing the Soviets as People: Reflections on a Journey for Peace," *Fellowship* 48, nos. 10–11 (1982): 4.

106. On the breadth and diversity of these programs, see the appendix in Gale Warner and Michael Shuman, *Citizen Diplomats: Pathfinders in Soviet-American Relations—and How You Can Join Them* (New York: Continuum, 1987), 305–81.

107. END order form, n.d., SCPC, END.

108. Mary Kaldor, "Beyond the Blocs: Defending Europe the Political Way," *World Policy Journal* 1, no. 1 (1983): 14.

109. Steven R. Reed, "Two British and an American Member of the Greenham . . . ," United Press International, May 27, 1983.

110. Wim Bartels and Ben Schennink, "The Dutch Peace Movement (IKV): Work, Results, Dilemmas and Search for New Alliances," n.d. [1981?], SCPC, IKV.

111. *END Journal* 15 (1985): 6.

112. Václav Havel, "The Anatomy of a Reticence," in "Dialogue in Process . . . Voices from the East," 1985, SCPC, END. The tensions between Eastern and Western understandings of peace are discussed in Idesbald Godderis and Małgorzata Świder, "Peace or Solidarity? Poland, the Euromissile Crisis, and the 1980s Peace Movement," in Nuti et al., *Euromissile Crisis*, 291–308.

113. On the dilemmas facing END, see Patrick Burke, "European Nuclear Disarmament: Transnational Peace Campaigning in the 1980s," in Conze, Klimke, and Varon, *Nuclear Threats*, 239; Stefan Berger and Norman LaPorte, "Between Scylla and Charybdis: END and Its Attempt to Overcome the Bipolar World Order in the 1980s," *Labour History* 111 (2016): 19–23.

114. Dan Smith, "Why We Must Talk Peace to Soviet Powermongers," letter to the editor, *Guardian*, January 15, 1983.

115. "Dialogue in Process . . . Voices from the East," 1985, SCPC, END.

116. On this point, see Holger Nehring, "The Last Battle of the Cold War: Peace Movements and German Politics in the 1980s," in Nuti et al., *Euromissile Crisis*, 319.

117. "The Peace Movement in Europe: Digging in for the Long Haul," *Fellowship* 49, no. 12 (1983): 16.

118. Michael Howard, "Deterrence, Consensus and Reassurance in the Defence of Europe," *Adelphi Papers* 23, no. 184 (1983): 20.

119. "Botschafter Weck, Brüssel (NATO), an das Auswärtige Amt," January 4, 1983, *AAPD 1983*, ed. Tim Geiger, Matthias Peter, and Mechthild Lindemann (Munich: Oldenbourg, 2014), doc. 2.

9. The Year of the Missile

1. James M. Markham, "Mitterrand, on Bonn Visit, Warns against Efforts to Divide the West," *New York Times*, January 21, 1983.

2. "No Drift toward Neutralism, Kohl Tells the French," *New York Times*, January 22, 1983.

3. John Vinocur, "Mitterrand Sees Test for the West's Unity: Debate on Europe's Missiles Widens," *New York Times*, January 24, 1983. See also Russell Watson, "An Arms Deal: Now or Never?," *Newsweek*, January 31, 1983.

4. Watson, "An Arms Deal."

5. Alfred Grosser, "Diese Krise ist die schwerste," *Der Spiegel*, October 19, 1981.

6. "Netherlands Affirms Cruise Missile Plan," *Chicago Tribune*, November 23, 1982.

7. "Van Agt Criticized for Vacillating on Cruise Issue," April 24, 1981, FBIS-WEU-81-085.

8. "Dutch Delay Cruise Missile Decision," *Guardian*, November 17, 1981.

9. Don Cook, "Voters Increase Odds against Cruise Missiles in Netherlands," *Los Angeles Times*, September 11, 1982.

10. "Opposition Attacks Euromissile Site Choice," June 30, 1983, FBIS-WEU-83-134.

11. William J. Dyess interview, March 29, 1989, FAOHP, 23.

12. Hugh De Santis interview, January 27, 2006, FAOHP, 34.

13. *Second Interim Report on Nuclear Weapons in Europe, Prepared by the North Atlantic Assembly's Special Committee on Nuclear Weapons in Europe: A Report to the Committee on Foreign Relations, United States Senate, January 1983* (Washington, DC: Government Printing Office, 1983), 53.

14. James Thomson to Zbigniew Brzezinski and David Aaron, "TNF—the Situation in Belgium," March 10, 1980, JCL, RAC, NLC-23-58-2-5-6.

15. *Second Interim Report on Nuclear Weapons in Europe*, 53.

16. State Department to US Embassy Brussels "TNF: Presidential Letter to PM Martens," May 6, 1980, JCL, RAC, NLC-6-6-2-8-9.

17. US Embassy Brussels to State Department, "Belgian Stance on TNF at Ankara: Meeting with Foreign Minister Nothomb," June 24, 1980, JCL, RAC, NLC-6-6-2-16-0.

18. *Second Interim Report on Nuclear Weapons in Europe*, 53.

19. *Second Interim Report on Nuclear Weapons in Europe*, 54.

20. Bradley Graham, "Kohl Meets Soviet Aide, Urges 'Genuine Détente'," *Washington Post*, October 8, 1982.

21. James M. Markham, "Germany's Volatile Greens," *New York Times*, February 13, 1983.

22. On the founding and early years of the West German Greens, see Silke Mende, *"Nicht rechts, nicht links, sondern vorn": Eine Geschichte der Gründungsgrünen* (Munich: Oldenbourg, 2011).

23. For details on the Green Party's concerts and their reception, see Martin Klimke and Laura Stapane, "From Artists for Peace to the Green Caterpillar: Cultural Activism and Electoral Politics in 1980s West Germany," in *Nuclear Threats, Nuclear*

Fear and the Cold War of the 1980s, ed. Eckart Conze, Martin Klimke, and Jeremy Varon (Cambridge: Cambridge University Press, 2017), 124–32.

24. Markham, "Germany's Volatile Greens."

25. "Petra Kelly interview | Helen John | Ann Pettitt | Nuclear Disarmament | Part 2 | 1982," ThamesTV, November 25, 1982, https://www.youtube.com/watch?v= GAbKZ5JroRo. On the many connections between the opposition to the Euromissiles and the memory of the Holocaust, see Eckart Conze, "Missile Bases as Concentration Camps: The Role of National Socialism, the Second World War, and the Holocaust in the West German Discourse on Nuclear Armament," in Conze, Klimke, and Varon, *Nuclear Threats*, 79–98.

26. James M. Markham, "The A-Bomb Is 'Convicted' in Nuremberg," *New York Times*, February 23, 1983.

27. "NSPG Meeting," January 13, 1983, RRL, ESNSC, box 91603, folder "NSPG 0050 13 Jan 1983 [Arms Control/INF]."

28. SPD election poster, "Vertragen statt rüsten," 1983, BA, Plak. 007-004-020.

29. "Haltet ein, macht Frieden," 1983, AdsD, 6/PLKA002747.

30. Bernard Gwertzman, "Rostow Defends Arms Agreement Disowned by U.S.," *New York Times*, January 17, 1983.

31. Frédéric Bozo, "France, the Euromissiles, and the End of the Cold War," in Nuti et al., *Euromissile Crisis*, 199–203.

32. James M. Markham, "Gromyko Warns Germans of Risk If New U.S. Missiles Are Deployed," *New York Times*, January 18, 1983.

33. "NSPG Meeting," January 13, 1983, RRL, ESNSC, MF, box 91603, folder "NSPG 0050 13 Jan 1983 [Arms Control/INF]."

34. On the Greens' entry into the Bundestag, see Silke Mende, "'Enemies at the Gate': The West German Greens and Their Arrival at the Bundestag—between Old Ideals and New Challenges," *German Politics and Society* 33, no. 4 (2015): 66–79.

35. Robert Gerald Livingston, "West Germany's Green Power," *Washington Quarterly* 6, no. 3 (1983): 175.

36. Jeffrey D. McCausland, "German Politics and Alliance Unity," *Parameters* 13, no. 4 (1983): 71.

37. Hella Pick, "Kohl's Victory Means Setback for Russia's Anti-cruise Campaign," *Guardian*, March 7, 1983.

38. Joseph Godson, "Euromissiles in the Aftermath of the West German Elections," *Washington Quarterly* 6, no. 3 (1983): 182.

39. David Binder, "Outcome Pleasing to Washington Because Kohl Backs A-Arm Plan," *New York Times*, March 7, 1983.

40. Ronald Reagan, "Remarks Announcing a Proposed Interim Intermediate-Range Nuclear Force Reduction Agreement," March 30, 1983, *PPP: Ronald Reagan 1983*, vol. 1, ed. Maxine L. Hill and Thomas D. Kevan (Washington, DC: Government Printing Office, 1984), 473.

41. "NSPG Meeting," January 13, 1983, RRL, ESNSC, MF, box 91603, folder "NSPG 0050 13 Jan 1983 [Arms Control/INF]."

42. "NSPG Meeting," January 13, 1983, RRL, ESNSC, MF, box 91603, folder "NSPG 0050 13 Jan 1983 [Arms Control/INF]."

43. George H. W. Bush, speech at the Royal Institute of International Affairs, Guildhall, London, February 9, 1983, GBL, VP, DGF, FTF, OA/ID 19791,

folder "[Vice President's Trip to Europe, January 30–February 10, 1983] London, United Kingdom."

44. Thatcher had urged Reagan to bring up his speech by a day to make sure it could be covered in the newspapers, because there would be no circulation on Good Friday. Kristan Stoddart, *Facing Down the Soviet Union: Britain, the USA, NATO and Nuclear Weapons, 1976–1983* (London: Palgrave Macmillan, 2014), 222.

45. John Tagliabue, "West Germans Protest Nuclear Missiles for 4th Day," *New York Times*, April 5, 1983.

46. The Campaign for Nuclear Disarmament suggested that a hundred thousand demonstrators were in attendance. Paul Brown, Shyama Perera, and Martin Wainwright, "Protest by CND Stretches 14 Miles," *Guardian*, April 2, 1983; Nicholas Timmins, "Thousands of Hands Link in CND rally," *Times* (London), April 2, 1983.

47. Brown, Perera, and Wainwright, "Protest by CND Stretches 14 Miles."

48. Alan Travis, "Revealed: Thatcher Aide Wanted to Use Prince William to Hobble CND," *Guardian*, July 20, 2016.

49. *Report of the Special Committee on Nuclear Weapons in the Atlantic Alliance* (Washington, DC: Government Printing Office, 1985), 104.

50. David McKie, "Voters Turn against Trident, Cruise," *Guardian*, January 21, 1983.

51. E. P. Thompson, *The Heavy Dancers* (New York: Pantheon, 1985), 69, 105.

52. Thompson, *Heavy Dancers*, 91.

53. Thompson, *Heavy Dancers*, 92.

54. John Nott to Margaret Thatcher, "Nuclear Issues," October 29, 1982, TNA, PREM 19/979.

55. "Heseltine Announces Arrival of Greenham Missiles," *Guardian*, November 15, 1983.

56. House of Lords, *Hansard*, May 11, 1983, 5th series, vol. 442, col. 462–65.

57. Ian Gow to Michael Jopling, March 7, 1983, MTFA, doc. 151111. Signatories made a direct comparison to the arrangement Harold Macmillan's government had negotiated for the Thor missiles in the late 1950s.

58. House of Commons *Hansard*, March 1, 1983, 6th series, vol. 38, col. 117–22

59. House of Commons *Hansard*, March 1, 1983, 6th series, vol. 38, col. 117–22.

60. Peter Jenkins, "Foot and Healey Out of Step?," *Guardian*, May 26, 1983.

61. Adam Roberts, "The Trouble with Unilateralism: The UK, the 1983 General Election, and Non-nuclear Defence," *Bulletin of Peace Proposals* 14, no. 4 (1983): 306.

62. *Report of the Special Committee on Nuclear Weapons in the Atlantic Alliance*, 106.

63. David Fairhall, "Mandate Given for Trident and Cruise—Heseltine," *Guardian*, June 17, 1983.

64. Aileen Ballantyne, "Mandate on Cruise Denied," *Guardian*, June 13, 1983.

65. Paul Brown, "The Women of Greenham Concede That Cruise Will Come," *Guardian*, July 8, 1983.

66. *Report of the Special Committee on Nuclear Weapons in the Atlantic Alliance*, 114. See also Leopoldo Nuti, "The Nuclear Debate in Italian Politics in the Late 1970s and Early 1980s," in Nuti et al., *Euromissile Crisis*, 242.

67. DPC final communiqué, Brussels, June 2, 1983, NATO, M-DPC-1(83)8. On the practice of footnoting, see Effie G. H. Pedaliu, "'Footnotes' as an Expression of Distrust? The United States and the NATO 'Flanks' in the Last Two Decades of the Cold War," in *Trust, but Verify: The Politics of Uncertainty and the Transformation of the Cold War Order, 1969–1991*, ed. Martin Klimke, Reinhild Kreis, and Christian F. Ostermann (Stanford, CA: Stanford University Press, 2016), 237–58.

68. "Summary Record of a Meeting of the Council Held at NATO Headquarters, Brussels on Wednesday, 13th April 1983 at 10.15 a.m.," April 18, 1983, NATO, C-R(83)15. For Papandreou's policy of peace, see Eirini Karamouzi and Dionysios Chourchoulis, "Troublemaker or Peacemaker? Andreas Papandreou, the Euromissile Crisis, and the Policy of Peace, 1981–86," *Cold War History* 19, no. 1 (2019): 39–61; Eirini Karamouzi, "'At Last, Our Voice Is Heard in the World': Andreas Papandreou, Greece and the Six Nation Initiative during the Euromissile Crisis," in *Margins for Manoeuvre in Cold War Europe: The Influence of Smaller Powers*, ed. Laurien Crump and Susanna Erlandsson (London: Routledge, 2019), 224–40.

69. John Birch to FCO, "Athens Telno 258 to FCO: Greek Prime Minister's Views on INF," June 10, 1983, TNA, PREM 19/979.

70. Richard Kinchen to Peter Ricketts, "The Greek Proposal to Postpone Deployment on INF Missiles," August 23, 1983, TNA, PREM 19/979.

71. NPG final communiqué, March 24, 1982, NATO, M-NPG(82)7. The Danish use of footnoting is also covered in Pedaliu, "'Footnotes' as an Expression of Distrust?"

72. *Intermediate-Range Nuclear Forces (INF): Progress Report to Ministers by the Special Consultative Group* (Brussels: NATO Information Service, 1983), 3.

73. John Weston to David Gillmore, "Danish Parliament Debate on Foreign Affairs and INF," May 26, 1983, TNA, PREM 19/979.

74. Canadian Embassy Copenhagen to External Affairs, "INF-Danish Policy," May 27, 1983, LAC, RG25, vol. 28252, file 27-4-NATO-1-INF, part 2.

75. "Verbatim Record of the Meeting of the Defence Planning Committee in Ministerial Session Held on Wednesday, 1st June 1983 at 11.30 a.m. and 3.15 p.m. at NATO Headquarters, Brussels," June 1, 1983, NATO, DPC-VR(83)6 2.

76. Peter Osnos, "Denmark Fails to Gain Backing for Euromissiles," *Washington Post*, May 9, 1983.

77. "October Days of Protest: NO to Euromissiles—YES to a Freeze," *Fellowship* 49, nos. 7–8 (1983): 11.

78. Kathrin Fahlenbrach and Laura Stapane, "Visual and Media Strategies of the Peace Movement," in Becker-Schaum et al., *Nuclear Crisis*, 232–34.

79. "Soviet Government Statement," September 7–8, 1983, *Current Digest of the Soviet Press* 35, no. 35 (1983): 9.

80. William Clark to Ronald Reagan, "NSPG Meeting: Soviet Shoot-Down of KAL Airliner," September 2, 1983, RRL, CMC, box 2, folder "KAL 007 1."

81. Margaret Thatcher, Ronald Reagan memorandum of conversation, 11:37 a.m., September 29, 1983, TNA, PREM 19/1153.

82. See, for example, Dusko Doder, "Andropov Said Seriously Ill, Misses Parade," *Washington Post*, November 8, 1983; Serge Schmemann, "Andropov, Reported Ill, Misses Fete," *New York Times*, November 6, 1983.

83. NSDD 104, "U.S. Approach to INF Negotiations," September 21, 1983, CREST, CIA-RDP10M02313R000100990001-1.

84. Ronald Reagan, "Radio Address to the Nation and Peoples of Other Countries on Peace," September 24, 1983, *PPP: Ronald Reagan 1983*, vol. 2, ed. Thomas D. Kevan (Washington, DC: Government Printing Office, 1985), 1344.

85. Ronald Reagan, "Address before the 38th Session of the United Nations General Assembly in New York, New York," September 26, 1983, *PPP: Ronald Reagan 1983*, vol. 2, 1350–51.

86. "*Pravda* Editorial on President Reagan's INF Proposals (Excerpts)," October 4, 1983, *Survival* 26, no. 1 (1984): 33–34.

87. William Drozdiak, "Geneva Chances Slim, Nitze Says," *Washington Post*, October 8, 1983.

88. Ronald D. Asmus, "Soviet Bloc Intensifies Campaign against Euromissiles," October 17, 1983, OSA, RFE/RL, HU OSA 300-8-3-13843.

89. "October Days of Protest," 11.

90. William Drozdiak, "More Than a Million Protest Missiles in Western Europe," *Washington Post*, October 23, 1983; Michael Binyon, "Cheers and Boos as Brandt Urges Rejection of New Weapons," *Times* (London), October 24, 1983. Despite these massive figures, internal assessments at the West German foreign ministry concluded that the "hot autumn" did not find the kind of support organizers had hoped. For a postmortem, see "Friedensbewegung," November 15, 1983, PA-AA, B150/581.

91. On the Spanish protest movement in the 1980s, see Giulia Quaggio, "Social Movements and Participatory Democracy: Spanish Protests for Peace during the Last Decade of the Cold War (1981–1986)," *Archiv für Sozialgeschichte* 58 (2018): 279–302.

92. "550.000!," *De waarheid*, October 31, 1983; "Verrassend optreden van prinses Irene," *De Telegraaf*, October 31, 1983.

93. "Refuse the Cruise International Day of Protest," 1983, MUL, MTF, box 20, folder "Other Organizations—Printed + Circulars—Disarmament." On Canadian opposition to cruise missile testing and its links to the Euromissiles, see Susan Colbourn, "'Cruising toward Nuclear Danger': Canadian Anti-nuclear Activism, Pierre Trudeau's Peace Mission, and the Transatlantic Partnership," *Cold War History* 18, no. 1 (2018): 19–36.

94. Freiwirth letter, August 13, 1983, SCPC, CSE.

95. Thomas E. Halverson, *The Last Great Nuclear Debate: NATO and Short-Range Nuclear Weapons in the 1980s* (Basingstoke, UK: Macmillan, 1995), 60.

96. "The Montebello Decision, on Reductions of Nuclear Forces," annex to NPG communiqué, October 28, 1983, NATO, M-NPG-2(83)23.

97. "Record of Office Meeting Held by the Secretary of State on 8 November," TNA, FCO 46/3082; "Brief for MISC 7," TNA, FCO 46/3555.

98. Pierre Elliott Trudeau, "Reflections on Peace and Security," October 27, 1983, Department of External Affairs Statements and Speeches no. 83/18.

99. On the origins and implementation of Pierre Trudeau's peace mission, see Brett Thompson, "Pierre Elliott Trudeau's Peace Initiative: 25 Years On," *International Journal* 64, no. 4 (2009): 1117–37; Luc-André Brunet, "Unhelpful Fixer? Canada, the Euromissile Crisis, and Pierre Trudeau's Peace Initiative, 1983–1984," *International*

History Review 41, no. 6 (2019): 1145–67. The connections between NATO's policies and Trudeau's thinking are highlighted in Colbourn, "'Cruising toward Nuclear Danger.'"

100. David Hoffman, "'I Had a Funny Feeling in My Gut," *Washington Post*, February 10, 1999.

101. See, for example, Aaron Donaghy, *The Second Cold War: Carter, Reagan, and the Domestic Politics of Foreign Policy* (Cambridge: Cambridge University Press, 2021).

102. Christopher Andrew and Oleg Gordievsky, *KGB: The Inside Story of Its Operations from Lenin to Gorbachev* (London: Hodder & Stoughton, 1990), 492–507; Nate Jones, *Able Archer: The Secret History of the NATO Exercise That Almost Triggered Nuclear War* (New York: New Press, 2016); Hal Brands, *What Good Is Grand Strategy? Power and Purpose in American Statecraft from Harry S. Truman to George W. Bush* (Ithaca, NY: Cornell University Press, 2014), 124; Campbell Craig and Frederik Logevall, *America's Cold War: The Politics of Insecurity* (Cambridge, MA: Belknap Press of Harvard University Press, 2010), 322; John Lewis Gaddis, *The Cold War: A New History* (New York: Penguin, 2007), 227–28; Don Oberdorfer, *From the Cold War to a New Era: The United States and the Soviet Union, 1983–1991* (Baltimore: Johns Hopkins University Press, 1998), 65–68.

103. Viktor Esin, in William C. Wohlforth, ed., *Witnesses to the End of the Cold War* (Baltimore: Johns Hopkins University Press, 1996), 72–73.

104. Simon Miles, "The War Scare That Wasn't: Able Archer 83 and the Myths of the Second Cold War," *Journal of Cold War Studies* 22, no. 3 (2020): 109–11.

105. Quoted in President's Foreign Intelligence Advisory Board, "The Soviet 'War Scare,'" February 15, 1990, ISCAP Release 2013-015-doc1, 69.

106. Directorate of Intelligence, "Soviet Thinking on the Possibility of Armed Confrontation with the United States," December 30, 1983, RRL, JFMF, box 3, folder "January 1984 (2)."

107. Scholars using sources from the Warsaw Pact tend to be much more skeptical that Able Archer 83 was a near-miss nuclear war than those who only use Western sources. See Dmitry Adamsky, "'Not Crying Wolf': Soviet Intelligence and the 1983 War Scare," in Nuti et al., *Euromissile Crisis*, 49–65; Gordon Barrass, *The Great Cold War: A Journey through the Hall of Mirrors* (Stanford, CA: Stanford University Press, 2009), 297–312; Beatrice Heuser, "Military Exercises and the Dangers of Misunderstandings: The East-West Crisis of the Early 1980s," in *Military Exercises: Political Messaging and Strategic Impact*, ed. Beatrice Heuser, Tormod Heier, and Guillaume Lasconjarias (Rome: NATO Defense College, 2018), 113–37; Mark Kramer, "Die Nicht-Krise um 'Able Archer 1983': Fürchtete die sowjetische Führung tatsächlich einen atomaren Großangriff im Herbst 1983?," in *Wege zur Wiedervereinigung: Die beiden deutschen Staaten in ihren Bündnissen 1970 bis 1990*, ed. Oliver Bange and Bernd Lemke (Munich: Oldenbourg, 2013), 129–49; Vojtech Mastny, "How Able Was 'Able Archer'? Nuclear Trigger and Intelligence in Perspective," *Journal of Cold War Studies* 11, no. 1 (2009): 108–23; Miles, "War Scare That Wasn't," 86–118.

108. Nicholas Meyers, dir., *The Day After* (ABC Circle, 1983).

109. Russell Watson, "Can We Cut the Risk?," *Newsweek*, December 5, 1983.

110. "Viewpoint," ABC, November 20, 1983, https://www.youtube.com/watch?v=PcCLZwU2t34. For more on the concept of nuclear winter, Sagan's role

promoting it, and questions about its scientific claims, see Carl Sagan and Richard Turco, *A Path Where No Man Thought: Nuclear Winter and the End of the Arms Race* (New York: Random House, 1990); Paul Rubinson, *Redefining Science: Scientists, the National Security State, and Nuclear Weapons in Cold War America* (Amherst: University of Massachusetts Press, 2016), 170–214; Wilfried Mausbach, "Nuclear Winter: Prophecies of Doom and Images of Desolation in the Second Cold War," in Conze, Klimke, and Varon, *Nuclear Threats*, 27–54.

111. House of Commons, *Hansard*, October 31, 1983, 6th series, vol. 47, col. 620–712.

112. Aileen Ballantyne and Jean Stead, "Police Arrest 187 as Greenham Women Pull Down Fences," *Guardian*, October 31, 1983.

113. Ballantyne and Stead, "Police Arrest 187."

114. Ian Aitken and David Fairhall, "Threat to Shoot at Cruise Protests," *Guardian*, November 2, 1983.

115. E. P. Thompson, "Why the Noes Have It at Greenham Common," letter to the editor, *Guardian*, November 5, 1983.

116. "Decision Launched a Peace Revival," *Guardian*, November 15, 1983.

117. Canadian Embassy Bonn to External Affairs, "PMs Initiative on East/West Relations—FRG Setting," November 3, 1983, LAC, RG25, vol. 25337, file 28-6-1-TRUDEAU PEACE MISSION, part 5. See also Arnaud to Claude Cheysson, "L'intervention américaine à la Grenade et le déploiement des FNI en Europe occidentale," November 5, 1983, AD, 1930INVA/5675.

118. "Heseltine Announces Arrival of Greenham Missiles."

119. House of Commons, *Hansard*, November 14, 1983, 6th series, vol. 48, col. 616–28.

120. Charles Ridley, "Government Wins Vote to Deploy Cruise Missiles," United Press International, November 16, 1983.

121. Washington to Auswärtiges Amt, "Sowjetische Demarche in Ottawa vom 18.11.1983," November 18, 1983, PA-AA, B150/581; "National Intelligence Daily," November 22, 1983, CREST, CIA-RDP85T01094R000500010007-4.

122. On the walk-in-the-park episode, see Paul H. Nitze, *From Hiroshima to Glasnost: At the Center of Decision—a Memoir*, with Ann M. Smith and Steven L. Rearden (New York: Grove Weidenfeld, 1989), 389–97.

123. "Speech by Helmut Schmidt to the S.P.D. Conference (Excerpt)," November 19–20, 1983, *Survival* 26, no. 2 (1984): 87–88.

124. UK Embassy Bonn to FCO, "SPD Vote against INF Stationing," November 20, 1983, TNA, FCO 33/6622.

125. For the full debates, see Deutscher Bundestag, Stenographischer Bericht, 35. Sitzung, 10. Wahlperiode, November 21, 1983; Deutscher Bundestag, Stenographischer Bericht, 36. Sitzung, 10. Wahlperiode, November 22, 1983. Kelly's remark is from Deutscher Bundestag, Stenographischer Bericht, 36. Sitzung, 10. Wahlperiode, November 22, 1983, 2521. For Schmidt's paper airplane, see Watson, "Can We Cut the Risk?"

126. Gregory Treverton testimony, *Political and Military Issues in the Atlantic Alliance: Hearings before the Subcommittee on Europe and the Middle East of the Committee on Foreign Affairs, House of Representatives, Ninety-Eighth Congress, Second Session, August 1, October 1, 1984* (Washington, DC: Government Printing Office, 1984), 2–10.

127. Italian officials concluded that the government's ability to hold firm had boosted the country's position within the alliance. Washington to Rome, "Prospettive per la Ripresa nel Negoziato sulle FNI," December 5, 1983, WCDA, doc. 155154.

128. Gregory Treverton testimony.

Part Three. Destroy

1. Margaret Thatcher, "Open Letter on Nuclear Disarmament," April 10, 1986, MTFA, doc. 106360.

2. Thatcher, "Open Letter," April 10, 1986, MTFA, doc. 106360.

3. "Margaret Thatcher Interviewed about Ronald Reagan," January 8, 1990, MTFA, doc. 109324.

4. "Thatcher Says British Nuclear Arms Deter Soviets," Associated Press, February 19, 1988.

5. "Thatcher Says British Nuclear Arms Deter Soviets."

6. George H.W. Bush, Margaret Thatcher memorandum of telephone conversation, January 23, 1989, GBL, MT.

7. Cabinet Office to the White House, April 1, 1987, NSA EBB544: The Gorbachev File, ed. Svetlana Savranskaya and Thomas Blanton, March 2, 2016, doc. 9.

8. Frank Carlucci to Ronald Reagan, "Mrs. Thatcher's View of Gorbachev—(Weekend Reading)," n.d. [April 1987], NSA EBB544, doc. 9.

9. Luke Harding, "Kohl Tells of Being Battered by Iron Lady," Guardian, November 2, 2005.

10. The Empty Chair

1. Maynard W. Glitman, The Last Battle of the Cold War: An Inside Account of Negotiating the Intermediate-Range Nuclear Forces Treaty (New York: Palgrave Macmillan, 2006), 95.

2. Glitman, Last Battle of the Cold War, 96.

3. George Russell, "A Soviet Walkout," Time, December 5, 1983.

4. See, for example, Russell, "Soviet Walkout."

5. John F. Burns, "The Walkout by Moscow," New York Times, November 26, 1983.

6. William Drozdiak, "West Germans Protest Missiles," Washington Post, October 21, 1984.

7. Report of the Special Committee on Nuclear Weapons in the Atlantic Alliance (Washington, DC: Government Printing Office, 1985), 102.

8. Drozdiak, "West Germans Protest Missiles."

9. "Menschen- und Aktionskette für Frieden und Arbeit von Duisburg nach Hasselbach 20. Oktober," 1984, BA, Plak. 007-021-040.

10. "100,000 in Europe Protest U.S. Missiles," Chicago Tribune, April 9, 1985.

11. CND press information, "Operation Christmas Card," December 3, 1984, LSE, CND/1993/2/6.

12. Quoted in Peter Grier, "The Short, Happy Life of the Glick-Em," Air Force Magazine, July 1, 2002.

13. Cruise Resistance Bulletin no. 1, 1985, LSE, CND/2008/8/4/65.

14. Paul H. Nitze, *From Hiroshima to Glasnost: At the Center of Decision—a Memoir*, with Ann M. Smith and Steven L. Rearden (New York: Grove Weidenfeld, 1989), 399.

15. Petra Kelly interview, December 16, 1986, WPNA.

16. *The MacNeil/Lehrer News Hour*, December 7, 1983, AAPB, cpb-aacip/507-2b8v98068c.

17. See, for example, "Chairman's Press Release," January 11, 1984, NATO, Press Release (84)1; "Chairman's Press Statement," February 20, 1984, NATO, Statement Burt 20/02/1984.

18. *Intermediate-Range Nuclear Forces (INF): Progress Report to Ministers by the Special Consultative Group* (Brussels: NATO Information Service, 1983), 41.

19. Margaret Thatcher, George Bush memorandum of conversation, June 24, 1983, TNA, PREM 19/1033.

20. Pierre Elliott Trudeau, "Reflections on Peace and Security," October 27, 1983, Department of External Affairs Statements and Speeches no. 83/18. See, for more details on the peace mission, Luc-André Brunet, "Unhelpful Fixer? Canada, the Euromissile Crisis, and Pierre Trudeau's Peace Initiative, 1983–1984," *International History Review* 41, no. 6 (2019): 1145–67; Susan Colbourn, "'Cruising toward Nuclear Danger': Canada, the Euromissile Crisis, and Pierre Trudeau's Peace Initiative, 1983–1984," *International History Review* 41, no. 6 (2019): 1145–67.

21. "Bundeskanzler Kohl an Präsident Reagan," December 1, 1983, *AAPD 1983*, ed. Tim Geiger, Matthias Peter, and Mechthild Lindemann (Munich: Oldenbourg, 2014), doc. 365.

22. "Declaration of Brussels," December 9, 1983, NATO, M-2(83)32.

23. Foreign Broadcast Information Service (FBIS) analysis report, "Moscow Projects Unyielding Stance in Reporting Gromyko Visit," October 5, 1984, RRL, JFMF, box 7, folder "Signals Oct–Dec 1984 1/3."

24. "Chairman's Press Statement," February 20, 1984, NATO, Statement Burt 20/02/1984.

25. "Notes on the INF Negotiations," March 13, 1984, LAC, RG25, vol. 22258, file 27-4-NATO-1-INF, part 7.

26. NPG final communiqué, October 12, 1984, NATO, M-NPG-2(84)20.

27. "Romania and West Germany on Missiles and Security," October 17, 1984, OSA, RFE/RL, HU OSA 300-8-3-13868.

28. William Drozdiak, "Kremlin Paralysis," *Washington Post*, September 9, 1984.

29. "FRG Approves DM950 Million Bank Loan to the GDR," July 26, 1984, FBIS-EEU-84-150. On the broader climate of German-German relations during this period, see Hermann Wentker, "NATO's Double-Track Decision and East-West German Relations," in Becker-Schaum et al., *Nuclear Crisis*, 91–99. For background on the ties between the two German governments, see Oliver Bange, "'Keeping Détente Alive': Inner-German Relations under Helmut Schmidt and Erich Honecker, 1974–1982," in *The Crisis of Détente in Europe: From Helsinki to Gorbachev, 1975–1985*, ed. Leopoldo Nuti (London: Routledge, 2009), 230–43.

30. "*Pravda* Sees Resurgence of Revanchism in FRG," May 17, 1984, FBIS-SOV-84-098.

31. Charles Gati, "Soviet Empire: Alive but Not Well," *Problems of Communism* 34 (1985): 78.

32. James M. Markham, "For Both East and West Two Germanys Is Better," *New York Times*, September 23, 1984.

33. Ronald Reagan, "Address to the Nation and Other Countries on United States–Soviet Relations," January 16, 1984, *PPP: Ronald Reagan 1984*, vol. 1, ed. Wilma P. Greene and William K. Banks (Washington, DC: Government Printing Office, 1986), 40–44.

34. Reagan, "Address to the Nation and Other Countries," 40–44.

35. Mary McGrory, "Despite His Handlers' Hype, Reagan Didn't Sound Converted," *Washington Post*, January 19, 1984.

36. The idea of a Reagan reversal is best summed up in Beth A. Fischer, *The Reagan Reversal: Foreign Policy and the End of the Cold War*. For recent assessments showing how the Reagan administration's Soviet policy developed and the relationship—and gaps—between public rhetoric and private deliberations, see Simon Miles, *Engaging the Evil Empire: Washington, Moscow, and the Beginning of the End of the Cold War* (Ithaca, NY: Cornell University Press, 2020), 57–84; Aaron Donaghy, *The Second Cold War: Carter, Reagan, and the Domestic Politics of Foreign Policy* (Cambridge: Cambridge University Press, 2021), 184–212, 216. Miles's and Donaghy's arguments emphasize different aspects of NATO's Able Archer exercise. Miles's focuses on how it was not a near-miss with war, whereas Donaghy's highlights how the Reagan White House responded to the prospect that it might have been a war scare. Often seen as incompatible, these two views can—and did—coexist. Able Archer might not have been a brush with nuclear war, but that did not stop those in the West from seeing it that way and acting based on that belief. I am grateful to Elizabeth Charles for our conversations on this point.

37. Ronald Reagan diary entry, October 10, 1983, *The Reagan Diaries*, vol. 1, ed. Douglas Brinkley (New York: HarperCollins, 2009), 273. See also Ronald Reagan, *An American Life: The Autobiography* (New York: Simon & Schuster, 1990), 585.

38. George Shultz to Ronald Reagan, "U.S.-Soviet Relations in 1983," January 19, 1983, RRL, JFMF, box 41, folder "US-USSR Relations January–February 1983." On Shultz's role in shaping Reagan's foreign policy, see Elizabeth C. Charles and James Graham Wilson, "Confronting the Soviet Threat: Reagan's Approach to Policymaking," in *The Reagan Moment: America and the World in the 1980s*, ed. Jonathan R. Hunt and Simon Miles (Ithaca, NY: Cornell University Press, 2021), 105–22.

39. William Clark to Ronald Reagan, "U.S.-Soviet Relations in 1983," n.d. [January 1983], RRL, JFMF, box 41, folder "US-USSR Relations January–February 1983"; William Clark to Ronald Reagan, "The Prospects for Progress in US-Soviet Relations," February 4, 1983, RRL, WPCF, box 8, folder "US-Soviet Relations Papers 2."

40. Reagan, *American Life*, 570; Jack F. Matlock Jr., *Autopsy on an Empire: The American Ambassador's Account of the Collapse of the Soviet Union* (New York: Random House, 1995), 86.

41. Jack Matlock to Robert McFarlane, "Presidential Speech on U.S.-Soviet Relations," December 20, 1983, RRL, JFMF, box 42, folder "US-USSR Relations Dec 1983–Jan 1984."

42. Ronald Reagan to Barney Oldfield, March 12, 1984, in *Reagan: A Life in Letters*, ed. Kiron K. Skinner, Annelise Anderson, and Martin Anderson (New York: Free Press, 2003), 735.

43. Reagan, *American Life*, 587.

44. Reagan's aides considered this question in advance, given the many signs of Andropov's poor health. Jack Matlock to Robert McFarlane, "What If Andropov Dies?," February 6, 1984, RRL, JFMF, box 3, folder "February 1984 (1)."

45. British Information Services news release, "Prime Minister Thatcher's Press Conference," February 14, 1984, LAC, RG25, vol. 26958, file 28-6-1-TRUDEAU PEACE MISSION, part 31.

46. Sessions dealt with East-West relations, Britain's global interests, arms control and disarmament issues, and the Middle East. "Strategy Meetings: Foreign Affairs," September 6, 1983, TNA, PREM 19/1155. See also Margaret Thatcher, *The Downing Street Years* (New York: HarperCollins, 1993), 450–53.

47. John Cole to Brian Fall, "Policy on East/West Relations," September 12, 1983, MTFA, doc. 111075. For more on this shift in the Thatcher government's Soviet policy, see Archie Brown, "The Change to Engagement in Britain's Cold War Policy: The Origins of the Thatcher-Gorbachev Relationship," *Journal of Cold War Studies* 10, no. 3 (2008): 3–47.

48. London to External Affairs, "East/West Relations: Change in British Emphasis," October 21, 1983, LAC, RG25, vol. 25336, file 28-6-1-TRUDEAU PEACE MISSION, part 2.

49. British, Canadian, French, West German, US, and Australian efforts are chronicled in Miles, *Engaging the Evil Empire*, 84–105. The Italians also pursued similar efforts to renew dialogue with the Soviet Union parallel to these other Western overtures. For an overview of détente's role in transatlantic relations, see Susan Colbourn and Mathias Haeussler, "Once More, With Feeling: Transatlantic Relations in the Reagan Years," in *The Reagan Moment: America and the World in the 1980s*, ed. Jonathan R. Hunt and Simon Miles (Ithaca, NY: Cornell University Press, 2021), 123–43.

50. Papandreou's five counterparts were Argentinian president Raúl Alfonsín, Mexico's Miguel de la Madrid, Julius Nyerere of Tanzania, Swedish prime minister Olof Palme, and Indian prime minister Indira Gandhi. Olafur Grimsson and Nicholas Dunlop, "Indira Gandhi and the Five Continent Initiative," *Bulletin of the Atomic Scientists* 45, no. 1 (1985): 46. On Papandreou's participation in the initiative, see Eirini Karamouzi, "'At Last, Our Voice Is Heard in the World': Andreas Papandreou, Greece and the Six Nation Initiative during the Euromissile Crisis," in *Margins for Manoeuvre in Cold War Europe: The Influence of Smaller Powers*, ed. Laurien Crump and Susanna Erlandsson (London: Routledge, 2019), 224–40. Pierre Trudeau was also invited to participate but declined.

51. "Declaration of Brussels," December 9, 1983, NATO, M-2(83)32.

52. "Summary Record of a Meeting of the Council Held at NATO Headquarters, Brussels on Wednesday, 25th April 1984 at 10.15 a.m.," May 30, 1984, NATO, C-R(84)24. A more detailed treatment of the drafting process and the Western allies' debates can be found in Susan Colbourn, "Debating Détente: NATO's Tindemans Initiative, or Why the Harmel Report Still Mattered in the 1980s," *Journal of Strategic Studies* 43, nos. 6–7 (2020): 897–919.

53. "Washington Statement on East-West Relations," May 31, 1984, NATO, M-1(84)11.

54. "Summary Record of a Meeting of the Council Held at NATO Headquarters, Brussels on Wednesday, 25th April 1984 at 10.15 a.m.," May 30, 1984, NATO, C-R(84)24.

55. *NATO Review* 32, no. 1 (1984).

56. Michael Heseltine, "The Atlantic Alliance: An Agenda for 1984," *NATO Review* 32, no. 1 (1984): 1.

57. Heseltine, "Atlantic Alliance," 1.

58. Daniel Charles and David Albright, "Europeanization of NATO," *Bulletin of the Atomic Scientists* 40, no. 9 (1984): 45. See also Peter Schmidt, *Europeanization of Defense: Prospects of Consensus?* (Santa Monica, CA: RAND Corp., 1984).

59. MAE note, "Riattivazione dell'UEO," December 13, 1984, WCDA, doc. 155163.

60. Jacques F. Poos, "Prospects for the WEU," *NATO Review* 35, no. 4 (1987): 16–19.

61. CIA Directorate of Intelligence assessment, "Status of the Western European Union Initiative," October 1984, CREST, CIA-RDP85S00316R00030002 0001-6.

62. Henry A. Kissinger, "A Plan to Reshape NATO," in *European Peace Movements and the Future of the Western Alliance*, ed. Walter Laqueur and Robert Hunter (New Brunswick, NJ: Transaction, 1985), 41–55. See also "Kissinger Appraises NATO," *New York Times*, February 27, 1984.

63. Phil Williams, "The Nunn Amendment, Burden-Sharing and US Troops in Europe," *Survival* 27, no. 1 (1985): 2–10.

64. Theodore Draper, "The Western Misalliance," in Laqueur and Hunter, *European Peace Movements*, 56–58.

65. Christopher Layne, "Neocons vs. Eurowimps," *Reason*, December 1986.

66. *Report of the Special Committee on Nuclear Weapons in the Atlantic Alliance*, 124.

67. Philip Mansfield to Geoffrey Howe, "The Netherlands Decision on INF Deployment," June 18, 1984, TNA, FCO 46/5269.

68. "Dutch Statement on Cruise Missile Deployment," *Survival* 26, no. 5 (1984): 238–39.

69. Quoted in *Report of the Special Committee on Nuclear Weapons in the Atlantic Alliance*, 124.

70. William J. Dyess interview, March 29, 1989, FAOHP, 24. See also Giles Scott-Smith, "The Netherlands between East and West," in Nuti et al., *Euromissile Crisis*, 262–63.

71. "Text of Soviet Statement on Space Weapons," *New York Times*, July 7, 1984.

72. Dusko Doder, "Howe Questions Intent of Soviets to Negotiate," *Washington Post*, July 4, 1984; "Interview with Andrew Neil and Jon Connell of the *Sunday Times* of London," September 9, 1984, *PPP: Ronald Reagan 1984*, vol. 2, ed. William K. Banks (Washington, DC: Government Printing Office, 1987), 1256.

73. Jack Matlock to Robert McFarlane, "The Soviets: Where We Stand," July 6, 1984, RRL, JFMF, box 5, folder "July 1984 [07/01/1984–07/14/1984]."

74. Ronald Reagan, Brian Mulroney memorandum of conversation, September 25, 1984, RRL, ESNSC, CF, box 12, folder "Canada 09/25/84–10/21/84."

75. Burns, "Walkout by Moscow."

76. Adelman's article appeared as Kenneth L. Adelman, "Arms Control with and without Agreements," *Foreign Affairs* 63, no. 2 (1984): 240–63.

77. George P. Shultz, *Turmoil and Triumph: My Years as Secretary of State* (New York: Charles Scribner's Sons, 1993), 497–98.

78. Konstantin Chernenko to Ronald Reagan, November 17, 1984, RRL, ESNSC, HOSF, box 39.

79. Shultz, *Turmoil and Triumph*, 500.

80. George Shultz, Andrei Gromyko memorandum of conversation, 9:40 a.m.–1:00 p.m., January 7, 1985, RRL, JFMF, box 8, folder "March 1985 (1)."

81. Shultz, Gromyko memorandum of conversation, 9:40 a.m.–1:00 p.m., 7 January 1985, RRL, JFMF, box 8, folder "March 1985 (1)."

82. George Shultz, Andrei Gromyko memorandum of conversation, 3:35 p.m.–6:55 p.m., January 8, 1985, RRL, JFMF, box 8, folder "March 1985 (1)."

83. Jack Matlock to Robert McFarlane, "Organizing for Arms Reduction Negotiations with the Soviets," January 12, 1985, RRL, JFMF, box 7, folder "January 1985 (2)."

84. "U.S. Soviet Negotiations on Space and Nuclear Arms, Interrelationship between the Questions Which Will Be the Subject of the Negotiations," February 5, 1985, LAC, RG25, vol. 28526, file 27-4-NATO-1-INF, part 10.

85. *Report of the Special Committee on Nuclear Weapons in the Atlantic Alliance*, 128.

86. *Report of the Special Committee on Nuclear Weapons in the Atlantic Alliance*, 129.

87. Ricketts to Budd, "Anglo-German Summit: Belgian INF Deployment," January 17, 1985, TNA, PREM 19/1765.

88. "Note for the Record of a Meeting with the German Defence Minister, Dr. Woerner at 9.25 am on Friday 18th January 1985," TNA, PREM 19/1764.

89. Gary Yerkey, "Belgium Pledges to Set Timetable for Deployment of US Missiles," *Christian Science Monitor*, January 21, 1985.

90. Canadian Embassy Brussels to External Affairs, "Belgian Missile Deployment," January 31, 1985, LAC, RG25, vol. 28526, file 27-4-NATO-1-INF, part 9.

91. Elizabeth Pond, "Future of the Atlantic Alliance: Unity . . . in Diversity?," *Christian Science Monitor*, March 12, 1985.

92. "Reagan Administration Secretary of State Reflects on His Tenure and Tillerson's," October 4, 2017, National Public Radio, https://www.npr.org/2017/10/04/555710502/reagan-administration-secretary-of-state-reflects-on-his-tenure-and-tillersons.

11. Who's Afraid of Gorbachev?

1. Canadian Embassy Moscow to External Affairs, "PM Mulroney Mtg with Gorbachev:14Mar85," March 15, 1985, LAC, RG25, vol. 8673, file 20-1-2-USSR, part 49.

2. Brian Fall interview, January 23, 2017, BDOHP, 51.

3. Ronald Reagan diary entry, March 11, 1985, *The Reagan Diaries*, vol. 1, ed. Douglas Brinkley (New York: HarperCollins, 2009), 434.

4. UK Embassy Moscow to FCO, "Election of Gorbachev," March 12, 1985, TNA, PREM 19/1646.

5. "Priorities/Opportunities for 1985," March 28, 1985, RRL, JFMF, box 8, folder "April 1985 (1)."

6. On the shift in Gorbachev's thinking, see Elizabeth C. Charles, "Gorbachev and the Decision to Decouple the Arms Control Package: How the Breakdown of the Reykjavik Summit Led to the Elimination of the Euromissiles," in Nuti et al., *Euromissile Crisis*, 66–84; Svetlana Savranskaya, "Learning to Disarm: Mikhail Gorbachev's Interactive Learning and Changes in the Soviet Negotiating Positions Leading to the INF Treaty," in Nuti et al., *Euromissile Crisis*, 85–103.

7. William Taubman, *Gorbachev: His Life and Times* (New York: W. W. Norton, 2017), esp. 7–157.

8. US Embassy London to State Department, "FCO Impressions of Gorbachev," December 20, 1984, RRL, JFMF, box 7, folder "Signals Oct–Dec 1984 3/3."

9. Andrei Grachev, *Gorbachev's Gamble: Soviet Foreign Policy and the End of the Cold War* (Cambridge: Polity, 2008), 62.

10. UK Embassy Moscow to FCO, "The Death of Chernenko and Gorbachev's Succession," March 21, 1985, TNA, PREM 19/1647.

11. Richard Burt to Louis Delvoie, April 10, 1985, LAC, RG25, vol. 28256, file 27-4-NATO-1-INF, part 10.

12. George Shultz, Andrei Gromyko memorandum of conversation, 9:40 a.m.–1:00 p.m., January 7, 1985, RRL, JFMF, box 8, folder "March 1985 (1)."

13. NSDD 165, "Instructions for the First Round of US/Soviet Negotiations in Geneva," RRL, https://www.reaganlibrary.gov/public/archives/reference/scanned-nsdds/nsdd165.pdf.

14. Jack Matlock to Robert McFarlane, "U.S.-Soviet Relations: Planning for 1985," n.d., RRL, JFMF, box 8, folder "April 1985 (2)."

15. Matlock to McFarlane, "U.S.-Soviet Relations: Planning for 1985," n.d., RRL, JFMF, box 8, folder "April 1985 (2)."

16. Canadian Delegation NATO to External Affairs, "INF: Special Consultative Group (SCG) Mtg: 13 Feb," February 13, 1985, LAC, RG25, vol. 28526, file 27-4-NATO-1-INF, part 10.

17. Canadian Delegation NATO to External Affairs, "INF: Special Consultative Group (SCG) Mtg: 23Apr," April 24, 1985, LAC, RG25, vol. 28526, file 27-4-NATO-1-INF, part 10.

18. Canadian Delegation NATO to External Affairs, "INF: Special Consultative Group (SCG) Mtg: 13 Feb," February 13, 1985, LAC, RG25, vol. 28526, file 27-4-NATO-1-INF, part 10.

19. "Draft SCG Progress Report," May 15, 1985, LAC, RG25, vol. 28526, file 27-4-NATO-1-INF, part 10.

20. "Aufzeichnung des Legationsrats I. Klasse Weiß," March 29, 1985, *AAPD 1985*, ed. Michael Ploetz, Mechthild Lindemann, and Christoph Johannes Franzen (Munich: Oldenbourg, 2016), doc. 84.

21. Edward Rowny draft article, "Gorbachev's First Hundred Days," n.d. [June 1985], RRL, JFMF, box 9, folder "June 1985 (3)."

22. "Action Memorandum from the Assistant Secretary of State for European and Canadian Affairs (Ridgway) to Secretary of State Shultz," n.d., *FRUS 1981–1988*, vol. 5: *Soviet Union, March 1985–October 1986*, ed. Elizabeth C. Charles (Washington, DC: Government Printing Office, 2020), doc. 68.

23. "Excerpts from Remarks of Gorbachev and Mitterrand to the Press in Paris," *New York Times*, October 5, 1985. On Gorbachev's concept of a common European home, see Marie-Pierre Rey, "'Europe Is Our Common Home': A Study of Gorbachev's Diplomatic Concept," *Cold War History* 4, no. 2 (2004): 33–65.

24. "Gorbachev and Europe," November 18, 1985, OSA, RFE/RL, HU OSA 300-8-3-8641.

25. "Dutch Statement on Cruise Missile Deployment," *Survival* 26, no. 5 (1984): 238–39.

26. James M. Markham, "Gorbachev Opens in Paris to Mixed Reviews," *New York Times*, October 6, 1985.

27. UK Embassy The Hague to FCO, "Netherlands/INF: The 'People's Petition,'" October 28, 1985, TNA, FCO 46/4738.

28. Jo Thomas, "100,000 in London Protest Arms Race," *New York Times*, October 27, 1985.

29. Markham, "Gorbachev Opens in Paris."

30. Maarten Huygen, "Dateline Holland: NATO's Pyrrhic Victory," *Foreign Policy* no. 62 (1986): 167.

31. Canadian Embassy The Hague to External Affairs, "Neths: Cruise Missiles," September 18, 1985, LAC, RG25, vol. 28526, file 27-4-NATO-1-INF, part 10.

32. "Prime Minister's Meeting with Dr Vogel: 2 July" [1985], TNA, PREM 19/1764.

33. Canadian Embassy Moscow to External Affairs, "CSCE 10th Anniversary: SSEA Bilateral Meeting with Shevardnadze," August 5, 1985, LAC, RG25, vol. 8673, file 20-1-2-USSR, part 49.

34. George Shultz to Ronald Reagan, "What to Expect from Gorbachev in Geneva," November 12, 1985, RRL, DTRF, box 7, folder "Memoranda to the President from Robert C. McFarlane (3)."

35. Jack Matlock to Robert McFarlane, "Gromyko's 'Elevation': First Thoughts," July 2, 1985, RRL, JFMF, box 10, folder "July 1985 (1)."

36. Jack F. Matlock Jr., *Autopsy on an Empire: The American Ambassador's Account of the Collapse of the Soviet Union* (New York: Random House, 1995), 74.

37. CIA Directorate of Intelligence, "Gorbachev, the New Broom," June 1985, RRL, JFMF, box 10, folder "June 1985 (4)."

38. Hedrick Smith, "Gorbachev on Stage," *New York Times*, April 9, 1985.

39. "Lord Carrington Asks Why Anti-nuclear Movements' Policy Should Be Considered Less Risky Than NATO's," May 24, 1985, NATO, Statement Carrington 24/05/1985.

40. Wilfried Loth, "The Cold War: What It Was About and Why It Ended," in *Perforating the Iron Curtain: European Détente, Transatlantic Relations, and the Cold War, 1965–1985*, ed. Poul Villaume and Odd Arne Westad (Copenhagen: Museum Tusculanum, 2010), 29. For the transnational circulation of ideas and its impact on Gorbachev's thinking, see Thomas Risse-Kappen, "Ideas Do Not Float Freely: Transnational

Coalitions, Domestic Structures, and the End of the Cold War," *International Organization* 48, no. 2 (1994): 185–214.

41. Grachev, *Gorbachev's Gamble*, 67.

42. Andrian Danilevich interview, September 21, 1992, in *Soviet Intentions 1965–1985*, vol. 2: *Soviet Post–Cold War Testimonial Evidence* (McLean, VA: BDM, 1995), 43.

43. Ronald Reagan to Suzanne Massie, February 10, 1986, in *Reagan: A Life in Letters*, ed. Kiron K. Skinner, Annelise Anderson, and Martin Anderson (New York: Free Press, 2003), 417.

44. George Shultz to Ronald Reagan, "Your October 23–24 Trip to the United Nations General Assembly: Scope Paper," October 7, 1985, RRL, DTRF, box 7, folder "Geneva Oversight Group."

45. "Statement by Soviet General Secretary Gorbachev," January 15, 1986," *DoD 1986*, doc. 5.

46. Anatoly Chernyaev, *My Six Years with Gorbachev*, trans. and ed. Robert D. English and Elizabeth Tucker (University Park: Pennsylvania State University Press, 2000), 45.

47. Mikhail Gorbachev, *Memoirs*, trans. Georges Peronansky and Tatjana Varsavsky (New York: Doubleday, 1995), 412.

48. Ronald Reagan diary entry, January 15, 1986, *The Reagan Diaries*, vol. 2, ed. Douglas Brinkley (New York: HarperCollins, 2009), 562.

49. Grachev, *Gorbachev's Gamble*, 68.

50. James Graham Wilson, *The Triumph of Improvisation: Gorbachev's Adaptability, Reagan's Engagement, and the End of the Cold War* (Ithaca, NY: Cornell University Press, 2014), 101–2.

51. Alexei Arbatov interview, December 30, 1987, WPNA.

52. Jack Matlock to John Poindexter, "Reply to Gorbachev's Handwritten Letter," February 1, 1986, RRL, JFMF, box 14, folder "February 1986 (1)."

53. Ronald Reagan diary entry, February 3, 1986, *Reagan Diaries*, vol. 2, 568.

54. George P. Shultz, *Turmoil and Triumph: My Years as Secretary of State* (New York: Charles Scribner's Sons, 1993), 701.

55. NSDD 210, "Allied Consultations on the US Response to General Secretary Gorbachev's January 14, 1986, Arms Control Proposal," February 4, 1986, RRL, https://www.reaganlibrary.gov/public/archives/reference/scanned-nsdds/nsdd 210.pdf.

56. Maynard W. Glitman, *The Last Battle of the Cold War: An Inside Account of Negotiating the Intermediate-Range Nuclear Forces Treaty* (New York: Palgrave Macmillan, 2006), 119.

57. "USSR: Gorbachev's New Style on Arms Control," n.d., RRL, JFMF, box 20, folder "Arms Control—USSR."

58. Mikhail Gorbachev to Ronald Reagan, September 15, 1986, NSA EBB203: The Reykjavik File: Previously Secret Documents from U.S. and Soviet Archives on the 1986 Reagan-Gorbachev Summit, ed. Svetlana Savranskaya and Thomas Blanton, October 13, 2006, doc. 1.

59. "Talking Points Prepared by the National Security Council Staff," October 7, 1986, *FRUS 1981–1988*, vol. 5, doc. 297.

60. Chernyaev, *My Six Years with Gorbachev*, 81. See also Taubman, *Gorbachev*, 295.

61. Shultz, *Turmoil and Triumph*, 760.

62. Ronald Reagan, Mikhail Gorbachev memorandum of conversation, 3:30–5:40 p.m., October 11, 1986, NSA EBB563: Gorbachev's Nuclear Initiative of January 1986 and the Road to Reykjavik, ed. Svetlana Savranskaya and Thomas Blanton, October 12, 2016, doc. 30.

63. Ronald Reagan, Mikhail Gorbachev memorandum of conversation, October 12, 1986, NSA EBB563, doc. 32.

64. Ronald Reagan, Mikhail Gorbachev memorandum of conversation, October 12, 1986, NSA EBB563, doc. 32.

65. Donald T. Regan, *For the Record: From Wall Street to Washington* (San Diego, CA: Harcourt Brace Jovanovich, 1988), 351–52.

66. Joseph Lelyveld, "Reykjavik Was a Shock at 10 Downing Street," *New York Times*, November 9, 1986.

67. James M. Markham, "Western Allies Grumble about Reykjavik Plans," *New York Times*, October 22, 1986.

68. James Schlesinger, "Reykjavik and Revelations: A Turn of the Tide?," *Foreign Affairs* 65, no. 3 (1986): 428.

69. "Ron, Be Patient," *Newsweek*, October 27, 1986.

70. Jane M. O. Sharp, "After Reykjavik: Arms Control and the Allies," *International Affairs* 63, no. 2 (1987): 242–45.

71. UK Embassy Moscow to FCO, "US/Soviet Relations," n.d., TNA, PREM 19/1759.

72. For an assessment of the split within the alliance post-Reykjavik, see Italian Delegation NATO to MAE, "Sessione Miniseriale del Consiglio Atlantico—Punto II Ordine del Giorno: Dibatto in Seduia Ristretta Sulle Prospettive Est-Ouest Nel Dopo Reykjavik," December 13, 1986, WCDA, doc. 155177.

73. Margaret Thatcher, *The Downing Street Years* (New York: HarperCollins, 1993), 471.

74. "Prime Minister's Talk with President Reagan," October 13, 1986, TNA, PREM 19/1759; "President's Telephone Conversation with Prime Minister," October 13, 1986, RRL, ESNSC, SF, 8607413.

75. Canadian Delegation NATO to External Affairs, "Zero Option and the Europeans," February 27, 1986, LAC, RG25, vol. 28672, file 27-4-NATO-1-INF, part 11.

76. UK Embassy Washington to FCO, "Reykjavik," October 18, 1986, TNA, PREM 19/1759.

77. "Gen Rogers Views Zero Option as 'Senseless,'" November 19, 1986, FBIS-WEU-86-229; UK Embassy Bonn to FCO, "NATO Generals on LRINF," November 21, 1986, TNA, FCO 46/5267.

78. "Testimony by the Supreme Allied Commander, Europe (Rogers) before a Panel of the House Committee on Armed Services: The Zero Option for Longer-Range Intermediate-Range Nuclear Forces in Europe [Extract]," December 10, 1986, *DoD 1986*, doc. 233.

79. Markham, "Western Allies Grumble."

80. "Address by ACDA Director Adelman: A World without Nuclear Weapons," November 13, 1986, *DoD 1986*, doc. 214.

81. How to calculate the balance of conventional forces between NATO and the Warsaw Pact was the subject of considerable debate. For contemporary assessments, see, for example, Jonathan Dean, *Watershed in Europe: Dismantling the East-West Military Confrontation* (Lexington, MA: Lexington, 1987), 29–59.

82. Canadian Delegation NATO to External Affairs, "SCG: 02Feb," January 28, 1987, LAC, RG25, vol. 28853, file 27-4-NATO-1-INF, part 12.

83. UK Embassy Moscow to FCO, "Reykjavik: INF/SDI Linkage," October 16, 1986, TNA, PREM 19/1759; "Television Address by Soviet General Secretary Gorbachev: Results of the Meeting in Reykjavik [Extracts]," October 22, 1986, *DoD 1986*, doc. 203.

84. "Session of the Politburo of the CC CPSU," October 14, 1986, NSA EBB203, doc. 21.

85. "USSR CC CPSU Politburo Session on Reparations for Reykjavik," October 8, 1986, NSA EBB203, doc. 8.

86. Anatoly Chernyaev, in William C. Wohlforth, ed., *Witnesses to the End of the Cold War* (Baltimore: Johns Hopkins University Press, 1996), 48.

87. Danilevich interview, September 21, 1992, 34; Alexei Arbatov, "What Lessons Learned?," in *Turning Points in Ending the Cold War*, ed. Kiron K. Skinner (Stanford, CA: Hoover Institution, 2007), 55.

88. Stanley R. Sloan, "NATO Nuclear Forces: Modernization and Arms Control," Congressional Research Service Issue Brief no. IB81128 (1983), 6.

89. Aleksandr Yakovlev to Mikhail Gorbachev, "Toward an Analysis of the Fact of the Visit of Prominent American Political Leaders to the USSR (Kissinger, Vance, Kirkpatrick, Brown, and others)," February 25, 1987, NSA EBB238: The INF Treaty and the Washington Summit: 20 Years Later, ed. Svetlana Savranskaya and Thomas Blanton, December 10, 2007, doc. 2.

90. Jack F. Matlock Jr., *Reagan and Gorbachev: How the Cold War Ended* (New York: Random House, 2004), 248; Svetlana Savranskaya, "Learning to Disarm: Mikhail Gorbachev's Interactive Learning and Changes in the Soviet Negotiating Positions Leading to the INF Treaty," in Nuti et al., *Euromissile Crisis*, 89–90.

91. Excerpt of Politburo minutes, "On Soviet-American Relations and Negotiations on Nuclear and Space Armaments," February 26, 1987, NSA EBB238, doc. 3.

92. Grachev, *Gorbachev's Gamble*, 96.

93. William E. Odom, *The Collapse of the Soviet Military* (New Haven, CT: Yale University Press, 1998), 110.

94. Ronald Reagan, "Remarks to Reporters on Intermediate-Range Nuclear Force Reductions," March 3, 1987, *PPP: Ronald Reagan 1987*, vol. 1, ed. William K. Banks (Washington, DC: Government Printing Office, 1989), 191–92.

95. "Telegram from Secretary of State Shultz to the Department of State and the White House," April 15, 1987, *FRUS 1981–1988*, vol. 6: *Soviet Union, October 1986–January 1989*, ed. James Graham Wilson (Washington, DC: Government Printing Office, 2016), doc. 43.

96. "Possible Soviet Proposal of Zero-Zero in SRINF Missiles of 500 to 1000 kms Range," n.d. [1987], TNA, FCO 46/5904.

97. Charles Powell to Margaret Thatcher, "Arms Control," April 24, 1987, TNA, PREM 19/2054.

98. UK Embassy Moscow to FCO, "Shultz's Meeting with Gorbachev: Comment," April 15, 1987, TNA, PREM 19/2172.

99. UK Delegation NATO to FCO, "Follow-On to Shultz's NAC Briefing: Future Alliance Work," April 16, 1987, TNA, PREM 19/5094.

100. Canadian Delegation NATO to External Affairs, "SCG Opening Statement," April 29, 1987, LAC, RG25, vol. 28853, file 27-4-NATO-1-INF, part 12.

101. Deutscher Bundestag, Stenographische Bericht, 11. Wahlperiode, 6. Sitzung, March 29, 1987, 258.

102. "Bundesminister Wörner an Bundeskanzler Kohl," April 19, 1987, *AAPD 1987*, ed. Tim Szatkowski, Tim Geiger, and Jens Jost Hofmann (Munich: Oldenbourg, 2018), doc. 116.

103. "Gespräch des Bundeskanzler Kohl mit Ministerpräsident Martens," May 6, 1987, *AAPD 1987*, doc. 125.

104. For a brief overview of these efforts, see Tim Geiger, "Controversies over the Double Zero Option: The Kohl-Genscher Government and the INF Treaty," in *The INF Treaty of 1987: A Reappraisal*, ed. Philipp Gassert, Tim Geiger, and Hermann Wentker (Göttingen, Germany: Vandenhoeck & Ruprecht, 2021), 139–40.

105. Deutscher Bundestag, Stenographischer Bericht, 11. Wahlperiode, 16. Sitzung, June 4, 1987, 923–28.

106. UK Delegation NATO to FCO, "LRINF/SRINF: SACEUR's Views," April 27, 1987, TNA, PREM 19/2054.

107. UK Delegation NATO to FCO, "LRINF/SRINF: Third Party Systems, Etc.," May 9, 1987, TNA, FCO 46/5905.

108. Geiger, "Controversies over the Double Zero Option," 147.

109. Hans-Dietrich Genscher, *Erinnerungen* (Berlin: Siedler, 1995), 572–73.

110. "Chancen für die Menschen in Deutschland und für Abrüstung und Rüstungskontrolle—Erklärungen des Bundeskanzlers," August 27, 1987, Bulletin 80–87.

111. Russell Watson, "A Rush to the Summit," *Newsweek*, September 7, 1987.

112. Charles Powell to Geoffrey Howe, "GLCM Related Activities following the Signature of an INF Treaty," October 26, 1987, TNA, PREM 19/2056.

113. CND flyer, "American Cruise Missiles Now at 2nd U.K. Base," n.d. [1987], LSE, CND/1993/6/7 [3 of 5].

114. Martin Nesirky, "Netherlands Prepares for U.S. Nuclear Mid-range Missiles That May Never Come," *Los Angeles Times*, June 21, 1987.

115. Shultz, *Turmoil and Triumph*, 996.

116. "Non-Paper Prepared by Secretary of State Shultz," November 18, 1987, *FRUS 1981–1988*, vol. 6, doc. 94.

117. The INF Treaty consisted of four parts: a treaty, a memorandum of understanding regarding the relevant data (system numbers, bases, storage sites, and the like), a protocol on the elimination of the missiles, and a protocol on inspections.

118. Ronald Reagan, "Address to the American and Soviet Peoples on the Soviet–United States Summit Meeting," December 8, 1987, *PPP: Ronald Reagan 1987*, vol. 2, ed. William K. Banks (Washington, DC: Government Printing Office, 1987), 1486; "Intermediate Range Nuclear Weapons Treaty Signing," C-SPAN, December 8, 1987, https://www.c-span.org/video/?652-1/intermediate-range-nuclear-weapons-treaty-signing.

119. Ronald Reagan, "Address to the American and Soviet Peoples," 1486; "Intermediate Range Nuclear Weapons Treaty Signing," December 8, 1987, https://www.c-span.org/video/?652-1/intermediate-range-nuclear-weapons-treaty-signing.

120. Robert Shogan, "Arms Pact Sparks Disagreement: Reagan-Conservative Gap Could Be Unbridgeable," *Los Angeles Times*, April 27, 1987; Hedrick Smith, "The Right against Reagan," *New York Times Magazine*, January 17, 1988.

121. Philip M. Kaiser, "Reagan Is No Chamberlain," *New York Times*, February 5, 1988.

122. Eugene V. Rostow, "Go Slow on Ratifying the I.N.F. Pact," *New York Times*, January 5, 1988.

123. Russell Watson, "The Right Wing Opens Fire," *Newsweek*, November 30, 1987.

124. "Dealing at Last," *Newsweek*, April 27, 1987.

125. Shultz, *Turmoil and Triumph*, 1085.

126. Ronald Reagan, "The President's News Conference Following the Soviet–United States Summit Meeting in Moscow," June 1, 1988, *PPP: Ronald Reagan 1988*, vol. 1, ed. William K. Banks (Washington, DC: Government Printing Office, 1990), 709. See also "Trip to Russia, President Reagan, General Secretary Mikhail Gorbachev Walking in Red Square Talking to Soviet Citizens. Moscow, Russia," May 31, 1988, RRL, master tape no. 559, https://www.youtube.com/watch?v=LZUu5WraroM.

127. Ronald Reagan, "Remarks and a Question-and-Answer Session with the Students and Faculty at Moscow State University," May 31, 1988, *PPP: Ronald Reagan 1988*, vol. 1, 686–87.

128. Bradley Lynn Coleman and Kyle Longley, introduction to *Reagan and the World: Leadership and National Security 1981–1989*, ed. Bradley Lynn Coleman and Kyle Longley (Lexington: University Press of Kentucky, 2017), 1.

129. Hans-Dietrich Genscher remarks, World Economic Forum, Davos, Switzerland, February 1, 1987, German Information Center Statements and Speeches 10, no. 3.

12. Blast from the Past

1. *END: Journal of European Nuclear Disarmament* 32 (1988).

2. John R. Galvin, "The INF Treaty—No Relief from the Burden of Defence," *NATO Review* 36, no. 1 (1988): 1.

3. Pat Dounoukos, "She Still Loves This Planet," *Peace Magazine*, June–July 1988, 16.

4. Bernard Rogers, prepared statement for the Committee on Foreign Relations, printed in *The INF Treaty: Hearings before the Committee on Foreign Relations, United States Senate, One Hundredth Congress, Second Session on the Treaty between the United States of America and the Union of Soviet Socialist Republics on the Elimination of their Intermediate-Range and Shorter-Range Missiles, February 16, 18, and 19, 1988, Part 3* (Washington, DC: Government Printing Office, 1988), 245.

5. Karen DeYoung, "Nuclear Issues Linger for NATO," *Washington Post*, December 23, 1987.

6. "The Montebello Decision on Reductions of Nuclear Forces," annex to NPG communiqué, October 28, 1983, NATO, M-NPG-2(83)23. On the links

between INF and SNF in West German thinking regarding the Montebello decision, see "Reduzeirung bzw. Abzug der nuklearen Kurzstreckensysteme (SNF) in Europea und künftiges Vertedigungskonzept der NATO," November 15, 1983, PA-AA, B150/581.

7. "The Montebello Decision," annex to NPG communiqué, October 28, 1983, NATO, M-NPG-2(83)23.

8. "Remarks by General Bernard W. Rogers, Supreme Allied Commander, Europe to the Dutch Atlantic Commission," December 5, 1985, *Atlantisch Nieuws* nos. 11/12 (1985): 4.

9. "Remarks by General Bernard W. Rogers," 5.

10. On flexible response as myth, with a focus on the 1960s and 1970s, see Francis J. Gavin, *Nuclear Statecraft: History and Strategy in America's Atomic Age* (Ithaca, NY: Cornell University Press, 2012), 30–56. Gavin's arguments emphasize the disconnect between flexible response in theory and in practice. Yet, however incredible the strategy was, the theory governed the strategic and political conversations within NATO circles, even as officials appreciated the clear limits of flexible response in purely military terms.

11. "Gen. Rogers: Time to Say 'Time Out,'" *Army*, September 1987, 27.

12. Jeffrey Arthur Larsen, "The Politics of NATO Short-Range Nuclear Modernization 1983–1990: The Follow-On-to-Lance Missile Decisions" (PhD diss., Princeton University, 1991), 203.

13. Frank Carlucci, "The Effective of NATO Strategy," remarks prepared for the Wehrkunde, Munich, February 7, 1988, *Defense Issues* 7, no. 3, 4.

14. Quoted in Ed Lion, "Thatcher Champions Nuclear Deterrent," United Press International, June 7, 1987.

15. "Statement on the Ministerial Meeting of the North Atlantic Council at Reykjavik," June 12, 1987, NATO, M-1(87)25.

16. Senate Republican Policy Committee memorandum, "Western Europe and the INF Treaty," February 2, 1988, CREST, CIA-RDP90M00005R000300070027-8.

17. Galvin, "The INF Treaty," 4.

18. Charles Powell to A. C. Galsworthy, "Prime Minister's Visit to NATO and SHAPE, 17 February," February 17, 1988, TNA, PREM 19/2365.

19. "Declaration of the Heads of State and Government Participating in the Meeting of the North Atlantic Council in Brussels," March 3, 1988, NATO, M-1(88)13.

20. House of Commons, *Hansard*, March 4, 1988, 6th series, vol. 128, col. 1280–95.

21. David Gore-Booth to David Dain, "Germany and SNF," December 11, 1987, TNA, FCO 46/5793.

22. "Declaration of the Heads of State and Government Participating in the Meeting of the North Atlantic Council in Brussels," March 3, 1988, NATO, M-1(88)13.

23. "German Press Review," *Week in Germany*, February 11, 1988, 3.

24. Deutscher Bundestag, Stenographischer Bericht, 243. Sitzung, 10. Wahlperiode, November 6, 1986, 18740.

25. Bullard to Fall, "German Views on SNF," September 18, 1987, TNA, FCO 46/5973.

26. *Discriminate Deterrence: Report of the Commission on Integrated Long-Term Strategy* (Washington, DC: Government Printing Office, 1988), 65. The commission was

made up of high-level experts and former officials and chaired by Fred Iklé and Albert Wohlstetter. The commission's other members included Anne L. Armstrong, Zbigniew Brzezinski, William P. Clark, W. Graham Claytor Jr., Andrew J. Goodpaster, James L. Holloway III, Samuel P. Huntington, Henry Kissinger, Joshua Lederberg, Bernard Schriever, and John Vessey.

27. US Embassy Bonn to State Department, "Report of the Commission on Integrated Long-Term Strategy: 'Discriminate Deterrence,'" January 6, 1988, RRL, WACF, RAC box 3, folder "NATO (January 1988)."

28. "Quadripartite Meeting: Ebenhausen: 21–23 March 1988 Discriminate Deterrence: The European Perspective," March 1988, TNA, FCO 46/6542.

29. Gregory F. Treverton, "This Time, NATO's Spat Hits a Nerve," *Los Angeles Times*, May 5, 1989.

30. Pierre Lellouche, "All This Talk of 'Singularity' Weakens the Alliance," *International Herald Tribune* (European ed.), February 17, 1988.

31. Brian Fall to John Boyd, "SNF Modernisation," November 1, 1988, TNA, FCO 46/6596.

32. Richard Owen, "West German Plea to Thatcher for Defence Sympathy," *Times*, December 17, 1987, clipping in TNA, FCO 46/5973.

33. Beattie to P. John Goulden, "Follow-Up to Chevening: Way Ahead on SNF," May 3, 1988, TNA, FCO 46/6568.

34. Brian Fall to John Boyd, "SNF Modernisation," November 1, 1988, TNA, FCO 46/6596.

35. Michael Alexander to John Boyd, "SNF, the Comprehensive Concept Etc.," September 16, 1988, TNA, FCO 46/6596.

36. NPG communiqué, October 28, 1988, NATO, M-NPG-2(88)63.

37. M. Glynne Evans to Paul Lever, "Belgian Defence Policy and SNF Modernisation," November 1988, TNA, FCO 46/6614.

38. FCO to UK Embassy Brussels, "Belgian Defence Policy and SNF Modernisation," November 22, 1988, TNA, FCO 46/6614.

39. John Boyd to Michael Alexander, "SNF Modernisation / Arms Control," November 3, 1988, TNA, FCO 46/6596.

40. George Bush, Margaret Thatcher memorandum of telephone conversation, January 23, 1989, GBL, MT.

41. Bush to Kohl, January 25, 1989, GBL, BSC, HSMF, OA/ID 91114, folder "Germany (Outgoing) 1989–1993."

42. Philip Zelikow to Brent Scowcroft, "The U.S. Message on SNF: Advice from USNATO," February 10, 1989, GBL, CRF, OA/ID CF00715, folder "Strategic Nuclear Force (SNF)."

43. "Gespräch des Bundesministers Genscher mit dem amerikanischen Außenminister Baker," February 12, 1989, *AAPD 1989*, ed. Daniela Taschler, Tim Szatkowski, and Christoph Johannes Franzen (Munich: Oldenbourg, 2020), doc. 40; Hans-Dietrich Genscher, *Rebuilding a House Divided: A Memoir by the Architect of Germany's Reunification*, trans. Thomas Thornton (New York: Broadway, 1998), 240–44.

44. George Bush, Francesco Cossiga memorandum of conversation, February 24, 1989, GBL, MT.

45. "Address by Mikhail Gorbachev at the UN General Assembly (Excerpts)," December 7, 1988, WCDA, doc. 116224.

46. Jim Hoagland, "The Issue in Europe Is Firstly Strategic," *International Herald Tribune* (European ed.), December 12, 1988.

47. UK Embassy Bonn to FCO, "Karpov's Visit to Bonn, 27–28 February: SNF," March 2, 1989, TNA, PREM 19/2611.

48. White House to Cabinet Office, "Letter from the President to Prime Minister Thatcher," March 9, 1989, GBL, BSC, HSMF, OA/ID 91115, folder "United Kingdom (Outgoing) 1989–1993 [1]."

49. Genscher, *Rebuilding a House Divided*, 244–45.

50. James A. Baker III, *The Politics of Diplomacy: Revolution, War and Peace, 1989–1992*, with Thomas M. DeFrank (New York: G. P. Putnam's Sons, 1995), 82.

51. FCO to UK Embassy The Hague, "SNF: Telephone Call from Dutch Foreign Minister," April 25, 1989, TNA, PREM 19/2617.

52. Charles Powell minute, "Bilateral with the Foreign Secretary, 23 March 1989," March 22, 1989, TNA, PREM 19/3340.

53. Robert J. McCartney, "Missile Rift Highlights NATO Split," *Washington Post*, April 26, 1989.

54. Deutscher Bundestag, Stenographischer Bericht, 140. Sitzung, 11. Wahlperiode, April 27, 1989, 10325.

55. George Bush, Helmut Kohl memorandum of telephone conversation, May 5, 1989, GBL, MT.

56. Charles Powell to Brent Scowcroft, May 4, 1989, TNA, PREM 19/2617.

57. Charles Powell to Stephen Wall, "SNF," May 3, 1989, TNA, PREM 19/2617.

58. Charles Powell to Brent Scowcroft, May 4, 1989, TNA, PREM 19/2617.

59. George Bush, Ruud Lubbers memorandum of conversation, May 9, 1989, GBL, MT.

60. Charles Powell minute, "Bilateral with the Foreign Secretary," May 9, 1989, TNA, PREM 19/3340.

61. P. John Goulden minute, "SNF: US Position," May 5, 1989, TNA, PREM 19/2617.

62. George Bush, "Remarks and a Question-and-Answer Session with Reporters Following a Luncheon with Prime Minister Brian Mulroney of Canada," May 4, 1989, *PPP: George Bush 1989*, vol. 1, ed. William K. Banks (Washington, DC: Government Printing Office, 1990), 515.

63. US Mission NATO to State Department, "Heads Up from Brussels: Germany, the United States and the Comprehensive Concept," February 9, 1989, GBL, CRF, OA/ID CF00715, folder "Strategic Nuclear Forces (SNF)."

64. British Military Government Berlin to FCO, "SNF: US/FRG Contacts," May 14, 1989, TNA, PREM 19/2617.

65. Carol Giacomo, "Baker Urges Deeper Short-Range Arms Cuts by Soviet Union," Reuters, May 12, 1989.

66. Percy Cradock to Charles Powell, "Gorbachev's Proposals on SNF and Conventional Force Cuts," May 12, 1989, TNA, PREM 19/2617.

67. UK Embassy Bonn to FCO, "SNF: German Views," 12 May 1989, TNA, PREM 19/2617.

68. George Bush, "Remarks at the Texas A&M Commencement Ceremony in College Station," May 12, 1989, *PPP: George Bush 1989*, vol. 1, 540–43.

69. Jeffrey A. Engel, *When the World Seemed New: George H. W. Bush and the End of the Cold War* (Boston: Houghton Mifflin Harcourt, 2017), 136–37.

70. Charles Powell to Stephen Wall, "SNF," May 22, 1989, TNA, PREM 19/2617.

71. Charles Powell to Stephen Wall, "SNF," May 19, 1989, TNA, PREM 19/2617.

72. Powell to Wall, "SNF," May 22, 1989, TNA, PREM 19/2617.

73. Powell to Wall, "SNF," May 22, 1989, TNA, PREM 19/2617.

74. George Bush to Helmut Kohl, May 23, 1989, GBL, BSC, HSMF, OA/ID 91114, folder "Germany (Outgoing) 1989–1993."

75. Bush to Kohl, May 23, 1989, GBL, BSC, HSMF, OA/ID 91114, folder "Germany (Outgoing) 1989–1993."

76. UK Embassy Rome to FCO, "NATO Summit: Bush's Visit to Rome," May 28, 1989, TNA, PREM 19/2617.

77. UK Embassy Rome to FCO, "NATO Summit: Bush's Visit to Rome," May 28, 1989, TNA, PREM 19/2617.

78. UK Embassy Rome to FCO, "NATO Summit: Bush's Visit to Rome," May 28, 1989, TNA, PREM 19/2617.

79. George Bush, "Remarks Announcing a Conventional Arms Control Initiative and a Question-and-Answer Session with Reporters in Brussels," May 29, 1989, *PPP: George Bush 1989*, vol. 1, 618–21.

80. "The Alliance's Comprehensive Concept of Arms Control and Disarmament," May 29, 1989, NATO, https://www.nato.int/cps/en/natohq/official_texts_23553.htm.

81. "Peace in Their Time, Trouble to Come," *Economist*, June 3, 1989.

82. John Dickie, "Your Move, Gorbachev," *Daily Mail*, May 30, 1989.

83. George Bush, "Remarks to the Citizens of Mainz, Federal Republic of Germany," May 31, 1989, *PPP: George Bush 1989*, vol. 1, 651.

84. Margaret Thatcher, *The Downing Street Years* (New York: HarperCollins, 1993), 789.

85. Brent Scowcroft to George Bush, "Dealing with the Germans," August 7, 1989, GBL, BSC, USSR, OA/ID 91120, folder "Soviet Power Collapse in Eastern Europe–SNF–May 1989 [1]."

86. Scowcroft to Bush, "Dealing with the Germans," August 7, 1989, GBL, BSC, USSR, OA/ID 91120, folder "Soviet Power Collapse in Eastern Europe–SNF–May 1989 [1]."

87. John Tagliabue, "East Germans Get Permission to Quit Prague for West," *New York Times*, October 1, 1989.

88. "Brezhnev Doctrine Dead: No More Invasions," August 16, 1989, OSA, RFE/RL, HU OSA 300-8-3-8759.

89. "1989: 'Wir sind das Volk'—Leipzig im Oktober," https://www.youtube.com/watch?v=2OjCesZRf_I.

90. Mary Elise Sarotte, *1989: The Struggle to Create Post–Cold War Europe* (Princeton, NJ: Princeton University Press, 2009), 36–45.

91. George Bush, "The President's News Conference," February 12, 1990, *PPP: George Bush 1990*, vol. 1, ed. Karen Howard Ashlin (Washington, DC: Government Printing Office, 1991), 215.

92. Thomas L. Friedman, "Clamor in the East," *New York Times*, November 21, 1989.

93. Michael Fry and Philip Zelikow to Brent Scowcroft, "Short-Range Nuclear Forces (SNF) Arms Control and Modernization," February 16, 1990, GBL, BSC, USSR, OA/ID 91120, folder "Soviet Power Collapse in Eastern Europe–SNF–February–May 1990."

94. "Meeting with Helmut Kohl, Chancellor of the Federal Republic of Germany," February 24, 1990, GBL, MT.

95. George Bush, "The President's News Conference," May 3, 1990, *PPP: George Bush 1990*, vol. 1, 608.

96. *The Future of Europe: Hearings before the Committee on Foreign Relations and the Subcommittee on European Affairs of the United States Senate, One Hundred First Congress, Second Session, December 13, 1989, January 17, February 1 and 22, March 1, 7, 21, 22, 28, and 29, May 9, and June 12, 1990* (Washington, DC: Government Printing Office, 1991), 582.

97. "Meeting with Chancellor Helmut Kohl of the Federal Republic of Germany," June 8, 1990, GBL, MT.

98. "Meeting with Chancellor Kohl, Federal Republic of Germany," May 17, 1990, GBL, MT.

99. "London Declaration on a Transformed North Atlantic Alliance," July 6, 1990, NATO, https://www.nato.int/docu/comm/49-95/c900706a.htm. See also Timothy Andrews Sayle, *Enduring Alliance: A History of NATO and the Postwar Global Order* (Ithaca, NY: Cornell University Press, 2019), 229–32.

100. For a similar argument, see Thomas E. Halverson, *The Last Great Nuclear Debate: NATO and Short-Range Nuclear Weapons in the 1980s* (Basingstoke, UK: Macmillan, 1995), 131.

101. Gregory F. Treverton, *America, Germany, and the Future of Europe* (Princeton, NJ: Princeton University Press, 1992), 3.

Conclusion

1. John Balzar and Norman Kempster, "US Destroys 1st Nuclear Missiles," *Los Angeles Times*, September 9, 1988.

2. "2 Cruise Missiles Removed in England," *Los Angeles Times*, September 9, 1988.

3. Quoted in Deborah Kirkhuff, "Molesworth and the INF," *Air Force Missileers* 27, no. 1 (2019): 9–10.

4. "London Declaration on a Transformed North Atlantic Alliance," June 5–6, 1990, NATO, https://www.nato.int/docu/comm/49-95/c900706a.htm.

5. Helmut Kohl, *Vom Mauerfall zur Wiedervereinigung: Meine Erinnerungen* (Munich: Droemer, 2014), 15.

6. Hans-Dietrich Genscher, *Rebuilding a House Divided: A Memoir by the Architect of Germany's Reunification*, trans. Thomas Thornton (New York: Broadway, 1998), 305.

7. Quoted in Peter Grier, "The Short, Happy Life of the Glick-Em," *Air Force Magazine*, July 1, 2002, 71.

8. Sarah Hipperson, "Greenham Common Women's Peace Camp," http://www.greenhamwpc.org.uk/index.htm.

9. Quoted in Mary Kaldor, *Europe from Below: An East-West Dialogue* (London: Verso, 1991), 16.

10. To what extent peace and antinuclear activists should be credited with shaping high-level policy and bringing about the end of the Cold War is the subject of considerable debate. See, as starting points, Matthew Evangelista, *Unarmed Forces: The Transnational Movement to End the Cold War* (Ithaca, NY: Cornell University Press, 1999); Lawrence S. Wittner, "Peace through Strength? The Impact of the Antinuclear Uprising on the Carter and Reagan Administrations," in *Nuclear Threats, Nuclear Fear and the Cold War of the 1980s*, ed. Eckart Conze, Martin Klimke, and Jeremy Varon (Cambridge: Cambridge University Press, 2017), 271–89; Tim Geiger and Jan Hansen, "Did Protest Matter? The Influence of the Peace Movement on the West German Government and the Social Democratic Party, 1977–1983," in Conze, Klimke, and Varon, *Nuclear Threats*, 290–315; Andrea Chiampan, "Nuclear Weapons, 'Nuclear Ideas,' and Protests: Did They Matter?," in *New Perspectives on the End of the Cold War*, ed. Bernhard Blumenau, Jussi M. Hanhimäki, and Barbara Zanchetta (London: Routledge, 2018), 46–68; Stephanie Freeman, "Ronald Reagan and the Nuclear Freeze Movement," in *The Reagan Moment: America and the World in the 1980s*, ed. Jonathan R. Hunt and Simon Miles (Ithaca, NY: Cornell University Press, 2021), 144–61; Henry Richard Maar III, *Freeze! The Grassroots Movement to Halt the Arms Race and End the Cold War* (Ithaca, NY: Cornell University Press, 2022).

11. Mikhail Gorbachev, *Memoirs*, trans. Georges Peronansky and Tatjana Varsavsky (New York: Doubleday, 1995), 443.

12. "With Lenin Watching," *New York Times*, June 1, 1988.

13. For a discussion of these comparative advantages, see John D. Maurer, "The Forgotten Side of Arms Control: Enhancing U.S. Competitive Advantage, Offsetting Enemy Strengths," *War on the Rocks*, June 27, 2018, https://warontherocks.com/2018/06/the-forgotten-side-of-arms-control-enhancing-u-s-competitive-advantage-offsetting-enemy-strengths/.

14. William Taubman, *Gorbachev: His Life and Times* (New York: W. W. Norton, 2017). On the shifting balance of power in US-Soviet relations and the asymmetrical nature of the deals reached in the 1980s, see Simon Miles, *Engaging the Evil Empire: Washington, Moscow, and the Beginning of the End of the Cold War* (Ithaca, NY: Cornell University Press, 2020), esp. 5–6; Joshua R. Itzkowitz Shifrinson, *Rising Titans, Falling Giants: How Great Powers Exploit Power Shifts* (Ithaca, NY: Cornell University Press, 2018), 119–59.

15. Sarah B. Snyder, *Human Rights Activism and the End of the Cold War: A Transnational History of the Helsinki Network* (Cambridge: Cambridge University Press, 2011). On the Helsinki Final Act's impact beyond the emergence of human rights monitoring groups, see Michael Cotey Morgan, *The Final Act: The Helsinki Accords and the Transformation of the Cold War* (Princeton, NJ: Princeton University Press, 2018).

16. On the creation of Live Oak, see Timothy Andrews Sayle, *Enduring Alliance: A History of NATO and the Postwar Global Order* (Ithaca, NY: Cornell University Press, 2019), 77–97. A comprehensive history of the organization can be found in Harald

van Nes, *Das Ringen um Berlin im Kalten Krieg: Die Geschichte von Live Oak* (Berlin: De Gruyter Oldenbourg, 2021).

17. "London Declaration."

18. Sayle, *Enduring Alliance*, 233.

19. George H. W. Bush, Václav Havel memorandum of conversation, November 18, 1990, GBL, MT.

20. "North Atlantic Cooperation Council Statement on Dialogue, Partnership and Cooperation," December 20, 1991, NATO, https://www.nato.int/docu/comm/49-95/c911220a.htm.

21. Stephen Flanagan to Dennis Ross and Robert Zoellick, "Developing Criteria for Future NATO Members: Now Is the Time," May 1, 1992, GBL, NSC, BLF, CF01526, folder "NATO Membership."

22. What is now possible for historians to reconstruct with the available documentary record is showcased in M. E. Sarotte, *Not One Inch: America, Russia, and the Making of Post–Cold War Stalemate* (New Haven, CT: Yale University Press, 2021), esp. 8–13.

23. NATO's official information dates US concerns back to May 23, 2013. See "NATO and the INF Treaty," August 2, 2019, NATO, https://www.nato.int/cps/en/natohq/topics_166100.htm. The Russians' intermediate-range missile is typically referred to as the 9M729 or SSC-8.

24. Michael R. Gordon, "U.S. Says Russia Tested Cruise Missile, Violating Treaty," *New York Times*, July 28, 2014.

25. See, for example, "Meeting on Defence Industry Development," May 13, 2016, Office of the President of Russia, http://en.kremlin.ru/events/president/news/51911.

26. "Meeting of the Valdai International Discussion Club," October 27, 2016, Office of the President of Russia, http://en.kremlin.ru/events/president/news/53151.

27. Zeke Miller and Michael Balsamo, "Trump Says US Will Pull Out of Intermediate Range Nuke Pact," Associated Press, October 20, 2018, https://apnews.com/article/north-america-donald-trump-ap-top-news-politics-russia-99ab3fb09bbe41a497db0162a3c213be.

28. Michael R. Pompeo, "Remarks to the Press," February 1, 2019, US State Department, https://2017-2021.state.gov/remarks-to-the-press-12/index.html.

29. Michael R. Pompeo, "U.S. Withdrawal from the INF Treaty on August 2, 2019, US Department of State, https://2017-2021.state.gov/u-s-withdrawal-from-the-inf-treaty-on-august-2-2019/index.html.

30. "INF Nuclear Treaty: US Pulls Out of Cold War–Era Pact with Russia," October 2, 2019, *BBC News*, https://www.bbc.com/news/world-us-canada-49198565.

31. See, for example, John D. Maurer, "The Dual-Track Approach: A Long-Term Strategy for a Post–INF Treaty World," War on the Rocks, April 10, 2019, https://warontherocks.com/2019/04/the-dual-track-approach-a-long-term-strategy-for-a-post-inf-treaty-world/; Luis Simón and Alexander Lanoszka, "The Post-INF European Missile Balance: Thinking about NATO's Deterrence Strategy," *Texas National Security Review* 3, no. 2 (2020): 12–30.

32. Nuclear Posture Review, February 2018, US Department of Defense, https://media.defense.gov/2018/Feb/02/2001872886/-1/-1/1/2018-nuclear-posture-review-final-report.pdf.

33. Contemporaries did take solace from this same thinking. "To recall that crisis-ridden past," Josef Joffe argued, "is to draw some reassurance from it." See Josef Joffe testimony, *Political and Military Issues in the Atlantic Alliance: Hearings before the Subcommittee on Europe and the Middle East of the Committee on Foreign Affairs, House of Representatives, Ninety-Eighth Congress, Second Session, August 1, October 1, 1984* (Washington, DC: Government Printing Office, 1984), 21.

BIBLIOGRAPHY

Archives

Belgium

Archives of the North Atlantic Treaty Organization, Brussels

Canada

Library and Archives Canada, Ottawa, Ontario
McMaster University Library, Hamilton, Ontario

France

Archives Diplomatiques, La Courneuve

Germany

Archiv der sozialen Demokratie, Bonn
Archiv Grünes Gedächtnis, Berlin
Bundesarchiv, Koblenz
Politisches Archiv des Auswärtigen Amts, Berlin

The Netherlands

International Institute for Social History, Amsterdam

United Kingdom

Liddell Hart Centre for Military Archives, King's College London, London
British Library of Political and Economic Sciences, London School of
    Economics and Political Science, London
National Archives, Kew

United States

David M. Rubenstein Rare Book and Manuscript Library, Duke Univer-
    sity, Durham, North Carolina
George Bush Presidential Library, College Station, Texas
Gerald R. Ford Presidential Library, Ann Arbor, Michigan
Hoover Institution Archives, Palo Alto, California

Jimmy Carter Presidential Library, Atlanta, Georgia
John F. Kennedy Presidential Library, Boston, Massachusetts
Library of Congress, Washington, DC
Lyndon Baines Johnson Presidential Library, Austin, Texas
National Archives and Records Administration, College Park, Maryland
Richard Nixon Presidential Library, Yorba Linda, California
Ronald Reagan Presidential Library, Simi Valley, California
Swarthmore College Peace Collection, Swarthmore, Pennsylvania
Yale University Archives, New Haven, Connecticut

Digital Collections

Access to Archival Databases, https://aad.archives.gov/aad/index.jsp
American Archive for Public Broadcasting, https://americanarchive.org
British Diplomatic Oral History Programme, Churchill Archives Centre, https://archivesearch.lib.cam.ac.uk/repositories/9/resources/1529
CIA Records Search Tool, https://www.cia.gov/readingroom/
Foreign Affairs Oral History Program, Association for Diplomatic Studies and Training, https://adst.org/oral-history/
GBH Archives, https://openvault.wgbh.org
Releases from the Interagency Security Classifications Appeals Panel, https://www.archives.gov/declassification/iscap/releases
Presidential Oral Histories, Miller Center of Public Affairs, University of Virginia, https://millercenter.org/
Margaret Thatcher Foundation Archive, https://www.margaretthatcher.org/archive
Vanderbilt Television News Archive, https://tvnews.vanderbilt.edu
Vera and Donald Blinken Open Society Archives, https://www.osaarchivum.org
Wilson Center Digital Archive, https://digitalarchive.wilsoncenter.org

Published Document Collections

Banks, William K., ed. *Public Papers of the Presidents of the United States: George Bush 1989*, vol. 1. Washington, DC: Government Printing Office, 1987.
——. *Public Papers of the Presidents of the United States: Ronald Reagan 1984*, vol. 2. Washington, DC: Government Printing Office, 1987.
——. *Public Papers of the Presidents of the United States: Ronald Reagan 1987*, vol. 1. Washington, DC: Government Printing Office, 1989.
——. *Public Papers of the Presidents of the United States: Ronald Reagan 1987*, vol. 2. Washington, DC: Government Printing Office, 1989.
——. *Public Papers of the Presidents of the United States: Ronald Reagan 1988*, vol. 1. Washington, DC: Government Printing Office, 1990.

Bennett, Gill, and Keith A. Hamilton, eds. *Documents on British Policy Overseas* series 3, vol. 2: *The Conference on Security and Cooperation in Europe, 1972–75*. London: Stationery Office, 1997.

Bennett, M. Todd, ed. *Foreign Relations of the United States 1969–1976*, vol. 34: *National Security Policy*. Washington, DC: Government Printing Office, 2011.

Bernbaum, John A., Lisle A. Rose, and Charles S. Sampson, eds. *Foreign Relations of the United States 1952–1954*, vol. 5, pt. 2: *Western European Security*. Washington, DC: Government Printing Office, 1983.

Burr, William, ed. National Security Archive Electronic Briefing Book no. 301: Thirtieth Anniversary of NATO's Dual-Track Decision: The Road to the Euromissiles Crisis and the End of the Cold War. December 10, 2009. https://nsarchive2.gwu.edu/nukevault/ebb301/index.htm.

Burr, William, and Robert Wampler, eds. National Security Archive Electronic Briefing Book no. 139: "The Master of the Game": Paul H. Nitze and U.S. Cold War Strategy from Truman to Reagan. October 27, 2004. https://nsarchive2.gwu.edu/NSAEBB/NSAEBB139/index.htm.

Chance, Dorothy G., and Peter J. Haley, eds. *Public Papers of the Presidents of the United States: Richard Nixon 1969*. Washington, DC: Government Printing Office, 1971.

Charles, Elizabeth C., ed. *Foreign Relations of the United States 1981–1988*, vol. 5: *Soviet Union, March 1985–October 1986*. Washington, DC: Government Printing Office, 2020.

Das Gupta, Amit, Tim Geiger, Matthias Peter, Fabian Hilfrich, and Mechthild Lindemann, eds. *Akten zur Auswärtigen Politik der Bundesrepublik Deutschland 1977*. Munich: Oldenbourg, 2008.

Donohoe, Margaret M., Richard L. Claypoole, Katherine A. Mellody, and Kenneth R. Payne, eds. *Public Papers of the Presidents of the United States: Jimmy Carter 1977*, vol 1. Washington, DC: Government Printing Office, 1977.

——. *Public Papers of the Presidents of the United States: Jimmy Carter 1977*, vol 2. Washington, DC: Government Printing Office, 1978.

Eibl, Franz, and Hubert Zimmerman, eds. *Akten zur Auswärtigen Politik der Bundesrepublik Deutschland 1969*. Munich: Oldenbourg, 2000.

Galdi, Ernest J., ed. *Public Papers of the Presidents of the United States: Richard Nixon 1971*. Washington, DC: Government Printing Office, 1972.

Geiger, Tim, Amit Das Gupta, and Tim Szatkowski, eds. *Akten zur Auswärtigen Politik der Bundesrepublik Deutschland 1980*. Munich: Oldenbourg, 2011.

Geiger, Tim, Matthias Peter, and Mechthild Lindemann, eds. *Akten zur Auswärtigen Politik der Bundesrepublik Deutschland 1983*. Munich: Oldenbourg, 2014.

Geyer, David C., and Douglas E. Selvage, eds. *Soviet-American Relations: The Détente Years, 1969–1972*. Washington, DC: Government Printing Office, 2007.

Greene, Wilma P., and William K. Banks, eds. *Public Papers of the Presidents of the United States: Ronald Reagan 1984*, vol. 1. Washington, DC: Government Printing Office, 1986.

Greene, Wilma P., Katherine A. Mellody, and Kenneth R. Payne, eds. *Public Papers of the Presidents of the United States: Ronald Reagan 1981*. Washington, DC: Government Printing Office, 1982.

——. *Public Papers of the Presidents of the United States: Ronald Reagan 1982*, vol 1. Washington, DC: Government Printing Office, 1983.

Hamilton, Keith A., and Patrick Salmon, eds. *Documents on British Policy Overseas*, series 3, vol. 4: *The Year of Europe: America, Europe and the Energy Crisis, 1972–1974*. London: Routledge, 2006.

Hill, Maxine L., and Thomas D. Kevan, eds. *Public Papers of the Presidents of the United States: Ronald Reagan 1983*, vol 1. Washington, DC: Government Printing Office, 1984.

Humphrey, David C., and Charles S. Sampson, eds. *Foreign Relations of the United States 1964–1968*, vol. 14: *Soviet Union*. Washington, DC: Government Printing Office, 2001.

Keefer, Edward C., Charles S. Sampson, and Louis J. Smith, eds. *Foreign Relations of the United States 1961–1963*, vol. 11: *Cuban Missile Crisis and Aftermath*. Washington, DC: Government Printing Office, 1996.

Kevan, Thomas D., ed. *Public Papers of the Presidents of the United States: Ronald Reagan 1983*, vol. 2. Washington, DC: Government Printing Office, 1985.

Koopmann, Martin, Matthias Peter, and Daniela Taschler, eds. *Akten zur Auswärtigen Politik der Bundesrepublik Deutschland 1971*. Munich: Oldenbourg, 2002.

Landa, Ronald D., James E. Miller, David S. Patterson, and Charles S. Sampson, eds. *Foreign Relations of the United States 1958–1960*, vol. 7: *Western Europe*. Washington, DC: Government Printing Office, 1993.

Mahan, Erin R., ed. *Foreign Relations of the United States 1969–1976*, vol. 12: *Soviet Union, January 1969–October 1970*. Washington, DC: Government Printing Office, 2006.

——. *Foreign Relations of the United States 1969–1976*, vol. 32: *SALT I, 1969–1972*. Washington, DC: Government Printing Office, 2010.

——. *Foreign Relations of the United States 1969–1976*, vol. 33: *SALT II, 1972–1980*. Washington, DC: Government Printing Office, 2013.

Mellody, Katherine A., Kenneth R. Payne, and Brian L. Hermes, eds. *Public Papers of the Presidents of the United States: Jimmy Carter 1978*, vol. 1. Washington, DC: Government Printing Office, 1979.

Miller, James E., and Laurie Van Hook, eds. *Foreign Relations of the United States 1969–1976*, vol. 41: *Western Europe; NATO, 1969–1972*. Washington, DC: Government Printing Office, 2012.

Nary, R. William, and Ruth Ihara, eds. *Documents on Disarmament 1977*. Washington, DC: Government Printing Office, 1979.

Pautsch, Ilse Dorothee, Daniela Taschler, Franz Eibl, Frank Heinlein, Mechthild Lindemann, and Matthias Peter, eds. *Akten zur Auswärtigen Politik der Bundesrepublik Deutschland 1970*. Munich: Oldenbourg, 2001.

Pedlow, Gregory W., ed. *NATO Strategy Documents, 1949–1969*. Brussels: Historical Office, Supreme Headquarters Allied Powers Europe, 1997.

Peter, Matthias, Michael Ploetz, and Tim Geiger, eds. *Akten zur Auswärtigen Politik der Bundesrepublik Deutschland 1976*. Munich: Oldenbourg, 2007.

Ploetz, Michael, Mechthild Lindemann, and Christoph Johannes Franzen, eds. *Akten zur Auswärtigen Politik der Bundesrepublik Deutschland 1985*. Munich: Oldenbourg, 2016.

Ploetz, Michael, Tim Szatkowski, and Judith Michel, eds. *Akten zur Auswärtigen Politik der Bundesrepublik Deutschland 1982*. Munich: Oldenbourg, 2013.

Plümer, Lutz, ed. *Positionen der Friedensbewegung: Die Auseinandersetzung um den US-Mittelstreckenraketenbeschluß: Dokumente, Appelle, Beiträge*. Frankfurt: Sendler, 1981.

Rasmussen, Kathleen B., ed. *Foreign Relations of the United States 1969–1976*, vol. E-15, pt. 2: *Western Europe, 1973–1976*. Washington, DC: Government Printing Office, 2014.

Reid, Warren R., ed. *Public Papers of the Presidents of the United States: Lyndon B. Johnson*, vol. 2. Washington, DC: Government Printing Office, 1967.

Sampson, Charles S., ed. *Foreign Relations of the United States 1964–1968*, vol. 13: *Western Europe Region*. Washington, DC: Government Printing Office, 1995.

Savranskaya, Svetlana, and Thomas Blanton, eds. National Security Archive Electronic Briefing Book no. 563: Gorbachev's Nuclear Initiative of January 1986 and the Road to Reykjavik. https://nsarchive.gwu.edu/briefing-book/nuclear-vault-russia-programs/2016-10-12/gorbachevs-nuclear-initiative-january-1986.

———. National Security Archive Electronic Briefing Book no. 544: The Gorbachev File. March 2, 2016. https://nsarchive.gwu.edu/briefing-book/2016-03-02/gorbachev-file.

———. National Security Archive Electronic Briefing Book no. 238: The INF Treaty and the Washington Summit: 20 Years Later. December 10, 2007. https://nsarchive2.gwu.edu/NSAEBB/NSAEBB238/index.htm.

Selvage, Douglas E., ed. *Foreign Relations of the United States 1969–1976*, vol. 39: *European Security*. Washington, DC: Government Printing Office, 2007.

Smith, Louis J., and David H. Herschler, eds. *Foreign Relations of the United States 1969–1976*, vol. 1: *Foundations of Foreign Policy, 1969–1972*. Washington, DC: Government Printing Office, 2003.

Szatkowski, Tim, Tim Geiger, and Jens Jost Hofmann, eds. *Akten zur Auswärtigen Politik der Bundesrepublik Deutschland 1987*. Munich: Oldenbourg, 2018.

Taschler, Daniela, Amit Das Gupta, and Michael Mayer, eds. *Akten zur Auswärtigen Politik der Bundesrepublik Deutschland 1978*. Munich: Oldenbourg, 2009.

Taschler, Daniela, Tim Szatkowski, and Christoph Johannes Franzen, eds. *Akten zur Auswärtigen Politik der Bundesrepublik Deutschland 1989*. Munich: Oldenbourg, 2020.

Wilson, James Graham, ed. *Foreign Relations of the United States 1981–1988*, vol. 3: *Soviet Union, January 1981–January 1983*. Washington, DC: Government Printing Office, 2016.

———. *Foreign Relations of the United States 1981–1988*, vol. 6: *Soviet Union, October 1986–January 1989*. Washington, DC: Government Printing Office, 2016.

Publications and Media

Adamsky, Dmitry. "'Not Crying Wolf': Soviet Intelligence and the 1983 War Scare." In Nuti et al., *Euromissile Crisis*, 49–65.

Ambrose, Matthew J. *The Control Agenda: A History of the Strategic Arms Limitation Talks*. Ithaca, NY: Cornell University Press, 2018.

Andrew, Christopher, and Oleg Gordievsky. *KGB: The Inside Story of Its Operations from Lenin to Gorbachev.* London: Hodder & Stoughton, 1990.

Arbatov, Alexei. "What Lessons Learned?" In *Turning Points in Ending the Cold War,* edited by Kiron K. Skinner, 40–62. Stanford, CA: Hoover Institution, 2007.

Auger, Vincent A. *The Dynamics of Foreign Policy Analysis: The Carter Administration and the Neutron Bomb.* Lanham, MD: Rowman & Littlefield, 1996.

Badham, John, dir. *WarGames.* United Artists and Sherwood Productions, 1983.

Baker, James A., III. *The Politics of Diplomacy: Revolution, War and Peace, 1989–1992.* With Thomas M. DeFrank. New York: G. P. Putnam's Sons, 1995.

Bange, Oliver. "'Keeping Détente Alive': Inner-German Relations under Helmut Schmidt and Erich Honecker, 1974–1982." In *The Crisis of Détente in Europe: From Helsinki to Gorbachev, 1975–1985,* edited by Leopoldo Nuti, 230–43. London: Routledge, 2009.

———. "SS-20 and Pershing II: Weapon Systems and the Dynamization of East-West Relations." In Becker-Schaum et al., *Nuclear Crisis,* 70–86.

Bange, Oliver, and Poul Villaume. Introduction to *The Long Détente: Changing Concepts of Security and Cooperation in Europe, 1950s–1980s,* edited by Oliver Bange and Poul Villaume, 1–15. Budapest: Central European University Press, 2017.

Barrass, Gordon. *The Great Cold War: A Journey through the Hall of Mirrors.* Stanford, CA: Stanford University Press, 2009.

Barton, Oliver. "'The Most Staunch and Dependable of the Allies'? Britain and the Zero Option." In *The INF Treaty of 1987: A Reappraisal,* edited by Philipp Gassert, Tim Geiger, and Hermann Wentker, 91–122. Göttingen, Germany: Vandenhoeck & Ruprecht, 2021.

Baur, Philipp. "Nuclear Doomsday Scenarios in Film, Literature, and Music." In Becker-Schaum et al., *Nuclear Crisis,* 322–37.

Becker-Schaum, Christoph. "The Institutional Organization of the Peace Movement." In Becker-Schaum et al., *Nuclear Crisis,* 154–72.

Becker-Schaum, Christoph, Philipp Gassert, Martin Klimke, Wilfried Mausbach, and Marianne Zepp, eds. *Entrüstet Euch! Nuklearkrise, NATO-Doppelbeschluss und Friedensbewegung.* Paderborn, Germany: Schöningh, 2012.

———. *The Nuclear Crisis: The Arms Race, Cold War Anxiety, and the German Peace Movement of the 1980s.* New York: Berghahn Books, 2016.

———. "Introduction: The Nuclear Crisis, NATO's Double-Track Decision, and the Peace Movement of the 1980s." In Becker-Schaum et al., *Nuclear Crisis,* 1–36.

Berger, Stefan, and Norman LaPorte. "Between Scylla and Charybdis: END and Its Attempt to Overcome the Bipolar World Order in the 1980s." *Labour History* 111 (2016): 11–25.

Binns, Peter. *Missile Madness: The New Weapons Systems and How They Threaten Your Life.* 2nd ed. London: East End Offset, 1981.

Bittman, Ladislav. *The KGB and Soviet Disinformation: An Insider's View.* Washington, DC: Pergamon-Brassey's, 1985.

Bluth, Christoph. "The Origins of MBFR: West German Policy Priorities and Conventional Arms Control." *War in History* 7, no. 2 (2000): 181–206.

———. *Two Germanies and Military Security in Europe.* Basingstoke, UK: Palgrave Macmillan, 2002.

Bowie, Robert R. "Tensions within the Alliance." *Foreign Affairs* 42, no. 1 (1963): 49–69.

Bozo, Frédéric. "Détente versus Alliance: France, the United States and the Politics of the Harmel Report (1964–1968)." *Contemporary European History* 7, no. 3 (1998): 343–60.

——. *Deux stratégies pour l'Europe. De Gaulle, les États-Unis et l'Alliance atlantique 1958–1969.* Paris: Plon, 1996.

——. "France, the Euromissiles, and the End of the Cold War." In Nuti et al., *Euromissile Crisis*, 196–212.

——. "The Sanctuary and the Glacis: France, the Federal Republic of Germany, and Nuclear Weapons in the 1980s (Part 1)." *Journal of Cold War Studies* 22, no. 3 (2020): 119–79.

Brands, Hal. *What Good Is Grand Strategy? Power and Purpose in American Statecraft from Harry S. Truman to George W. Bush.* Ithaca, NY: Cornell University Press, 2014.

Brosio, Manlio. "NATO and East-West Détente." *NATO Letter* 15, no. 12 (1967): 2–9.

Brown, Archie. "The Change to Engagement in Britain's Cold War Policy: The Origins of the Thatcher-Gorbachev Relationship." *Journal of Cold War Studies* 10, no. 3 (2008): 3–47.

Brunet, Luc-André. "Unhelpful Fixer? Canada, the Euromissile Crisis, and Pierre Trudeau's Peace Initiative, 1983–1984." *International History Review* 41, no. 6 (2019): 1145–67.

Brzezinski, Zbigniew. *Power and Principle: Memoirs of the National Security Adviser 1977–1981.* New York: Farrar, Strauss and Giroux, 1983.

Bundy, McGeorge. "'No First Use' Needs Careful Study." *Bulletin of the Atomic Scientists* 38, no. 6 (1982): 6–8.

Bundy, McGeorge, George F. Kennan, Robert S. McNamara, and Gerard Smith. "Nuclear Weapons and the Atlantic Alliance." *Foreign Affairs* 60, no. 4 (1982): 753–68.

Burke, Patrick. "European Nuclear Disarmament: Transnational Peace Campaigning in the 1980s." In Conze, Klimke, and Varon, *Nuclear Threats*, 227–50.

Burr, William. "The Nixon Administration, the 'Horror Strategy,' and the Search for Limited Nuclear Options, 1969–1972." *Journal of Cold War Studies* 7, no. 3 (2005): 34–78.

——. "A Question of Confidence: Theater Nuclear Forces, US Policy toward Germany, and the Origins of the Euromissile Crisis, 1975–1976." In Nuti et al., *Euromissile Crisis*, 123–38.

Caldicott, Helen. *Missile Envy: The Arms Race and Nuclear War.* New York: William Morrow, 1984.

Callaghan, James. *Time and Chance.* London: Collins, 1987.

Cameron, James. *The Double Game: The Demise of America's First Missile Defense System and the Rise of Strategic Arms Limitation.* New York: Oxford University Press, 2017.

——. "Moscow, 1972." In *Transcending the Cold War: Summits, Statecraft, and the Dissolution of Bipolarity in Europe*, edited by Kristina Spohr and David Reynolds, 67–91. Oxford: Oxford University Press, 2016.

Carr, Jonathan. *Helmut Schmidt: Helmsman of Germany*. London: Wiedenfeld & Nicolson, 1985.

Carter, Jimmy. *Keeping Faith: Memoirs of a President*. New York: Bantam, 1982.

——. *White House Diary*. New York: Farrar, Straus and Giroux, 2010.

Carver, Michael. "No First Use: A View from Europe." *Bulletin of the Atomic Scientists* 39, no. 3 (1983): 22–26.

Černy, Vladimír, and Petr Suchý. "Spies and Peaceniks: Czechoslovak Intelligence Attempts to Thwart NATO's Dual-Track Decision." *Cold War History* 20, no. 3 (2020): 273–91.

Chamberlin, Paul Thomas. *The Cold War's Killing Fields: Rethinking the Long Peace*. New York: HarperCollins, 2018.

Charles, Elizabeth C. "Gorbachev and the Decision to Decouple the Arms Control Package: How the Breakdown of the Reykjavik Summit Led to the Elimination of the Euromissiles." In Nuti et al., *Euromissile Crisis*, 66–84.

Charles, Elizabeth C., and James Graham Wilson. "Confronting the Soviet Threat: Reagan's Approach to Policymaking." In *The Reagan Moment: America and the World in the 1980s*, edited by Jonathan R. Hunt and Simon Miles, 105–22. Ithaca, NY: Cornell University Press, 2021.

Chernyaev, Anatoly. *My Six Years with Gorbachev*. Translated and edited by Robert D. English and Elizabeth Tucker. University Park: Pennsylvania State University Press, 2000.

Chiampan, Andrea. "Nuclear Weapons, 'Nuclear Ideas,' and Protests: Did They Matter?" In *New Perspectives on the End of the Cold War*, edited by Bernhard Blumenau, Jussi M. Hanhimäki, and Barbara Zanchetta, 46–68. London: Routledge, 2018.

——. "The Origins of the Euromissile Crisis, 1969–1979." PhD diss., Graduate Institute of International and Development Studies, 2017.

——. "The Reagan Administration and the INF Controversy, 1981–83." *Diplomatic History* 44, no. 5 (2020): 860–84.

——. "'Those European Chicken Littles': Reagan, NATO, and the Polish Crisis, 1981–2." *International History Review* 37, no. 4 (2015): 682–99.

The CIA and the Media: Hearings before the Subcommittee on Oversight of the Permanent Select Committee on Intelligence, House of Representatives, Ninety-Fifth Congress, First and Second Sessions, December 27, 28, 29, 1977, January 4, 5, and April 20, 1978. Washington, DC: Government Printing Office, 1978.

Coates, Ken. *No Cruise Missiles, No SS20's: European Nuclear Disarmament*. Nottingham, UK: Russell, 1981.

Colbourn, Susan. "'Cruising toward Nuclear Danger': Canadian Anti-nuclear Activism, Pierre Trudeau's Peace Mission, and the Transatlantic Partnership." *Cold War History* 18, no. 1 (2018): 19–36.

——. "Debating Détente: NATO's Tindemans Initiative, or Why the Harmel Report Still Mattered in the 1980s." *Journal of Strategic Studies* 43, nos. 6–7 (2020): 897–919.

——. "The Elephant in the Room: Rethinking Cruise Missile Testing and Pierre Trudeau's Peace Mission." In *Undiplomatic History: The New Study of Canada and the World*, edited by Asa McKercher and Philip van Huizen, 253–76. Montreal: McGill–Queen's University Press, 2019.

———. "An Interpreter or Two: Defusing NATO's Siberian Pipeline Dispute, 1981–1982." *Journal of Transatlantic Studies* 18, no. 2 (2020): 131–51.

Colbourn, Susan, and Mathias Haeussler. "Once More, With Feeling: Transatlantic Relations in the Reagan Years." In *The Reagan Moment: America and the World in the 1980s*, edited by Jonathan R. Hunt and Simon Miles, 123–43. Ithaca, NY: Cornell University Press, 2021.

Coleman, Bradley Lynn, and Kyle Longley. Introduction to *Reagan and the World: Leadership and National Security 1981–1989*, edited by Bradley Lynn Coleman and Kyle Longley, 1–10. Lexington: University Press of Kentucky, 2017.

Conze, Eckart. "Missile Bases as Concentration Camps: The Role of National Socialism, the Second World War, and the Holocaust in the West German Discourse on Nuclear Armament." In Conze, Klimke, and Varon, *Nuclear Threats*, 79–98.

Conze, Eckart, Martin Klimke, and Jeremy Varon, eds. *Nuclear Threats, Nuclear Fear and the Cold War of the 1980s*. Cambridge: Cambridge University Press, 2017.

Craig, Campbell, and Fredrik Logevall. *America's Cold War: The Politics of Insecurity*. Cambridge, MA: Belknap Press of Harvard University Press, 2010.

Critchley, Julian. "Should the First Use of Nuclear Arms Be Renounced?" *RUSI Journal* 127, no. 4 (1982): 32–34.

Daalder, Ivo H. *The Nature and Practice of Flexible Response: NATO Strategy and Theater Nuclear Forces since 1967*. New York: Columbia University Press, 1991.

Danielsen, Helge. "Norway and the Dual-Track Decision: The Role of Johan Jørgen Holst." In Nuti et al., *Euromissile Crisis*, 213–30.

Davis, Lynn E. "NATO's Requirements and Policy for LRTNF." In Rinne, *History of NATO TNF Policy*, 169–94.

de Graaf, Beatrice. "Stasi Operations in the Netherlands, 1979–89." *Studies in Intelligence* 52, no. 1 (2008): 1–16.

Dean, Jonathan. *Watershed in Europe: Dismantling the East-West Military Confrontation*. Lexington, MA: Lexington, 1987.

Deats, Richard Baggett. "Seeing the Soviets as People: Reflections on a Journey for Peace." *Fellowship* 48, nos. 10–11 (1982): 3–7.

Del Pero, Mario. "Henry Kissinger's Three Europes." *Journal of Transatlantic Studies* 17, no. 1 (2019): 5–21.

Discriminate Deterrence: Report of the Commission on Integrated Long-Term Strategy. Washington, DC: Government Printing Office, 1988.

Dobrynin, Anatoly. *In Confidence: Moscow's Ambassador to America's Six Cold War Presidents (1962–1986)*. New York: Random House, 1995.

Dobson, Alan P. "The Reagan Administration, Economic Warfare, and Starting to Close Down the Cold War." *Diplomatic History* 29, no. 3 (2005): 531–56.

Donaghy, Aaron. *The Second Cold War: Carter, Reagan, and the Domestic Politics of Foreign Policy*. Cambridge: Cambridge University Press, 2021.

Dougherty, James E. "The Atlantic Community—the Psychological Milieu." In *Atlantic Community in Crisis: A Redefinition of the Transatlantic Relationship*, edited by Walter F. Hahn and Robert L. Pfaltzgraff Jr., 30–51. New York: Pergamon, 1979.

———. "Strategy, Politics, and Ethical Feelings: A Perspective of the Protest Movement." In *Shattering Europe's Defense Consensus: The Antinuclear Protest Movement and the Future of NATO*, edited by James E. Dougherty and Robert Pfaltzgraff Jr., 1–14. Washington, DC: Pergamon-Brassey's, 1985.

Draper, Theodore. "The Western Misalliance." In *European Peace Movements and the Future of the Western Alliance*, edited by Walter Laqueur and Robert Hunter, 56–111. New Brunswick, NJ: Transaction, 1985.

Duchêne, François. "SALT, the *Ostpolitik*, and the Post–Cold War Context." *World Today* 26, no. 12 (1970): 500–11.

Dujardin, Vincent. "From Helsinki to the Missiles Question: A Minor Role for Small Countries? The Case of Belgium (1973–1985)." In Nuti, *Crisis of Détente in Europe*, 72–85.

"Dutch Statement on Cruise Missile Deployment." *Survival* 26, no. 5 (1984): 238–39.

Eagleburger, Lawrence S. "The US Approach to the Negotiations on Intermediate-Range Nuclear Forces." *NATO Review* 1 (1982): 7–11.

Ellison, James. "Defeating the General: Anglo-American Relations, Europe and the NATO Crisis of 1966." *Cold War History* 6, no. 1 (2006): 85–111.

Engel, Jeffrey A. *When the World Seemed New: George H. W. Bush and the End of the Cold War*. Boston: Houghton Mifflin Harcourt, 2017.

Esnos, Tyler. "Reagan's Economic War on the Soviet Union." *Diplomatic History* 42, no. 2 (2018): 281–304.

European Nuclear Disarmament. "A Nuclear Free Europe." Insert in E. P. Thompson, *Protest and Survive*. London: Campaign for Nuclear Disarmament and Bertrand Russell Peace Foundation, 1980.

European Security Study. *Strengthening Conventional Deterrence in Europe: Proposals for the 1980's*. London: Macmillan, 1983.

Evangelista, Matthew. *Unarmed Forces: The Transnational Movement to End the Cold War*. Ithaca, NY: Cornell University Press, 1999.

Fahlenbrach, Kathrin, and Laura Stapane. "Visual and Media Strategies of the Peace Movement." In Becker-Schaum et al., *Nuclear Crisis*, 222–41.

Fairbairns, Zoë, James Cameron, and Ed Barber. *Peace Moves: Nuclear Protest in the 1980s: Photographs by Ed Barber*. London: Chatto & Windus, Hogarth, 1984.

Fearon, James D. "Domestic Political Audiences and the Escalation of International Disputes." *American Political Science Review* 88, no. 3 (1994): 577–92.

Finan, James S. "Europe, the Super Powers and SALT." *Queen's Quarterly* 78, no. 3 (1971): 456–61.

Fink, Carole, and Bernd Schaefer. "Introduction." In *Ostpolitik, 1969–1974: European and Global Responses*, edited by Carole Fink and Bernd Schaefer, 1–11. Washington, DC, and Cambridge: German Historical Institute and Cambridge University Press, 2009.

Fischer, Beth A. *The Reagan Reversal: Foreign Policy and the End of the Cold War*. Columbia: University of Missouri Press, 1997.

Ford, Gerald. *A Time to Heal: The Autobiography of Gerald R. Ford*. New York: Harper & Row, 1979.

Freedman, Lawrence. "The First Two Generations of Nuclear Strategy." In *Makers of Modern Strategy: From Machiavelli to the Nuclear Age*, edited by Peter Paret, 735–78. Princeton, NJ: Princeton University Press, 1986.

———. "The Wilderness Years." In *The Nuclear Confrontation in Europe*, edited by Jeffrey D. Boutwell, Paul Doty, and Gregory F. Treverton, 44–66. London: Croom Helm, 1985.

Freeman, Stephanie. "The Making of an Accidental Crisis: The United States and the NATO Dual-Track Decision of 1979." *Diplomacy & Statecraft* 25 (2014): 331–55.

———. "Ronald Reagan and the Nuclear Freeze Movement." In *The Reagan Moment: America and the World in the 1980s*, edited by Jonathan R. Hunt and Simon Miles, 144–61. Ithaca, NY: Cornell University Press, 2021.

Fursenko, Aleksandr, and Timothy Naftali. *"One Hell of a Gamble": Khrushchev, Castro, and Kennedy, 1958–1964*. New York: W. W. Norton, 1997.

The Future of Europe: Hearings before the Committee on Foreign Relations and the Subcommittee on European Affairs of the United States Senate, One Hundred First Congress, Second Session, December 13, 1989, January 17, February 1 and 22, March 1, 7, 21, 22, 28, and 29, May 9, and June 12, 1990. Washington, DC: Government Printing Office, 1991.

The Future Tasks of the Alliance: NATO "Harmel Report." Brussels: NATO Information Service, 1968.

Gaddis, John Lewis. *The Cold War: A New History*. New York: Penguin, 2007.

———. *The Long Peace: Inquiries into the History of the Cold War*. Oxford: Oxford University Press, 1987.

Gaffney, Henry H. "Euromissiles as the Ultimate Evolution of Theater Nuclear Forces in Europe." *Journal of Cold War Studies* 16, no. 1 (2014): 180–99.

———. "The History of the Euromissiles." World Security Network, March 25, 2004. http://www.worldsecuritynetwork.com/NATO/Gaffney-H.-H/The-History-of-the-Euromissiles.

Gala, Marilena. "The Euromissile Crisis and the Centrality of the 'Zero Option.'" In Nuti et al., *Euromissile Crisis*, 158–75.

Garthoff, Raymond L. *Détente and Confrontation: American-Soviet Relations from Nixon to Reagan*. Rev. ed. Washington, DC: Brookings Institution, 1994.

———. "The Soviet SS-20 Decision." *Survival* 25, no. 3 (1983): 110–19.

Gati, Charles. "Soviet Empire: Alive but Not Well." *Problems of Communism* 34 (1985): 73–86.

Gavin, Francis J. "NATO's Radical Response to the Nuclear Revolution." In *Charter of the North Atlantic Treaty Organization: Together with Scholarly Commentaries and Essential Historical Documents*, edited by Ian Shapiro and Adam Tooze, 177–92. New Haven, CT: Yale University Press, 2018.

———. *Nuclear Statecraft: History and Strategy in America's Atomic Age*. Ithaca, NY: Cornell University Press, 2012.

Geiger, Tim. "Controversies over the Double Zero Option: The Kohl-Genscher Government and the INF Treaty." In *The INF Treaty of 1987: A Reappraisal*, edited by Philipp Gassert, Tim Geiger, and Hermann Wentker, 123–54. Göttingen, Germany: Vandenhoeck & Ruprecht, 2021.

Geiger, Tim, and Jan Hansen. "Did Protest Matter? The Influence of the Peace Movement on the West German Government and the Social Democratic Party, 1977–1983." In Conze, Klimke, and Varon, *Nuclear Threats*, 290–315.

Genest, Marc A. *Negotiating in the Public Eye: The Impact of the Press on the Intermediate-Range Nuclear Force Negotiations*. Stanford, CA: Stanford University Press, 1995.

Genscher, Hans-Dietrich. *Erinnerungen*. Berlin: Siedler Verlag, 1995.

——. *Rebuilding a House Divided: A Memoir by the Architect of Germany's Reunification*. Translated by Thomas Thornton. New York: Broadway, 1998.

Gillessen, Günther. "Countering Soviet Nuclear Supremacy in Europe: Security Policy with Intermediate-Range Missiles." *NATO Review* 30, no. 2 (1982): 18–22.

Giscard d'Estaing, Valéry. *Le pouvoir et la vie*, vol. 2: *L'affrontement*. Paris: Cie 12, 1991.

Glen, John, dir. *Octopussy*. Eon Productions and United Artists, 1983.

Glitman, Maynard W. *The Last Battle of the Cold War: An Inside Account of Negotiating the Intermediate-Range Nuclear Forces Treaty*. New York: Palgrave Macmillan, 2006.

Godderis, Idesbald, and Małgorzata Świder. "Peace or Solidarity? Poland, the Euromissile Crisis, and the 1980s Peace Movement." In Nuti et al., *Euromissile Crisis*, 291–308.

Gorbachev, Mikhail. *Memoirs*. Translated by Georges Peronansky and Tatjana Varsavsky. New York: Doubleday, 1995.

Gotlieb, Allan. *The Washington Diaries, 1981–1989*. Toronto: McClelland & Stewart, 2007.

Grachev, Andrei. *Gorbachev's Gamble: Soviet Foreign Policy and the End of the Cold War*. Cambridge: Polity, 2008.

Graham, Thomas, Jr. *Disarmament Sketches: Three Decades of Arms Control and International Law*. Seattle: University of Washington Press, 2002.

Gray, William Glenn. *Germany's Cold War: The Global Campaign to Isolate East Germany, 1949–1969*. Chapel Hill: University of North Carolina Press, 2003.

"Great Confrontations at the Oxford Union: Caspar Weinberger vs. E. P. Thompson." February 27, 1984. https://www.youtube.com/watch?v=wMdTJJa3kVo.

Grinevsky, Oleg. "The Crisis That Didn't Erupt: The Soviet-American Relationship." In *Turning Points in Ending the Cold War*, edited by Kiron K. Skinner, 63–92. Stanford, CA: Hoover Institution, 2007.

Guasconi, Maria Eleonora. "Public Opinion and the Euromissile Crisis." In Nuti et al., *Euromissile Crisis*, 271–90.

Haftendorn, Helga. "The Link between CSCE and MBFR: Two Sprouts from One Bulb." In *Origins of the European Security System: The Helsinki Process Revisited, 1965–75*, edited by Andreas Wenger, Vojtech Mastny, and Christian Nuenlist, 237–58. London: Routledge, 2008.

——. *NATO and the Nuclear Revolution: A Crisis of Credibility, 1966–1967*. Oxford: Oxford University Press, 1996.

Haig, Alexander M., Jr. *Caveat: Realism, Reagan, and Foreign Policy*. New York: Macmillan, 1984.

——. *Inner Circles: How America Changed the World—a Memoir*. With Charles McCarry. New York: Warner, 1992.

Halliday, Fred. *The Making of the Second Cold War*. London: Verso, 1983.

Halverson, Thomas E. *The Last Great Nuclear Debate: NATO and Short-Range Nuclear Weapons in the 1980s*. Basingstoke, UK: Macmillan, 1995.

Hanhimäki, Jussi M. "Conservative Goals, Revolutionary Outcomes: The Paradox of Détente." *Cold War History* 8, no. 4 (2008): 503–12.

Hansen, Jan. Untitled review in H-Diplo Roundtable 28, no. 30 (June 23, 2017). https://networks.h-net.org/system/files/contributed-files/roundtable-xviii-30.pdf.

Harvey, Kyle. "The Promise of Internationalism: US Anti-nuclear Activism and the European Challenge." In *Making Sense of the Americas: How Protest Related to America in the 1980s and Beyond*, edited by Jan Hansen, Christian Helm, and Frank Reichherzer, 225–44. Frankfurt: Campus, 2015.

Haslam, Jonathan. "Moscow's Misjudgment in Deploying SS-20 Missiles." In Nuti et al., *Euromissile Crisis*, 31–48.

———. *The Soviet Union and the Politics of Nuclear Weapons in Europe, 1969–87: The Problem of the SS-20*. London: Macmillan, 1989.

Hassner, Pierre. "Pacifism and East-West Relations." In *European Peace Movements and the Future of the Western Alliance*, ed. Walter Laqueur and Robert Hunter, 112–43. New Brunswick, NJ: Transaction, 1985.

Heinemann, Winfried. "'Learning by Doing': Disintegrating Factors and the Development of Political Cooperation in Early NATO." In *NATO and the Warsaw Pact: Intrabloc Conflicts*, edited by Mary Ann Heiss and S. Victor Papacosma, 43–57. Kent, OH: Kent State University Press, 2008.

Herf, Jeffrey. *War by Other Means: Soviet Power, West German Resistance, and the Battle of the Euromissiles*. New York: Free Press, 1991.

Hershberg, Jim. "Anatomy of a Controversy: Anatoly F. Dobrynin's Meeting with Robert F. Kennedy, Saturday, October 27, 1962." *Cold War International History Bulletin* 5 (1995): 75–80.

Heseltine, Michael. "The Atlantic Alliance: An Agenda for 1984." *NATO Review* 32, no. 1 (1984): 1–3.

Heuser, Beatrice. "Military Exercises and the Dangers of Misunderstandings: The East-West Crisis of the Early 1980s." In *Military Exercises: Political Messaging and Strategic Impact*, edited by Beatrice Heuser, Tormod Heier, and Guillaume Lasconjarias, 113–37. Rome: NATO Defense College, 2018.

Hobbs, David. *Cruise Missiles: Facts and Issues*. Aberdeen, UK: Centre for Defence Studies, 1982.

Hoffmann, Stanley. "Nuclear Weapons and NATO: Reasons and Unreason," *Foreign Affairs* 60, no. 2 (1981): 327–46.

Hofmann, Arne. *The Emergence of Détente in Europe: Brandt, Kennedy and the Formation of Ostpolitik*. London: Routledge, 2007.

Hogan, J. Michael, and Ted J. Smith III. "Polling on the Issues: Public Opinion and the Nuclear Freeze." *Public Opinion Quarterly* 55, no. 4 (1991): 534–69.

Holloway, David. "The Dynamics of the Euromissile Crisis, 1977–1983." In Nuti et al., *Euromissile Crisis*, 11–28.

Howard, Michael. "Deterrence, Consensus and Reassurance in the Defence of Europe." *Adelphi Papers* 23, no. 184 (1983): 17–26.

Huntington, Samuel P. "Conventional Deterrence and Conventional Retaliation in Europe." *International Security* 8, no. 3 (1983): 32–56.

Inboden, William. "Grand Strategy and Petty Squabbles: The Paradox and Lessons of the Reagan NSC." In *The Power of the Past: History and Statecraft*, edited by Hal Brands and Jeremi Suri, 151–80. Washington, DC: Brookings Institution, 2015.

Independent Commission for Disarmament and Security Issues. *Common Security: A Blueprint for Survival*. New York: Simon & Schuster, 1982.

The INF Treaty: Hearings before the Committee on Foreign Relations, United States Senate, One Hundredth Congress, Second Session on the Treaty between the United States of America and the Union of Soviet Socialist Republics on the Elimination of Their Intermediate-Range and Shorter-Range Missiles, February 16, 18, and 19, 1988, Part 3. Washington, DC: Government Printing Office, 1988.

Inglehart, Ronald. "Postmaterialism in an Environment of Insecurity." *American Political Science Review* 75, no. 4 (1981): 880–900.

——. *The Silent Revolution: Changing Values and Political Styles among Western Publics.* Princeton, NJ: Princeton University Press, 1977.

——. "The Silent Revolution in Europe: Intergenerational Change in Post-Industrial Societies." *American Journal of Political Science* 65 (1971): 991–1017.

Interim Report on Nuclear Weapons in Europe, Prepared by the North Atlantic Assembly's Special Committee on Nuclear Weapons in Europe: A Report to the Committee on Foreign Relations, United States Senate, December 1981. Washington, DC: Government Printing Office, 1981.

Intermediate-Range Nuclear Forces (INF): Progress Report to Ministers by the Special Consultative Group. Brussels: NATO Information Service, 1983.

Ireland, Timothy. "Building NATO's Nuclear Posture 1950–65." In *The Nuclear Confrontation in Europe*, edited by Jeffrey D. Boutwell, Paul Doty, and Gregory F. Treverton, 5–43. London: Croom Helm, 1985.

Jervis, Robert. *Perception and Misperception in International Politics.* New ed. Princeton, NJ: Princeton University Press, 2017.

Jones, Nate. *Able Archer 83: The Secret History of the NATO Exercise That Almost Triggered Nuclear War.* New York: New Press, 2016.

Kaiser, Karl, Georg Leber, Alois Mertes, and Franz-Josef Schulze. "Nuclear Weapons and the Preservation of Peace: A Response to an American Proposal for Renouncing the First Use of Nuclear Weapons." *Foreign Affairs* 60, no. 5 (1982): 1157–70.

Kaiser, Karl, Winston Lord, Thierry de Montbrial, and David Watt. *Western Security: What Has Changed? What Should Be Done?* New York: Council on Foreign Relations, 1981.

Kalden, Sebastian. "A Case of 'Hollanditis': The Interchurch Peace Council in the Netherlands and the Christian Peace Movement in Western Europe." In Conze, Klimke, and Varon, *Nuclear Threats*, 251–68.

Kaldor, Mary. "Beyond the Blocs: Defending Europe the Political Way." *World Policy Journal* 1, no. 1 (1983): 1–21.

——. *Europe from Below: An East-West Dialogue.* London: Verso, 1991.

Kalinovsky, Artemy. *A Long Goodbye: The Soviet Withdrawal from Afghanistan.* Cambridge, MA: Harvard University Press, 2011.

Kampelman, Max. *Entering New Worlds: The Memoirs of a Private Man in Public Life.* New York: HarperCollins, 1991.

Karamouzi, Eirini. "'At Last, Our Voice Is Heard in the World': Andreas Papandreou, Greece and the Six Nation Initiative during the Euromissile Crisis." In *Margins for Manoeuvre in Cold War Europe: The Influence of Smaller Powers*, edited by Laurien Crump and Susanna Erlandsson, 224–40. London: Routledge, 2019.

——. "'Out with the Bases of Death': Civil Society and Peace Mobilization in Greece during the 1980s." *Journal of Contemporary History* 56, no. 3 (2021): 617–38.

Karamouzi, Eirini, and Dionysios Chourchoulis. "Troublemaker or Peacemaker? Andreas Papandreou, the Euromissile Crisis, and the Policy of Peace, 1981–86." *Cold War History* 19, no. 1 (2019): 39–61.

Kelly, Petra. *Fighting for Hope*. Translated by Marianne Howarth. Boston: South End, 1984.

Kemper, Claudia. "More Than a FREEZE: Political Mobilization and the Peace Movement in 1980s U.S. Society." In *The INF Treaty of 1987: A Reappraisal*, edited by Philipp Gassert, Tim Geiger, and Hermann Wentker, 237–58. Göttingen, Germany: Vandenhoeck & Ruprecht, 2021.

Kennan, George F. *The Nuclear Delusion: Soviet-American Relations in the Atomic Age*. New York: Pantheon, 1982.

Kieninger, Stephan. *Dynamic Détente: The United States and Europe, 1964–1975*. Lanham, MD: Lexington, 2016.

Kissinger, Henry A. "A Plan to Reshape NATO." In *European Peace Movements and the Future of the Western Alliance*, edited by Walter Laqueur and Robert Hunter, 41–55. New Brunswick, NJ: Transaction, 1985.

———. "The Unsolved Problems of European Defense." *Foreign Affairs* 40, no. 4 (1962): 515–41.

———. *The White House Years*. Boston: Little, Brown, 1979.

Klimke, Martin, and Laura Stapane. "From Artists for Peace to the Green Caterpillar: Cultural Activism and Electoral Politics in 1980s West Germany." In Conze, Klimke, and Varon, *Nuclear Threats*, 116–42.

Knoblauch, William M. "Will You Sing About the Missiles?" In Conze, Klimke, and Varon, *Nuclear Threats*, 101–15.

Kohl, Helmut. *Vom Mauerfall zur Wiedervereinigung: Meine Erinnerungen*. Munich: Droemer, 2014.

Kramer, Mark. "Die Nicht-Krise um 'Able Archer 1983': Fürchtete die sowjetische Führung tatsächlich einen atomaren Großangriff im Herbst 1983?" In *Wege zur Wiedervereinigung: Die beiden deutschen Staaten in ihren Bündnissen 1970 bis 1990*, edited by Oliver Bange and Bernd Lemke, 129–49. Munich: Oldenbourg, 2013.

Krell, Gert. "The Controversy about 'Flexible Response.'" *Bulletin of Peace Proposals* 17, no. 2 (1986): 131–40.

Krell, Gert, Harald Müller, Matthew Evangelista, and Jeffrey Herf. "Correspondence." *International Security* 11, no. 2 (1986): 193–215.

Lacouture, Jean. *De Gaulle*, vol. 3: *Le souverain, 1951–1970*. Paris: Éditions du Seuil, 1986.

Lall, Betty Goetz. "A NATO-Warsaw Détente?" *Bulletin of the Atomic Scientists* 20, no. 9 (1964): 37–39.

Lamb, Christopher Jon. "Public Opinion and Nuclear Weapons in Europe: A Report on the 27th Annual Session of the North Atlantic Assembly." *NATO Review* 29, no. 6 (1981): 27–31.

Laqueur, Walter, and Robert Hunter. Introduction to *European Peace Movements and the Future of the Western Alliance*, edited by Walter Laqueur and Robert Hunter, 1–12. New Brunswick, NJ: Transaction, 1985.

Larsen, Jeffrey Arthur. "The Politics of NATO Short-Range Nuclear Modernization 1983–1990: The Follow-On-to-Lance Missile Decisions." PhD diss., Princeton University, 1991.

Lee, Wayne E. *Waging War: Conflict, Culture, and Innovation in World History.* Oxford: Oxford University Press, 2016.

Legge, J. Michael. *Theater Nuclear Weapons and the NATO Strategy of Flexible Response.* Santa Monica, CA: RAND Corp., 1983.

Lindsay, Jon R. and Erik Gartzke. "Introduction: Cross-Domain Deterrence, from Practice to Theory." In *Cross-Domain Deterrence: Strategy in an Era of Complexity,* edited by Jon R. Lindsay and Erik Gartzke, 1–23. Oxford: Oxford University Press, 2019.

Lippert, Werner D. *The Economic Diplomacy of Ostpolitik: Origins of NATO's Energy Dilemma.* New York: Berghahn Books, 2011.

Locher, Anna, and Christian Nuenlist. "What Role for NATO? Conflicting Western Perceptions of Détente, 1963–65." *Journal of Transatlantic Studies* 2, no. 2 (2004): 185–208.

Lofland, John. *Polite Protestors: The American Peace Movement of the 1980s.* Syracuse, NY: Syracuse University Press, 1993.

Long, Austin, and Brendan Rittenhouse Green. "Stalking the Secure Second Strike: Intelligence, Counterforce, and Nuclear Strategy." *Journal of Strategic Studies* 38, nos. 1–2 (2015): 38–73.

Loth, Wilfried. "The Cold War: What It Was About and Why It Ended." In *Perforating the Iron Curtain: European Détente, Transatlantic Relations, and the Cold War, 1965–1985,* edited by Poul Villaume and Odd Arne Westad, 19–34. Copenhagen: Museum Tusculanum, 2010.

Lucas, W. Scott. *Divided We Stand: Britain, the US and the Suez Crisis.* London: Hodder & Stoughton, 1991.

Lutsch, Andreas. "In Favor of 'Effective' and 'Non-discriminatory' Non-dissemination Policy: The FRG and the NPT Negotiation Process (1962–1966)." In *Negotiating the Nuclear Non-proliferation Treaty: Origins of the Nuclear Order,* edited by Roland Popp, Liviu Horovitz, and Andreas Wenger, 36–57. London: Routledge, 2017.

——. "The Zero Option and NATO's Dual-Track Decision: Rethinking the Paradox." *Journal of Strategic Studies* 43, nos. 6–7 (2020): 957–89.

Lyakhovskiy, Aleksandr Antonovich. "Inside the Soviet Invasion of Afghanistan and the Seizure of Kabul, December 1979." Translated by Gary Goldberg and Artemy Kalinovsky. Cold War International History Project Working Paper 51. Washington, DC: Woodrow Wilson Center for International Scholars, 2007.

Maar, Henry Richard, III. *Freeze! The Grassroots Movement to Halt the Arms Race and End the Cold War.* Ithaca, NY: Cornell University Press, 2022.

Martin, Garrett. "Towards a New Concert of Europe: De Gaulle's Vision of a Post–Cold War Europe." In *Visions of the End of the Cold War in Europe, 1945–1990,* edited by Frédéric Bozo, Marie-Pierre Rey, Bernd Rother, and N. Piers Ludlow, 91–104. New York: Berghahn Books, 2012.

Mastny, Vojtech. "How Able Was 'Able Archer'? Nuclear Trigger and Intelligence in Perspective." *Journal of Cold War Studies* 11, no. 1 (2009): 108–23.

Matlock, Jack F., Jr. *Autopsy on an Empire: The American Ambassador's Account of the Collapse of the Soviet Union.* New York: Random House, 1995.

——. *Reagan and Gorbachev: How the Cold War Ended*. New York: Random House, 2004.

Mausbach, Wilfried. "Nuclear Winter: Prophecies of Doom and Images of Desolation in the Second Cold War." In Conze, Klimke, and Varon, *Nuclear Threats*, 27–54.

——. "Vereint marschieren, getrennt schlagen? Die amerikanische Friedensbewegung und der Widerstand gegen den NATO-Doppelbeschluss." In *Zweiter Kalter Krieg und Friedensbewegung: Der NATO-Doppelbeschluss in deutsch-deutscher und internationaler Perspektive*, edited by Philipp Gassert, Tim Geiger, and Hermann Wentker, 283–304. Munich: Oldenbourg, 2011.

McCausland, Jeffrey D. "German Politics and Alliance Unity." *Parameters* 13, no. 4 (1983): 69–77.

McNamara, Robert S. "The Military Role of Nuclear Weapons: Perceptions and Misperceptions." *Foreign Affairs* 62, no. 1 (1983): 59–80.

Mearsheimer, John J. "Prospects for Conventional Deterrence in Europe." *Bulletin of the Atomic Scientists* 41, no. 7 (1985): 158–62.

Mende, Silke. "'Enemies at the Gate': The West German Greens and Their Arrival at the Bundestag—between Old Ideals and New Challenges." *German Politics and Society* 33, no. 4 (2015): 66–79.

——. "*Nicht rechts, nicht links, sondern vorn*": *Eine Geschichte der Gründungsgrünen*. Munich: Oldenbourg, 2011.

Meyers, Nicholas, dir. *The Day After*. ABC Circle, 1983.

Michaels, Jeffrey H. "Visions of the Next War or Reliving the Last One? Early Alliance Views of War with the Soviet Bloc." *Journal of Strategic Studies* 43, nos. 6–7 (2020): 990–1013.

Milder, Stephen. "The 'Example of Wyhl': How Grassroots Protest in the Rhine Valley Shaped West Germany's Antinuclear Movement." In Conze, Klimke, and Varon, *Nuclear Threats*, 167–85.

Miles, Simon. *Engaging the Evil Empire: Washington, Moscow, and the Beginning of the End of the Cold War*. Ithaca, NY: Cornell University Press, 2020.

——. "Envisioning Détente: The Johnson Administration and the October 1964 Khrushchev Ouster." *Diplomatic History* 40, no. 4 (2016): 722–49.

——. "The War Scare That Wasn't: Able Archer 83 and the Myths of the Second Cold War." *Journal of Cold War Studies* 22, no. 3 (2020): 86–118.

The Military Balance 1975–1976. London: International Institute for Strategic Studies, 1976.

Morgan, Michael Cotey. *The Final Act: The Helsinki Accords and the Transformation of the Cold War*. Princeton, NJ: Princeton University Press, 2018.

"NATO and Public Opinion." *NATO Letter* 16, no. 1 (1968): inside cover.

NATO: Can the Alliance Be Saved? Report of Senator Sam Nunn to the Committee on Armed Services, United States Senate, May 13, 1982. Washington, DC: Government Printing Office, 1982.

NATO's Future Role: Hearings before the Subcommittee on Europe and the Middle East of the Committee on Foreign Affairs, House of Representatives, Ninety-Seventh Congress, Second Session, May 20, June 3, and 9, 1982. Washington, DC: Government Printing Office, 1982.

Nehring, Holger. "The Last Battle of the Cold War: Peace Movements and German Politics in the 1980s." In Nuti et al., *Euromissile Crisis*, 309–30.

——. "A Transatlantic Security Crisis? Transnational Relations between the West German and the U.S. Peace Movements, 1977–1985." In *European Integration and the Atlantic Community in the 1980s*, edited by Kiran Klaus Patel and Kenneth Weisbrode, 177–200. Cambridge: Cambridge University Press, 2013.

Nena, "99 Red Balloons." Track 1 on *99 Luftballons*. Spliff Studios, 1984.

Niedhart, Gottfried. "Ostpolitik: Transformation through Communication and the Quest for Peaceful Change." *Journal of Cold War Studies* 18, no. 3 (2016): 14–59.

——. "U.S. Détente and West German *Ostpolitik*: Parallels and Frictions." In *The Strained Alliance: U.S.-European Relations from Nixon to Carter*, edited by Matthias Schulz and Thomas A. Schwartz, 23–44. Washington, DC, and Cambridge: German Historical Institute and Cambridge University Press, 2010.

Nitze, Paul H. *From Hiroshima to Glasnost: At the Center of Decision—a Memoir*. With Ann M. Smith and Steven L. Rearden. New York: Weidenfeld, 1989.

Nixon, Richard M. "Asia after Viet Nam." *Foreign Affairs* 46, no. 1 (1967): 111–25.

——. *R. N.: The Memoirs of Richard Nixon*. New York: Simon & Schuster.

No First Use: A Report by the Union of Concerned Scientists. Cambridge, MA: Union of Concerned Scientists, 1983.

Nuclear Posture Review. Washington, DC: Office of the Secretary of Defense, 2018.

Nunn, Sam. "NATO: Saving the Alliance." *Washington Quarterly* 5, no. 3 (1982): 19–29.

Nuti, Leopoldo. "The Nuclear Debate in Italian Politics in the Late 1970s and Early 1980s." In Nuti et al., *Euromissile Crisis*, 231–50.

——. "The Origins of the 1979 Dual Track Decision—a Survey." In *The Crisis of Détente in Europe: From Helsinki to Gorbachev, 1975–1985*, edited by Leopoldo Nuti, 57–71. London: Routledge, 2009.

Nuti, Leopoldo, Frédéric Bozo, Marie-Pierre Rey, and Bernd Rother, eds. *The Euromissile Crisis and the End of the Cold War*. Washington, DC, and Stanford, CA: Woodrow Wilson Center Press and Stanford University Press, 2015.

——. "Editors' Introduction." In Nuti et al., *Euromissile Crisis*, 1–9.

Oberdorfer, Don. *From the Cold War to a New Era: The United States and the Soviet Union, 1983–1991*. Baltimore: Johns Hopkins University Press, 1998.

Odom, William E. *The Collapse of the Soviet Military*. New Haven, CT: Yale University Press, 1998.

Painter, David S. "Energy and the End of the Evil Empire." In *The Reagan Moment: America and the World in the 1980s*, edited by Jonathan R. Hunt and Simon Miles, 43–63. Ithaca, NY: Cornell University Press, 2021.

Parisi, Ilaria. "'Pacifism Does Not Ensure Peace': Explaining the Low Profile of the French Pacifist Movement." In *Making Sense of the Americas: How Protest Related to America in the 1980s*, edited by Jan Hansen, Christian Helm, and Frank Reichherzer, 89–108. Frankfurt: Campus Verlag, 2015.

Pedaliu, Effie G. H. "'Footnotes' as an Expression of Distrust? The United States and the NATO 'Flanks' in the Last Two Decades of the Cold War." In *Trust, but Verify: The Politics of Uncertainty and the Transformation of the Cold War Order, 1969–1991*, edited by Martin Klimke, Reinhild Kreis, and Christian F. Ostermann, 237–58. Stanford, CA: Stanford University Press, 2016.

Pfaltzgraff, Robert L., and Jacquelyn K. Davis. *The Cruise Missile: Bargaining Chip or Defense Bargain?* Cambridge, MA: Institute for Foreign Policy Analysis, 1977.

Pierre, Andrew J. "The SALT Agreement and Europe." *World Today* 28, no. 7 (1972): 281–88.

Political and Military Issues in the Atlantic Alliance: Hearings before the Subcommittee on Europe and the Middle East of the Committee on Foreign Affairs, House of Representatives, Ninety-Eighth Congress, Second Session, August 1, October 1, 1984. Washington, DC: Government Printing Office, 1984.

Pons, Silvio. "The Rise and Fall of Eurocommunism." In *The Cambridge History of the Cold War*, vol. 3: *Endings*, edited by Melvyn P. Leffler and Odd Arne Westad, 45–65. Cambridge: Cambridge University Press, 2010.

"*Pravda* Editorial on President Reagan's INF Proposals (Excerpts)," October 4, 1983. *Survival* 26, no. 1 (1984): 33–34.

"President Brezhnev's Speech to the 17th Congress of Soviet Trade Unions (Excerpts)," March 16, 1982. *Survival* 24, no. 4 (1982): 184–85.

Priest, Andrew. "'In Common Cause': The NATO Multilateral Force and Mixed-Manning Demonstration on USS *Claude V. Ricketts*, 1964–1965." *Journal of Military History* 69, no. 3 (2005): 759–88.

Quaggio, Giulia. "Social Movements and Participatory Democracy: Spanish Protests for Peace during the Last Decade of the Cold War (1981–1986)." *Archiv für Sozialgeschichte* 58 (2018): 279–302.

Reagan, Ronald. *An American Life: The Autobiography.* New York: Simon & Schuster, 1990.

———. *Reagan: A Life in Letters.* Edited by Kiron K. Skinner, Annelise Anderson, and Martin Anderson. New York: Free Press, 2003.

———. *The Reagan Diaries.* Edited by Douglas Brinkley. 2 vols. New York: HarperCollins, 2009.

Regan, Donald T. *For the Record: From Wall Street to Washington.* San Diego: Harcourt Brace Jovanovich, 1988.

Report of the Special Committee on Nuclear Weapons in the Atlantic Alliance. Washington, DC: Government Printing Office, 1985.

Report on the Future Tasks of the Alliance. Brussels: NATO Information Service, 1968.

Rey, Marie-Pierre. "'Europe Is Our Common Home': A Study of Gorbachev's Diplomatic Concept." *Cold War History* 4, no. 2 (2004): 33–65.

———. "Gorbachev's New Thinking and Europe, 1985–1989." In *Europe and the End of the Cold War: A Reappraisal*, edited by Frédéric Bozo, Marie-Pierre Rey, N. Piers Ludlow, and Leopoldo Nuti, 23–35. London: Routledge, 2008.

Richardson, D. E. "The Cruise Missile: A Strategic Weapon for the 1980s." *Electronics & Power* 23, nos. 11–12 (1977): 896–901.

Richter, Saskia. *Die Aktivistin: Das Leben der Petra Kelly.* Munich: Deutsche Verlags-Anstalt, 2010.

Rid, Thomas. *Active Measures: The Secret History of Disinformation and Political Warfare.* New York: Farrar, Straus and Giroux, 2020.

Rinne, Robert L., ed. *The History of NATO TNF Policy: The Role of Studies, Analysis and Exercises Conference Proceedings.* 3 vols. Livermore, CA: Sandia National Laboratories, 1994.

Risse-Kappen, Thomas. "Ideas Do Not Float Freely: Transnational Coalitions, Domestic Structures, and the End of the Cold War." *International Organization* 48, no. 2 (1994): 185–214.

——. *The Zero Option: INF, West Germany, and Arms Control.* Translated by Lesley Booth. Boulder, CO: Westview, 1988.

Roberts, Adam. "The Trouble with Unilateralism: The UK, the 1983 General Election, and Non-nuclear Defence." *Bulletin of Peace Proposals* 14, no. 4 (1983): 305–12.

Rochon, Thomas R. *Mobilizing for Peace: The Antinuclear Movements in Western Europe.* Princeton, NJ: Princeton University Press, 1988.

Rose, Clive. *Campaigns against Western Defence: NATO's Adversaries and Critics.* New York: St. Martin's, 1985.

Rubinson, Paul. *Redefining Science: Scientists, the National Security State, and Nuclear Weapons in Cold War America.* Amherst: University of Massachusetts Press, 2016.

Rücker, Katrin. "Why Was There No 'Accidental Armageddon' Discourse in France? How Defense Intellectuals, Peace Movements, and Public Opinion Rethought the Cold War during the Euromissile Crisis." In Conze, Klimke, and Varon, *Nuclear Threats*, 316–34.

Sagan, Carl, and Richard Turco. *A Path Where No Man Thought: Nuclear Winter and the End of the Arms Race.* New York: Random House, 1990.

SALT and the NATO Allies: A Staff Report to the Subcommittee on European Affairs of the Committee on Foreign Relations, United States Senate, October 1979. Washington, DC: Government Printing Office, 1979.

Sargent, Daniel J. *A Superpower Transformed: The Remaking of American Foreign Relations in the 1970s.* Oxford: Oxford University Press, 2015.

Sarotte, Mary Elise. *1989: The Struggle to Create Post–Cold War Europe.* Princeton, NJ: Princeton University Press, 2009.

——. *Not One Inch: America, Russia, and the Making of Post–Cold War Stalemate.* New Haven, CT: Yale University Press, 2021.

Savel'yev, Aleksandr' G., and Nikolay N. Detinov. *The Big Five: Arms Control Decision-Making in the Soviet Union.* Edited by Gregory Varhall. Translated by Dmitriy Trenin. Westport, CT: Praeger, 1995.

Savranskaya, Svetlana. "Learning to Disarm: Mikhail Gorbachev's Interactive Learning and Changes in the Soviet Negotiating Positions Leading to the INF Treaty." In Nuti et al., *Euromissile Crisis*, 85–103.

Sayle, Timothy Andrews. *Enduring Alliance: A History of NATO and the Postwar Global Order.* Ithaca, NY: Cornell University Press, 2019.

——. "A Nuclear Education: The Origins of NATO's Nuclear Planning Group." *Journal of Strategic Studies* 43, no. 6–7 (2020): 920–56.

——. "'We Do Not Wish to Be Obstructionist': How Canada Took and Kept a Seat on NATO's Nuclear Planning Group." In *The Nuclear North: Histories of Canada in the Atomic Age,* edited by Susan Colbourn and Timothy Andrews Sayle, 40–64. Vancouver: UBC Press, 2020.

Schelling, Thomas C. *Arms and Influence with a New Preface and Afterword.* New Haven, CT: Yale University Press, 2008.

Schmidt, Helmut. *Menschen und Mächte*. Berlin: Siedler, 1987.

——. "The 1977 Alastair Buchan Memorial Lecture." *Survival* 20, no. 1 (1978): 2–10.

——. "Perspectives of the Alliance." *Survival* 12, no. 2 (1970): 43–45.

——. *Strategie des Gleichgewichts: Deutsche Friedenspolitik und die Westmächte*. Stuttgart, Germany: Seewald Verlag, 1969.

——. *Verteidigung oder Vergeltung: Ein deutscher Beitrag zum strategischen Problem der NATO*. Stuttgart, Germany: Seewald Verlag, 1961.

Schmidt, Helmut, and Giovanni di Lorenzo. *Auf eine Zigarette mit Helmut Schmidt*. Cologne, Germany: Kiepenheuer and Witsch, 2010.

Schmidt, Peter. *Europeanization of Defense: Prospects of Consensus?* Santa Monica, CA: RAND Corp., 1984.

Schmidt, Wolfgang. "The Euromissile Crisis, the Palme Commission, and the Search for a New Security Model." In Nuti et al., *Euromissile Crisis*, 348–66.

Schregel, Susanne. "Global Micropolitics: Toward a Transnational History of Grassroots Nuclear-Free Zones." In Conze, Klimke, and Varon, *Nuclear Threats*, 206–26.

Schwartz, David N. *NATO's Nuclear Dilemmas*. Washington, DC: Brookings Institution, 1983.

Schwartz, Thomas A. *Henry Kissinger and American Power: A Political Biography*. New York: Hill & Wang, 2020.

——. *Lyndon Johnson and Europe: In the Shadow of Vietnam*. Cambridge, MA: Harvard University Press, 2003.

——. "Moving beyond the Cold War: The Johnson Administration, Bridge-Building, and Détente." In *Beyond the Cold War: Lyndon Johnson and the New Global Challenges of the 1960s*, edited by Francis J. Gavin and Mark Atwood Lawrence, 76–94. Oxford: Oxford University Press, 2014.

Scott-Smith, Giles. "Maintaining Transatlantic Community: US Public Diplomacy, the Ford Foundation and the Successor Generation Concept in US Foreign Affairs, 1960s–1980s." *Global Society* 28, no. 1 (2014): 90–103.

——. "The Netherlands between East and West." In Nuti et al., *Euromissile Crisis*, 251–68.

——. "Searching for the Successor Generation: Public Diplomacy, the US Embassy's International Visitor Program and the Labour Party in the 1980s." *British Journal of Politics and International Relations* 8, no. 2 (2006): 214–37.

Second Interim Report on Nuclear Weapons in Europe, Prepared by the North Atlantic Assembly's Special Committee on Nuclear Weapons in Europe: A Report to the Committee on Foreign Relations, United States Senate, January 1983. Washington, DC: Government Printing Office, 1983.

Sharp, Jane M. O. "After Reykjavik: Arms Control and the Allies." *International Affairs* 63, no. 2 (1987): 239–57.

——. "Reshaping NATO Nuclear Policy." *Bulletin of the Atomic Scientists* 41, no. 4 (1985): 38–44.

Shifrinson, Joshua R. Itzkowitz. *Rising Titans, Falling Giants: How Great Powers Exploit Power Shifts*. Ithaca, NY: Cornell University Press, 2018.

Shultz, George P. *Turmoil and Triumph: My Years as Secretary of State*. New York: Charles Scribner's Sons, 1993.

Simón, Luis, and Alexander Lanoszka. "The Post-INF European Missile Balance: Thinking about NATO's Deterrence Strategy." *Texas National Security Review* 3, no. 3 (2020). http://dx.doi.org/10.26153/tsw/10224.

Sloan, Stanley R. "NATO Nuclear Forces: Modernization and Arms Control." Congressional Research Service Issue Brief no. IB81128 (1983).

Slocombe, Walter. "Extended Deterrence." *Washington Quarterly* 7, no. 4 (1984): 93–103.

Smith, Gerard. *Doubletalk: The Story of SALT I.* Lanham, MD: University Press of America, 1995.

Snyder, Sarah B. *Human Rights Activism and the End of the Cold War: A Transnational History of the Helsinki Network.* Cambridge: Cambridge University Press, 2011.

——. "'Jerry, Don't Go': Domestic Opposition to the 1975 Helsinki Final Act." *Journal of American Studies* 44, no. 1 (2010): 67–81.

Sommer, Theo. "For an Atlantic Future." *Foreign Affairs* 43, no. 1 (1964): 112–25.

Soviet Covert Action (the Forgery Offensive): Hearings before the Subcommittee on Oversight of the Permanent Select Committee on Intelligence, House of Representatives, Ninety-Sixth Congress, Second Session, February 6, 19, 1980. Washington, DC: Government Printing Office, 1980.

Soviet Military Power. Washington, DC: Government Printing Office, 1981.

Spohr, Kristina. "Bonn, Guadeloupe, and Vienna, 1978–9." In *Transcending the Cold War: Summits, Statecraft, and the Dissolution of Bipolarity in Europe, 1970–1990,* edited by Kristina Spohr and David Reynolds, 122–44. Oxford: Oxford University Press, 2016.

——. "NATO's Nuclear Politics and the Schmidt-Carter Rift." In Nuti et al., *Euromissile Crisis,* 139–57.

Spohr-Readman, Kristina. "Germany and the Politics of the Neutron Bomb, 1975–1979." *Diplomacy & Statecraft* 21 (2010): 259–85.

"Statement on a European Nuclear-Free Zone." *Security Dialogue* 11, no. 2 (1980): 109.

Sting, "Russians." Track 3 on *The Dream of the Blue Turtles.* Sony Music, 1985.

Stoddart, Kristan. "Creating the 'Seamless Robe of Deterrence': Great Britain's Role in NATO's INF Debate." In Nuti et al., *Euromissile Crisis,* 176–95.

——. *Facing Down the Soviet Union: Britain, the USA, NATO and Nuclear Weapons, 1976–1983.* London: Palgrave Macmillan, 2014.

Stromseth, Jane E. *The Origins of Flexible Response: NATO's Debate over Strategy in the 1960s.* Houndmills, UK: Macmillan, 1988.

Strong, Robert A. *Working in the World: Jimmy Carter and the Making of American Foreign Policy.* Baton Rouge: Louisiana State University Press, 2000.

Suri, Jeremi. *Power and Protest: Global Revolution and the Rise of Détente.* Cambridge, MA: Harvard University Press, 2003.

Tal, David. *US Strategic Arms Policy in the Cold War: Negotiations and Confrontation over SALT, 1969–1979.* London: Routledge, 2017.

Talbott, Strobe. *Deadly Gambits: The Reagan Administration and the Stalemate in Nuclear Arms Control.* New York: Vintage, 1985.

——. *Endgame: The Inside Story of SALT II.* New York: HarperCollins, 1979.

Taubman, William. *Gorbachev: His Life and Times*. New York: W. W. Norton, 2017.

———. *Khrushchev: The Man and His Era*. New York: W. W. Norton, 2003.

Terriff, Terry. *The Nixon Administration and the Making of U.S. Nuclear Strategy*. Ithaca, NY: Cornell University Press, 1995.

Thatcher, Margaret. *The Downing Street Years*. New York: HarperCollins, 1993.

Thies, Wallace J. *Why NATO Endures*. Cambridge: Cambridge University Press, 2009.

Thompson, Brett. "Pierre Elliott Trudeau's Peace Initiative: 25 Years On." *International Journal* 64, no. 4 (2009): 1117–37.

Thompson, E. P. *The Heavy Dancers*. New York: Pantheon, 1985.

———. "A Letter to America." In *Protest and Survive*, edited by E. P. Thompson and Dan Smith, 3–52. New York: Monthly Review, 1981.

———. *Protest and Survive*. 2nd ed. Nottingham, UK: Russell, 1980.

Thomson, James A. "The LRTNF Decision: Evolution of US Theatre Nuclear Policy, 1975–9." *International Affairs* 60, no. 4 (1984): 601–14.

Torigian, Joseph. "'You Don't Know Khrushchev Well': The Ouster of the Soviet Leader as a Challenge to Recent Scholarship on Authoritarian Politics." *Journal of Cold War Studies* 24, no. 1 (2022): 78–115.

Tornetta, Vincenzo. "The Nuclear Strategy of the Atlantic Alliance and the 'No-First-Use' Debate." *NATO Review* 30, no. 5 (1982): 1–7.

Trachtenberg, Marc A. *A Constructed Peace: The Making of the European Settlement, 1945–1963*. Princeton, NJ: Princeton University Press, 1999.

———. *History and Strategy*. Princeton, NJ: Princeton University Press, 1991.

Treverton, Gregory F. *America, Germany, and the Future of Europe*. Princeton, NJ: Princeton University Press, 1992.

———. *Making the Alliance Work: The United States and Western Europe*. Ithaca, NY: Cornell University Press, 1985.

———. "NATO Alliance Politics." In *Cruise Missiles: Technology, Strategy, Politics*, edited by Richard K. Betts, 415–42. Washington, DC: Brookings Institution, 1981.

———. "Nuclear Weapons and the 'Gray Area.'" *Foreign Affairs* 57, no. 5 (1979): 1075–89.

Tsipis, Kosta. "The Long-Range Cruise Missile." *Bulletin of the Atomic Scientists* 31, no. 4 (1975): 12–26.

Twenty-Fifth Meeting of the North Atlantic Assembly Held at Ottawa, Canada, October 22 to October, 1979. Report of the U.S. Delegation. Washington, DC: Committee on Foreign Relations, 1980.

"US State Department Statement on Soviet INF Position (Excerpts)." December 21, 1982, *Survival* 25, no. 2 (1983): 88.

Vaïsse, Justin. *Neoconservatism: The Biography of a Movement*. Translated by Arthur Goldhammer. Cambridge, MA: Belknap Press of Harvard University Press, 2010.

Vaïsse, Maurice. "De Gaulle's Handling of the Berlin and Cuban Crises." In *Europe, Cold War and Coexistence, 1955–1965*, edited by Wilfried Loth, 63–75. London: Routledge, 2004.

van Dijk, Ruud. "'A Mass Psychosis': The Netherlands and NATO's Dual-Track Decision, 1978–1979." *Cold War History* 12, no. 3 (2012): 381–405.

van Nes, Harald. *Das Ringen um Berlin im Kalten Krieg: Die Geschichte von Live Oak.* Berlin: De Gruyter Oldenbourg, 2021.

Vance, Cyrus. *Hard Choices: Critical Years in America's Foreign Policy.* New York: Simon & Schuster, 1983.

Vershbow, Alexander R. "The Cruise Missile: The End of Arms Control?" *Foreign Affairs* 55, no. 1 (1976): 133–46.

Vigil, David Nathaniel. "Elusive Equality: The Nuclear Arms Race in Europe and the History of the INF Treaty, 1969–1988." PhD diss., Emory University, 2014.

von Hassel, Kai-Uwe. "Organizing Western Defense: The Search for Consensus," *Foreign Affairs* 43, no. 2 (1965): 209–16.

Wampler, Robert A. "Ambiguous Legacy: The United States, Great Britain and the Foundations of NATO Strategy, 1948–1957." PhD diss., Harvard University, 1991.

Warner, Gale, and Michael Shuman. *Citizen Diplomats: Pathfinders in Soviet-American Relations—and How You Can Join Them.* New York: Continuum, 1987.

Wasserman, Sherri L. *The Neutron Bomb Controversy: A Study in Alliance Politics.* New York: Praeger, 1983.

Wenger, Andreas. "NATO's Transformation in the 1960s and the Ensuing Political Order in Europe." In *Transforming NATO in the Cold War: Challenges beyond Deterrence in the 1960s,* edited by Andreas Wenger, Christian Nuenlist, and Anna Locher, 221–42. Abingdon, UK: Routledge, 2006.

Wentker, Hermann. "NATO's Double-Track Decision and East-West German Relations." In Becker-Schaum et al., *Nuclear Crisis,* 871–73.

Werrell, Kenneth P. *The Evolution of the Cruise Missile.* Maxwell Air Force Base, AL: Air University Press, 1985.

Wettig, Gerhard. "The Last Soviet Offensive in the Cold War: Emergence and Development of the Campaign against NATO Euromissiles, 1979–1983." *Cold War History* 9, no. 1 (2009): 79–110.

Why NATO? Brussels: NATO Information Service, 1968.

Wiegrefe, Klaus. *Das Zerwürfnis: Helmut Schmidt, Jimmy Carter und die Krise der deutsch-amerikanischen Beziehungen.* Berlin: Propyläen, 2005.

Williams, Phil. "The Nunn Amendment, Burden-Sharing and US Troops in Europe." *Survival* 27, no. 1 (1985): 2–10.

Wilson, James Graham. *The Triumph of Improvisation: Gorbachev's Adaptability, Reagan's Engagement, and the End of the Cold War.* Ithaca, NY: Cornell University Press, 2014.

Windsor, Philip. "Current Tensions in NATO." *World Today* 26, no. 7 (1970): 289–95.

Wittner, Lawrence S. "Peace through Strength? The Impact of the Antinuclear Uprising on the Carter and Reagan Administrations." In Conze, Klimke, and Varon, *Nuclear Threats,* 271–89.

———. *Toward Nuclear Abolition: A History of the World Nuclear Disarmament Movement, 1971–Present.* Stanford, CA: Stanford University Press, 2003.

Wohlforth, William C., ed. *Witnesses to the End of the Cold War.* Baltimore: Johns Hopkins University Press, 1996.

World Peace Council. *In the Name of Life Itself Ban the Neutron Bomb!* Helsinki: Information Centre of the World Peace Council, 1977.

Zelizer, Julian E. "Détente and Domestic Politics." *Diplomatic History* 33, no. 4 (2009): 653–70.

Ziemann, Benjamin. "A Quantum of Solace? European Peace Movements during the Cold War and Their Elective Affinities." *Archiv für Sozialgeschichte* 49 (2009): 351–89.

Zimmerman, Hubert. *Money and Security: Troops, Monetary Policy, and West Germany's Relations with the United States and Britain, 1950–1971.* Washington, DC, and Cambridge: German Historical Institute and Cambridge University Press, 2002.

Zubok, Vladislav M., and Constantin Pleshakov. *Inside the Kremlin's Cold War: From Stalin to Khrushchev.* Cambridge, MA: Harvard University Press, 1996.

INDEX